WRITING LIVES
EXPLORING LITERACY AND COMMUNITY

WRITING LIVES
EXPLORING LITERACY
AND COMMUNITY

EDITORS

Sara Garnes
David Humphries
Vic Mortimer
Jennifer Phegley
Kathleen R. Wallace

THE OHIO STATE UNIVERSITY

ST. MARTIN'S PRESS • New York

EDITOR-IN-CHIEF: Steve Debow
MANAGER, PUBLISHING SERVICES: Emily Berleth
PUBLISHING SERVICES ASSOCIATE: Meryl Gross
PROJECT MANAGEMENT: Richard Steins
PRODUCTION SUPERVISOR: Kurt Nelson
COMPOSITION: Jan Ewing, EWING SYSTEMS
COVER DESIGN: Patricia McFadden
COVER ART: Untitled (Why Are You Here?) by Barbara Kruger, 1990. Silkscreen on paper commissioned by the Wexner Center for the Arts, The Ohio State University, Columbus, Ohio.

Manufactured in the United States of America.
0 9 8 7 6
f e d c b a

For information, write:
St. Martin's Press, Inc.
175 Fifth Avenue
New York, NY 10010

ISBN: 0-312-14979-4

Acknowledgments

"Why I Write," from SUCH, SUCH WERE THE JOYS by George Orwell. Copyright © 1953 by Sonia Brownell Orwell and renewed 1981 by Mrs. George K. Perutz, Mrs. Miriam Gross, & Dr. Michael Dickson, Executors of the Estate of Sonia Brownell Orwell. Reprinted by permission of Harcourt Brace & Company.
"Turning Topsy Turvey" by Mary Ann Williams. Reprinted with permission from Kojo Kamau.
"Literacy in Three Metaphors" by Sylvia Scribner. Published in *The American Journal of Education* 93:1 (1984). Reprinted with permission from The University of Chicago Press.
"The Things They Carried," from THE THINGS THEY CARRIED. Copyright © 1990 by Tim O'Brien. Reprinted by permission of Houghton Mifflin Co./Seymour Lawrence. All rights reserved.

Acknowledgments and copyrights are continued at the back of the book on pages 456–458, which constitute an extension of the copyright page.

CONTENTS

PREFACE TO INSTRUCTORS

Writing Lives: Exploring Literacy and Community promotes critical reading, writing, and discussion as means of inquiry. While students may be familiar with literacy through public debates on illiteracy or functional literacy, our goal is to have students identify and understand their participation within various *literacies*. We have intentionally complicated the issue by focusing on *literacies* in the plural rather than on a single *literacy*. The readings themselves illustrate this complexity: No single definition sufficiently describes the many ways in which individuals come to understand the most effective means of reading, writing, speaking, listening, or behaving within a given community. The impact of social situation upon literacy, then, is a central focus of this text.

The pedagogy that informs this reader espouses a student-centered classroom where writing is taught as a process with multiple opportunities for drafting, receiving responses from peers and instructors before revising, and eventually developing a final draft. We also provide plenty of opportunities for writing informally, so that students can reflect upon and challenge their ideas as they think through their writing. As Donald Murray and others might put it, we intend to give students the opportunity to write to learn. We see reading and writing as related activities, and we encourage our students to approach these readings as writers themselves. Learning to read actively and critically encourages students to read for the details, generalizations, voice, tone, and style that can enrich their own resources as writers.

Since *Writing Lives: Exploring Literacy and Community* was developed primarily by and for a community of writing instructors, we invite new instructors to enter into a dialogue with the book and with their students. While the emphasis throughout the book is on the readings, Part 1, "The Practice of Literacy," provides a pedagogical apparatus that gives new instructors a flexible, supportive structure for adapting the readings and assignments to their own needs and interests.

The "Explorations" sections that appear at the end of each reading, for example, are meant to spur students to think about their own writing and reading processes, to generate class discussion, to introduce concepts, to direct students' attention to rhetorical strategies used in the essays, to help students consider a particular theme in a reading, or to assist students in comparing how similar themes are treated differently by various authors. To reach these goals, instructors can use "Explorations" in a variety of ways. They can be used as in-class discussion questions, as the basis for small-group work or collaborative projects, as short writing assignments, as part of an ongoing writer's notebook, or as the starting point for longer writing projects.

The "Writing before Reading" prompts that are found before each selection are meant to generate student inquiry about issues raised in the reading. Students may respond to these prompts in a writer's notebook, which we discuss in Part 1, or in a class discussion.

The sections titled "Further Suggestions for Writing," which appear at the end of Parts 2, 3, and 4, can also be modified by instructors. These writing suggestions are deliberately complex, encouraging students to find their own way into a topic of inquiry or research. These suggestions offer general guidelines, and they are meant to be suggestive, not prescriptive. Instructors may assign these prompts as they are written and let students decide which aspects of the assignment to focus on, or they may discuss the prompts with their students and together construct a revised approach. Instructors might also work with their students in rewriting a particular part of a prompt to emphasize one of the many aspects that the prompt addresses.

Part 1 of *Writing Lives: Exploring Literacy and Community* introduces strategies for reading and writing that are central to our approach in teaching first-year writing. While we expect that many instructors will supplement *Writing Lives* with a rhetoric, Part 1, "The Practice of Literacy," provides a context for the readings and accompanying suggestions for writing and discussion that follow. It is a resource that students and instructors can return to as they move through the readings and writing activities. The section on peer response, for example (pp. 16–19), is designed to help students become better peer responders and to help them learn how to incorporate feedback from their peers into their revised work. Since participation in peer responding groups or workshops is a progressive activity, students may return to this section to reflect on their own experiences and to continue to refine their own skills as peer responders and writers.

The next three parts contain selected readings, contextual information, "Writing before Reading," "Explorations," and "Further Suggestions for Writing." If used in the order in which the readings are presented, the book moves the student writer through three distinct but interrelated sections devoted to personal literacies, academic literacies, and public literacies.

The readings in Part 2, "Personal Literacies," were selected to prompt students to recollect and analyze their past literacy experiences within the context of particular communities. This unit encourages students to practice a stance they will develop during the course—that of a self-reflexive reader and writer—as they integrate the aims of the personal narrative with more common academic forms such as the expository essay. While Part 2 encourages students to see the value of their own experiences with literacy, it also suggests that they incorporate other voices—the voices of their communities and the voices of the authors they are reading—into their writing on literacy.

Part 3, "Academic Literacies," builds on the definitions of personal and communal literacies by examining what it means to be literate in an academic institution. Students consider social, political, and economic factors that influence how they negotiate the often difficult boundaries between home communities and the academy. In their writing, students examine multiple literacies at work in the university, including those not tied to a specific discipline or academic discourse. The "Writing before Reading," "Explorations," and "Suggestions for Further Writing" prompts in Part 3 ask students to use ethnographic methods to "read" specific sites and their attendant texts and develop analytic and persuasive essays presenting their interpretations.

Part 4, "Public Literacies," promotes further attention to audience and point of view by examining the significance of public discourse. The readings in this part examine how public images and media messages represent institutions and ideas and influence their intended audiences. The readings offer students ways of effectively engaging with and using public discourse in the academic sphere. While many students are familiar with the examples of public literacy described in the readings, instructors may also want to direct students beyond the readings to conduct research on particular examples of public literacy. A central goal of Part 4 is to help students participate in public literacies and negotiate representations of meaning in larger social contexts.

In taking such a broad view of literacy, *Writing Lives: Exploring Literacy and Community* provides a rich resource on the topic of literacy that can be used by students and instructors as a springboard for further research. We invite instructors and students to use the book to enter the ongoing conversations about literacy.

The idea for *Writing Lives: Exploring Literacy and Community* originated in 1993 with the staff of the First-Year Writing Program at The Ohio State University for use in its first-year writing courses. The reader was reorganized in 1995 to focus on the theme of literacy. We selected this topic for its obvious links to the study of reading and writing, and because it allows us to value the knowledge students bring to a first-year course while also encouraging them to examine critically how knowledge is constructed and used within various communities.

Writing Lives: Exploring Literacy and Community is unique in other ways: It was largely developed and written by graduate-student writing program administrators for incoming graduate teaching associates in the First-Year Writing Program at Ohio State. It was designed and tested to be used in a one-quarter long writing course, but it can also be adapted to semester systems.

The Ohio State University, like many other academic institutions, relies heavily on graduate student instructors and adjunct faculty to teach first-year writing. We have kept these instructors in mind as we developed this reader, and we hope that *Writing Lives: Exploring Literacy and Community* and its instructor's handbook will be particularly useful in programs with similar staffing demographics. We have attempted to provide first-year writing students and their instructors with a range of materials that illuminate the relationships between various literacy practices and individuals, communities, and cultures. While the readings explore the connections among culture and context evident in various language practices, the pedagogical apparatus of *Writing Lives: Exploring Literacy and Community* challenges students to recognize the ways in which language carries values and power and, in turn, to use this knowledge as writers themselves. The organization of the readings and pedagogical apparatus emphasizes this invitation to students to enter into a dialogue with their instructors, with the readings, and with each other.

ACKNOWLEDGMENTS

Writing Lives: Exploring Literacy and Community is the result of a collaborative work in progress carried out among graduate teaching associates, faculty, and staff associated with the First-Year Writing Program at The Ohio State University. In 1993, and under the leadership and inspiration of Suellynn Duffey, the program reexamined its rationale and approach to first-year writing courses and the professional development of graduate-student instructors. *Writing Lives: Exploring Literacy and Community* and the writing course it suggests have their roots in the first set of readings that were used and two subsequent custom-published editions.

Writing Lives: Exploring Literacy and Community reflects the ideas and hard work of many current and former writing instructors, including Victoria Dunn, Carrie Dirmeikis, Natalie Fields, Nathan Grey, Paul Hanstedt, Carrie Leverenz, Gianna Marsella, Chuck Schroeder, Melinda Turnley, Teresa Doerfler, Jane Greer, Amy Goodburn, and Lori Mathis.

Graduate students, who teach the majority of first-year writing sections at The Ohio State University, were instrumental in the development of this reader and all of its prior incarnations. These instructors selected most of the essays, developed and tested the pedagogical apparatus, and wrote most of the supplementary material.

Many others have helped in a variety of ways: Andrea Lunsford, vice-chair of composition and rhetoric; Carla Wilks, the Writing Program secretary; Sheila Craft and Tan Le, undergraduate work-study students who provided research support; and Jim Phelan, the chair of the Department of English, all provided encouragement throughout this project. Especially important to the development of this reader are the hundreds of graduate teaching associates at Ohio State who taught first-year writing and offered their suggestions and feedback. Their advice has been indispensable. The following graduate teaching associates deserve special acknowledgment: Janet Badia, Jennifer Cognard-Black, Tinitia Coleman, Ben Feigert, Natalie Fields, Melissa Goldthwaite, Sandee McGlaun, and Jean Williams.

We are grateful for the many suggestions we received from instructors at other institutions across the country. We heartily acknowledge and thank the following colleagues: John Alberti, Northern Kentucky University; Valerie Balester, Texas A & M University; Jane Duga, Cleveland State University; Patricia E. Eney, Miami University, Middletown Campus; Kevin Griffith, Capital University; Christine W. Heilman; Cynthia Lewieki-Wilson, Miami University; Margaret Lindgren, University of Cincinnati; Marilyn Palkovacs, University of Cincinnati; Crystal R. Robinson, Columbus State Community College; Kathleen A. Welsch, Xavier University; Betty Youngkin, University of Dayton.

Thanks also to Meg Spilleth, Steve Debow, and Keith Mullins of St. Martin's Press for their persistence and assistance in getting this book to press.

We hope that *Writing Lives: Exploring Literacy and Community* will serve well all those teachers and students who use it to examine the shared knowledge that contributes to their diverse literacies.

Sara Garnes
David Humphries
Vic Mortimer
Jennifer Phegley
Kathleen R. Wallace

WRITING LIVES
EXPLORING LITERACY AND COMMUNITY

1
THE PRACTICE
OF LITERACY

ENTERING THE CONVERSATION

As its title suggests, the selections in *Writing Lives: Exploring Literacy and Community* explore the themes of literacy and community. But more specifically, this book encourages *you* to explore these themes through your own writing. Take a moment to look at the cover art by Barbara Kruger. This piece asks you, quite emphatically, "Why are you here?" Kruger's work, which combines language with visual imagery, takes up an entire wall at the bottom of the main staircase at The Ohio State University's Wexner Center for the Arts. It is usually the first piece of art that a visitor encounters at the Wexner, and it sets a definite tone for the rest of the visit. The visitor feels compelled to respond by reflecting upon the reasons why she or he is visiting this particular art center.

We selected this piece of art to encourage you to ask the same question of your participation in a college first-year writing course. Why are you taking this course? Why are you attending college? We admit that these are big questions with many implications. If you have trouble coming up with answers, consider the witty possibilities that Kruger included in her work. Look closely at the cover, and you will find even more text just below the figure's mouth. Are you here:

to kill time?
to get cultured?
to widen your world?
to think good thoughts?
to improve your social life?

As you can see, questions lead to more questions, a process that may lead you as a student (or museum visitor!) to come up with answers to the question "Why are you here?" Take some time to explore your responses to this question in writing. You will find that you will gain valuable insight into how and why you write.

We have provided you with numerous opportunities to write as you work through Part 1 and the subsequent selections on personal, academic, and public literacies. We have labeled these sections "Writing before Reading" and "Explorations." They are designed to help you explore your thoughts in writing as well as generate class discussion both before and after you read the selections. We explain these types of writing in more detail later in this chapter. But before you read what we have to say about literacy, we invite you to begin your work as a writer by responding to the prompt below. Keep copies of what you write in a folder or in a notebook. Your response will become the basis for some of your written work on invention, composition, and revision techniques throughout the rest of this chapter.

WRITING BEFORE READING

How do you define literacy? Who and what helped you to arrive at that definition? Is literacy learned? Can it be measured? How do we recognize a literate person?

LITERACY AND COMMUNITY

When you wrote about literacy in response to the "Writing before Reading" exercise above, you probably wrote about how literacy is connected to reading and writing. Literacy refers to the ability to read and write, but it is also about recognizing, valuing, and using many different kinds of knowledge, or what we call in this book *literacies.*

As a first-year writing student in college, you already possess tremendous abilities in reading, writing, and other language practices. But you may not be as aware of the other ways in which you are literate. Perhaps you are especially adept at deciphering the conventions of Hollywood movies or the intricacies of major league sports. Perhaps you are a member of two different language communities, conversing with your grandparents in Vietnamese while using English on campus and your job. Perhaps you are particularly aware of the differences between various places and their physical and cultural environments. These are all examples of the range of literacies you will explore in this book.

We mean to give you a sense of how literacy, in all its complexity, involves our ability to recognize the communities we belong to and the knowledge that they value. Literacy is generally thought of as something we acquire in our homes, schools, and communities. However, we find that it is more accurate to say that we also *practice* literacy. Literacy demands that we negotiate between communities while recognizing that not all communities value the same kinds of knowledge or behaviors.

As you read, write, and take part in classroom discussions about the topics raised by these selections, you will notice that many people, including some of the writers included here, find *literacy* difficult to define. Different cultures value literacy for many reasons. In the United States, we hear much talk about *functional literacy*, a type of literacy that ensures that people can read and write well enough to participate in the political process and the economic system. When most of us think of literacy, we often define it in these terms. We usually define *illiteracy* as the inability to read or write; this aspect of literacy is most often covered by the media. These definitions of literacy are popular, but they are also limited. Literacy, or even better, *literacies*, is a necessarily broad concept. Different literacies require different abilities. Being literate in the United States includes things as seemingly mundane as understanding driving conventions and as politically relevant as understanding the basics of the U.S. Constitution. The former is important for navigating roadways and the latter for understanding the nuances of the latest presidential campaign as it is covered, for instance, in *The New York Times* or discussed in on-line chat rooms.

Literacy, then, can be broadly interpreted. It includes knowing printed texts as well as understanding practices, rituals, traditions, and even the layout of physical space and how it is used. If you want a quick experience of this extended sense of literacy, visit a service of a religious denomination that is not your own. You will probably notice some similarities; but you will also notice that the regular members of the congregation are much more in tune—or literate—about what is happening in that space than you are.

The selections in *Writing Lives: Exploring Literacy and Community* share a thematic concern with literacy, broadly defined. For some of these writers, for example George Orwell, literacy is tied primarily to the acts of reading and writing. For other authors, for example bell hooks, access to literacy also involves questioning access to power and privilege. Still other writers write about practices—such as Dumpster diving (described by Lars Eighner) or using computer technology (described by Barbara Kantrowitz)—that can also be understood as instances of literacy.

READING AS A WRITER

We wrote earlier that literacy is practiced within the contexts of various communities and social situations. If you start thinking of academic literacies as knowledge shared by certain groups in certain situations, you will begin to see how many literacies are at work on college campuses. Some of the literacies you practice while in college include those of your chosen major. Consider, for instance, how engineering majors and history majors use different professional jargon in their respective fields. But academic literacies also include learning how to participate in activities such as lectures and seminars as well as in college football games, fraternity or sorority parties, and other experiences unique to college settings. Academic literacies also include the lore, traditions, and values of particular institutions and of education in general.

Reading plays an essential part in your acquisition of these and other college literacies, and it also plays a significant role in how you acquire and participate in literacies (such as ecological and public literacies) that have application beyond your years in formal education. You already read for many reasons: to discover meaning and purpose, to observe organization and style, to reflect upon the relationships between others' and your own writing, to determine where you stand in relation to an author's argument, and to build common ground for class discussions of both reading and writing. You may even read and write for the sheer pleasure of it. When we use the word *reading* in this book, we are referring to *active reading*. Active reading is the form of reading all your professors will expect you to carry out. When you read actively, your purpose may be to clarify your thinking, to further develop an assignment, or to answer a question.

Active reading requires that you read with a questioning mind. Your professors will expect you to come to class with well-thought out questions about your reading. Learning to ask productive questions is part of acquiring the literacies prized in higher education. In your writing classroom, practicing your ability to ask questions of your instructors, peers, and the material you read will help you become a better writer. As you practice the art of asking questions, you will, among other things:

1. become more engaged with your reading and class discussions,
2. develop more focused papers, and
3. carry out more productive and, ultimately, more interesting research projects.

Reading and writing are interdependent activities. When you read with a questioning mind, you take part in a conversation with an author and his or her ideas. As you become more involved with your reading, you will find ways to *apply* what you read to your own writing projects. Your least successful work will occur when you "read up" on a subject and plunk down a string of quotes from established "authorities." Your best written work comes about when you reflect upon what you read and use it to support *your* ideas.

Reading actively and critically will help you write papers that you and your audience will find more engaging. Throughout *Writing Lives* we offer questions about readings to encourage you to think critically about the reading selections and your own writing. You will find "Writing before Reading" prompts throughout Part 1 and preceding each selection in Parts 2, 3, and 4. These questions are meant to engage your own thoughts and experiences *before* you read. We also include questions called "Explorations" after each selection. These questions are designed to help you prepare for class discussion as well as explore, through your own writing, your responses to what you read. "Explorations" typically direct your attention to specific features or themes central to each selection while inviting you to reflect upon your own writing processes. At the end of Parts 2, 3, and 4, we include "Further Suggestions for Writing." These suggestions often take the form of extended questions. You should use our questions to develop your own inquiry about a topic, an inquiry which will lead to your own essays, research papers, or other forms of writing.

Use the following guidelines to prompt your active reading:

- Read to understand the writer's message.
- Use the reading to explore your own thinking about the topic.
- Question the material and the writer's point of view.
- Measure the writer's experiences against your own.
- Identify the writer's audience.
- Explain why a writer uses certain examples to support his or her purpose in writing.
- Ask why the writer selected a particular form of writing.
- Question the writer's use of certain words or special jargon.

Writing in Response to Reading

You will generate a wealth of material and insights into what you read if you read actively. Writing as you read will help you keep track of and develop your thoughts. We call this type of writing *informal* because it is not meant to be as polished as the papers you turn in for a grade. Informal writing lets you explore your thinking, develop new ideas, or experiment with different writing styles. As you read *Writing Lives*, we recommend that you practice regularly at least two types of informal writing: 1) Taking notes in the margins of the selections as you read and 2) using a writer's notebook to develop longer ideas and thoughts about your reading and writing.

Taking notes in the margins helps you carry on a running conversation with the author of the piece you are reading. This type of note taking is essential to active reading. Practice the following note taking activities while you read:

- Write directly in the book. (If this makes you squeamish, use an erasable pen or pencil.)
- Highlight, underline, or circle passages or phrases you think are important.
- Pay attention to language. If you like the way the author wrote a passage or phrase, make a note of it.

Keeping a writer's notebook helps you keep track of your responses to your reading and to explore your thinking about your own development as a writer. Your writer's notebook can take many forms. You might want to use a spiral notebook, loose-leaf paper bound in a three-ring binder, or you might decide to produce your writer's notebook directly on a personal computer.

There are many uses for your writer's notebook. We have set up the "Writing before Reading" and "Explorations" sections in this book to prompt entries in your writer's notebook. Your instructor might present another model for you to follow or may not assign such a notebook at all. Either way, we strongly recommend that you keep a writer's notebook to collect your ideas. We asked you earlier to write about literacy. If you haven't already done so, make that entry the first one in your writing journal.

Your writer's notebook is a valuable aid as you participate in class discussions and as you begin longer writing assignments. Use your writer's notebook to write about your responses to the reading selections. You might begin by describing your gut level reaction to a text or by describing its formal features. Reflect upon the following questions:

- What is my emotional response to this piece of writing? Does it make me angry, enthusiastic, bored? Which passages seem to contribute most directly to this response?
- What did I find interesting about the piece, either in terms of the topic, the writer's point of view, or the writer's style?
- How well are the ideas developed?
- How well are the claims supported with details and examples?
- How well is the essay organized?
- Do the tone and style of the essay seem appropriate for the writer's purpose and audience?

EXPLORING THE WRITING PROCESS

Before we offer suggestions about the writing process, take a few minutes and remember times when you were writing or were expected to write.

Writing before Reading

How you write is often directly related to how you feel about writing. Perhaps you were a reporter, or you had to prepare a senior project in high school. Do you remember writing in grade school? Have you ever had to write on the job? Perhaps your supervisor asked you to write a description of your job responsibilities. Using specific memories and concrete details, write in response to any or all of the following questions: How do you feel about your writing and writing in general? How do these feelings affect how you respond to a writing assignment? Do you feel differently about writing that is not assigned for a class? How would you describe good or bad writing? What is good or bad about your writing? Who gave you this kind of feedback about your work?

Most writing tasks come in the form of assignments. In college, you will be expected to write many types of assignments, but the academic paper is the most prevalent. Academic writing, unlike the informal writing you do for exploration, is directed outward toward other people who will respond to and evaluate your work.

Deciding what to write about is one of the most significant challenges associated with academic writing. Most instructors will give you general guidelines for assignments, but they probably will not tell you exactly what to write about. An instructor might ask you to write a first-person narrative essay about personal literacy, but you will need to determine your focus within that large subject area. You will also need to determine your point of view.

Much of the work of writing is in exploring a subject to locate your focus and point of view. You can start this work right away by using the active reading techniques we discussed in the previous section. If your instructor supplies a written prompt, read it actively, marking questions in the margins and underlining significant passages. Then write about the assignment in your writer's notebook, recording your initial thoughts and generating more questions. Think about this early writing as a "writing to discover" exercise that will eventually lead you to a topic to explore further in your essay.

Invention Techniques:
Brainstorming, Freewriting, Clustering

Generating ideas is hard work. In the past, you may have found yourself stymied by the blank page or computer screen in front of you as you struggled to get a paper written. Those first words are often the hardest to produce, and writers often get into trouble by thinking that these first words have to be perfect. Professional and practiced writers, however, know that writing involves many false starts. These false starts are productive parts of the writing process because they help you discover both your true interests and the direction your final draft should take.

In this section, we introduce you to several *invention techniques* that will help you generate material about your assignment *before* you start composing a draft. You might also use these techniques to generate responses to the "Writing before Reading" and "Explorations" prompts throughout *Writing Lives*. The techniques we discuss here are brainstorming, clustering, and freewriting. In addition to helping you start an assignment, these techniques are also useful throughout the composing and revising process because they help you develop more material and think through connections in your paper. These invention techniques may at times overlap as you use them.

Brainstorming: Brainstorming is the process of generating ideas. It is focused writing you do by yourself or with a group of writers. For instance, you could brainstorm about possible topics for an assignment. All ideas are useful ideas while you are brainstorming. Sometimes the ones that seem least productive at first may actually contain the seeds of your final essay.

To use brainstorming as an invention strategy, write nonstop for at least 10 to 15 minutes in response to a word or idea. Try to write continuously, without pausing to check your spelling or edit your thoughts. Do not consider whether your ideas are "good" or "bad" at this point. The purpose of brainstorming is to get ideas out of your head and onto paper or into a word processing program where you can work with them.

We have included an example of brainstorming on the topic of "literacy" below.

BRAINSTORMING ON LITERACY:

--Things you do: Literacy is about reading and
writing.
--Things you have: Literacy is about books,
computers, libraries.
--Society: Literacy is a social issue; people
worry about literacy the way they worry about
heart disease, immunization shots, drug problems.
--Literacy is personal: Reading and writing are
usually done alone. When I think of reading, I
think of my favorite spots to read, and I
always picture myself alone, reading. When I
think of writing, I think of a writer up late,
alone.
--But reading is about society: Again, it's a
social issue. Also, reading and writing,
although done alone, involve communication
between two or more people.
--Issue: Does literacy help society or individuals more? Is that a fair distinction?
--Communication is good for society; it holds
people together.

```
--Literacy is a skill that helps individuals
get ahead.
--What do we do with literacy? Can we decide on
our own?
--Pictures: I'm thinking of those cash regis-
ters with little pictures of soft-drinks and
french fries. Is that literacy? What about
knowing which picture to click on on the com-
puter? Is that literacy?
--Big Issue: Words always seem to be involved
with literacy. Why are words better than pic-
tures or other things? I'm thinking of talking
in a second language: For a beginner, like me,
it's almost impossible to talk on the phone; in
person, I can get my ideas across. So communi-
cation is more than words?
-- Ranking: I'm wondering why we rank things
the way we do. Should we measure literacy by
happiness (???), dollars, books read, kindness?
I mean, what good does literacy REALLY do for
people. If it's important, why is it important?
-- From the last point:  What values are behind
literacy?  What do we imagine when we imagine
that everyone is literate?
```

Notice that this brainstorming looks a lot like a list, but it includes both one-word items and full sentences. Your own brainstorm might look more like a piece of prose, running from one side of the page to another in continuous sentences. But the effect is roughly the same. Read your brainstorming out loud. Now read the example above out loud. Did you notice how you started to associate certain words and images with others? That's the beauty of brainstorming—it creates meaning by creating associations.

Freewriting: Freewriting is an invention technique that gives you practice in writing freely and quickly. When you freewrite, you write so quickly that the editor in your mind, that critical voice that tells you that none of the words or sentences sound right, has no chance to slow you down. Freewriting will help you produce something that you can then work with. You can also use focused freewriting as an invention strategy. When you freewrite, you write about anything that comes to mind. When you do focused freewriting, you start with a topic or idea.

Use focused freewriting in your writer's notebook to further develop the subject of "literacy." Write nonstop for 10-15 minutes. Even if you get stuck and cannot think of something to say, just keep writing, even if you only write "I can't think of anything, I can't think ..." for a minute or two. Eventually, you will get back to the subject, and you will probably find that your writing got easier, more free, as you wrote along.

Here is an example of freewriting prompted by the word "literacy." The author of this freewrite wrote it on a computer.

```
        TEN MINUTES OF FREE-WRITING ON "LITERACY"
                      (AS WRITTEN)

    Literacy is something that everyone should
have, like immunization shots. I say immuniza-
tion shots because that's the kind of thing you
see posters for, and you also see posters some-
times for literacy. Everyone should be liter-
ate/or everyone should be immunized. This makes
it seem like everyone, almost, is literate, but
I don't know if that's true. I don't know how
they pick those people in the posters, either.
Usually they are either race car drivers or
basketball players.
    Literacy is also something that you should
have, like books. I mean, it's hard to think of
literacy without thinking of books and
libraries. The thing is, where do you go from
there? Books you can see, touch, hold, accumu-
late. I personally like to keep books so that I
can feel like I really know what's in them. If
I get a book from the library, I worry that
some day I will forget everything and wonder if
I ever understood what was in it. I don't usu-
ally look at my old books, though.
    Literacy is books. I say that because books
are something you hold onto and they are easy
to describe. I noticed that I just wrote "say."
I could have written "wrote." That's confusing.
Confusing, confusing. Literacy is confusing. I
think it's confusing because it's not just
something you have but something you do. That's
abstract--doing is abstract. How do you do lit-
eracy?
    Maybe it's not just something you do, but a
skill. That's also abstract, but it's something
that you CAN do whenever you have to. Like
free-throw shooting. I just noticed, as I
paused for a second (ok, I know that I should
continuously type, but I pursed, just for a
second), I just noticed that I have been break-
ing this up into paragraphs. I don't know why--
```

I think that I just did that whenever it looked
like I had typed a paragraph. I think that's
kind of skill, like literacy, because I have
been typing papers for a long time, and now I
just know some things, I have some skills, but
I don't even know exactly what they are.
    When I write something that's creative, I
try to tie things up. That's what's hard about
this kind of free-floating. I want to say something about literacy that I can use... Literacy
is, literacy is, literacy is about books and
other things. What other things? Computers,
paper, notebooks, journals, sign-language, I
don't know what else. I always used to hate to
go into the computer lab because there were
those guys (usually guys, I just edited that on
the spot) who would snicker when you would say
how do I print from this program? They would
say things that I wouldn't understand, usually,
or talk about computer things that I didn't
understand. They usually were playing games or
something and they intimidated me whenever I
asked them how to print or why something wasn't
working.
    I guess that's literacy, too. I have been
thinking about literacy for a long time, I
think. Why is everything confusing? I am about
to finish this, but I don't know how, in the
next thirty seconds can I think of something...
Literacy, race-car drivers, books. There is a
lot to this literacy thing.

Notice how the author of this focused freewriting example keeps
a running commentary going on his thoughts. Compare what you
wrote to this exercise by reading it out loud. Use the active reading
strategies we discussed in the previous section to identify passages
you believe are significant or that you might want to explore further.
You can then use these passages as prompts for additional rounds of
freewriting.

Clustering: Another invention strategy is clustering. Like brainstorming and freewriting, clustering can be used at various times: as
a first step in invention, as a way to further work with a bit of
freewriting, or to identity and develop key ideas in a completed draft.
Clustering is different from the other invention techniques because
it creates a visual map of your ideas. When you cluster, you start with
a key word, circle it, and then you let that first word suggest related

words and images. As you fill up the page, circle your key words and use lines to link them to related ones.

While you practice clustering, let your "right brain" take over. The right hemisphere of the brain is commonly associated with pattern making and creativity. The right brain sees the whole picture; the left brain sees parts. The right brain synthesizes; the left brain analyzes. The right brain is intuitive; the left brain is logical. In clustering, the right brain develops a pattern and sparks a piece of writing. Once the writing is completed, the left brain edits, revises, and so on. Of course, we alternate between logic and intuition all the time, and not always predictably; clustering will help you begin to see patterns. Clustering works well for some people, while for others it does not work at all. Practice it a few times, at various stages of the writing process and for different kinds of assignments, to see if it can be useful to you.

The next step is to write down all of the words and phrases triggered by the keyword. Cluster until you get an "aha" feeling; at that point, begin writing. The writing is what completes the process of clustering. Here is an example of clustering:

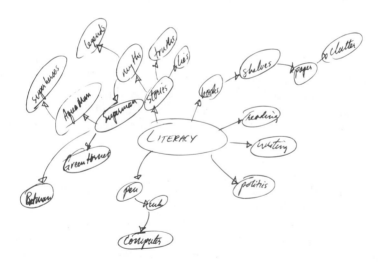

I like to tell myself that my first encounter with print involved books, like the biographies of famous Americans I read when I was in second and third grade. Those books focused on the boyhoods of people like Benjamin Franklin, George Washington, and Francis Marion (the Swamp Fox). There were probably books about women, too, but if there were, I didn't read them.

But I also read comic books – Superman (kind of dull), Aqua Man, Batman, and the Green Hornet. Each These stories fired my imagination, at least for a time. Perhaps they fed on fantasies of power and dominance in imaginary worlds where it was always clear who the good guys and bad guys were, and where the good guys always won. So if I want to forget that I ever read and enjoyed comic books, perhaps it is because I do not want to acknowledge that I, once upon a time, read anything as "naive" as comic books...

Our clustering exercise began with the key word *literacy*. Note that only some of the ideas that appear in the cluster made it into the writing that followed. That is not unusual. In fact, sometimes none of the words in an original cluster make it to a final draft. The example of clustering that we have included here was done as an exploratory exercise. The writer who did the cluster had spent a year thinking about literacy, especially about the books he had read in grade school. This writer was surprised that comic books came up in connection with literacy. Clustering can create conditions that lead to such surprises in your writing by helping you uncover ideas and experiences that you might otherwise have overlooked.

Clustering can also lead you to perspectives that you might otherwise miss. You might see and develop relationships among things and ideas. Clustering is also useful after you finish a freewriting exercise. Reread what you wrote and circle those ideas or thoughts or words that seem significant. Cluster those ideas and key terms that seem connected. Copy these items onto another piece of paper and try to extend the connections further.

In your writer's notebook, try to cluster your freewriting on "literacy." Once you have copied the first cluster from the freewrite onto a clean sheet of paper, extend the cluster out further. Explore the connections which emerge among these ideas. Notice that the cluster above is asymmetrical. Pay attention to places where your own cluster is crowded. Because they are more developed, such areas may indicate ideas that could become the focus of a paper.

Composing a Draft

We have offered several suggestions for generating material that you can use in your written work. Of course, not all composing processes work equally well for all writers. You may already have a process that works well for you. If you like to crash through a first draft and then restructure it later, go ahead. If you like to use a formal outline, go ahead. If you find, however, that your current method does not produce the results you want, try something else, or ask your instructor and classmates for advice.

We cannot help but make patterns of the information we take in. In fact, making meaning involves putting together, finding, or creating patterns. Clustering is a visual way of mapping these thought patterns. When you compose a draft, you are making meaning. When you sit down to write a draft, you might think that you have your paper all mapped out. Be willing, though, to accept some surprise developments.

Always assume that you will write more than one draft. Some people call the first draft the "discovery draft" in which writers make their first attempts at moving from writing for themselves to writing for others. By writing drafts, you free yourself from the need to make your writing perfect the first time around. When you write drafts, you also give yourself the opportunity to incorporate feedback from others into your work.

If you've taken the time to read actively and do some invention work, you are ready to compose the draft of a formal essay. The "blank" page or computer screen is not really blank at all. You have all your margin notes, the reflections in your writer's notebook, and discussions with classmates as resources. Before you begin to write, take time to review what you've already written. You might find interconnected ideas that you want to explore further. You might also make an outline of major points that you want to follow.

First drafts are often a swirl of ideas, some more developed than others. Expect less than perfection at this early stage. Just as you used invention exercises to produce a lot of potential material, you should look at the composing process as your opportunity to produce lots of text. Try not to be overly critical of your work as you compose. It is best to be more critical during revision, when you actually have paragraphs and pages to work with. The longer you can delay that criticism, the more time you have to generate and explore ideas. Your goal while composing is to create a draft that you can later mine for the ideas, illustrations, and turns of phrase that will provide the foundations for a polished essay.

As you plan your first draft, consider two important elements of your rhetorical situation: the audience and the purpose of your paper. In your writer's notebook, brainstorm about how you might best reach your audience with your message. Consider using some of the tools of the writer's trade: narration (telling a story), description (providing concrete, sensory detail), exposition (using comparison and contrast, analogies, examples, process analysis, classification, enumeration, causation, effects, definition), and persuasion. Throughout the composing and revising process you will reassess this material.

Peer Response: The Writer's Community

It's a myth that writing is a completely solitary activity. Parts of writing, such as those late nights spent revising, can be solitary, but writing also has its social aspects. Your writing is always dependent upon audience and is influenced by a variety of social contexts. But the process works both ways. You have probably already found that reading the work of others sparks new ideas and perspectives that enrich your own writing.

After you compose a draft, ask for feedback from someone who will give you an honest and helpful appraisal of your work. Requesting, giving, and evaluating such responses to your writing is essential to your growth as a writer and is the foundation of the process we call peer response. You will participate in peer response groups as a reader and as a writer. Reading your classmates' work gives you another opportunity to communicate your ideas to others. And, when your work is discussed by your peers, you have the opportunity to talk about your writing in new and specific ways.

Writing courses often incorporate peer response. You might find yourself working one-on-one with a classmate, or you might work in small groups. Both models require that you actively read each other's work and offer suggestions for further development.

Peer response groups vary in structure and procedure. You might stay in one group all term. In such a group, you have a chance to get to know each writer better, and you may become more comfortable sharing your writing and offering honest responses. Other models for peer response rotate members from group to group. This method might expose you to a greater range of writing in your class, provide you with a wider variety of responses to your own writing, and give you the opportunity to get to know more of your classmates. You might take copies of your peers' drafts home, respond to them in writing, and discuss them during the next class meeting. You might read the drafts during class and respond to them verbally. Your instructor might or might not participate in your group.

In whatever fashion peer response is handled in your course, you have multiple opportunities to practice active reading and writing strategies as you participate. As a reader of your peers' writing, you will need to read actively, responsively, and responsibly. In the process, you will find ways to develop your own work while you assist your peers.

Suggestions for Responding to the Work of Your Peers

Remember that the characteristics of good writing vary according to the assignment or the writer's intended audience and purpose. Useful peer response also varies accordingly. Your instructor may have your class develop a list of desirable traits that characterize a strong draft for a particular writing assignment. If your instructor does not lead such a group activity, brainstorm in your writer's notebook about such traits. In doing so, you will find that your suggestions during peer response will be more focused and ultimately helpful to the writers in your group.

Read each draft thoroughly: Read each draft once, straight through, without a pen in hand so that you get a sense of the paper as a whole before you respond to it in writing. Then, reread it actively, making specific comments in the margins and final comments on the final page. You want to give the writer a sense of your overall view of the paper. Write a sentence or two summarizing what you see as the main purpose of the essay. The writer will then be able to compare your response to what she or he had attempted to do.

How to respond to grammar issues: If you are responding to a first draft, keep your focus on helping your peers develop their ideas and structure and wait until you see another draft before you offer suggestions about grammar. However, if you only see one draft of a paper, or if the paper contains repeated mistakes in grammar or usage that make it difficult for you to follow the writer's train of thought, point these errors out to the writer and indicate how they might be corrected.

Talk about the written work, not the writer: Avoid personal attacks. Remember that you are trying to help the writer express his or her point of view, which may not be one that you agree with. If you see faulty logic, point it out. Remember that your group members will also be responding to your work. Approach their writing as you would want them to approach yours.

Keep your responses focused on writing issues: Explain your responses thoroughly. Avoid saying something is "good" or "bad" or "confusing" unless you explain specifically what you mean.

Be honest: Your responses to the work in front of you should point specifically to the strengths and weaknesses of the paper. For example, if a writer sets forth a convincing argument with relevant, supporting details, point this out. If you find that a writer needs to describe a procedure more clearly so you can follow it, point that out too. You should also try to indicate what sections made the paper interesting and which could be improved. Try to tell the writer what is most effective in his or her paper. By pointing out what works, you also help a writer understand why other sections may not have been as effective.

What to Do When Your Work Is Being Discussed

You can prepare for your turn during peer response by writing in your writer's notebook before your peer response meeting. Before you meet with your response group, assess your draft by recalling your audience and purpose for writing. Describe your audience and purpose for writing this particular essay, and describe what you like best and least about this particular draft. You might decide to distribute a copy of what you wrote to your peers with your draft. If you do so, you can guide their reading of your work and you might find their comments more helpful as a result.

Before your paper is the focus of peer response:

- Prepare a few questions about parts of your essay that you are concerned about or that you would like your peers to address.

- Identify the strongest and weakest areas of your essay and compare your opinions with those of your readers.

- Take notes so that you remember the suggestions you are given. You might also ask for written comments from your group members. It is helpful to have all these comments when you begin to revise.

- Be prepared to ask respondents to clarify their comments and to give concrete examples from your essay. You should not, however, automatically argue or enter into a prolonged discussion with a respondent if you disagree. Instead, think about why that respondent might disagree or be confused. Ask yourself if your paper supports or explains your point sufficiently.

- Try to separate yourself from your ego as much as possible. Because written work seems to be a personal representation of who we are, it is often difficult to make this separation. In order for peer response to be beneficial, try not to view criticism of your work as criticism of yourself. Avoid defensiveness by listening to responses first and then evaluating them before you respond verbally.

After each peer response session, write about your experience in your writer's notebook. Use these entries to help you prepare for future peer response sessions. Consider the following questions to get started on your entry: What did you find helpful during the session? What do you wish had gone differently? What kinds of questions did you and your group members ask about the essays? Did you give and receive the kinds of comments you expected? Or, were you surprised by some of the comments that your group made? How does this experience compare to times when you alone critiqued your drafts?

When you revise, consider the merit of the feedback you received. Incorporate only those suggestions that help you develop the paper in the ways you want it to go. Remember that you are the authority, the *author* of the essay, and it is up to you to make the final decisions as to what goes in and what does not.

REVISION

Feedback from others is a significant part of revision. It may help to think of revision as *re-vision*: looking at something again, as though for the first time. But even *re-vision* does not completely express all the work that goes into writing another draft. While revising, you do not just look at your draft again. You also must completely rethink your ideas. The words *pruning* and *shaping* better describe the process of revision. Although you may have to cut back on some parts of your work, other parts of your work that appeared only as the faint promise of buds in your first draft may start to grow. This type of revision is very different from *editing*, an activity that is concerned primarily with the final preparation of a manuscript.

The goal of revision is to produce a draft that is directed toward your audience. Drafts that successfully accomplish this goal are characterized by reader-based prose. This type of writing consciously anticipates the reader's expectations. Take time to reconsider your assignment and think through the original purpose in writing your paper. Reconsider your potential audience for your paper.

To do this, you need to anticipate questions your audience might have. You will also have to make decisions (such as how to organize your essay or how to choose the best examples to support your controlling idea) with your reader in mind. For example, if you are writing to an audience of geodetic science professors, you probably do not have to define "GPS." However, if you are writing for an audience of nonscientists, you might have to explain that the Global Positioning System (GPS) is a network of navigational satellites.

Effective revision demands that you become an active reader of your own work and that you evaluate and incorporate the suggestions of those who gave you feedback. In asking the following questions of your work, you may find that you need more feedback.

- Does the message you intended to write come across in the paper?

- Have you clearly conveyed your ideas to the audience that will read your paper?

- Are there significant and relevant ideas that still need development?
- Have you made sure that all your evidence and discussion support your paper's thesis or controlling idea?
- Do you need more detail?
- Do you need more or different types of evidence to support your ideas or arguments?
- Do the general tone and language you use create the effect you want?
- Do you need to do some more research? Check some facts?
- Do you need more or different evidence to support your claims?
- Would you enjoy reading this?

If you uncovered weak spots in your paper while considering these questions, you still have some revision to do. Reread your assignment, but also reconsider the topic you have decided to explore. As you worked through the inventing, composing, and drafting stages, you probably discovered questions that you needed to address to make your paper solid. Question-driven research is the sort of research that is expected on the college level. Determine where you would be most likely to find the information you need: You might use reference materials from the library, search the World Wide Web, post questions on an electronic bulletin board, conduct a site visit, or arrange an interview.

After you receive responses to your drafts, map out a revision plan in your writer's notebook. You might start your plan by describing what you usually do when you revise. If the course and your participation in peer response have given you ideas about approaching revision, say so. Writing this plan should keep you from feeling overwhelmed by the number of revisions you are considering. You might, for instance, respond to three or four of the most common comments from your peers or instructor. Try categorizing the suggestions for revision you received, responding to the ones that require the most work first. Respond to comments and questions about your essay with direct notes to yourself such as "I want to add this quote here, I need an example there."

Preparing the Final Draft

After you finish revising, you are ready to edit your work. Final editing includes making sure that the format of your work is appropriate for the assignment. Read your paper carefully during final editing. Check your spelling, proofread your grammar, and change phrasing where needed to clarify your meaning. Then, read your paper again, but out loud. By reading out loud, you will notice passages that you stumble over. Rewrite these passages so you can read them smoothly.

Appearances matter in written work. Follow your instructor's guidelines for preparing the draft you turn in for evaluation. Some will expect you to follow a specific style guide such as the MLA or Chicago Manual of Style. Remember, however, that the conventions for manuscript preparation vary among disciplines and among journals, magazines, and newspapers. If you follow the expected conventions, your intended audience will respond more favorably to your work

When You Receive a Grade and Written Responses

Your instructor may review a draft of your essay. His or her responses, like those of your peer group, should be considered as you prepare a revised version of the paper. You should also use these responses as you prepare your next assignment. Ask questions if you need clarification, or you might want to schedule a conference with your instructor to talk about your work. Prepare for such a conference as you would for your peer response group, and take some time after the conference to jot down your thoughts in your writer's notebook.

After you've completed an essay assignment and have received a grade, you might be asked to reflect on the process of the paper from the first brainstorming to the final, polished draft. Even if you don't receive such an assignment, this kind of reflection can be very useful to you as you chart your growth as a writer. In your writer's notebook, consider the following questions:

- What decisions did you make as you wrote and revised? What factors led to the choices you made?

- How did the responses of your peers and instructor influence your writing process and the final draft of your paper?

- What, if any, were the relationships between other texts you read while researching your paper and the process of writing your paper?

- In what ways did your previous experience as a student and your expectations about college writing and reading influence your drafts?

What do you think about your paper now that it has been evaluated?

2
PERSONAL LITERACIES

After years of working with words, writers often reflect on how they first became acquainted with language and how they came to understand language through their writing and experiences. These reflections, or personal literacy narratives, encourage writers to examine how their identity has been expressed and shaped through language. Writers, like all of us, explore and express their individuality through language. The literacy narrative, however, gives writers a vehicle for their examinations of how the values and beliefs of communities influence the rules and boundaries of language use and personal behavior. Personal literacy narratives, then, are stories of individual growth that reflect upon the factors that shaped that growth.

Consider for a moment how you have come to understand language. Perhaps as a child you had a favorite book or story that your parents read to you. This book or story may have helped you to learn about language by sparking your imagination or by making you curious about learning to read and write. While this story may be an intimate part of your personal history of becoming literate, it originated in a broader community. Children's stories such as "Little Red Riding Hood," "Br'er Rabbit," and those of Dr. Seuss all reflect different communities and values that may or may not overlap. For example, several of the Dr. Seuss stories teach fundamental skills in counting and identifying colors. The story of "Little Red Riding Hood" teaches the lesson that appearances may be deceiving. The tales of "Br'er Rabbit" show how cleverness allows the seemingly weak to triumph over the strong but stupid.

Different communities, different eras, and different authors are likely to have varied perspectives on the same issue, and in choosing to read or to tell particular stories, parents express their own sets of values. Your appreciation of a story's "importance" expresses both your own values and those of the communities to which you belong.

Understanding the language of a community and learning to read and write, then, are basic components of acquiring literacy. But to become truly literate, you also need to know the values of your community. Lars Eighner illustrates this kind of literacy in his essay "On Dumpster Diving." Eighner has the literacy necessary to "read" Dumpsters as well as the literacy to "read" the values of the society that produces the Dumpsters. This literacy allows Eighner to survive and succeed in this society. Frederick Douglass also suggests that literacy is intertwined with society and its values. His access to education is limited by the society in which he lived. In order for him to acquire and use the skills of reading and writing, he had to identify and challenge the values of society and place his acquisition of literacy within the context of the communities to which he belonged.

Our memories and our histories are often housed in our stories, which we share through different uses of language. In some sense, we *are* the stories we create and tell; we are the language we use to understand and express ourselves. Literacy is more than simply reading and writing. To be literate requires that we grasp the complexity of how language functions in communities.

The following readings illustrate these complex understandings of literacy. Some authors focus more on their own experiences with language and literacy. Others focus more on communities and the values behind different kinds of literacy. Each reading, though, will challenge you to consider not only *how* an author acquired a certain kind of literacy, but also *why* that literacy was valued by a particular community. In turn, you will be asked to reflect on your own process of acquiring literacies and how this process is intertwined with your membership in different communities.

EXPLORATION

Think about your favorite childhood book. Which communities does it most reflect? Describe the community values or desires expressed by this book.

Why I Write

GEORGE ORWELL

George Orwell (1903–1950) was the pseudonym used by
Eric Blair, a writer best known for his novels Animal Farm
(1945) and 1984 (1949). The son of a low-level British official, Orwell was born in India. As a young man, Orwell served
five years as a member of the Indian Imperial Police in Burma.
Although his experiences in Burma formed the basis for
Orwell's first published novel, Burmese Days (1934), and
several prominent essays, including "Shooting an Elephant"
and "A Hanging," Orwell did not achieve enduring prominence as a writer until Animal Farm was published. As Orwell
notes in "Why I Write," his success as a writer was closely
linked to his sense of political purpose. A self-described
"democratic Socialist," Orwell often alienated himself from
the British left through his outspoken critiques of left-wing
politics, including Animal Farm, which satirizes the rise and
decline of socialism in the former Soviet Union.

WRITING BEFORE READING

*How would you answer the question "Why do I write?" Other than
writing assigned for school or work, what other kinds of writing do you
do? Do people have to consider themselves writers in order to write?*

From a very early age, perhaps the age of five or six, I knew that   1
when I grew up I should be a writer. Between the ages of about seventeen and twenty-four I tried to abandon this idea, but I did so
with the consciousness that I was outraging my true nature and that
sooner or later I should have to settle down and write books.

I was the middle child of three, but there was a gap of five years   2
on either side, and I barely saw my father before I was eight. For this
and other reasons I was somewhat lonely, and I soon developed disagreeable mannerisms which made me unpopular throughout my
schooldays. I had the lonely child's habit of making up stories and
holding conversations with imaginary persons, and I think from the
very start my literary ambitions were mixed up with the feeling of
being isolated and undervalued. I knew that I had a facility with
words and a power of facing unpleasant facts, and I felt that this created a sort of private world in which I could get my own back for my
failure in everyday life. Nevertheless the volume of serious—i.e. seriously intended—writing which I produced all through my childhood

and boyhood would not amount to half a dozen pages. I wrote my
first poem at the age of four or five, my mother taking it down to dic-
tation. I cannot remember anything about it except that it was about
a tiger and the tiger had "chair-like teeth"—a good enough phrase,
but I fancy the poem was a plagiarism of Blake's "Tiger, Tiger." At
eleven, when the war of 1914–18 broke out, I wrote a patriotic
poem which was printed in the local newspaper, as was another, two
years later, on the death of Kitchener. From time to time, when I was
a bit older, I wrote bad and usually unfinished "nature poems" in
the Georgian style. I also, about twice, attempted a short story which
was a ghastly failure. That was the total of the would-be serious work
that I actually set down on paper during all those years.

However, throughout this time I did in a sense engage in literary   3
activities. To begin with there was the made-to-order stuff which I
produced quickly, easily and without much pleasure to myself. Apart
from school work, I wrote *vers d'occasion*, semi-comic poems which
I could turn out at what now seems to me astonishing speed—at fourteen I wrote a whole rhyming play, in imitation of Aristophanes, in
about a week—and helped to edit school magazines, both printed and
in manuscript. These magazines were the most pitiful burlesque stuff
that you could imagine, and I took far less trouble with them than I
now would with the cheapest journalism. But side by side with all this,
for fifteen years or more, I was carrying out a literary exercise of
a quite different kind: this was the making up of a continuous "story"
about myself, a sort of diary existing only in the mind. I believe this is
a common habit of children and adolescents. As a very small child I
used to imagine that I was, say, Robin Hood, and picture myself as the
hero of thrilling adventures, but quite soon my "story" ceased to be
narcissistic in a crude way and became more and more a mere description of what I was doing and the things I saw. For minutes at a time
this kind of thing would be running through my head: "He pushed
the door open and entered the room. A yellow beam of sunlight, fil-
tering through the muslin curtains, slanted on to the table, where a
matchbox, half open, lay beside the inkpot. With his right hand in his
pocket he moved across to the window. Down in the street a tortoise-
shell cat was chasing a dead leaf," etc etc. This habit continued till I
was about twenty-five, right through my non-literary years. Although
I had to search, and did search, for the right words, I seemed to be
making this descriptive effort almost against my will, under a kind of
compulsion from outside. The "story" must, I suppose, have reflected the styles of the various writers I admired at different ages, but so far
as I remember it always had the same meticulous descriptive quality.

When I was about sixteen I suddenly discovered the joy of mere   4
words, i.e. the sounds and associations of words. The lines from
Paradise Lost,

> So hee with difficulty and labour hard
> Moved on: with difficulty and labour hee,

which do not now seem to me so very wonderful, sent shivers down my backbone; and the spelling "hee" for "he" was an added pleasure. As for the need to describe things, I knew all about it already. So it is clear what kind of books I wanted to write, in so far as I could be said to want to write books at that time. I wanted to write enormous naturalistic novels with unhappy endings, full of detailed descriptions and arresting similes, and also full of purple passages in which words were used partly for the sake of their sound. And in fact my first completed novel, *Burmese Days*, which I wrote when I was thirty but projected much earlier, is rather that kind of book.

I give all this background information because I do not think one can assess a writer's motives without knowing something of his early development. His subject matter will be determined by the age he lives in—at least this is true in tumultuous, revolutionary ages like our own—but before he ever begins to write he will have acquired an emotional attitude from which he will never completely escape. It is his job, no doubt, to discipline his temperament and avoid getting stuck at some immature stage, or in some perverse mood: but if he escapes from his early influences altogether, he will have killed his impulse to write. Putting aside the need to earn a living, I think there are four great motives for writing, at any rate for writing prose. They exist in different degrees in every writer, and in any one writer the proportions will vary from time to time, according to the atmosphere in which he is living. They are:

1. Sheer egoism. Desire to seem clever, to be talked about, to be remembered after death, to get your own back on grown-ups who snubbed you in childhood, etc etc. It is humbug to pretend that this in not a motive, and a strong one. Writers share this characteristic with scientists, artists, politicians, lawyers, soldiers, successful businessmen—in short, with the whole top crust of humanity. The great mass of human beings are not acutely selfish. After the age of about thirty they abandon individual ambition—in many cases, indeed, they almost abandon the sense of being individuals at all—and live chiefly for others, or are simply smothered under drudgery. But there is also the minority of gifted, wilful people who are determined to live their own lives to the end, and writers belong in this class. Serious writers, I should say, are on the whole more vain and self-centred than journalists, though less interested in money.

2. Aesthetic enthusiasm. Perception of beauty in the external world, or, on the other hand, in words and their right arrangement. Pleasure in the impact of one sound on another, in the firmness of good prose or the rhythm of a good story. Desire to share an expe-

rience which one feels is valuable and ought not to be missed. The aesthetic motive is very feeble in a lot of writers, but even a pamphleteer or a writer of textbooks will have pet words and phrases which appeal to him for non-utilitarian reasons; or he may feel strongly about typography, width of margins, etc. Above the level of a railway guide, no book is quite free from aesthetic considerations.

    3. Historical impulse. Desire to see things as they are, to find out true facts and store them up for the use of posterity.   8

    4. Political purpose—using the word "political" in the widest possible sense. Desire to push the world in a certain direction, to alter other people's idea of the kind of society that they should strive after. Once again, no book is genuinely free from political bias. The opinion that art should have nothing to do with politics is itself a political attitude.   9

    It can be seen how these various impulses must war against one another, and how they must fluctuate from person to person and from time to time. By nature—taking your "nature" to be the state you have attained when you are first adult—I am a person in whom the first three motives would outweigh the fourth. In a peaceful age I might have written ornate or merely descriptive books, and might have remained almost unaware of my political loyalties. As it is I have been forced into becoming a sort of pamphleteer. First I spent five years in an unsuitable profession (the Indian Imperial Police, in Burma), and then I underwent poverty and the sense of failure. This increased my natural hatred of authority and made me for the first time fully aware of the existence of the working classes, and the job in Burma had given me some understanding of the nature of imperialism: but these experiences were not enough to give me an accurate political orientation. Then came Hitler, the Spanish civil war, etc. By the end of 1935 I had still failed to reach a firm decision. I remember a little poem that I wrote at that date, expressing my dilemma: 10

> A happy vicar I might have been
> Two hundred years ago,
> To preach upon eternal doom
> And watch my walnuts grow;
>
> But born, alas, in an evil time,
> I missed that pleasant haven,
> For the hair has grown on my upper lip
> And the clergy are all clean-shaven.
>
> And later still the times were good,
> We were so easy to please,
> We rocked our troubled thoughts to sleep
> On the bosoms of the trees.

All ignorant we dared to own
The joys we now dissemble;
The greenfinch on the apple bough
Could make my enemies tremble.

But girls' bellies and apricots,
Roach in a shaded stream,
Horses, ducks in flight at dawn,
All these are a dream.

It is forbidden to dream again;
We maim our joys or hide them;
Horses are made of chromium steel
And little fat men shall ride them.

I am the worm who never turned,
The eunuch without a harem;
Between the priest and the commissar
I walk like Eugene Aram;

And the commissar is telling my fortune
While the radio plays,
But the priest has promised an Austin Seven,
For Duggie always pays.

I dreamed I dwelt in marble halls,
And woke to find it true;
I wasn't born for an age like this;
Was Smith? Was Jones? Were you?[1]

The Spanish war and other events in 1936–37 turned the scale and thereafter I knew where I stood. Every line of serious work that I have written since 1936 has been written, directly or indirectly, *against* totalitarianism and *for* democratic Socialism, as I understand it. It seems to me nonsense, in a period like our own, to think that one can avoid writing of such subjects. Everyone writes of them in one guise or another. It is simply a question of which side one takes and what approach one follows. And the more one is conscious of one's political bias, the more chance one has of acting politically without sacrificing one's aesthetic and intellectual integrity.

What I have most wanted to do throughout the past ten years is 11 to make political writing into an art. My starting point is always a feeling of partisanship, a sense of injustice. When I sit down to write a book, I do not say to myself, "I am going to produce a work of art." I write it because there is some lie that I want to expose, some fact to which I want to draw attention, and my initial concern is to get a hearing. But I could not do the work of writing a book, or even a long magazine article, if it were not also an aesthetic experience.

---

[1] This poem first appeared in the *Adelphi*, December 1936.

Anyone who cares to examine my work will see that even when it is downright propaganda it contains much that a full-time politician would consider irrelevant. I am not able, and I do not want, completely to abandon the world-view that I acquired in childhood. So long as I remain alive and well I shall continue to feel strongly about prose style, to love the surface of the earth, and to take pleasure in solid objects and scraps of useless information. It is no use trying to suppress that side of myself. The job is to reconcile my ingrained likes and dislikes with the essentially public, non-individual activities that this age forces on all of us.

It is not easy. It raises problems of construction and of language, 12 and it raises in a new way the problem of truthfulness. Let me give just one example of the cruder kind of difficulty that arises. My book about the Spanish civil war, *Homage to Catalonia*, is, of course, a frankly political book, but in the main it is written with a certain detachment and regard for form. I did try very hard in it to tell the whole truth without violating my literary instincts. But among other things it contains a long chapter, full of newspaper quotations and the like, defending the Trotskyists who were accused of plotting with Franco. Clearly such a chapter, which after a year or two would lose its interest for any ordinary reader, must ruin the book. A critic whom I respect read me a lecture about it. "Why did you put in all that stuff?" he said. "You've turned what might have been a good book into journalism." What he said was true, but I could not have done otherwise. I happened to know, what very few people in England had been allowed to know, that innocent men were being falsely accused. If I had not been angry about that I should never have written the book.

In one form or another this problem comes up again. The prob- 13 lem of language is subtler and would take too long to discuss. I will only say that of late years I have tried to write less picturesquely and more exactly. In any case I find that by the time you have perfected any style of writing, you have always outgrown it. *Animal Farm* was the first book in which I tried, with full consciousness of what I was doing, to fuse political purpose and artistic purpose into one whole. I have not written a novel for seven years, but I hope to write another fairly soon. It is bound to be a failure, every book is a failure, but I know with some clarity what kind of book I want to write.

Looking back through the last page or two, I see that I have 14 made it appear as though my motives in writing were wholly public-spirited. I don't want to leave that as the final impression. All writers are vain, selfish and lazy, and at the very bottom of their motives there lies a mystery. Writing a book is a horrible, exhausting struggle, like a long bout of some painful illness. One would never undertake such a thing if one were not driven on by some demon whom one can neither resist nor understand. For all one knows that demon is simply the same instinct that makes a baby squall for attention. And yet it is also true that one can write nothing readable unless one constantly struggles to efface one's own personality. Good prose is like a window pane. I cannot say with certainty which of my motives are the strongest, but I know which of them deserve to be followed. And looking back through my work, I see that it is invariably where I lacked a *political* purpose that I wrote lifeless books and was betrayed into purple passages, sentences without meaning, decorative adjectives and humbug generally.

EXPLORATIONS

1. In what ways is writing a solitary act for Orwell? In what ways is it a communal or public act? What do you think?

2. What does "the importance of the age" mean to Orwell? How important do you think it is for writers to characterize their own age in some way?

3. Orwell suggests that all writing is political. Following his argument, explain how this might be so. Then, discuss your own point of view.

4. Orwell lists four motivations for becoming a writer. Which, if any, of these seem important to you? Can you think of any other motivations for writing?

5. Since many high schools use *Animal Farm* and *1984* , you may already be familiar with Orwell's writing. How does being familiar with an author affect the way you read his or her work?

Turning Topsy Turvey

MARY ANN WILLIAMS

Mary Ann Sheridan Williams (1945–1991) was born in Delaware County, Ohio. She earned her B.A. at Wilmington College, her M.A. at The Ohio State University, and her Ph.D. from the Union for Experimenting Colleges and Universities in Cincinnati. She was a poet, playwright, solo actress, and theatrical director. Williams was also an important part of The Ohio State University, where she was a faculty member, chair, and coordinator of broadcast productions for the Department of Black Studies. The following poem was written for the dedication of the Shepard Library in Columbus, Ohio.

WRITING BEFORE READING

Notice the different kinds of language that Williams uses in her poem. Can you identify some of the sources from which she gets particular words and expressions?

Mary had a little lamb   1
    Who said so?
Its fleece were white as snow
    What happened to all the cute Black lambs?
Little Miss muffet sat on a tuffet   5
    Say, Man, doesn't Topsy have a leading role?

All the school books that I saw cried jungle savages and lifetime
        primitives
    when it came to my kind
But now more books talk about me.   10
    Phillis Wheatley and Paul Lawrence D
        Paved the way for the writing of Black Like Me

When I scan the packed shelves of Shepard I'm proud to see
    Maya Angelou and good ol' Alex Haley lookin' right back
        as determined as can be   15

These polished books have neat pages and the pages, long and
        short words and the words, friendly letters
My Black people shuffled, cried and died to learn those strange
        letters, study those long words, turn the endless
        pages and fondle the worn covers of books with   20
        trembling but with the steadfast stubborness of a
        mule who will work no more

My strawhatted and bandana covered Black people shined with
          quiet folk wisdom in the days when Death was the
          grader of all who dared to read   25
Swift Death pranced by with each Black letter committed to
          memory and each ragged book that these brave
          poets of life hid in the rhythms of their curious
          souls

Tender thoughts met Death's whip and hooves with a relentless   30
          hope of freeing the mind as well as the body
Death trampled many on the backroad to learning

Unlike the story of Jesus of Nazareth, they did not rise on the
          third day
          They yet cry from their unmarked graves   35
          to all mothers and fathers of would-be literates:
          "Teach your children to read and write. You must live
              for the answer to ignorance. You must twist each
              darkened hollow stare into a glimmer of knowing.
              Each little face must feel the joy of unlocking the   40
              ageless secrets of the written word . "
These impressionable bits of human clay can travel without
          leaving your doorstep.
They can unravel the countless mysteries of their sorrow-
          filled past and cloudy future.   45
They can rush into the arms of God by understanding the
          many voices of the past who leave their marks in the
          Holy Book
Teach these young Black children to laugh at themselves
          through our tales of long ago   50
Teach them to love letters, words, pages, books————so that
          when they look at you, they will know that you
          care.

EXPLORATIONS

1. What are some of the connections that Williams makes between literacy and a sense of history? How does she make these connections?

2. What kind of power does Williams see in the act of reading and writing?

3. Why does Williams value the contents of books as well as their actual
   physical qualities? What are some of the descriptions she uses to
   describe books?

Literacy in Three Metaphors

SYLVIA SCRIBNER

Sylvia Scribner (1923–) received her B.A. from Smith College in 1943 and her Ph.D. from the New School for Social Research in 1970. A social scientist who has spent a great deal of time in West Africa and who is currently affiliated with the Graduate Center of the City University of New York, Scribner is the co-author of The Psychology of Literacy *and other works in which she examines the complex relationships between social factors and the growth and development of individuals. The following essay begins with a similar examination and addresses how various definitions of literacy affect how individuals are perceived and how they respond to the world around them.*

WRITING BEFORE READING

Think back to the first days of your writing course. In what ways has your idea of literacy changed since then?

Although literacy is a problem of pressing national concern, we have yet to discover or set its boundaries. This observation, made several years ago by a leading political spokesman (McGovern 1978), echoes a long-standing complaint of many policymakers and educators that what counts as literacy in our technological society is a matter "not very well understood" (Advisory Committee on National Illiteracy 1929).

A dominant response of scholars and researchers to this perceived ambiguity has been to pursue more rigorously the quest for definition and measurement of the concept. Many approaches have been taken (among them, Adult Performance Level Project 1975; Bormuth 1975; Hillerich 1976; Kirsch and Guthrie 1977–78; Miller 1973; Powell 1977), and at least one attempt (Hunter and Harman 1979) has been made to put forward an "umbrella definition." Each of these efforts has identified important parameters of literacy, but none has yet won consensual agreement (for a thoughtful historical and conceptual analysis of shifting literacy definitions, see Radwin [1978]).

The definitional controversy has more than academic significance. Each formulation of an answer to the question "What is literacy?" leads to a different evaluation of the scope of the problem (i.e., the extent of *il*literacy) and to different objectives for programs aimed at the formation of a literate citizenry. Definitions of literacy shape our perceptions of individuals who fall on either side of the standard (what a "literate" or "nonliterate" is like) and thus in a deep way affect both the substance and style of educational programs. A chorus of clashing answers also creates problems for literacy planners and educators. This is clearly evident in the somewhat acerbic comments of Dauzat and Dauzat (1977, p. 37), who are concerned with adult basic education: "In spite of all of the furor and the fervor for attaining literacy . . . few have undertaken to say what they or anyone else means by literacy. Those few professional organizations, bureaus and individuals who have attempted the task of explaining 'what is literacy?' generate definitions that conflict, contradict but rarely complement each other. . . . These 'champions of the cause of literacy' crusade for a national effort to make literacy a reality without establishing what that reality is."

What lies behind the definitional difficulties this statement decries? The authors themselves provide a clue. They suggest that literacy is a kind of reality that educators should be able to grasp and explain, or, expressed in more classical terms, that literacy has an "essence" that can be captured through some Aristotelian-like enterprise. By a rational process of discussion and analysis, the "t rue" criterial components of literacy will be identified, and these in turn can become the targets of education for literacy.

Many, although by no means all, of those grappling with the problems of definition and measurement appear to be guided by such a search for the "essence"—for the "one best" way of conceptualizing literacy. This enterprise is surely a useful one and a necessary component of educational planning. Without denigrating its contribution, I would like to suggest, however, that conflicts and contradictions are intrinsic to such an essentialist approach.

Consider the following. Most efforts at definitional determination are based on a conception of literacy as an attribute of *individuals;* they aim to describe constituents of literacy in terms of individual abilities. But the single most compelling fact about literacy is that it is a *social* achievement; individuals in societies without writing systems do not become literate. Literacy is an outcome of cultural transmission; the individual child or adult does not extract the meaning of written symbols through personal interaction with the physical objects that embody them. Literacy abilities are acquired by individuals only in the course of participation in socially organized activities with written language (for a theoretical analysis of literacy as a set of socially organized practices, see Scribner and Cole [1981]). It follows that individual literacy is relative to social literacy. Since social literacy practices vary in time (Resnick [1983] contains historical studies) and space (anthropological studies are in Goody [1968]), what qualifies as individual literacy varies with them. At one time, the ability to write one's name was a hallmark of literacy; today in some parts of the world, the ability to memorize a sacred text remains the modal literacy act. Literacy has neither a static nor a universal essence.

The enterprise of defining literacy, therefore, becomes one of [7] assessing what counts as literacy in the modern epoch in some given social context. If a nation-society is the context, this enterprise requires that consideration be given to the functions that the society in question has invented for literacy and their distribution throughout the populace. Grasping what literacy "is" inevitably involves social analysis: What activities are carried out with written symbols? What significance is attached to them, and what status is conferred on those who engage in them? Is literacy a social right or a private power? These questions are subject to empirical determination. But others are not: Does the prevailing distribution of literacy conform to standards of social justice and human progress? What social and educational policies might promote such standards? Here we are involved, not with fact but with considerations of value, philosophy, and ideology similar to those that figure prominently in debates about the purposes and goals of schooling. Points of view about literacy as a social good, as well as a social fact, form the ground of the definitional enterprise. We may lack consensus on how best to define literacy because we have differing views about literacy's social purposes and values.

These differing points of view about the central meaning of literacy warrant deeper examination. In this essay, I will examine some [8] of them, organizing my discussion around three metaphors: literacy as adaptation, literacy as power, and literacy as a state of grace. Each of these metaphors is rooted in certain assumptions about the social motivations for literacy in this country, the nature of existing literacy practices, and judgments about which practices are critical for individual and social enhancement. Each has differing implications for educational policies and goals. I will be schematic in my discussion; my purpose is not to marshal supporting evidence for one or the other metaphor but to show the boundary problems of all. My argument is that any of the metaphors, taken by itself, gives us only a partial grasp of the many and varied utilities of literacy and of the complex social and psychological factors sustaining aspirations for and achievement of individual literacy. To illustrate this theme, I will draw on the literacy experiences of a Third World people who, although remaining at an Iron Age level of technology, have nevertheless evolved varied functions for written language; their experience demonstrates that, even in some traditional societies, literacy is a "many-meaninged thing."

LITERACY AS ADAPTATION

This metaphor is designed to capture concepts of literacy that   9
emphasize its survival or pragmatic value. When the term "functional literacy" was originally introduced during World War I (Harman 1970), it specified the literacy skills required to meet the tasks of modern soldiering. Today, functional literacy is conceived broadly as the level of proficiency necessary for effective performance in a range of settings and customary activities.

This concept has a strong commonsense appeal. The necessity   10
for literacy skills in daily life is obvious; on the job, riding around town, shopping for groceries, we all encounter situations requiring us to read or produce written symbols. No justification is needed to insist that schools are obligated to equip children with the literacy skills that will enable them to fulfill these mundane situational demands. And basic educational programs have a similar obligation to equip adults with the skills they must have to secure jobs or advance to better ones, receive the training and benefits to which they are entitled, and assume their civic and political responsibilities. Within the United States, as in other nations, literacy programs with these practical aims are considered efforts at human resource development and, as such, contributors to economic growth and stability.

In spite of their apparent commonsense grounding, functional   11
literacy approaches are neither as straightforward nor as unproblematic as they first appear. Attempts to inventory "minimal functional competencies" have floundered on lack of information and divided perceptions of functionality. Is it realistic to try to specify some uniform set of skills as constituting functional literacy for all adults? Two subquestions are involved here. One concerns the choice of parameters for defining a "universe of functional competencies." Which literacy tasks (e.g., reading a newspaper, writing a check) are "necessary," and which are "optional"? The Adult Performance Level Project test (1975), one of the best conceptualized efforts to specify and measure competencies necessary for success in adult life, has been challenged on the grounds that it lacks content validity: "The APL test fails to meet this [validity] criterion . . . not necessarily because test development procedures were technically faulty, but because it is not logically possible to define this universe of behaviors [which compose functional competence] without respect to a value position which the test developers have chosen not to discuss" (Cervero 1980, p. 163).

An equally important question concerns the concept of uniformity. Do all communities and cultural groups in our class-based and   12
heterogeneous society confront equivalent functional demands? If

not, how do they differ? Some experts (e.g., Gray 1965; Hunter and
Harman 1979) maintain that the concept of functional literacy
makes sense only with respect to the proficiencies required for participation in the actual life conditions of particular groups or
communities. But how does such a relativistic approach mesh with
larger societal needs? If we were to consider the level of reading and
writing activities carried out in small and isolated rural communities
as the standard for functional literacy, educational objectives would
be unduly restricted. At the other extreme, we might not want to use
literacy activities of college teachers as the standard determining the
functional competencies required for high school graduation. Only
in recent years has research been undertaken on the range of literacy activities practiced in different communities or settings within the
United States (e.g., Heath 1980, 1981; Scribner 1982a), and we still
know little about how, and by whom, required literacy work gets
done. Lacking such knowledge, public discussions fluctuate between
narrow definitions of functional skills pegged to immediate vocational and personal needs, and sweeping definitions that virtually
reinstate the ability to cope with college subject matter as the hallmark of literacy. On the other hand, adopting different criteria for
different regions or communities would ensure the perpetuation of
educational inequalities and the differential access to life opportunities with which these are associated.

Adapting literacy standards to today's needs, personal or social,   13
would be shortsighted. The time-limited nature of what constitutes
minimal skill is illustrated in the "sliding scale" used by the U. S.
Bureau of Census to determine literacy. During World War I, a
fourth-grade education was considered sufficient to render one literate; in 1947, a U. S. Census sample survey raised that figure to five
years; and by 1952 six years of school was considered the minimal
literacy threshold. Replacing the school-grade criterion with a functional approach to literacy does not eliminate the time problem.
Today's standards for functional competency need to be considered
in the light of tomorrow's requirements. But not all are agreed as
to the nature or volume of literacy demands in the decades ahead.
Some (e.g., Naisbitt 1982) argue that, as economic and other activities become increasingly subject to computerized techniques of
production and information handling, even higher levels of literacy
will be required of all. A contrary view, popularized by McLuhan
(1962, 1964) is that new technologies and communication media
are likely to reduce literacy requirements for all. A responding argument is that some of these technologies are, in effect, new systems of
literacy. The ability to use minicomputers as information storage and
retrieval devices requires mastery of symbol systems that build on
natural language literacy; they are second-order literacies as it were.

One possible scenario is that in coming decades literacy may be increased for some and reduced for others, accentuating the present uneven, primarily class-based distribution of literacy functions.

From the perspective of social needs, the seemingly well-defined 14 concept of functional competency becomes fuzzy at the edges. Equally as many questions arise about functionality from the individual's point of view. Functional needs have not yet been assessed from the perspective of those who purportedly experience them. To what extent do adults whom tests assess as functionally illiterate perceive themselves as lacking the necessary skills to be adequate parents, neighbors, workers? Inner-city youngsters may have no desire to write letters to each other; raising one's reading level by a few grades may not be seen as a magic ticket to a job; not everyone has a bank account that requires the mastery of unusual forms (Heath 1980). Appeals to individuals to enhance their functional skills might founder on the different subjective utilities communities and groups attach to reading and writing activities.

The functional approach has been hailed as a major advance over 15 more traditional concepts of reading and writing because it takes into account the goals and settings of people's activities with written language. Yet even tender probing reveals the many questions of fact, value, and purpose that complicate its application to educational curricula.

We now turn to the second metaphor. 16

LITERACY AS POWER

While functional literacy stresses the importance of literacy to 17 the adaptation of the individual, the literacy-as-power metaphor emphasizes a relationship between literacy and group or community advancement.

Historically, literacy has been a potent tool in maintaining the 18 hegemony of elites and dominant classes in certain societies, while laying the basis for increased social and political participation in others (Resnick 1983; Goody 1968). In a contemporary framework, expansion of literacy skills is often viewed as a means for poor and politically powerless groups to claim their place in the world. The International Symposium for Literacy, meeting in Persepolis, Iran (Bataille 1976), appealed to national governments to consider literacy as an instrument for human liberation and social change. Paulo Freire (1970) bases his influential theory of literacy education on the need to make literacy a resource for fundamental social transformation. Effective literacy education, in his view, creates a critical consciousness through which a community can analyze its conditions of social existence and engage in effective action for a just society. Not to be literate is a state of victimization.

Yet the capacity of literacy to confer power or to be the primary [19] impetus for significant and lasting economic or social change has proved problematic in developing countries. Studies (Gayter, Hall, Kidd, and Shivasrava 1979; United Nations Development Program 1976) of UNESCO's experimental world literacy program have raised doubts about earlier notions that higher literacy rates automatically promote national development and improve the social and material conditions of the very poor. The relationship between social change and literacy education, it is now suggested (Harman 1977), may be stronger in the other direction. When masses of people have been mobilized for fundamental changes in social conditions—as in the USSR, China, Cuba, and Tanzania—rapid extensions of literacy have been accomplished (Gayter et al. 1979; Hammiche 1976; Scribner 1982*b*). Movements to transform social reality appear to have been effective in some parts of the world in bringing whole populations into participation in modern literacy activities. The validity of the converse proposition—that literacy per se mobilizes people for action to change their social reality—remains to be established.

What does this mean for us? The one undisputed fact about illit- [20] eracy in America is its concentration among poor, black, elderly, and minority-language groups—groups without effective participation in our country's economic and educational institutions (Hunter and Harman 1979). Problems of poverty and political powerlessness are, as among some populations in developing nations, inseparably intertwined with problems of access to knowledge and levels of literacy skills. Some (e.g., Kozol 1980) suggest that a mass and politicized approach to literacy education such as that adopted by Cuba is demanded in these conditions. Others (e.g., Hunter and Harman 1979) advocate a more action-oriented approach that views community mobilization around practical, social, and political goals as a first step in creating the conditions for effective literacy instruction and for educational equity.

The possibilities and limits of the literacy-as-power metaphor [21] within our present-day social and political structure are not at all clear. To what extent can instructional experiences and programs be lifted out of their social contexts in other countries and applied here? Do assumptions about the functionality and significance of literacy in poor communities in the United States warrant further consideration? Reder and Green's (1984) research and educational work among West Coast immigrant communities reveals that literacy has different meanings for members of different groups. How can these cultural variations be taken into account? How are communities best mobilized for literacy—around local needs and small-scale activism?

or as part of broader political and social movements? If literacy has not emerged as a priority demand, should government and private agencies undertake to mobilize communities around this goal? And can such efforts be productive without the deep involvement of community leaders?

LITERACY AS A STATE OF GRACE

Now we come to the third metaphor. I have variously called it 22 literacy as salvation and literacy as a state of grace. Both labels are unsatisfactory because they give a specific religious interpretation to the broader phenomenon I want to depict—that is, the tendency in many societies to endow the literate person with special virtues. A concern with preserving and understanding scripture is at the core of many religious traditions, Western and non-Western alike. As studies by Resnick and Resnick (1977) have shown, the literacy-as-salvation metaphor had an almost literal interpretation in the practice of post-Luther Protestant groups to require of the faithful the ability to read and remember the Bible and other religious material. Older religious traditions—Hebraic and Islamic—have also traditionally invested the written word with great power and respect. "This is a perfect book. There is no doubt in it," reads a passage from the Qur'an. Memorizing the Qur'an—literally taking its words into you and making them part of yourself—is simultaneously a process of becoming both literate and holy.

The attribution of special powers to those who are literate has its 23 ancient secular roots as well. Plato and Aristotle strove to distinguish the man of letters from the poet of oral tradition. In the perspective of Western humanism, literateness has come to be considered synonymous with being "cultured," using the term in the old-fashioned sense to refer to a person who is knowledgeable about the content and techniques of the sciences, arts, and humanities as they have evolved historically. The term sounds elitist and archaic, but the notion that participation in a literate—that is, bookish—tradition enlarges and develops a person's essential self is pervasive and still undergirds the concept of a liberal education (Steiner 1973). In the literacy-as-a-state-of-grace concept, the power and functionality of literacy is not bounded by political or economic parameters but in a sense transcends them; the literate individual's life derives its meaning and significance from intellectual, aesthetic, and spiritual participation in the accumulated creations and knowledge of humankind, made available through the written word.

The self-enhancing aspects of literacy are often given a cognitive 24 interpretation (Greenfield and Bruner 1969; Olson 1977). For

centuries, and increasingly in this generation, appeals have been
made for increased attention to literacy as a way of developing
minds. An individual who is illiterate, a UNESCO (1972) publication states, is bound to concrete thinking and cannot learn new
material. Some teachers of college English in the United States (e.g.,
Farrell 1977) urge greater prominence for writing in the curriculum
as a way of promoting logical reasoning and critical thinking.
Literate and nonliterate individuals presumably are not only in different states of grace but in different stages of intellectual development as well. Although evidence is accumulating (Scribner and Cole
1981) refuting this view, the notion that literacy per se creates a
great divide in intellectual abilities between those who have and
those who have not mastered written language is deeply entrenched
in educational circles of industrialized countries.

The metaphor of literacy-as-grace, like the others, has boundary   25
problems. For one thing, we need to know how widely dispersed this
admiration of book knowledge is in our society. To what extent are
beliefs about the value of literateness shared across social classes and
ethnic and religious groups? How does book culture—more accurately, how do book cultures—articulate with the multiple and
diverse oral cultures flourishing in the United States? Which people
value literacy as a preserver of their history or endow their folk
heroes with book learning? Are there broad cultural supports for
book learning among wide sectors of the population? McLuhan and
others have insisted that written literacy is a vestige of a disappearing
"culture." Is this point of view defensible? And if so, what implications does it pose for our educational objectives?

I have described some current views of the meaning of literacy in   26
terms of three metaphors. I have tried to indicate that each metaphor
embraces a certain set of, sometimes unexamined, values; moreover,
each makes assumptions about social facts in our society—the utilities
of literacy and the conditions fostering individual attainment of literacy status. These metaphors are often urged on us as competitive;
some choice of one or the other does in fact seem a necessary starting point for a definitional enterprise. But for purposes of social and
educational planning, none need necessarily become paramount
at the expense of the others; all may have validity. To illustrate this
argument, I will briefly describe research on the social meaning of literacy among a West African people. Learning how literacy functions
among a people far removed from us culturally and geographically
may help us take a new look at its functions here at home.

SOCIAL MEANING OF LITERACY: A CASE STUDY

My own consideration of the question "What is literacy?" was 27 prompted by research experiences in a traditional West African society. Together with colleagues, I spent five years studying the social and intellectual consequences of literacy among the Vai people of West Africa (Scribner and Cole 1981). The material conditions of Vai life are harsh. Rural villages lack electricity and public water supplies; clinics and schools are scarce; dirt roads, often impassable in the rainy season, restrict social and economic exchanges. To the casual observer, Vai society is the very prototype of traditional nonliterate subsistence farming societies. Yet the Vai have practiced literacy for over 150 years, initially in a syllabic writing system of their own invention. The Vai script has been passed on from one generation to another in tutorial fashion without benefit of a formal institution such as a school and without the constitution of a professional teacher group. In addition to this indigenous script, literacy in the Arabic and Roman alphabets also flourishes in the countryside. The Vai are a Muslim people, and the Arabic script is the literacy for religious practice and theological learning. Missionaries and, more recently, the Liberian government have been disseminating English literacy, the official government literacy, through the establishment of Western-style schools. About one-third of the Vai male population is literate in one of these scripts, the majority in the Vai script. Many read and write both Vai and Arabic, and some outstanding scholars are literate in all three scripts. Since each writing system has a different orthography, represents a different language and is learned in a different setting, becoming literate in two or more scripts is an impressive intellectual accomplishment. Why do people take the trouble to do it?

Certain obvious answers are ruled out. Literacy is not a necessity 28 for personal survival. As far as we could determine, nonliteracy status does not exclude a person from full participation in economic activities or in town or society life. As we look around Vai country and see major activities and institutions continuing to function in the traditional oral mode, we are at a loss to define the literacy competencies that might be useful in everyday life. But Vai literates have not been at such a loss and have found no end of useful functions for writing.

Commonly they engage in extensive personal correspondence, 29 which for some involves the composition of 30–40 letters per month. Since Vai society, like other traditional societies, maintains an effective oral grapevine system, reasons for the popularity of letter writing are not self-evident, especially since all letters must be personally sent and hand-delivered. Yet literates find the advantage of secrecy and guarantee of delivery more than compensation for the time and trouble spent in writing. Scholars (Hair 1963; Holsoe 1967) speculate that the usefulness of the Vai script in protecting secrets and allowing clandestine resistance to the central governing machinery of Liberia, whose official literacy was English, were important factors in its invention and longevity.

On closer study, we find that Vai script literacy also serves many   30 personal and public record-keeping functions. Household heads keep albums for family births, deaths, and marriages; some maintain lists of dowry items and death feast contributions that help to regulate kinship exchanges. Records also enlarge the scope and planful aspects of commercial transactions. Artisans maintain lists of customers; farmers record the yield and income from cash-crop farming. The script also serves a variety of administrative purposes such as recording house tax payments and political contributions. Some fraternal and religious organizations maintain records in Vai script. All of these activities fit nicely into the metaphor of literacy as functional adaptation; the only surprising aspect is that so many varieties of pragmatic uses occur in an economic and social milieu in which modern institutions (schools, cash markets) still play a limited role.

Not all literacy uses are devoted to practical ends. Although the   31 Vai script has not been used to produce public books or manuscripts, in the privacy of their homes, many Vai literates engage in creative acts of composition. Almost everyone keeps a diary; some write down maxims and traditional tales in copybooks; others maintain rudimentary town histories; some record their dreams and tales of advice to children; a few who might qualify as scholars produce extended family and clan histories. Townspeople, when questioned about the value of the script, will often cite its utilitarian functions, but will equally as often speak about its importance for self-education and knowledge. Vai script literates are known in the community, are accorded respect, and are sought out for their information and help as personal scribes or as town clerks. A Vai parable about the relative merits of money, power, and book learning for success in this world concludes with the judgment that the "man who knoweth book passeth all."

Why this excursion into a case of African literacy after our   32 metaphoric discussion of the goals of literacy education in a technological society? Perhaps because Vai society, much simpler than ours in the range of literacy functions it calls for, nonetheless serves to highlight unnecessary simplicities in our attempts to define the one best set of organizing principles for literacy education. If we were called on as experts to devise literacy education programs for the Vai people, which metaphor would dominate our recommendations? Would we emphasize the spread of functional competencies, urging all farmers to keep crop records and all carpenters to list customers? This would be an effective approach for some, but it would neglect the interests and aspirations of others. Should we appeal to the cultural pride of the populace, suggesting Vai script literacy be extended as an instrument for group cohesion and social change? We might count on support for this appeal, but resistance as well; Qur'anic schools and the network of Muslim teachers and scholars are a powerful counterforce to the Vai script and a countervailing center for cultural cohesion. Moreover, families participating in the Vai script tradition do not necessarily repudiate participation in English literacy; some find it prudent to have one or more children in English school as well as Qur'anic school. As for literacy as a state of grace, aspirations for self-improvement and social status clearly sustain many aspects of Vai literacy both in the Arabic religious and Vai secular traditions. A diversity of pragmatic, ideological, and intellectual factors sustains popular literacy among the Vai.

The sociohistorical processes leading to multiple literacies 33 among the Vai are not unique. In their research in Alaska, Reder and Green (1983) found community members practicing literacy in any one (or, occasionally, a combination) of three languages. Some used the Cyrillic script, introduced by the Russian Orthodox Church, for reading and writing Russian; others used that script for literacy activities in their native Eskimo language; and still others participated in English literacy. Each of these literacies, they report, occurred through distinct socialization processes and in well-defined nonoverlapping domains of activity, and each had a distinctive social meaning. Wagner (in press) similarly documents the multiple meanings of literacy in contemporary Moroccan society, and other reports might be cited.

This is not to suggest, of course, that all cultural groups have 34 elaborated rich functions for literacy, nor that all groups strive for participation in the official literacy of their state (as, for example, English in Alaska and throughout the United States). The value of the growing body of ethnographic studies for the "What is literacy?" question is twofold. First, it promotes skepticism of the "one best answer" approach to the improvement of literacy in our society. Second, it urges the need for understanding the great variety of beliefs and aspirations that various people have developed toward literacy in their particular historical and current life circumstances.

What implications does this analysis have for literacy policy and 35 education? This is a question that calls for the continued, sustained, and thoughtful attention of educators and others in our society. One implication that I find compelling is the need to "disaggregate" various levels and kinds of literacy. If the search for an essence is futile, it might appropriately be replaced by serious attention to varieties of literacy and their place in social and educational programs. In this disentangling process, I would place priority on the need to extricate matters of value and policy from their hidden position in the definitional enterprise and to address them head on. The International Symposium for Literacy, closing UNESCO's Experimental World Literacy Program, declared that literacy is a fundamental human right (Bataille 1976). Literacy campaigns need no other justification. Setting long-range social and educational goals, however, pushes us farther toward an inquiry into the standard of literacy that is a desirable (valued) human right in our highly developed technological society, whose policies have such a powerful impact on the world's future. What is *ideal* literacy in our society? If the analysis by metaphor presented here contributes some approach to that question, it suggests that ideal literacy is simultaneously adaptive, socially empowering, and self-enhancing. Enabling youth and adults to progress toward that ideal would be a realization of the spirit of the symposium in Persepolis reflective of the resources and literacy achievements already available in our society. This suggests that long-term social and educational policies might be directed at maximum literacy objectives; minimal literacy standards would serve a useful function, not as goals but as indicators of our progress in equipping individuals and communities with the skills they need for "takeoff" in continuing literacy careers.

Recognition of the multiple meanings and varieties of literacy [36] also argues for a diversity of educational approaches, informal and community-based as well as formal and school-based. As ethnographic research and practical experience demonstrate, effective literacy programs are those that are responsive to perceived needs, whether for functional skills, social power, or self-improvement. Individual objectives may be highly specific: to qualify for a promotion at work, to help children with their lessons, to record a family history. Anzalone and McLaughlin (1982) have coined the term "specific literacies" to designate such special-interest or special-purpose literacy skills. The road to maximal literacy may begin for some through the feeder routes of a wide variety of specific literacies.

These are speculative and personal views; others will have differ- [37] ent conceptions. The notions offered here of ideal and specific literacies do not simplify the educational issues nor resolve the definitional dilemmas. I hope, however, that these concepts and the metaphoric analysis from which they flowed suggest the usefulness of "dissecting literacy" into its many forms and, in the process, clarifying the place of fact and value in discussions of the social meaning of literacy.

NOTE

This paper is based on a planning document for research on literacy that I prepared when associate director of the National Institute of Education. Eugene Radwin made many helpful comments on that document and contributed a number of bibliographic references cited here.

REFERENCES

Adult Performance Level Project. *Adult Functional Competency: A Summary.* Austin: University of Texas, Division of Extension, 1975.

Advisory Committee on National Illiteracy. "Report." *School and Society* 30 (1929): 708.

Anzalone, S., and S. McLaughlin. *Literacy for Specific Situations.* Amherst: University of Massachusetts, Center for International Education, 1982.

Bataille, L., ed. *A Turning Point for Literacy: Proceedings of the International Symposium for Literacy, Persepolis, Iran, 1975.* Oxford: Pergamon Books, 1976.

Bormuth, J. R. "Reading Literacy: Its Definition and Assessment." In *Toward a Literate Society: The Report of the Committee on Reading of the National Academy of Education,* edited by J. B. Carroll and J. S. Chall. New York: McGraw-Hill Book Co., 1975.

Cervero, R. M. "Does the Texas Adult Performance Level Test Measure Functional Competence?" *Adult Education* 30 (1980): 152–65.

Dauzat, S. J., and J. Dauzat. "Literacy in Quest of a Definition." *Convergence* 10 (1977): 37–41.

Farrell, L. J. "Literacy, the Basics, and All that Jazz." *College English* 38 (1977): 443–59.

Freire, P. *Cultural Action for Freedom* (Monograph Series no. 1). Cambridge, Mass.: Harvard Educational Review, 1970.

Cayter, M., B. Hall, J. R. Kidd, and V. Shivasrava. *The World of Literacy: Policy, Research and Action.* Toronto: International Development Centre, 1979.

Goody, J., ed. *Literacy in Traditional Societies.* Cambridge: Cambridge University Press, 1968.

Gray, W. *The Teaching of Reading and Writing: An International Survey.* Chicago: Scott, Foresman & Co./UNESCO, 1965.

Greenfield, P. M., and J. S. Bruner. "Culture and Cognitive Growth." In *Handbook of Socialization: Theory and Research,* edited by D. A. Goslin. New York: Rand McNally & Co., 1969.

Hair, P. E. H. "Notes on the Discovery of the Vai Script." *Sierra Leone Language Review* 2 (1963): 36–49.

Hammiche, B. "Functional Literacy and Educational Revolution." In *A Turning Point for Literacy: Proceedings of the International Symposium for Literacy, Persepolis Iran, 1975,* edited by L. Bataille. Oxford: Pergamon Press, 1976.

Harman, D. "Review of *The Experimental World Literacy Program.*" *Harvard Educational Review* 47 (1977): 444–46.

Heath, S. B. "The Functions and Uses of Literacy." *Journal of Communication* 30 (1980): 123–33.

Heath, S. B. "Toward an Ethnohistory of Writing in American Education." In *Writing: The Nature, Development and Teaching of Written Communication,* vol. 1, edited by M. F. Whiteman. Hillsdale, N. J.: Lawrence Erlbaum Associates, 1981.

Hillerich, R. L. "Toward an Assessable Definition of Literacy." *English Journal* 65 (1976): 50–55.

Holsoe, S. E. "Slavery and Economic Response among the Vai." In *Slavery in Africa: Historical and Anthropological Perspectives,* edited by S. Miers and I. Kopytoff. Madison: University of Wisconsin Press, 1977.

Hunter, C. S. J., and D. Harman. *Adult Illiteracy in the United States.* New York: McGraw-Hill Book Co., 1979.

Kirsch, I., and J. T. Guthrie. "The Concept and Measurement of Functional Literacy." *Reading Research Quarterly* 13 (1977–78): 485–507.

Kozol, J. *Prisoners of Silence: Breaking the Bonds of Adult Illiteracy in the United States.* New York: Continuum Publishing Corp., 1980.

McGovern, G. *Congressional Record* (September 1978), p. 14,834.

McLuhan, M. *The Gutenberg Galaxy.* Toronto: University of Toronto Press, 1962.

McLuhan, M. *Understanding Media: The Extensions of Man.* New York: McGraw-Hill Book Co., 1964

Miller, G. A., ed. *Linguistic Communication: Perspectives for Research.* Newark, Del.: International Reading Association, 1973.

Naisbett, J. *Megatrends: Ten New Directions Transforming Our Lives.* New York: Warner Books, 1982.

Olson, D. R. "From Utterance to Text: The Bias of Language in Speech and Writing." *Harvard Educational Review* 47 (1977): 257–81.

Powell, W. R. "Levels of Literacy." *Journal of Reading* 20 (1977): 488–92.

Radwin, E. "Literacy—What and Why." Unpublished manuscript, Harvard University, 1978.

Reder, S., and K. R. Green. "Literacy as a Functional Component of Social Structure in an Alaska Fishing Village." *International Journal of the Sociology of Language* 42 (1983): 122–41.

Resnick, D. P., ed. *Literacy in Historical Perspective.* Washington, D. C.: Library of Congress, 1983.

Resnick, D. P., and L. B. Resnick. "The Nature of Literacy: An Historical Exploration." *Harvard Educational Review* 47 (1977): 370–85.

Scribner, S. "Industrial Literacy" (Final Report to the Ford Foundation). New York: CUNY, Graduate School and University Center, 1982. (a)

Scribner, S. "Observations on Literacy Education in China." *Linguistic Reporter* 25 (1982): 1–4. (b)

Scribner, S., and M. Cole. *The Psychology of Literacy.* Cambridge, Mass.: Harvard University Press, 1981.

Steiner, G. "After the Book." In *The Future of Literacy,* edited by R. Disch. Englewood Cliffs, N. J.: Prentice-Hall, Inc. 1973.

United Nations Development Program. *The Experimental World Literacy Programme: A Critical Assessment.* Paris: UNESCO, 1976.
UNESCO. *Regional Report on Literacy.* Teheran: UNESCO, 1972.
Wagner, D. A., B. M. Messick, and J. Spratt. "Studying Literacy in Morocco." In *The Acquisition of Literacy: Ethnographic Perspectives,* edited by B. B. Schieffelin and P. Gilmore. Norwood, N. J.: Ablex, in press.

EXPLORATIONS

1. How would Scribner answer the question "Why do I write?"

2. In what ways does Scribner move beyond traditional definitions of literacy that are limited to reading and writing?

3. How do you think Scribner's ideas of literacy are affected by a specific place (such as Cisneros's third-floor flats) or a particular time (such as Orwell's importance of the age)?

4. Which metaphor seemed most compelling to you? What metaphor or metaphors can you think of to explain or shed light on a broadening definition of literacy?

5. Sylvia Scribner is known primarily as a social scientist and nonfiction writer, but she uses the idea of metaphor, which is normally associated with fiction and poetry, to organize this nonfiction essay. Why do you think she chose to do this? What does her use of metaphor imply about the distinctions we make about different kinds of writing and the different ways that writers use various kinds of language? How did the idea of metaphor help her organize her essay? Do you think that metaphors allowed you to better understand her ideas and purpose for writing this essay?

6. Who do you think Scribner had in mind when she wrote this essay? Do you think she had a particular audience in mind?

The Things They Carried

Tim O'Brien

---

*Tim O'Brien (1946–) graduated from Macalester College
in 1968, was drafted into the U.S. Army, and served in
Vietnam. Best known for his fictional writing on the
Vietnam conflict, O'Brien has explored a variety of narrative techniques.* Going After Cacciato *(1978) and* The
Things They Carried: A Work of Fiction *(1990), from which
the following story of the same name is taken, have similar
structures. Both are works of fiction with individual chapters
that can stand alone as independent short stories.* The
Things They Carried *is narrated by a character named "Tim
O'Brien," and although the author states that he is not
this character, O'Brien brings the passion and details from
personal experiences and memories to his carefully crafted
and intricately connected stories.*

WRITING BEFORE READING

*Although Tim O'Brien's writing is largely based on his own experi-
ences, he subtitled* The Things They Carried *as "A Work of Fiction."
What are some of the things that you think go into the making of a good
story? What expectations do you bring with you to a work of fiction?*

First Lieutenant Jimmy Cross carried letters from a girl named   1
Martha, a junior at Mount Sebastian College in New Jersey. They
were not love letters, but Lieutenant Cross was hoping, so he kept
them folded in plastic at the bottom of his rucksack. In the late afternoon, after a day's march, he would dig his foxhole, wash his hands
under a canteen, unwrap the letters, hold them with the tips of his
fingers, and spend the last hour of light pretending. He would imagine romantic camping trips into the White Mountains in New
Hampshire. He would sometimes taste the envelope flaps, knowing
her tongue had been there. More than anything, he wanted Martha
to love him as he loved her, but the letters were mostly chatty,
elusive on the matter of love. She was a virgin, he was almost sure.
She was an English major at Mount Sebastian, and she wrote beautifully about her professors and roommates and midterm exams,
about her respect for Chaucer and her great affection for Virginia
Woolf. She often quoted lines of poetry; she never mentioned the
war, except to say, Jimmy, take care of yourself. The letters weighed
ten ounces. They were signed "Love, Martha," but Lieutenant

Cross understood that "Love" was only a way of signing and did not mean what he sometimes pretended it meant. At dusk, he would carefully return the letters to his rucksack. Slowly, a bit distracted, he would get up and move among his men, checking the perimeter, then at full dark he would return to his hole and watch the night and wonder if Martha was a virgin.

The things they carried were largely determined by necessity. Among the necessities or near necessities were P-38 can openers, pocket knives, heat tabs, wrist watches, dog tags, mosquito repellent, chewing gum, candy, cigarettes, salt tablets, packets of Kool-Aid, lighters, matches, sewing kits, Military Payment Certificates, C rations, and two or three canteens of water. Together, these items weighed between fifteen and twenty pounds, depending upon a man's habits or rate of metabolism. Henry Dobbins, who was a big man, carried extra rations; he was especially fond of canned peaches in heavy syrup over pound cake. Dave Jensen, who practiced field hygiene, carried a toothbrush, dental floss, and several hotel-size bars of soap he'd stolen on R&R in Sydney, Australia. Ted Lavender, who was scared, carried tranquilizers until he was shot in the head outside the village of Than Khe in mid-April. By necessity, and because it was SOP, they all carried steel helmets that weighed five pounds including the liner and camouflage cover. They carried the standard fatigue jackets and trousers. Very few carried underwear. On their feet they carried jungle boots—2.1 pounds—and Dave Jensen carried three pairs of socks and a can of Dr. Scholl's foot powder as a precaution against trench foot. Until he was shot, Ted Lavender carried six or seven ounces of premium dope, which for him was a necessity. Mitchell Sanders, the RTO, carried condoms. Norman Bowker carried a diary. Rat Kiley carried comic books. Kiowa, a devout Baptist, carried an illustrated New Testament that had been presented to him by his father, who taught Sunday school in Oklahoma City, Oklahoma. As a hedge against bad times, however, Kiowa also carried his grandmother's distrust of the white man, his grandfather's old hunting hatchet. Necessity dictated. Because the land was mined and booby-trapped, it was SOP for each man to carry a steel-centered, nylon-covered flak jacket, Simonov carbines and black-market Uzis and .38-caliber Smith & Wesson handguns and 66 mm LAWs and shotguns and silencers and blackjacks and bayonets and C-4 plastic explosives. Lee Strunk carried a slingshot; a weapon of last resort, he called it. Mitchell Sanders carried brass knuckles. Kiowa carried his grandfather's feathered hatchet. Every third or fourth man carried a Claymore antipersonnel mine—3.5 pounds with its firing device. They all carried at least one M-18 colored smoke grenade—twenty-four ounces. Some carried CS or teargas grenades. Some carried white-phosphorus grenades. They carried all they could bear, and then some, including a silent awe for the terrible power of the things they carried.

In the first week of April, before Lavender died, Lieutenant 3 Jimmy Cross received a good-luck charm from Martha. It was a simple pebble, an ounce at most. Smooth to the touch, it was a milky-white color with flecks of orange and violet, oval-shaped, like a miniature egg. In the accompanying letter, Martha wrote that she had found the pebble on the Jersey shoreline, precisely where the land touched water at high tide, where thing came together but also separated. It was this separate-but-together quality, she wrote, that had inspired her to pick up the pebble and to carry it in her breast pocket for several days, where it seemed weightless, and then to send it through the mail, by air, as a token of her truest feelings for him. Lieutenant Cross found this romantic. But he wondered what her truest feelings were, exactly, and what she meant by separate-but-together. He wondered how the tides and waves had come into play on that afternoon along the Jersey shoreline when Martha saw the pebble and bent down to rescue it from geology. He imagined bare feet. Martha was a poet, with the poet's sensibilities, and her feet would be brown and bare, the toenails unpainted, the eyes chilly and somber like the ocean in March, and though it was painful, he wondered who had been with her that afternoon. He imagined a pair of shadows moving along the strip of sand where things came together but also separated. It was phantom jealousy, he knew, but he couldn't help himself. He loved her so much. On the march, through the hot days of early April, he carried the pebble in his mouth, turning it with his tongue, battery-powered clackers. Dave Jensen carried earplugs. Most often, before blowing the tunnels, they were ordered by higher command to search them, which was considered bad news, but by and large they just shrugged and carried out orders. Because he was a big man, Henry Dobbins was excused from tunnel duty. The others would draw numbers. Before Lavender died there were seventeen men in the platoon, and whoever drew the number seventeen would strip off his gear and crawl in head first with a flashlight and Lieutenant Cross's .45-caliber pistol. The rest of them would fan out as security. They would sit down or kneel, not facing the hole, listening to the ground beneath them, imagining cobwebs and ghosts, whatever was down there—the tunnel walls squeezing in—how the flashlight seemed impossibly heavy in the hand and how it was tunnel vision in the very strictest sense, compression in all ways, even time, and how you had to wiggle in—ass and elbows—a swallowed-up feeling—will your flashlight go dead? Do rats carry rabies? If you screamed, how far would the sound carry? Would your buddies hear it? Would they have the courage to drag you out? In some respects, though not many, the waiting was worse than the tunnel itself. Imagination was a killer.

On April 6, when Lee Strunk drew the number seventeen, he laughed and muttered something and went down quickly. The morning was hot and very still. Not good, Kiowa said. He looked at the tunnel opening, then out across a dry paddy toward the village of Than Khe. Nothing moved. No clouds or birds or people. As they waited, the men smoked and drank Kool-Aid, not talking much, feeling sympathy for Lee Strunk but also feeling the luck of the draw. You win some, you lose some, said Mitchell Sanders, and sometimes you settle for a rain check. It was a tired line and no one laughed.

Henry Dobbins ate a tropical chocolate bar. Ted Lavender popped a tranquilizer and went off to pee.

After five minutes, Lieutenant Jimmy Cross moved to the tunnel, leaned down, and examined the darkness. Trouble, he thought—a cave-in maybe. And then suddenly, without willing it, he was thinking about Martha. The stresses and fractures, the quick collapse, the two of them buried alive under all that weight. Dense, crushing love. Kneeling, watching the hole, he tried to concentrate on Lee Strunk and the war, all the dangers, but his love was too much for him, he felt paralyzed, he wanted to sleep inside her lungs and breathe her blood and be smothered. He wanted her to be a virgin and not a virgin, all at once. He wanted to know her. Intimate secrets—why poetry? Why so sad? Why that grayness in her eyes? Why so alone? Not lonely, just alone—riding her bike across campus or sitting off by herself in the cafeteria. Even dancing, she danced alone—and it was the aloneness that filled him with love. He remembered telling her that one evening. How she nodded and looked away. And how, later, when he kissed her, she received the kiss without returning it, her eyes wide open, not afraid, not a virgin's eyes, just flat and uninvolved.

Lieutenant Cross gazed at the tunnel. But he was not there. He was buried with Martha under the white sand at the Jersey shore. They were pressed together, and the pebble in his mouth was her tongue. He was smiling. Vaguely, he was aware of how quiet the day was, the sullen paddies, yet he could not bring himself to worry about matters of security. He was beyond that. He was just a kid at war, in love. He was twenty-two years old. He couldn't help it.

A few moments later Lee Strunk crawled out of the tunnel. He came up grinning, filthy but alive. Lieutenant Cross nodded and closed his eyes while the others clapped Strunk on the back and made jokes about rising from the dead.

Worms, Rat Kiley said. Right out of the grave. Fuckin' zombie.

The men laughed. They all felt great relief.

Spook City, said Mitchell Sanders.

Lee Strunk made a funny ghost sound, a kind of moaning, yet 12
very happy, and right then, when Strunk made that high happy
moaning sound, when he went *Ahhooooo*, right then Ted Lavender
was shot in the head on his way back from peeing. He lay with his
mouth open. The teeth were broken. There was a swollen black
bruise under his left eye. The cheekbone was gone. Oh shit, Rat
Kiley said, the guy's dead. The guy's dead, he kept saying, which
seemed profound—the guy's dead. I mean really.

*

The things they carried were determined to some extent by supersti- 13
tion. Lieutenant Cross carried his good-luck pebble. Dave Jensen
carried a rabbit's foot. Norman Bowker, otherwise a very gentle
person, carried a thumb that had been presented to him as a gift by
Mitchell Sanders. The thumb was dark brown, rubbery to the touch,
and weighed four ounces at most. It had been cut from a VC corpse,
a boy of fifteen or sixteen. They'd found him at the bottom of an
irrigation ditch, badly burned, flies in his mouth and eyes. The boy
wore black shorts and sandals. At the time of his death he had been
carrying a pouch of rice, a rifle, and three magazines of ammunition.
    You want my opinion, Mitchell Sanders said, there's a definite 14
moral here.
    He put his hand on the dead boy's wrist. He was quiet for a 15
time, as if counting a pulse, then he patted the stomach, almost
affectionately, and used Kiowa's hunting hatchet to remove the
thumb.
    Henry Dobbins asked what the moral was. 16
    Moral? 17
    You know. *Moral*. 18
    Sanders wrapped the thumb in toilet paper and handed it across 19
to Norman Bowker. There was no blood. Smiling, he kicked the
boy's head, watched the flies scatter, and said, It's like with that
old TV show—Paladin. Have gun, will travel.
    Henry Dobbins thought about it. 20
    Yeah, well, he finally said. I don't see no moral. 21
    There it *is*, man. 22
    Fuck off. 23

They carried USO stationery and pencils and pens. They carried 24
Sterno, safety pins, trip flares, signal flares, spools of wire, razor
blades, chewing tobacco, liberated joss sticks and statuettes of the
smiling Buddha, candles, grease pencils, *The Stars and Stripes*, fin-
gernail clippers, Psy Ops leaflets, bush hats, bolos, and much more.
Twice a week, when the resupply choppers came in, they carried hot
chow in green Mermite cans and large canvas bags filled with iced

beer and soda pop. They carried plastic water containers, each with a two-gallon capacity. Mitchell Sanders carried a set of starched tiger fatigues for special occasions. Henry Dobbins carried Black Flag insecticide. Dave Jensen carried empty sandbags that could be filled at night for added protection. Lee Strunk carried tanning lotion. Some things they carried in common. Taking turns, they carried the big PRC-77 scrambler radio, which weighed thirty pounds with its battery. They shared the weight of memory. They took up what others could no longer bear. Often, they carried each other, the wounded or weak. They carried infections. They carried chess sets, basketballs, Vietnamese-English dictionaries, insignia of rank, Bronze Stars and Purple Hearts, plastic cards imprinted with the Code of Conduct. They carried diseases, among them malaria and dysentery. They carried lice and ringworm and leeches and paddy algae and various rots and molds. They carried the land itself— Vietnam, the place, the soil—a powdery orange-red dust that covered their boots and fatigues and faces. They carried the sky. The whole atmosphere, they carried it, the humidity, the monsoons, the stink of fungus and decay, all of it, they carried gravity. They moved like mules. By daylight they took sniper fire, at night they were mortared, but it was not battle, it was just the endless march, village to village, without purpose, nothing won or lost. They marched for the sake of the march. They plodded along slowly, dumbly, leaning forward against the heat, unthinking, all blood and bone, simple grunts, soldiering with their legs, toiling up the hills and down into the paddies and across the rivers and up again and down, just humping, one step and then the next and then another, but no volition, no will, because it was automatic, it was anatomy, and the war was entirely a matter of posture and carriage, the hump was everything, a kind of inertia, a kind of emptiness, a dullness of desire and intellect and conscience and hope and human sensibility. Their principles were in their feet. Their calculations were biological. They had no sense of strategy or mission. They searched the villages without knowing what to look for, not caring, kicking over jars of rice, frisking children and old men, blowing tunnels, sometimes setting fires and sometimes not, then forming up and moving on to the next village, then other villages, where it would always be the same. They carried their own lives. The pressures were enormous. In the heat of early afternoon, they would remove their helmets and flak jackets, walking bare, which was dangerous but which helped ease the strain. They would often discard things along the route of march. Purely for comfort, they would throw away rations, blow their Claymores and grenades, no matter, because by nightfall the resupply choppers would arrive with more of the same, then a day or two later still more, fresh watermelons and crates of ammunition and sunglasses and woolen sweaters—the resources were stunning—sparklers for the Fourth of July, colored eggs for Easter. It was the great American war chest—the fruits of science, the smokestacks, the canneries, the arsenals at Hartford, the Minnesota forests, the machine shops, the vast fields of corn and wheat—they carried like freight trains; they carried it on their backs and shoulders—and for all the ambiguities of Vietnam, all the mysteries and unknowns, there was at least the single abiding certainty that they would never be at a loss for things to carry.

After the chopper took Lavender away, Lieutenant Jimmy Cross   25
led his men into the village of Than Khe. They burned everything. They shot chickens and dogs, they trashed the village well, they called in artillery and watched the wreckage, then they marched for several hours through the hot afternoon, and then at dusk, while Kiowa explained how Lavender died, Lieutenant Cross found himself trembling.

He tried not to cry. With his entrenching tool, which weighed   26
five pounds, he began digging a hole in the earth.

He felt shame. He hated himself. He had loved Martha more   27
than his men, and as a consequence Lavender was now dead, and this was something he would have to carry like a stone in his stomach for the rest of the war.

All he could do was dig. He used his entrenching tool like an ax,   28
slashing, feeling both love and hate, and then later, when it was full dark, he sat at the bottom of his foxhole and wept. It went on for a long while. In part, he was grieving for Ted Lavender, but mostly it was for Martha, and for himself, because she belonged to another world, which was not quite real, and because she was a junior at Mount Sebastian college in New Jersey, a poet and a virgin and uninvolved, and because he realized she did not love him and never would.

*

Like cement, Kiowa whispered in the dark. I swear to God—   29
boom-down. Not a word.

I've heard this, said Norman Bowker.   30

A pisser, you know? Still zipping himself up. Zapped while   31
zipping.

All right, fine. That's enough.   32

Yeah, but you had to see it, the guy just—   33

I *heard*, man. Cement. So why not shut the fuck *up?*   34

Kiowa shook his head sadly and glanced over at the hole where   35
Lieutenant Jimmy Cross sat watching the night. The air was thick and wet. A warm, dense fog had settled over the paddies and there was the stillness that precedes rain.

After a time Kiowa sighed. 36

One thing for sure, he said. The Lieutenant's in some deep 37
hurt. I mean that crying jag—the way he was carrying on—it wasn't
fake or anything, it was real heavy-duty hurt. The man cares.

Sure, Norman Bowker said. 38

Say what you want, the man does care. 39

We all got problems. 40

Not Lavender. 41

No, I guess not. Bowker said. Do me a favor, though. 42

Shut up? 43

That's a smart Indian. Shut up. 44

Shrugging, Kiowa pulled off his boots. He wanted to say more, 45
just to lighten up his sleep, but instead he opened his New Testament
and arranged it beneath his head as a pillow. The fog made things
seem hollow and unattached. He tried not to think about Ted
Lavender, but then he was thinking how fast it was, no drama, down
and dead, and how it was hard to feel anything except surprise. It
seemed un-Christian. He wished he could find some great sadness, or
even anger, but the emotion wasn't there and he couldn't make it
happen. Mostly he felt pleased to be alive. He liked the smell of the
New Testament under his cheek, the leather and ink and paper and
glue, whatever the chemicals were. He liked hearing the sounds of
night. Even his fatigue, it felt fine, the stiff muscles and the prickly
awareness of his own body, a floating feeling. He enjoyed not being
dead. Lying there, Kiowa admired Lieutenant Jimmy Cross's capacity for grief. He wanted to share the man's pain, he wanted to care
as Jimmy Cross cared. And yet when he closed his eyes, all he could
think was Boom-down, and all he could feel was the pleasure of
having his boot off and the fog curling in around him and the damp
soil and the Bible smells and the plush comfort of night.

After a moment Norman Bowker sat up in the dark. 46

What the hell, he said. You want to talk, *talk*. Tell it to me. 47

Forget it. 48

No, man, go on. One thing I hate, it's a silent Indian. 49

For the most part they carried themselves with poise, a kind of 50
dignity. Now and then, however, there were times of panic, when
they squealed or wanted to squeal but couldn't, when they twitched
and made moaning sounds and covered their heads and said Dear
Jesus and flopped around on the earth and fired their weapons blind-
ly and cringed and sobbed and begged for the noise to stop and went
wild and made stupid promises to themselves and to God and to
their mothers and fathers, hoping not to die. In different ways, it
happened to all of them. Afterward, when the firing ended, they
would blink and peek up. They would touch their bodies, feeling

shame, then quickly hiding it. They would force themselves to stand. As if in slow motion, frame by frame, the world would take on the old logic—absolute silence, then the wind, then sunlight, then voices. It was the burden of being alive. Awkwardly, the men would reassemble themselves, first in private, then in groups, becoming soldiers again. They would repair the leaks in their eyes. They would check for casualties, call in dust-offs, light cigarettes, try to smile, clear their throats and spit and begin cleaning their weapons. After a time someone would shake his head and say, No lie, I almost shit my pants, and someone else would laugh, which meant it was bad, yes, but the guy had obviously not shit his pants, it wasn't that bad, and in any case nobody would ever do such a thing and then go ahead and talk about it. They would squint into the dense, oppressive sunlight. For a few moments, perhaps, they would fall silent, lighting a joint and tracking its passage from man to man, inhaling, holding in the humiliation. Scary stuff, one of them might say. But then someone else would grin or flick his eyebrows and say, Roger-dodger, almost cut me a new asshole, *almost.*

There were numerous such poses. Some carried themselves with a sort of wistful resignation, others with pride or stiff soldierly discipline or good humor or macho zeal. They were afraid of dying but they were even more afraid to show it. [51]

They found jokes to tell. [52]

They used a hard vocabulary to contain the terrible softness. [53] *Greased,* they'd say. *Offed, lit up, zapped while zipping.* It wasn't cruelty, just stage presence. They were actors and the war came at them in 3-D. When someone died, it wasn't quite dying, because in a curious way it seemed scripted, and because they had their lines mostly memorized, irony mixed with tragedy, and because they called it by other names, as if to encyst and destroy the reality of death itself. They kicked corpses. They cut off thumbs. They talked grunt lingo. They told stories about Ted Lavender's supply of tranquilizers, how the poor guy didn't feel a thing, how incredibly tranquil he was.

There's a moral here, said Mitchell Sanders. [54]

They were waiting for Lavender's chopper, smoking the dead [55] man's dope.

The moral's pretty obvious, Sanders said, and winked. Stay [56] away from drugs. No joke, they'll ruin your day every time.

Cute, said Henry dobbins. [57]

Mind-blower, get it? Talk about wiggy—nothing left, just blood [58] and brains.

They made themselves laugh. [59]

There it is, they'd say, over and over, as if the repetition itself [60] were an act of poise, a balance between crazy and almost crazy, knowing without going. There it is, which meant be cool, let it ride, because oh yeah, man, you can't change what can't be changed, there it is, there it absolutely and positively and fucking well *is*.

They were tough.   61

They carried all the emotional baggage of men who might die.   62
Grief, terror, love, longing—these were intangibles, but the intangibles had their own mass and specific gravity, they had tangible weight. They carried shameful memories. They carried the common secret of cowardice barely restrained, the instinct to run or freeze or hide, and in many respects this was the heaviest burden of all, for it could never be put down, it required perfect balance and perfect posture. They carried their reputations. They carried the soldier's greatest fear, which was the fear of blushing. Men killed, and died, because they were embarrassed not to. It was what had brought them to the war in the first place, nothing positive, no dreams of glory or honor, just to avoid the blush of dishonor. They died so as not to die of embarrassment. They crawled into tunnels and walked point and advanced under fire. Each morning, despite the unknowns, they made their legs move. They endured. They kept humping. They did not submit to the obvious alternative, which was simply to close the eyes and fall. So easy, really. Go limp and tumble to the ground and let the muscles unwind and not speak and not budge until your buddies picked you up and lifted you into the chopper that would roar and dip its nose and carry you off to the world. A mere matter of falling, yet no one ever fell. It was not courage, exactly; the object was not valor. Rather, they were too frightened to be cowards.

By and large they carried these things inside, maintaining the   63
masks of composure. They sneered at sick call. They spoke bitterly about guys who had found release by shooting off their own toes or fingers. Pussies, they'd say. Candyasses. It was fierce, mocking talk, with only a trace of envy or awe, but even so, the image played itself out behind their eyes.

They imagined the muzzle against flesh. They imagined the   64
quick, sweet pain, then the evacuation to Japan, then a hospital with warm beds and cute geisha nurses.

They dreamed of freedom birds.   65

At night, on guard, staring into the dark, they were carried away   66
by jumbo jets. They felt the rush of takeoff. *Gone!* they yelled. And then velocity, wings and engines, a smiling stewardess—but it was more than a plane, it was a real bird, a big sleek silver bird with feathers and talons and high screeching. They were flying. The weights fell off, there was nothing to bear. They laughed and held on tight, feeling the cold slap of wind and altitude, soaring, thinking *It's over, I'm gone!*—they were naked, they were light and free—it was

all lightness, bright and fast and buoyant, light as light, a helium buzz in the brain, a giddy bubbling in the lungs as they were taken up over the clouds and the war, beyond duty, beyond gravity and mortification and global entanglements—*Sin loi!* they yelled, *I'm sorry, motherfuckers, but I'm out of it, I'm goofed, I'm on a space cruise, I'm gone!*—and it was a restful, disencumbered sensation, just riding the light waves, sailing that big silver freedom bird over the mountains and oceans, over America, over the farms and great sleeping cities and cemeteries and highways and the golden arches of McDonald's. It was flight, a kind of fleeing, a kind of falling, falling higher and higher, spinning off the edge of the earth and beyond the sun and through the vast, silent vacuum <u>where there were no burdens and where everything weighed exactly nothing.</u> *Gone!* they screamed, *I'm sorry but I'm gone!* And so at night, not quite dreaming, they gave themselves over to lightness, they were carried, they were purely borne.

On the morning after Ted Lavender died, First Lieutenant Jimmy 67
Cross crouched at the bottom of his foxhole and burned Martha's letters. Then he burned the two photographs. There was a steady rain falling, which made it difficult, but he used heat tabs and Sterno to build a small fire, screening it with his body, holding the photographs over the tight blue flame with the tips of his fingers.

He realized it was only a gesture. Stupid, he thought. 68
Sentimental, too, but mostly just stupid.

Lavender was dead. You couldn't burn the blame. 69

Besides, the letters were in his head. And even now, without 70
photographs, Lieutenant Cross could see Martha playing volleyball in her white gym shorts and yellow T-shirt. He could see her moving in the rain.

When the fire died out, Lieutenant Cross pulled his poncho over 71
his shoulders and ate breakfast from a can.

There was no great mystery, he decided. 72

In those burned letters Martha had never mentioned the war, 73
except to say, Jimmy, take care of yourself. She wasn't involved. She signed the letters "Love," but it wasn't love, and all the fine lines and technicalities did not matter.

The morning came up wet and blurry. Everything seemed part 74
of everything else, the fog and Martha and the deepening rain.

It was a war, after all. 75

Half smiling, Lieutenant Jimmy Cross took out his maps. He 76
shook his head hard, as if to clear it, then bent forward and began planning the day's march. In ten minutes, or maybe twenty, he would rouse the men and they would pack up and head west, where the maps showed the country to be green and inviting. They would

do what they had always done. The rain might add some weight, but otherwise it would be one more day layered upon all the other days.

He was realistic about it. There was that new hardness in his 77 stomach.

No more fantasies, he told himself. 78

Henceforth, when he thought about Martha, it would be only 79 to think that she belonged elsewhere. He would shut down the daydreams. This was not Mount Sebastian, it was another world, where there were no pretty poems or midterm exams, a place where men died because of carelessness and gross stupidity. Kiowa was right. Boom-down, and you were dead, never partly dead.

Briefly, in the rain, Lieutenant Cross saw Martha's gray eyes 80 gazing back at him.

He understood. 81

It was very sad, he thought. The things men carried inside. The 82 things men did or felt they had to do.

He almost nodded at her, but didn't. 83

Instead he went back to his maps. He was now determined to 84 perform his duties firmly and without negligence. It wouldn't help Lavender, he knew that, but from this point on he would comport himself as a soldier. He would dispose of his good-luck pebble. Swallow it, maybe, or use Lee Strunk's slingshot, or just drop it along the trail. On the march he would impose strict field discipline. He would be careful to send out flank security, to prevent straggling or bunching up, to keep his troops moving at the proper pace and at the proper interval. He would insist on clean weapons. He would confiscate the remainder of Lavender's dope. Later in the day, perhaps, he would call the men together and speak to them plainly. He would accept the blame for what had happened to Ted Lavender. He would be a man about it. He would look them in the eyes, keeping his chin level, and he would issue the new SOPs in a calm, impersonal tone of voice, an officer's voice, leaving no room for argument or discussion. Commencing immediately, he'd tell them, they would no longer abandon equipment along the route of march. They would police up their acts. They would get their shit together, and keep it together, and maintain it neatly and in good working order.

He would not tolerate laxity. He would show strength, distanc- 85 ing himself. 86

Among the men there would be grumbling, of course, and maybe worse, because their days would seem longer and their loads heavier, but Lieutenant Cross reminded himself that his obligation was not to be loved but to lead. He would dispense with love; it was not now a factor. And if anyone quarreled or complained, he would simply tighten his lips and arrange his shoulders in the correct command posture. He might give a curt little nod. Or he might not. He might just shrug and say Carry on, then they would saddle up and form into a column and move out toward the villages west of Than Khe.

EXPLORATIONS

1. In what ways are the characters in O'Brien's story literate? How are their ideas of literacy shaped by their particular time, place, and community?

2. How does O'Brien use the words *reading*, *writing*, and *story-telling* in his story?

3. Which of Scribner's three metaphors of literacy seem most applicable to the characters in the story?

4. How does O'Brien use lists of objects to organize his narrative? How do you think he might have used these lists in the process of invention?

5. How do you think O'Brien would answer the question "Why do you write?" Which passages in O'Brien's essay support your opinion?

On Dumpster Diving

LARS EIGHNER

Lars Eighner was born in Corpus Christi, Texas, in 1946, and he later studied at the University of Texas. He worked as an attendant and ward worker in a mental institution from 1980 to 1987 before finding himself homeless for three years. Travels with Lizbeth *(1993), the book that includes "On Dumpster Diving," recounts these years. It began as letters to friends explaining his circumstances and evolved into a series of essays on equipment that he had found in the garbage. Eighner later sent the essays to the* Threepenny Review *for publication. "On Dumpster Diving" shows Eighner's uniquely powerful insights and unconventional, yet elegant, prose style, which is similar in some ways to the nineteenth-century fiction he enjoys.*

WRITING BEFORE READING

Think about a subject or activity about which you could consider yourself an expert. How did you become an expert? How would you go about explaining this expertise to someone else?

Long before I began Dumpster diving I was impressed with Dumpsters, enough so that I wrote the Merriam-Webster research service to discover what I could about the word "Dumpster." I learned from them that "Dumpster" is a proprietary word belonging to the Dempsey Dumpster company. (private, owned) 1

Since then I have dutifully capitalized the word although it was lowercased in almost all of the citations Merriam-Webster photocopied for me. Dempsey's word is too apt. I have never heard these things called anything but Dumpsters. I do not know anyone who knows the generic name for these objects. From time to time, however, I hear a wino or hobo give some corrupted credit to the original and call them Dipsy Dumpsters. 2

I began Dumpster diving about a year before I became homeless. 3

I prefer the term "scavenging" and use the word "scrounging" when I mean to be obscure. I have heard people, evidently meaning to be polite, using the word "foraging," but I prefer to reserve that word for gathering nuts and berries and such which I do also according to the season and the opportunity. "Dumpster diving" seems to me to be a little too cute and, in my case, inaccurate 4 because I lack the athletic ability to lower myself into the Dumpsters as the true divers do, much to their increased profit.

I like the frankness of the word "scavenging," which I can 5 hardly think of without picturing a big black snail on an aquarium wall. I live from the refuse of others. I am a scavenger. I think it a sound and honorable niche, although if I could I would naturally prefer to live the comfortable consumer life, perhaps—and only perhaps—as a slightly less wasteful consumer owing to what I have learned as a scavenger.

While my dog Lizbeth and I were still living in the house on 6 Avenue B in Austin, as my savings ran out, I put almost all of my sporadic income into rent. The necessities of daily life I began to extract from Dumpsters. Yes, we ate from Dumpsters. Except for jeans, all my clothes came from Dumpsters. Boom boxes, candles, bedding, toilet paper, medicine, books, a typewriter, a virgin male love doll, change sometimes amounting to many dollars: I have acquired many things from the Dumpsters.

I have learned much as a scavenger. I mean to put some of what 7 I have learned down here, beginning with the practical art of dumpster diving and proceeding to the abstract.

What is safe to eat?   8

After all, the finding of objects is becoming something of an 9 urban art. Even respectable employed people will sometimes find something tempting sticking out of a Dumpster or standing beside one. Quite a number of people, not all of them of the bohemian type, are willing to brag that they found this or that piece in the trash. But eating from Dumpsters is the thing that separates the dilettanti from the professionals.

Eating safely from the Dumpsters involves three principles: using 10 the senses and common sense to evaluate the condition of the found materials, knowing the Dumpsters of a given area and checking them regularly, and seeking always to answer the question, "Why was this discarded?"

Perhaps everyone who has a kitchen and a regular supply of 11 groceries has, at one time or another, made a sandwich and eaten half of it before discovering mold on the bread or got a mouthful of milk before realizing the milk had turned. Nothing of the sort is likely to happen to a Dumpster diver because he is constantly reminded that most food is discarded for a reason. Yet a lot of perfectly good food can be found in Dumpsters.

Canned goods, for example, turn up fairly often in the 12 Dumpsters I frequent. All except the most phobic people would be willing to eat from a can even if it came from a Dumpster. Canned goods are among the safest of foods to be found in Dumpsters, but are not utterly foolproof.

Although very rare with modern canning methods, botulism is a 13 possibility. Most other forms of food poisoning seldom do lasting harm to a healthy person. But botulism is almost certainly fatal and often the first symptom is death. Except for carbonated beverages, all canned goods should contain a slight vacuum and suck air when first punctured. Bulging, rusty, dented cans and cans that spew when punctured should be avoided, especially when the contents are not very acidic or syrupy.

Heat can break down the botulin, but this requires much more 14 cooking than most people do to canned goods. To the extent that botulism occurs at all, of course, it can occur in cans on pantry shelves as well as in cans from Dumpsters. Need I say that home-canned goods found in Dumpsters are simply too risky to be recommended.

From time to time one of my companions, aware of the source of 15 my provisions, will ask, "Do you think these crackers are really safe to eat?" For some reason it is most often the crackers they ask about.

The question always makes me angry. Of course I would not 16 offer my companion anything I had doubts about. But more than that I wonder why he cannot evaluate the condition of the crackers for himself. I have no special knowledge and I have been wrong before. Since he knows where the food comes from, it seems to me he ought to assume some of the responsibility for deciding what he will put in his mouth.

For myself I have few qualms about dry foods such as crackers, 17 cookies, cereal, chips, and pasta if they are free of visible contaminates and still dry and crisp. Most often such things are found in the original packaging, which is not so much a positive sign as it is the absence of a negative one.

Raw fruits and vegetables with intact skins seem perfectly safe to 18 me, excluding of course the obviously rotten. Many are discarded for minor imperfections which can be pared away. Leafy vegetables, grapes, cauliflower, broccoli, and similar things may be contaminated by liquids and may be impractical to wash.

Candy, especially hard candy, is usually safe if it has not drawn 19 ants. Chocolate is often discarded only because it has become discolored as the cocoa butter de-emulsified. Candying after all is one method of food preservation because pathogens do not like very sugary substances.

All of these foods might be found in any Dumpster and can be 20 evaluated with some confidence largely on the basis of appearance. Beyond these are foods which cannot be correctly evaluated without additional information.

I began scavenging by pulling pizzas out of the Dumpster 21
behind a pizza delivery shop. In general prepared food requires
caution, but in this case I knew when the shop closed and went to
the Dumpster as soon as the last of the help left.

Such shops often get prank orders, called "bogus." Because 22
help seldom stays long at these places pizzas are often made with the
wrong topping, refused on delivery for being cold, or baked incor-
rectly. The products to be discarded are boxed up because inventory
is kept by counting boxes: a boxed pizza can be written off; an
unboxed pizza does not exist.

I never placed a bogus order to increase the supply of pizzas and 23
I believe no one else was scavenging in this Dumpster. But the
people in the shop became suspicious and began to retain their
garbage in the shop overnight.

While it lasted I had a steady supply of fresh, sometimes warm 24
pizza. Because I knew the Dumpster I knew the source of the pizza,
and because I visited the Dumpster regularly I knew what was fresh
and what was yesterday's.

The area I frequent is inhabited by many affluent college 25
students. I am not here by chance; the Dumpsters in this area are
very rich. Students throw out many good things, including food. In
particular they tend to throw everything out when they move at the
end of a semester, before and after breaks, and around midterm
when many of them despair of college. So I find it advantageous to
keep an eye on the academic calendar.

The students throw food away around the breaks because they 26
do not know whether it has spoiled or will spoil before they return.
A typical discard is a half jar of peanut butter. In fact nonorganic
peanut butter does not require refrigeration and is unlikely to spoil
in any reasonable time. The student does not know that, and since it
is Daddy's money, the student decides not to take a chance.

Opened containers require caution and some attention to the 27
question "Why was this discarded?" But in the case of discards from
student apartments, the answer may be that the item was discarded
through carelessness, ignorance, or wastefulness. This can sometimes
be deduced when the item is found with many others, including
some that are obviously perfectly good.

Some students, and others, approach defrosting a freezer by 28
chucking out the whole lot. Not only do the circumstances of such
a find tell the story, but also the mass of frozen goods stays cold for
a long time and items may be found still frozen or freshly thawed.

Yogurt, cheese, and sour cream are items that are often thrown 29
out while they are still good. Occasionally I find a cheese with a spot
of mold, which of course I just pare off, and because it is obviously

why such a cheese was discarded, I treat it with less suspicion than an apparently perfect cheese found in similar circumstances. Yogurt is often discarded, still sealed, only because the expiration date on the carton has passed. This is one of my favorite finds because yogurt will keep for several days, even in warm weather.

Students throw out canned goods and staples at the end of 30 semesters and when they give up college at midterm. Drugs, pornography, spirits, and the like are often discarded when parents are expected—Dad's day, for example. And spirits also turn up after big party weekends, presumably discarded by the newly reformed. Wine and spirits, of course, keep perfectly well even after opened.

My test for carbonated soft drinks is whether they still fizz 31 vigorously. Many juices or other beverages are too acid or too syrupy to cause much concern provided they are not visibly contaminated. Liquids, however, require some care.

One hot day I found a large jug of Pat O'Brien's Hurricane 32 mix. The jug had been opened, but it was still ice cold. I drank three large glasses before it became apparent to me that someone had added the rum to the mix, and not a little rum. I never tasted the rum and by the time I began to feel the effects I had already ingested a very large quantity of the beverage. Some divers would have considered this a boon, but being suddenly and thoroughly intoxicated in a public place in the early afternoon is not my idea of a good time.

I have heard of people maliciously contaminating discarded food 33 and even handouts, but mostly I have heard of this from people with vivid imaginations who have had no experience with Dumpsters themselves. Just before the pizza shop stopped discarding its garbage at night, jalapeños began showing up on most of the discarded pizzas. If indeed this was meant to discourage me it was a wasted effort because I am a native Texan.

For myself, I avoid game, poultry, pork, and egg-based foods 34 whether I find them raw or cooked. I seldom have the means to cook what I find, but when I do I avail myself of plentiful supplies of beef which is often in very good condition. I suppose fish becomes disagreeable before it becomes dangerous. The dog is happy to have any such thing that is past its prime and, in fact, does not recognize fish as food until it is quite strong.

Home leftovers, as opposed to surpluses from restaurants, are 35 very often bad. Evidently, especially among students, there is a common type of personality that carefully wraps up even the smallest leftover and shoves it into the back of the refrigerator for six months or so before discarding it. Characteristic of this type are the reused jars and margarine tubs which house the remains.

I avoid ethnic foods I am unfamiliar with. If I do not know what 36
it is supposed to look like when it is good, I cannot be certain I will
be able to tell if it is bad.

No matter how careful I am I still get dysentery at least once 37
a month, oftener in warm weather. I do not want to paint too
romantic a picture. Dumpster diving has serious drawbacks as a way
of life.

I learned to scavenge gradually, on my own. Since then I have initi- 38
ated several companions into the trade. I have learned that there is
a predictable series of stages a person goes through in learning to
scavenge.

At first the new scavenger is filled with disgust and self-loathing. 39
He is ashamed of being seen and may lurk around, trying to duck
behind things, or he may try to dive at night.

(In fact, most people instinctively look away from a scavenger. 40
By skulking around, the novice calls attention to himself and arouses
suspicion. Diving at night is ineffective and needlessly messy.)

Every grain of rice seems to be a maggot. Everything seems to 41
stink. He can wipe the egg yolk off the found can, but he cannot
erase the stigma of eating garbage out of his mind.

That stage passes with experience. The scavenger finds a pair of 42
running shoes that fit and look and smell brand new. He finds
a pocket calculator in perfect working order. He finds pristine
ice cream, still frozen, more than he can eat or keep. He begins
to understand: people do throw away perfectly good stuff, a lot of
perfectly good stuff.

At this stage, Dumpster shyness begins to dissipate. The diver, 43
after all, has the last laugh. He is finding all manner of good things
which are his for the taking. Those who disparage his profession are
the fools, not he.

He may begin to hang onto some perfectly good things for 44
which he has neither a use nor a market. Then he begins to take note
of the things which are not perfectly good but are nearly so. He
mates a Walkman with broken earphones and one that is missing a
battery cover. He picks up things which he can repair.

At this stage he may become lost and never recover. Dumpsters 45
are full of things of some potential value to someone and also of
things which never have much intrinsic value but are interesting. All
the Dumpster divers I have known come to the point of trying to
acquire everything they touch. Why not take it, they reason, since it
is all free.

This is, of course, hopeless. Most divers come to realize that they 46
must restrict themselves to items of relatively immediate utility. But

in some cases the diver simply cannot control himself. I have met several of these pack-rat types. Their ideas of the values of various pieces of junk verge on the psychotic. Every bit of glass may be a diamond, they think, and all that glistens, gold.

I tend to gain weight when I am scavenging. Partly this is 47 because I always find far more pizza and doughnuts than water-packed tuna, nonfat yogurt, and fresh vegetables. Also I have not developed much faith in the reliability of Dumpsters as a food source, although it has been proven to me many times. I tend to eat as if I have no idea where my next meal is coming from. But mostly I just hate to see food go to waste and so I eat much more than I should. Something like this drives the obsession to collect junk.

As for collecting objects, I usually restrict myself to collecting 48 one kind of small object at a time, such as pocket calculators, sunglasses, or campaign buttons. To live on the street I must anticipate my needs to a certain extent: I must pick up and save warm bedding I find in August because it will not be found in Dumpsters in November. But even if I had a home with extensive storage space I could not save everything that might be valuable in some contingency.

I have proprietary feelings about my Dumpsters. As I have sug- 49 gested, it is no accident that I scavenge from Dumpsters where good finds are common. But my limited experience with Dumpsters in other areas suggests to me that it is the population of competitors rather than the affluence of the dumpers that most affects the feasibility of survival by scavenging. The large number of competitors is what puts me off the idea of trying to scavenge in places like Los Angeles.

Curiously, I do not mind my direct competition, other scav- 50 engers, so much as I hate the can scroungers.

People scrounge cans because they have to have a little cash. I 51 have tried scrounging cans with an able-bodied companion. Afoot a can scrounger simply cannot make more than a few dollars a day. One can extract the necessities of life from the Dumpsters directly with far less effort than would be required to accumulate the equivalent value in cans.

Can scroungers, then, are people who *must* have small amounts 52 of cash. These are drug addicts and winos, mostly the latter because the amounts of cash are so small.

Spirits and drugs do, like all other commodities, turn up in 53 dumpsters and the scavenger will from time to time have a half bottle of a rather good wine with his dinner. But the wino cannot survive on these occasional finds; he must have his daily dose to stave off the DTs. All the cans he can carry will buy about three bottles of Wild Irish Rose.

I do not begrudge them the cans, but can scroungers tend to 54
tear up the Dumpster, mixing the contents and littering the area.
They become so specialized that they can see only cans. They earn
my contempt by passing up change, canned goods, and readily hock-
able items.

There are precious few courtesies among scavengers. But is a com- 55
mon practice to set aside surplus items: pairs of shoes, clothing, canned
goods, and such. A true scavenger hates to see good stuff go to waste
and what he cannot use he leaves in good condition in plain sight.

Can scroungers lay waste to everything in their path and will stir 56
one of a pair of good shoes to the bottom of a Dumpster, to be lost
or ruined in the muck. Can scroungers will even go through individual garbage cans, something I have never seen a scavenger do.

Individual garbage cans are set out on the public easement only 57
on garbage days. On other days going through them requires tres-
passing close to a dwelling. Going through individual garbage cans
without scattering litter is almost impossible. Litter is likely to reduce
the public's tolerance of scavenging. Individual garbage cans are
simply not as productive as Dumpsters; people in houses and duplex-
es do not move as often and for some reason do not tend to discard
as much useful material. Moreover, the time required to go through
one garbage can that serves one household is not much less than the
time required to go through a Dumpster that contains the refuse of
twenty apartments.

But my strongest reservation about going through individual 58
garbage cans is that this seems to me a very personal kind of invasion
to which I would object if I were a householder. Although many
things in Dumpsters are obviously meant never to come to light, a
Dumpster is somehow less personal.

I avoid trying to draw conclusions about the people who dump in 59
the Dumpsters I frequent. I think it would be unethical to do so,
although I know many people will find the idea of scavenger ethics
too funny for words.

Dumpsters contain bank statements, bills, correspondence, and 60
other documents, just as anyone might expect. But there are also less
obvious sources of information. Pill bottles, for example. The labels
on pill bottles contain the name of the patient, the name of the
doctor, and the name of the drug. AIDS drugs and antipsychotic
medicines, to name but two groups, are specific and are seldom prescribed for any other disorders. The plastic compacts for birth control pills usually have complete label information.

Despite all of this sensitive information, I have had only one 61
apartment resident object to my going through the Dumpster. In

that case it turned out the resident was a university athlete who was taking bets and was afraid I would turn up his wager slips.

Occasionally a find tells a story. I once found a small paper bag 62 containing some unused condoms, several partial tubes of flavored sexual lubricant, a partially used compact of birth control pills, and the torn pieces of a picture of a young man. Clearly she was through with him and planning to give up sex altogether.

Dumpster things are often sad—abandoned teddy bears, shred- 63 ded wedding books, despaired-of sales kits. I find many pets lying in state in Dumpsters. Although I hope to get off the streets so that Lizbeth can have a long and comfortable old age, I know this hope is not very realistic. So I suppose when her time comes she too will go into a Dumpster. I will have no better place for her. And after all, for most of her life her livelihood has come from the Dumpster. When she finds something I think is safe that has been spilled into the Dumpster I let her have it. She already knows the route around the best Dumpsters. I like to think that if she survives me she will have a chance of evading the dog catcher and of finding her suste- nance on the route.

Silly vanities also come to rest in the Dumpsters. I am a rather 64 accomplished needleworker. I get a lot of materials from the Dumpsters. Evidently sorority girls, hoping to impress someone, perhaps themselves, with their mastery of a womanly art, buy a lot of embroider-by-number kits, work a few stitches horribly, and eventu- ally discard the whole mess. I pull out their stitches, turn the canvas over, and work original design. Do not think I refrain from chuck- ling as I make original gifts from these kits.

I find diaries and journals. I have often thought of compiling a 65 book of literary found objects. And perhaps I will one day. But what I find is hopelessly commonplace and bad without being, even unconsciously, camp. College students also discard their papers. I am horrified to discover the kind of paper which now merits an A in an undergraduate course. I am grateful, however, for the number of good books and magazines the students throw out.

In the area I know best I have never discovered vermin in the 66 Dumpster, but there are two kinds of kitty surprise. One is alley cats which I meet as they leap, claws first, out of Dumpsters. This is espe- cially thrilling when I have Lizbeth in tow. The other kind of kitty surprise is a plastic garbage bag filled with some ponderous, amor- phous mass. This always proves to be used cat litter.

City bees harvest doughnut glaze and this makes the Dumpster 67 at the doughnut shop more interesting. My faith in the instinctive wisdom of animals is always shaken whenever I see Lizbeth attempt to catch a bee in her mouth, which she does whenever bees are present. Evidently some birds find Dumpsters profitable, for birdie surprise is almost as common as kitty surprise of the first kind. In hunting season all kinds of small game turn up in Dumpsters, some of it, sadly, not entirely dead. Curiously, summer and winter, maggots are uncommon.

The worst of the living and near-living hazards of the Dumpsters 68 are the fire ants. The food that they claim is not much of a loss, but they are vicious and aggressive. It is very easy to brush against some surface of the Dumpster and pick up half a dozen or more fire ants, usually in some sensitive area such as the underarm. One advantage of bringing Lizbeth along as I make Dumpster rounds is that, for obvious reasons, she is very alert to ground-based fire ants. When Lizbeth recognizes the signs of fire ant infestation around our feet she does the Dance of the Zillion Fire Ants. I have learned not to ignore this warning from Lizbeth, whether I perceive the tiny ants or not, but to remove ourselves at Lizbeth's first pas de bourrée. All the more so because the ants are the worst in the months I wear flip-flops, if I have them.

(Perhaps someone will misunderstand the above. Lizbeth does 69 the Dance of the Zillion Fire Ants when she recognizes more fire ants than she cares to eat, not when she is being bitten. Since I have learned to react promptly, she does not get bitten at all. It is the isolated patrol of fire ants that falls in Lizbeth's range that deserve pity. Lizbeth finds them quite tasty.)

By far the best way to go through a Dumpster is to lower your- 70 self into it. Most of the good stuff tends to settle at the bottom because it is usually weightier than the rubbish. My more athletic companions have often demonstrated to me that they can extract much good material from a Dumpster I have already been over.

To those psychologically or physically unprepared to enter a 71 Dumpster, I recommend a stout stick, preferably with some barb or hook at one end. The hook can be used to grab plastic garbage bags. When I find canned goods or other objects loose at the bottom of a Dumpster I usually can roll them into a small bag that I can then hoist up. Much Dumpster diving is a matter of experience for which nothing will do except practice.

Dumpster diving is outdoor work, often surprisingly pleasant. It 72 is not entirely predictable; things of interest turn up every day and some say there are finds of great value. I am always very pleased when I can turn up exactly the thing I most wanted to find. Yet in spite of the element of chance, scavenging more than most other pursuits tends to yield returns in some proportion to the effort and intelligence brought to bear. It is very sweet to turn up a few dollars in change from a Dumpster that has just been gone over by a wino.

The land is now covered with cities. The cities are full of 73
Dumpsters. I think of scavenging as a modern form of self-reliance.
In any event, after ten years of government service, where everything
is geared to the lowest common denominator, I find work that
rewards initiative and effort refreshing. Certainly I would be happy
to have a sinecure again, but I am not heartbroken not to have one
anymore.

I find from the experience of scavenging two rather deep lessons. 74
The first is to take what I can use and let the rest go by. I have come
to think that there is no value in the abstract. A thing I cannot use
or make useful, perhaps by trading, has no value however fine or rare
it may be. I mean useful in a broad sense—so, for example, some art
I would think useful and valuable, but other art might be otherwise
for me.

I was shocked to realize that some things are not worth acquir- 75
ing, but now I think it is so. Some material things are white
elephants that eat up the possessor's substance.

The second lesson is of the transience of material being. This has 76
not quite converted me to a dualist, but it has made some headway
in that direction. I do not suppose that ideas are immortal, but certainly mental things are longer-lived than other material things.

Once I was the sort of person who invests material objects with 77
sentimental value. Now I no longer have those things, but I have the
sentiments yet.

Many times in my travels I have lost everything but the clothes 78
I was wearing and Lizbeth. The things I find in Dumpsters, the love
letters and ragdolls of so many lives, remind me of this lesson. Now
I hardly pick up a thing without envisioning the time I will cast it
away. This I think is a healthy state of mind. Almost everything I
have now has already been cast out at least once, proving that what
I own is valueless to someone.

Anyway, I find my desire to grab for the gaudy bauble has been 79
largely sated. I think this is an attitude I share with the very
wealthy—we both know there is plenty more where what we have
came from. Between us are the rat-race millions who have con-
founded their selves with the objects they grasp and who nightly
scavenge the cable channels looking for they know not what.

I am sorry for them. 80

EXPLORATIONS

1. Think about the literacies described and deployed in "On Dumpster
   Diving." What does Eighner think you need to know to become a

successful, literate Dumpster diver? What values do you need to assume? Why is Eighner a successful Dumpster diver?

2. How would you describe Eighner's writing style? How does this style contribute to his aims in writing this piece? Why do you think Eighner uses a number of precise terms to describe Dumpster diving? In what ways did these terms affect your understanding of Dumpster diving?

3. How would you describe Eighner's attitude towards students? Do you think he was writing specifically to students in this essay?

4. In what ways did Eighner meet or change your expectations about Dumpster divers? Why do you think that Eighner ended his essay by expressing sympathy for other kinds of scavengers?

5. Compare Eighner's and Tim O'Brien's essays for their use of lists. What is the effect of listing?

From Outside, In

BARBARA MELLIX

Barbara Mellix received her M.F.A. in creative writing in 1986 from the University of Pittsburgh. She is currently the assistant dean of the College of Arts and Sciences at the University of Pittsburgh, where she also teaches composition.

WRITING BEFORE READING

Think of a time when you changed or adjusted your language practices for a given setting. Why did you make these changes?

Two years ago, when I started writing this paper, trying to bring order out of chaos, my ten-year-old daughter was suffering from an acute attack of boredom. She drifted in and out of the room complaining that she had nothing to do, no one to "be with" because none of her friends were at home. Patiently I explained that I was working on something special and needed peace and quiet, and I suggested that she paint, read, or work with her computer. None of these interested her. Finally, she pulled up a chair to my desk and watched me, now and then heaving long, loud sighs. After two or three minutes (nine or ten sighs), I lost my patience. "Looka here, Allie," I said, "you are too old for this kinda carryin' on. I done told you this is important. You wronger than dirt to be in here haggin' me like this and you know it. Now git on outta here and leave me off before I put my foot all the way down."

I was at home, alone with my family, and my daughter understood that this way of speaking was appropriate in that context. She knew, as a matter of fact, that it was almost inevitable; when I get angry at home, I speak some of my finest, most cherished black English. Had I been speaking to my daughter in this manner in certain other environments, she would have been shocked and probably worried that I had taken leave of my sense of propriety.

Like my children, I grew up speaking what I considered two distinctly different languages—black English and standard English (or as I thought of them then, the ordinary everyday speech of "country" coloreds and "proper" English)—and in the process of acquiring these languages, I developed an understanding of when, where, and how to use them. But unlike my children, I grew up in a world that was primarily black. My friends, neighbors, minister, teachers— almost everybody I associated with every day—were black.

And we spoke to one another in our own special language: *That sho
is a pretty dress you got on. If she don' soon leave me off I'm gon
tell her head a mess. I was so mad I could'a pissed a blue rod. He
all the time trying to low-rate somebody. Ain't that just about the
nastiest thing you ever set ears on?*

Then there were the "others," the "proper" blacks, trans-   4
planted relatives and one-time friends who came home from the city
for weddings, funerals, and vacations. To these we spoke standard
English. "Ain't?" my mother would yell at me when I used the
term in the presence of "others." "You *know* better than that."
And I would hang my head in shame and say the "proper" word.

I remember one summer sitting in my grandmother's house in   5
Greeleyville, South Carolina, when it was full of the chatter of city
relatives who were home on vacation. My parents sat quietly, only
now and then volunteering a comment or answering a question. My
mother's face took on a strained expression when she spoke. I could
see that she was being careful to say just the right words in just the
right way. Her voice sounded thick, muffled. And when she finished
speaking, she would lapse into silence, her proper smile on her face.
My father was more articulate, more aggressive. He spoke quickly,
his words sharp and clear. But he held his proud head higher, a
signal that he, too, was uncomfortable. My sisters and brothers and
I stared at our aunts, uncles, and cousins, speaking only when
prompted. Even then, we hesitated, formed our sentences in our
minds, then spoke softly, shyly.

My parents looked small and anxious during those occasions,   6
and I waited impatiently for our leave-taking when we would mock
our relatives the moment we were out of their hearing. "Reeely, "
we would say to one another, flexing our wrists and rolling our eyes,
"how dooo you stan' this heat? Chile, it just too hyooo-mid for
words." Our relatives had made us feel "country," and this was our
way of regaining pride in ourselves while getting a little revenge in
the bargain. The words bubbled in our throats and rolled across our
tongues, a balming.

As a child I felt this same doubleness in uptown Greeleyville   7
where the whites lived. "Ain't that a pretty dress you're wearing!" Toby, the town policeman, said to me one day when I was
fifteen. "Thank you very much," I replied, my voice barely audible
in my own ears. The words felt wrong in my mouth, rigid, foreign.
It was not that I had never spoken that phrase before—it was common in black English, too—but I was extremely conscious that this
was an occasion for proper English. I had taken out my English and
put it on as I did my church clothes, and I felt as if I were wearing
my Sunday best in the middle of the week. It did not matter that

Toby had not spoken grammatically correct English. He was white
and could speak as he wished. I had something to prove. Toby did
not.

Speaking standard English to whites was our way of demonstrat-   8
ing that we knew their language and could use it. speaking it to
standard-English-speaking blacks was our way of showing them that
we, as well as they, could "put on airs." But when we spoke
standard English, we acknowledged (to ourselves and to others—but
primarily to ourselves) that our customary way of speaking was inferior. We felt foolish, embarrassed, somehow diminished because we
were ashamed to be our real selves. We were reserved, shy in the
presence of those who owned and/or spoke *the* language.

My parents never set aside time to drill us in standard English.   9
Their forms of instruction were less formal. When my father was feeling particularly expansive, he would regale us with tales of his
exploits in the outside world. In almost fluent English, complete
with dialogue and flavored with gestures and embellishment, he told
us about his attempt to get a haircut at a white barbershop; his
refusal to acknowledge one of the town merchants until the man
addressed him as "Mister"; the time he refused to step off the sidewalk uptown to let some whites pass; his airplane trip to New York
City (to visit a sick relative) during which the stewardess and
porters—recognizing that he was a "gentleman"—addressed him as
"Sir." I did not realize then—nor, I think, did my father—that he
was teaching us, among other things, standard English and the relationship between language and power.

My mother's approach was different. Often, when one of us   10
said, "I'm gon wash off my feet," she would say, "And what will
you walk on if you wash them off?" Everyone would laugh at the
victim of my mother's "proper" mood. But it was different when
one of us children was in a proper mood. "You think you are so
superior," I said to my oldest sister one day when we were arguing
and she was winning. "Superior!" my sister mocked. "You mean I
am acting 'biggidy'? My sisters and brothers sniggered, then
joined in teasing me. Finally, my mother said, "Leave your sister
alone. There's nothing wrong with using proper English." There
was a half-smile on her face. I had gotten "uppity," had "put on
airs" for no good reason. I was at home, alone with the family, and
I hadn't been prompted by one of my mother's proper moods.
But there was also a proud light in my mother's eyes; her children
were learning English very well.

Not until years later, as a college student, did I begin to under-   11
stand our ambivalence toward English, our scorn of it, our need
to master it, to own and be owned by it—an ambivalence that

extended to the public-school classroom. In our school, where there were no whites, my teachers taught standard English but used black English to do it. When my grammar-school teachers wanted us to write, for example, they usually said something like, "I want y'all to write five sentences that make a statement. Anybody get done before the rest can color." It was probably almost those exact words that led me to write these sentences in 1953 when I was in the second grade:

> The white clouds are pretty.
> There are only 15 people in our room.
> We will go to gym.
> We have a new poster.
> We may go out doors.

Second grade came after "Little First" and "Big First," so by then I knew the implied rules that accompanied all writing assignments. Writing was an occasion for proper English. I was not to write in the way we spoke to one another: The white clouds pretty; There ain't but 15 people in our room; We going to gym; We got a new poster; We can go out in the yard. Rather I was to use the language of "other": clouds *are*, there *are*, we *will*, we *may*.

My sentences were short, rigid, perfunctory, like the letters my   12
mother wrote to relatives:

> Dear Papa,
> How are you? How is Mamie? Fine I hope. We are fine. We will come
> to see you Sunday. Cousin Ned will give us a ride.
>   Love,
>   Daughter

The language was not ours. It was something from outside us, something we used for special occasions.

But my coloring on the other side of that second-grade paper is   13
different. I drew three hearts and a sun. The sun has a smiling face that radiates and envelops everything it touches. And although the sun and its world are enclosed in a circle, the colors I used—red, blue, green, purple, orange, yellow, black—indicates that I was less restricted with drawing and coloring than I was with writing standard English. My valentines were not just red. My sun was not just a yellow ball in the sky.

By the time I reached the twelfth grade, speaking and writing   14
standard English had taken on new importance. Each year, about half of the newly graduated seniors of our school moved to large cities—particularly in the North—to live with relatives and find work. Our English teacher constantly corrected our grammar: "Not 'ain't,' but 'isn't.'" We seldom wrote papers, and even those few

were usually plot summaries of short stories. When our teacher returned the papers, she usually lectured on the importance of using standard English: "I *am;* you *are;* he, she, or it *is*," she would say, writing on the chalkboard as she spoke. "How you gon git a job talking about 'I is,' or 'I isn't' or 'I ain't' ? "

In Pittsburgh, where I moved after graduation, I watched my aunt and uncle—who had always spoken standard English when in Greeleyville—switch from black English to standard English to a mixture of the two, according to where they were or who they were with. At home and with certain close relatives, friends, and neighbors, they spoke black English. With those less close, they spoke a mixture. In public and with strangers, they generally spoke standard English. 15

In time, I learned to speak standard English with ease and to switch smoothly from black to standard or a mixture, and back again. But no matter where I was, no matter what the situation or occasion, I continued to write as I had in school: 16

> Dear Mommie,
> How are you? How is everybody else? Fine I hope. I am fine. So are Aunt and Uncle. Tell everyone I said hello. I will write again soon.
> Love,
> Barbara

At work, at a health insurance company, I learned to write letters to customers. I studied form letters and letters written by co-workers, memorizing the phrases and the ways in which they were used. I dictated:

> Thank you for your letter of January 5. We have made the changes in your coverage you requested. Your new premium will be $150 every three months. We are pleased to have been of service to you.

In a sense, I was proud of the letters I wrote for the company: they were proof of my ability to survive in the city, the outside world—an indication of my growing mastery of English. But they also indicate that writing was still mechanical for me, something that didn't require much thought.

Reading also became a more significant part of my life during those early years in Pittsburgh. I had always liked reading, but now I devoted more and more of my spare time to it. I read romances, mysteries, popular novels. Looking back, I realized that the books I liked best were simple, unambiguous: good versus bad and right versus wrong with right rewarded and wrong punished, mysteries unraveled and all set right in the end. It was how I remembered life in Greeleyville. 17

Of course I was romanticizing. Life in Greeleyville had not been   18
so very uncomplicated. Back there I had been—first as a child, then
as a young woman with limited experience in the outside world—
living in a relatively closed-in society. But there were implicit and
explicit principles that guided our way of life and shaped our relationships with one another and the people outside—principles that a
newcomer would find elusive and baffling. In Pittsburgh, I had
matured, become more experienced: I had worked at three different
jobs, associated with a wider range of people, married, had children.
This new environment with different prescripts for living required
that I speak standard English much of the time, and slowly, imper-
ceptibly, I had ceased seeing a sharp distinction between myself and
"others." Reading romances and mysteries, characterized by
dichotomy, was a way of shying away from change, from the person
I was becoming.

But that other part of me—that part which took great pride in   19
my ability to hold a job writing business letters—was increasingly
drawn to the new developments in my life and the attending possibilities, opportunities for even greater change. If I could write letters
for a nationally known business, could I not also do something better, more challenging, more important? Could I not, perhaps, go to
college and become a school teacher? For years, afraid and a little
embarrassed, I did no more than imagine this different me, this
possible me. But sixteen years after coming north, when my younger
daughter entered kindergarten, I found myself unable—or unwilling—to resist the lure of possibility. I enrolled in my first college
course: Basic Writing, at the University of Pittsburgh.

For the first time in my life, I was required to write extensively   20
about myself. Using the most formal English at my command, I
wrote these sentences near the beginning of the term:

> One of my duties as a homemaker is simply picking up after others. A
> day seldom passes that I don't search for a mislaid toy, book, or gym
> shoe, etc. I change the Ty-D-Bol, fight "ring around the collar," and
> keep our laundry smelling "April fresh." Occasionally, I settle argu-
> ments between my children and suggest things to do when they're
> bored. Taking telephone messages for my oldest daughter is my newest
> (and sometimes most aggravating) chore. Hanging the toilet paper is
> my most insignificant.

My concern was to use "appropriate" language, to sound as if I
belonged in a college classroom. But I felt separate from the
language—as if it did not and could not belong to me. I couldn't
think and feel genuinely in that language, couldn't make it express
what I thought and felt about being a housewife. A part of me
resented, among other things, being judged by such things as the

appearance of my family's laundry and toilet bowl, but in that language I could only imagine and write about a conventional housewife.

For the most part, the remainder of the term was a period of 21 adjustment, a time of trying to find my bearings as a student in a college composition class, to learn to shut out my black English whenever I composed, and to prevent it from creeping into my formulations; a time for trying to grasp the language of the classroom and reproduce it in my prose; for trying to talk about myself in that language, reach others through it. Each experience of writing was like standing naked and revealing my imperfection, my "otherness." And each new assignment was another chance to make myself over in language, reshape myself, make myself "better" in my rapidly changing image of a student in a college composition class.

But writing became increasingly unmanageable as the term pro- 22 gressed, and by the end of the semester, my sentences sounded like this:

> My excitement was soon dampened, however, by what seemed like a small voice in the back of my head saying that I should be careful with my long awaited opportunity. I felt frustrated and this seemed to make it difficult to concentrate.

There is a poverty of language in these sentences. By this point, I knew that the clichéd language of my Housewife essay was unacceptable, and I generally recognized trite expressions. At the same time, I hadn't yet mastered the language of the classroom, hadn't yet come to see it as belonging to me. Most notable is the lifelessness of the prose, the apparent absence of a person behind the words. I wanted those sentences—and the rest of the essay—to convey the anguish of yearning to, at once, become something more and yet remain the same. I had the sensation of being split in two, part of me going into a future the other part didn't believe possible. As that person, the student writer at that moment, I was essentially mute. I could not—in the process of composing—use the language of the old me, yet I couldn't imagine myself in the language of "others."

I found this particularly discouraging because at midsemester I 23 had been writing in a much different way. Note the language of this introduction to an essay I had written then, near the middle of the term:

> Pain is a constant companion to the people in "Footwork." Their jobs are physically damaging. Employers are insensitive to their feelings and in many cases add to their problems. The general public wounds them further by treating them with disgrace because of what they do for a liv-

ing. Although the workers are as diverse as they are similar, there is a definite link between them. They suffer a great deal of abuse.

The voice here is stronger, more confident, appropriate terms like "physically damaging," "wounds them further," "insensitive," "diverse"—terms I couldn't have imagined using when writing about my own experience—and shaping them into sentences like "Although the workers are as diverse as they are similar, there is a definite link between them." And there is the sense of a personality behind the prose, someone who sympathizes with the workers. "The general public wounds them further by treating them with disgrace because of what they do for a living."

What causes these differences? I was, I believed, explaining other people's thoughts and feelings, and I was free to move about in the language of "others" so long as I was speaking *of* others. I was unaware that I was transforming into my best classroom language my own thoughts and feelings about people whose experiences and ways of speaking were in many ways similar to mine.   24

The following year, unable to turn back or to let go of what had become something of an obsession with language (and hoping to catch and hold the sense of control that had eluded me in Basic Writing), I enrolled in a research writing course. I spent most of the term learning how to prepare for and write a research paper. I chose sex education as my subject and spent hours in libraries, searching for information, reading, taking notes. Then (not without messiness and often demoralizing frustration) I organized my information into categories, wrote a thesis statement, and composed my paper—a series of paragraphs and quotations spaced between carefully constructed transitions. The process and results felt artificial, but as I would later come to realize I was passing through a necessary stage. My sentences sounded like this: 25

> This reserve becomes understandable with examination of who the abusers are. In an overwhelming number of cases, they are people the victims know and trust. Family members, relatives, neighbors, and close family friends commit seventy-five percent of all reported sex crimes against children, and parents, parent substitutes and relatives are the offenders in thirty to eighty percent of all reported cases. While assault by strangers does occur, it is less common, and is usually a single episode. But abuse by family members, relatives and acquaintances may continue for an extended period of time. In cases of incest, for example, children are abused repeatedly for an average of eight years. In such cases, "the use of physical force is rarely necessary because of the child's trusting, dependent relationship with the offender. The child's cooperation is often facilitated by the adult's position of dominance, an offer of material goods, a threat of physical violence, or a misrepresentation of moral standards."

The completed paper gave me a sense of profound satisfaction, 26
and I read it often after my professor returned it. I know now that
what I was pleased with was the language I used and the professional voice it helped me maintain. "Use better words," my teacher had
snapped at me one day after reading the notes I'd begun accumulating from my research, and slowly I began taking on the language
of my sources. In my next set of notes, I used the word "vacillat-
ing"; my professor applauded. And by the time I composed the final
draft, I felt at ease with terms like "overwhelming number of
cases," "single episode," and "reserve," and I shaped them into
sentences similar to those of my "expert" sources.

If I were writing the paper today, I would of course do some 27
things differently. Rather than open with an anecdote—as my teacher
suggested—I would begin simply with a quotation that caught my
interest as I was researching my paper (and which I scribbled, without its source, in the margin of my notebook): "Truth does not do
so much good in the world as the semblance of truth does evil." The
quotation felt right because it captured what was for me the central
idea of my essay—an idea that emerged gradually during the making
of my paper—and expressed it in a way I would like to have said it.
The anecdote, a hypothetical situation I invented to conform to the
information in the paper, felt forced and insincere because it represented—to a great degree—my teacher's understanding of the essay,
her idea of what in it was most significant. Improving upon my previous experiences with writing, I was beginning to think and feel in
the language I used, to find my own voices in it, to sense that how
one speaks influences how one means. But I was not yet secure
enough, comfortable enough with the language to trust my intuition.

Now that I know that to seek knowledge, freedom, and autono- 28
my means always to be in the concentrated process of becoming—
always to be venturing into new territory, feeling one's way at first,
then getting one's balance, negotiating, accommodating, discovering
one's self in ways that previously defined "others"—I sometimes get
tired. And I ask myself why I keep on participating in this highbrow
form of violence, this slamming against perplexity. But there is no real
futility in the question, no hint of that part of the old me who stood
outside standard English, hugging to herself a disabling mistrust of a
language she thought could not represent a person with her history
and experience. Rather, the question represents a person who feels the
consequences of her education, the weight of her possibilities as a
teacher and writer and human being, a voice in society. And I would
not change that person, would not give back the good burden that
accompanies my growing expertise, my increasing power to shape
myself in language and share that self with "others."

"To speak," says Frantz Fanon, "means to be in a position to   29
use a certain syntax, to grasp the morphology of this or that language, but it means above all to assume a culture, to support the
weight of civilization."[1] To write means to do the same, but in a
more profound sense. However, Fanon also says that to achieve
mastery means to "get" in a position of power, to "grasp," to
"assume." This I have learned both as a student and subsequently
as a teacher—can involve tremendous emotional and psychological
conflict for those attempting to master academic disclosure.
Although as a beginning student writer I had a fairly good grasp of
ordinary spoken English and was proficient at what Labov calls
"code-switching" (and what John Baugh in *Black Street Speech*
terms "style shifting"), when I came face to face with the demands
of academic writing, I grew increasingly self-conscious, constantly
aware of my status as a black and a speaker of one of the many black
English vernaculars—a traditional outsider. For the first time, I experienced my sense of doubleness as something menacing, a built-in
enemy. Whenever I turned inward for salvation, the balm so available
during my childhood, I found instead this new fragmentation which
spoke to me in many voices. It was the voice of my desire to prosper,
but at the same time it spoke of what I had relinquished and could
not regain: a safe way of being, a state of powerlessness which
exempted me from responsibility for who I was and might be. And
it accused me of betrayal, of turning away from blackness. To recover balance, I had to take on the language of the academy, the
language of "others." And to do that, I had to learn to imagine
myself as a part of the culture of that language, and therefore someone free to manage that language, to take liberties with it. Writing
and rewriting, practicing, experimenting, I came to comprehend
more fully the generative power of language. I discovered—with the
help of some especially sensitive teachers—that through writing one
can continually bring new selves into being, each with new responsibilities and difficulties, but also with new possibilities. Remarkable
power, indeed. I write and continually give birth to myself.

NOTE

[1] *Black Skin, White masks* (1952; rpt. New York: Grove Press, 1967), pp.
     17–18.

EXPLORATIONS

1. As a child, Mellix's choice of how and when to speak is governed more
   by her community's sense of "propriety" than by her sense of what

constitutes effective or expressive speech. Who determines what this proper speech is, and how does Mellix come to know this? In what ways does Mellix distinguish when to use different kinds of language?

2. In what ways does Mellix come to feel a sense of ownership and belonging for different kinds of language? Can you choose which kinds of language she would like to "own"?

3. Mellix says she realized "the implied rules that accompany all writing assignments," namely that they require standard American English. What do you think the rules are for language in this class and what are some of the ways that you have become familiar with them?

4. As the writer of "From Outside, In," what is Barbara Mellix's rhetorical situation? In other words, how has Mellix written her speaking "selves" into this essay? How does her position as speaker/writer affect how she deals with the subjects of language and literacy? Who seems to be included in Mellix's primary audience for this essay?

Aria: A Memoir of a Bilingual Childhood

RICHARD RODRIGUEZ

Born the son of Mexican immigrants in Sacramento, California, Richard Rodriguez describes his experiences with language and education in his autobiographical book Hunger of Memory *(1982). For Rodriguez, the transition from Spanish (the private language of his home and family) to English (the public language of the school) was necessary for his growth as an individual. In the following essay he examines both the losses and gains of this transition.*

WRITING BEFORE READING

Have you ever been in a situation where you did not speak the language being used by most of the people? How did you communicate?

I remember, to start with, that day in Sacramento, in a California now nearly thirty years past, when I first entered a classroom—able to understand about fifty stray English words. The third of four children, I had been preceded by my older brother and sister to a neighborhood Roman Catholic school. But neither of them had revealed very much about their classroom experiences. They left each morning and returned each afternoon, always together, speaking Spanish as they climbed the five steps to the porch. And their mysterious books, wrapped in brown shopping-bag paper, remained on the table next to the door, closed firmly behind them.

An accident of geography sent me to a school where all my classmates were white and many were the children of doctors and lawyers and business executives. On that first day of school, my classmates must certainly have been uneasy to find themselves apart from their families, in the first institution of their lives. But I was astonished. I was fated to be the "problem student" in class.

The nun said, in a friendly but oddly impersonal voice: "Boys and girls, this is Richard Rodriguez." (I heard her sound it out: *Rich-heard Road-ree-guess.*) It was the first time I had heard anyone say my name in English. "Richard," the nun repeated more slowly, writing my name down in her book. Quickly I turned to see my mother's face dissolve in a watery blur behind the pebbled-glass door.

Now, many years later, I hear of something called "bilingual education"—a scheme proposed in the late 1960s by Hispanic-

American social activists, later endorsed by a congressional vote. It is a program that seeks to permit non-English-speaking children (many from lower class homes) to use their "family language" as the language of school. Such, at least, is the aim its supporters announce. I hear them, and am forced to say no: It is not possible for a child, any child, ever to use his family's language in school. Not to understand this is to misunderstand the public uses of schooling and to trivialize the nature of intimate life.

Memory teaches me what I know of these matters. The boy reminds the adult. I was a bilingual child, but of a certain kind: "socially disadvantaged," the son of working-class parents, both Mexican immigrants.

In the early years of my boyhood, my parents coped very well in America. My father had steady work. My mother managed at home. They were nobody's victims. When we moved to a house many blocks from the Mexican-American section of town, they were not intimidated by those two or three neighbors who initially tried to make us unwelcome. ("Keep your brats away from my sidewalk!") But despite all they achieved, or perhaps because they had so much to achieve, they lacked any deep feeling of ease, of belonging in public. They regarded the people at work or in crowds as being very distant from us. Those were the others, *los gringos*. That term was interchangeable in their speech with another, even more telling: *los americanos*.

I grew up in a house where the only regular guests were my relations. On a certain day, enormous families of relatives would visit us, and there would be so many people that the noise and the bodies would spill out to the backyard and onto the front porch. Then for weeks no one would come. (If the doorbell rang, it was usually a salesman.) Our house stood apart—gaudy yellow in a row of white bungalows. We were the people with the noisy dog, the people who raised chickens. We were the foreigners on the block. A few neighbors would smile and wave at us. We waved back. But until I was seven years old, I did not know the name of the old couple living next door or the names of the kids living across the street.

In public, my father and mother spoke a hesitant, accented, and not always grammatical English. And then they would have to strain, their bodies tense, to catch the sense of what was rapidly said by *los gringos*. At home, they returned to Spanish. The language of their Mexican past sounded in counterpoint to the English spoken in public. The words would come quickly, with ease. Conveyed through those sounds was the pleasing, soothing, consoling reminder that one was at home.

During those years when I was first learning to speak, my mother and father addressed me only in Spanish; in Spanish I learned to

reply. By contrast, English (*inglés*) was the language I came to associate with gringos, rarely heard in the house. I learned my first words
of English overhearing my parents speaking to strangers. At six years
of age, I knew just enough words for my mother to trust me on
errands to stores one block away—but no more.

I was then a listening child, careful to hear the very different   10
sounds of Spanish and English. Wide-eyed with hearing, I'd listen
to sounds more than to words. First, there were English (gringo)
sounds. So many words still were unknown to me that when the
butcher or the lady at the drugstore said something, exotic polysyl-
labic sounds would bloom in the midst of their sentences. Often the
speech of people in public seemed to me very loud, booming with
confidence. The man behind the counter would literally ask, "What
can I do for you?" But by being so firm and clear, the sound of his
voice said that he was a gringo; he belonged in public society. There
were also the high, nasal notes of middle-class American speech—
which I rarely am conscious of hearing today because I hear them so
often, but could not stop hearing when I was a boy. Crowds at
Safeway or at bus stops were noisy with the birdlike sounds of *los
gringos*. I'd move away from them all—all the chirping chatter
above me.

My own sounds I was unable to hear, but I knew that I spoke   11
English poorly. My words could not extend to form complete
thoughts. And the words I did speak I didn't know well enough to
make distinct sounds. (Listeners would usually lower their heads to
hear better what I was trying to say.) But it was one thing for *me*
to speak English with difficulty; it was more troubling to hear my
parents speaking in public: their high-whining vowels and guttural
consonants; their sentences that got stuck with "eh" and "ah"
sounds; the confused syntax; the hesitant rhythm of sounds so
different from the way gringos spoke. I'd notice, moreover, that my
parents' voices were softer than those of gringos we would meet.

I am tempted to say now that none of this mattered. (In adult-   12
hood I am embarrassed by childhood fears.) And, in a way, it didn't
matter very much that my parents could not speak English with ease.
Their linguistic difficulties had no serious consequences. My mother
and father made themselves understood at the county hospital clinic
and at government offices. And yet, in another way, it mattered very
much. It was unsettling to hear my parents struggle with English.
Hearing them, I'd grow nervous, and my clutching trust in their
protection and power would be weakened.

There were many times like the night at a brightly lit gasoline   13
station (a blaring white memory) when I stood uneasily hearing my
father talk to a teenage attendant. I do not recall what they were saying, but I cannot forget the sounds my father made as he spoke. At

one point his words slid together to form one long word—sounds as confused as the threads of blue and green oil in the puddle next to my shoes. His voice rushed through what he had left to say. Toward the end, he reached falsetto notes, appealing to his listener's understanding. I looked away at the lights of passing automobiles. I tried not to hear any more. But I heard only too well the attendant's reply, his calm, easy tones. Shortly afterward, headed for home, I shivered when my father put his hand on my shoulder. The very first chance that I got, I evaded his grasp and ran on ahead into the dark, skipping with feigned boyish exuberance.

But then there was Spanish: *español,* the language rarely heard   14
away from the house; *español,* the language which seemed to me therefore a private language, my family's language. To hear its sounds was to feel myself specially recognized as one of the family, apart from *los otros.* A simple remark, an inconsequential comment could convey that assurance. My parents would say something to me and I would feel embraced by the sounds of their words. Those sounds said: *I am speaking with ease in Spanish. I am addressing you in words I never use with los gringos. I recognize you as someone special, close, like no one outside. You belong with us. In the family. Ricardo.*

At the age of six, well past the time when most middle-class   15
children no longer notice the difference between sounds uttered at home and words spoken in public, I had a different experience. I lived in a world compounded of sounds. I was a child longer than most. I lived in a magical world, surrounded by sounds both pleasing and fearful. I shared with my family a language enchantingly private—different from that used in the city around us.

Just opening or closing the screen door behind me was an   16
important experience. I'd rarely leave home all alone or without feeling reluctance. Walking down the sidewalk, under the canopy of tall trees, I'd warily notice the (suddenly) silent neighborhood kids who stood warily watching me. Nervously, I'd arrive at the grocery store to hear there the sounds of the gringo, reminding me that in this so-big world I was a foreigner. But if leaving home was never routine, neither was coming back. Walking toward our house, climbing the steps from the sidewalk, in summer when the front door was open, I'd hear voices beyond the screen door talking in Spanish. For a second or two I'd stay, linger there listening. Smiling, I'd hear my mother call out, saying in Spanish, "Is that you, Richard?" Those were her words, but all the while her sounds would assure me: *You are home now. Come closer inside. With us.* "*Sí,* " I'd reply.

Once more inside the house, I would resume my place in the   17
family. The sounds would grow harder to hear. Once more at home, I would grow less conscious of them. It required, however, no more than the blurt of the doorbell to alert me all over again to listen to

sounds. The house would turn instantly quiet while my mother went to the door. I'd hear her hard English sounds. I'd wait to hear her voice turn to soft-sounding Spanish, which assured me, as surely as did the clicking tongue of the lock on the door, that the stranger was gone.

Plainly, it is not healthy to hear such sounds often. It is not healthy to distinguish public from private sounds so easily. I remained cloistered by sounds, timid and shy in public, too dependent on the voices at home. And yet I was a very happy child when I was at home. I remember many nights when my father would come back from work, and I'd hear him call out to my mother in Spanish, sounding relieved. In Spanish, his voice would sound the light and free notes that he never could manage in English. Some nights I'd jump up just hearing his voice. My brother and I would come running into the room where he was with our mother. Our laughing (so deep was the pleasure!) became screaming. Like others who feel the pain of public alienation, we transformed the knowledge of our public separateness into a consoling reminder of our intimacy. Excited, our voices joined in a celebration of sounds. *We are speaking now the way we never speak out in public—we are together,* the sounds told me. Some nights no one seemed willing to loosen the hold that sounds had on us. At dinner we invented new words that sounded Spanish, but made sense only to us. We pieced together new words by taking, say, an English verb and giving it Spanish endings. My mother's instructions at bedtime would be lacquered with mock-urgent tones. Or a word like *sí*, sounded in several notes, would convey added measures of feeling. Tongues lingered around the edges of words, especially fat vowels, and we happily sounded that military drum roll, the twirling roar of the Spanish *r*. Family language, my family's sounds: the voices of my parents and sisters and brother. Their voices insisting: *You belong here. We are family members. Related. Special to one another. Listen!* Voices singing and sighing, rising and straining, then surging, teeming with pleasure which burst syllables into fragments of laughter. At times it seemed there was steady quiet only when, from another room, the rustling whispers of my parents faded and I edged closer to sleep.

Supporters of bilingual education imply today that students like me miss a great deal by not being taught in their family's language. What they seem not to recognize is that, as a socially disadvantaged child, I regarded Spanish as a private language. The odd truth is that my first-grade classmates could have become bilingual, in the conventional sense of the word, more easily than I. Had they been taught early (as upper middle-class children often are taught) a "second language" like Spanish or French, they could have regarded it simply as another public language. In my case, such bilingualism could not have been so quickly achieved. What I did not believe was that I could speak a single public language.

Without question, it would have pleased me to have heard my teachers address me in Spanish when I entered the classroom. I would have felt much less afraid. I would have imagined that my instructors were somehow "related" to me: I would indeed have heard their Spanish as my family's language. I would have trusted them and responded with ease. But I would have delayed—postponed for how long?—having to learn the language of public society. I would have evaded—and for how long?—learning the great lesson of school: that I had a public identity.

Fortunately, my teachers were unsentimental about their responsibility. What they understood was that I needed to speak public English. So their voices would search me out, asking me questions. Each time I heard them I'd look up in surprise to see a nun's face frowning at me. I'd mumble, not really meaning to answer. The nun would persist. "Richard, stand up. Don't look at the floor. Speak up. Speak to the entire class, not just to me!" But I couldn't believe English could be my language to use. (In part, I did not want to believe it.) I continued to mumble. I resisted the teacher's demands. (Did I somehow suspect that once I learned this public language my family life would be changed?) Silent, waiting for the bell to sound, I remained dazed, diffident, afraid.

Because I wrongly imagined that English was intrinsically a public language and Spanish was intrinsically private, I easily noted the difference between classroom language and the language at home. At school, words were directed to a general audience of listeners. ("Boys and girls . . .") Words were meaningfully ordered. And the point was not self-expression alone, but to make oneself understood by many others. The teacher quizzed: "Boys and girls, why do we use that word in this sentence? Could we think of a better word to use there? Would the sentence change its meaning if the words were differently arranged? Isn't there a better way of saying much the same thing?" (I couldn't say. I wouldn't try to say.)

Three months passed. Five. A half year. Unsmiling, ever watchful, my teachers noted my silence. They began to connect my behavior with the slow progress my brother and sisters were making. Until, one Saturday morning, three nuns arrived at the house to talk to our parents. Stiffly they sat on the blue living-room sofa. From the doorway of another room, spying on the visitors, I noted the incongruity, the clash of two worlds, the faces and voices of school intruding upon the familiar setting of home. I overheard one voice gently wondering, "Do your children speak only Spanish at home, Mrs. Rodriguez?" While another voice added, "That Richard especially seems so timid and shy. "

That Rich-heard!   24

With great tact, the visitors continued, "Is it possible for you   25
and your husband to encourage your children to practice their
English when they are home?" Of course my parents complied.
What would they not do for their children's well-being? And how
could they question the Church's authority which those women
represented? In an instant they agreed to give up the language (the
sounds) which had revealed and accentuated our family's closeness.
The moment after the visitors left, the change was observed.
"Ahora, speak to us only *en inglés*, "my father and mother told us.

At first, it seemed a kind of game. After dinner each night, the   26
family gathered together to practice "our" English. It was still then
inglés, a language foreign to us, so we felt drawn to it as strangers.
Laughing, we would try to define words we could not pronounce.
We played with strange English sounds, often overanglicizing our
pronunciations. And we filled the smiling gaps of our sentences with
familiar Spanish sounds. But that was cheating, somebody shouted,
and everyone laughed.

In school, meanwhile, like my brother and sister, I was required   27
to attend a daily tutoring session. I needed a full year of this special
work. I also needed my teachers to keep my attention from straying
in class by calling out, *"Rich-heard"*—their English voices slowly
loosening the ties to my other name, with its three notes, *Ri-car-do*.
Most of all, I needed to hear my mother and father speak to me in a
moment of seriousness in "broken"— suddenly heartbreaking—
English. This scene was inevitable. One Saturday morning I entered
the kitchen where my parents were talking, but I did not realize that
they were talking in Spanish until, the moment they saw me, their
voices changed and they began speaking English. The gringo sounds
they uttered startled me. Pushed me away. In that moment of trivial
misunderstanding and profound insight, I felt my throat twisted by
unsounded grief. I simply turned and left the room. But I had no
place to escape to where I could grieve in Spanish. My brother and
sisters were speaking English in another part of the house.

Again and again in the days following, as I grew increasingly   28
angry, I was obliged to hear my mother and father encouraging me:
"Speak to us *en inglés*. " Only then did I determine to learn classroom English. Thus, sometime afterward it happened: one day in
school, I raised my hand to volunteer an answer to a question. I
spoke out in a loud voice and I did not think it remarkable when the
entire class understood. That day I moved very far from being the
disadvantaged child I had been only days earlier. Taken hold at last
was the belief, the calming assurance, that I *belonged* in public.

Shortly after, I stopped hearing the high, troubling sounds of *los*   29
gringos. A more and more confident speaker of English, I didn't

listen to how strangers sounded when they talked to me. With so many English-speaking people around me, I no longer heard American accents. Conversations quickened. Listening to persons whose voices sounded eccentrically pitched, I might note their sounds for a few seconds, but then I'd concentrate on what they were saying. Now when I heard someone's tone of voice—angry or questioning or sarcastic or happy or sad—I didn't distinguish it from the words it expressed. Sound and word were thus tightly wedded. At the end of each day I was often bemused, and always relieved, to realize how "soundless," though crowded with words, my day in public had been. An eight-year-old boy, I finally came to accept what had been technically true since my birth: I was an American citizen.

But diminished by then was the special feeling of closeness at home. Gone was the desperate, urgent, intense feeling of being at home among those with whom I felt intimate. Our family remained a loving family, but one greatly changed. We were no longer so close, no longer bound tightly together by the knowledge of our separateness from *los gringos*. Neither my older brother nor my sisters rushed home after school any more. Nor did I. When I arrived home, often there would be neighborhood kids in the house. Or the house would be empty of sounds.

Following the dramatic Americanization of their children, even my parents grew more publicly confident—especially my mother. First she learned the names of all the people on the block. Then she decided we needed to have a telephone in our house. My father, for his part, continued to use the word gringo, but it was no longer charged with bitterness or distrust. Stripped of any emotional content, the word simply became a name for those Americans not of Hispanic descent. Hearing him, sometimes, I wasn't sure if he was pronouncing the Spanish word *gringo*, or saying gringo in English.

There was a new silence at home. As we children learned more and more English, we shared fewer and fewer words with our parents. Sentences needed to be spoken slowly when one of us addressed our mother or father. Often the parent wouldn't understand. The child would need to repeat himself. Still the parent misunderstood. The young voice, frustrated, would end up saying, "Never mind"—the subject was closed. Dinners would be noisy with the clinking of knives and forks against dishes. My mother would smile softly between her remarks; my father, at the other end of the table, would chew and chew his food while he stared over the heads of his children.

My mother! My father! After English became my primary language, I no longer knew what words to use in addressing my parents. The old Spanish words (those tender accents of sound) I had earlier

used—*mamá* and *papá*—I couldn't use any more. They would have
been all-too-painful reminders of how much had changed in my life.
On the other hand, the words I heard neighborhood kids call their
parents seemed equally unsatisfactory. "Mother" and "father, "
"ma," "papa," "pa," "dad," "pop" (how I hated the all-
American sound of that last word)—all these I felt were unsuitable
terms of address for *my* parents. As a result, I never used them at
home. Whenever I'd speak to my parents, I would try to get their
attention by looking at them. In public conversations, I'd refer to
them as my "parents" or my "mother" and "father. "

My mother and father, for their part, responded differently, as   34
their children spoke to them less. My mother grew restless, seemed
troubled and anxious at the scarceness of words exchanged in the
house. She would question me about my day when I came home
from school. She smiled at my small talk. She pried at the edges of
my sentences to get me to say something more. ("What . . . ?")
She'd join conversations she overheard, but her intrusions often
stopped her children's talking. By contrast, my father seemed to
grow reconciled to the new quiet. Though his English somewhat
improved, he tended more and more to retire into silence. At dinner
he spoke very little. One night his children and even his wife helplessly giggled at his garbled English pronunciation of the Catholic
"Grace Before Meals." Thereafter he made his wife recite the
prayer at the start of each meal, even on formal occasions when there
were guests in the house.

Hers became the public voice of the family. On official business   35
it was she, not my father, who would usually talk to strangers on the
phone or in stores. We children grew so accustomed to his silence
that years later we would routinely refer to his "shyness." (My
mother often tried to explain: both of his parents died when he was
eight. He was raised by an uncle who treated him as little more than
a menial servant. He was never encouraged to speak. He grew up
alone—a man of few words.) But I realized my father was not shy
whenever I'd watch him speaking Spanish with relatives. Using
Spanish, he was quickly effusive. Especially when talking with other
men, his voice would spark, flicker, flare alive with varied sounds. In
Spanish he expressed ideas and feeling he rarely revealed when speaking English. With firm Spanish sounds he conveyed a confidence and
authority that English would never allow him.

The silence at home, however, was not simply the result of fewer   36
words passing between parents and children. More profound for me
was the silence created by inattention to sounds. At about the time
I no longer bothered to listen with care to the sounds of English in
public, I grew careless about listening to the sounds made by the
family when they spoke. Most of the time I would hear someone

speaking at home and didn't distinguish his sounds from the words people uttered in public. I didn't even pay much attention to my parents' accented and ungrammatical speech—at least not at home. Only when I was with them in public would I become alert to their accents. But even then their sounds caused me less and less concern. For I was growing increasingly confident of my own public identity.

I would have been happier about my public success had I not 37 recalled, sometimes, what it had been like earlier, when my family conveyed its intimacy through a set of conveniently private sounds. Sometimes in public, hearing a stranger, I'd hark back to my lost past. A Mexican farm worker approached me one day downtown. He wanted directions to some place. "*Hijito,* . . ." he said. And his voice stirred old longings. Another time I was standing beside my mother in the visiting room of a Carmelite convent, before the dense screen which rendered the nuns shadowy figures. I heard several of them speaking Spanish in their busy, singsong, overlapping voices, assuring my mother that yes, yes, we were remembered, all our family was remembered, in their prayers. Those voices echoed faraway family sounds. Another day a dark-faced old woman touched my shoulder lightly to steady herself as she boarded a bus. She murmured something to me I couldn't quite comprehend. Her Spanish voice came near, like the face of a never-before-seen relative in the instant before I was kissed. That voice, like so many of the Spanish voices I'd hear in public, recalled the golden age of my childhood.

Bilingual educators say today that children lose a degree of 38 "individuality" by becoming assimilated into public society. (Bilingual schooling is a program popularized in the seventies, that decade when middle-class "ethnics" began to resist the process of assimilation—the "American melting pot.") But the bilingualists oversimplify when they scorn the value and necessity of assimilation. They do not seem to realize that a person is individualized in two ways. So they do not realize that, while one suffers a diminished sense of *private* individuality by being assimilated into public society, such assimilation makes possible the achievement of *public* individuality.

Simplistically again, the bilingualists insist that a student should 39 be reminded of his difference from others in mass society, of his "heritage." But they equate mere separateness with individuality. The fact is that only in private—with intimates—is separateness from the crowd a prerequisite for individuality; an intimate "tells" me that I am unique, unlike all others, apart from the crowd. In public, by contrast, full individuality is achieved, paradoxically, by those who are able to consider themselves members of the crowd. Thus it happened for me. Only when I was able to think of myself as an American, no longer an alien in gringo society, could I seek the rights and opportunities necessary for full public individuality. The social and political advantages I enjoy as a man began on the day I came to believe that my name is indeed *Rich-heard Road-ree-guess.* It is true that my public society today is often impersonal; in fact, my public society is usually mass society. But despite the anonymity of the crowd, and despite the fact that the individuality I achieve in public is often tenuous—because it depends on my being one in a crowd—I celebrate the day I acquired my new name. Those middle-class ethnics who scorn assimilation seem to me filled with decadent self-pity, obsessed by the burden of public life. Dangerously, they romanticize public separateness and trivialize the dilemma of those who are truly socially disadvantaged.

If I rehearse here the changes in my private life after my   40
Americanization, it is finally to emphasize a public gain. The loss implies the gain. The house I returned to each afternoon was quiet. Intimate sounds no longer greeted me at the door. Inside there were other noises. The telephone rang. Neighborhood kids ran past the door of the bedroom where I was reading my schoolbooks—covered with brown shopping-bag paper. Once I learned the public language, it would never again be easy for me to hear intimate family voices. More and more of my day was spent hearing words, not sounds. But that may only be a way of saying that on the day I raised my hand in class and spoke loudly to an entire roomful of faces, my childhood started to end.

EXPLORATIONS

1. In responding to the proponents of "bilingual education," Rodriguez writes: "It is not possible for a child, any child, ever to use his family's language in school." Do you agree with this statement? Why or why not?

2. How does Rodriguez associate language and power with his parents?

3. Rodriguez makes a clear distinction between the private aspects of Spanish as opposed to the public nature of English. Do you agree with this distinction? Do you think that it's true in all cases?

4. Rodriguez wonders how long he would have postponed learning English if his teachers had not forced him to use English in class. How long do you think he would have postponed learning English if he had been educated in a bilingual school?

5. If the nuns had not talked to his parents and brought the public language of English into the home, do you think Rodriguez would have still learned English? Beyond school, what are some of the other factors that might have encouraged him to learn English?

Kentucky Home

BETHANY CRABTREE

Bethany Crabtree is a former student at The Ohio State University.

WRITING BEFORE READING

Have you ever visited a place after hearing a lot about it? In what ways did your expectations shape your experiences of that place?

As I was sitting listening to the radio the other day, one of my favorite songs by the Judds, "Guardian Angels," began to play. If I had to choose a song that expressed my feelings about myself, it would be this song. Every time I hear it, I cannot help wondering at the amazing role that my own Kentucky heritage has played in my life; and I still remember the day when I discovered exactly how much it has played.

"Bethany, if you ever get married, be sure to ask your husband where he was born and if he ever intends to go back again!" My mother's admonition was given to me as our eyes followed the spectacle that was slowly making his way down the side of the hill.

I laughed at my mother's remark but I, too, in all of my fifteen-year-old tomboyish bravery, was now having second thoughts about the wisdom of coming to this place. The Beverly Hillbillies had nothing on this man, and my words do little justice in describing him. He was the classic embodiment of an Appalachian backwoodsman in a dirty camouflage "monkey suit," an ill-trimmed beard, and—to accent his look—a double-barrel shotgun slung "fashionably" over one shoulder as only a "redneck" can do.

As I said a silent prayer for my life and pleaded with my daddy to let us turn back before it was too late, realization hit me; and I thought, "Welcome to Kentucky, Crabtree!" Well, to be more specific, it was not *just* Kentucky but, as my father would say, "East'rn Kentucky, up around Louisa, at the corner of Fortieth 'n Plum. That's forty miles from nowhere 'n plum back in the sticks, in Crabtree Holler, just outside o' Webbv'l." I must agree that this would be the most accurate description, since we had to park our car a mile back where the road ended and walk to the green two-story house that we were now standing beside.

"This was the house that my fam'ly bilt 'n moved into once we got 'nuff money to move closer to the road," my father reminisced. By this time, the man with the shotgun was standing in front of us, chewing tobacco and wondering exactly what business had brought us here. My father explained that his family used to live here long ago and that they still owned it, and he was bringing his wife and children to see where he was born and raised. At this clarification of our presence and identity, the man's whiskers spread to make way for a big friendly grin.

" Well, mighty glad to meet ya'!" he exclaimed with a hillbilly drawl. "Th' name's Hatfield. I'm the caretaker. "   6

"Hatfield?" I asked, "Of the Hatfields and McCoys?"   7

" Yep!" He puffed up with pride at the recognition. I, on the other hand, was not so honored and had seen enough to last me a lifetime; I wanted to go home. Home, as in back to Columbus, Ohio, where at least if I got shot someone could hear me scream and a hospital was around the corner. But we were staying. It was alright if we wandered around the grounds and went back to where the log cabins from the first Crabtree settlement stood, on one condition: "Y'all might wanna tawlk kinda loud out there," Hatfield called after us. "It's deer season 'n if'n ya' don't, ya'all's lible t' git shot at!"   8

As my mother and I paled, I heard my father chuckle, "Deer season! Whadda ya' know! When I was a boy, a deer'd had t' pack his own lunch t' a-crossed our land! Ha!" And then we were off, talking very loudly.   9

For two miles we climbed over rocks, walked down the middle of a creek (the trail leading back to the cabin having long since been reclaimed by nature), shimmied up small waterfalls, and trekked through weeds that made my six-foot-one-inch tall father seem short in comparison. As I followed, hoping that he remembered the way, I witnessed the transformation of my father from a fifty-three-year-old man into a thirteen-year-old boy. He pointed out different places and retold stories from his boyhood that I had heard dozens of times before but had never tired of hearing. These were my favorite stories—stories about a mischievous little boy from 'way back in the hills growing up in a land that progress had failed to visit. Sure, I liked hearing about princesses, knights, and dragons; but I could relate to that imaginative little boy in my father's tales because, like me, he was ornery to the bone.   10

But, on that October day when I was fifteen, I saw those stories in a whole new light. I was standing in the ravine where he used to swing across on grapevines. I could see the field where he and one of his little brothers had set fire to haystacks and then watched helplessly as their mama had tried to fight the fire by herself—the field where Billy, the family's little red pony, had run across when he had   11 gotten spooked after a plane had flown over their land for the first time. I giggled as a picture flashed through my mind of my grandpa in his younger days running across the field after the poor animal, cussing him out for all he was worth. Maybe, I thought, this trip wouldn't turn out so bad after all.

My brother's voice calling to us snapped me back into the pre- 12 sent. "Mom! Beth! Dad's lost!" I groaned as my brother ran to catch up with my father. A few moments later he called back again, "No, he's not—the cabins are just ahead."

Before we knew it, we were approaching several stone chimneys 13 that served as landmarks of what, forty years prior, had been the homes of my ancestors. Besides the chimneys, only a few rotting logs outlined what would have been the frames of the cabins. They were small, one-room cabins made of hand-hewn logs; and soot from the cooking fires still stained the stones in the chimneys. My father said that the one to the left was where he, his parents, and his brothers and sister had lived; but the one we were standing next to was where he was born, in his grandparents' cabin.

My father then bent down to pick up a stone that had fallen 14 loose from the chimney. As he looked at it, I caught the glimmer of a tear in his eye. Here we were, standing in a place that to a passer-by might have been a remnant from Abraham Lincoln's day; but, until forty or so years ago, it had been the backwoods community of a close-knit extended family, held together by love and the pioneer philosophy of "taking care of your own." But this was not just any family—it was my family, my father's birthplace.

For the first time in my life, I realized that this wasn't just the 15 site of amusing bedtime stories: this was my heritage, the story of one-half of my family and where they and I came from. I had always poked fun at my father when we would visit historic farms from the 1800's and he would remember using the vast majority of the archaic farm machinery. I would tease and tell my friends that he had been close personal friends with Abraham Lincoln, but now my laughter was quickly fading. I was contemplating how this all tied into who I was because of this country boy from the back hills of Eastern Kentucky.

This was no longer the uncivilized territory that my "city-girl 16 snobbery" had viewed it as back at the green house that was closer to the road—it was an unwritten story of a family that had made its way to Kentucky from Ireland when the United States was just being born. They had explored and fought for freedom with Daniel Boone and had eventually come to settle this place at the "corner of Fortieth 'n Plum." Then, on April 9, 1936, they produced one of the kindest-hearted men I know, Carl Jackson Crabtree, my father.

They were poor and often had no idea where the next meal 17
would come from, but they survived the Depression, the Second
World War, and then saved enough money to move to a two-story
home closer to the road. What kept them going was love, pride, and
faith in God above. My father said that he didn't even know that he
was poor until someone told him one day.

Of course, my father's come a long way since that humble 18
beginning, but I would not call it a rags-to-riches story because they
never allowed themselves to succumb to self-pity.

In this age of computers, progress, and life-on-the-go, we tend 19
to look down on people whom we classify as hillbillies. We say that
they are stupid and shiftless; but, if there was anything that I learned
from that trip, it is that being a hillbilly is not a shameful thing.
These people who were my ancestors were smart enough to build
homes and families in a wilderness and were hard-working pioneers
who knew that work meant the difference between surviving or per-
ishing. I am now in college but, no matter how educated or affluent
I ever become, I will always carry with me the pride of my hillbilly
heritage.

I have been instilled with the Crabtree's never die, always stand 20
tall and come-out-fighting-no-matter-what-the-odds stubbornness;
and it is how I live my life. If my opinion is in the minority and I
truly believe in it, my opinion will not change. Today, if a circumstance arises that seems unconquerable, I take a deep breath and
remember that I am a Crabtree to the end; and that means approaching the obstacle as a leader victorious: an overcomer. I know that, if
I plan to succeed in life, I must never forget my Eastern Kentucky
roots because they have provided me with the key to live my
dreams.

I try to live by one Crabtree philosophy that always comes in 21
handy in my day-to-day life: "If ya' cain't whip yer bully cousin
'cause he's bigger 'n you, put Ben Gay on his dog's nose, tell a
joke, laugh, and continue with yer life."

The "Ben Gay on the dog's nose" is another story for anoth- 22
er time; but, basically what it boils down to is that learning comes in
all forms: not just in a classroom and not just as facts and figures.
Pride, respectability, the ability to stand up for what you believe in,
and the strength to laugh when you have made a mistake and then
to correct it and start over are all major aspects of learning. But,
not only that, they are lessons that I had to learn and goals that I
needed to achieve before I could even start on that long road to
becoming a successful scholar.

Now that I look back, it seems as though my hillbilly philosophy 23
of life has helped me through some difficult times in my life—both

as a student and as a person. I have always been an excellent student and a die-hard competitor in all of my endeavors; and, like any strong-willed person, I focus on winning, perfection, and first-rate success. Unfortunately, life isn't always like that; and sometimes it appears that I'm taking one step forward and two steps back, so I learned to take tumbles with grace and dignity. Of course, I also learned to bounce back, try once more, and then say with glee to those who doubted me, "In your face!"

No time in my life could have proven my hillbilly unwillingness 24 to do what was socially acceptable over what I felt in my heart was right than when I was making plans for my senior year.

I was ranked third in my class, had a 4.156 GPA, and was on my 25 way to law school. Since I was an excellent debator, this was, to my teachers, my tailor-made "path of righteousness." That was why my announcement to attend a career center came as such a shock. They brushed it off as a big hoax and then began to realize that I was serious. I was bombarded with protest upon protest.

"But you're college prep," they would say.   26

"I want to be a nurse," would come my retort.   27

"Why not realize your potential to become a doctor?"   28

"I have, but my mind is made up."   29

"Do you realize what the colleges will say when they read 'Fort 30 Hayes Career Center' on your application?"

"Yes. They will say, 'My, what a focused young girl!' and then 31 accept me."

Arguments such as this one with my teachers would always end 32 with a desperate sigh of resignation on their part and a comment made under their breath to the effect that, "She won't last a week before she'll be begging to drop that Clinical Laboratory course."

They were right, I didn't last a week: I lasted thirty-six weeks 33 and then became a certified phlebotomist with a good-paying job, a number three ranking in my high school graduating class (college prep, with honors, thank you!), and several colleges vying for my attention.

What it all boils down to is that I cannot allow myself or my 34 dreams to be set back because of what others might say or do. If I am going to learn and achieve, it will be in a way that suits God and me. In order to learn it, I have to earn it.

I hold no hard feelings toward my teachers because I know that 35 they were only concerned about what would be best for me, and they now understand why I had to do what I did in order to accomplish what I, in my heart, knew was best for me.

As I walked across that stage at Veterans' Memorial Auditorium 36 to receive my high school graduation diploma, I could see my

Eastern Kentucky ancestors fill up with pride at the sight of what had come of the children of the hillbillies of Crabtree Holler. I owe many of my accomplishments in life to the power of spirit that they have instilled in me. I have no idea what tomorrow holds for me but, as long as I remember the pride in my heritage and try to live up to that standard, combined with my faith in God, there's not going to be anything that I cannot handle.

EXPLORATIONS

1. What are some of the ways Crabtree uses language to create a sense of her Kentucky home? In particular, how does she incorporate other voices and dialogue into her writing?

2. What kinds of literacy does Crabtree attribute to her ancestors? What values do these kinds of literacy reflect? What kind of literacy does she seek as a student? What kind of literacy do her teachers encourage her to accept, and what are the values behind this kind of literacy? How does she resolve the tension between these different value systems?

3. In what ways has Crabtree's academic success changed her understanding of her Kentucky family community?

4. Were your expectations for this essay different because you knew that Bethany Crabtree was a student? Did you read her essay differently? Do these distinctions matter? Explain your point of view.

Chapter VII from Narrative of the Life of Frederick Douglass, an American Slave: Written by Himself

FREDERICK DOUGLASS

Frederick Douglass was born a slave in Maryland in 1818. Originally named Frederick Bailey, he was the son of Harriet Bailey, whom he saw only a few times before her death. His father was a white man, probably the plantation overseer. While in Baltimore, he taught himself to read and write and in 1838 escaped to the North, where he renamed himself Frederick Douglass. In 1841, Douglass gave his first abolitionist speech, and he soon achieved acclaim as a powerful speaker. After he published the first edition of his Narrative *in 1845, he also became recognized as one the great American intellectuals of the nineteenth century. In 1847, Douglass founded his own abolitionist newspaper, and he continued to be a voice of leadership in the African-American community both before and after the Civil War.*

WRITING BEFORE READING

Education is often considered to be empowering. Is this necessarily true? Why or why not?

I lived in Master Hugh's family about seven years. During this 1
time, I succeeded in learning to read and write. In accomplishing this, I was compelled to resort to various stratagems. I had no regular teacher. My mistress, who had kindly commenced to instruct me, had, in compliance with the advice and direction of her husband, not only ceased to instruct, but had set her face against my being instructed by any one else. It is due, however, to my mistress to say of her, that she did not adopt this course of treatment immediately. She at first lacked the depravity indispensable to shutting me up in mental darkness. It was at least necessary for her to have some training in the exercise of irresponsible power, to make her equal to the task of treating me as though I were a brute.

My mistress was, as I have said, a kind and tender-hearted 2
woman; and in the simplicity of her soul she commenced, when I first went to live with her, to treat me as she supposed one human being ought to treat another. In entering upon the duties of a slaveholder, she did not seem to perceive that I sustained to her the

relation of a mere chattel, and that for her to treat me as a human being was not only wrong, but dangerously so. Slavery proved as injurious to her as it did to me. When I went there, she was a pious, warm, and tender-hearted woman. There was no sorrow or suffering for which she had not a tear. She had bread for the hungry, clothes for the naked, and comfort for every mourner that came within her reach. Slavery soon proved its ability to divest her of these heavenly qualities. Under its influence, the tender heart became stone, and the lamblike disposition gave way to one of tiger-like fierceness. The first step in her downward course was in her ceasing to instruct me. She now commenced to practise her husband's precepts. She finally became even more violent in her opposition than her husband himself. She was not satisfied with simply doing as well as he had commanded; she seemed anxious to do better. Nothing seemed to make her more angry than to see me with a newspaper. She seemed to think that here lay the danger. I have had her rush at me with a face made all up of fury, and snatch from me a newspaper, in a manner that fully revealed her apprehension. She was an apt woman; and a little experience soon demonstrated, to her satisfaction, that education and slavery were incompatible with each other.

From this time I was most narrowly watched. If I was in a ₃ separate room any considerable length of time, I was sure to be suspected of having a book, and was at once called to give an account of myself. All this, however, was too late. The first step had been taken. Mistress, in teaching me the alphabet, had given me the *inch*, and no precaution could prevent me from taking the *ell*.

The plan which I adopted, and the one by which I was most ₄ successful, was that of making friends of all the little white boys whom I met in the street. As many of these as I could, I converted into teachers. With their kindly aid, obtained at different times and in different places, I finally succeeded in learning to read. When I was sent of errands, I always took my book with me, and by going one part of my errand quickly, I found time to get a lesson before my return. I used also to carry bread with me, enough of which was always in the house, and to which I was always welcome; for I was much better off in this regard than many of the poor white children in our neighborhood. This bread I used to bestow upon the hungry little urchins, who, in return, would give me that more valuable bread of knowledge. I am strongly tempted to give the names of two or three of those little boys, as a testimonial of the gratitude and affection I bear them; but prudence forbids;—not that it would injure me, but it might embarrass them; for it is almost an unpardonable offence to teach slaves to read in this Christian country. It is enough to say of the dear little fellows, that they lived on Philpot

Street, very near Durgin and Bailey's ship-yard. I used to talk this matter of slavery over with them. I would sometimes say to them, I wished I could be as free as they would be when they got to be men. "You will be free as soon as you are twenty-one, *but I am a slave for life!* Have not I as good a right to be free as you have?" These words used to trouble them; they would express for me the liveliest sympathy and console me with the hope that something might occur by which I might be free.

I was now about twelve years old, and the thought of being a slave for life began to bear heavily upon my heart. Just about this time, I got hold of a book entitled "The Columbian Orator." Every opportunity I got, I used to read this book. Among much of other interesting matter, I found in it a dialogue between a master and his slave. The slave was represented as having run away from his master three times. The dialogue represented the conversation which took place between them, when the slave was retaken the third time. In this dialogue, the whole argument in behalf of slavery was brought forward by the master, all of which was disposed of by the slave. The slave was made to say some very smart as well as impressive things in reply to his master—things which had the desired though unexpected effect; for the conversation resulted in the voluntary emancipation of the slave on the part of the master.

In the same book, I met with one of Sheridan's mighty speeches on and in behalf of Catholic emancipation. These were choice documents to me. I read them over and over again with unabated interest. They gave tongue to interesting thoughts of my own soul, which had frequently flashed through my mind, and died away for want of utterance. The moral which I gained from the dialogue was the power of truth over the conscience of even a slaveholder. What I got from Sheridan was a bold denunciation of slavery, and a powerful vindication of human rights. The reading of these documents enabled me to utter my thoughts, and to meet the arguments brought forward to sustain slavery; but while they relieved me of one difficulty, they brought on another even more painful than the one of which I was relieved. The more I read, the more I was led to abhor and detest my enslavers. I could regard them in no other light than a band of successful robbers, who had left their homes, and gone to Africa, and stolen us from our homes, and in a strange land reduced us to slavery. I loathed them as being the meanest as well as the most wicked of men. As I read and contemplated the subject, behold! that very discontentment which Master Hugh had predicted would follow my learning to read had already come, to torment and sting my soul to unutterable anguish. As I writhed under it, I would at times feel that learning to read had been a curse rather than a blessing. It had given me a view of my wretched condition, without the remedy. It opened my eyes to the horrible pit, but to no ladder upon which to get out. In moments of agony, I envied my fellow-slaves for their stupidity. I have often wished myself a beast. I preferred the condition of the meanest reptile to my own. Any thing, no mater what, to get rid of thinking! It was this everlasting thinking of my condition that tormented me. There was no getting rid of it. It was pressed upon me by every object within sight or hearing, animate or inanimate. The silver trump of freedom had roused my soul to eternal wakefulness. Freedom now appeared, to disappear no more forever. It was heard in every sound, and seen in every thing. It was ever present to torment me with a sense of my wretched condition. I saw nothing without seeing it, I heard nothing without hearing it, and felt nothing without feeling it. It looked from every star, it smiled in every calm, breathed in every wind, and moved in every storm.

I often found myself regretting my own existence, and wishing myself dead; and but for the hope of being free, I have no doubt but that I should have killed myself, or done something for which I should have been killed. While in this state of mind, I was eager to hear any one speak of slavery. I was a ready listener. Every little while, I could hear something about the abolitionists. It was some time before I found what the word meant. It was always used in such connections as to make it an interesting word to me. If a slave ran away and succeeded in getting clear, or if a slave killed his master, set fire to a bar, or did any thing very wrong in the mind of a slave-holder, it was spoken of as the fruit of *abolition*. Hearing the word in this connection very often, I set about learning what it meant. The dictionary afforded me little or no help. I found it was "the act of abolishing;" but then I did not know what was to be abolished. Here I was perplexed. I did not dare to ask any one about its meaning, for I was satisfied that it was something they wanted me to know very little about. After a patient waiting, I got one of our city papers, containing an account of the number of petitions from the north, praying for the abolition of slavery in the District of Columbia, and of the slave trade between the States. From this time I understood the words *abolition* and *abolitionist*, and always drew near when that word was spoken, expecting to hear something of importance to myself and fellow-slaves. The light broke in upon me by degrees. I went one day down on the wharf of Mr. Waters; and seeing two Irishmen unloading a scow of stone, I went, unasked, and helped them. When we had finished, one of them came to me and asked me if I were a slave. I told him I was. He asked, "Are ye a slave for life?" I told him I was. The good Irishman seemed to be deeply affected by the statement. He said to the other that it was a pity so fine a little fellow as myself should be a slave for life. He said it was a shame to hold me. They both advised me to run away to the north; that I should find friends there, and that I should be free. I pretended not to be interested in what they said, and treated them as if I did not understand them; for I feared they might be treacherous. White men have been known to encourage slaves to escape, and then, to get the reward, catch them and return them to their masters. I was afraid that these seemingly good men might use me so; but I nevertheless remembered their advice, and from that time I resolved to run away. I looked forward to a time at which it would be safe for me to escape. I was too young to think of doing so immediately; besides, I wished to learn how to write, as I might have occasion to write my own pass. I consoled myself with the hope that I should one day find a good chance. Meanwhile, I would learn to write.

The idea as to how I might learn to write was suggested to me 8 by being in Durgin and Bailey's ship-yard, and frequently seeing the ship carpenters, after hewing, and getting a piece of timber ready for use, write on the timber the name of that part of the ship for which it was intended. When a piece of timber was intended for the larboard side, it would be marked thus—" L." When a piece was for the starboard side, it would be marked thus—"S."A piece for the larboard side forward, would be marked thus—" L. F." When a piece was for starboard side forward, it would be marked thus—" S. F." For larboard aft, it would be marked thus—" L. A." For star-board aft, it would be marked thus—" S. A." I soon learned the names of these letters, and for what they were intended when placed upon a piece of timber in the ship-yard. I immediately commenced copying them, and in a short time was able to make the four letters named. After that, when I met with any boy who I knew could write, I would tell him I could write as well as he. The next word would be, "I don't believe you. Let me see you try it." I would then make the letters which I had been so fortunate as to learn, and ask him to beat that. In this way I got a good many lessons in writing, which it is quite possible I should never have gotten in any other way. During this time, my copy-book was the board fence, brick wall, and pave-ment; my pen and ink was a lump of chalk. With these, I learned mainly how to write. I then commenced and continued copying the Italics in Webster's Spelling Book, until I could make them all with-out looking on the book. By this time, my little Master Thomas had gone to school, and learned how to write, and had written over a number of copy-books. These had been brought home, and shown to some of our near neighbors, and then laid aside. My mistress used to go to class meeting at the Wilk Street meetinghouse every

Monday afternoon, and leave me to take care of the house. When left thus, I used to spend the time in writing in the spaces left in Master Thomas's copy-book, copying what he had written. I continued to do this until I could write a hand very similar to that of Master Thomas. Thus, after a long, tedious effort for years, I finally succeeded in learning how to write.

EXPLORATIONS

1. Why is Mistress Hugh so violently opposed to Douglass learning to read and write? Why does she think that education and slavery are incompatible? How does the book Douglass reads, *The Columbian Orator*, corroborate this view?

2. Why does Douglass initially have misgivings about his ability to read and the way it affects his view of freedom?

3. How does he come to understand the word *abolition* and what power does it have for him?

4. Why is it significant that Douglass teaches himself to write? How do others help him with his efforts? Although he is a slave and an outsider in Baltimore, in what ways does Douglass exemplify some of the typical American qualities such as self-reliance and independence?

On Being White, Female, and Born in Bensonhurst

MARIANNA DEMARCO TORGOVNICK

Marianna DeMarco Torgovnick was born in Brooklyn, New York, in 1949, the daughter of Salvatore, a clerk, and Rose, a garment worker. She earned her B.A. at New York University and her M.A. and Ph.D. at Columbia University. Currently a professor of English at Duke University, she is known primarily as a literary and cultural critic. In "On Being White, Female, and Born in Bensonhurst," which was recognized as one of the best American essays of 1991, she explores the culture of Bensonhurst (where she grew up) and the ways in which this culture continues to shape her identity as a member of the academic community.

WRITING BEFORE READING

Which community do you consider to be your home community? Do you think that you will always belong to this community? Do you have a choice in belonging to this community?

The Mafia protects the neighborhood, our fathers say, with that peculiar satisfied pride with which law-abiding Italian Americans refer to the Mafia: the Mafia protects the neighborhood from "the coloreds." In the fifties and sixties, I heard that information repeated, in whispers, in neighborhood parks and in the yard at school in Bensonhurst. The same information probably passes today in the parks (the word now "blacks," not "colored") but perhaps no longer in the schoolyards. From buses each morning, from neighborhoods outside Bensonhurst, spill children of all colors and backgrounds—American blacks, West Indian black, Hispanic, and Asian. But the blacks are the only ones especially marked for notice. Bensonhurst is no longer entirely protected from "the coloreds." But in a deeper sense, at least for Italian Americans, Bensonhurst never changes.

Italian-American life continues pretty much as I remember it. Families with young children live side by side with older couples whose children are long gone to the suburbs. Many of those families live "down the block" from the last generation or, sometimes still, live together with parents or grandparents. When a young family leaves, as sometimes happens, for Long Island or New Jersey or (very

109

common now) for Staten Island, another arrives, without any special effort being required, from Italy or a poorer neighborhood in New York. They fill the neat but anonymous houses that make up the mostly tree-lined streets: two-, three-, or four-family houses for the most part (this is a working, lower to middle-middle class area, and people need rents to pay mortgages), with a few single family or small apartment houses tossed in at random. Tomato plants, fig trees, and plaster madonnas often decorate small but well-tended yards which face out onto the street; the grassy front lawn, like the grassy back yard, is relatively uncommon.

Crisscrossing the neighborhood and marking out ethnic zones—   3
Italian, Irish, and Jewish, for the most part, though there are some Asian Americans and some people (usually Protestants) called simply Americans—are the great shopping streets: Eighty-sixth Street, Kings Highway, Bay Parkway, Eighteenth Avenue, each with its own distinctive character. On Eighty-sixth Street, crowds bustle along sidewalks lined with ample, packed fruit stands. Women wheeling shopping carts or baby strollers check the fruit carefully, piece by piece, and often bargain with the dealer, cajoling for a better price or letting him know that the vegetables, this time, aren't up to snuff. A few blocks down, the fruit stands are gone and the streets are lined with clothing and record shops, mobbed by teenagers. Occasionally, the el rumbles overhead, a few stops out of Coney Island on its way to the city, a trip of around one hour.

On summer nights, neighbors congregate on stoops which   4
during the day serve as play yards for children. Air conditioning exists everywhere in Bensonhurst, but people still sit outside in the summer—to supervise children, to gossip, to stare at strangers. *"Buona sera,"* I say, or *"Buona notte,"* as I am ritually presented to Sal and Lily and Louie, the neighbors sitting on the stoop. *"Grazie,"* I say when they praise my children or my appearance. It's the only time I use Italian, which I learned at high school, although my parents (both second-generation Italian Americans, my father Sicilian, my mother Calabrian) speak it at home to each other but never to me or my brother. My accent is the Tuscan accent taught at school, not the southern Italian accents of my parents and the neighbors.

It's important to greet and please the neighbors; any break in   5
this decorum would seriously offend and aggrieve my parents. For the neighbors are the stern arbiters of conduct in Bensonhurst. Does Mary keep a clean house? Did Gina wear black long enough after her mother's death? Was the food good at Tony's wedding? The neighbors know and pass judgment. Any news of family scandal (my brother's divorce, for example) provokes from my mother the ago-

nized words: "But what will I *tell* people?" I sometimes collaborate in devising a plausible script.

A large sign on the church I attended as a child sums up for me   6 the ethos of Bensonhurst. The sign urges contributions to the church building fund with the message, in huge letters: " EACH YEAR ST. SIMON AND JUDE SAVES THIS NEIGHBORHOOD ONE MILLION DOLLARS IN TAXES. " Passing the church on the way from largely Jewish and middle-class Sheepshead Bay (where my in-laws live) to Bensonhurst, year after year, my husband and I look for the sign and laugh at the crass level of its pitch, its utter lack of attention to things spiritual. But we also understand exactly the values it represents.

In the summer of 1989, my parents were visiting me at my house   7 in Durham, North Carolina, from the apartment in Bensonhurst where they have lived since 1942: three small rooms, rent-controlled, floor clean enough to eat off, every corner and crevice known and organized. My parents' longevity in a single apartment is unusual even for Bensonhurst, but not that unusual; many people live for decades in the same place or move within a ten-block radius. When I lived in this apartment, there were four rooms, one has since been ceded to a demanding landlord, one of the various landlords who have haunted my parents' life and must always be appeased lest the ultimate threat—removal from the rent-controlled apartment— be brought into play. That summer, during their visit, on August 23 (my younger daughter's birthday) a shocking, disturbing, news report issued from the neighborhood: it had become another Howard Beach.

Three black men, walking casually through the streets at night,   8 were attacked by a group of whites. One was shot dead, mistaken, as it turned out, for another black youth who was dating a white, although part-Hispanic, girl in the neighborhood. It all made sense: the crudely protective men, expecting to see a black arriving at the girl's house and overreacting; the rebellious girl dating the outsider boy; the black dead as a sacrifice to the feelings of the neighborhood.

I might have felt outrage, I might have felt guilt or shame, I   9 might have despised the people among whom I grew up. In a way I felt all four emotions when I heard the news. I expect that there were many people in Bensonhurst who felt the same rush of emotions. But mostly I felt that, given the set-up, this was the only way things could have happened. I detested the racial killing, but I also understood it. Those streets, which should be public property available to all, belong to the neighborhood. All the people sitting on the stoops on August 23 knew that as well as they knew their own names. The black men walking through probably knew it too—though their casual walk sought to deny the fact that, for the neighbors, even the

simple act of blacks walking through the neighborhood would be
seen as invasion.

Italian Americans in Bensonhurst are notable for their cohesive-   10
ness and provinciality; the slightest pressure turns those qualities into
prejudice and racism. Their cohesiveness is based on the stable
economic and ethical level that links generation to generation, keeping Italian Americans in Bensonhurst and the Italian-American
community alive as the Jewish-American community of my youth is
no longer alive. (Its young people routinely moved to the suburbs or
beyond and were never replaced, so that Jews in Bensonhurst today
are almost all very old people.) Their provinciality results from the
Italian Americans' devotion to jealous distinctions and discrimina-
tions. Jews are suspect, but (the old Italian women admit) "they
make good husbands." The Irish are okay, fellow Catholics, but not
really "like us"; they make bad husbands because they drink and
gamble. Even Italians come in varieties, by region (Sicilian,
Calabrian, Neapolitan, very rarely any region further north) and by
history in this country (the newly arrived and ridiculed "gaffoon"
versus the second or third generation).

Bensonhurst is a neighborhood dedicated to believing that its   11
values are the only values; it tends toward certain forms of inertia.
When my parents visit me in Durham, they routinely take chairs from
the kitchen and sit out on the lawn in front of the house, not on the
chairs on the back deck; then they complain the streets are too quiet.
When they walk around my neighborhood (these De Marcos who
have friends named Travaglianti and Occhipinti), they look at the
mailboxes and report that my neighbors have strange names. Prices
at my local supermarket are compared, in unbelievable detail, with
prices on Eighty-sixth Street. Any rearrangement of my kitchen since
their last visit is registered and criticized. Difference is not only
unwelcome, it is unacceptable. One of the most characteristic things
my mother ever said was in response to my plans for renovating my
house in Durham. When she heard my plans, she looked around,
crossed her arms, and said, "If it was me, I wouldn't change nothing." My father once asked me to level with him about a Jewish
boyfriend who lived in a different part of the neighborhood, react-
ing to his Jewishness, but even more to the fact that he often wore
Bermuda shorts: "Tell me something, Marianna. Is he a
Communist?" Such are the standards of normality and political
thinking in Bensonhurst.

I often think that one important difference between Italian   12
Americans in New York neighborhoods like Bensonhurst and Italian
Americans elsewhere is the others moved on—to upstate New York,
to Pennsylvania, to the Midwest. Though they frequently settled in

communities of fellow Italians, they did move on. Bensonhurst Italian Americans seem to have felt that one large move, over the ocean, was enough. Future moves could be only local: from the Lower East Side, for example, to Brooklyn, or from one part of Brooklyn to another. Bensonhurst was for many of these people the summa of expectations. If their America were to be drawn as a *New Yorker* cover, Manhattan itself would be tiny in proportion to Bensonhurst and to its satellites, Staten Island, New Jersey, and Long Island.

"Oh, no" my father says when he hears the news about the 13 shooting. Though he still refers to blacks as "coloreds," he's not really a racist and is upset that this innocent youth was shot in his neighborhood. He has no trouble acknowledging the wrongness of the death. But then, like all the news accounts, he turns to the fact, repeated over and over, that the blacks had been on their way to look at a used car when they encountered the hostile mob of whites. The expectation is right before him but, "Yeah," he says, still shaking his head, "yeah, but what were they *doing* there? They didn't belong."

Over the next few days, the television news is even more 14 disturbing. Rows of screaming Italians lining the streets, most of them looking like my relatives. I focus especially on one woman who resembles almost completely my mother: stocky but not fat, mid-seventies but well preserved, full face showing only minimal wrinkles, ample steel-gray hair neatly if rigidly coiffed in a modified beehive hairdo left over from the sixties. She shakes her fist at the camera, protesting the arrest of the Italian-American youths in the neighborhood and the incursion of more blacks into the neighborhood, protesting the shooting. I look a little nervously at my mother (the parent I resemble), but she has not even noticed the woman and stares impassively at the television.

What has Bensonhurst to do with what I teach today and write? 15 Why did I need to write about this killing in Bensonhurst, but not in the manner of a news account or a statistical sociological analysis? Within days of hearing the news, I began to plan this essay, to tell the world what I knew, even though I was aware that I could publish the piece only someplace my parents or their neighbors would never see or hear about it. I sometimes think that I looked around from my baby carriage and decided that someday, the sooner the better, I would get out of Bensonhurst. Now, much to my surprise, Bensonhurst—the antipode of the intellectual life I sought, the least interesting of places—had become a respectable intellectual topic. People would be willing to hear about Bensonhurst—and all by the dubious virtue of a racial killing in the streets.

The story as I would have to tell it would be to some extent a   16
class narrative: about the difference between working class and upper
middle class, dependence and a profession, Bensonhurst and a posh
suburb. But I need to make it clear that I do not imagine myself as
writing from a position of enormous self-satisfaction, or even enormous distance. You can take the girl out of Bensonhurst (that much
is clear), but you may not be able to take Bensonhurst out of the girl.
And upward mobility is not the essence of the story, though it is an
important marker and symbol.

In Durham today, I live in a twelve-room house surrounded by   17
an acre of trees. When I sit on my back deck on summer evenings,
no houses are visible through the trees. I have a guaranteed income,
teaching English at an excellent university, removed by many years of
education from the fundamental economic and social conditions of
Bensonhurst. The only time my mother ever expressed pleasure at
my work was when I got tenure, what my father still calls, with no
irony intended, "ten years." "What does that mean?" my mother
asked when she heard the news. Then she reached back into her
experience as a garment worker, subject to periodic layoffs. "Does it
mean they can't fire you just for nothing and can't lay you off?"
When I said that was exactly what it means, she said, "Very good.
Congratulations. That's *wonderful.*" I was free from the *padrones*,
from the network of petty anxieties that had formed, in large part,
her very existence. Of course, I wasn't really free of petty anxieties:
would my salary increase keep pace with my colleagues', how would
my office compare, would this essay be accepted for publication, am
I happy? The line between these worries and my mother's is the line
between the working class and the upper middle class.

But getting out of Bensonhurst never meant to me a big house,   18
or nice clothes, or a large income. And it never meant feeling good
about looking down on what I left behind or hiding my background.
Getting out of Bensonhurst meant freedom—to experiment, to grow,
to change. It also meant knowledge in some grand, abstract way. All
the material possessions I have acquired, I acquired simply along the
way—and for the first twelve years after I left Bensonhurst, I chose to
acquire almost nothing at all. Now, as I write about the neighborhood, I recognize that although I've come far in physical and material distance, the emotional distance is harder to gauge. Bensonhurst
has everything to do with who I am and even with what I write.
Occasionally I get reminded of my roots, of their simultaneously
choking and nutritive power.

Scene one: It's after a lecture at Duke, given by a visiting   19
professor from Princeton. The lecture was long and a little dull and
—bad luck—I had agreed to be one of the people having dinner with

the lecturer afterward. We settle into our table at the restaurant: this man, me, the head of the comparative literature program (also a professor of German), and a couple I like who teach French, the husband at my university, the wife at one nearby. The conversation is sluggish, as it often is when a stranger, like the visiting professor, has to be assimilated into a group, so I ask the visitor from Princeton a question to personalize things a bit. "How did you get interested in what you do? What made you become a professor of German?" The man gets going and begins talking about how it was really unlikely that he, a nice Jewish boy from Bensonhurst, would have chosen, in the mid-fifties, to study German. Unlikely indeed.

I remember seeing *Judgment at Nuremburg* in a local movie 20 theater and having a woman in the row in back of me get hysterical when some clips of a concentration camp were shown. "My God," she screamed in a European accent, "look at what they did. Murderers, MURDERERS!"—and she had to be supported out by her family. I couldn't see, in the dark, whether her arm bore the neatly tattooed numbers that the arms of some of my classmates' parents did—and that always affected me with a thrill of horror. Ten years older than me, this man had lived more directly through those feelings, lived with and *among* those feelings. The first chance he got, he raced to study in Germany. I myself have twice chosen not to visit Germany, but I understand his impulse to identify with the Other as a way of getting out of the neighborhood.

At the dinner, the memory about the movie pops into my mind 21 but I pick up instead on the Bensonhurst—I'm also from there, but Italian American. Like a flash, he asks something I haven't been asked in years: Where did I go to high school and (more common question) what was my maiden name? I went to Lafayette High School, I say, and my name was De Marco. Everything changes: his facial expression, his posture, his accent, his voice. "Soo, Dee Maw-ko," he says, "dun anything wrong at school today—got enny pink slips? Wanna meet me later at the park or maybe bye the Baye?" When I laugh, recognizing the stereotype that Italians get pink slips for misconduct at school and the notorious chemistry between Italian women and Jewish men, he says, back in his Princetonian voice: "My God, for a minute I felt like I was turning into a were-wolf."

It's odd that although I can remember almost nothing else 22 about this man—his face, his body type, even his name—I remember this lapse into his "real self" with enormous vividness. I am especially struck by how easily he was able to slip into the old, generic Brooklyn accent. I myself have no memory of ever speaking in that accent, though I also have no memory of trying not to speak it, except for teaching myself, carefully, to say "oil" rather than "earl."

But the surprises aren't over. The female French professor, 23 whom I have known for at least five years, reveals for the first time that she is also from the neighborhood, though she lived across the other side of Kings Highway, went to a different, more elite high school, and was Irish American. Three of six professors, sitting at an eclectic vegetarian restaurant in Durham, all from Bensonhurst—a neighborhood where (I swear) you couldn't get the *New York Times* at any of the local stores.

Scene two: I still live in Bensonhurst. I'm waiting for my par- 24 ents to return from a conference at my school, where they've been summoned to discuss my transition from elementary to junior high school. I am already a full year younger than any of my classmates, having skipped a grade, a not uncommon occurrence for "gifted" youngsters. Now the school is worried about putting me in an accel- erated track through junior high, since that would make me two years younger. A compromise was reached: I would be put in a special program for gifted children, but one that took three, not two, years. It sounds okay.

Three years later, another wait. My parents have gone to school 25 this time to make another decision. Lafayette High School has three tracks: academic, for potentially college-bound kids; secretarial, mostly for Italian-American girls or girls with low aptitude-test scores (the high school is de facto segregated, so none of the tracks is as yet racially coded, though they are coded by ethnic group and gender); and vocational, mostly for boys with the same attributes, ethnic or intellectual. Although my scores are superb, the guidance counselor has recommended the secretarial track; when I protested, the conference with my parents was arranged. My mother's prefer- ence is clear: the secretarial track—college is for boys; I will need to make a "good living" until I marry and have children. My father also prefers the secretarial track, but he wavers, half proud of my aberrantly high scores, half worried. I press the attack, saying that if I were Jewish I would have been placed, without question, in the academic track. I tell him I have sneaked a peek at my files and know that my IQ is at genius level. I am allowed to insist on the change into the academic track.

What I did, and I was ashamed of it even then, was to play upon 26 my father's competitive feelings with Jews: his daughter could and should be as good as theirs. In the bank where he was a messenger, and at the insurance company where he worked in the mailroom, my father worked with Jews, who were almost always his immediate supervisors. Several times, my father was offered the supervisory job but turned it down after long conversations with my mother about the dangers of making a change, the difficulty of giving orders to friends. After her work in a local garment shop, after cooking dinner and washing the floor each night, my mother often did piecework making bows; sometimes I would help her for fun, but it *wasn't* fun, I was free to stop while she continued for long, tedious hours to increase the family income. Once a week, her part-time boss, Dave, would come by to pick up the boxes of bows. Short, round, with his shirttails sloppily tucked into his pants and a cigar almost always dangling from his lips, Dave was a stereotyped Jew but also, my parents always said, a nice guy, a decent man.

Years after, similar choices come up, and I show the same 27 assertiveness I showed with my father, the same ability to deal for survival, but tinged with Bensonhurst caution. Where will I go to college? Not to Brooklyn College, the flagship of the city system—I know that, but don't press the invitations I have received to apply to prestigious schools outside of New York. The choice comes down to two: Barnard, which gives me a full scholarship, minus five hundred dollars a year that all scholarship students are expected to contribute from summer earnings, or New York University, which offers me one thousand dollars above tuition as a bribe. I waver. My parents stand firm: they are already losing money by letting me go to college; I owe it to the family to contribute the extra thousand dollars plus my summer earnings. Besides, my mother adds, harping on a favorite theme, there are no boys at Barnard; at NYU I'm more likely to meet someone to marry. I go to NYU and do marry in my senior year, but he is someone I didn't meet at college. I was secretly relieved, I now think (though at the time I thought I was just placating my parents' conventionality), to be out of the marriage sweepstakes.

The first boy who ever asked me for a date was Robert Lubitz, 28 in eighth grade: tall and skinny to my average height and teenage chubbiness. I turned him down, thinking we would make a ridiculous couple. Day after day, I cast my eyes at stylish Juliano, the class cutup; day after day, I captivated Robert Lubitz. Occasionally, one of my brother's Italian-American friends would ask me out, and I would go, often to ROTC dances. My specialty was making political remarks so shocking that the guys rarely asked me again. After a while I recognized destiny: the Jewish man was a passport out of Bensonhurst. I of course did marry a Jewish man, who gave me my freedom and, very important, helped remove me from the expectations of Bensonhurst. Though raised in a largely Jewish section of Brooklyn, he had gone to college in Ohio and knew how important it was, as he put it, "to get past the Brooklyn Bridge." We met on neutral ground, in Central Park, at a performance of Shakespeare. The Jewish-Italian marriage is a common enough catastrophe in Bensonhurst for my parents to have accepted, even welcomed, mine—though my parents continued to treat my husband like an outsider for the first twenty years ("Now Marianna. Here's what's going on with you brother. But don't tell-a you husband").

Along the way I make other choices, more fully marked by 29 Bensonhurst cautiousness. I am attracted to journalism or the arts as careers, but the prospects for income seem iffy. I choose instead to imagine myself as a teacher. Only the availability of NDEA fellowships when I graduate, with their generous terms, propels me from high school teaching (a thought I never much relished) to college teaching (which seems like a brave new world). Within the college teaching profession, I choose offbeat specializations: the novel, interdisciplinary approaches (not something clear and clubby like Milton or the eighteenth century). Eventually I write the book I like best about primitive others as they figure within Western obsessions: my identification with "the Other," my sense of being "Other, " surfaces at last. I avoid all mentoring structures for a long time but accept aid when it comes to me on the basis of what I perceive to be merit. I'm still, deep down, Italian-American Bensonhurst, though by this time I'm a lot of other things as well.

Scene three: In the summer of 1988, a little more than a year 30 before the shooting in Bensonhurst, my father woke up trembling and in what appeared to be a fit. Hospitalization revealed that he had a pocket of blood on his brain, a frequent consequence of falls for older people. About a year earlier, I had stayed home, using my children as an excuse, when my aunt, my father's much loved sister, died, missing her funeral; only now does my mother tell me how much my father resented my taking his suggestion that I stay home. Now, confronted with what is described as brain surgery but turns out to be less dramatic than it sounds, I fly home immediately.

My brother drives three hours back and forth from New Jersey 31 every day to chauffeur me and my mother to the hospital: he is being a fine Italian-American son. For the first time in years, we have long conversations alone. He is two years older than I am, a chemical engineer who has also left the neighborhood but has remained closer to its values, with a suburban, Republican inflection. He talks a lot about New York, saying that (except for neighborhoods like Bensonhurst) it's a "third-world city now." It's the summer of the Tawana Brawley incident, when Brawley accused white men of abducting her and smearing racial slurs on her body with her own excrement. My brother is filled with dislike for Al Sharpton and Brawley's other vocal supporters in the black community—not because they're black, he says, but because they're troublemakers, stirring things up. The city is drenched in racial hatred that makes itself felt in the halls of the hospital: Italians and Jews in the beds and as doctors: blacks as nurses and orderlies.

This is the first time since I left New York in 1975 that I have 32 visited Brooklyn without once getting into Manhattan. It's the first time I have spent several days alone with my mother, living in her apartment in Bensonhurst. My every move is scrutinized and commented on. I feel like I am going to go crazy.

Finally, it's clear that my father is going to be fine, and I can go 33 home. She insists on accompanying me to the travel agent to get my ticket for home, even though I really want to be alone. The agency (a Mafia front?) has no one who knows how to ticket me for the exotic destination of North Carolina and no computer for doing so. The one person who can perform this feat by hand is out. I have to kill time for an hour and suggest to my mother that she go home, to be there for my brother when he arrives from Jersey. We stop in a Pork Store, where I buy a stash of cheeses, sausages, and other delicacies unavailable in Durham. My mother walks home with the shopping bags, and I'm on my own.

More than anything I want a kind of *sorbetto* or ice I remember 34 from my childhood, a *cremolata*, almond-vanilla-flavored with large chunks of nuts. I pop into the local bakery (at the unlikely hour of 11 A.M.) and ask for a *cremolata*, usually eaten after dinner. The woman—a younger version of my mother—refuses: they haven't made a fresh ice yet, and what's left from the day before is too icy, no good. I explain that I'm about to get on a plane for North Carolina and want that ice, good or not. But she has her standards and holds her ground, even though North Carolina has about the same status in her mind as Timbuktu and she knows I will be banished, perhaps forever, from the land of *cremolata*.

Then, while I'm taking a walk, enjoying my solitude, I have 35 another idea. On the block behind my parents' house, there's a club for men, for men from a particular town or region in Italy: six or seven tables, some on the sidewalk beneath a garish red, green, and white sign; no women allowed or welcome unless they're with men, and no women at all during the day when the real business of the club—a game of cards for old men—is in progress. Still, I know that inside the club would be coffee and a *cremolata* ice. I'm thirty-eight, well-dressed, very respectable looking; I know what I want. I also know I'm not supposed to enter that club. I enter anyway, asking the teenage boy behind the counter firmly, in my most professional tones, for a *cremolata* ice. Dazzled, he complies immediately. The old men at the card table have been staring at this scene, unable to place me exactly, though my facial type is familiar. Finally, a few old men's hisses pierce the air. *"Strega,"* I hear as I leave, *"mala strega"*—"witch," or "brazen whore." I have been in Bensonhurst less than a week, but I have managed to reproduce, on my final day there for this visit, the conditions of my youth. Knowing the rules, I have broken them. I shake hands with my discreetly rebellious past, still an outsider walking through the neighborhood, marked and insulted—though unlikely to be shot.

EXPLORATIONS

1. How does Torgovnick adjust her use of language in response to different communities and their values? Why do you think Torgovnick's accent is so important in the neighborhood of her childhood?

2. In what ways does Torgovnick's present position in the university allow her to understand Bensonhurst differently from when when she was living there? In what ways does it separate her from Bensonhurst? Does she ever really get away from Bensonhurst?

3. What does it mean to be literate in Bensonhurst? What expectations for behavior and language use exist in the Bensonhurst community? How do these expectations organize the community? How do they limit and damage them? Put your discussion in the context of your own experience as a member of a community, and consider how such expectations originate and are perpetuated or resisted.

4. How can Torgovnick say that the Bensonhurst killing "made sense"? What community assumptions must be validated for it to make sense? Is Torgovnick condoning the violence?

5. No one directly told Torgovnick that she shouldn't go to the club and order a *cremolata*. How did she come to know that she should not? Why did she act as if she were "illiterate" in this instance?

6. Torgovnick writes about the complexity of language and its simultaneous ability and inability to convey what we actually mean, as well as its tendency to convey meanings other than those we intend. Torgovnick is concerned with the ways in which communities use language. To what extent does she conform to community expectations? In terms of her rhetorical situation, why does she act as an "illiterate"?

Literacy and the Lesbian/Gay Learner

ELLEN LOUISE HART

When this essay was published in 1988, Ellen Louise Hart was teaching writing at the University of California—Santa Cruz. She was also doing graduate work in literature, with special interests in lesbian poetry and the representations of lesbians and gay men in fiction. Hart was born in Maine and has lived in Vermont and California. In this essay, which appeared in the collection The Lesbian in Front of the Classroom *(1988), Hart advances literacy "beyond the performance of concrete tasks to the creation of self, world, and identity."*

WRITING BEFORE READING

How do you express yourself differently in the classroom from the ways you do in other situations? Why do you choose to express yourself in this way? Do you always feel safe in voicing your opinions? If not, why not?

Millions of Americans have never learned to read and write. 1
How many are lesbians and gay men and how might homophobia be helping to enforce their illiteracy? As teachers what can we do? Before I address these questions I want to present some premises about homosexuality and education[1] and follow with a definition of literacy. I want to make clear that homosexuality is not a "controversial issue"; it is a way of loving, living, creating homes and rituals, communities, cultures and cultural artifacts. Homosexuality can not be reduced to a private act that belongs in the bedroom and not in the classroom. Sexuality is much more than sex; it is integral to identity, culture, and all of life. It is personal, and the personal, as we know, is the political. Then, as teachers it is essential for us to recognize that since an estimated ten per cent of the population is lesbian or gay, at any given time in any given classroom, from kindergarten to the university, ten percent of our students will be, or will become, lesbian or gay. Others will be bisexual, and twenty-five per cent will have a lesbian or gay family member. Education that is true to its name presents accurate information about homosexuality and includes lesbian, gay, and bisexual perspectives throughout the entire curriculum. This integration provides opportunity for our

students to raise their self-esteem, to develop values based on knowledge rather than prejudice and dogma, and to learn.

By literacy I mean the ability to function independently in the [2] society as a reader and writer, not only being able to read road signs and the ingredients on packages of food, to read bills and write checks, but to read, with comprehension and ease, newspapers and magazines, stories and poems and textbooks, to write, fluently, letters, journals, stories, and papers. Then there is another level of literacy that moves beyond the performance of concrete tasks to the creation of self, world, and identity. What is different about this process of becoming literate for a lesbian or gay man? The most fundamental difference is the need for particular texts that represent lesbian and gay experience and consciousness, the experience and consciousness of individual lesbians and gay men. Our lesbian and gay students need to know that they exist and that they exist in print. Literacy also requires the writing skills to enable the continuing creation of these representations. The claims I bring to this discussion of literacy are that the acts of reading and writing are acts of creation, not peripheral but essential to all education and all learning. Gay and lesbian students have special needs as learners in a patriarchal, heterosexist, homophobic society where their lives and experience are largely absent or misrepresented.

A Classroom Climate Survey, conducted in 1984 at Berkeley by [3] the Associated Students of the University of California (ASUC), found that lesbian and gay students were the most uncomfortable in class, more than any other ethnic minority group, women, or the disabled. While I am ill at ease with this comparison of oppressions and do not believe that this kind of suffering can ever be measured, the ASUC study supports my claim that throughout elementary, secondary, and post-secondary education, lesbian and gay students are deeply hurt. Like any other people, lesbians and gay men have an overwhelming need to see themselves made visible. Not only are these needs not being attended to, lesbian and gay students frequently must sit in silence while abusive comments about homosexuality and homosexuals made by their peers are tolerated, condoned, echoed by their teachers. The same ASUC study found that "82% of lesbian and gay students surveyed had been subjected to pejorative stereotypical comments about homosexuals by instructors."[2] A 1983 University of California Lesbian and Gay Intercampus Network (UCLGIN) study found that only thirteen per cent of student, faculty, staff, and alumni surveyed at the nine U. C. campuses considered that lesbian and gay topics "had been adequately covered in courses where they should have been treated."[3] The Berkeley Multicultural Lesbian and Gay Studies Program

(MLGS), a student organization, has been working for the past five years to encourage faculty to develop courses and curriculum on lesbian and gay issues. They argue:

> The lesbian and gay perspective has been systematically omitted from the University's course offerings . . . The roots of the omission . . . are not hard to find. The UCLGIN survey revealed that thirty-six per cent of the faculty responding that lesbian/gay topics were appropriate to their fields had refrained from doing research on these topics because of fear of negative reaction from colleagues, while forty-one per cent had refrained from including such material in their courses. Forty-four percent of students refrained from doing research or coursework for the same reason, and fourteen per cent were advised by faculty not to pursue these topics.[4]

These UC surveys are useful for establishing a view of the censorship and the suffering of lesbian and gay students. And yet, it is at this end of the educational process, a place only the most select group ever reaches, where it is possible to find any opportunity to take a course and engage in a discussion concerning homosexuality; the picture in elementary and secondary schools is far worse.

I now want to turn to the classroom to consider the contradic- 4 tions of a theory of teaching writing based on the idea of freedom of expression for a student, lesbian or gay, who is not free, who is taboo, silenced and made invisible. In *Writing Without Teachers* (1973) and *Writing With Power* (1981), Peter Elbow pioneered the technique of an automatic, nonstop, timed, restrictionless writing called "free writing." "Even if someone reads it, it doesn't send any ripples," Elbow writes.[5] "Free" is also a key word for educator John Holt: "People get better at using language when they use it to say things they really want to say to people they really want to say them to, in a context in which they can express themselves freely and honestly."[6] On the one hand how "free" is any student ever in a class that is part of a program that is part of an institution that is part of a system that is hierarchical, authoritarian, racist, classist, sexist, and so on? Still, for some students there can be something freeing about freewriting, particularly because students need not share the ideas they have generated with an audience. But this exercise is often followed by a sharing exercise that is part of the process of developing the idea. As Elbow puts it, the next step after freewriting, sharing, is the "essential human act at the heart of writing."[7]

My point here is that a student who is lesbian or gay may not feel 5 that she can express herself freely and honestly and she will therefore censor herself. She may fear "ripples" from the teacher or even more from her peers in the class. And so she will divert her first and best, her most vital idea, and the work of getting better at using language is getting undone. A non-gay student may be more likely than the gay student to feel free. To illustrate this point I will use an experience I had teaching in a community college adult literacy program.

A woman came into my beginning writing class. I gave her paper   6
and asked her to write a letter introducing herself. She began to write and by the end of the class had four or five pages to read to me. She had written about a man in the Navy she'd married, about how unhappy she'd been cooped up alone when he wouldn't let her go out at night, how he brought his friends home and demanded she fix dinner for them, how she began to break away from him, had a relationship secretly with another man and finally left her husband, how he tried to get her back and she wouldn't go. "Whew!" she said as she went out the door. "I just had to get that down on paper. " I never saw the student again. But somehow this had been an important moment for her. She felt the need to tell her story in writing and she had presumed that she would be free to do it.

How many of my students did not feel free? How many censored   7
their topics? Kept their journal writing secret or separate from school writing? Gave up on their writing because they didn't know what to say? In the literacy program students first learning to write describe family reunions and wedding anniversaries (some community college writing programs actually call a section of their program emphasizing personal experience writing "the engagement ring unit"), but they do not write coming out stories or portraits of gay relationships. And I know there are gay and lesbian students in the class, not only because of statistics, but because gays are not as invisible to themselves as they are to others. I decide that the man getting teased by other students in the class, who is thrilled to be interviewing someone who used to know Prince (the pre-"Purple Rain" androgynous Prince), has to be gay; that the teacher and counselor who helped Gina get off drugs and finish high school was a woman and Gina is probably a lesbian. And sure enough. There they are in the gay bar, at the gay pride and freedom day parade, along with others I've recognized, none of whom ever wrote anything explicit about being gay. I don't know if that was a conscious decision or how painful it was, how much it hurt their development as a writer, when the split between the speakable and the unspeakable will catch up with them, how much longer they will stay in school, keep writing, keep reading, keep encouraging their children, their parents to read and to write.

Luis, who dropped out of the program, sees me one morning in   8
a local, lesbian owned and operated breakfast spot. "I'm thinking of coming back to school," he tells me. "I can't understand what

I read in the newspaper. And I talk so fast I can't write. This is the right time for me. You know, I've got no kids, no wife—he's talking fast and watching me—"no husband to support." Luis is coming out to me. And he's checking out how safe and comfortable my classroom might be.

Another example of how self-censorship affects a gay student is 9 Walter, whose work I followed over a period of several years. He repeatedly cycled through the college writing courses, dropping out at the highest level and re-enrolling himself in entry level classes. In my intermediate course, he wrote his papers in the third person, referring to himself as "junior." His first essay described a suicide attempt which he explained was a plea for attention from his father. In his last essay he researched the founding of the Sears Roebuck Company. (His reason for the project was to find out whether or not Roebuck was black since he had found contradictory information about this.) The essay took him a year to write; he took an incomplete in the course and finally turned in a report that said very little. A year later Walter came into a beginning writing class I was teaching because he had taken an incomplete in a literature course and he wanted an opportunity to work on an essay on *Huckleberry Finn.* After two weeks of pouring over criticism, unable to put a word of his own on paper, he dropped out.

I use Walter as an example of a motivated and ambitious student 10 (he often talked about transferring to a four year university and becoming a teacher) afraid to have an idea of his own. I don't want to appear to be simplifying the complexity of his problems with school and with writing which clearly amount to a deeply rooted psychological block. I would like research to be available that will help to explain how his position in the world as a gay man—and as a gay black man—influences his ability to write and to learn.

I want to use one more example from my teaching—a University 11 of California student enrolled in a composition and rhetoric course. On the first day of class Nathan is describing a night at a gay bar, responding to an assignment to describe a recent event showing something about his values, traditions, or culture. He watches closely as I glance over the paper, measuring my reaction to his subject, a topic he can censor in the future depending on my response. Later he writes essays, oblique, and convoluted about "universal oppressions" and how we all "have to struggle against them," until I call him into a writing conference. "Why don't you be more clear?" I ask him. "I've been afraid to," he says. While others lucidly defend abortion rights, civil rights, religious freedom, only Nathan is writing about gay rights, and he writes vaguely and self-consciously.

Homophobia advises our students not to write clearly. Self- 12
censorship and fear of our response keep lesbian and gay students
from "getting power through voice."[8] "Real voice," Peter Elbow
calls it. "Nothing stops you," he writes, "from writing now, today
words that people will want to read. Nothing stops you, that is, but
your fear or unwillingness or lack of familiarity with what I am calling your real voice." As the quarter progressed Nathan became
increasingly vocal about his politics, in class discussions never specifically mentioning gay issues, but coming close as he spoke about
gender stereotyping and oppression. Neither did I encourage him to
be more specific in these discussions, even though I know that specificity is at the root of critical thinking.

How might things have been different for Nathan, Walter, Gina, 13
Luis, and others? For one thing, I was not "out" in the classroom;
I included no readings on lesbian and gay issues; I reinforced their
silence as well as the split in their lives: for them, like them, I was gay
in the bars and at the parades, but never in the classroom. As I write
this, I'm aware of a sense that I failed these students and that I now
must ask myself—that as lesbian and gay teachers and academics we
all must ask ourselves: what are our attitudes toward our gay and lesbian students? What kind of responsibility do we have? How are we
similar to and different from other members of the profession who
identify with students like themselves; male teachers, male students;
feminist teachers, feminist students; black teachers, black students?
As lesbian and gay teachers how does our invisibility affect our teaching and our students' lives?

I am reminded of an English professor I had in the mid- 14
seventies, a formidable woman who lived with another formidable
woman, also of the English Department. This professor raised an
eyebrow at me one morning as I excused myself from her survey of
great literature (all of it written by men) in order to attend
" Women's Day" activities. On the program I held out to her, she
pointed first to the "Lesbian Workshop" at the college that day,
then to the "Lesbian Workshop" to follow during "Women's
Weekend" at a neighboring college. "I see you're both using the
same language," she said, her face a mask. Puzzled and embarrassed, I hastily assured her we didn't want to exclude anyone, and
she nodded me away.

Looking back I would say that in three years I read two pieces of 15
"lesbian literature" with this professor who travelled to far way
midwestern universities to lecture on Willa Cather and Gertrude
Stein. Our class session on *Three Women* was devoted entirely to
Stein's use of grammar. During our discussion of Henry James'
The Bostonians—her favorite women's writer, she told us—there

was no mention of the lesbian relationship between the two main characters, and I could only get up the nerve, finally, to approach her after class one day to ask if she would please stop using the term "women's lib." Her housemate and colleague used similar tactics: she was primarily responsible for the department's veto of Virginia Woolf as required reading. When I asked about some earlier writing she had done on Edna St. Vincent Millay, she told me shortly that she preferred to disclaim it. The picture of these two women shows most poignantly my experience with teachers who refrain from openly conducting or encouraging discussion of love between women. When I speak of the intellectual growth denied lesbian and gay students, I speak from my own memory of suffocating censorship.

In her "Foreword" to *The Coming Out Stories*, Adrienne Rich [16] asks the reader to view in her mind millions of pages of women's writing censored, concealed, lost, burned:

> As you read the stories in this book I would like you to think of those piles of ash, those cages behind which women's words, lesbian words, lie imprisoned. . . . This is poverty. This is starvation. This is cultural imperialism—the decision made by one group of people that another group shall be cut off from their past, shall be kept from the power of memory, context, continuity. This is why lesbians, meeting, need to tell and retell stories like the ones in this book. In the absence of the books we needed, the knowledge of women whose lives were like our own, an oral tradition—here set down on paper—has sustained us.[9]

Like Rich I believe that the "coming out story," the lesbian narrative, has a central position in the making of lesbian history and culture. (An interesting question, and subject for research, is whether the coming out story has a similar role in the making of gay male culture.) But I wonder about the notion of an oral tradition. Lesbians do tell their stories to each other, in small private circles; yet it seems to me that peculiar to lesbian culture is its extreme dependence on writing.

Because of the taboo surrounding lesbian experience and the [17] profound isolation surrounding many lesbian women, writing has a special place in the coming out process, and this is not only true for women who have access to education. I suspect that the coming out story is shared with one other, the woman with whom the experience is lived, and then very often the story is put down in writing—in the form of a poem, journal entry, a letter. I believe that lesbians rarely have access to the power Paule Marshall attributes to "the poets in the kitchen," the "set of giants" who taught "the first lesson in the narrative art."[10] Describing her mother and her mother's friends who "suffered a triple invisibility, being black, female and foreigner," Marshall writes: "Given the kind of women they were,

they couldn't tolerate the fact of their invisibility, their powerlessness. And they fought back using the only weapon at their
command: the spoken word."[11] Lesbians do not have the kitchen
table tradition Marshall shows us here, or Cherríe Moraga describes
in "La Güera," "the sounds of my mother and aunts gossiping—
half in English, half in Spanish—while drinking cerveza in the
kitchen."[12] We do not have the words of our mothers, aunts, grand-
mothers around us. We inherit invisibility and silence.

There *is* a shared language among lesbians and often it originates   18
from books. In the "Preface" to *Another Mother Tongue: Gay
Words, Gay Worlds,* Judy Grahn, lesbian poet and cultural worker,
describes sources for her research:

> I have recalled my utter isolation at sixteen, when I looked up *Lesbian*
> in the dictionary, having no one to ask about such things,
> terrified, elated, painfully self-aware, grateful it was there at all. Feeling
> the full weight of the social silence surrounding it. I have gone over and
> over in my mind the careful teaching my first lover Von gave me, as she
> recited in strictest secrecy the litany of words and phrases related to the
> forbidden subject of our being.[13]

This list, Grahn remembers, included a "mysterious word she had
no definition for: *catafoil.* . . . *Catafoil,* I now believe, came from a
Gay book Von read while standing in a drugstore—a habit she had,
especially with Gay books since it was socially embarrassing if not
dangerous to buy them."[14] Grahn argues that an oral tradition
exists among lesbians and she traces origins of that tradition. What is
striking is that much of the oral tradition has its roots in writing.

Grahn followed *Another Mother Tongue* with *The Highest*   19
Apple: Sappho and the Lesbian Poetic Tradition, which began as a
chapter of the first book and grew too large. In her introduction she
writes:

> Poetry is important to women, and it is especially important to
> Lesbians. More than one Lesbian has been kept from floundering on
> the rocks of alienation from her own culture, her own center, by having
> access, at least, to lesbian poetry. We owe a great deal to poetry; two of
> our most important names, for instance: Lesbian and Sapphic. When
> has a larger group of humans, more pervasive behavior, and much more
> than this, the tradition of women's secret powers that such names
> imply, ever been named for a single poet?[15]

Writing sustains lesbians. Our "weapon" against our isolation and
oppression has traditionally been the written word. For lesbians,
then, the consistent culture is the written culture—and we have had
to be very vigilant to keep that culture consistent, to sift through the
ashes of women's writing, to piece together Sappho's fragments,

to keep the books on our kitchen tables and beside our beds. Lesbian and gay cultures have a unique dependency on literacy, and lesbians and gay men must be able to read and to write their own stories if the culture and the people are to survive.

Finally, I want to focus on necessity. There are many questions I 20 can explore here about how need manifests itself for lesbian and gay learners. Jonathan Kozol writes about the cycle of illiteracy in *Illiterate America*. How many of those parents who pass illiteracy on to their children are gay and lesbian? What might the relationship be of illiteracy to the spread of AIDS in terms of accessibility to information about the disease? And what about the relationship of literacy to healing? Journal writing is often used in workshops for incest survivors. (see Ellen Bass's work, especially *I Never Told Anyone: Writings by Women Survivors of Child Sexual Abuse*) and in work on recovering from alcoholism and substance abuse (see Jean Swallow, ed., *Out From Under: Sober Dykes and Our Friends*) and in work on healing from abusive relationships (see *Naming the Violence: Speaking Out About Lesbian Battering*, ed. Kerry Lobel for the National Coalition Against Domestic Violence Lesbian Task Force). And what role might literacy have in healing from Sex and Love Addiction, from depression? (I think of the last verse of a song Bonnie Raitt has recorded:

> Tonight I'm sitting learning how to read
> Because in school I never liked to
> It's just one of the little things I'm going to need
> As I go on living my life without you.)

These are questions that can open up new areas in the study of literacy in America.

I want to end with the words of two participants in a summer 21 writing workshop for teachers who expressed their need when I pushed the group to begin to think about how lesbian and gay students are being censored. What I wanted to do as a member of that group was create a space in which the lesbian and gay students (there were five of us in a class of twenty) could voice our particular concerns, could speak and write our experience as gay and lesbian teachers. What happened was that I tried for three days in a row to bring the issue to the table. The first day no one responded. The second day someone agreed that it was an important subject but it then got lost. On the third day, late in the morning, the group leader asked me to bring the matter up after a break. Here are two freewritings that came out of that moment. Sam wrote:

> My father is gay. He has lived with the same man for almost four-teen years, one year less than my parents' marriage lasted. Ellen tells

me that 25% of the population has an immediate family member who is gay, 10% are gay themselves. I never knew this as a teenager. No one ever talked about it. We never dealt with it in school.

For me, in adolescence—a time of great pain and change for even the happiest of us, my father's homosexuality was something I had to bear alone. It was something I discussed with no one. It increased my sense of isolation. Running was my place of belonging and to a great extent my coach played the role of my father. I believe if I could have written about this, it would have helped me to accept my father on his own terms much sooner.

Homophobia is a prejudice that must be dealt with in the classroom. To ignore it is criminal.

Alice wrote:

The room grew strangely silent. This group of expressive, committed, open-minded people seemed suddenly uncomfortable. My heart leaped into my throat, all my blood began to tingle. And I too remained silent. I who love to say what I think, especially regarding issues I know something about.

They have murdered us, burned us at the stake and in the gas chambers. They have taken our children from us. They have fired us from jobs and blacklisted us. They have cross-referenced us in the card catalogs with abnormal psychology, "see also suicide and depression." They have separated us from our mates, our lovers. They have arrested and incarcerated us. They have banned us from public participation. They have silenced us.

And that's the overt oppression.

The covert oppression is standing next to my lover at my brother's wedding and having to listen to my uncle making cracks about my not being married. Or watching a young person in school struggle with her sexual identity, wanting to offer myself as an example, but remaining mute.

Realizations are stirring me to the core. I can no longer sit here in silence.

Gay issues are issues which affect us all. These are issues not of sexuality and lifestyle alone. They are issues of political, religious and intellectual freedom.

The writings by these two teachers are coming out stories, just [22] as the writing I am doing now is part of my own continuing story. Clearly, we can not tell or teach any one else's story until we are free to tell and to be told our own.

NOTES

1 Helping to inform these premises are *Demystifying Homosexuality: A Teaching Guide about Lesbians and Gay Men*, published by the Human Rights Foundation, and Alicia Abramson's "TA's Guide for Overcoming Homophobia in the Classroom," UC Berkeley.

2 Proposal to Vice-Chancellor Roderic Park for campus funding of the Multicultural Lesbian and Gay Studies Program, UC Berkeley, June 30, 1986.

3 Ibid.

4 Ibid.

5 Peter Elbow, *Writing Without Teachers* (New York: Oxford University Press, 1973) p. 3.

6 *Handbook for Planning An Effective Writing Program* (California State Department of Education, 1983) p. 69.

7 Peter Elbow, *Writing With Power* (New York: Oxford University Press, 1981) p. 20.

8 Ibid. p. 304.

9 Adrienne Rich, "Foreword," *The Coming Out Stories*, eds. Julia Penelope Stanley and Susan J. Wolfe, (Watertown, Massachusetts: Persephone Press, 1980) xi-xii.

10 Paule Marshall, from "The Poets in the Kitchen," *The Borzoi College Reader*, eds. Charles Muscatine and Marlene Griffith (New York: Alfred Knopf, 1984) p. 81.

11 Marshall, p. 78.

12 Cherríe Moraga, "La Güera," *This Bridge Called My Back: Writings By Radical Women of Color*, eds. Cherríe Moraga and Gloria Anzaldúa (New York: Kitchen Table Women of Color Press, 1981) p. 31.

13 Judy Grahn, *Another Mother Tongue: Gay Words, Gay Worlds* (Boston: Beacon Press, 1984) xii.

14 Ibid.

15 Judy Grahn, *The Highest Apple: Sappho and the Lesbian Poetic Tradition* (San Francisco: Spinsters Ink, 1985) xii.

EXPLORATIONS

1. How does Hart define literacy? How does she link literacy with identity?

2. How does Hart define freedom in the classroom? In what ways is the freedom of gay and lesbian students limited in the classroom?

3. Compare your definition of the "voice" you use in writing with Hart's. In what ways do you think this voice is shaped by the values you encounter in the classroom?

4. According to Hart, why is writing particularly important in the lesbian community? In what ways does silence restrict individuals and the power of a community? How does writing allow Hart to identify with the values of a certain community? In the communities to which you belong, does language act to create a sense of cohesion and belonging?

If so, how? You might also consider how silence functions within these communities.

5. This essay was originally published in a collection entitled *The Lesbian in Front of the Classroom*. Basing your argument on evidence from the text, did Hart intend her essay exclusively for a lesbian audience, or did she anticipate other audiences for her work?

FURTHER SUGGESTIONS
FOR WRITING: PERSONAL LITERACIES

The writing assignments that follow are complex because they list numerous invention strategies, that is, ways of coming up with material to write about. As Part 1 of this book explained, writing is a way of discovering your thoughts. As you write in response to the suggestion questions and activities here, you will generate a great deal of material. Explore that material for significant insights that you can develop into an essay, a research paper, or another style of prose.

1. **Writing a Personal Literacy Narrative:** Writing a literacy narrative will help you clarify your own experience of the relationship between literacy and community. In this narrative, you will do two interrelated things: 1) focus on one or several literacy experiences you've had within a particular community and 2) describe the significance of those experiences in making you a literate person.

   This assignment encourages you to rely upon and critique your personal memories, develop and use rich detail as supporting material in your writing, and develop your skills in narration and description. It's not a research paper in the sense that you'll be using the library. You will, however, draw upon your own vast store of memory and knowledge to develop your essay. As you begin to write and set in motion the continual process of revision, use the following questions and activities to help you generate material and organize your thoughts:

   - What are the earliest memories you have of speaking, reading, or writing? Try to recreate those memories. Describe the contexts within which they occurred.

   - List and describe those people and/or communities that have influenced your sense of literacy.

   - Describe the texts that have been most important to you. Why were they important? Are they still important? Why or why not?

   - List the times when you realized that you did not have the literacy necessary to participate fully. Describe how you felt; describe actions that you may have taken because of these experiences.

   - Explain how your sense of who you are has shaped your experiences of listening, speaking, reading, or otherwise behaving according to the expectations of the community about which you're writing.

   - Describe how you became literate and/or how you learned to understand the most effective language or behaviors in a particular community.

   - Explain why you wanted to belong to a certain community.

Reread passages of the selections that you highlighted or marked as important. Reread any responses to your reading that you may have included in your writer's notebook. Perhaps you strongly agreed or disagreed with the author or authors. Use a quotation or paraphrase a passage that supports or explains a point that you want to make. Remember to attribute the source accurately in your paper.

2. **Considering the Implications of Becoming Literate:** In his *Narrative*, Frederick Douglass writes: "I would at times feel that learning to read had been a curse rather than a blessing. It had given me a view of my wretched condition, without the remedy. It opened my eyes to the horrible pit, but upon which no ladder to get out." Many other writers, such as Richard Rodriguez and Bethany Crabtree, describe the process of becoming literate as a transition involving a sense of gain as well as of loss. In preparing your paper, do the following: 1) Analyze how one or more of the authors describe the contradictions associated with becoming literate, and 2) connect their observations to your own experiences of becoming literate.

This essay asks you to consider critically some of the selections you have read in Part 2 and your responses to them. It also asks you to reconsider your own experiences with literacy and the communities and values that shaped and informed these experiences. To help you begin the process of organizing and revising your thoughts, you may want to consider some of the following issues and questions:

- When have you been encouraged to become literate in a particular community? Who encouraged you to do so, and what do you think their motives were?

- Identify some of the communities in which you have tried to become literate. Why did you want to become literate in these communities?

- Literacy is often associated with power. As Douglass points out, some kinds of literacy can also cause a sense of being powerless or helpless. Have you ever had a similar experience with learning a new kind of literacy? If so, describe the connections you see between literacy and power.

- In American society, the goal of 100 percent literacy is often proposed by various groups. What kind of literacy does this refer to? Who would benefit from this literacy? What does this suggest about the general way that literacy is valued in our society?

- George Orwell talks about writing as a kind of literacy that deals with private ghosts and demons as well as larger communities and public politics. In your experience, how has literacy been both a way of expressing your own personality as well as a way to participate in certain communities or groups? Has becoming literate ever brought these two parts of your life into tension?

- Richard Rodriguez writes that with every gain in literacy there is a loss. Do you agree? If so, discuss a time in your life when becoming literate in one community seemed to exclude you from another community.

3. **Writing about Other's Literacy Experiences:** Discuss literacy experiences with other members of your class, with immigrants living in your community, or with instructors in your school. Explain how they agree or disagree with the views expressed by the writers included in Part 2, for example, with George Orwell or Barbara Mellix. To prepare for your interviews and discussions, refer to the reading selections and to your writer's notebook. Prepare several questions, even though you may not ask all of them. You may choose to interview people about practices, rituals, and traditions necessary to gain membership in a community. To what extent do the results of your interviews allow you to extend the discussion of personal literacies begun in Part 2?

3

ACADEMIC LITERACIES

Although most Americans would probably agree that education is necessary for the well-being of both individuals and society as a whole, the history of American education has been characterized by contending visions of the purposes of education. In Part 2, for example, Richard Rodriguez and Frederick Douglass portray education as part of the American ideal of self-reliance and progress. At the same time, many of the writers in Part 3, such as Cherríe Moraga, Zitkala-Sa, and Mike Rose, suggest that teachers and schools often fail to accept and learn from the literate practices that many students bring with them to classrooms. The selections in "Academic Literacies" discuss and challenge the purposes of education, its importance in American culture, and the different literacies that are learned at the college level. Part 3 asks you to consider why you are in college, how you will benefit from your time there, and whether or not you and society benefit from your being a student.

What does it mean to be "literate" within an academic institution? Are different literacies at work at different kinds of community colleges, four-year colleges, and universities? Being literate in a college or university setting involves *becoming* literate in the particular language practices of an academic discipline. Academic literacy also includes becoming literate in the traditions and lore of an institution as well as its natural and constructed environments. As you become part of an academic community, you will undoubtedly find yourself negotiating the differences between the literacies of your home communities and those of the university. The literate practices of our home communities are not always valued by colleges and universities, as many writers in Part 3 will argue and as Marianna DeMarco Torgovnick and Richard Rodriguez implied in Part 2. How, then, are we to succeed in college without losing touch with the places where we grew up? Just as important, how can a college or university learn from the variety of literacies that teachers *and* students bring with them to campus?

The readings in Part 3 ask you to consider these "boundary crossings" between home communities and the academy. They also encourage you to reflect critically on education and educational settings, to look at *what* you are being taught, *how* you are being taught, and *where* you are being taught. In his essay "The Banking Concept of Education," Paulo Freire argues against teaching methods that assume students are little more than passive receptacles for the knowledge of their teachers. bell hooks examines the tensions that can arise when students from working class and minority backgrounds learn to speak the language of the academy. And David Orr advocates that our universities and colleges teach ecological literacy, a literacy that encourages making links between the natural world and our intellectual work.

On the other hand, E. D. Hirsch argues that we need to pay more attention to the content of education, that there are certain ideas and traditions that all Americans must know if they are to read and write effectively. Allan Bloom asserts that a liberal education should expose students to timeless, unchanging truths in an effort to make students more fully human before they enter the "intellectual wasteland" of professional work. But as Jacqueline Jones Royster, Zitkala-Sa, and Langston Hughes argue, the question of whose traditions and stories are taught in schools involves a difficult and often painful political and social struggle.

You will notice that all of the writers in Part 3 argue that the process of education should be changed. You might want to consider the following questions as you read: What kinds of changes do they advocate? On which issues do they agree or disagree? How are these writers defining "academic literacy"? Is a single definition even possible or desirable? Do you think that there will always be a need to change the process of education in the United States? These readings are often deliberately provocative, and you will probably find yourself applying these writers' observations and arguments to your own experience of education. You may find that your goals and expectations for college have been affirmed, changed, or complicated. Are there any changes in educational processes or institutions you would like to see made? If so, who would benefit from such changes? What would have to happen for such change to occur?

EXPLORATION

Drawing on your own experiences as a college student, develop a definition of academic literacy. Is it in conflict with what your college defines as academic literacy? You might consider the following questions before you begin: What were your own expectations of higher education? In what ways have they been met, challenged, or modified? What does your institution expect from you as a student? What does it mean to be college educated? What do you need to know to succeed in college?

Theme for English B

LANGSTON HUGHES

One of the central figures of the Harlem Renaissance of the 1920s, Langston Hughes (1902-1967) was initially criticized by African-American intellectuals for his portrayal of what they considered to be troublesome views of African-American life. Hughes wrote about regular folk, people he described as "workers, roustabouts, and singers, and job hunters on Lenox Avenue in New York, or Seventh Street in Washington or South State in Chicago—people up today and down tomorrow, working this week and fired the next, beaten and baffled, but determined not to be wholly beaten, buying furniture on the installment plan, filling the house with roomers to help pay the rent, hoping to get a new suit for Easter—and pawning that suit before the Fourth of July." Hughes is also known for the idiom and rhythm he expressed in his work. He incorporated colloquial speech and the rhythms of jazz in attempting to express the lives of African Americans.

WRITING BEFORE READING

Reflect on a time when you tried to fulfill an assignment in ways that kept your own identity in the writing.

The instructor said,

> Go home and write
> a page tonight.
> And let that page come out of you—
> Then, it will be true.

I wonder if it's that simple?   5
I am twenty-two, colored, born in Winston-Salem.
I went to school there, then Durham, then here
to this college on the hill above Harlem.
I am the only colored student in my class.
The steps from the hill lead down into Harlem,   10
through a park, then I cross St. Nicholas,
Eighth Avenue, Seventh, and I come to the Y,
the Harlem Branch Y, where I take the elevator
up to my room, sit down, and write this page:

It's not easy to know what is true for you or me   15
at twenty-two, my age. But I guess I'm what
I feel and see and hear, Harlem, I hear you:
hear you, hear me—we two—you, me, talk on this page.

I feel and see and hear, Harlem, I hear you:
hear you, hear me—we two—you, me, talk on this page.
(I hear New York, too.) Me—who?   20

Well, I like to eat, sleep, drink, and be in love.
I like to work, read, learn and understand life.
I like a pipe for a Christmas present,
or records—Bessie, bop, or Bach.
I guess being colored doesn't make me *not* like   25
the same things other folks like who are other races.
So will my page be colored that I write?

Being me, it will not be white.
But it will be
a part of you, instructor.   30
You are white—
yet a part of me, as I am a part of you.
That's American.
Sometimes perhaps you don't want to be a part of me.
Nor do I often want to be a part of you.   35
But we are, that's true!
As I learn from you,
I guess you learn from me—
although you're older—and white—
and somewhat more free.   40

This is my page for English B.

EXPLORATIONS

1. List some of the themes that Hughes develops in this poem. How does
   he link them? How does the structure of the poem work to support and
   highlight these themes and their relationships?
2. Why is it not so simple to write "a page that comes out of you," especially one that is "true"? How is Hughes "true" to himself in this
   poem? How does Hughes include the various aspects of his identity
   (race, ability, goals) as he completes his assignment?
3. Identify elements of Hughes's "theme" that stand out as poetic.
   What effect do they create in you as a reader?
4. Hughes wrote his theme as a poem. Rewrite his poem in prose. Does
   the change in form create a change in meaning? How would you evaluate this "theme" if you received a copy of it in your peer-response
   group?

The Fourth Vision:
Literate Language at Work

SHIRLEY BRICE HEATH

Shirley Brice Heath is a professor of English and linguistics at Stanford University. She has also taught in bilingual class-rooms in southern California, an experience that led her to study the ways that people link their language to their different cultural backgrounds. Heath is best known for Ways with Words: Language, Life and Work in Communities and Classrooms, *which was published in 1983. For nearly a decade (1969–1978), Heath lived, worked, and played with the children and families whose stories she tells in* Ways with Words. *In the book, Heath describes the literate practices in the homes and schools of two working-class communities in the Piedmont region of the Carolinas, where she grew up. A profile of Heath in* Language Arts, *a journal for elementary school English teachers, notes that she has contributed significantly to our understanding of "the complexity of language learning and of the importance of understanding the social context of language development and use." "The Fourth Vision" is the concluding essay in* The Right to Literacy *(1990).*

WRITING BEFORE READING

How would you describe an ideal school? What would people learn and how would they learn it? How would this ideal school serve both the individual and the community?

In the 24 November 1985 issue of the *New York Times* book review section, Harold Brodkey, novelist and short story writer, wrote an essay entitled "Reading, the Most Dangerous Game." To his readers he gave this warning:

> I think reading and writing are the most dangerous human things because they operate on and from that part of the mind in which judgments of reality are made; and because of the authority language has from when we learn to speak and use its power as a family matter, as an immediate matter, and from when we learn to read and see its modern middle-class power as a public matter establishing our rank in the world. (45)

Brodkey, as a literary writer, wishes, of course, to promote, encourage, and enrich what he calls "the most dangerous human things" of reading and writing. In analyzing how reading and writing are dangerous, he gives us three visions, which precede a fourth of my devising, to which the title of this chapter refers. Brodkey reminds us that reading and writing operate on and intensify "judgments of reality—the abilities we have to imagine and then to bestow the authority that language can have. He terms reading and writing dangers because they must bring unpredictability, change, reassessment, redefinition. Brodkey tells us:

> novels, plays, essays, fact pieces, poems, through conversion or in the process of argument with them, change you or else—to use an idiom— you haven't listened. If the reader is not at risk, he is not reading. And if the writer is not at risk, he is not writing. (44)

Reading and writing thus remove us from ordinariness, commonalities, uniformities. They bring about and, most frequently, are our only ways to ensure the creation and the exchange of ideas. Hence, a central danger within reading and writing is the growth and spread of ideas, as well as the power of problem identifying and problem solving that can come through speaking about and acting on their imperatives. The conversion or process of argument that changes us as we read and write leads us to have to place first ourselves in authority and then, immediately after, others with whom we want to extend the argument. As Deborah Brandt points out in this volume, literate knowledge has to become a craft knowledge, because what sustains literateness is not the *what* but the *who*.

Brodkey speaks directly of the authority in the first three visions of literate language—the authority we have when we learn to speak and use its power—as a family matter, immediate matter, and public matter establishing our rank beyond primary associates to our rank in the larger world. To these three visions I add a fourth—its authority and power as a work matter. Within American society, this fourth vision has risen in authority and power in the past decade, while the first three visions have diminished. Perhaps not surprisingly, the literate language of reading and writing at work now draws on the manners and methods through which such language used to work in the first three—family, daily life of schooling, and public matters of leisure and religious life. For some, the literate language of work now provides in some cases models for talk and idea exchange that home, school, and community provided in earlier eras.

Let's look briefly at the first three visions and where they stand today in American life. How do their conditions affect the fourth vision?

LANGUAGE WITHIN THE FAMILY

Language as a family matter includes those uses of spoken and   6
written language that scholars and laymen alike have long argued
should help establish our identity, our referencing to the world, and
our ways of both seeking solitude and putting ourselves forward to
the world beyond the family. It is that language through which children are nurtured and play games, explore their immediate physical
and social world, and express curiosity, emotion, and basic needs.
The average American thinks of young children learning language
within a rich, stable network of interactions with parents, siblings,
playmates, and family friends.

But rapidly changing patterns of employment and child-care   7
arrangements are not compatible with idealized images of consistent,
verbally supportive care givers. All families—mainstream and
nonmainstream—are in constant states of change, and the leisure
patterns, family mealtime exchanges, and joint adult-child projects of
several decades ago face considerable competition in households of
single parents and families in which both parents work full-time
(Suransky). In 1986 only seven percent of the families in the United
States could be described as the traditional ideal or typical family—a
two-parent family in which working fathers and homemaking mothers provided sustenance, structure, and support for children
(Hodgkinson). Single-parent households, dual-career families, and
extended households made up of nonkin and nonconjugally linked
temporary residents give little time to extended spoken or written
language interactions with children. As a result, America's children
receive far less language for learning in families and through family
events than in the decades that preceded the 1970s.

America's children are silent and lonely across socioeconomic   8
classes and in cultural and linguistic memberships. Evidence for this
silent loneliness comes from a number of sources. In the late 1970s
a team of psychologists in Chicago enlisted seventy-five adolescents
of middle-class families to take part in a study of their daily lives
(Csikszentmihalyi and Larson). Researchers collected data through
the experience sample method; for one week the participants carried
electronic pagers and responded during one random moment within each two-hour period to a pager beep. The responses consisted of
the adolescents' filling out self-report forms to record their activities, feelings, and thoughts at that moment. These high school students continued their normal activities during the week of recording
and participated as well in follow-up individual interviews about
their daily experiences.

The teenagers indicated that leisure time with their families   9
consisted primarily of noninteractive, unchallenging, passive activi-

ties. The warmest memories these adolescents had were of family times together that involved a trip. At home, the parents and the children rarely did things together, so they seemed to have to leave home to be together as a family. The typical happy-memory scenario pictured relatives around a fireplace after a day of active winter sports, eating and joking or singing and playing games together. These memories were of structured times for talk and interactions that served as cornerstones for the adolescents' self-concepts and projections of their own preferred future family habits.

Being alone was the context in which teenagers felt the worst. They confessed that they were unable to fill solitude with any productive activities. For them thinking took the form of worrying. When teenagers could not do anything, they questioned their own existence. For them the unstated rule of living was "to *be* one must *do*. To know that we exist and that we matter in the world, we must act in ways that prove our existence" (Csikszentmihalyi and Larson 197). Talk is a key feature of this doing-being, and talk and athletic activities take up the bulk of time that adolescents spend with their friends. However, these teenagers spent less than five percent of their time exclusively with a parent or parents; among a sample of one thousand self-reports, they reported being alone with their fathers only ten times, and five of those times included watching television. The adolescents spent approximately half an hour a week, less than five minutes a day, interacting exclusively with their fathers and less than fifteen minutes a day with their mothers.

But we must look at patterns in families of other social classes and cultural-linguistic membership to avoid drawing the conclusion that the patterns of life implied by these teenagers' reports occur only in middle-class families driven by perceived economic pressures and aspirations of upward mobility. An ethnography of Trackton, a black working-class community in the Piedmont Carolinas in the 1970s and early 1980s, pictured families and friends spending long hours outdoors or on porches that looked onto the plazalike center of the neighborhood (Heath, *Ways with Words*). Children and young people moved on and off this stage, always likely targets for jests, conversations, and teasing challenges. In the late 1980s, as the children of Trackton moved away to urban centers to establish independent households, the language environment of their children bore little resemblance to that of their own childhood. Highrise public housing projects, often poorly maintained and heavily targeted for criminal activities, provided few public stages on which children could perform for and interact with familiar caring adults. Young mothers tended to stay shut up in their own apartments, passing their days by watching television and waiting and hoping for some bureaucratic miracle that would bring a change in their lives.

For example, detailed notes and tape recordings kept by one for-   12
mer Trackton child, the single parent of three children in the late
1980s, revealed that she spent most of her waking hours as a passive
spectator of television and reader of magazines featuring the lives of
movie or television stars. During the occasional visits from her girlfriends, they talked nearly eighty percent of the time. In a random
selection of twenty hours of tapes made over two years, approximately fourteen percent of the recording sessions included talk
between the mother and her children. She asked direct questions
about the children's immediate actions, offered comments on those
actions, and gave directions or requested certain changes in behavior; these exchanges of talk usually lasted less than one minute. Of
course occasions when the talk of mother and child continued for as
much as four turns, ninety-two percent took place when someone
else—usually a girlfriend or the neighbor girl who served as a baby-
sitter—was in the room. In thirteen instances in twenty hours of
taping, the mother initiated nondirective talk to one of the children.
On nine occasions, she used some written artifact, a newspaper or
magazine advertisement, as the basis of her talk to her children
(Heath, "Children").

The spatial, occupational, and temporal changes in the lives of   13
Trackton's children who later located in project housing in urban
centers dramatically constrain talk and other interactions between
adults and children. In Trackton, from infancy to young adulthood,
everyone had immediate access to family and neighborhood friends.
Living and talking were largely public affairs, involving many speak-
ers of varied ages, goals, and affiliations. In the late 1980s, public
housing, new types of threats from drug-related criminal activities,
and the absence of extended families or close friends walled young
mothers and their children in urban centers into self-protective noninteractive isolation.

Patterns of daily life that cut the young off from supportive talk   14
that recognizes their roles and responses appear in families at all
points along the continuum from middle class to the poor of inner-
city high-rise housing projects. A mid-1980s study of nearly 500
teenagers from a wide range of classes and regions of the country
who left home between the ages of twelve and nineteen reported
that approximately sixty percent of the youngsters who left home felt
compelled to do so (Lefkowitz). They felt that they had no support
for the numerous responsibilities they had taken on in their daily
lives: care for younger siblings, jobs outside of school, moderate
school achievement against peer pressures to goof off. These young
people reported leaving in the hope of finding supportive listeners
and occasions for telling their stories and for taking in others'
stories.

LANGUAGE IN SCHOOL

Where were the teachers of these students? Were there not   15
teachers who saw them daily and provided some forms of verbal support? Public promotions of literacy and basic skills in the 1980s and
issues of accountability have worked to silence teachers and students
in many ways. Across the United States, school districts, individual
schools and their teachers, as well as their students, face assessment
by standardized tests that ask students to manipulate discrete isolated elements of written texts. Relatively little class time can go into
students' and teachers' talking together about any topic. Thus,
back-to-basics programs, oral and written fill-in-the-blank exercises,
and teacher-dominated classrooms focus primarily on the mechanics
of language and remediation at the sentence level. Under most
dominant philosophies of pedagogy at the end of the twentieth
century, classrooms cannot foster teacher-student relationships that
build a sense of expertise and responsibility in students. Numerous
studies indicate the brevity and the limited scope of language in
classrooms that set the teacher as the question asker and the student
as the responder: Applebee tells us that students spend only three
percent of their time in secondary English classes writing discourse
that extends to a paragraph's length; studies of classroom language
use repeatedly illustrate the limited amount of oral participation
students have (e.g., Cazden). Guidance counselors have their attention turned almost exclusively to students headed for college; in
addition, in many urban schools there is a ratio of one counselor for
every 500 students (Lefkowitz).

Textbooks and tests do not, with rare exceptions, ask students to   16
identify problems; instead, they ask students to *solve* problems
already identified and stated by others. Requests for direct action
research that would require speaking and listening skills (e.g., interviews with local figures and comparisons of radio and television
coverage of current events) usually come primarily in extra-credit
sections of textbooks or from teachers of advanced placement or
honors sections. Numerous studies of classroom language report the
scarcity of occasions on which teachers sit back and let the students
talk or ask open-ended questions; even teachers who express the goal
of wanting to improve their students'oral language skills find it
extremely difficult to give up their central position as talkers in the
classroom. Perhaps somewhat paradoxically, in the past decade those
occasions of the greatest amount of talk by students interacting with
each other have come from the introduction of computers. With this
event, many teachers felt free to admit that some of their students
had more knowledge and expertise than their elders; thus, students
and their teacher often worked together as experts and novice.

In earlier eras, in spite of the prevalence of rote memorization   17
and recitation, the blending of different grades and ages in the same
classroom offered occasions for cross-age talk on academic topics.
Students were asked to prepare speeches on topics that related to the
values of civic life; they participated in planning and producing
school programs for affairs that drew a large portion of the community to the school. Textbooks and teaching materials, in contrast
to later patterns, provided questions that drew from students'
experiences, asked for argumentation, counterpropositions, and
comparisons of one's own experiences with those of characters presented in the textbooks (deCastell, Luke, and Luke).

LANGUAGE IN THE COMMUNITY

It is within the community—usually in our leisure activities and   18
in community organizations, such as the church—that we first learn
to contend with language, in Brodkey's terms, "as a public matter
establishing our rank in the world" (45). When we leave our homes
to explore play and to find recreation in our communities, we first
meet the need to explain ourselves through language, to acknowledge that it is possible that our familial nonverbal and verbal habits
will not be understood by those beyond our households. For many
young Americans of the late 1980s, the first such venture into organized patterns of leisure came from participation on neighborhood
basketball courts and baseball fields. Youngsters learned early
to align themselves with a team, a group for affiliation beyond the
family. Occasionally, for big games or special events, members of the
family came to watch, and there could follow considerable talk about
the who, what, why, and how of the game. But, in the main, leisure-
time activities brought together only those of the same age group,
and cross-age talk with adults, with the exceptions of coaches and
community park directors, rarely occurred.

Adult Americans spent an extraordinary amount of their leisure   19
time as either sports spectators or sports participants. They watched
experts of professional or collegiate affiliation, and they took up individual pursuits of athletics, often as a form of physical exercise.
Neither as spectators nor as participants, however, did adults find
many occasions to talk with the young about these events. National
team sports, such as football and basketball, focused the attention of
the spectators on events planned, administered, and monitored by
others. Audience members for these games were strangers who
focused their observations on the game. For events such as tennis
matches and golf tournaments, the spectators centered their attention
on celebrity players and observed strict rules of silence during play.

Exceptions to these spectator sports were local events, such as   20
high school basketball games, Little League baseball, and neighborhood soccer games. These games often brought together fans who
were not strangers to each other, and much talk by participants and
spectators alike surrounded the planning, execution, and follow-up
appraisal of these events. The patterns of interaction parallel those of
earlier years, when a weekend baseball game, church supper, or town
parade could involve nearly every member of the community in
arranging and successfully carrying off the event. For these events
and for some of the most commonly played outdoor games (croquet,
horseshoes, sack races), some role for participants of all ages was
usually assured. In the stories that circulated after such family or
community events, everyone could share in the telling, since all had
various degrees of experience and points of view from which they
had experienced the occasion.

In an earlier era, indoor leisure activities across classes and eth-   21
nic groups often centered on building the mind and the wits. Labor
outside the home—whether for pioneers, farmers, sailors, or merchants—provided substantial amounts of exercise for their bodies.
Spending time at home and in neighborhood activities to sharpen
the wits and to expand knowledge about the world held considerable
attraction for men and women, old and young. Throughout the
centuries of American history, men and women wrote in their diaries
and letters about the ways in which family activities around games,
photographs, and books centered on talk that would build the mind
and hone the wits. Parlors were made for talking, reading, and playing games that were often word challenges, tests of memory and
interpretation, and ways of practicing negotiation (consider the
game Monopoly, for example). In addition, a considerable amount
of what contemporary psychologists call "reciprocal teaching" (see
Brown and Palincsar) went on during these cross-age family events.

At the end of the twentieth century, a large portion of leisure   22
time for the middle class centers on developing the body and not the
mind. Participation in these activities is, more often than not, guided in large part through specialized books, magazines, audio tapes
and videotapes, and advertising that insists on the "proper" shoes,
clothing, and equipment for these activities. Moreover, the majority
of these activities are age-graded and gender-segregated. Men run
and play golf with male colleagues and not with their children or
female associates; similarly, women find female associates to share
their activities, and the most affluent hire baby-sitters to care for
their children while they work out at the gym or join an aerobics
class. Jogging, walking, biking, and playing tennis or racquetball take
on a hyperreality—outside actual participation—through the accou-
trements and sources of professional knowledge and institutions

(clubs, weight rooms) that surround these activities. The former habits of learning by listening to the experiences of close associates have given way to heeding the advice of professional models, advisers, and promoters. Thus, the ready give-and-take of extended occasions for talk that formerly accompanied leisure events in the family and the neighborhood have almost passed from the everyday experiences of middle-class Americans.

At home these changes in preferred leisure activities have come   23
with rearrangements in the organization of both time and space. The living room has replaced the parlor of earlier days, and it is now often the location of the television set and the video recorder. If the living room is not the location of these artifacts, they are in the family room—a paradoxical name since the family as a unit rarely gathers there. In many upper-middle-class families, children and adults have their separate spaces for their preferred leisure activities. Teenagers have a computer and a stereo in their room, while adults may have small television sets or portable compact disc players in several rooms of the house. Games are age-graded and kept in separate locations, so there may be no central site for storing family games.

Throughout American history the church has been a central   24
institution of community life. In the first two centuries of United States history, temples, churches, synagogues, and mosques in towns and cities served not only as religious centers but also as education- al, recreational, and social avenues beyond the family. Protestant church activities tended to center on texts—biblical, instructional, and musical; reading, talking about, and listening to written texts took up much of the time spent in religious activities. Implicit in many of these occasions of interpretation was the expectation that reading and talking about written texts would lead to altered actions and reformed views of one's own performances in the public world.

Beginning in the 1920s and with a dramatic increase in the 1970s   25
and 1980s, churches that took a hostile view of diversity in cultures moved to restrict their parishioners' access to various interpretations of the Bible, instructional materials, and music. The separation from the world that came from being born again led to a reliance on ministers as leaders and interpreters; the chosen followed the ministers' words (Marty). Institutions of fundamentalism and neoorthodoxy drew their congregations close to reading—to the written word—but without open interpretation through speaking about the word. Ritualized language in the words of authoritarian leaders and through recommended study sessions made sure that readers knew how and what to speak about the texts. Institutions increasingly prescribed actions for their congrega- tions, discouraged wide reading, and accepted only approved religious materials prepared for their specific groups. The goal seemed to be to fix a boundary on belief and on practice (Goody xvii).

Decidedly anti-intellectual and fearful of examinations of alter-   26
native premises of decision making, fundamentalists helped spread
throughout the public a resurgence of faith in educational basics to
reinforce children's learning of fundamental reading and mathematical skills. Opposed to open-ended interpretations of literature,
personal writing, and textbooks that encouraged alternative view-
points and stressed America's pluralistic culture, fundamentalists
came in the 1980s to be highly influential in designing the curricula
of language arts and science in public schools (see Moffett).

In short, from family life and our immediate daily life in school   27
to the more public institutional domains of leisure and religion, children in the United States in the late 1980s, in comparison with their
counterparts in earlier decades, had fewer opportunities to follow a
single topic or line of thought through a sustained conversation with
adults. Extended occasions for talk between those of different levels
and perspectives of expertise diminished in the home, the church,
and the school. In earlier eras it was commonplace for families to
insist on the presence of the young for family dinnertime, parlor
games, and numerous other occasions attended by family members
of different ages. These occasions provided numerous multiply
patterned, redundant opportunities for the young to hear debates,
stories, and long explanations of ways to accomplish certain feats.
The adage "children are to be seen and not heard" attests to long
hours of enforced listening skills. In addition, well into the 1950s,
radio programs, such as the *Jack Benny Show*, depended for their
entertainment value on long, involved verbal arguments, puns, and
wordplays.

The philosopher Walter Benjamin has lamented the decline of   28
storytelling that began with the rise of the novel and greatly acceler-
ated with the newspaper. He claims that the grip of the press on the
middle class lies primarily in the centering of the press on information: "the information which supplies a handle for what is nearest
gets the readiest hearing" (89). Benjamin goes on to remind us that
the art of listening has receded as the middle class has come to focus
primarily on information that can lay claim to immediate verifiabili-
ty, to being "understandable in itself" (89). Every reported event
from the news media comes wrapped in a simple explanation that
does not have to rely on readers' having "intelligence coming from
afar," either geographical or historical (89).

In contrast, storytelling and conversation laced through with   29
mininarratives allow listeners to interpret, to give tales amplitude and
extensions in time and space. Information that aims to explain itself
without losing time does so through explicit tellings of psychological and social connections that stories never release directly. Lived
and relived experiences communicated in stories become remem-

bered experiences, repeated over time and space by a community of listeners. Those who listen, truly listen, know they are the remakers of knowledge through the shared experiences of not only the stories heard but also their stories remembered, related, and released on other occasions that remind the listeners of old stories and analogous times, places, or situations.

LANGUAGE AT WORK

What of the fourth vision, literate language at work? How does this language relate to the diminished habits of conversation, story-telling, and communicating experiences in the home, in immediate life, and in the public world? Ironically, in the late 1980s, situations in which work took place increasingly provided occasions in which we could create narratives and share our observing, thinking, and listening with those with whom we worked. The example most immediately at hand is that of those teachers who worked then to promote and extend literate behaviors and not just the basic skills of literacy. My discussion of language at work focuses primarily on teachers who have acknowledged the power of expanding spoken and written genres in their work and then offers a brief comparison with other workplaces. 30

Numerous portions of this volume tell the stories of teachers who call on students to pool, share, and compare their everyday knowledge before they move on to taking in new information. Moreover, many of those whose work is represented in this volume are fringe dwellers, professionals who cling to the edges of institutions in part-time jobs and in programs that claim no place in the regular catalog of institutional activities. Those who teach basic English, study skills, adult basic education, remedial reading, and English as a second language always stand astride the theory and the practice of both politics and pedagogy. 31

Yet, as the essays in this volume illustrate, these teachers have visions with their students not of literacy skills but of literate behaviors. Within the programs and the philosophies included here, being literate means "having counsel" for oneself and for others through communicable experience (Benjamin 86). Being literate means being able to talk with and listen with others to interpret texts, say what they mean, link them to personal experience and with other texts, argue with them and make predictions from them, develop future scenarios, compare and evaluate related situations, and know that the practice of all these literate abilities is practical. Counsel is practical advice, but it is often "less an answer to a question than a proposal concerning the continuation of a story which is just unfolding" 32

(Benjamin 86). Thus, counsel depends on our ability to let ourselves and our situations speak to identify problems, to hypothesize futures, and to compare experiences.

How paradoxical it is that, within those institutions of home and school on which the United States has historically depended for instilling literate behaviors, we can find few extended occasions for literate behaviors. There are few occasions for learning through social interactions to provide reinforcement and to assure us that our knowledge is appropriate. Without extended opportunities to talk through and about what we know and have experienced, we have little hope of writing extended coherent prose. Repeatedly, research on writing in the world of work beyond school tells us that the vast majority of writing is first draft only—jottings and incomplete messages to ourselves or intimates to record, remind, or prod us (Mikulecky and Winchester). The relatively small percentage of writing that goes beyond the first draft emerges from a considerable amount of thinking and talking, both self-talk and social exchange with others. Subsequent drafts, especially those of institutions, move through talking and responding before final execution. Much of the talk that surrounds such writing is that of "having counsel"— considering at a practical level questions or possible scenarios—about the purposes of this writing or its continuation as part of a larger story (Flower).

Several essays in this volume illustrate how these literate language behaviors at work can reenter those classrooms in which teachers and students see themselves as members of a learning community. For example, the adult basic education and English as a second language teachers featured on the *Teacher to Teacher* videotape series produced at City University of New York demonstrate four major features of literate language at work: (1) The students and teachers are highly interactive; they compare and evaluate real-world knowledge and information reported in written texts. (2) They look behind the surface information, a characteristic that can spring up readily within those who have developed habits of storytelling. (3) The storytellers tend to begin their stories with the circumstances of their own learning by locating themselves in relation to the experiences of the story. (4) These students and teachers demonstrate repeatedly how a collective of learners sharing responsibility for building and analyzing bodies of experience "move up and down the rungs of their experience as on a ladder" (Benjamin 102).

Other essays reflecting the whole language approaches inspired by the work of Kenneth and Yetta Goodman echo across age levels the interactive nature of learning. Bringing young students into literature studies validates their life experiences and enables them to include the reactions and the realities of others within their own responses. The experience of the self and its communication to steady listeners enable students to let their own life habits become the net with which they sweep in information from beyond their daily spatial and temporal worlds.

Several essays in this volume illustrate ways in which we can   36 engage students in assessment. The predominant pattern in most schools reflects dependency on assessment tools that come from beyond the teacher and the students. Reported in this volume are numerous efforts to involve students in analyzing their own spoken and written products. Students examine papers written at different times for various purposes and with different kinds of support. They create portfolios of the writing they consider best, and they consider what goes into the making of particular pieces of writing for different audiences, purposes, and topic knowledge. These students go far beyond receiving assessment from others; they take the principles and practices of assessment as part of their own daily monitoring system. Students learn to observe, reflect, analyze, and report on their own selections of the evidence they produced through their own writing, reading, speaking, and listening.

Teachers of these students are learners. They need environments   37 in which together they can exhibit healthy skepticism about too narrow a range of ways of assessing their students' growth. Teachers need to feel free to turn their own and their colleagues' attention to ways they can learn about their own teaching. Currently, assessment tools beyond the teacher and students' construction hold both accountable. This situation reinforces the view that knowledge is simply accounted for, that it is a commodity of one-way transmission, and that it is not interactive. Common sense tells us otherwise. Conjoined learning at the task and with others of similar intention or social engagement provides the bulk of lifelong learning. Thus, learners—students and teachers alike—need consistent and intense attention to their own growth in the accumulation of facts and the awareness of ways of knowing (collections of accounts of such teachers include Newkirk and Atwell; Goswami and Stillman; Lightfoot and Martin).

Aside from such evidence that some groups of teachers and   38 students are working together in collective efforts to further their literate behaviors, what encouragement comes from the world of work beyond these classrooms? Increasingly, American businesses look ahead to the dramatic increase in jobs that require independent problem-identifying skills, oral communication abilities, and experience in collaboration. In several ways some corporations are trying to reshape their own institutions and to reorient their approaches to workers. One example comes from the Creative Education Foundation, an independent, not-for-profit foundation in Buffalo,

New York, that became in the late 1980s a strong influence on American corporations. Business executives and managers joined musicians, teachers, scientists, and physicians in seminars that led the participants to talk, exchange ideas, and seek ways of making new connections by interacting with others from different experiences. Regional meetings throughout the year enabled workers to stay in touch with creative approaches to their work and to communicating experiences within their work. Fundamental within the approach was the need to intensify common approaches to everyday experience: to observe with new concentration, to imagine situations, to bring unlikely concepts together, and to listen.

Beyond the learning activities of the Creative Education 39
Foundation itself lay recommendations about patience and common sense in expecting institutions to change. For some corporations the return of managers from creativity education was not always immediately well received or even acknowledged. The recommendation of the Creative Education Foundation to those returning to their jobs sounded similar to what teachers give each other after attendance at especially effective workshops and regional and national conventions: put new creative skills to work quietly in one's own area of responsibility and be willing to share with others who notice and ask about changes.

Another creative approach to collaboration and problem identi- 40
fication comes from leadership seminars provided by the United Auto Workers at Fremont, California, General Motors-Toyota plant. Several hours each week, workers from the plant came together with other workers across sections and levels of the automotive plant to identify problems; to consider ways of collecting evidence that could suggest solutions; and to record, analyze, and compare collectively their observations, talks with other workers, and deliberations in their own problem-identifying and problem-solving setting. These leadership seminars stood in the place of literacy classes that other automotive plants offered. Here a work center put into action the belief that literate behaviors, through commitment and responsibility to group efforts, bring greater returns than individually acquired literacy skills that may be gained in a traditional classroom approach.

Numerous research studies and panels of corporate executives 41
reported in the 1980s the need for workers to organize tasks verbally, communicate directions to colleagues, and generate coherent spoken and written texts for a variety of audiences (Carnegie Forum on Education and the Economy; Mikulecky and Winchester; Mikulecky and Ehlinger; Scribner; Sticht). Former low-level white-collar jobs are now combining traditional clerical functions with professional activities that formerly belonged to management. What is being predicted for clerical workers, for example, is "more sophis-

ticated reasoning ability [and] a wide understanding of company policy and procedures" without the degree of autonomy that formerly attached to managerial and professional positions (Feldberg and Glenn 96). One of the ironies often overlooked in the discussions about the deskilling of the American work force through computers is the way in which the demands of computers parallel those of humans: computers at work have had to become multifunctional and highly interactive (Bair). Humans must now follow this pattern to improve information accessibility, sharing, and collaborative problem identification and solution. Researchers within and outside industry and technology increasingly reported in the late 1980s that taking full advantage of technology would require closer attention to the social significance of human-machine interactions "embedded in on-going human interactions" (Blomberg 195).

These interactions work, both literally and figuratively, because   42
they provide occasions for socially distributed cognition that brings human minds and machines together to solve increasingly challenging problems. From such collaboration by those in medicine, aviation, space control, ship navigation, and law enforcement, each of us benefits daily. Our initial challenge is to see the communication of experience and the collaborative problem-solving spirit behind these advances as the key components of literate behaviors. A second challenge is to expand the learning strategies and situations described in this volume and to cooperate with those representatives of the education and business sectors who share humanistic goals. Researchers from a variety of sectors began in the late 1980s to acknowledge the power of such concepts as socially distributed cognition (see Wertsch) and ensembled individualism (see Sampson). Other researchers reinforced these theoretical notions with close examinations of what happened in a variety of workplaces (e.g., Odell and Goswami; Blomberg; Forsythe; Helander). Perhaps most important for direct effects on rethinking literate behaviors is the renewed interest in communication in the workplace (e.g., Porter and Roberts).

All these institutional changes and research efforts appear to be   43
coming together to diminish the focus on the autonomous person working in isolation at discrete mechanistic tasks. Within academic psychology and sociology, proponents for ensembled individualism began in the mid 1980s to argue against either the historical or the sociopsychological validity of self-contained individualism. To those who argue that firm boundaries, personal control, and an exclusionary concept of the person are necessary to support the core American cultural values of freedom, responsibility, and achievement, others point out that ensembled individualism is supported by cross-cultural, historical, and intracultural evidence. This work

demonstrated the achievements of cooperative groups who engaged in mutually obligatory communal relationships and should lead to the reconsideration of case histories that heretofore seemed to highlight self-contained individual efforts (Clark, Mills, and Powell).

The fourth vision is, then, one of learners talking and considering together. Three conclusions seem to point to past achievements that we must use to challenge both the future organization of institutions and simplistic definitions of literacy: 44

1. All of us—children and adults, students and teachers, shop workers and supervisors, clerical workers and managers—learn most successfully with and from each other when we have full access to looking, listening, talking, and taking part in authentic tasks we understand. 45

2. We can complement each other in particular areas of expertise if we learn to communicate our experiences; sharing what we know helps bring the group to higher performance than private reflections of individuals do. 46

3. Humans must move beyond information and skills to meaning and interpretation for learning to take place and to extend itself. So-called at-risk or slow learners frequently have learned in out-of-school experience a multitude of approaches that allow them to move away from the mere display of learning to the creation of learning. Schools too often demonstrate in their assignments that the meaning is that there is no meaning to be interpreted from self-experiences or comparisons between direct learning and the knowledge found in books. The clear message often seems to be that the meaning lies in the text and not in the active engagement of text and reader together. 47

SEEING HOW WE SEE

There is a Socratic parable, well-known in some quarters, about a teacher who gives students two magnifying glasses and invites them to look at the one through the other. When each student has told all that he or she has learned, the sage delivers the lesson in the form of a question: "Of what have you told me—the thing you have seen or the other thing through which you have seen it?" 48

This same conundrum lurks behind the study of literacy. Is it an object of analysis through which we circumscribe our examinations of it, or is it an experience that will, when we look closely, point out beyond the mere direct image of text and reader or writer to illuminate significant aspects of human existence? Brodkey's reflections on reading and writing, along with some comparative framing of the 49 uses of leisure time in families and an examination of the nature of interactions in the lives of schools and churches, have led us to look beyond these three visions to that of a fourth—literate language at work. In so doing, we find that collective bonds and shared goals in work settings from adult basic education classrooms to clerical offices can facilitate oral collaboration to identify and solve problems creatively. Groups, more easily than individuals, can move beyond simplistic single-cause explanations to multiple causes that are context-dependent. Moreover, facilitating opportunities for workers to observe, record, retell, and compare stories in groups with different levels and kinds of expertise promotes rapid learning.

The major institutions of literate behaviors in American life, the   50
school and the church, have in the past decade increasingly chosen to play it safe by restricting, limiting, and even punishing those who speak too much or too freely and those who act beyond the words of their leaders. These institutions have attempted to eliminate, it seems, the dangers but also the creativity that come from reading in any follow-up through speaking and acting. Those social institutions historically responsible in the American context for the care of the mind and the body of the young have seemed to lose their literate behaviors. It is as though these organizations have chosen to leave aside any responsibility for creating and re-creating information and interpretations. The full meaning of *responsible*—being able to respond in something other than a prescripted formulaic and almost ritualistic manner—is not easily found in schools. Other institutions historically promoting such responsiveness and responsibility, religious organizations and families, have also altered their earlier functions and priorities. The major places of such responsibility are businesses that reorient to involve workers in leadership and some neighborhood-based organizations, such as youth centers, Boy Scouts, junior Sierra Clubs, and Future Farmers of America.

This volume brings together several accounts of the efforts of   51
those who focus on reading, writing, speaking, and listening as the bases of learning. Most of the accounts contained here are, however, alternative or marginal programs and practices within their institutions. The philosophies, actions, and results presented here do not easily simplify into programs, step-by-step methods, or simple pedagogical recommendations. A public that wants to simplify the literacy problem will find extraordinarily complex the theories of learning, human interaction, and understanding of socioeconomic forces and their relation to power that underlie these alternatives. But resistance or misunderstanding from the public must not tempt those who are involved in the theory and the practice of literate behaviors to become reductionists. We must be cautious that the flexible, dynamic, and highly creative approaches to reading, writing, listening, and

speaking represented in this volume do not become reinterpreted as simplified ready-made teacher-proof programs. The overwhelming tendency of education today is to simplify, standardize, and make predictable. What society must recognize is that literate behaviors allow us to address complexities, promote creative problem identification and solution, and chart new directions for learning.

We have numerous magnifying glasses by which we look at other 52 magnifying glasses. We have numerous ways of reading and of reading literacy. Our theories and our research become more elaborate, more sophisticated, and often more specialized as we look more microscopically at some elements of reading or of literacy. But perhaps the sage's simple lesson of the conundrum—"Of what have you told me—the thing you have seen or the other thing through which you have seen it?"—is the best lesson. Without acknowledging before and during our look through the magnifying glass its larger context and the value system we have adopted that forces much of the community to look at only the smallness of reading, we cannot know what we have seen.

It is a fourth vision then—one beyond that of the mere labeling 53 and numbering of literacy, beyond that of preserving and transmitting, and even beyond expanding what we must work for. We must decide that we wish to use literate behaviors to create and re-create beyond our current authority and power. It is in our ensembled individualism that we can be free from the limitations of ourselves as individuals and bound into a new condition of creation and re-creation of literateness and humaneness.

WORKS CITED

Applebee, Arthur. *Writing in the Secondary School: English and the Content Areas.* Urbana: NCTE, 1981.

Bair, James H. "User Needs for Office Systems Solutions." Kraut 177–94.

Benjamin, Walter. *Illuminations.* New York: Schocken, 1968.

Blomberg, Jeanette L. "Social Interaction and Office Communication: Effects on User's Evaluation of New Technologies." Kraut 195–210.

Brodkey, Harold. "Reading, the Most Dangerous Game." *New York Times Book Review* 24 Nov. 1985: 1, 44, 45.

———. *Stories in an Almost Classical Mode.* New York: Knopf, 1988.

Brown, Ann, and Annemarie Sullivan Palincsar. "Reciprocal Teaching of Comprehension Strategies: A Natural History of One Program for Enhancing Learning." *Intelligence and Exceptionality: New Directions for Theory, Assessment, and Instructional Practice.* Ed. Jeanne D. Day and John G. Borkowski. Norwood: Ablex, 1987. 81–132.

Carnegie Forum on Education and the Economy. *A Nation Prepared: Teachers for the Twenty-First Century.* Washington: Task Force on Teaching as a Profession, 1986.

Cazden, Courtney. *Classroom Discourse: The Language of Teaching and Learning.* Portsmouth: Heinemann, 1988.

Clark, Margaret S., Judson Mills, and Martha C. Powell. "Keeping Track of Needs in Communal and Exchange Relationships." *Journal of Personality and Social Psychology* 51 (1986): 333–38.

Csikszentmihalyi, Mihaly, and Reed Larson. *Being Adolescent: Conflict and Growth in the Teenage Years.* New York: Basic, 1984.

deCastell, Suzanne, Alan Luke, and Carmen Luke, eds. *Language, Authority, and Criticism: Readings on the School Textbook.* London: Falmer, 1989.

Feldberg, Roslyn L., and Evelyn Nakano Glenn. "Technology and the Transformation of Clerical Work." Kraut 77–97.

Flower, Linda. *The Construction of Purpose in Writing and Reading.* Working Paper 4. Berkeley: Center for the Study of Writing, 1988.

Forsythe, Diana. "Engineering Knowledge: An Anthropological Study of an Artificial Laboratory." Twelfth annual meeting of the Society for Social Studies of Science. Worcester, Mass., 12 Nov. 1987.

Goodlad, John I. *A Place Called School: Prospects for the Future.* New York: McGraw, 1984.

Goodman, Kenneth. *What's Whole in Whole Language?* Portsmouth: Heinemann, 1986.

Goody, Jack. *The Logic of Writing and the Organization of Society.* Cambridge: Cambridge UP, 1986.

Goswami, Dixie, and Peter R. Stillman, eds. *Reclaiming the Classroom: Teachers' Research as an Agency for Change.* Portsmouth: Heinemann, 1987.

Heath, Shirley Brice. "The Children of Trackton's Children: Spoken and Written Language in Social Change." *Cultural Psychology: Essays on Comparative Human Development.* Ed. James W. Stigler, Richard Shweder, and Gilbert S. Herdt. Cambridge: Cambridge UP, 1990. 496–519.

———. *Ways with Words: Language, Life, and Work in Communities and Classrooms.* Cambridge: Cambridge UP, 1983.

Helander, Martin, ed. *Handbook of Human-Computer Interaction.* Amsterdam: North-Holland, 1988.

Hodgkinson, Harold. "What's Ahead for Education." *Principal* (Jan. 1986): 6–11.

Kraut, Robert E., ed. *Technology and the Transformation of White-Collar Work.* Hillsdale: Erlbaum, 1987.

Lefkowitz, Bernard. *Tough Change: Growing Up on Your Own in America.* New York: Free, 1987.

Lightfoot, Martin, and Nancy Martin, eds. *The Word for Teaching Is Learning: Essays for James Britton.* Portsmouth: Heinemann, 1988.

Marty, Martin E. *Religion and Republic: The American Circumstance.* Boston: Beacon, 1987.

Mikulecky, Larry, and Jeanne Ehlinger. "The Influence of Metacognitive Aspects of Literacy on Job Performance of Electronics Technicians." *Journal of Reading Behavior* 18 (1986): 41–62.

Mikulecky, Larry, and David Winchester. "Job Literacy and Job Performance among Nurses at Varying Employment Levels." *Adult Education Quarterly* 34 (1983): 1–15.

Moffett, James. *Storm in the Mountains: A Case Study of Censorship, Conflict, and Consciousness.* Carbondale: Southern Illinois UP, 1988.

Newkirk, Thomas, and Nancie Atwell, eds. *Understanding Writing: Ways of Observing, Learning, and Teaching.* Portsmouth: Heinemann, 1988.

Odell, Lee, and Dixie Goswami, eds. *Writing in Non-Academic Settings.* New York: Guilford, 1985.

Porter, Lyman W., and Karlene H. Roberts. "Communication in Organizations." *Handbook of Industrial and Organizational Psychology.* Ed. Marvin D. Dunnette. Chicago: Rand, 1987. 1553–85.

Sampson, Edward E. "The Debate on Individualism: Indigenous Psychologies of the Individual and Their Role in Personal and Societal Functioning." *American Psychologist* 43 (1988): 15–22.

Scribner, Sylvia. "Studying Working Intelligence." *Everyday Cognition: Its Development in Social Context.* Ed. Barbara Rogoff and Jean Lave. Cambridge: Harvard UP, 1984. 9–40.

Smith, Joel D. "Literacy in the Workplace." Conference Broadening the Definition of Literacy. Center for the Study of Writing. Berkeley, 5 May 1988.

Sticht, Thomas G. *Reading for Working: A Functional Literacy Anthology.* Alexandria: Human Resources Research Assn., 1975.

Suransky, Valerie Polakow. *The Erosion of Childhood.* Chicago: U of Chicago P, 1982.

Wertsch, James V., ed. *Culture, Communication, and Cognition: Vygotskian Perspectives.* Cambridge: Cambridge UP, 1985.

EXPLORATIONS

1. Heath begins her article by suggesting (along with writer Harold Brodkey) that reading and writing are the most dangerous games. How does she develop this notion in the article?

2. Heath makes a number of comparisons between literate practices in the past and in the present. Which time does she seem to prefer? How do you know?

3. What kind of activities might take place in Heath's ideal school? In other words, what would Heath like to see teachers and students do differently in schools?

4. How does Heath define her "fourth vision" of literate language? From what kinds of sources does she draw her evidence?

5. Heath claims that the "overwhelming tendency of education today is to simplify, standardize, and make predictable." Based on your own experiences in school and on the evidence presented by Heath, to what extent is her claim persuasive?

6. How does Heath's article extend or complicate the definitions of literacy you developed in Part 2?

Crossing Boundaries

MIKE ROSE

*Mike Rose holds a Ph.D. in educational psychology and is on
the faculty of the UCLA Graduate School of Education and
Information Studies and UCLA Writing Programs.* Lives on
the Boundary *(1989), from which the chapter "Crossing
Boundaries" is excerpted, chronicles Rose's own difficult
journey through the public schools and the university. But
the book is also an argument against viewing underprepared
students as "remedial," "illiterate," and "intellectually
deficient." Instead, Rose argues that the difficulties that
many students face in school have as much to do with the
cycles of despair and defeat in which they are trapped as they
do with the ways teachers and schools respond to underprepared students. Rose combines his serious critique of education in America with demonstrations of what is possible at all
levels of education and with all students.*

WRITING BEFORE READING

*All of us, in some significant ways, are underprepared for college and
university work. Describe a way in which you have felt underprepared
for college.*

Through all my experiences with people struggling to learn, the   1
one thing that strikes me most is the ease with which we misperceive
failed performance and the degree to which this misperception both
reflects and reinforces the social order. Class and culture erect
boundaries that hinder our vision—blind us to the logic of error and
the everpresent stirring of language—and encourage the designation
of otherness, difference, deficiency. And the longer I stay in education, the clearer it becomes to me that some of our basic orientations
toward the teaching and testing of literacy contribute to our inability to see. To truly educate in America, then, to reach the full sweep
of our citizenry, we need to question received perception, shift
continually from the standard lens. The exploratory stories that
bring this book to its close encourage us to sit close by as people use
language and consider, as we listen, the orientations that limit our
field of vision.

The humanities presume particular methods of expression and
inquiry—language, dialogue, reflection, imagination, and
metaphor. . . . [and] remain dedicated to the disciplined develop-

ment of verbal, perceptual, and imaginative skills needed to
understand experience.

–*The Humanities in American Life*, Report of the Rockefeller
Commission on the Humanities

Two young men have walked in late and are standing around 2
the back of the classroom, halfheartedly looking for seats. One
wears a faded letterman's jacket, the other is bundled up in a
bright red sweater and a long overcoat. A third student has
plopped his books by the door and is hunkering down against the
wall. This is Developmental English in a state college in Ohio. It is
December, and the radiators are turned up high. Occasional clanks
are emitted by some distant valve. The room is stuffy with dry heat.
The teacher directs the latecomers to some seats in the front, and
he begins the lesson. The class is working on pronoun agreement.
They have worked on it for a week and will continue to work on it
for another. The windows are frosted at the edges. In the distance,
a tall smokestack releases a curling black stream diagonally across
the sky.

Students designated "developmental" at this school must take 3
a year's worth of very basic English before they can move into standard Freshman Comp. Their year is broken into two semesters.
During the first semester they inch through a thick workbook filled
with grammar exercises: "Circle the correct pronoun in this sentence: That was her/she in the lecture hall" or "Supply the correct
pronoun for the following sentence: the recruits were upset by _____
scores on the fitness tests." Some of this they do at home. Most of
it they do in class. That way, the teacher can be sure they are doing
it. They hand in their workbooks regularly to have the teacher check
their answers.

The course involves very little writing, except for words and 4
phrases the students must scribble in the blanks on the pages. Some
class discussion is generated when the teacher has the students read
their answers. Periodically he will explain a rule or illustrate its use
on the blackboard. Young men along the back wall fill in a blank now
and then; the rest of the time, they're eyeballing the teacher and
talking softly. A girl is filing her nails. Students in the middle of the
room are bent over their workbooks, penciling in answers, erasing
them, looking up and out the frosted windows. A skinny boy in the
front is going down the page as mechanically as Melville's pallid
scrivener.

There are sentences being written in this class, but not by 5
mandate of the dean of instruction. Two girls close to the door have
been passing notes all hour; they are producing the class's most
extended discourse. Students are not asked to write here because it

is assumed—as it is assumed in many such basic courses—that they
must first get all their workbook pronouns to agree with their workbook antecedents. When they reach the second semester, they will,
for fifteen weeks, do some small amount of writing, but that writing
will be limited to single sentences. At this school, and many others,
the English Department and the program that coordinates remedial
courses are philosophically and administratively separated. Different
schools have different histories, but often—as was the case here—the
separation was strongly influenced by the English Department's
desire to be freed from basic instruction. The two departments at
this school, though, have an unusually stringent agreement:
Anything longer than the sentence (even two or three sentences
strung together) is considered *writing*, and the teaching of writing
shall be the province of the English Department. Anything at the
sentence level or smaller (like filling words and phrases into a workbook) is to be considered grammar review, and that falls within the
domain of the remedial program. For one academic year, then,
students who desperately need to improve their writing will not be
writing anything longer than the sentence. This particular slicing of
the pedagogical pie is extreme in its execution, but the assumptions
about error, remediation, and the linguistic capabilities of poorly
prepared students that undergird it remain widespread in America—
and they influence everything from lesson plans to the sectioning of
academic territory. Given the pervasiveness of these assumptions, it
would be valuable to consider, for a moment, their origins.

A good place to begin is with the encounter of educational   6
psychology and schooling. Turn-of-the-century English education
was built on a Latin and Greek-influenced grammar, primarily a set
of prescriptions for conducting socially acceptable discourse. So
when psychologists began investigating the teaching of writing, they
found a pedagogy of memory and drill, one concentrating on the
often arcane dos and don'ts of usage. They also found reports like
those issuing from the Harvard faculty in the 1890s that called attention to the presence of errors in handwriting, spelling, and grammar
in the writing of that university's entering freshmen. The twentieth-
century writing curriculum, then, was focused on the particulars of
usage, grammar, and mechanics. Correctness became, in James
Berlin's words, the era's "most significant measure of accomplished prose."

Such a focus suited educational researchers' approach to lan-   7
guage: a mechanistic orientation that studied language by reducing it
to discrete behaviors and that defined growth as the accretion of these
particulars. Quantification and measurement were central
to the researchers' method, so the focus on error—which seemed
eminently measurable—found justification in a model of mind that was

ascending in American academic psychology. This approach was further supported and advanced by what Raymond Callahan has called "the cult of efficiency," a strong push to apply to education the principles of industrial scientific management. Educational gains were defined as products, and the output of products could be measured. Pedagogical effectiveness—which meant cost-effectiveness—could be determined with "scientific" accuracy. What emerges, finally, is a combination of positivism, efficiency, and a focus on grammar that would have a profound influence on pedagogy and research.

Textbooks as well as workbooks reflected this orientation. One 8 textbook for teachers presented an entire unit on the colon. A text for students devoted seven pages to the use of a capital letter to indicate a proper noun. Research, too, focused on the details of language, especially on listing and tabulating error. You rarely find consideration of the social context of error, or of its significance in the growth of the writer. Instead you find studies like those of W. S. Guiler's tally of the percentages of 350 students who, in misspelling *mortgage*, erred by omitting the *t* versus those who dropped the first *g*.

Despite the fact that the assumptions about language and learn- 9 ing informing these approaches to teaching and research began to be challenged by the late 1930s, the procedures of the earlier era have remained with us. This trend has the staying power it does for a number of reasons: It gives a method—a putatively objective one—to the strong desire of our society to maintain correct language use. It is very American in its seeming efficiency. And it offers a simple, understandable view of complex linguistic problems. The trend reemerges most forcefully in times of crisis: when budgets crunch and accountability looms or, particularly, when "nontraditional" students flood our institutions. A reduction of complexity has great appeal in institutional decision making, especially in difficult times: a scientific-atomistic approach to language, with its attendant tallies and charts, nicely fit an economic decision-making model. When in doubt or when scared or when pressed, count.

This orientation to language complements the way we conceive 10 of remediation.

The designation *remedial* has powerful implications in educa- 11 tion—to be remedial is to be substandard, inadequate—and, because of the origins of the term, the inadequacy is metaphorically connected to disease and mental defectiveness. The etymology of the word *remedial* places its origins in law and medicine, and by the late nineteenth century the term generally fell into the medical domain. It was then applied to education, to children who were thought to have neurological problems. But *remedial* quickly generalized beyond the description of such students to those with broader, though special, educational problems and then to those learners who were from backgrounds that did not provide optimal environmental and educational opportunities.

As increasing access to education brought more and more 12 children into the schools, the medical vocabulary—with its implied medical model—remained dominant. People tried to *diagnose* various *disabilities, defects, deficits, deficiencies,* and *handicaps,* then tried to *remedy* them. So you start to see all sorts of reading and writing problems clustered together and addressed with this language. For example, William S. Gray's important monograph, *Remedial Cases in Reading: Their Diagnosis and Treatment,* listed as "specific causes of failure in reading" inferior learning capacity, congenital word blindness, poor auditory memory, defective vision, a narrow span of recognition, ineffective eye movements, inadequate training in phonetics, inadequate attention to the content, an inadequate speaking vocabulary, a small meaning vocabulary, speech defects, lack of interest, and timidity. The remedial paradigm was beginning to include those who had troubles as varied as bad eyes, second language interference, and shyness. The semantic net of *remedial* was expanding and expanding.

It is likely that the appeal of medical-remedial language had 13 much to do with its associations with scientific objectivity and accuracy—powerful currency in the efficiency-minded 1920s and 1930s. Consider, as illustration, this passage from Albert Lang's 1930 textbook, *Modern Methods in Written Examinations.* The medical model is explicit:

> Teaching bears a resemblance to the practice of medicine. Like a successful physician, the good teacher must be something of a diagnostician. The physician by means of a general examination singles out the individual whose physical defects require a more thorough testing. He critically scrutinizes the special cases until he recognized the specific troubles. After a careful diagnosis he is able to prescribe intelligently the best remedial or corrective measures.

The theoretical and pedagogical model that was available for "corrective teaching" led educators to view literacy problems from a medical-remedial perspective. Thus they set out to diagnose as precisely as possible the errors (defects) in a student's paper—which they saw as symptomatic of equally isolable defects in the student's linguistic capacity—and devise drills and exercises to remedy them. (One of the 1930s nicknames for remedial sections was "sick sections." During the next decade they would be tagged "hospital sections.") Such corrective teaching was, in the words of one educator, "the most logical as well as the most scientific method."

Though we have, over the last fifty years, developed a richer 14 understanding of reading and writing difficulties, the reductive view of error and the language of medicine is still with us. A recent letter from the senate of a local liberal arts college is sitting on my desk. It discusses a "program in remedial writing for . . . [those] entering freshmen suffering from severe writing handicaps." We seem entrapped by this language, this view of students and learning. We still talk of writers as suffering from specifiable, locatable defects, deficits, and handicaps that can be localized, circumscribed, and remedied. Such talk carries with it the etymological wisps and traces of disease and serves to exclude from the academic community those who are so labeled. They sit in scholastic quarantine until their disease can be diagnosed and remedied.

This atomistic, medical model of language is simply not supported by more recent research in language and cognition. But because the teaching of writing—particularly teaching designated remedial—has been conceptually and, as with the Ohio program, administratively segmented from the rich theoretical investigation that characterizes other humanistic study, these assumptions have rarely been subjected to rigorous and comprehensive scrutiny. *The Humanities in American Life*, the important position paper from which the epigraph to this section is drawn, argues passionately for the wide relevance of the humanities and urges the serious engagement of humanists in teacher training, industry, and adult basic education—areas they, for the most part, have abandoned. But until the traditional orientations to error and remediation are examined to their core, until the teaching of writing and reading to underprepared students is fundamentally reconceived, then the spirited plea of the Rockefeller Commission will be, for many in America, just another empty homiletic. Consider, after all, what those students in Developmental English are really learning.

The curriculum in Developmental English breeds a deep social and intellectual isolation from print; it fosters attitudes and beliefs about written language that, more than anything, *keep* students from becoming fully, richly literate. The curriculum teaches students that when it comes to written language use, they are children: they can only perform the most constrained and ordered of tasks, and they must do so under the regimented guidance of a teacher. It teaches them that the most important thing about writing—the very essence of writing—is grammatical correctness, not the communication of something meaningful, or the generative struggle with ideas . . . not even word play. It's a curriculum that rarely raises students' heads from the workbook page to consider the many uses of written language that surround them in their schools, jobs, and neighborhoods. Finally, by its tedium, the curriculum teaches them that writing is a crushing bore. These students traverse course after remedial course, becoming increasingly turned off to writing, increasingly convinced that they are hopelessly inadequate. "Writing," one of the students tells me. "Man, I've never been any good at writing." "English," says another, "is not my thing." This last comment comes from the latecomer in the letterman's   17 jacket. I've caught up with him after class, and as we walk outside the building, our breath turns to steam. He carries a radio, turned on now, on which a smitten rapmaster is trying to convince someone named Roxanne that he is a "debonair doc": "There's anesthesiology," he rhythmically intones, "ophthalmology, in-ternal medicine, and plastic sur-ger-y." The young man, his name is Melvyn, is moving as we talk, and I ask him about the song. He likes rap music best, he says, because the speaker, the M. C., handles words so well, uses them to build him-self up, to get women, to express his ideas about things. Three good reasons to write, I think. Good old-fashioned motives for putting pen to paper. In a 1934 report on the teaching of college English, a Nebraska professor pleaded for "ceaseless, brutal drill on mechanics. . . . Never mind imagination, the soul, literature, for at least one semester, but pray for literacy and fight for it." The twisted logic of this exasperated cry lives on—it informs Melvyn's curriculum. Literacy can be gained by brutalizing the imagination. A linguistic version of burning the village to save it. The M. C., meanwhile, has swayed Roxanne and moves on to his peroration:

> It's only customary
> to give this commentary.
> You'll never find a rap
> like this in *any* dictionary.

"The humanities presume particular methods of expression and   18 inquiry—language, dialogue, reflection, imagination, and meta-phor." The primary, even the sole, manifestation of the humanities that many lower-class and underprepared students encounter in high school, community, and state college is their English class. Considering the yearlong course of study laid out for Melvyn, his M. C. might be right. The instruction in language use he confronts strips away the vibrancy and purpose, the power and style, the mean-ing of the language that swirls around him. The dictionary, and all that represents written language, is rendered sterile. Literacy, as that Nebraska professor recommended, is severed from imagination. Is it any wonder that so many see school approaches to language as a source of consternation, as tedious and dulling, as a rebuff rather than an invitation?

> I myself I thank God for the dream to come back to school and to be able to seek the dream I want, because I know this time I will try and make my dream come true.

Each semester the staff of the Bay Area literacy program we're   19
about to visit collects samples of their students' writing and makes
books for them. You can find an assortment on an old bookshelf by
the coordinator's desk. The booklets are simple: mimeographed,
faint blue stencil, stapled, dog-eared. There are uneven drawings on
the thin paper covers: a bicycle leaning against a tree, the Golden
Gate Bridge, an Aubrey Beardsley sketch. The stories are about
growing up, raising children, returning—sadly or with anticipation—
to hometowns, to Chicago or St. Louis or to a sweep of rural communities in the South. Many of the stories are about work: looking
for work, losing work, wanting better work. And many more are
about coming back to school. Coming back to school. Some of these
writers haven't been in a classroom in thirty years.

The stories reveal quite a range. Many are no longer than a para-   20
graph, their sentences simple and repetitive, tenuously linked by *and*
and *then* and *anyway.* There are lots of grammar and spelling errors
and problems with sentence boundaries—in a few essays, periods
come where commas should be or where no punctuation is needed
at all: "It was hard for me to stay in school because I was allway sick.
and that was verry hard for me." Or, "I sound better. now that my
boys are grown." Papers of this quality are written, for the most
part, by newcomers, people at the end of their first semester. But
other papers—quite a few, actually—are competent. They tend to
come from those who have received a year or more of instruction.
There are still problems with grammar and sentence fragments
and with spelling, since the writers are using a wider, more ambitious
vocabulary. Problems like these take longer to clear up, but the writers are getting more adept at rendering their experience in print, at
developing a narrative, at framing an illustration, at turning a phrase
in written language:

> The kitchen floor was missing some of its tiles and had not been kissed
> with water and soap for a long time.

> The [teacher] looked for a moment, and then said, "All the students
> wishing to be accounted for, please be seated."

> A minute went by, then a tough looking Mexican boy got up, and
> walked to the teacher with a knife in his hand. When he got to the desk
> he said, "I'm here teacher! My name is Robert Gomez." With that
> he put the knife away, and walked over and found a seat.

> Back in the jaws of dispair, pain, and the ugly scars of the defeated par-
> ents he loved. Those jaws he had struggled free of when he had moved
> out and away when he was eighteen years old.

> . . . the wind was howling, angry, whirling.

A few new students also created such moments, indicators of   21
what they'll be able to do as they become more fluent writers, as
they develop some control over and confidence in establishing themselves on paper:

> [I used to have] light, really light Brown eyes, like Grasshopper eyes.
> which is what some peoples used to call me. Grasshopper, or
> Grasshopper eyes. . . . I decided one Day to catch a Grasshopper. and
> look at its eye to be sure of the color.

> It was early in the morning just before dawn. Big Red, the sun hasen't
> showed its face in the heaven. The sky had that midnight blue look. The
> stars losing their shine.

There are about eight or ten of these stapled collections, a hun-   22
dred and fifty or so essays. Five years' worth. An archive scattered
across an old bookcase. There's a folding chair close by. I've been
sitting in it for some time now, reading one book, then another,
story after story. Losing track. Drifting in and out of lives.
Wondering about grasshopper eyes, about segregated schools, wanting to know more about this journey to the West looking for work.
Slowly something has been shifting in my perception: the errors—the
weird commas and missing letters, the fragments and irregular punctuation—they are ceasing to be slips of the hand and brain. They are
becoming part of the stories themselves. They are the only fitting
way, it seems, to render dislocation—shacks and field labor and
children lost to the inner city—to talk about parents you long for,
jobs you can't pin down. Poverty has generated its own damaged
script, scars manifest in the spelling of a word.

This is the prose of America's underclass. The writers are those   23
who got lost in our schools, who could not escape neighborhoods
that narrowed their possibilities, who could not enter the job market
in any ascendent way. They are locked into unskilled and semiskilled
jobs, live in places that threaten their children, suffer from disorders
and handicaps they don't have the money to treat. Some have been
unemployed for a long time. But for all that, they remain hopeful,
have somehow held onto a deep faith in education. They have come
back to school. Ruby, the woman who wrote the passage that opens
this section, walks unsteadily to the teacher's desk—the arthritis in
her hip goes unchecked—with a paper in her hand. She looks over
her shoulder to her friend, Alice: "I ain't givin' up the ship this
time," she says and winks, "though, Lord, I might drown with it."
The class laughs. They understand.

It is a very iffy thing, this schooling. But the participants put a lot   24
of stock in it. They believe school will help them, and they are very
specific about what they want: a high school equivalency, or the ability to earn seven dollars an hour. One wants to move from being a

nurse's aide to a licensed vocational nurse, another needs to read and write and compute adequately enough to be self-employed as a car painter and body man. They remind you of how fundamentally important it is—not just to your pocket but to your soul as well—to earn a decent wage, to have a steady job, to be just a little bit in control of your economic life. The goals are specific, modest, but they mean a tremendous amount for the assurance they give to these people that they are still somebody, that they can exercise control. Thus it is that talk of school and a new job brings forth such expansive language, as soaring as any humanist's testament to the glory of the word: "I thank God to be able to seek the dream I want. . . ." For Ruby and her classmates the dream deferred neither dried up like a raisin in the sun, nor has it exploded. It has emerged again—for it is so basic—and it centers on schooling. "I admire and respect knowledge and thoes that have it are well blessed," writes another student. "My classmates are a swell group becaus they too have a dream and they too are seeking knowledge and I love them for that."

Sitting in the classroom with Ruby, Alice, and the rest, you   25 think, at times, that you're at a revival meeting. There is so much testifying. Everybody talks and writes about dreams and goals and "doing better for myself." This is powerful, edifying—but something about it, its insistence perhaps, is a little discordant. The exuberance becomes jittery, an almost counterphobic boosting and supporting. It is no surprise, then, that it alternates with despair. In their hearts, Ruby and her classmates know how tenuous this is, how many times they've failed before. Somebody says something about falling down. Sally says, "I've felt that too. Not falling down on my legs or knees, but falling down within me." No wonder they sermonize and embrace. It's not just a few bucks more a week that's at stake; literacy, here, is intimately connected with respect, with a sense that they are not beaten, the mastery of print revealing the deepest impulse to survive.

When they entered the program, Ruby and Alice and Sally and all the   26 rest were given several tests, one of which was a traditional reading inventory. The test had a section on comprehension—relatively brief passages followed by multiple-choice questions—and a series of sections that tested particular reading skills: vocabulary, syllabication, phonics, prefixes and roots. The level of the instrument was pretty sophisticated, and the skills it tested are the kind you develop in school: answering multiple-choice questions, working out syllable breaks, knowing Greek and Latin roots, all that. What was interesting about this group of test takers was that—though a few were barely literate—many could read and write well enough to get along, and, in some cases, to help those in their communities who were less

skilled. They could read, with fair comprehension, simple news articles, could pay bills, follow up on sales and coupons, deal with school
forms for their kids, and help illiterate neighbors in their interactions
with the government. Their skills were pretty low-level and limited
profoundly the kinds of things they could read or write, but they
lived and functioned amid print. The sad thing is that we don't really have tests of such naturally occurring competence. The tests we do
have, like the one Ruby and the others took, focus on components
of reading ability tested in isolation (phonetic discrimination, for
example) or on those skills that are school-oriented, like reading a
passage on an unfamiliar topic unrelated to immediate needs: the
mating habits of the dolphin, the Mayan pyramids. Students then
answer questions on these sorts of passages by choosing one of four
or five possible answers, some of which may be purposely misleading.

To nobody's surprise, Ruby and her classmates performed   27
miserably. The tasks of the classroom were as unfamiliar as could be.
There is a good deal of criticism of these sorts of reading tests, but
one thing that is clear is that they reveal how well people can
perform certain kinds of school activities. The activities themselves
may be of questionable value, but they are interwoven with instruction and assessment, and entrance to many jobs is determined by
them. Because of their centrality, then, I wanted to get some sense
of how the students went about taking the tests. What happened as
they tried to meet the test's demands? How was it that they failed?

My method was simple. I chose four students and had each of   28
them take sections of the test again, asking them questions as they
did so, encouraging them to talk as they tried to figure out an item.

The first thing that emerged was the complete foreignness of the   29
task. A sample item in the prefixes and roots section (called Word
Parts) presented the word "<u>un</u>happy," and asked the test-taker to
select one of four other words "which gives the meaning of the
underlined part of the first word." The choices were *very, glad, sad,
not.* Though the person giving the test had read through the instructions with the class, many still could not understand, and if they
chose an answer at all, most likely chose *sad,* a synonym for the
whole word *unhappy.*

Nowhere in their daily reading are these students required to   30
focus on parts of words in this way. The multiple-choice format is also
unfamiliar—it is not part of day-to-day literacy—so the task as well as
the format is new, odd. I explained the directions again—read them
slowly, emphasized the sample item—but still, three of the four students continued to fall into the test maker's trap of choosing syn-
onyms for the target word rather than zeroing in on the part of the
word in question. Such behavior is common among those who fail in
our schools, and it has led some commentators to posit that students

like these are cognitively and linguistically deficient in some fundamental way: they process language differently, or reason differently
from those who succeed in school, or the dialect they speak in some
basic way interferes with their processing of Standard Written English.

Certainly in such a group—because of malnourishment, trauma, 31
poor health care, environmental toxins—you'll find people with
neurolinguistic problems or with medical difficulties that can affect
perception and concentration. And this group—ranging in age from
nineteen to the mid-fifties—has a wide array of medical complications:
diabetes, head injury, hypertension, asthma, retinal deterioration, and
the unusual sleep disorder called narcolepsy. It would be naive to
deny the effect of all this on reading and writing. But as you sit alongside these students and listen to them work through a task, it is not
damage that most strikes you. Even when they're misunderstanding
the test and selecting wrong answers, their reasoning is not distorted
and pathological. Here is Millie, whose test scores placed her close to
the class average— and average here would be very low just about
anywhere else.

Millie is given the word "kilometer" and the following list of 32
possible answers:

  a. thousand
  b. hundred
  c. distance
  d. speed

She responds to the whole word—*kilometer*—partially because she
still does not understand how the test works, but also, I think,
because the word is familiar to her. She offers *speed* as the correct
answer because: "I see it on the signs when I be drivin'." She
starts to say something else, but stops abruptly. "Whoa, it don't
have to be 'speed'—it could be 'distance.' "

"It could be 'distance,' couldn't it?" I say. 33
"Yes, it coud be one or the other. " 34
"Okay. " 35
"And then again," she says reflectively, "it could be a number. " 36
Millie tapped her knowledge of the world—she had seen *kilome-* 37
ter on road signs—to offer a quick response: *speed*. But she saw just
as quickly that her knowledge could logically support another answer
(*distance*), and, a few moments later, saw that what she knew could
also support a third answer, one related to number. What she lacked
was specific knowledge of the Greek prefix *kilo*, but she wasn't
short on reasoning ability. In fact, reading tests like the one Millie
took are constructed in such a way as to trick you into relying on
commonsense reasoning and world knowledge—and thereby choosing a *wrong* answer. Take, for example, this item:

Cardiogram
a. heart
b. abnormal
c. distance
d. record

Millie, and many others in the class, chose *heart*. To sidestep that answer, you need to know something about the use of *gram* in other such words (versus its use as a metric weight), but you need to know, as well, how these tests work.

After Millie completed five or six items, I had her go back over   38
them, talking through her answers with her. One item that had originally given her trouble was "<u>extra</u>ordinary": a) "beyond"; b) "acute"; c) "regular"; d) "imagined." She had been a little rattled when answering this one. While reading the four possible answers, she stumbled on "imagined": "I . . . im . . ."; then, tentatively, "imaged"; a pause again, then "imagine," and, quickly, "I don't know that word."

I pronounce it.   39
She looks up at me, a little disgusted: "I said it, didn't I?"   40
"You did say it."   41
"I was scared of it."   42
Her first time through, Millie had chosen *regular*, the wrong   43
answer—apparently locking onto *ordinary* rather than the underlined prefix *extra*—doing just the opposite of what she was supposed to do. It was telling, I thought, that Millie and two or three others talked about words scaring them.

When we came back to "<u>extra</u>ordinary" during our review,   44
I decided on a strategy, "Let's try something," I said. "These tests are set up to trick you, so let's try a trick ourselves." I take a pencil and do something the publishers of the test tell you not to do: I mark up the test booklet. I slowly begin to circle the prefix *extra*, saying, "this is the part of the word we're concerned with, right?" As soon as I finish she smiles and says "beyond," the right answer.

"Did you see what happened there?" I said. "As soon as I   45
circled the part of the word, you saw what it meant."
"I see it," she says. "I don't be thinking about what I'm   46
doing."
I tell her to try what I did, to circle the part of the word in ques-   47
tion, to remember that trick, for with tests like this, we need a set of tricks of our own.
"You saw it yourself," I said.   48
"Sure did. It was right there in front of me—'cause the rest of   49
them don't even go with 'extra.'"

I had been conducting this interview with Millie in between her 50
classes, and our time was running out. I explained that we'd pick this
up again, and I turned away, checking the wall clock, reaching to turn
off the tape recorder. Millie was still looking at the test booklet.

"What is this word right here?" she asked. She had gone ahead 51
to the other, more difficult, page of the booklet and was pointing to
" egocentric."

I take my finger off the recorder's STOP button. "Let's circle 52
it," I say. "What's that word? Say it."

"Ego." 53

"What's that mean?" 54

"Ego. Oh my." She scans the four options—*self, head, mind,* 55
kind—and says "self."

"Excellent!" 56

" You know, when I said 'ego,' I tried to put it in a sentence: 57
'My ego,' I say. That's *me.*"

I ask her if she wants to look at one more. She goes back to 58
"cardio<u>gram</u>," which she gets right this time. Then to "<u>thermome</u>-
ter," which she also gets right. And "<u>bi</u>focal," which she gets right
without using her pencil to mark the prefix. Once Millie saw and
understood what the test required of her, she could rely on her world
knowledge to help her reason out some answers. Cognitive psychologists talk about task representation, the way a particular problem is
depicted or reproduced in the mind. Something shifted in Millie's
conception of her task, and it had a powerful effect on her performance.

It was common for nineteenth-century American educators to see 59
their mission with the immigrant and native-born urban poor as a fundamentally moral one. Historian Michael Katz quotes from the Boston
school committee's description of social and spiritual acculturation:

> . . . taking children at random from a great city, undisciplined, unin-
> structed, often with inveterate forwardness and obstinacy, and with the
> inherited stupidity of centuries of ignorant ancestors; forming them
> from animals into intellectual beings, and . . . from intellectual beings
> into spiritual beings; giving to many their first appreciation of what is
> wise, what is true, what is lovely and what is pure.

In our time, educators view the effects of poverty and cultural 60
dislocation in more enlightened ways; though that moralistic strain
still exists, the thrust of their concern has shifted from the spiritual
to the more earthly realm of language and cognition. Yet what
remains is the disturbing tendency to perceive the poor as *different*
in some basic way from the middle and upper classes—the difference
now being located in the nature of the way they think and use

language. A number of studies and speculations over the past twenty-five years has suggested that the poor are intellectually or linguistically deficient or, at the least, different: They lack a logical language or reason in ways that limit intellectual achievement or, somehow, process information dysfunctionally. If we could somehow get down to the very basic loops and contours of their mental function, we would find that theirs are different from ours. There's a huge literature on all this and, originating with critics like linguist William Labov, a damning counterliterature. This is not the place to review that work, but it would be valuable to consider Millie against the general outlines of the issue.

Imagine her in a typical classroom testing situation. More dra- 61 matically, imagine her in some university laboratory being studied by one or two researchers—middle class and probably white. Millie is a strong woman with a tough front, but these would most likely be uncomfortable situations for her. And if she were anxious, her performance would be disrupted: as it was when she didn't identi- ty *imagined*—a word she pronounced and knew—because she was "scared of it." Add to this the fact that she is very much adrift when it comes to school-based tests: She simply doesn't know how to do them. What would be particularly damning for her would be the fact that, even with repeated instruction and illustration, she failed to catch on to the way the test worked. You can see how an observer would think her unable to shift out of (inadequate) performance, unable to understand simple instructions and carry them out. Deficient or different in some basic way: nonlogical, nonrational, unable to think analytically. It would be from observations like this that a theory of fundamental cognitive deficiency or difference would emerge.

We seem to have a need as a society to explain poor performance 62 by reaching deep into the basic stuff of those designated as other: into their souls, or into the deep recesses of their minds, or into the very ligature of their language. It seems harder for us to keep focus on the politics and sociology of intellectual failure, to keep before our eyes the negative power of the unfamiliar, the way information poverty constrains performance, the effect of despair on cognition.

"I was so busy looking for 'psychopathology,' . . ." says 63 Robert Coles of his early investigations of childhood morality, "that I brushed aside the most startling incidents, the most instructive examples of ethical alertness in the young people I was getting to know." How much we don't see when we look only for deficiency, when we tally up all that people can't do. Many of the students in this book display the gradual or abrupt emergence of an intellectual acuity or literate capacity that just wasn't thought to be there. This is not to deny that awful limits still exist for those like Millie: so much knowledge and so many procedures never learned; such a long, cumbersome history of relative failure. But this must not obscure the equally important fact that if you set up the right conditions, try as best you can to cross class and cultural boundaries, figure out what's needed to encourage performance, that if you watch and listen, again and again there will emerge evidence of ability that escapes those who dwell on differences.

Ironically, it's often the reports themselves of our educational   64
inadequacies—the position papers and media alarms on illiteracy in America—that help blind us to cognitive and linguistic possibility. Their rhetorical thrust and their metaphor conjure up disease or decay or economic and military defeat: A malignancy has run wild, an evil power is consuming us from within. (And here reemerges that nineteenth-century moral terror.) It takes such declamation to turn the moneyed wheels of government, to catch public attention and entice the givers of grants, but there's a dark side to this political reality. The character of the alarms and, too often, the character of the responses spark in us the urge to punish, to extirpate, to return to a precancerous golden age rather than build on the rich capacity that already exists. The reports urge responses that reduce literate possibility and constrain growth, that focus on pathology rather than on possibility. Philosophy, said Aristotle, begins in wonder. So does education.

> You know, Mike, people always hold this shit over you, make you . . . make you feel stupid with their fancy talk. But now *I've* read it, I've read shakespeare, I can say I, *Olga*, have read it. I won't tell you I like it, 'cause I don't know if I do or I don't. But I like knowing what it's about.

I have a vivid memory of sitting on the edge of my bed—I was   65
twelve or thirteen maybe—and listening with unease to a minute or so of classical music. I don't know if I found it as I was turning the dial, searching for the Johnny Otis Show or the live broadcast from Scribner's Drive-in, or if the tuner had simply drifted into another station's signal. Whatever happened, the music caught me in a disturbing way, and I sat there, letting it play. It sounded like the music I heard in church, weighted, funereal. Eerie chords echoing from another world. I leaned over, my fingers on the tuner, and, in what I remember as almost a twitch, I turned the knob away from the melody of these strange instruments. My reaction to the other high culture I encountered—*The Iliad* and Shakespeare and some schoolbook poems by Longfellow and Lowell—was similar, though less a visceral rejection and more a rejecting disinterest, a sense of irrelevance. The few Shakespearean scenes I did know—saw on television, or read or heard in grammar school—seemed snooty and put-on, kind of dumb. Not the way I wanted to talk. Not interesting to me.

There were few books in our house: a couple of thin stories read   66
to me as a child in Pennsylvania (*The Little Boy who Ran Away*, an
Uncle Remus sampler), the *M* volume of the *World Book
Encyclopedia* (which I found one day in the trash behind the
secondhand store), and the Hollywood tabloids my mother would
bring home from work. I started buying lots of Superman and
Batman comic books because I loved the heroes' virtuous omnipo-
tence—comic books, our teachers said, were bad for us—and, once I
discovered them, I began checking out science fiction novels from
my grammar school library. Other reading material appeared: the
instructions to my chemistry set, which I half understood and only
half followed, and, eventually, my astronomy books, which seemed
to me to be magical rather than discursive texts. So it was that my
early intrigue with literacy—my lifts and escapes with language and
rhythm—came from comic books and science fiction, from the
personal, nonscientific worlds I created with bits and pieces of laboratory and telescopic technology, came, as well, from the Italian
stories I heard my uncles and parents tell. It came, too, from the
music my radio brought me: music that wove in and out of my days,
lyrics I'd repeat and repeat—"gone, gone, gone, jumpin' like a
catfish on a pole"—wanting to catch that sound, seeking other emotional frontiers, other places to go. Like rocker Joe Ely, I picked up
Chicago on my transistor radio.

    Except for school exercises and occasional cards my mother   67
made me write to my uncles and aunts, I wrote very little during my
childhood; it wasn't until my last year in high school that Jack
MacFarland sparked an interest in writing. And though I developed
into a good reader, I performed from moderately well to terribly on
other sorts of school literacy tasks. From my reading I knew vocabulary words, and I did okay on spelling tests—though I never lasted
all that long in spelling bees—but I got C's and D's on the everpresent requests to diagram sentences and label parts of speech. The
more an assignment was related to real reading, the better I did; the
more analytic, self-contained, and divorced from context, the lousi-
er I performed. Today some teachers would say I was a concrete
thinker. To be sure, the development of my ability to decode words
and read sentences took place in school, but my orientation to reading—the way I conceived of it, my purpose for doing it—occurred
within the tight and untraditional confines of my home. The quirks
and textures of my immediate environment combined with my
escapist fantasies to draw me to books. "It is what we are excited
about that educates us," writes social historian Elizabeth Ewen. It is
what taps our curiosity and dreams. Eventually, the books that
seemed so distant, those Great Books, would work their way into my
curiosity, would influence the way I framed problems and the way I

wrote. But that would come much later—first with Jack MacFarland (mixed with his avant-garde countertradition), then with my teachers at Loyola and UCLA—an excitement and curiosity shaped by others and connected to others, a cultural and linguistic heritage received not from some pristine conduit, but exchanged through the heat of human relation.

A friend of mine recently suggested that education is one culture 68 embracing another. It's interesting to think of the very different ways that metaphor plays out. Education can be a desperate, smothering embrace, an embrace that denies the needs of the other. But education can also be an encouraging, communal embrace—at its best an invitation, an opening. Several years ago, I was sitting in a workshop conducted by the Brazilian educator Paulo Freire. It was the first hour or so and Freire, in his sophisticated, accented English, was establishing the theoretical base of his literacy pedagogy—heady stuff, a blend of Marxism, phenomenology, and European existentialism. I was two seats away from Freire; in front of me and next to him was a younger man, who, puzzled, finally interrupted the speaker to ask a question. Freire acknowledged the question and, as he began answering, he turned and quickly touched the man's forearm. Not patronizing, not mushy, a look and a tap as if to say: "You and me right now, let's go through this together." Embrace. With Jack MacFarland it was an embrace: no-nonsense and cerebral, but a relationship in which the terms of endearment were the image in a poem, a play's dialogue, the winding narrative journey of a novel.

More often than we admit, a failed education is social more than 69 intellectual in origin. And the challenge that has always faced American education, that it has sometimes denied and sometimes doggedly pursued, is how to create both the social and cognitive means to enable a diverse citizenry to develop their ability. It is an astounding challenge: the complex and wrenching struggle to actualize the potential not only of the privileged but, too, of those who have lived here for a long time generating a culture outside the mainstream and those who, like my mother's parents and my father, immigrated with cultural traditions of their own. This painful but generative mix of language and story can result in clash and dislocation in our communities, but it also gives rise to new speech, new stories, and once we appreciate the richness of it, new invitations to literacy.

Pico Boulevard, named for the last Mexican governor of California, 70 runs an immense stretch west to east: from the wealth of the Santa Monica beaches to blighted Central Avenue, deep in Los Angeles. Union Street is comparatively brief, running north to south, roughly from Adams to Temple, pretty bad off all the way. Union intersects

Pico east of Vermont Avenue and too far to the southwest to be touched by the big-money development that is turning downtown Los Angeles into a whirring postmodernist dreamscape. The Pico-Union district is very poor, some of its housing as unsafe as that on Skid Row, delapidated, overcrowded, rat-infested. It used to be a working-class Mexican neighborhood, but for about ten years now it has become the concentrated locale of those fleeing the political and economic horror in Central America. Most come from El Salvador and Guatemala. One observer calls the area a gigantic refugee camp.

As you move concentrically outward from Pico-Union, you'll 71 encounter a number of other immigrant communities: Little Tokyo and Chinatown to the northeast, Afro-Caribbean to the southwest, Koreatown to the west. Moving west, you'll find Thai and Vietnamese restaurants tucked here and there in storefronts. Filipinos, Southeast Asians, Armenians, and Iranians work in the gas stations, the shoe-repair stores, the minimarts. A lawnmower repair shop posts its sign in Korean, Spanish, and English. A Korean church announces "Jesus Loves You" in the same three languages. "The magnitude and diversity of immigration to Los Angeles since 1960," notes a report from UCLA's Graduate School of Architecture and Urban Planning, "is comparable only to the New York-bound wave of migrants around the turn of the century." It is not at all uncommon for English composition teachers at UCLA, CalState L.A., Long Beach State—the big urban universities and colleges—to have, in a class of twenty-five, students representing a dozen or more linguistic backgrounds: from Spanish and Cantonese and Farsi to Hindi, Portuguese, and Tagalog. Los Angeles, the new Ellis Island.

On a drive down the Santa Monica Freeway, you exit on 72 Vermont and pass Rick's Mexican Cuisine, Hawaii Discount Furniture, The Restaurant Ecuatoriano, Froggy's Children's Wear, Seoul Autobody, and the Bar Omaha, Turn east on Pico, and as you approach Union, taking a side street here and there, you'll start seeing the murals: The Virgin of Guadalupe, Steve McQueen, a scene resembling Siqueiros's heroic workers, the Statue of Liberty, Garfield the Cat. Graffiti are everywhere. The dreaded Eighteenth Street gang—an established Mexican gang—has marked its turf in Arabic as well as Roman numerals. Newer gangs, a Salvadoran gang among them, are emerging by the violent logic of territory and migration; they have Xed out the Eighteenth Street *placas* and written their own threatening insignias in place. Statues of the Blessed Mother rest amid potted plants in overgrown front yards. There is a rich sweep of small commerce: restaurants, markets, bakeries, legal services ("Income Tax y Amnestia"), beauty salons ("Lolita's Magic Touch—Salon de Belleza—Unisex"). A Salvadoran restaurant sells teriyaki burgers. A "Discoteca Latina" advertises "great rap hits." A clothing store has a Dick Tracy sweatshirt on a half mannequin; a boy walks out wearing a blue t-shirt that announces "Life's a Beach." Culture in a Waring blender.

There are private telegram and postal services: messages sent straight to "domicilio a CentroAmerica." A video store advertises a comedy about immigration: *Ni de Aqui/Ni de Alla*, "Neither from Here nor from There." The poster displays a Central American Indian caught on a wild freeway ride: a Mexican in a sombrero is pulling one of the Indian's pigtails, Uncle Sam pulls the other, a border guard looks on, ominously suspended in air. You see a lot of street vending, from oranges and melons to deco sunglasses: rhinestones and plastic swans and lenses shaped like a heart. Posters are slapped on posters: one has rows of faces of the disappeared. Santa Claus stands on a truck bumper and waves drivers into a ninety-nine cent outlet. 73

Families are out shopping, men loiter outside a cafe, a group of young girls collectively count out their change. You notice, even in the kaleidoscope you pick out his figure, you notice a dark-skinned boy, perhaps Guatemalan, walking down Pico with a cape across his shoulders. His hair is piled in a four-inch rockabilly pompadour. He passes a dingy apartment building, a *pupuseria*, a body shop with no name, and turns into a storefront social services center. There is one other person in the sparse waiting room. She is thin, her gray hair pulled back in a tight bun, her black dress buttoned to her neck. She will tell you, if you ask her in Spanish, that she is waiting for her English class to begin. She might also tell you that the people here are helping her locate her son—lost in Salvadoran resettlement camps—and she thinks that if she can learn a little English, it will help her bring him to America. 74

The boy is here for different reasons. He has been causing trouble in school, and arrangements are being made for him to see a bilingual counselor. His name is Mario, and he immigrated with his older sister two years ago. His English is halting, unsure; he seems simultaneously rebellious and scared. His caseworker tells me that he still has flashbacks of Guatemalan terror: his older brother taken in the night by death squads, strangled, and hacked apart on the road by his house. Then she shows me his drawings, and our conversation stops. Crayon and pen on cheap paper: blue and orange cityscapes, eyes on billboards, in the windshields of cars, a severed hand at the bus stop. There are punks, beggars, piñatas walking the streets—upright cows and donkeys—skeletal homeboys, corseted girls carrying sharpened bones. "He will talk to you about these," the caseworker tells me. "They're scary, aren't they? The school doesn't know what the hell to do with him. I don't think he really knows what to do with all that's in him either." 75

In another part of the state, farther to the north, also rich in immi-   76
gration, a teacher in a basic reading and writing program asks his
students to interview one another and write a report, a capsule of a
classmate's life. Caroline, a black woman in her late forties, chooses Thuy Anh, a Vietnamese woman many years her junior. Caroline
asks only five questions—Thuy Anh's English is still difficult to
understand—simple questions: What is your name? Where were you
born? What is your education? Thuy Anh talks about her childhood
in South Vietnam and her current plans in America. She is the
oldest of nine children, and she received a very limited Vietnamese
education, for she had to spend much of her childhood caring for her
brothers and sisters. She married a serviceman, came to America,
and now spends virtually all of her time pursuing a high school
equivalency, struggling with textbook descriptions of the American
political process, frantically trying to improve her computational
skills. She is not doing very well at this. As one of her classmates
observed, she might be trying too hard.

Caroline is supposed to take notes while Thuy Anh responds to   77
her questions, and then use the notes to write her profile, maybe
something like a reporter would do. But Caroline is moved to do
something different. She's taken by Thuy Anh's accounts of
watching over babies. "Mother's little helper," she thinks. And
that stirs her, this woman who has never been a mother. Maybe, too,
Thuy Anh's desire to do well in school, her driven eagerness, the
desperation that occasionally flits across her face, maybe that moves
Caroline as well. Over the next two days, Caroline strays from the
assignment and writes a two-and-a-half-page fiction that builds to a
prose poem. She recasts Thuy Anh's childhood into an American
television fantasy.

Thuy Anh is "Mother's little helper." Her five younger sisters   78
"are happy and full of laughter . . . their little faces are bright with
eyes sparkling." The little girls' names are "Hellen, Ellen, Lottie,
Alice, and Olie"—American names—and they "cook and sew and
make pretty doll dresses for their dolls to wear." Though the family
is Buddhist, they exchange gifts at Christmas and "gather in the
large living room to sing Christmas carols." Thuy Anh "went to
school every day she could and studied very hard." One day, Thuy
Anh was "asked to wright a poem and to recite it to her classmates." And, here, Caroline embeds within her story a prose
poem—which she attributes to Thuy Anh:

> My name is Thuy Anh I live near the Ocean. I see the waves boisterous
> and impudent bursting and splashing against the huge rocks. I see the
> white boats out on the blue sea. I see the fisher men rapped in heavy
> coats to keep their bodys warm while bringing in large fishes to sell to
> the merchants, Look! I see a larg white bird going on its merry way.

Then I think of how great God is for he made this great sea for me to see and yet I stand on dry land and see the green and hillie side with flowers rising to the sky. How sweet and beautiful for God to have made Thuy Anh and the sea.

I interview Caroline. When she was a little girl in Arkansas, she 79 "would get off into a room by myself and read the Scripture." The "poems in King Solomon" were her favorites. She went to a segregated school and "used to write quite a bit" at home. But she "got away from it" and some years later dropped out of high school to come west to earn a living. She's worked in a convalescent hospital for twenty years, never married, wishes she had, comes, now, back to school and is finding again her love of words. "I get lost . . . I'm right in there with my writing, and I forget all my surroundings." She is classified as a basic student—no diploma, low-level employment, poor test scores—had been taught by her grandmother that she would have to earn her living "by the sweat of my brow. "

Her work in the writing course had been good up to the point 80 of Thuy Anh's interview, better than that of many classmates, adequate, fairly free of error, pretty well organized. But the interview triggered a different level of performance. Caroline's early engagement with language reemerged in a lyrical burst: an evocation of an imagined childhood, a curious overlay of one culture's fantasy over another's harsh reality. Caroline's longing reshaped a Vietnamese girlhood, creating a life neither she nor Thuy Anh ever had, an intersection of biblical rhythms and *Father Knows Best.*

Over Chin's bent head arches a trellis packed tight with dried 81 honeysuckle and chrysanthemum, sea moss, mushrooms, and ginseng. His elbow rests on the cash register—quiet now that the customers have left. He shifts on the stool, concentrating on the writing before him: "A young children," he scribbles, and pauses. "Young children," that doesn't sound good, he thinks. He crosses out "children" and sits back. A few seconds pass. He can't think of the right way to say it, so he writes "children" again and continues: "a young children with his grandma smail . . ." "Smail," He pulls a Chinese-English dictionary from under the counter.

In front of the counter and extending down the aisle are boxes 82 of dried fish: shark fins, mackerel, pollock. They give off a musky smell. Behind Chin are rows of cans and jars: pickled garlic, pickled ginger, sesame paste. By the door, comic books and Chinese weeklies lean dog-eared out over the thin retaining wire of a dusty wooden display. Chin has found his word: It's not *smail,* it's *smile.* "A young children with his grandma smile . . ." He reaches in the pocket of his jeans jacket, pulls out a piece of paper, and unfolds it.

There's a word copied on it he has been wanting to use. A little bell over the door jingles. An old man comes in, and Chin moves his yellow pad aside.

Chin remembers his teacher in elementary school telling him   83
that his writing was poor, that he didn't know many words. He went to middle school for a few years but quit before completing it. Very basic English—the ABCs and simple vocabulary—was, at one point, part of his curriculum, but he lived in a little farming community, so he figured he would never use it. He did, though, pick up some letters and a few words. He immigrated to America when he was seventeen, and for the two years since has been living with his uncle in Chinatown. His uncle signed him up for English classes at the community center. He didn't like them. He did, however, start hanging out in the recreation room, playing pool and watching TV. The English on TV intrigued him. And it was then that he turned to writing. He would "try to learn to speak something" by writing it down. That was about six months ago. Now he's enrolled in a community college literacy program and has been making strong progress. He is especially taken with one tutor, a woman in her mid-thirties who encourages him to write. So he writes for her. He writes stories about his childhood in China. He sneaks time when no one is in the store or when customers are poking around, writing because he likes to bring her things, writing, too, because "sometime I think writing make my English better. "

The old man puts on the counter a box of tea guaranteed to help   84
you stop smoking. Chin rings it up and thanks him. The door jingles and Chin returns to his writing, copying the word from his folded piece of paper, a word he found in *People* magazine: "A young children with his grandma smile *gleefully*."

Frank Marell, born Meraglio, my oldest uncle, learned his   85
English as Chin is learning his. He came to America with his mother and three sisters in September 1921. They came to join my grandfather who had immigrated long before. They joined, as well, the millions of Italian peasants who had flowed through Customs with their cloth-and-paper suitcases, their strange gestural language, and their dark, empty pockets. Frank was about to turn eight when he immigrated, so he has faint memories of Calabria. They lived in a one-room stone house. In the winter, the family's scrawny milk cow was brought inside. By the door there was a small hole for a rifle barrel. Wolves came out of the hills. He remembers the frost and burrs stinging his feet as he foraged the countryside for berries and twigs and fresh grass for the cow. *Chi esce riesce*, the saying went— "he who leaves succeeds"—and so it was that my grandfather left when he did, eventually finding work amid the metal and steam of the Pennsylvania Railroad.

My uncle remembers someone giving him bread on the [86] steamship. He remembers being very sick. Once in America, he and his family moved into the company housing projects across from the stockyard. The house was dirty and had gouges in the wood. Each morning his mother had to sweep the soot from in front of the door. He remembers rats. He slept huddled with his father and mother and sisters in the living room, for his parents had to rent out the other rooms in order to buy clothes and shoes and food. Frank never attended school in Italy. He was eight now and would enter school in America. America, where eugenicists were attesting, scientifically, to the feeblemindedness of his race, where the popular press ran articles about the immorality of these swarthy exotics. Frank would enter school here. In many ways, you could lay his life like a template over a current life in the Bronx, in Houston, in Pico-Union.

He remembers the embarrassment of not understanding the [87] teacher, of not being able to read or write. Funny clothes, oversize shoes, his hair slicked down and parted in the middle. He would lean forward—his assigned seat, fortunately, was in the back—and ask other Italian kids, ones with some English, to tell him what for the love of God was going on. He had big, sad eyes, thick hands, skin dark enough to yield the nickname Blacky. Frank remembers other boys—Carmen Santino, a kid named Hump, Bruno Tucci—who couldn't catch on to this new language and quit coming to school. Within six months of his arrival, Frank would be going after class to the back room of Pete Mastis's Dry Cleaners and Shoeshine Parlor. He cleaned and shined shoes, learned to operate a steam press, ran deliveries. He listened to the radio, trying to mimic the harsh complexities of English. He spread Pete Mastis's racing forms out before him, copying words onto the margins of newsprint. He tried talking to the people whose shoes he was shining, exchanging tentative English with the broken English of Germans and Poles and other Italians.

Eventually, Frank taught his mother to sign her name. By the [88] time he was in his teens, he was reading flyers and announcements of sales and legal documents to her. He was also her scribe, doing whatever writing she needed to have done. Frank found himself immersed in the circumstance of literacy.

With the lives of Mario and Caroline and Chin and Frank Marell as [89] a backdrop, I want to consider a current, very powerful set of proposals about literacy and culture.

There is a strong impulse in American education—curious in a [90] country with such an ornery streak of antitraditionalism—to define achievement and excellence in terms of the acquisition of a historically validated body of knowledge, an authoritative list of books and allusions, a canon. We seek a certification of our national intelligence, indeed, our national virtue, in how diligently our children can display this central corpus of information. This need for certification tends to emerge most dramatically in our educational policy debates during times of real or imagined threat: economic hard times, political crises, sudden increases in immigration. Now is such a time, and it is reflected in a number of influential books and commission reports. E. D. Hirsch argues that a core national vocabulary, one oriented toward the English literate tradition—Alice in Wonderland to zeitgeist—will build a knowledge base that will foster the literacy of all Americans. Diane Ravitch and Chester Finn call for a return to a traditional historical and literary curriculum: the valorous historical figures and the classical literature of the once-elite course of study. Allan Bloom, Secretary of Education William Bennett, Mortimer Adler and the Paideia Group, and a number of others have affirmed, each in their very different ways, the necessity of the Great Books: Plato and Aristotle and Sophocles, Dante and Shakespeare and Locke, Dickens and Mann and Faulkner. We can call this orientation to educational achievement the canonical orientation.

At times in our past, the call for a shoring up of or return to a 91
canonical curriculum was explicitly elitist, was driven by a fear that the education of the select was being compromised. Today, though, the majority of the calls are provocatively framed in the language of democracy. They assail the mediocre and grinding curriculum frequently found in remedial and vocational education. They are disdainful of the patronizing perceptions of student ability that further restrict the already restricted academic life of disadvantaged youngsters. They point out that the canon—its language, conventions, and allusions—is central to the discourse of power, and to keep it from poor kids is to assure their disenfranchisement all the more. The books of the canon, claim the proposals, the Great Books, are a window onto a common core of experience and civic ideals. There is, then, a spiritual, civic, and cognitive heritage here, and *all* our children should receive it. If we are sincere in our desire to bring Mario, Chin, the younger versions of Caroline, current incarnations of Frank Marell, and so many others who populate this book—if we truly want to bring them into our society—then we should provide them with this stable and common core. This is a forceful call. It promises a still center in a turning world.

I see great value in being challenged to think of the curriculum 92
of the many in the terms we have traditionally reserved for the few; it is refreshing to have common assumptions about the capacities of underprepared students so boldly challenged. Many of the people we have encountered in these pages have displayed the ability to engage books and ideas thought to be beyond their grasp. There were the

veterans: Willie Oates writing, in prison, ornate sentences drawn from *The Mill on the Floss*. Sergeant Gonzalez coming to understand poetic ambiguity in "Butch Weldy." There was the parole aide Olga who no longer felt walled off from *Macbeth*. There were the EOP students at UCLA, like Lucia who unpackaged *The Myth of Mental Illness* once she had an orientation and overview. And there was Frank Marell who, later in his life, would be talking excitedly to his nephew about this guy Edgar Allan Poe. Too many people are kept from the books of the canon, the Great Books, because of misjudgments about their potential. Those books eventually proved important to me, and, as best I know how, I invite my students to engage them. But once we grant the desirability of equal curricular treatment and begin to consider what this equally distributed curriculum would contain, problems arise: If the canon itself is the answer to our educational inequities, why has it historically invited few and denied many? Would the canonical orientation provide adequate guidance as to how a democratic curriculum should be constructed and how it should be taught? Would it guide us in opening up to Olga that "fancy talk" that so alienated her?

Those who study the way literature becomes canonized, how linguistic creations are included or excluded from a tradition, claim that the canonical curriculum students would most likely receive would not, as is claimed, offer a common core of American experience. Caroline would not find her life represented in it, nor would Mario. The canon has tended to push to the margin much of the literature of our nation: from American Indian songs and chants to immigrant fiction to working-class narratives. The institutional messages that students receive in the books they're issued and the classes they take are powerful and, as I've witnessed since my Voc. Ed. days, quickly internalized. And to revise these messages and redress past wrongs would involve more than adding some new books to the existing canon—the very reasons for linguistic and cultural exclusion would have to become a focus of study in order to make the canon act as a democratizing force. Unless this happens, the democratic intent of the reformers will be undercut by the content of the curriculum they propose. [93]

And if we move beyond content to consider basic assumptions about teaching and learning, a further problem arises, one that involves the very nature of the canonical orientation itself. The canonical orientation encourages a narrowing of focus from learning to that which must be learned: It simplifies the dynamic tension between student and text and reduces the psychological and social dimensions of instruction. The student's personal history recedes as the what of the classroom is valorized over the how. Thus it is that the encounter of student and text is often portrayed by canonists as [94] a transmission. Information, wisdom, virtue will pass from the book to the student if the student gives the book the time it merits, carefully traces its argument or narrative or lyrical progression. Intellectual, even spiritual growth will *necessarily* result from an encounter with Roman mythology, *Othello*, and "I heard a Fly buzz—when I died—," with biographies and historical sagas and patriotic lore. Learning is stripped of confusion and discord. It is stripped, as well, of strong human connection. My own initiators to the canon—Jack MacFarland, Dr. Carothers, and the rest—knew there was more to their work than their mastery of a tradition. What mattered most, I see now, were the relationships they established with me, the guidance they provided when I felt inadequate or threatened. This mentoring was part of my entry into that solemn library of Western thought—and even with such support, there were still times of confusion, anger, and fear. It is telling, I think, that once that rich social network slid away, once I was in graduate school in intense, solitary encounter with that tradition, I abandoned it for other sources of nurturance and knowledge.

The model of learning implicit in the canonical orientation   95 seems, at times, more religious than cognitive or social: Truth resides in the printed texts, and if they are presented by someone who knows them well and respects them, that truth will be revealed. Of all the advocates of the canon, Mortimer Adler has given most attention to pedagogy—and his Paideia books contain valuable discussions of instruction, coaching, and questioning. But even here, and this is doubly true in the other manifestos, there is little acknowledgment that the material in the canon can be not only difficult but foreign, alienating, overwhelming.

We need an orientation to instruction that provides guidance on   96 how to determine and honor the beliefs and stories, enthusiasm, and apprehensions that students reveal. How to build on them, and when they clash with our curriculum—as I saw so often in the Tutorial Center at UCLA—when they clash, how to encourage a discussion that will lead to reflection on what students bring and what they're currently confronting. Canonical lists imply canonical answers, but the manifestos offer little discussion of what to do when students fail. If students have been exposed to at least some elements of the canon before—as many have—why didn't it take? If they're encountering it for the first time and they're lost, how can we determine where they're located—and what do we do then?

Each member of a teacher's class, poor *or* advantaged, gives rise   97 to endless decisions, day-to-day determinations about a child's reading and writing: decisions on how to tap strength, plumb confusion, foster growth. The richer your conception of learning and your understanding of its social and psychological dimensions, the more insightful and effective your judgments will be. Consider the sources of literacy we saw among the children in El Monte: shop-keepers' signs, song lyrics, auto manuals, the conventions of the Western family stories and tales, and more. Consider Chin's sources—television and *People* magazine—and Caroline's oddly generative mix of the Bible and an American media illusion. Then there's the jarring confluence of personal horror and pop culture flotsam that surfaces in Mario's drawings, drawings that would be a rich, if volatile, point of departure for language instruction. How would these myriad sources and manifestations be perceived and evaluated if viewed within the framework of a canonical tradition, and what guidance would the tradition provide on how to understand and develop them? The great books and central texts of the canon could quickly become a benchmark against which the expressions of student literacy would be negatively measured, a limiting band of excellence that, ironically, could have a dispiriting effect on the very thing the current proposals intend: the fostering of mass literacy.

To understand the nature and development of literacy we need ⁹⁸ to consider the social context in which it occurs—the political, economic, and cultural forces that encourage or inhibit it. The canonical orientation discourages deep analysis of the way these forces may be affecting performance. The canonists ask that schools transmit a coherent traditional knowledge to an ever-changing, frequently uprooted community. This discordance between message and audience is seldom examined. Although a ghetto child can rise on the lilt of a Homeric line—books *can* spark dreams—appeals to elevated texts can also divert attention from the conditions that keep a population from realizing its dreams. The literacy curriculum is being asked to do what our politics and our economics have failed to do: diminish differences in achievement, narrow our gaps, bring us together. Instead of analysis of the complex web of causes of poor performance, we are offered a faith in the unifying power of a body of knowledge, whose infusion will bring the rich and the poor, the longtime disaffected and the uprooted newcomers into cultural unanimity. If this vision is democratic, it is simplistically so, reductive, not an invitation for people truly to engage each other at the point where cultures and classes intersect.

I worry about the effects a canonical approach to education ⁹⁹ could have on cultural dialogue and transaction—on the involvement of an abandoned underclass and on the movement of immigrants like Mario and Chin into our nation. A canonical uniformity promotes rigor and quality control; it can also squelch new thinking, diffuse the generative tension between the old and the new. It is significant that the canonical orientation is voiced with most force during times

of challenge and uncertainty, for it promises the authority of tradition, the seeming stability of the past. But the authority is fictive,
gained from a misreading of American cultural history. No period of
that history was harmoniously stable; the invocation of a golden age
is a mythologizing act. Democratic culture is, by definition, vibrant
and dynamic, discomforting and unpredictable. It gives rise to apprehension; freedom is not always calming. And, yes, it can yield
fragmentation, though often as not the source of fragmentation is
intolerant misunderstanding of diverse traditions rather than the
desire of members of those traditions to remain hermetically separate. A truly democratic vision of knowledge and social structure
would honor this complexity. The vision might not be soothing, but
it would provide guidance as to how to live and teach in a country
made up of many cultural traditions.

We are in the middle of an extraordinary social experiment: the 100
attempt to provide education for all members of a vast pluralistic
democracy. To have any prayer of success, we'll need many conceptual blessings: A philosophy of language and literacy that affirms the
diverse sources of linguistic competence and deepens our understanding of the ways class and culture blind us to the richness of
those sources. A perspective on failure that lays open the logic of
error. An orientation toward the interaction of poverty and ability
that undercuts simple polarities, that enables us to see simultaneously the constraints poverty places on the play of mind and the actual
mind at play within those constraints. We'll need a pedagogy that
encourages us to step back and consider the threat of the standard
classroom and that shows us, having stepped back, how to step forward to invite a student across the boundaries of that powerful
room. Finally, we'll need a revised store of images of educational
excellence, ones closer to egalitarian ideals—ones that embody the
reward and turmoil of education in a democracy, that celebrate the
plural, messy human reality of it. At heart, we'll need a guiding set
of principles that cannot encourage us to retreat from, but move us
closer to, an understanding of the rich mix of speech and ritual and
story that is America.

EXPLORATIONS

1. Throughout *Lives on the Boundary* (the book from which this piece is
   excerpted), Rose uses a mixture of vignettes, personal narrative, and
   argument. How do the vignettes influence you as a reader? What might
   be Rose's purpose in using them?

2. With the example of Millie taking and failing a reading test that
   required knowledge of prefixes, Rose illustrates that much of education
   and test taking is not about knowing what's expected of you but about

knowing what the "tricks" are and then using a few tricks of your own. What does he mean? What tricks have you acquired, and why (and in which circumstances) do you use them?

3. Rose describes the debilitating focus on deficiency, error, and patholo-gy in education. How might focusing on abilities and possibilities work better? Could such a focus work in American education? Why or why not?

4. Rose emphasizes his borrowed concept of "Education as Embrace." What do you think he means by this phrase? What are some of the ben-efits and drawbacks of this metaphor? Can you think of other metaphors for education?

5. What does Rose mean by what he calls the "canonical orientation" toward literacy? What are his arguments against it? How would you dis-agree with his arguments? How would you agree with them? What per-sonal examples are you able to offer to support or refute his claims and your own?

It's the Poverty

CHERRÍE MORAGA

*In This Bridge Called My Back: Writings by Radical Women
of Color, a 1981 book that Moraga co-edited with Gloria
Anzaldúa, Moraga described herself as "a very tired
Chicana/half-breed/feminist/lesbian/writer/teacher/talk-
er/waitress." Her plays and poetry have won several awards,
including the Before Columbus American Book Award, the
Fund for New American Plays Award, and the National
Endowment for the Arts Theatre Playwrights' Fellowship.
"It's the Poverty" is from her collection of poetry and
prose entitled* Loving in the War Years, Lo Que Nunca Pasó
por Sus Labios.

WRITING BEFORE READING

*Reflect on a time when you had to struggle to find the words to say
what you meant.*

for Kim   1

You say to me.
"Take a drive with me
up the coast, babe
and bring your typewriter."   5

All the way down the coast
you and she stopped at motels
your typewriters tucked under your free arm
dodging the rain fast to the shelter
of metal awnings, red and white   10
I imagine them—you two
snorting brandy in those vinyl rooms
propping your each machine onto an end table.

. . .

This story becomes you.
A fiction I invent with my ears   15
evoking heroism in the first
description of the weather.

I say
my typewriter sticks in the wet.
I have been using the same ribbon   20
over and over and over again.
Yes, we both agree I could use

192

a new ribbon. But it's the poverty
the poverty of my imagination, we agree.
I lack imagination you say.   25

No. I lack language.

The language to clarify
my resistance to the literate.
Words are a war to me.
They threaten my family.   30

To gain the word to describe the loss,
I risk losing everything.
I may create a monster,
the word's length and body
swelling up colorful and thrilling   35
looming over my *mother*, characterized.
Her voice in the distance
unintelligible   illiterate.

These are the monster's words.

. . .

Understand.   40
My family is poor.
Poor. I can't afford
a new ribbon. The risk
of this one
is enough   45
to keep me moving
through it, accountable.
The repetition, like my mother's stories retold,
each time reveals more particulars
gains more familiarity.   50
You can't get me in your car so fast.

. . .

You tell me how you've learned
to write while you drive
how I can leave my droning machine behind
for all   55
you care.

I say, not-so-fast
not
so
fast. The drone   60
a chant to my ears
a common blend of histories
repeatedly inarticulate.

Not so fast.
I am poorer than you.   65

In my experience, fictions
are for hearing about,
not living.

EXPLORATIONS

1. How is writing—or finding words—a struggle for the speaker in the poem?

2. What is at stake for the speaker in this poem? Against what is the speaker struggling?

3. Who seems to have the most power to define such words as "imagination" and "illiterate" in this poem?

70

75

80

Cultural Literacy

E. D. HIRSCH, JR.

E. D. Hirsch is a professor of English at the University of Virginia. He has published several scholarly books and articles about literary theory, but he is perhaps best known for his notion of "cultural literacy." The essay printed here first appeared in The American Scholar *in 1983. Four years later, he published* Cultural Literacy: What Every American Needs to Know. *The book was a bestseller that sparked a heated debate about the purposes of education. Hirsch argues that readers and writers must share a body of core knowledge if they are to be understood, and that many Americans do not have that knowledge. A 63-page appendix to the book lists 5,000 names, terms, and phrases that Hirsch believes are essential to cultural literacy. He has also published* The Dictionary of Cultural Literacy, *which provides brief definitions of the terms he introduced in the earlier book.*

WRITING BEFORE READING

How do you define "good style" in writing?

For the past twelve years I have been pursuing technical research in the teaching of reading and writing. I now wish to emerge from my closet to declare that technical research is not going to remedy the national decline in our literacy that is documented in the decline of verbal SAT scores. We already know enough about methodology to do a good job of teaching reading and writing. Of course we would profit from knowing still more about teaching methods, but better teaching techniques alone would produce only a marginal improvement in the literacy of our students. Raising their reading and writing levels will depend far less on our methods of instruction (there are many acceptable methods) than on the specific contents of our school curricula. Commonsensical as this proposition might seem to the man in the street, it is regarded as heresy by many (I hope by ever fewer) professional educators. The received and dominant view of educational specialists is that the specific materials of reading and writing instruction are interchangeable so long as they are "appropriate," and of "high quality. "

But consider this historical fact. The national decline in our 2
literacy has accompanied a decline in our use of common, nationwide materials in the subject most closely connected with literacy,
"English." From the 1890s to 1900 we taught in English courses
what amounted to a national core curriculum. As Arthur Applebee
observes in his excellent book *Tradition and Reform in the Teaching
of English*, the following texts were used in those days in more than
25 percent of our schools: *The Merchant of Venice*, *Julius Caesar*,
"First Bunker Hill Oration," *The Sketch Book*, *Evangeline*, "The
Vision of Sir Launfal," "Snow-Bound," *Macbeth*, "The Lady of
the Lake," *Hamlet*, "The Deserted Village," Gray's "Elegy,"
"Thanatopsis," *As You Like It*. Other widely used works will strike
a resonance in those who are over fifty: "The Courtship of Miles
Standish," "Il Penseroso," *Paradise Lost*, "L'Allegro,"
"Lycidas," *Ivanhoe*, *David Copperfield*, *Silas Marner*, etc., etc.
Then in 1901 the College Entrance Examinations Board issued its
first "uniform lists" of texts required to be known by students in
applying to colleges. This core curriculum, though narrower,
became even more widespread than the earlier canon. Lest anyone
assume that I shall urge a return to those particular texts, let me at
once deny it. By way of introducing my subject, I simply want to
claim that the decline in our literacy and the decline in commonly
shared knowledge that we acquire in school are causally related facts.
Why this should be so and what we might do about it are my twin
subjects.

That a decline in our national level of literacy has occurred few 3
will serious doubt. The chief and decisive piece of evidence for it is
the decline in verbal SAT scores among the white middle class. (This
takes into account the still greater lowering of scores caused by an
increased proportion of poor and minority students taking the tests.)
Now scores on the verbal SAT show a high correlation with reading
and writing skills that have been tested independently by other
means. So, as a rough index to the literacy levels of our students, the
verbal SAT is a reliable guide. That is unsurprising if we accept the
point made by John Carroll and others that the verbal SAT is chiefly
a vocabulary test, for no one is surprised by a correlation between a
rich vocabulary and a high level of literacy. A rich vocabulary is not
a purely technical or rote-learnable skill. Knowledge of words is an
adjunct to knowledge of cultural realities signified by words, and to
whole domains of experience to which words refer. Specific words go
with specific knowledge. And when we begin to contemplate how to
teach specific knowledge, we are led back inexorably to the contents
of the school curriculum, whether or not those contents are linked,
as they used to be, to specific texts.

From the start of our national life, the school curriculum has 4
been an especially important formative element of our national
culture. In the schools we not only tried to harmonize the various
traditions of our parent cultures, we also wanted to strike out on our
own within the dominant British heritage. Being rebellious children,
we produced our own dictionary, and were destined, according to
Melville, to produce our own Shakespeare. In this self-conscious job
of culture making, the schools played a necessary role. That was
especially true in the teaching of history and English, the two
subjects central to culture making. In the nineteenth century we held
national conferences on school curricula. We formed the College
Board, which created the "uniform lists" already referred to. The
dominant symbol for the role of the school was the symbol of the
melting pot.

But from early times we have also resisted this narrow uniformi- 5
ty in our culture. The symbol of the melting pot was opposed by the
symbol of the stew pot, where our national ingredients kept their
individual characteristics and contributed to the flavor and vitality of
the whole. That is the doctrine of pluralism. It has now become the
dominant doctrine in our schools, especially in those subjects,
English and history, that are closest to culture making. In math and
science, by contrast, there is wide agreement about the contents of a
common curriculum. But in English courses, diversity and pluralism
now reign without challenge. I am persuaded that if we want to
achieve a more literate culture than we now have, we shall need to
restore the balance between these two equally American traditions of
unity and diversity. We shall need to restore certain common
contents to the humanistic side of the school curriculum. But before
we can make much headway in that direction, we shall also need to
modify the now-dominant educational principle that holds that any
suitable materials of instruction can be used to teach the skills of
reading and writing. I call this the doctrine of educational formalism.

The current curriculum guide to the study of English in the state 6
of California is a remarkable document. In its several pages of advice
to teachers I do not find the title of a single recommended work.
Such "curricular guides" are produced on the theory that the
actual contents of English courses are simply vehicles for inculcating
formal skills, and that contents can be left to local choice. But
wouldn't even a dyed-in-the-wool formalist concede that teachers
might be saved time if some merely illustrative, non-compulsory
titles were listed? Of course; but another doctrine, in alliance with
formalism, conspires against even that concession to content—the
doctrine of pluralism. An illustrative list put out by the state would

imply official sanction of the cultural and ideological values expressed by the works on the list. The California Education Department is not in the business of imposing cultures and ideologies. Its business is to inculcate "skills" and "positive self-concepts," regardless of the students' cultural backgrounds. The contents of English should be left to local communities.

This is an attractive theory to educators in those places where   7
spokesmen for minority cultures are especially vocal in their attack on the melting-pot idea. That concept, they say, is nothing but cultural imperialism (true), which submerges cultural identities (true) and gives minority children a sense of inferiority (often true). In recent years such attitudes have led to attacks on teaching school courses exclusively in standard English; in the bilingual movement (really a monolingual movement) it has led to attacks on an exclusive use of the English language for instruction. This kind of political pressure has encouraged a retreat to the extreme and untenable educational formalism reflected in the California curriculum guide.

What the current controversies have really demonstrated is a truth   8
that is quite contrary to the spirit of neutrality implied by educational formalism. Literacy is not just a formal skill; it is also a political deci-sion. The decision to *want* a literate society is a value-laden one that carries costs as well as advantages. English teachers by profession are committed to the ideology of literacy. They cannot successfully avoid the political implications of that ideology by hiding behind the skirts of methodology and research. Literacy implies specific contents as well as formal skills. Extreme formalism is misleading and evasive. But allow me to illustrate that point with some specific examples.

During most of the time that I was pursuing research in literacy I   9
was, like others in the field, a confirmed formalist. In 1977 I came out with a book on the subject, *The Philosophy of Composition*, that was entirely formalistic in outlook. One of my arguments, for instance, was that the effectiveness of English prose as an instrument of communi-cation gradually increased, after the invention of printing, through a trial-and-error process that slowly uncovered some of the psycholin-guistic principles of efficient communication in prose. I suggested that freshmen could learn in a semester what earlier writers had taken centuries to achieve, if they were directly taught those underlying psycholinguistic principles. (With respect to certain formal structures of clauses, this idea still seems valid.) I predicted fur-ther that we could learn how to teach those formal principles still more effectively if we pursued appropriately controlled pedagogical research.

So intent was I upon this idea that I undertook some arduous   10
research into one of the most important aspects of writing pedagogy—

evaluation. After all, in order to decide upon the best methods of inculcating the skills of writing, it was essential to evaluate the results of using the different teaching methods. For that we needed non-arbitrary, reliable techniques for evaluating student writing. In my book I had made some suggestions about how we might do this, and those ideas seemed cogent enough to a National Endowment for the Humanities panel to get me a grant to go forward with the research. For about two years I was deeply engaged in this work. It was this detailed engagement with the realities of reading and writing under controlled conditions that caused me finally to abandon my formalistic assumptions. (Later I discovered that experimentation on a much bigger scale had brought Richard C. Anderson, the premier scholar in reading research, to similar conclusions.)

The experiments that changed my mind were, briefly, these: To 11 get a non-arbitrary evaluation of writing, we decided to base our evaluations on actual audience effects. We devised a way of comparing the effects of well-written and badly written versions of the same paper. Our method was to pair off two large groups of readers (about a hundred in each group), each of which, when given the *same* piece of writing, would read it collectively with the same speed and comprehension. In other words, we matched the reading skills of these two large groups. Then, when one group was given a good version and the other given a degraded version, we measured the overall effect of these stylistic differences on speed and accuracy of comprehension. To our delight, we discovered that good style did make an appreciable difference, and that the degree of difference was replicable and predictable. So far so good. But what became very disconcerting about these results was that they came out properly only when the subjects of the papers were highly familiar to our audiences. When, later in the experiments, we introduced unfamiliar materials, the results were not only messy, they were "counterintuitive," the term of art for results that go against one's expectations. (Real scientists generally like to get counterintuitive results, but we were not altogether disinterested onlookers and were dismayed.) For what we discovered was that good writing makes very little difference when the subject is unfamiliar. We English teachers tend to believe that a good style is all the more helpful when the content is difficult, but it turns out that we are wrong. The reasons for this unexpected result are complex, and I will not pause to discuss them at length, since the important issues lie elsewhere.

Briefly, good style contributes little to our reading of unfamiliar 12 material because we must continually backtrack to test out different hypotheses about what is being meant or referred to. Thus, a reader of a text about Grant and Lee who is unsure just who Grant and Lee are would have to get clues from later parts of the text, and then go back to re-read earlier parts in the light of surer conjectures. This trial-and-error backtracking with unfamiliar material is so much more time-consuming than the delays caused by a bad style alone that style begins to lose its importance as a factor in reading unfamiliar material. The contribution of style in such cases can no longer be measured with statistical confidence.

The significance of this result is, first of all, that one cannot, even   13
in principle, base writing evaluations on audience effects—the only non-arbitrary principle that makes any sense. The reading skill of an audience is not a constant against which prose can be reliably measured. Audience reading skills vary unpredictably with the subject matter of the text. Although we were trying to measure our prose samples with the yardstick of paired audiences, the contrary had, in effect, occurred; our carefully contrived prose samples were measuring the background knowledge of our audiences. For instance, if the subject of a text was "Friendship," all audience pairs, everywhere we gave the trials, exhibited the same differentials. Also, for all audiences, if the subject was "Hegel's Metaphysics," the differential between good and bad writing tended to disappear. Also, so long as we used university audiences, a text on Grant and Lee gave the same sort of appropriate results as did a text on friendship. But for one community college audience (in, no less, Richmond, Virginia) "Grant and Lee" turned out to be as unfamiliar as "Hegel's Metaphysics"—a complacency-shattering result.

While the variability of reading skills within the same person was   14
making itself disconcertingly known to me, I learned that similar variability was showing up in formal writing skills—and for the same reasons. Researchers at the City University of New York were finding that when a topic is unfamiliar, writing skill declines in all of its dimensions—including grammar and spelling—not to mention sentence structure, parallelism, unity, focus, and other skills taught in writing courses. One part of the explanation for such results is that we all have limited attention space, and cannot pay much heed to form when we are devoting a lot of our attention to unfamiliar content. But another part of the explanation is more interesting. Part of our skill in reading and in writing is skill not just with linguistic structures but with words. Words are not purely formal counters of language; they represent large underlying domains of content. Part of language skill is content skill. As Apeneck Sweeney profoundly observed: "I gotta use words when I talk to you."

When I therefore assert that reading and writing skills are   15
content-bound, I mean also to make the corollary assertion that important aspects of reading and writing skills are *not* transferable.

Of course some skills *are* carried over from task to task; we know that broad strategies of reading and writing can become second nature, and thereby facilitate literary skills at all levels. But the content-indifferent, how-to approach to literacy skills is enormously oversimplified. As my final example of this, I shall mention an ingenious experiment conducted by Richard C. Anderson and his colleagues at the University of Illinois. It, too, was an experiment with paired audiences and paired texts. The texts were two letters, each describing a wedding, each of similar length, word-familiarity, sentence complexity, and number of idea units. Each audience was similarly paired according to age, educational level, marital status, sex, professional specialty, etc. Structurally speaking, the texts were similar and the audiences were similar. The crucial variables were these: one letter described a wedding in America, the other a wedding in India. One audience was American, the other Indian. Both audiences read both letters. The results were that the reading skills of the two groups—their speed and accuracy of comprehension—were very different in reading the two linguistically similar letters. The Americans read about an American wedding skillfully, accurately, and with good recall. They did poorly with the letter about the Indian wedding. The reverse was the case with the group of Indian readers. Anderson and his colleagues concluded that reading is not just a linguistic skill, but involves translinguistic knowledge beyond the abstract sense of words. They suggested that reading involves both "linguistic-schemata" (systems of expectation) and "content-schemata" as well. In short, the assumptions of educational formalism are incorrect.

Every writer is aware that the subtlety and complexity of what can 16 be conveyed in writing depends on the amount of relevant tacit knowledge that can be assumed in readers. As psycholinguists have shown, the explicitly stated words on the page often represent the smaller part of the literary transaction. Some of this assumed knowledge involves such matters as generic conventions, that is, what to expect in a business letter, a technical report, a detective story, etc. An equally significant part of the assumed knowledge—often a more significant part—concerns tacit knowledge of the experiential realities embraced by the discourse. Not only have I gotta use words to talk to you, I gotta assume you know *something* about what I am saying. If I had to start from scratch, I couldn't start at all.

We adjust for this in the most casual talk. It has been shown that 17 we always explain ourselves more fully to strangers than to intimates. But, when the strangers being addressed are some unknown collectivity to whom we are writing, how much shall we then need to explain? This was one of the most difficult authorial problems that arose with the advent of printing and mass literacy. Later on, in the eighteenth century, Dr. Johnson confidently assumed he could predict the knowledge possessed by a personage whom he called "the common reader." Some such construct is a necessary fiction for every writer in every literate culture and subculture. Even a writer for an astrophysics journal must assume a "common reader" for the subculture being addressed. A newspaper writer must also assume a "common reader" but for a much bigger part of the culture, perhaps for the literate culture as a whole. In our own culture, Jefferson wanted to create a highly informed "common reader," and he must have assumed the real existence of such a personage when he said he would prefer newspapers without government to government without newspapers. But, without appropriate, tacitly shared background knowledge, people cannot understand newspapers. A certain extent of shared, canonical knowledge is inherently necessary to a literate democracy.

For this canonical information I have proposed the term 18 "cultural literacy." It is the translinguistic knowledge on which linguistic literacy depends. You cannot have the one without the other. Teachers of foreign languages are aware of this interdependency between linguistic proficiency and translinguistic, cultural knowledge. To get very far in reading or writing French, a student must come to know facets of French culture quite different from his own. By the same token, American children learning to read and write English get instruction in aspects of their own national culture that are as foreign to them as French. National culture always has this "foreignness" with respect to family culture alone. School materials contain unfamiliar materials that promote the "acculturation" that is a universal part of growing up in any tribe or nation. Acculturation into a national literate culture might be defined as learning what the "common reader" of a newspaper in a literate culture could be expected to know. That would include knowledge of certain values (whether or not one accepted them), and knowledge of such things as (for example) the First Amendment, Grant and Lee, and DNA. In our own culture, what should these contents be? Surely our answer to that should partly define our school curriculum. Acculturation into a literate culture (the minimal aim of schooling; we should aim still higher) could be defined as the gaining of cultural literacy.

Such canonical knowledge could not be fixed once and for all. 19 "Grant and Lee" could not have been part of it in 1840, or "DNA" in 1940. The canon changeth. And in our media-paced era, it might change from month to month—faster at the edges, more slowly at the center, and some of its contents would be connected to events beyond our control. But much of it is within our control and is part of our traditional task of culture making. One reassuring feature of our responsibilities as makers of culture is the implicit and automatic character of most canonical cultural knowledge; we get it through the pores. Another reassuring aspect is its vagueness. How much do I *really* have to know about DNA in order to comprehend a newspaper text directed to the common reader? Not much. Such vagueness in our background knowledge is a feature of cultural literacy that Hilary Putnam has analyzed brilliantly as "the division of linguistic labor." An immensely literate person, Putnam claims that he does not know the difference between a beech tree and an elm. Still, when reading those words he gets along acceptably well because he knows that under the division of linguistic labor somebody in the culture could supply more precise knowledge if it should be needed. Putnam's observation suggests that the school curriculum can be vague enough to leave plenty of room for local choice regarding what things shall be studied in detail, and what things shall be touched on just far enough to get us by. This vagueness in cultural literacy permits a reasonable compromise between lockstep, Napoleonic prescription of texts on the one side, and extreme laissez-faire pluralism on the other. Between these two extremes we have a national responsibility to take stock of the contents of schooling.

Although I have argued that a literate society depends upon 20 shared information, I have said little about what that information should be. This is chiefly a political question. Estimable cultures exist that are ignorant of Shakespeare and the First Amendment. Indeed, estimable cultures exist that are entirely ignorant of reading and writing. On the other hand, no culture exists that is ignorant of its own traditions. In a literate society, culture and cultural literacy are nearly synonymous terms. American culture, always large and heterogeneous, and increasingly lacking a common acculturative curriculum, is perhaps getting fragmented enough to lose its coherence as a culture. Television is perhaps our only national curriculum, despite the justified complaints against it as a partial cause of the literacy decline. My hunch is that this complaint is overstated. The decline in literacy skills, I have suggested, is mainly a result of cultural fragmentation. Within black culture, for instance, blacks are more literate than whites, a point that was demonstrated by Robert L. Williams, as I learned from a recent article on the SAT by Jay Amberg (THE AMERICAN SCHOLAR, Autumn 1982). The big political question that has to be decided is whether we *want* a broadly literate culture that unites our cultural fragments enough to allow us to write to one another and read what our fellow citizens have written. Our traditional, Jeffersonian answer has been yes. But even if that political decision remains the dominant one, as I very much hope, we still face the much more difficult political decision of choosing the contents of cultural literacy.

The answer to this question is not going to be supplied by the- 21 oretical speculation and educational research. It will be worked out, if at all, by discussion, argument, and compromise. Professional educators have understandably avoided this political arena. Indeed, educators should *not* be left to decide so momentous an issue as the canonical contents of our culture. Within a democracy, educational technicians do not want and should not be awarded the function that Plato reserved for philosopher kings. But who is making such decisions at a national level? Nobody, I fear, because we are transfixed by the twin doctrines of pluralism and formalism.

Having made this technical point where I have some expertise, I 22 must now leave any pretense of authority, except as a parent and citizen. The question of guidance for our national school curriculum is a political question on which I have only a citizens's opinion. For my own part, I wish we could have a National Board of Regents— our most successful and admirable body for educational leadership. This imposing body of practical idealists is insulated by law from short-term demagogic pressures. It is a pluralistic group, too, with representation for minority as well as majority cultures. Its influence for good may be gauged by comparing the patterns of SAT scores in New York with those in California, two otherwise comparable states. To give just one example of the Regents' leadership in the field of writing, they have instituted a requirement that no New Yorker can receive a high school diploma before passing a statewide writing test that requires three types of prose composition.

Of course I am aware that the New York Regents have powers 23 that no National Board in this country could possibly gain. But what a National Board could hope to achieve would be the respect of the country, a respect that could give it genuine influence over our schools. Such influence, based on leadership rather than compulsion, would be quite consistent with our federalist and pluralist principles. The Board, for instance, could present broad lists of suggested literary works for the different grades, lists broad enough to yield local freedom but also to yield a measure of commonality in our literary heritage. The teachers whom I know, while valuing their independence, are eager for intelligent guidance in such matters.

But I doubt that such a Curriculum Board would ever be estab- 24 lished in this country. So strong is our suspicion of anything like a central "ministry of culture," that the Board is probably not a politically feasible idea. But perhaps a consortium of universities, or of national associations, or of foundations could make ongoing recommendations that arise from broadly based discussions of the national curriculum. In any case, we need leadership at the national level, and we need specific guidance.

It would be useful, for instance, to have guidance about the 25 *words* that high school graduates ought to know—a lexicon of cultural literacy. I am thinking of a special sort of lexicon that would include not just ordinary dictionary words, but would also include proper names, important phrases, and conventions. Nobody likes word lists as objects of instruction; for one thing, they don't work. But I am not thinking of such a lexicon as an object of instruction. I am thinking of it rather as a guide to objects of instruction. Take the phrase "First Amendment," for instance. That is a lexical item that can hardy be used without bringing in a lot of associated information. Just what *are* the words and phrases that our school graduates should know? Right now, this seems to be decided by the makers of the SAT, which is, as I have mentioned, chiefly a vocabulary test. The educational technicians who choose the words that appear on the SAT are already the implicit makers of our national curriculum. Is then the Educational Testing Service our hidden National Board of Education? Does it sponsor our hidden national curriculum? If so, the ETS is rather to be praised than blamed. For if we wish to raise our national level of literacy, a hidden national curriculum is far better than no curriculum at all.

Where does this leave us? What issues are raised? If I am right in 26 my interpretation of the evidence—and I have seen no alternative interpretation in the literature—then we can only raise our reading and writing skills significantly by consciously redefining and extending our cultural literacy. And yet our current national effort in the schools is largely run on the premise that the best way to proceed is through a culturally neutral, skills-approach to reading and writing. But if skill in writing and in reading comes about chiefly through what I have termed cultural literacy, then radical consequences follow. These consequences are not merely educational but social and political in their scope—and that scope is vast. I shall not attempt to set out these consequences here, but it will be obvious that acting upon them would involve our dismantling and casting aside the leading educational assumptions of the past half century.

EXPLORATIONS

1. How does Hirsch seem to be defining "literacy"?

2. Hirsch asserts that "culture making" is the function of literacy. What kind of culture does Hirsch seem to think we should be making?

3. Choose a college textbook and use some of the following questions to analyze the textbook. Consider the textbook carefully. What does the cover look like? Does the body of the text contain pictures, charts, diagrams? Does it have a preface, appendix, or glossary? What effect does the overall appearance of the textbook have on a reader? Describe the organization of the textbook. How is the information contained in it presented and organized? Sequentially, categorically, hierarchically? Are there sections, subheadings, boldfaced words? Why might the authors of the book have organized it as they did? Based on your analysis of this textbook, what kind of knowledge do you think is most valued in the class in which it is used? And, how does it appear that you are expected to go about learning the information contained in this text?

4. Hirsch claims that "we have a national responsibility to take stock of the contents of schooling." Whom does he mean by "we"?

5. Who is Hirsch's audience? Like many of the writers in Part 3, Hirsch is a college professor; unlike Shirley Brice Heath, Jacqueline Jones Royster, and Jean Anyon, however, he does not use footnotes or provide a list of works cited. Speculate about why this might be so. What does that say about his intended audience and about his purposes in writing this particular essay?

6. Hirsch suggests that there is a body of knowledge that every American must know in order to read and write well. How would such content be determined? Who would decide? What are the political, social, and economic stakes involved in such decisions?

Final Exam: American Renaissance

WILLIAM STAFFORD

William Stafford (1914–1993) was born in Hutchison, Kansas, received his B.A. and M.A. from the University of Kansas, and a Ph.D. from the State University of Iowa in 1955. A professor of English at Lewis and Clark College in Portland, Oregon, Stafford also held other jobs during his lifetime, including several positions with the Church of the Brethren and other peace churches. All these interests as well as the places where he lived appear as major themes in Stafford's poetry and nonfiction. Stafford is known in part for his composition habits; he wrote daily and produced over 30 collections of poetry and nonfiction. In Writing the Australian Crawl: Views of the Writer's Vocation *(1978), Stafford wrote that "A writer is not so much someone who has something to say as he is someone who has found a process that will bring about new things he would not have thought of if he had not started to say them."*

WRITING BEFORE READING

Reflect on multiple choice, fill-in-the-blank, and short answer tests. What do such tests imply about the nature and purpose of learning in schools?

Fill in blanks: Your name is   1
_____ _____ ldo Emerson. Your friend
Thor _____ lives at _____ Pond; he owes
you rent and an ax. Your
neighbor in a house with _____ gables   5
won't respond to another neighbor, Herman
_____, who broods about a whale colored _____
You think it is time for America to _____ .

In a few choice words, tell why.

EXPLORATIONS

1. What kind of "exam" does Stafford describe? Can you "fill in the blanks"? In what sense might filling in the blanks be what the poem is about?

2. Describe the tone Stafford adopts in this poem and its affect on you as a reader and student. What do you think is the point of the poem? Does this tone support this point?

3. What makes this piece of writing a poem rather than an essay? Compare Stafford's poem with Hughes's poem.

4. Remember that Stafford is a poet and a college English professor. What is he spoofing in this poem? In answering this question, try to respond to the last line of the poem. What relationship does this line have to the rest of the poem?

The Banking Concept of Education

PAULO FREIRE

Paulo Freire (pronounced "Frair-uh") was born in 1921 in Recife, Brazil. In the course of his long career as a teacher and a writer, he has served as the secretary of education and general coordinator of the National Plan of Adult Literacy in Brazil, has been a visiting professor at Harvard, and has worked as a consultant to the Office of Education at the World Council of Churches in Geneva, Switzerland. Freire has been a professor of education at Catholic University of Sao Paulo, Brazil, since 1981. Much of his early career was spent working in poverty-stricken areas of Brazil, where he developed methods for teaching illiterate adults to read and write and, in the process, to take power over their own lives by learning to think critically. Freire argues that teachers have a simple choice: They can either work to liberate and humanize their students, or they can work to dominate them. In his view, education should be a collaborative process in which teachers and students work together on an equal footing. "The Banking Concept of Education" is a chapter in what is perhaps his best known book, The Pedagogy of the Oppressed *(1970).*

WRITING BEFORE READING

Would you consider yourself to be an active or a passive student, or does this vary depending on the course or the teacher?

A careful analysis of the teacher-student relationship at any level, 1 inside or outside the school, reveals its fundamentally *narrative* character. This relationship involves a narrating Subject (the teacher) and patient, listening objects (the students). The contents, whether values or empirical dimensions of reality, tend in the process of being narrated to become lifeless and petrified. Education is suffering from narration sickness.

The teacher talks about reality as if it were motionless, static, 2 compartmentalized, and predictable. Or else he expounds on a topic completely alien to the existential experience of the students. His task is to "fill" the students with the contents of his narration— contents which are detached from reality, disconnected from the totality that engendered them and could give them significance.

209

Words are emptied of their concreteness and become a hollow, alienated, and alienating verbosity.

The outstanding characteristic of this narrative education, then,   3
is the sonority of words, not their transforming power. "Four times
four is sixteen; the capital of Pará is Belém." The student records,
memorizes, and repeats these phrases without perceiving what four
times four really means, or realizing the true significance of "capital" in the affirmation "the capital of Pará is Belém," that is, what
Belém means for Pará and what Pará means for Brazil.

Narration (with the teacher as narrator) leads the students to   4
memorize mechanically the narrated content. Worse yet, it turns
them into "containers," into "receptacles" to be "filled" by the
teacher. The more completely he fills the receptacles, the better a
teacher he is. The more meekly the receptacles permit themselves to
be filled, the better students they are.

Education thus becomes an act of depositing, in which the   5
students are the depositories and the teacher issues communiqués
and makes deposits which the students patiently receive, memorize,
and repeat. This is the "banking" concept of education, in which
the scope of action allowed to the students extends only as far as
receiving, filing, and storing the deposits. They do, it is true, have
the opportunity to become collectors or cataloguers of the things
they store. But in the last analysis, it is men themselves who are filed
away through the lack of creativity, transformation, and knowledge
in this (at best) misguided system. For apart from inquiry, apart from
the praxis, men cannot be truly human. Knowledge emerges only
through invention and re-invention, through the restless, impatient,
continuing, hopeful inquiry men pursue in the world, with the
world, and with each other.

In the banking concept of education, knowledge is a gift   6
bestowed by those who consider themselves knowledgeable upon
those whom they consider to know nothing. Projecting an absolute
ignorance onto others, a characteristic of the ideology of oppression,
negates education and knowledge as processes of inquiry. The teacher
presents himself to his students as their necessary opposite; by considering their ignorance absolute, he justifies his own existence. The
students, alienated like the slave in the Hegelian dialectic, accept their
ignorance as justifying the teacher's existence—but, unlike the slave,
they never discover that they educate the teacher.

The *raison d'étre* of libertarian education, on the other hand,   7
lies in its drive towards reconciliation. Education must begin with
the solution of the teacher-student contradiction, by reconciling the
poles of the contradiction so that both are simultaneously teachers
and students.

This solution is not (nor can it be) found in the banking con- 8
cept. On the contrary, banking education maintains and even stimulates the contradiction through the following attitudes and practices,
which mirror oppressive society as a whole:

(a) the teacher teaches and the students are taught;
(b) the teacher knows everything and the students know nothing;
(c) the teacher thinks and the students are thought about;
(d) the teacher talks and the students listen—meekly;
(e) the teacher disciplines and the students are disciplined;
(f) the teacher chooses and enforces his choice, and the students
    comply;
(g) the teacher acts and the students have the illusion of acting
    through the action of the teacher;
(h) the teacher chooses the program content, and the students
    (who were not consulted) adapt to it;
(i) the teacher confuses the authority of knowledge with his own
    professional authority, which he sets in opposition to the free-
    dom of the students;
(j) the teacher is the Subject of the learning process, while the
    pupils are mere objects

It is not surprising that the banking concept of education re- 9
gards men as adaptable, manageable beings. The more students work
at storing the deposits entrusted to them, the less they develop the
critical consciousness which would result from their intervention in
the world as transformers of that world. The more completely they
accept the passive role imposed on them, the more they tend simply
to adapt to the world as it is and to the fragmented view of reality
deposited in them.

The capability of banking education to minimize or annul the 10
students' creative power and to stimulate their credulity serves the
interests of the oppressors, who care neither to have the world
revealed nor to see it transformed. The oppressors use their
"humanitarianism" to preserve a profitable situation. Thus they
react almost instinctively against any experiment in education which
stimulates the critical faculties and is not content with a partial view
of reality but always seeks out the ties which link one point to another and one problem to another.

Indeed, the interests of the oppressors lie in "changing the 11
consciousness of the oppressed, not the situation which oppresses
them";[1] for the more the oppressed can be led to adapt to that situation, the more easily they can be dominated. To achieve this end, the
oppressors use the banking concept of education in conjunction with
a paternalistic social action apparatus, within which the oppressed

receive the euphemistic title of "welfare recipients." They are treated as individual cases, as marginal men who deviate from the general configuration of a "good, organized, and just" society. The oppressed are regarded as the pathology of the healthy society, which must therefore adjust these "incompetent and lazy" folk to its own patterns by changing their mentality. These marginals need to be "integrated," "incorporated" into the healthy society they have "forsaken."

The truth is, however, that the oppressed are not "marginals," 12 are not men living "outside" society. They have always been "inside"—inside the structure which made them "beings for others." The solution is not to "integrate" them into the structure of oppression, but to transform that structure so that they can become "beings for themselves." Such transformation, of course, would undermine the oppressors' purposes; hence their utilization of the banking concept of education to avoid the threat of student *conscientização.*

The banking approach to adult education, for example, will 13 never propose to students that they critically consider reality. It will deal instead with such vital questions as whether Roger gave green grass to the goat, and insist upon the importance of learning that, on the contrary, *Roger* gave green grass to the rabbit. The "humanism" of the banking approach masks the effort to turn men into automatons—the very negation of their ontological vocation to be more fully human.

Those who use the banking approach, knowingly or unknow- 14 ingly (for there are innumerable well-intentioned bank-clerk teachers who do not realize that they are serving only to dehumanize), fail to perceive that the deposits themselves contain contradictions about reality. But, sooner or later, these contradictions may lead formerly passive students to turn against their domestication and the attempt to domesticate reality. They may discover through existential experience that their present way of life is irreconcilable with their vocation to become fully human. They may perceive through their relations with reality that reality is really a *process,* undergoing constant transformation. If men are searchers and their ontological vocation is humanization, sooner or later they may perceive the contradiction in which banking education seeks to maintain them, and then engage themselves in the struggle for their liberation.

But the humanist, revolutionary educator cannot wait for this 15 possibility to materialize. From the outset, his efforts must coincide with those of the students to engage in critical thinking and the quest for mutual humanization. His efforts must be imbued with a profound trust in men and their creative power. To achieve this, he must be a partner of the students in his relations with them.

The banking concept does not admit to such partnership—and 16 necessarily so. To resolve the teacher-student contradiction, to exchange the role of depositor, prescriber, domesticator, for the role of student among students would be to undermine the power of oppression and serve the cause of liberation.

Implicit in the banking concept is the assumption of a dichoto- 17 my between man and the world: man is merely *in* the world, not *with* the world or with others; man is spectator, not re-creator. In this view, man is not a conscious being (*corpo consciente*); he is rather the possessor of *a* consciousness: an empty "mind" passively open to the reception of deposits of reality from the world outside. For example, my desk, my books, my coffee cup, all the objects before me—as bits of the world which surrounds me—would be "inside" me, exactly as I am inside my study right now. This view makes no distinction between being accessible to consciousness and entering consciousness. The distinction, however, is essential: the objects which surround me are simply accessible to my consciousness, not located within it. I am aware of them, but they are not inside me.

It follows logically from the banking notion of consciousness 18 that the educator's role is to regulate the way the world "enters into" the students. His task is to organize a process which already occurs spontaneously, to "fill" the students by making deposits of information which he considers to constitute true knowledge.[2] And since men "receive" the world as passive entities, education should make them more passive still, and adapt them to the world. The educated man is the adapted man, because he is better "fit" for the world. Translated into practice, this concept is well suited to the purposes of the oppressors, whose tranquility rests on how well men fit the world the oppressors have created, and how little they question it.

The more completely the majority adapt to the purposes which 19 the dominant minority prescribe for them (thereby depriving them of the right to their own purposes), the more easily the minority can continue to prescribe. The theory and practice of banking education serve this end quite efficiently. Verbalistic lessons, reading require-ments,[3] the methods for evaluating "knowledge," the distance between the teacher and the taught, the criteria for promotion: everything in this ready-to-wear approach serves to obviate thinking.

The bank-clerk educator does not realize that there is no true 20 security in his hypertrophied role, that one must seek to live *with* others in solidarity. One cannot impose oneself, nor even merely co-exist with one's students. Solidarity requires true communication, and the concept by which such an educator is guided fears and pro-scribes communication.

Yet only through communication can human life hold meaning.   21
The teacher's thinking is authenticated only by the authenticity of
the students' thinking. The teacher cannot think for his students,
nor can he impose his thought on them. Authentic thinking, thinking that is concerned about *reality*, does not take place in ivory tower
isolation, but only in communication. If it is true that thought has
meaning only when generated by action upon the world, the subor-
dination of students to teachers becomes impossible.

Because banking education begins with a false understanding of   22
men as objects, it cannot promote the development of what Fromm
calls "biophily," but instead produces its opposite: "Necrophily. "

> While life is characterized by growth in a structured, functional manner,
> the necrophilous person loves all that does not grow, all that is mechan-
> ical. The necrophilous person is driven by the desire to transform the
> organic into the inorganic, to approach life mechanically, as if all living
> persons were things. . . . Memory, rather than experience; having, rather
> than being, is what counts. The necrophilous person can relate to an
> object—a flower or a person—only if he possesses it; hence a threat to
> his possession is a threat to himself; if he loses possession he loses con-
> tact with the world. . . . He loves control, and in the act of controlling
> he kills life.[4]

Oppression—overwhelming control—is necrophilic; it is nour-   23
ished by love of death, not life. The banking concept of education,
which serves the interests of oppression, is also necrophilic. Based on
a mechanistic, static, naturalistic, spatialized view of consciousness, it
transforms students into receiving objects. It attempts to control
thinking and action, leads men to adjust to the world, and inhibits
their creative power.

When their efforts to act responsibly are frustrated, when they   24
find themselves unable to use their faculties, men suffer. "This suffering due to impotence is rooted in the very fact that the human
equilibrium has been disturbed."[5] But the inability to act which
causes men's anguish also causes them to reject their impotence, by
attempting

> . . . to restore [their] capacity to act. But can [they], and how? One way
> is to submit to and identify with a person or group having power. By
> this symbolic participation in another person's life, [men have] the
> illusion of acting, when in reality [they] only submit to and become a
> part of those who act.[6]

Populist manifestations perhaps best exemplify this type of behav-   25
ior by the oppressed, who, by identifying with charismatic leaders,
come to feel that they themselves are active and effective. The rebellion they express as they emerge in the historical process is motivated

by that desire to act effectively. The dominant elites consider the remedy to be more domination and repression, carried out in the name of freedom, order, and social peace (that is, the peace of the elites). Thus they can condemn—logically, from their point of view—"the violence of a strike by workers and [can] call upon the state in the same breath to use violence in putting down the strike."[7]

Education as the exercise of domination stimulates the credulity of students, with the ideological intent (often not perceived by educators) of indoctrinating them to adapt to the world of oppression. This accusation is not made in the naïve hope that the dominant elites will thereby simply abandon the practice. Its objective is to call the attention of true humanists to the fact that they cannot use banking educational methods in the pursuit of liberation. For they would only negate that very pursuit. Nor may a revolutionary society inherit these methods from an oppressor society. The revolutionary society which practices banking education is either misguided or mistrusting of men. In either event, it is threatened by the specter of reaction.

Unfortunately, those who espouse the cause of liberation are themselves surrounded and influenced by the climate which generates the banking concept, and often do not perceive its true significance or its dehumanizing power. Paradoxically, then, they utilize this same instrument of alienation in what they consider an effort to liberate. Indeed, some "revolutionaries" brand as "innocents," "dreamers," or even "reactionaries" those who would challenge this educational practice. But one does not liberate men by alienating them. Authentic liberation—the process of humanization—is not another deposit to be made in men. Liberation is a praxis: the action and reflection of men upon their world in order to transform it. Those truly committed to the cause of liberation can accept neither the mechanistic concept of consciousness as an empty vessel to be filled, nor the use of banking methods of domination (propaganda, slogans—deposits) in the name of liberation.

Those truly committed to liberation must reject the banking concept in its entirety, adopting instead a concept of men as conscious beings, and consciousness as consciousness intent upon the world. They must abandon the educational goal of deposit-making and replace it with the posing of the problems of men in their relations with the world. "Problem-posing" education, responding to the essence of consciousness—*intentionality*—rejects communiqués and embodies communication. It epitomizes the special characteristic of consciousness: being *conscious of,* not only as intent on objects but as turned in upon itself in a Jasperian "split"—consciousness as consciousness *of* consciousness.

Liberating education consists in acts of cognition, not transfer- 29
rals of information. It is a learning situation in which the cognizable
object (far from being the end of the cognitive act) intermediates the
cognitive actors— teacher on the one hand and students on the
other. Accordingly, the practice of problem-posing education entails
at the outset that the teacher-student contradiction be resolved.
Dialogical relations—indispensable to the capacity of cognitive actors
to cooperate in perceiving the same cognizable object—are otherwise
impossible.

Indeed, problem-posing education, which breaks with the vertical 30
patterns characteristic of banking education, can fulfill its functions
as the practice of freedom only if it can overcome the above contradiction. Through dialogue, the teacher-of-the-students and the
students-of-the-teacher cease to exist and a new term emerges:
teacher-student with students-teachers. The teacher is no longer merely the-one-who-teaches, but one who is himself taught in dialogue
with the students, who in turn while being taught also teach. They
become jointly responsible for a process in which all grow. In this
process, arguments based on "authority" are no longer valid; in order
to function, authority must be *on the side of* freedom, not *against* it.
Here, no one teaches another, nor is anyone self-taught. Men teach
each other, mediated by the world, by the cognizable objects which in
banking education are "owned" by the teacher.

The banking concept (with its tendency to dichotomize every- 31
thing) distinguishes two stages in the action of the educator. During
the first, he cognizes a cognizable object while he prepares his
lessons in his study or his laboratory; during the second, he
expounds to his students about that object. The students are not
called upon to know, but to memorize the contents narrated by the
teacher. Nor do the students practice any act of cognition, since the
object towards which that act should be directed is the property of
the teacher rather than a medium evoking the critical reflection of
both teacher and students. Hence in the name of the "preservation
of culture and knowledge" we have a system which achieves neither
true knowledge nor true culture.

The problem-posing method does not dichotomize the activity 32
of the teacher-student: he is not "cognitive" at one point and
"narrative" at another. He is always "cognitive," whether preparing a project or engaging in dialogue with the students. He does not
regard cognizable objects as his private property, but as the object
of reflection by himself and the students. In this way, the problem-
posing educator constantly re-forms his reflections in the reflection
of the students. The students—no longer docile listeners— are now
critical co-investigators in dialogue with the teacher. The teacher

presents the material to the students for their consideration, and re-considers his earlier considerations as the students express their own. The role of the problem-posing educator is to create, together with the students, the conditions under which knowledge at the level of the *doxa* is superseded by true knowledge, at the level of the *logos.*

Whereas banking education anesthetizes and inhibits creative power, problem-posing education involves a constant unveiling of reality. The former attempts to maintain the *submersion* of consciousness; the latter strives for the *emergence* of consciousness and *critical intervention* in reality. 33

Students, as they are increasingly posed with problems relating to themselves in the world and with the world, will feel increasingly challenged and obliged to respond to that challenge. Because they apprehend the challenge as interrelated to other problems within a total context, not as a theoretical question, the resulting comprehension tends to be increasingly critical and thus constantly less alienated. Their response to the challenge evokes new challenges, followed by new understandings; and gradually the students come to regard themselves as committed. 34

Education as the practice of freedom—as opposed to education as the practice of domination—denies that man is abstract, isolated, independent, and unattached to the world; it also denies that the world exists as a reality apart from men. Authentic reflection considers neither abstract men nor the world without men, but *men in their relations with the world*. In these relations consciousness and world are simultaneous: consciousness neither precedes the world nor follows it. 35

> La conscience et le monde sont dormés d'un même coup: extérieur par essence à la conscience, le monde est, par essence relatif à elle.[8]

In one of our culture circles in Chile, the group was discussing (based on a codification[9]) the anthropological concept of culture. In the midst of the discussion, a peasant who by banking standards was completely ignorant said: "Now I see that without man there is no world." When the educator responded: "Let's say, for the sake of argument, that all the men on earth were to die, but that the earth itself remained, together with trees, birds, animals, rivers, seas, the stars . . . wouldn't all this be a world?" "Oh no," the peasant replied emphatically. "There would be no one to say: 'This is a world'."

The peasant wished to express the idea that there would be lacking the consciousness of the world which necessarily implies the world of consciousness. *I* cannot exist without a *not-I*. In turn, the *not-I* depends on that existence. The world which brings conscious- 36 ness into existence becomes the world *of* that consciousness. Hence, the previously cited affirmation of Sartre: *"La conscience et le monde sont dormés d'un même coup."*

As men, simultaneously reflecting on themselves and on the world, increase the scope of their perception, they begin to direct their observations toward previously inconspicuous phenomena:

> In perception properly so-called, as an explicit awareness [*Gewahren*], I am turned towards the object, to the paper, for instance. I apprehend it as being this here and now. The apprehension is a singling out, every object having a background in experience. Around and about the paper lie books, pencils, ink-well, and so forth, and these in a certain sense are also "perceived," perceptually there, in the "field of intuition"; but whilst I was turned towards the paper there was no turning in their direction, nor any apprehending of them, not even in a secondary sense. They appeared and yet were not singled out, were not posited on their own account. Every perception of a thing has such a zone of background intuitions or background awareness, if "intuiting" already includes the state of being turned towards, and this also is a "conscious experience," or more briefly a "consciousness of" all indeed that in point of fact lies in the co-perceived objective background.[10]

That which had existed objectively but had not been perceived in its deeper implications (if indeed it was perceived at all) begins to "stand out," assuming the character of a problem and therefore of challenge. Thus, men begin to single out elements from their "background awareness" and to reflect upon them. These elements are not objects of men's consideration, and, as such, objects of their actions and cognition.

In problem-posing education, men develop their power to perceive critically *the way they exist* in the world *with which* and *in which* they find themselves; they come to see the world not as a static reality, but as a reality in process, in transformation. Although the dialectical relations of men with the world exist independently of how these relations are perceived (or whether or not they are perceived at all), it is also true that the form of action men adopt is to a large extent a function of how they perceive themselves in the world. Hence, the teacher-student and the students-teachers reflect simultaneously on themselves and the world without dichotomizing this reflection from action, and thus establish an authentic form of thought and action.

Once again, the two educational concepts and practices under analysis come into conflict. Banking education (for obvious reasons) attempts, by mythicizing reality, to conceal certain facts which explain the way men exist in the world; problem-posing education sets itself the task of demythologizing. Banking education resists dialogue; problem-posing education regards dialogue as indispensable to the act of cognition which unveils reality. Banking education treats students as objects of assistance; problem-posing education makes them critical thinkers. Banking education inhibits creativity and domesticates (although it cannot completely destroy) the *intentionality* of consciousness by isolating consciousness from the world, thereby denying men their ontological and historical vocation of becoming more fully human. Problem-posing education bases itself on creativity and stimulates true reflection and action upon reality, thereby responding to the vocation of men as beings who are authentic only when engaged in inquiry and creative transformation. In sum: banking theory and practice, as immobilizing and fixating forces, fail to acknowledge men as historical beings; problem-posing theory and practice take man's historicity as their starting point.

Problem-posing education affirms men as being in the process 40 of *becoming*—as unfinished, uncompleted beings in and with a likewise unfinished reality. Indeed, in contrast to other animals who are unfinished, but not historical, men know themselves to be unfinished; they are aware of their incompletion. In this incompletion and this awareness lie the very roots of education as an exclusively human manifestation. The unfinished character of men and the transformational character of reality necessitate that education be an ongoing activity.

Education is thus constantly remade in the praxis. In order to *be*, 41 it must *become*. Its "duration" (in the Bergsonian meaning of the word) is found in the interplay of the opposites *permanence* and *change*. The banking method emphasizes permanence and becomes reactionary; problem-posing education—which accepts neither a "well-behaved" present nor a predetermined future—roots itself in the dynamic present and becomes revolutionary.

Problem-posing education is revolutionary futurity. Hence it is 42 prophetic (and, as such, hopeful). Hence, it corresponds to the historical nature of man. Hence, it affirms men as beings who transcend themselves, who move forward and look ahead, for whom immobility represents a fatal threat, for whom looking at the past must only be a means of understanding more clearly what and who they are so that they can more wisely build the future. Hence, it identifies with the movement which negates men as being aware of their incompletion—an historical movement which has its point of departure, its Subjects and its objective.

The point of departure of the movement lies in men themselves. 43 But since men do not exist apart from the world, apart from reality, the movement must begin with the men-world relationship. Accordingly, the point of departure must always be with men in the "here and now," which constitutes the situation within which they are submerged, from which they emerge, and in which they intervene. Only by starting from this situation—which determines their perception of it—can they begin to move. To do this authentically they must perceive their state not as fated and unalterable, but merely as limiting—and therefore challenging.

Whereas the banking method directly or indirectly reinforces 44 men's fatalistic perception of their situation, the problem-posing method presents this very situation to them as a problem. As the situation becomes the object of their cognition, the naïve or magical perception which produced their fatalism gives way to perception which is able to perceive itself even as it perceives reality, and can thus be critically objective about that reality.

A deepened consciousness of their situation leads men to 45 apprehend that situation as an historical reality susceptible of transformation. Resignation gives way to the drive for transformation and inquiry, over which men feel themselves to be in control. If men, as historical beings necessarily engaged with other men in a movement of inquiry, did not control that movement, it would be (and is) a violation of men's humanity. Any situation in which some men prevent others from engaging in the process of inquiry is one of violence. The means used are not important; to alienate men from their own decision-making is to change them into objects.

This movement of inquiry must be directed towards humaniza- 46 tion—man's historical vocation. The pursuit of full humanity, however, cannot be carried out in isolation or individualism, but only in fellowship and solidarity; therefore it cannot unfold in the antagonistic relations between oppressors and oppressed. No one can be authentically human while he prevents others from being so. Attempting *to be more* human, individualistically, leads to *having more*, egotistically: a form of dehumanization. Not that it is not fundamental *to have* in order *to be* human. Precisely because it *is* necessary, some men's *having* must not be allowed to constitute an obstacle to others' *having*, must not consolidate the power of the former to crush the latter.

Problem-posing education, as a humanist and liberating praxis, 47 posits as fundamental that men subjected to domination must fight for their emancipation. To that end, it enables teachers and students to become Subjects of the educational process by overcoming authoritarianism and an alienating intellectualism; it also enables men to overcome their false perception of reality. The world—no longer something to be described with deceptive words—becomes the object of that transforming action by men which results in their humanization.

Problem-posing education does not and cannot serve the inter- 48
ests of the oppressor. No oppressive order could permit the
oppressed to begin to question: Why? while only a revolutionary
society can carry out this education in systematic terms, the revolutionary leaders need not take full power before they can employ the
method. In the revolutionary process, the leaders cannot utilize
the banking method as an interim measure, justified on grounds
of expediency, with the intention of *later* behaving in a genuinely
revolutionary fashion. They must be revolutionary—that is to say,
dialogical—from the outset.

NOTES

1 Simone de Beauvoir, *La Pensée de Droite, Aujord'hui* Paris; ST, *El
Pensamiento Politico de la Derecha* (Buenos Aires, 1963), p. 34.
2 This concept corresponds to what Sartre calls the "digestive" or
"nutritive" concept of education, in which knowledge is "fed" by
the teacher to the students to "fill them out." See Jean-Paul Sartre,
"Une idée fundamentale de la phénomenologie de Husserl:
L'internationalité," *Situations* I (Paris, 1947).
3 For example, some professors specify in their reading lists that a book
should be read from pages 10 to 15—and do this to "help" their students!
4 Fromm, *op. cit.*, p. 41.
5 *Ibid.*, p. 31.
6 *Ibid.*
7 Reinhold Niebuhr, *Moral Man and Immoral Society* (New York,
1960), p. 130.
8 Sartre, *op. cit.*, p. 32.
9 See Chapter 3.—Translator's note.
10 Edmund Husserl, *Ideas—General Introduction to Pure
Phenomenology* (London, 1969), pp. 105–106.

EXPLORATIONS

1. Freire says that the traditional classroom is based on the "banking concept of education." What is the banking concept of education? In a
"banking" classroom, what are the roles of the participants?
2. "Problem-posing education" is introduced as the opposite of the
banking concept. What is the purpose of problem-posing education?
What is the problem-posing teacher's role? What are the students'
roles? How are "students" and "teachers" redefined in problem-posing education?
3. In claiming that the teacher is a "subject" while students are
"objects," what is Freire saying about the teacher-student relationship? Consider your definition of "relationship." What is the "rela-

tionship" between teachers and students in "banking" education? How would schools and classrooms be affected if students became "subjects"? How might such a change occur? Who would benefit from such a change? Who wouldn't?

4. The banking concept, Freire says, is an adaptive tool that makes students fill the societal roles assigned to them. Can education *not* be adaptive? Can change occur without adaptation? What might Sylvia Scribner (in Part 1) say about education as adaptation?

5. Freire writes that "Solidarity requires true communication." What is this "solidarity"? What is "true communication" and why is it necessary for the development of solidarity? What, to Freire, does it mean to be "truly human"? How do you define "truly human"? How does this compare with Scribner's "literacy as a state of grace" metaphor?

6. Both Freire and Rose (as well as other writers in Part 3) discuss how education has traditionally worked against the needs of many working-class and other "underprepared" students. What are the attitudes and principles that uphold the traditional system? Is the traditional system as easy to identify as Freire seems to imply?

Perspectives on the Intellectual Tradition of Black Women Writers

JACQUELINE JONES ROYSTER

Jacqueline Jones Royster is an associate professor of English at The Ohio State University. She has published numerous articles on composition, rhetoric, and the history of African-American women. While a professor at Spelman College, she helped to found SAGE: A Scholarly Journal on Black Women, *which was the first journal to provide a forum for critical discussions of issues relating to African-American women and to disseminate new knowledge about them to a broad audience. This essay was first delivered as a speech at the 1988 Right to Literacy Conference, and was published in* The Right to Literacy *in 1990.*

WRITING BEFORE READING

What qualities of character or personality do you associate with someone described as an "intellectual"?

In her 1974 essay "In Search of Our Mothers' Gardens," ₁ Alice Walker issued the scholarly community a challenge, as pointedly articulated in this passage:

> What did it mean for a Black woman to be an artist in our grandmothers' time? In our great-grandmothers' day? It is a question with an answer cruel enough to stop the blood. . . . How was the creativity of the Black woman kept alive, year after year and century after century, when for most of the years Black people have been in America, it was a punishable crime for a Black person to read or write? And the freedom to paint, to sculpt, to expand the mind with action did not exist. Consider, if you can bear to imagine it, what might have been the result if singing, too, had been forbidden by law. Listen to the voices of Bessie Smith, Billie Holiday, Nina Simone, Robert Flack, and Aretha Franklin, among others, and imagine those voices muzzled for life. (233–34)

Walker paints a provocative image of the creative and intellectual ₂ impulses of African American women and raises questions that cut to the core of concepts like justice, equity, empowerment, and the actualization of potential. What she demonstrates through this milestone literary event is that—despite the bonds of slavery, despite laws that forbade basic literacy skills, despite incomprehensible barriers in all dimensions of their lives—black women were still bold enough to keep raising their voices. And, despite a myth that still dies hard, many of them wrote down their words. By doing so, they helped fashion a creative and intellectual authority, a garden that has yielded models of productivity and achievement for black women who are continuing to define and redefine intellectual possibilities.

Worth noting is the rarity of encountering the words *intellectu-* 3 *al* and *black women* in the same sentence. The rarity, though, is not the fault of black women. It is the fault of entrenched systems of racism, sexism, and classism that do not permit justice, equity, or the freedom to see worth and value from whichever quarter they arise. Consequently, any analysis of the lives and the achievements of black women but clearly an analysis of their intellectual tradition must provide a conscious crediting of the effects of interlocking systems of oppression.

When we look with an informed eye at the ways in which black 4 women have used writing over time, it should be immediately obvious that there was a struggle for basic literacy. All black people had to struggle for the right to learn, for the right to have access to the tools of learning, of empowerment, of privilege. Black women have had to struggle in desperation not just against racist and economic barriers but also against sexist barriers. Even so, a historical view of the ways in which African American women have used writing assures us that we are not looking at just a struggle for basic literacy. Over the centuries, there has been more going on in what black women write than just novice beginnings, practice, or five-finger exercises in thought and expression. In acknowledging a literacy continuum that distinguishes between the basically literate and those who accomplish stellar feats in using their literacy skills, we see that black women have gone well beyond the first spirals of hierarchical notions of literacy. They have established themselves not just as readers and writers but as master artisans and visionaries—that is, they belong to the central traditions of the literate world at its best.

In trying to establish a firm basis for making such an assertion, we 5 can look synchronically at the diverse literary achievements of contemporary black women writers to identify connections across their lives and works, and we can look at the diverse literary achievements of black women historically. In addition, we can look diachronically at the resonating threads that speak to connections among current achievements, lives, conditions, and circumstances and their antecedents. With such information, we can begin to reconstruct a full image of our mothers' gardens—that is, the origins of the creative and intellectual authority of black women writers, as Hazel V. Carby has done in her pacesetting analysis, *Reconstructing Womanhood: The Emergence of the Afro-American Woman Novelist.*

The collective visions of writers like Gwendolyn Brooks, Alice　6
Walker, Toni Morrison, Gloria Naylor, Paule Marshall, and Lorraine
Hansberry have demonstrated that black women have a unique view
and understanding of the human condition. They have chronicled
lives, perspectives, and circumstances in ways that we have not known
before. As evidenced by their receiving of prestigious awards and
prizes in the literary world, black women writers are acknowledged as
among the best writers in the United States, even in the world. They
have a way with words, and both popular and scholarly critics have
hailed these days to be a renaissance for black women writers.

In the tradition of scholarship, the acknowledgment of a renais-　7
sance carries with it an imperative to be mindful that nothing
happens in a vacuum. The imperative dictates that we must search for
origins, foundations, precedents, and foreshadowings, so that we
have a substantive sense of what the renaissance is. These women did
not spring forth from nothing and nowhere. Instead, they have been
instrumental in continuing a creative trust, a tradition established by
earlier black women writers. They join their predecessors in forming
a continuous community of creativity and productivity from the
1700s to the present.

The voices of African American women have been a part of the　8
American literary scene since the days of the black and unknown
bards of spirituals and folklore, although they have not always been
credited. As Louis Gates, Jr., and Ann Allen Shockley have pointed
out, black women launched the African American literate tradition:
Phillis Wheatley with the first volume of poetry in 1773; Ann Plato
with the first book of essays in 1841; Harriet E. Wilson with the first
novel in 1859; Frances Ellen Watkins Harper with the first short
story during that same year; Frances Anne Rollins, using the pseudonym Frank A. Rollins, with the first biography in 1868; and so on.
Over the centuries the voices of black women have been raised and,
within marginalized contexts, occasionally have been heard, though
categorized most often as minor voices, not major ones. This cate-
gorization was created and continues to exist in spite of a rising
mound of evidence documenting the critical roles that black women
have filled socially, culturally, and artistically.

Regardless of how others have seen them and their efforts,　9
however, over the centuries black women have demonstrated systematically the central place that literacy has held in their lives. They
have continued to write. They have articulated lives and conditions
with courage, compassion, insight. They have offered to the world
more than it has been willing to receive.

In essence, though, black women writers have for all practical　10
purposes met the same fate as other women. They have been

ignored, disregarded, marginalized, trampled, neglected, devalued, and forgotten. After all, as Mary Helen Washington contends,

> What we have to recognize is that the creation of the fiction of tradition is a matter of power, not justice, and that that power has always been in the hands of men—mostly white but some black. Women are the disinherited. (xvii–xviii)

For no one is that statement more true than for black women.

What does this perspective indicate about the intellectual capacities of black women or about them not just as creative beings but as intellectual beings who engage in activities that demonstrate the higher literacy skills of problem finding and problem solving? How have they contributed to the world of ideas and the progress of humanity in understanding ourselves and the universe? What is the tradition of black feminist thought? 11

To see and to understand the tradition of black women's intellectualism, we must enrich our definitions of *tradition*, *literacy*, and *intellectualism*, and then we must use this enriched vision to look again at the historical evidence of the ways in which black women have used their literacy. This framework can help us distinguish the significant threads and begin a thorough documentation of the nature of black women's intellectualism. 12

Tradition is defined by *Webster's Ninth New Collegiate Dictionary* as 13

> **1:** an inherited, established, or customary pattern of thought, action, or behavior (as a religious practice or a social custom) **2:** the handing down of information, beliefs, and customs by word of mouth or by example from one generation to another without instruction **3:** cultural continuity in social attitudes and institutions **4:** characteristic manner, method, or style.

Such definitions, however, do not go far enough in establishing what manner of circumstance a tradition is. What does it mean to claim a history? How are we empowered to see patterns and to assign value? By what manner and mechanisms are we authorized to count time or to credit experience?

Historically, the institutions of power and prestige have not afforded the experiences and contributions of black women the privilege of being considered for entry into a dialogue on historical or traditional values and contributions. The assumption was that there is no such history, no such tradition, no such value, and, of course, no such contributions. Consequently, the claiming of the status of tradition for black women's intellectualism is an act that goes radically against the tide. It is an act of empowerment. The power comes from having access to what Deirdre David terms "intellectual ancestry " 14

(226). Emphatically, contemporary black women writers did not just spring forth; they evolved from prior communities of remarkably active women who created, preserved, nurtured, and passed along a rich legacy of habits of mind, spirit, and action.

The process of revealing the tradition of black feminist thought is   15 a process of placing the historical events of black women's intellectually based activities within the meaningful scheme of their lives. It means coming to an understanding of their particular habits of mind, spirit, and action, and it means demonstrating that these particular events are recurrent, reflective, resonant and that there are echoes and reverberations throughout the totality of their experiences in this country.

At this point, we can place the definition of *tradition* against   16 predominant visions of literacy. Too often, definitions of *literacy* are simplistic, referring generally to the ability to read and write as isolated activities. These definitions often do not take into account the complexities of the context in which literacy acts take place. Fortunately, the efforts of scholar-activists like Paolo Freire and Geneva Smitherman are bringing light to the dialogue, but threads recognizing the implications of narrow frames for concepts like literacy are not new. For example, during the struggle for women's suffrage and in response particularly to literacy requirements for the right to vote, Sojourner Truth said, "You know, children, I don't read such small stuff as letters, I read men and nations" (Lowenberg and Bogin 239). Truth could not read or write texts, but she did see that being unlettered does not automatically indicate an inability to think or to understand or to operate rationally. What her statement implies is that one set of tools for reading was not available to her, but other tools were, and she was able to use the available tools with power and authority.

From this point of departure, our visions of literacy can   17 be enriched. As Jerrie Cobb Scott has conceptualized it, literacy includes at the core our ways of knowing, our multisensory ways of coming to awareness. It means developing the ability to gain access to information—for example, by being able to read, write, and see what is there and not there—and also developing the ability to use the information well, as in analytically and creatively finding and solving problems. It is more than deciphering and producing little letters on a page. Literacy is the skill, the process, the practice of "reading" and being articulate about "men and nations," which is more than just simplistic, isolated decoding and encoding skills.

Sojourner Truth was not literate enough to read "such small   18 stuff as letters," but she was able to see what was there and not there, to grapple with complex situations, and to emerge as a rational and capable thinker. With the changing literacy demands of current cultural contexts, however, becoming literate does mean gaining the skills to read and to write; beyond that, it also means taking the power and the authority to know in multisensory ways and to act with authority based on that knowing. Knowledge is indeed power. In our day and time, literacy is indeed power. It allows us, as Mary Helen Washington weaves the notion throughout much of her analysis of black women writers, to write ourselves into being and, by doing so, to claim creative and intellectual power over information and experience. Like the claiming of a tradition, a move toward literacy is a political act.

Next is the pivotal centerpiece of black feminist thought, the   19 concept of intellectualism. The politics of tradition claiming and the politics of literacy, with their ties to power and empowerment, often pale against the politics of claiming the self as an intellectual being. *Webster's Ninth New Collegiate Dictionary* defines *intellect* as

> **1a:** the power of knowing as distinguished from the power to feel and to will: the capacity for knowledge **b:** the capacity for rational or intelligent thought esp. when highly developed **2:** a person with great intellectual powers.

A contrasting view of intellectualism has been put forth by other scholars. bell hooks explains that the intellectual is a whole person, one centered in a life of the spirit, body, and mind and one who brings the possibility of wholeness and nonfragmentation to bear on experience, integrating intellect and passion. This more holistic view of intellectualism does not allow for the separation of analytical and creative thought from an ethical core or physical existence. This view takes into account what Lowenberg and Bogin explain as "psychic wholeness," from which a person is able to fashion an inner core that is capable of being used to "take soundings, establish directions, discern the self"—in other words, to operate as an intellectual being (8–14, 9).

The lives of black women in America are a testament to   20 "psychic wholeness," to the way in which the experience of fragmentation, particularly the horrors and the remnants of the institution of slavery, can be defeated by persistence, resiliency, and an ability to remain whole. As Paula Giddings points out, black women were able to emerge from fragmentation, "whole, courageous, and loving." They were also able to emerge moving and shaking the world around them. If we start with the documentary evidence of the nineteenth century, text after text demonstrates that black women put their minds to the task of living lives after slavery, envisioning wide-ranging possibilities, creating multifaceted options, conceptualizing ways of reifying ideas and ideals, and putting thought into action.

If we examine the body of nineteenth- and early twentieth- 21 century texts that are becoming available, we can easily see patterns emerging that highlight the tradition of black feminist thought. These women played critical roles as the interpreters and as the articulators of experiences. They had a penchant for contextualizing and centering pieces of the puzzle of black people's lives in the United States that did not fit. They had the capacity to imagine doable things within adverse circumstances. They were committed to putting thought into meaningful action, doing so in response to issues related to the abolition of slavery and racism and to education, economic opportunity, religion, lynchings, women's rights, the moral integrity of black women. Generally, they were the champions of truth, justice, and equality. They transmitted black American culture as mothers (actual and fictive), teachers, and social activists. They demonstrated a fully developed range of intellectual activity. In an adaptation of Joseph Williams's definition of critical thinking (Royster 3), they looked at the world, saw what was there and not there, were articulate about their visions of reality, and worked tirelessly to get things done that they thought would bring their ideals to life.

The validation for these assertions lies in the indisputable 22 evidence of the lives of the women who set the standard. Fortunately, we know about their activities, their thoughts, and their feelings because they wrote them down. Some of them chose to express themselves through creative writing: Lucy Terry, Phillis Wheatley, Sarah Forten, and Harriet E. Wilson, each of whom wrote before 1860, and Frances E. W. Harper, Alice Dunbar Nelson, and Pauline Hopkins, each of whom were first published before 1900. Through poetry, short stories, plays, and novels, these early black women writers raised the banner of sociopolitical activism, condemning the injustice and the inequities of racist, sexist, and economic oppressions. They expressed themselves beautifully and insightfully on the misery and the misfortune of black people and on their strength and beauty. They used their writing to appreciate the people and the world around them, to discover personal identity by race and gender, to define and label relationships, to address sociocultural issues, to respond to power, and to offer solutions to pressing problems. From this body of texts, we have much to learn about black women's ways of knowing, thinking, and operating.

In their creative works, writers take on the facades of character, 23 persona, and narrator, distancing themselves from their texts by the fact of the fiction-ness, regardless of the representativeness of the creative vision. In contrast, in their nonfiction works, writers have the privilege of speaking more candidly as themselves and not just as their creative-intellectual inventions. Fortunately, in documenting the tradition of black women's intellectualism, we have the advantage of a relatively large pool of nonfiction texts. Whether as creative writers or as writers of nonfiction prose, black women established their intellectual worth through persistent and courageous action. They spoke up and out, and they spoke often.

Like Sojourner Truth, several black women made speeches to 24 carry the abolitionist message (see Quarles), but not all were unlettered, like Truth. The first black female public speaker was Maria Stewart in 1832 (see Giddings, *When and Where I enter;* Quarles). A freeborn woman from Connecticut, Stewart was sponsored by the Afric-American Female Intelligence Society of Boston, one of the early black female literary societies (see Porter). Against societal norms, this organization boldly invited not just a woman but a black woman to speak before a mixed audience of men and women on the substantive issues of civil and women's rights. This act made Stewart the first American- born woman to give public speeches and to leave extant copies of the texts. According to Giddings, Stewart's speeches "articulated the precepts upon which the future activism of Black women would be based. Her ideas reflected both the fundamentals of the Victorian ethic and criticism of its inherent biases" (*When and Where* 50). Stewart was followed by Nancy Prince, Harriet Tubman, Sarah Parker Remond, Sojourner Truth, Frances Ellen Watkins Harper, Ida Wells-Barnett, Fannie Barrier Williams, and a continuing cadre of others (Lowenberg and Bogin 6).

Despite these individual achievements, however, literacy was still 25 exceptional. The struggle for educational opportunities was constant. In the racist and sexist realities of the nineteenth- and early twentieth-century publishing world, there was a critical lack of systems and resources designed to nurture talent among women generally and black women in particular. As Anna Julia Cooper—who was born a slave but who became a scholar, an educator, a pioneer in the black club women's movement, and a social activist—wrote, "I constantly felt (as I suppose many an ambitious girl has felt) a thumping from within unanswered by any beckoning from without" (76). In *A Voice from the South,* published in 1892, Cooper appeals to American society to make, in her words, "not the boys less, but the girls more" (79). As a single text, *A Voice from the South* remains Cooper's most representative effort, and it stands today as one of the earliest and best historical resources for black feminist thought. It give much sustenance to the contemplative mind and challenges any scholar who may question the historical depth of an intellectual tradition for black American women.

In a section of the book entitled "The Status of Woman in   26
America," Cooper explains that even her black male contempo-
raries—who, she believed, should be more sensitive to the conditions
of black women and more supportive of their efforts—would not
admit a need for the voice of black women. She presents a long list
of social and economic debates in American life from which black
women are excluded. While Cooper identifies the political advantage
of men, she also points out that

> politics, and surely American politics, is hardly a school for great minds.
> Sharpening rather than deepening, it develops the faculty of taking
> advantage of present emergencies rather than the insight to distinguish
> between the true and the false, the lasting and the ephemeral advantage.
> Highly cultivated selfishness rather than consecrated benevolence is its
> passport to success. (137)

Her insightful argument is grounded in both a breadth and a depth
of knowledge. Her words are rationally ordered and developed. Her
language is powerful, and her images are compelling. Most of all, her
insights are fired by her belief in her position. The book is her
attempt to help a troubled nation see its problems more clearly and
her attempt to offer solutions that she believed to be reasonable and
productive.

In Cooper's estimation, "The world has had to limp along   27
with the wobbling gait and one-sided hesitancy of a man with one
eye" (122), with the bandaged eye symbolizing the feminine
perspective. She speaks of black women as the "muffled chord," the
"mute and voiceless note" (i), and she insists that they be heard:

> The colored woman, then, should not be ignored because her bark is
> resting in the silent waters of the sheltered cove. She is watching the
> movements of the contestants none the less and is all the better quali-
> fied, perhaps, to weigh and judge and advise because not herself in the
> excitement of the race. Her voice, too, has always been heard in clear,
> unfaltering tones, ringing the changes on those deeper interests which
> make for permanent good. (138)

A Voice from the South, as the preeminent historical text in   28
black feminist thought, is enlightening, but Cooper was not the only
early standard-bearer of this intellectual tradition. Our visions of the
history of black women's literacy and intellectualism can benefit
even more from an examination of a wide-ranging body of early
texts. The list of women who wrote speeches, essays, journals,
biographies, autobiographies, and newspaper and magazine articles
is an impressive one that includes, in addition to the names mentioned earlier, Charlotte Forten Grimké, Lucy Craft Laney, Fanny
Jackson Coppin, Amanda Berry Smith, Mary Church Terrell,

Josephine St. Pierre Ruffin, Nanny Burroughs, and Amy Jacques Garvey.

In producing both creative and nonfiction texts, these early 29 black women writers passed on the intellectual torch. They demonstrated by their examples what it means to live a committed life, what it means to think and to act from the same body, to operate with reason, passion, and compassion. They gave evidence of the creativity and the productivity of an attitude that nurtures not only the notion of being thoughtful and rational but also the notion of the obligation to act in ways that make a positive difference in the lives of human beings.

A major dimension of their intellectual legacy is the notion of 30 psychic wholeness. As a culture, we have reaped the rewards of this wholeness. We have benefited from their thoughts and actions, as evidenced, for example, by the number of their social, economic, and political programs that have changed, often in unacknowledged ways, the course of our modern lives. We have failed, however, to give credit to the quality of their intellectual, creative, and socially conscious vision.

At the 1851 Women's Rights Convention in Akron, Ohio, 31 Sojourner Truth said:

> they talk about this thing in the head; what's this they call it? ["Intellect," whispered someone near.] That's it, honey. What's that got to do with women's rights or negro rights? If my cup won't hold but a pint, and yours holds a quart, wouldn't you be mean not to let me have my little half-measure full? (Lowenberg and Bogin 236)

Similarly, in *A Voice from the South*, Cooper urges the nation to forget about the problem of race and to concentrate on encouraging all members of the races to do their best. She says:

> God and time will work the problem. You and I are only to stand for the quantities *at their best*, which he means for us to represent . . . and so if a few are determined to be white—amen, so be it; but don't let them argue as if there were no part to be played in life by black men and black women, and as if to become white were the sole specific and panacea for all the ills that flesh is heir to—the universal solvent for all America's irritations. (171–72)

Today especially, we need the full potential of all our diverse 32 citizenry, male and female, regardless of race, creed, color, cultural orientation, or background. What is certain is that, to take advantage of these wide-ranging possibilities, we must have the types of mental constructs that allow the envisioning of human diversity as a positive and productive fact of contemporary life. In the case of black women's literacy and intellectualism, the evidence speaks for itself.

Black women have offered to this culture more than just a "half-measure." If we can right the injustice of their exclusion from intellectual domains, the process of our rectification may allow us to envision more productively other persons whom we now categorize as marginal, nontraditional, or illiterate.

Another of Cooper's statements in 1892 is all the more relevant [33] for us almost a century later: "We need men and women who do not exhaust their genius splitting hairs on aristocratic distinctions and thanking God they are not as others" (33). At this critical point in our nation's history, we need people to recognize that difference and diversity constitute opportunities for richness and that the acknowledgment of any potential does not lessen the value of the whole but strengthens it.

WORKS CITED

Carby, Hazel V. *Reconstructing Womanhood: The Emergence of the Afro-American Woman Novelist.* New York: Oxford UP, 1987.

Cooper, Anna Julia. *A Voice from the South.* New York: Oxford UP, 1988.

David, Deirdre. *Intellectual Women and Victorian Patriarchy: Harriet Martineau, Elizabeth Barrett Browning, George Eliot.* Ithaca: Cornell UP, 1987.

Freire, Paolo. *Pedagogy of the Oppressed.* New York: Continuum, 1988.

Gates, Henry Louis, Jr. "Foreword: In Her Own Write." Cooper vii–xxii.

Giddings, Paula. Panelist. Forum on Black Women's Intellectualism. Spelman College. Atlanta, 24 Nov. 1986. Forum proceedings forthcoming. *Sage: A Scholarly Journal on Black Women.*

——. *When and Where I Enter: The Impact of Black Women on Race and Sex in America.* New York: Morrow, 1984.

hooks, bell. Panelist. Forum on Black Women's Intellectualism. Spelman College. Atlanta, 24 Nov. 1986. Forum proceedings forthcoming. *Sage: A Scholarly Journal on Black Women.*

Lowenberg, Bert J., and Ruth Bogin, eds. *Black Women in Nineteenth Century American Life: Their Words, Their Thoughts, Their Feelings.* University Park: Pennsylvania State UP, 1976.

Porter, Dorothy. "The Organized Educational Activities of Negro Literary Societies, 1828–1846." *Journal of Negro Education* 5.4 (1936): 555–76.

Quarles, Benjamin. *Black Abolitionists.* New York: Oxford UP, 1969.

Royster, Jacqueline Jones. *Critical Thinking Pilot Project: Summary Report.* Atlanta: Spelman Coll. Comprehensive Writing Program, 1987.

Scott, Jerrie Cobb. Coordinator. A Literacy across the Disciplines Workshop for Faculty and Administrators. Central State University. Wilberforce, Ohio, 28 Jan. 1988.

234 PART THREE: *Academic Literacies*

Scott, Jerrie Cobb, and Bing Davis. "A Picture Is Worth a Thousand Words: The Visual-Print Connection." *Dialogue: Arts in the Midwest* (Nov.-Dec. 1989): 19–21.

Shockley, Ann Allen. *Afro-American Women Writers, 1746–1933.* Boston: Hall, 1988.

Smitherman, Geneva. "Toward a National Public Policy on Language." *College English* 49.1 (1987): 29–36.

Walker, Alice. "In Search of Our Mothers' Garden." *In Search of Our Mothers' Gardens.* New York: Harcourt, 1983. 231–243.

Washington, Mary Helen. *Invented Lives: Narratives of Black Women 1860–1960.* Garden City: Anchor, 1987.

Webster's Ninth New Collegiate Dictionary. 1986 edition.

EXPLORATIONS

1. How does Royster define "literacy"? Compare her definition with Hirsch's. Do you see similarities or differences? Explain.

2. How does Royster define "intellectual"? In what ways does her definition differ from the dictionary definition?

3. How does Royster work against dictionary definitions in order to develop her ideas about literacy and intellectualism?

4. What are Royster's purposes in writing this essay? Where, in the text, does she make her purposes clear?

5. How does Royster establish her authority as a writer?

Confronting Class in the Classroom

BELL HOOKS

bell hooks (1955–) is the pen name of Gloria Watkins; "bell hooks" was the name of her great-grandmother, whose wisdom Watkins wanted to honor. She is currently Distinguished Professor of English at City College in New York. Her work has explored how factors such as African-American womanhood, feminism, the civil rights movement, and critical theory clash in the world at large and in her own life. Responses to her essays and books have included both high praise and stark controversy. In "Confronting Class in the Classroom," which appeared in Teaching to Transgress *in 1994, hooks asks us to address how class boundaries and conflicts affect and are affected by what happens in college and university classrooms.*

WRITING BEFORE READING

In what social class would you place yourself? In what ways does this classification shape the way that you view society?

Class is rarely talked about in the United States; nowhere is there 1 a more intense silence about the reality of class differences than in educational settings. Significantly, class differences are particularly ignored in classrooms. From grade school on, we are all encouraged to cross the threshold of the classroom believing we are entering a democratic space—a free zone where the desire to study and learn makes us all equal. And even if we enter accepting the reality of class differences, most of us still believe knowledge will be meted out in fair and equal proportions. In those rare cases where it is acknowledged that students and professors do not share the same class backgrounds, the underlying assumption is still that we are all equally committed to getting ahead, to moving up the ladder of success to the top. And even though many of us will not make it to the top, the unspoken understanding is that we will land somewhere in the middle, between top and bottom.

Coming from a nonmaterially privileged background, from the 2 working poor, I entered college acutely aware of class. When I received notice of my acceptance at Stanford University, the first question that was raised in my household was how I would pay for it. My parents understood that I had been awarded scholarships, and allowed to take out loans, but they wanted to know where the money would come from for transportation, clothes, books. Given these concerns, I went to Stanford thinking that class was mainly about materiality. It only took me a short while to understand that class was more than just a question of money, that it shaped values, attitudes, social relations, and the biases that informed the way knowledge would be given and received. These same realizations about class in the academy are expressed again and again by academics from working-class backgrounds in the collection of essays *Strangers in Paradise* edited by Jake Ryan and Charles Sackrey.

During my college years it was tacitly assumed that we all agreed that class should not be talked about, that there would be no critique of the bourgeois class biases shaping and informing pedagogical process (as well as social etiquette) in the classroom. Although no one ever directly stated the rules that would govern our conduct, it was taught by example and reinforced by a system of rewards. As silence and obedience to authority were most rewarded, students learned that this was the appropriate demeanor in the classroom. Loudness, anger, emotional outbursts, and even something as seemingly innocent as unrestrained laughter were deemed unacceptable, vulgar disruptions of classroom social order. These traits were also associated with being a member of the lower classes. If one was not from a privileged class group, adopting a demeanor similar to that of the group could help one to advance. It is still necessary for students to assimilate bourgeois values in order to be deemed acceptable.

Bourgeois values in the classroom create a barrier, blocking the possibility of confrontation and conflict, warding off dissent. Students are often silenced by means of their acceptance of class values that teach them to maintain order at all costs. When the obsession with maintaining order is coupled with the fear of "losing face," of not being thought well of by one's professor and peers, all possibility of constructive dialogue is undermined. Even though students enter the "democratic" classroom believing they have the right to "free speech," most students are not comfortable exercising this right to "free speech." Most students are not comfortable exercising this right—especially if it means they must give voice to thoughts, ideas, feelings that go against the grain, that are unpopular. This censoring process is only one way bourgeois values overdetermine social behavior in the classroom and undermine the democratic exchange of ideas. Writing about his experience in the section of *Strangers in Paradise* entitled "Outsiders," Karl Anderson confessed:

Power and hierarchy, and not teaching and learning, dominated the graduate school I found myself in. "Knowledge" was one-upmanship, and no one disguised the fact. . . . The one thing I learned absolutely was the inseparability of free speech and free thought. I, as well as some of my peers, were refused the opportunity to speak and sometimes to ask questions deemed "irrelevant" when the instructors didn't wish to discuss or respond to them.

Students who enter the academy unwilling to accept without question the assumptions and values held by privileged classes tend to be silenced, deemed troublemakers.

Conservative discussions of censorship in contemporary university settings often suggest that the absence of constructive dialogue, enforced silencing, takes place as a by-product of progressive efforts to question canonical knowledge, critique relations of domination, or subvert bourgeois class biases. There is little or no discussion of the way in which the attitudes and values of those from materially privileged classes are imposed upon everyone via biased pedagogical strategies. Reflected in choice of subject matter and the manner in which ideas are shared, these biases need never be overtly stated. In his essay Karl Anderson states that silencing in "the most oppressive aspect of middle-class life." He maintains; 5

> It thrives upon people keeping their mouths shut, unless they are actually endorsing whatever powers exist. The free marketplace of "ideas" that is so beloved of liberals is as much a fantasy as a free marketplace in oil or automobiles; a more harmful fantasy, because it breeds even more hypocrisy and cynicism. Just as teachers can control what is said in their classrooms, most also have ultra-sensitive antennae as to what will be rewarded or punished that is said outside them. And these antennae control them.

Silencing enforced by bourgeois values is sanctioned in the classroom by everyone.

Even those professors who embrace the tenets of critical pedagogy (many of whom are white and male) still conduct their classrooms in a manner that only reinforces bourgeois models of decorum. At the same time, the subject matter taught in such classes might reflect professorial awareness of intellectual perspectives that critique domination, that emphasize an understanding of the politics of difference, of race, class, gender, even though classroom dynamics remain conventional, business as usual. When contemporary feminist movement made its initial presence felt in the academy there was both an ongoing critique of conventional classroom dynamics and an attempt to create alternative pedagogical strategies. However, as feminist scholars endeavored to make Women's Studies a discipline administrators and peers would respect, there was a shift in perspective. 6

Significantly, feminist classrooms were the first spaces in the   7
university where I encountered any attempt to acknowledge class
difference. The focus was usually on the way class differences were
structured in the larger society, not on our class position. Yet the
focus on gender privilege in patriarchal society often meant that
there was a recognition of the ways women were economically
disenfranchised and therefore more likely to be poor or working
class. Often, the feminist classroom was the only place where
students (mostly female) from materially disadvantaged circumstances would speak from that class positionality, acknowledging
both the impact of class on our social status as well as critiquing the
class biases of feminist thought.

When I first entered university settings I felt estranged from this   8
new environment. Like most of my peers and professors, I initially
believed those feelings were there because of differences in racial and
cultural background. However, as time passed it was more evident
that this estrangement was in part a reflection of class difference. At
Stanford, I was often asked by peers and professors if I was there on
a scholarship. Underlying this question was the implication that
receiving financial aid "diminished" one in some way. It was not just
this experience that intensified my awareness of class difference, it was
the constant evocation of materially privileged class experience (usually that of the middle class) as a universal norm that not only set
those of us from working-class backgrounds apart but effectively
excluded those who were not privileged from discussions, from social
activities. To avoid feelings of estrangement, students from working-
class backgrounds could assimilate into the mainstream, change
speech patterns, points of reference, drop any habit that might reveal
them to be from a nonmaterially privileged background.

Of course I entered college hoping that a university degree   9
would enhance my class mobility. Yet I thought of this solely in economic terms. Early on I did not realize that class was much more
than one's economic standing, that it determined values, standpoint, and interests. It was assumed that any student coming from a
poor or working-class background would willingly surrender all values and habits of being associated with this background. Those of us
from diverse ethnic/racial backgrounds learned that no aspect of our
vernacular culture could be voiced in elite settings. This was especially the case with vernacular language or a first language that was
not English. To insist on speaking in any manner that did not conform to privileged class ideals and mannerisms placed one always in
the position of interloper.

Demands that individuals from class backgrounds deemed unde-   10
sirable surrender all vestiges of their past create psychic turmoil. We

were encouraged, as many students are today, to betray our class origins. Rewarded if we chose to assimilate, estranged if we chose to maintain those aspects of who we were, some were all too often seen as outsiders. Some of us rebelled by clinging to exaggerated manners and behavior clearly marked as outside the accepted bourgeois norm. During my student years, and now as a professor, I see many students from "undesirable" class backgrounds become unable to complete their studies because the contradictions between the behavior necessary to "make it" in the academy and those that allowed them to be comfortable at home, with their families and friends, are just too great.

Often, African Americans are among those students I teach from 11 poor and working-class backgrounds who are most vocal about issues of class. They express frustration, anger, and sadness about the tensions and stress they experience trying to conform to acceptable white, middle-class behaviors in university settings while retaining the ability to "deal" at home. Sharing strategies for coping from my own experience, I encourage students to reject the notion that they must choose between experiences. They must believe they can inhabit comfortably two different worlds, but they must make each space one of comfort. They must creatively invent ways to cross borders. They must believe in their capacity to alter the bourgeois settings they enter. All too often, students from nonmaterially privileged backgrounds assume a position of passivity—they behave as victims, as though they can only be acted upon against their will. Ultimately, they end up feeling they can only reject or accept the norms imposed upon them. This either/or often sets them up for disappointment and failure.

Those of us in the academy from working-class backgrounds are 12 empowered when we recognize our own agency, our capacity to be active participants in the pedagogical process. This process is not simple or easy: it takes courage to embrace a vision of wholeness of being that does not reinforce the capitalist version that suggests that one must always give something up to gain another. In the introduction to the section of their book titled "Class Mobility and Internalized Conflict," Ryan and Sackrey remind readers that "the academic work process is essentially antagonistic to the working class, and academics for the most part live in a different world of culture, different ways that make it, too, antagonistic to working class life." Yet those of us from working-class backgrounds cannot allow class antagonism to prevent us from gaining knowledge, degrees and enjoying the aspects of higher education that are fulfilling. Class antagonism can be constructively used, not made to reinforce the notion that students and professors from working-class backgrounds are "outsiders" and "interlopers," but to subvert and challenge the existing structure.

When I entered my first Women's Studies classes at Stanford, 13 white professors talked about "women" when they were making the experience of materially privileged white women a norm. It was both a matter of personal and intellectual integrity for me to challenge this biased assumption. By challenging, I refused to be complicit in the erasure of black and/or working-class women of all ethnicities. Personally, that meant I was not able just to sit in class, grooving on the good feminist vibes—that was a loss. The gain was that I was honoring the experience of poor and working-class women in my own family, in that very community that had encouraged and supported me in my efforts to be better educated. Even though my intervention was not wholeheartedly welcomed, it created a context for critical thinking, for dialectical exchange.

Any attempt on the part of individual students to critique 14 the bourgeois biases that shape pedagogical process, particularly as they relate to epistemological perspectives (the points from which information is shared) will, in most cases, no doubt, be viewed as negative and disruptive. Given the presumed radical or liberal nature of early feminist classrooms, it was shocking to me to find those settings were also often closed to different ways of thinking. While it was acceptable to critique patriarchy in that context, it was not acceptable to confront issues of class, especially in ways that were not simply about the evocation of guilt. In general, despite their participation in different disciplines and the diversity of class backgrounds, African American scholars and other nonwhite professors have been no more willing to confront issues of class. Even when it became more acceptable to give at least lip service to the recognition of race, gender, and class, most professors and students just did not feel they were able to address class in anything more than a simplistic way. Certainly, the primary area where there was the possibility of meaningful critique and change was in relation to biased scholarship, work that used the experiences and thoughts of materially privileged people as normative.

In recent years, growing awareness of class differences in 15 progressive academic circles has meant that students and professors committed to critical and feminist pedagogy have the opportunity to make spaces in the academy where class can receive attention. Yet there can be no intervention that challenges the status quo if we are not willing to interrogate the way our presentation of self as well as our pedagogical process is often shaped by middle-class norms. My awareness of class has been continually reinforced by my efforts to remain close to loved ones who remain in materially underprivileged class positions. This has helped me to employ pedagogical strategies that create ruptures in the established order, that promote modes of learning which challenge bourgeois hegemony.

One such strategy has been the emphasis on creating in class- 16 rooms learning communities where everyone's voice can be heard, their presence recognized and valued. In the section of *Strangers in Paradise* entitled "Balancing Class Locations," Jane Ellen Wilson shares the way an emphasis on personal voice strengthened her.

> Only by coming to terms with my own past, my own background, and seeing that in the context of the word at large, have I begun to find my true voice and to understand that, since it is my own voice, that no pre-cut niche exists for it; that part of the work to be done is making a place, with others, where my and our voices, can stand clear of the background noise and voice our concerns as part of a larger song.

When those of us in the academy who are working class or from working-class backgrounds share our perspectives, we subvert the tendency to focus only on the thoughts, attitudes, and experiences of those who are materially privileged. Feminist and critical pedagogy are two alternative paradigms for teaching which have really empha- sized the issue of coming to voice. That focus emerged as central, precisely because it was so evident that race, sex, and class privilege empower some students more than others, granting "authority" to some voices more than others.

A distinction must be made between a shallow emphasis on 17 coming to voice, which wrongly suggests there can be some democ- ratization of voice wherein everyone's words will be given equal time and be seen as equally valuable (often the model applied in feminist classrooms), and the more complex recognition of the uniqueness of each voice and a willingness to create spaces in the classroom where all voices can be heard because all students are free to speak, knowing their presence will be recognized and valued. This does not mean that anything can be said, no matter how irrelevant to classroom subject matter, and receive attention—or that some- thing meaningful takes place if everyone has equal time to voice an opinion. In the classes I teach, I have students write short paragraphs that they read aloud so that we all have a chance to hear unique perspectives and we are all given an opportunity to pause and listen to one another. Just the physical experience of hearing, of listening intently, to each particular voice strengthens our capacity to learn together. Even though a student may not speak again after this moment, that student's presence has been acknowledged.

Hearing each other's voices, individual thoughts, and some- 18 times associating theses voices with personal experience makes us

more acutely aware of each other. That moment of collective participation and dialogue means that students and professor respect—and
here I invoke the root meaning of the word, "to look at"—each
other, engage in acts of recognition with one another, and do not
just talk to the professor. Sharing experiences and confessional
narratives in the classroom helps establish communal commitment to
learning. These narrative moments usually are the space where the
assumption that we share a common class background and perspective is disrupted. While students may be open to the idea that they
do not all come from a common class background, they may still
expect that the values of materially privileged groups will be the
class's norm.

Some students may feel threatened if awareness of class differ-   19
ence leads to changes in the classroom. Today's students all dress
alike, wearing clothes from stores such as the Gap and Benetton; this
acts to erase the markers of class difference that older generations of
students experienced. Young students are more eager to deny the
impact of class and class differences in our society. I have found that
students from upper- and middle-class backgrounds are disturbed if
heated exchange takes place in the classroom. Many of them equate
loud talk or interruptions with rude and threatening behavior. Yet
those of us from working-class backgrounds may feel that discussion
is deeper and richer if it arouses intense responses. In class, students
are often disturbed if anyone is interrupted while speaking, even
though outside class most of them are not threatened. Few of us are
taught to facilitate heated discussions that may include useful interruptions and digressions, but it is often the professor who is most
invested in maintaining order in the classroom. Professors cannot
empower students to embrace diversities of experience, standpoint,
behavior, or style if our training has disempowered us, socialized us
to cope effectively only with a single mode of interaction based on
middle-class values.

Most progressive professors are more comfortable striving to   20
challenge class biases through the material studied than they are with
interrogating how class biases shape conduct in the classroom and
transforming their pedagogical process. When I entered my first
classroom as a college professor and a feminist, I was deeply afraid of
using authority in a way that would perpetuate class elitism and other
forms of domination. Fearful that I might abuse power, I falsely pretended that no power difference existed between students and
myself. That was a mistake. Yet it was only as I began to interrogate
my fear of "power"—the way that fear was related to my own class
background where I had so often seen those with class power coerce,
abuse, and dominate those without—that I began to understand that

power was not itself negative. It depended what one did with it. It was up to me to create ways within my professional power constructively, precisely because I was teaching in institutional structures that affirm it is fine to use power to reinforce and maintain coercive hierarchies.

Fear of losing control in the classroom often leads individual 21 professors to fall into a conventional teaching pattern wherein power is used destructively. It is this fear that leads to collective professorial investment in bourgeois decorum as a means of maintaining a fixed notion of order, of ensuring that the teacher will have absolute authority. Unfortunately, this fear of losing control shapes and informs the professorial pedagogical process to the extent that it acts as a barrier preventing any constructive grappling with issues of class.

Sometimes students who want professors to grapple with class 22 differences often simply desire that individuals from less materially privileged backgrounds be given center stage so that an inversion of hierarchical structures takes place, not a disruption. One semester, a number of black female students from working-class backgrounds attended a course I taught on African American women writers. They arrived hoping I would use my professorial power to decenter the voices of privileged white students in nonconstructive ways so that those students would experience what it is like to be an outsider. Some of these black students rigidly resisted attempts to involve the others in an engaged pedagogy where space is created for everyone. Many of the black students feared that learning new terminology or new perspectives would alienate them from familiar social relations. Since these fears are rarely addressed as part of progressive pedagogical process, students caught in the grip of such anxiety often sit in classes feeling hostile, estranged, refusing to participate. I often face students who think that in my classes they will "naturally" not feel estranged and that part of this feeling of comfort, or being "at home," is that they will not have to work as hard as they do in other classes. These students are not expecting to find alternative pedagogy in my classes but merely "rest" from the negative tensions they may feel in the majority of other courses. It is my job to address these tensions.

If we can trust the demographics, we must assume that the acad- 23 emy will be full of students from diverse classes, and that more of our students than ever before will be from poor and working-class backgrounds. This change will not be reflected in the class background of professors. In my own experience, I encounter fewer and fewer academics from working-class backgrounds. Our absence is no doubt related to the way class politics and class struggle shapes who will receive graduate degrees in our society. However, constructively confronting issues of class is not simply a task for those of us who came from working-class and poor backgrounds; it is a challenge for all professors. Critiquing the way academic settings are structured to reproduce class hierarchy, Jake Ryan and Charles Sackrey emphasize "that no matter what the politics or ideological stripe of the individual professor, or what the content of his or her teaching, Marxist, anarchist, or nihilist, he or she nonetheless participates in the reproduction of the cultural and class relations of capitalism." Despite this bleak assertion they are willing to acknowledge that "nonconformist intellectuals can, through research and publication, chip away with some success at the conventional orthodoxies, nurture students with comparable ideas and intentions, or find ways to bring some fraction of the resources of the university to the service of the . . . class interests of the workers and others below." Any professor who commits to engaged pedagogy recognizes the importance of constructively confronting issues of class. That means welcoming the opportunity to alter our classroom practices creatively so that the democratic ideal of education for everyone can be realized.

EXPLORATIONS

1. hooks claims that class is rarely talked about in classrooms. In what ways does your own experience support or contradict hooks' claim?

2. hooks argues that "[e]ven those professors who embrace the tenets of critical pedagogy (many of whom are white and male) will conduct their classrooms in a manner that only reinforces bourgeois models of decorum." What does she mean? How does this argument compare with Freire's?

3. Based on your reading of Freire (with whom hooks once studied) and hooks, what might critical pedagogy look like? What might it feel like for students and teachers? What might it mean to "hear each others' voices" in the classroom?

4. Can a teacher believe in critical pedagogy and still teach in traditional ways? Put another way, how do teaching practices reinforce or resist certain societal values?

5. How might teachers and their students go about critiquing and attempting to change particular social values? What are the ethics of attempting to do this?

6. Map the rhetorical situation in one of your classrooms. This map should include the following information: a floor plan that indicates the arrangement of desks, students, teachers, and any special equipment; charts that indicate who talks and how much; lists of activities, materials, and so on; and notes on what kinds of writing, speaking, listening,

and reading occur. Once you have mapped the classroom, speculate on what the map might mean. For example, what does your map say about authority and where it is located? What does it say about the roles that are available to students and teachers?

M. Degas Teaches Art & Science at Durfee Intermediate School

PHILIP LEVINE

Philip Levine (born 1928) was born in Detroit and received his formal education there in the public schools and at Wayne State University. He worked at "a succession of stupid jobs" for industrial companies in Detroit before spending years as a visiting professor and writer at universities across the country. His poetry has often chronicled the lives of the working class, in part because he wants to provide a voice for people whom he sees as all too often "voiceless." Levine's What Work Is, the collection in which "M. Degas Teaches Art & Science at Durfee Intermediate School" appears, won the National Book Award for Poetry in 1991.

WRITING BEFORE READING

What makes a teacher effective or ineffective?

He made a line on the blackboard,
one bold stroke from right to left
diagonally downward and stood back
to ask, looking as always at no one
in particular, "What have I done?"
From the back of the room Freddie
shouted, "You've broken a piece
of chalk." M. Degas did not smile.
"What have I done?" he repeated.
The most intellectual students
looked down to study their desks
except for Gertrude Bimmler, who raised
her hand before she spoke. "M. Degas,
you have created the hypotenuse
of an isosceles triangle." Degas mused.
Everyone knew that Gertrude could not
be incorrect. "It is possible,"
Louis Warshowsky added precisely,
"that you have begun to represent
the roof of a barn." I remember
that it was exactly twenty minutes
past eleven, and I thought at worst
this would go on another forty
minutes. It was early April,

1

5

10

15

20

246

the snow had all but melted on   25
the playgrounds, the elms and maples
bordering the cracked walks shivered
in the new winds, and I believed
that before I knew it I'd be
swaggering to the candy store   30
for a Milky Way. M. Degas
pursed his lips, and the room
stilled until the long hand
of the clock moved to twenty one
as though in complicity with Gertrude,   35
who added confidently, "You've begun
to separate the dark from the dark."
I looked back for help, but now
the trees bucked and quaked, and I
knew this could go on forever.   40

EXPLORATIONS

1. Students offer various interpretations of the line that M. Degas draws
   on a chalkboard. What do those interpretations tell us about those students? About how they see the world?

2. What does the narrator of the poem know "could go on forever"?

3. How would you describe M. Degas' "teaching methods"? How is
   knowledge created in the classroom described in the poem?

Social Class and the Hidden Curriculum of Work

JEAN ANYON

Jean Anyon is an associate professor and chairperson of the department of education at Rutgers University. She has published several scholarly articles on social class, gender, and race in education. She is completing a book entitled Race, Social Class, and Urban School Reform.

WRITING BEFORE READING

Reflect on the "work" you do in a classroom and the "work" you do on the job. Do you notice any similarities or differences?

Scholars in political economy and the sociology of knowledge have recently argued that public schools in complex industrial societies like our own make available different types of educational experience and curriculum knowledge to students in different social classes. Bowles and Gintis (1976), for example, have argued that students from different social class backgrounds are rewarded for classroom behaviors that correspond to personality traits allegedly rewarded in the different occupational strata—the working classes for docility and obedience, the managerial classes for initiative and personal assertiveness. Basil Bernstein (1977), Pierre Bourdieu (Bourdieu and Passeron 1977), and Michael W. Apple (1979), focusing on school knowledge, have argued that knowledge and skills leading to social power and reward (e.g., medical, legal, managerial) are made available to the advantaged social groups but are withheld from the working classes, to whom a more "practical" curriculum is offered (e.g., manual skills, clerical knowledge). While there has been considerable argumentation of these points regarding education in England, France, and North America, there has been little or no attempt to investigate these ideas empirically in elementary or secondary schools and classrooms in this country.[1]

This article offers tentative empirical support (and qualification) of the above arguments by providing illustrative examples of differences in student *work* in classrooms in contrasting social class communities. The examples were gathered as part of an ethnographical study of curricular, pedagogical and pupil evaluation practices in five elementary schools. The article attempts a theoretical approach to social class analysis.

· · · ·

THE SAMPLE OF SCHOOLS

The social class designation of each of the five schools will be iden-   3
tified, and the income, occupation, and other relevant available social
characteristics of the students and their parents will be described. The
first three schools are in a medium-sized city district in northern New
Jersey, and the other two are in a nearby New Jersey suburb.

The first two schools I will call *Working-class Schools*. Most of   4
the parents have blue-collar jobs. Less than a third of the fathers are
skilled, while the majority are in unskilled or semiskilled jobs. During
the period of the study (1978-1979) approximately 15 percent of
the fathers were unemployed. The large majority (85 percent) of the
families are white. The following occupations are typical: platform,
storeroom, and stockroom workers; foundrymen, pipe welders, and
boilermakers; semiskilled and unskilled assembly-line operatives;
gas station attendants, auto mechanics, maintenance workers,
and security guards. Less than 30 percent of the women work, some
part-time and some full-time, on assembly lines, in storerooms and
stockrooms, as waitresses, barmaids, or sales clerks. Of the fifth grade
parents, none of the wives of the skilled workers had jobs.
Approximately 15 percent of the families in each school are at or
below the federal "poverty" level;[2] most of the rest of the family
incomes are at or below $12,000, except some of the skilled workers
whose incomes are higher. The incomes of the majority of the families in these two schools (i.e., at or below $12,000) are typical of
38.6 percent of the families in the United States (U. S. Bureau of the
Census, 1979, p. 2, table A).

The third school is called the *Middle-class School*, although   5
because of neighborhood residence patterns, the population is a
mixture of several social classes. The parents' occupations can be
divided into three groups: a small group of blue-collar "rich," who
are skilled, well-paid workers such as printers, carpenters, plumbers,
and construction workers. The second group is composed of parents
in working-class and middle-class while-collar jobs: women in office
jobs, technicians, supervisors in industry, and parents employed by
the city (such as firemen, policemen, and several of the school's
teachers). The third group is composed of occupations such as
personnel directors in local firms, accountants, "middle management," and a few small capitalists (owners of shops in the area). The
children of several local doctors attend this school. Most family
incomes are between $13,000 and $25,000 with a few higher. This
income range is typical of 38.9 percent of the families in the United
States (U. S. Bureau of the Census, 1979, p. 2, table A).

The fourth school has a parent population that is at the upper   6
income level of the upper middle class, and is predominantly profes-

sional. This school will be called the *Affluent Professional School.*
Typical jobs are: cardiologist, interior designer, corporate lawyer or
engineer, executive in advertising or television. There are some families who are not as affluent as the majority (e.g., the family of the
superintendent of the district's schools, and the one or two families
in which the fathers are skilled workers). In addition, a few of the
families are more affluent than the majority, and can be classified in
the capitalist class (e.g., a partner in a prestigious Wall Street stock
brokerage firm). Approximately 90 percent of the children in this
school are white. Most family incomes are between $40,000 and
$80,000. This income span represents approximately 7 percent of
the families in the United States.[3]

In the fifth school the majority of the families belong to the   7
capitalist class. This school will be called the *Executive Elite School*
because most of the fathers are top executives (e.g., presidents and
vice presidents) in major U. S.-based multinational corporations—for
example, ATT, RCA, City Bank, American Express, U.S. Steel.
A sizable group of fathers are top executives in financial firms on
Wall Street. There are also a number of fathers who list their occupations as "general counsel" to a particular corporation, and these
corporations are also among the large multinationals. Many of the
mothers do volunteer work in the Junior League, Junior Fortnightly,
or other service groups; some are intricately involved in town politics; and some are themselves in well-paid occupations. There are no
minority children in the school. Almost all family incomes are over
$100,000 with some in the $500,000 range. The incomes in this
school represent less than 1 percent of the families in the United
States (see Smith and Franklin, 1974).

Since each of the five schools is only one instance of elementary   8
education in a particular social class context, I will not generalize
beyond the sample. However, the examples of school work which
follow will suggest characteristics of education in each social setting
that appear to have theoretical and social significance and to be
worth investigation in a larger number of schools.

. . . .

The Working-Class School. In the two working-class schools,   9
work is following the steps of a procedure. The procedure is usually
mechanical, involving rote behavior and very little decision making
or choice. The teachers rarely explain why the work is being
assigned, how it might connect to other assignments, or what the
idea is that lies behind the procedure or gives it coherence and perhaps meaning or significance. Available textbooks are not always
used, and the teachers often prepare their own dittoes or put work
examples on the board. Most of the rules regarding work are desig-

nations of what the children are to do; the rules are steps to follow. These steps are told to the children by the teachers and often written on the board. The children are usually told to copy the steps as notes. These notes are to be studied. Work is often evaluated not according to whether it is right or wrong, but according to whether the children followed the right steps.

The following examples illustrate these points. In math, when 10 two-digit division was introduced, the teacher in one school gave a four-minute lecture on what the terms are called (i.e., which number is the divisor, dividend, quotient, and remainder). The children were told to copy these names in their notebooks. Then the teacher told them the steps to follow to do the problems, saying, "This is how you do them." The teacher listed the steps on the board, and they appeared several days later as a chart hung in the middle of the front wall: "Divide; Multiply; Subtract; Bring Down." The children often did examples of two-digit division. When the teacher went over the examples with them, he told them for each problem what the procedure was, rarely asking them to conceptualize or explain it themselves: "3 into 22 is 7; do your subtraction and one is left over." During the week that two-digit division was introduced (or at any other time), the investigator did not observe any discussion of the idea of grouping involved in division, any use of manipulables, or any attempt to relate two-digit division to any other mathematical process. Nor was there any attempt to relate the steps to an actual or possible thought process of the children. The observer did not hear the terms dividend, quotient, etc., used again. The math teacher in the other working-class school followed similar procedures regarding two-digit division, and at one point her class seemed confused. She said, "You're confusing yourselves. You're tensing up. Remember, when you do this, it's the same steps over and over again—and that's the way division always is." Several weeks later, after a test, a group of her children "still didn't get it," and she made no attempt to explain the concept of dividing things into groups, or to give them manipulables for their own investigation. Rather, she went over the steps with them again and told them that they "needed more practice."

In other areas of math, work is also carrying out often unex- 11 plained, fragmented procedures. For example, one of the teachers led the children through a series of steps to make a one-inch grid on their paper *without* telling them that they were making a one-inch grid, or that it would be used to study scale. She said, "Take your ruler. Put it across the top. Make a mark at every number. Then move your ruler down to the bottom. No, put it across the bottom. Now make a mark on top of every number. Now draw a line from. . . ." At this point a girl said that she has a faster way to do it and the teacher said, "No, you don't; you don't even know what I'm making yet. Do it this way, or it's wrong." After they had made the lines up and down and across, the teacher told them she wanted them to make a figure by connecting some dots and to measure that, using the scale of one inch equals one mile. Then they were to cut it out. She said, "Don't cut until I check it."

In both working-class schools, work in language arts is mechan-   12
ics of punctuation (commas, periods, question marks, exclamation points), capitalization, and the four kinds of sentences. One teacher explained to me, "Simple punctuation is all they'll ever use." Regarding punctuation, either a teacher or a ditto stated the rules for where, for example, to put commas. The investigator heard no class-room discussion of the aural context of punctuation (which, of course, is what gives each mark its meaning). Nor did the investiga-tor hear any statement or inference that placing a punctuation mark could be a decision-making process, depending, for example, on one's intended meaning. Rather, the children were told to follow the rules. Language arts did not involve creative writing. There were several writing assignments throughout the year, but in each instance the children were given a ditto, and they wrote answers to questions on the sheet. For example, they wrote their "autobiography" by answering such questions as "Where were you born?" "What is your favorite animal?" on a sheet entitled, "All About Me."

In one of the working-class schools the class had a science   13
period several times a week. On the three occasions observed, the children were not called upon to set up experiments or to give expla-nations for facts or concepts. Rather, on each occasion the teacher told them in his own words what the book said. The children copied the teacher's sentences from the board. Each day that preceded the day they were to do a science experiment, the teacher told them to copy the directions from the book for the procedure they would carry out the next day, and to study the list at home that night. The day after each experiment, the teacher went over what they had "found" (they did the experiments as a class, and each was actually a class demonstration led by the teacher). Then the teacher wrote what they "found" on the board, and the children copied that in their notebooks. Once or twice a year there are science projects. The project is chosen and assigned by the teacher from a box of three-by-five-inch cards. On the card the teacher has written the question to be answered, the books to use, and how much to write. Explaining the cards to the observer, the teacher said, "It tells them exactly what to do, or they couldn't do it."

Social studies in the working-class schools is also largely mechan-   14
ical, rote work that was given little explanation or connection to larger contexts. In one school, for example, although there was a

book available, social studies work was to copy the teacher's notes from the board. Several times a week for a period of several months, the children copied these notes. The fifth grades in the district were to study U. S. history. The teacher used a booklet she had purchased called "The Fabulous Fifty States." Each day she put information from the booklet in outline form on the board and the children copied it. The type of information did not vary: the name of the state, its abbreviation, state capital, nickname of the state, its main products, main business, and a "Fabulous Fact" (e.g., "Idaho grew 27 billion potatoes in one year. That's enough potatoes for each man, woman and . . ."). As the children finished copying the sentences, the teacher erased them and wrote more. Children would occasionally go to the front to pull down the wall map in order to locate the states they were copying, and the teacher did not dissuade them. But the observer never saw her refer to the map; nor did the observer ever hear her make other than perfunctory remarks concerning the information the children were copying. Occasionally the children colored in a ditto and cut it out to make a stand-up figure (representing, for example, a man roping a cow in the Southwest). These were referred to by the teacher as their social studies "projects."

Rote behavior was often called for in classroom oral work. When   15
going over math and language arts skills sheets, for example, as the teacher asked for the answer to each problem, he fired the questions rapidly, staccato, and the scene reminded the observer of a sergeant drilling recruits: above all, the questions demanded that you stay at attention: "the next one? What do I put here? . . . Here? Give us the next." Or "How many commas in this sentence? Where do I put them . . . The next one?"

The (four) fifth grade teachers observed in the working-class   16
schools attempted to control classroom time and space by making decisions without consulting the children and without explaining the basis for their decisions. The teacher's control thus often seemed capricious. Teachers, for instance, very often ignored the bells to switch classes—deciding among themselves to keep the children after the period was officially over, to continue with the work, or for disciplinary reasons, or so they (the teachers) could stand in the hall and talk. There were no clocks in the rooms in either school, and the children often asked, "What period is this?" "When do we go to gym?" The children had no access to materials. These were handed out by teachers and closely guarded. Things in the room "belonged" to the teacher: "Bob, bring me my garbage can." The teachers continually gave the children orders. Only three times did the investigator hear a teacher in either working-class school preface a directive with an unsarcastic "please," or "let's" or "would

you." Instead, the teachers said, "Shut up," " Shut your mouth," "Open your books," "Throw your *gum* away—if you want to rot your teeth, do it on your *own* time." Teachers made every effort to control the movement of the children, and often shouted, "Why are you out of your *seat??!!* " If the children got permission to leave the room they had to take a written pass with the date and time.

The control that the teachers have is less than they would like.   17 It is a result of constant struggle with the children. The children continually resist the teachers' orders and the work itself. They do not directly challenge the teachers' authority or legitimacy, but they make indirect attempts to sabotage and resist the flow of assignments:

TEACHER:	I will put some problems on the board. You are to divide.
CHILD:	We got to divide?
TEACHER:	Yes.
SEVERAL CHILDREN:	(Groan) Not again. Mr. B., we done this yesterday.
CHILD:	Do we put the date?
TEACHER:	Yes. I hope we remember we work in silence. You' re supposed to do it on white paper. I' ll explain it later.
CHILD:	Somebody broke my pencil. (Crash—a child falls out of his chair.)
CHILD:	(repeats) Mr. B., somebody broke my *pencil!*
CHILD:	Are we going to be here all morning?
	(Teacher comes to the observer, shakes his head and grimaces, then smiles.)

The children are successful enough in their struggle against work that there are long periods where they are not asked to *do* any work, but just to sit and be quiet. Very often the work that the teachers assign is "easy," that is, not demanding, and thus receives less resistance. Sometimes a compromise is reached where, although the teachers insist that the children continue to work, there is a constant murmur of talk. The children will be doing arithmetic examples, copying social studies notes, or doing punctuation or other dittoes, and all the while there is muted but spirited conversation—about somebody's broken arm, an afterschool disturbance of the day before, etc. Sometimes the teachers themselves join in the conversation because, as one teacher explained to me, "It's a relief from the routine."

Middle-class School. In the middle-class school, work is getting   18
the right answer. If one accumulates enough right answers one gets
a good grade. One must follow the directions in order to get the
right answers, but the directions often call for some figuring, some
choice, some decision making. For example, the children must often
figure out by themselves what the directions ask them to do, and
how to get the answer: what do you do first, second, and perhaps
third? Answers are usually found in books or by listening to the
teacher. Answers are usually words, sentences, numbers, or facts and
dates; one writes them on paper, and one should be neat. Answers
must be in the right order, and one can not make them up.

The following activities are illustrative. Math involves some   19
choice: one may do two-digit division the long way, or the short way,
and there are some math problems that can be done "in your
head." When the teacher explains how to do two-digit division,
there is recognition that a cognitive process is involved; she gives
several ways, and says, "I want to make sure you understand what
you're doing—so you get it right"; and, when they go over the
homework, she asks the *children* to tell how they did the problem
and what answer they got.

In social studies the daily work is to read the assigned pages in   20
the textbook and to answer the teacher's questions. The questions
are almost always designed to check on whether the students have
read the assignment and understood it: who did so-and-so; what
happened after that; when did it happen, where, and sometimes, why
did it happen? The answers are in the book and in one's understanding of the book; the teacher's hints when one doesn't know
the answer are to "read it again," or to look at the picture or at the
rest of the paragraph. One is to search for the answer in the "context," in what is given.

Language arts is "simple grammar, what they need for everyday   21
life." The language arts teacher says, "They should learn to speak
properly, to write business letters and thank-you letters, and to
understand what nouns and verbs and simple subjects are." Here, as
well, the actual work is to choose the right answers, to understand
what is given. The teacher often says, "Please read the next sentence
and then I'll question you about it." One teacher said in some
exasperation to a boy who was fooling around in class, "If you
don't know the answers to the questions I ask, then you can't stay
in this *class!* (pause) You *never* know the answers to the questions I
ask, and it's not fair to me—and certainly not to you!"

Most lessons are based on the textbook. This does not involve a   22
critical perspective on what is given there. For example, a critical
perspective in social studies is perceived as dangerous by these teachers because it may lead to controversial topics; the parents might

complain. The children, however, are often curious, especially in social studies. Their questions are tolerated, and usually answered perfunctorily. But after a few minutes the teacher will say, "All right, we're not going any farther. Please open your social studies workbook." While the teachers spend a lot of time explaining and expanding on what the textbooks say, there is little attempt to analyze how or why things happen, or to give thought to how pieces of a culture, or, say, a system of numbers or elements of a language fit together or can be analyzed. What has happened in the past, and what exists now may not be equitable or fair, but (shrug) that is the way things are, and one does not confront such matters in school. For example, in social studies after a child is called on to read a passage about the pilgrims, the teacher summarizes the paragraph and then says, "So you can see how strict they were about everything." A child asks, "Why?" "Well, because they felt that if you weren't busy you'd get into trouble." Another child asks, "Is it true that they burned women at the stake?" The teacher says, "Yes, if a woman did anything strange, they handed them. [sic] What would a woman do, do you think, to make them burn them? [sic] See if you can come up with better answers than my other [social studies] class." Several children offer suggestions, to which the teacher nods but does not comment. Then she says, "OK, good," and calls on the next child to read.

Work tasks do not usually request creativity. Serious attention is 23 rarely given in school work to *how* the children develop or express their own feelings and ideas, either linguistically or in graphic form. On the occasions when creativity or self-expression is requested, it is peripheral to the main activity, or it is "enrichment," or "for fun." During a lesson on what similes are, for example, the teacher explains what they are, puts several on the board, gives some other examples herself, and then asks the children if they can "make some up." She calls on three children who give similes, two of which are actually in the book they have open before them. The teacher does not comment on this, and then asks several others to choose similes from the list of phrases in the book. Several do so correctly, and she says, "Oh good! You're picking them out! See how *good* we are?" Their homework is to pick out the rest of the similes from the list.

Creativity is not often requested in social studies and science 24 projects, either. Social studies projects, for example, are given with directions to "find information on your topic," and write it up. The children are not supposed to copy, but to "put it in your own words." Although a number of the projects subsequently went beyond the teacher's direction to find information and had quite expressive covers and inside illustrations, the teacher's evaluative comments had to do with the amount of information, whether they had "copied," and if their work was neat.

The style of control of the three fifth grade teachers observed in   25
this school varied from somewhat easygoing to strict, but in contrast
to the working-class schools, the teachers' decisions were usually
based on external rules and regulations, for example, on criteria that
were known or available to the children. Thus, the teachers always
honor the bells for changing classes, and they usually evaluate children's work by what is in the textbooks and answer booklets.

There is little excitement is school work for the children, and the   26
assignments are perceived as having little to do with their interests
and feelings. As one child said, what you do is "store facts in your
head like cold storage—until you need it later for a test, or your
job." Thus, doing well is important because there are thought to be
other likely rewards: a good job, or college.[4]

Affluent Professional School. In the affluent professional school,   27
work is creative activity carried out independently. The students are
continually asked to express and apply ideas and concepts. Work
involves individual thought and expressiveness, expansion and illustration of ideas, and choice of appropriate method and material.
(The class is not considered an open classroom, and the principal
explained that because of the large number of discipline problems in
the fifth grade this year they did not departmentalize. The teacher
who agreed to take part in the study said she is "more structure d "
this year than she usually is.) The products of work in this class are
often written stories, editorials and essays, or representations of ideas
in mural, graph, or craft form. The products of work should not be
like everybody else's and should show individuality. They should
exhibit good design, and (this is important), they must also fit
empirical reality. Moreover, one's work should attempt to interpret
or "make sense" of reality. The relatively few rules to be followed
regarding work are usually criteria for, or limits on, individual
activity. One's product is usually evaluated for the quality of its
expression and for the appropriateness of its conception to the task.
In many cases one's own satisfaction with the product is an important criterion for its evaluation. When right answers are called for, as
in commercial materials like SRA (Science Research Associates) and
math, it is important that the children decide on an answer as a result
of thinking about the idea involved in what they're being asked to
do. Teacher's hints are to "think about is some more."

The following activities are illustrative. The class takes home a   28
sheet requesting each child's parents to fill in the number of cars
they have, the number of television sets, refrigerators, games, or
rooms in the house, etc. Each child is to figure the average number
of a type of possession owned by the fifth grade. Each child must
compile the "data" from all the sheets. A calculator is available in
the classroom to do the mechanics of finding the average. Some

children decide to send sheets to the fourth grade families for comparison. Their work should be "verified" by a classmate before it is handed in.

Each child and his or her family has made a geoboard. The 29 teacher asks the class to get their geoboards from the side cabinet, to take a handful of rubber bands, and then to listen to what she would like them to do. She says, "I would like you to design a figure and then find the perimeter and area. When you have it, check with your neighbor. After you've done that, please transfer it to graph paper and tomorrow I'll ask you to make up a question about it for someone. When you hand it in, please let me know whose it is, and who verified it. Then I have something else for you to do that's really fun. (pause) Find the average number of chocolate chips in three cookies. I'll give you three cookies, and you'll have to *eat* your way through, I'm afraid!" Then she goes around the room and gives help, suggestions, praise, and admonitions that they are getting noisy. They work sitting, or standing up at their desks, at benches in the back, or on the floor. A child hands the teacher his paper and she comments, "I'm not accepting this paper. Do a better design." To another child she says, "That's fantastic! But you'll never find the area. Why don't you draw a figure inside [the big one] and subtract to get the area?"

The school district requires the fifth grades to study ancient 30 civilizations (in particular, Egypt, Athens, and Sumer). In this classroom, the emphasis is on illustrating and re-creating the culture of the people of ancient times. The following are typical activities: The children made an 8mm film on Egypt, which one of the parents edited. A girl in the class wrote the script, and class acted it out. They put the sound on themselves. They read stories of those days. They wrote essays and stories depicting the lives of the people and the societal and occupational divisions. They chose from a list of projects, all of which involved graphic representations of ideas: for example, "Make a mural depicting the division of labor in Egyptian society. "

Each child wrote and exchanged a letter in hieroglyphics with a 31 fifth grader in another class, and they also exchanged stories they wrote in cuneiform. They made a scroll and singed the edges so it looked authentic. They each chose an occupation and made an Egyptian plaque representing that occupation, simulating the appropriate Egyptian design. They carved their design on a cylinder of wax, pressed the wax into clay, and then baked the clay. Although one girl did not choose an occupation, but carved instead a series of gods and slaves, the teacher said, "That's all right, Amber, it's beautiful." As they were working the teacher said, "don't cut into your clay until you're satisfied with your design."

Social studies also involves almost daily presentation by the chil- 32
dren of some event from the news. The teacher's questions ask the
children to expand what they say, to give more details, and to be
more specific. Occasionally she adds some remarks to help them see
connections between events.

The emphasis on expressing and illustrating ideas in social 33
studies is accompanied in language arts by an emphasis on creative
writing. Each child wrote a rhebus story for a first grader whom they
had interviewed to see what kind of story the child liked best. They
wrote editorials on pending decisions by the school board, and radio
plays, some of which were read over the school intercom from the
office, and one of which was performed in the auditorium. There is
no language arts textbook because, the teacher said, "The principal
wants us to be creative." There is not much grammar, but there is
punctuation. One morning when the observer arrived the class was
doing a punctuation ditto. The teacher later apologized for using the
ditto. "It's just for review," she said. "I don't teach punctuation
that way. We use their language." The ditto had three unambiguous
rules for where to put commas in a sentence. As the teacher was
going around to help the children with the ditto, she repeated several times, "Where you put commas depends on how you say the
sentence; it depends on the situation and what you want to say. "
Several weeks later the observer saw another punctuation activity.
The teacher had printed a five-paragraph story on an oak tag and
then cut it into phrases. She read the whole story to the class from
the book, then passed out the phrases. The group had to decide how
the phrases could best be put together again. (They arranged the
phrases on the floor.) The point was not to replicate the story,
although that was not irrelevant, but to "decide what you think the
best way is." Punctuation marks on cardboard pieces were then
handed out and the children discussed, and then decided, what mark
was best at each place they though one was needed. At the end of
each paragraph the teacher asked, "Are you satisfied with the way
the paragraphs are now? Read it to yourself and see how it sounds."
Then she read the original story again, and they compared the two.

Describing her goals in science to the investigator, the teacher 34
said, "We use ESS (Elementary Science Study). It's very good
because it gives a hands-on experience—so they can make *sense* out
of it. It doesn't matter whether it [what they find] is right or
wrong. I bring them together and there's value in discussing their
ideas."

The products of work in this class are often highly valued by the 35
children and the teacher. In fact, this was the only school in which
the investigator was not allowed to take original pieces of the children's work for her files. If the work was small enough, however,

and was on paper, the investigator could duplicate it on the copying machine in the office.

The teacher's attempt to control the class involves constant [36] negotiation. She does not give direct orders unless she is angry because the children have been too noisy. Normally, she tries to get them to foresee the consequences of their actions and to decide accordingly. For example, lining them up to go see a play written by the sixth graders, she says, "I presume you're lined up by someone with whom you want to sit. I hope you're lined up by someone you won't get in trouble with." The following two dialogues illustrate the process of negotiation between student and teacher.

TEACHER: Tom, you're behind in your SRA this marking period.

TOM: So what!

TEACHER: Well, last time you had a hard time catching up.

TOM: But I have my [music] lesson at 10:00.

TEACHER: Well, that doesn't mean you're going to sit here for twenty minutes.

TOM: Twenty minutes! OK. (He goes to pick out a SRA booklet and chooses one, puts it back, then takes another, and brings it to her.)

TEACHER: OK, this is the one you want, right?

TOM: Yes.

TEACHER: OK, I'll put tomorrow's date on it so you can take it home tonight or finish it tomorrow if you want.

TEACHER: (to a child who is wandering around during reading) Kevin, why don't you do *Reading for Concepts?*

KEVIN: No, I don't like *Reading for Concepts.*

TEACHER: Well, what are you going to do?

KEVIN: (pause) I'm going to work on my DAR. (The DAR had sponsored an essay competition on "Life in the American Colonies.")

One of the few rules governing the children's movement is that [37] no more than three children may be out of the room at once. There is a school rule that anyone can go to the library at any time to get a book. In the fifth grade I observed, they sign their name on the chalkboard and leave. There are no passes. Finally, the children have a fair amount of officially sanctioned say over what happens in the class. For example, they often negotiate what work is to be done. If the teacher wants to move on to the next subject, but the children say they are not ready, they want to work on their present projects some more, she very often lets them do it.

Executive Elite School. In the executive elite school, work is 38 developing one's analytical intellectual powers. Children are continually asked to reason through a problem, to produce intellectual products that are both logically sound and of top academic quality. A primary goal of thought is to conceptualize rules by which elements may fit together in systems, and then to apply these rules in solving a problem. School work helps one to achieve, to excel, to prepare for life.

The following are illustrative. The math teacher teaches area and 39 perimeter by having the children derive formulae for each. First she helps them, through discussion at the board, to arrive at A = W x L as a formula (not *the* formula) for area. After discussing several, she says, "Can anyone make up a formula for perimeter? Can you figure that out yourselves? (pause) Knowing what we know, can we think of a formula?" She works out three children's suggestions at the board, saying to two, "Yes, that's a good one," and then asks the class if they can think of any more. No one volunteers. To prod them, she says, "If you use rules and good reasoning, you get many ways. Chris, can you think up a formula?"

She discusses two-digit division with the children as a decision- 40 making process. Presenting a new type of problem to them, she asks, "What's the *first* decision you'd make if presented with this kind of example? What is the first thing you'd *think?* Craig?" Craig says, "To find my first partial quotient." She responds, "Yes, that would by your first decision. How would you do that?" Craig explains, and then the teacher says, "OK, we'll see how that works for you." The class tries his way. Subsequently, she comments on the merits and shortcomings of several other children's decisions. Later, she tells the investigator that her goals in math are to develop their reasoning and mathematical thinking and that, unfortunately, "there's no *time* for manipulables."

While right answers are important in math, they are not 41 "given" by the book or by the teacher, but may be challenged by the children. Going over some problems in late September the teacher says, "Raise your hand if you do not agree." A child says, "I don't agree with 64." the teacher responds, "OK, there's a question about 64. (to class) Please check it. Owen, they're disagreeing with you. Kristen, they're checking yours." The teacher emphasized this repeatedly during September and October with statements like, "Don't be afraid to say if you disagree. In the last [math] class, somebody disagreed, and they were right. Before you disagree, check yours, and if you still think we're wrong, then we'll check it out." By Thanksgiving, the children did not often speak in terms of right and wrong math problems, but of whether they agreed with the answer that had been given.

There are complicated math mimeos with many word problems. 42 Whenever they go over the examples, they discuss how each child has set up the problem. The children must explain it precisely. On one occasion the teacher said, "I'm more—just as interested in *how* you set up the problem as in what answer you find. If you set up a problem in a good way, the answer is *easy* to find."

Social studies work is most often reading and discussion of con- 43 cepts and independent research. There are only occasional artistic, expressive, or illustrative projects. Ancient Athens and Sumer are, rather, societies to analyze. The following questions are typical of those which guide the children's independent research: "What mistakes did Pericles make after the war?" "What mistakes did the citizens of Athens make?" "What are the elements of a civilization?" "How did Greece build an economic empire?" "Compare the way Athens chose its leaders with the way we choose ours." Occasionally the children are asked to make up sample questions for their social studies tests. On an occasion when the investigator was present the social studies teacher rejected a child's question by saying, "That's just fact. If I asked you that question on a test, you'd complain it was just memory! Good questions ask for concepts."

In social studies—but also in reading, science, and health—the 44 teachers initiate classroom discussions of current social issues and problems. These discussions occurred on every one of the investigator's visits, and a teacher told me, "These children's opinions are important—it's important that they learn to reason things through." The classroom discussions always struck the observer as quite realistic and analytical, dealing with concrete social issues like the following: "Why do workers strike?" "Is that right or wrong?" "Why do we have inflation, and what can be done to stop it?" "Why do companies put chemicals in food when the natural ingredients are available?" etc. Usually the children did not have to be prodded to give their opinions. In fact, their statements and the interchanges between them struck the observer as quite sophisticated conceptually and verbally, and well-informed. Occasionally the teachers would prod with statements such as, "Even if you don't know [the answers], if you think logically about it, you can figure it out." And "I'm asking you [these] questions to help you think this through."

Language arts emphasizes language as a complex system, one 45 that should be mastered. The children are asked to diagram sentences of complex grammatical construction, to memorize irregular verb conjugations (he lay, he has lain, etc. . . .), and to use the proper participles, conjunctions, and interjections in their speech. The teacher (the same one who teaches social studies) told them, "It is not enough to get these right on tests; you must use what you learn [in grammar classes] in your written and oral work. I will grade you on that."

Most writing assignments are either research reports and essays for social studies, or experiment analyses and write-ups for science. There is only an occasional story or other "creative writing" assignment. On the occasion observed by the investigator (the writing of a Halloween story), the points the teacher stressed in preparing the children to write involved the structural aspects of a story rather than the expression of feelings or other ideas. The teacher showed them a filmstrip, "The Seven Parts of a Story," and lectured them on plot development, mood setting, character development, consistency, and the use of a logical or appropriate ending. The stories they subsequently wrote were, in fact, well-structured, but many were also personal and expressive. The teacher's evaluative comments, however, did not refer to the expressiveness or artistry, but were all directed toward whether they had "developed" the story well.

Language arts work also involved a large amount of practice in presentation of the self and in managing situations where the child was expected to be in charge. For example, there was a series of assignments in which each child had to be a "student teacher." The child had to plan a lesson in grammar, outlining, punctuation, or other language arts topics and explain the concept to the class. Each child was to prepare a worksheet or game and a homework assignment as well. After each presentation, the teacher and other children gave a critical appraisal of the "student teacher's" performance. Their criteria were: whether the student spoke clearly; whether the lesson was interesting; whether the student made any mistakes; and whether he or she kept control of the class. On an occasion when a child did not maintain control, the teacher said, "When you're up there, you have authority, and you have to use it. I'll back you up."

The teacher of math and science explained to the observer that she likes the ESS program because "the children can manipulate variables. They generate hypotheses and devise experiments to solve the problem. They have to explain what they found."

The executive elite school is the only school where bells do not demarcate the periods of time. The two fifth grade teachers were very strict about changing classes on schedule, however, as specific plans for each session had been made. The teachers attempted to keep tight control over the children during lessons, and the children were sometimes flippant, boisterous, and occasionally rude. However, the children may be brought into line by reminding them that "it is up to you." "You must control yourself," "you are responsible for your work," you must "set your priorities." One teacher told a child, "You are the only driver of your car—and only you can regulate your speed." A new teacher complained to the observer that she had thought "these children" would have more control.

While strict attention to the lesson at hand is required, the teach- 50 ers make relatively little attempt to regulate the movement of the children at other times. For example, except for the kindergartners, the children in this school do not have to wait for the bell to ring in the morning; they may go to their classroom when they arrive at school. Fifth graders often came early to read, to finish work, or to catch up. After the first two months of school the fifth grade teachers did not line the children up to change classes or to go to gym, etc., but, when the children were ready and quiet, they were told they could go—sometimes without the teachers.

In the classroom, the children could get materials when they 51 needed them and took what they needed from closets and from the teacher's desk. They were in charge of the office at lunchtime. During class they did not have to sign out or ask permission to leave the room; they just got up and left. Because of the pressure to get work done, however, they did not leave the room very often. The teachers were very polite to the children, and the investigator heard no sarcasm, no nasty remarks, and few direct orders. The teachers never called the children "honey," or "dear," but always called them by name. The teachers were expected to be available before school, after school, and for part of their lunch time to provide extra help if needed.

. . . .

The foregoing analysis of differences in school work in contrasting 52 social class contexts suggests the following conclusion: the "hidden curriculum" of school work is tacit preparation for relating to the process of production in a particular way. Differing curricular, peda-gogical, and pupil evaluation practices emphasize different cognitive and behavioral skills in each social setting and thus contribute to the development in the children of certain potential relationships to phys-ical and symbolic capital, to authority, and to the process of work. School experience, in the sample of schools discussed here, differed qualitatively by social class. These differences may not only contribute to the development in the children in each social class of certain types of economically significant relationships and not others, but would thereby help to *reproduce* this system of relations in society. In the contribution to the reproduction of unequal social relations lies a the-oretical meaning, and social consequence, of classroom practice.

The identification of different emphases in classrooms in a sam- 53 ple of contrasting social class contexts implies that further research should be conducted in a large number of schools to investigate the types of work tasks and interactions in each, to see if they differ in the ways discussed here, and to see if similar potential relationships are uncovered. Such research could have as a product the further elucidation of complex but not readily apparent connections between everyday activity in schools and classrooms and the unequal structure of economic relationships in which we work and live.

NOTES

[1] But see, in a related vein, Apple and King (1977) and Rist (1973).
[2] The U. S. Bureau of the Census defines "poverty" for a nonfarm family of four as a yearly income of $6,191 a year or less. U.S. Bureau of the Census, *Statistical Abstract of the United States: 1978* (Washington, D.C.: U.S. Government Printing Office, 1978, p. 465, table 754).
[3] This figure is an estimate. According to the Bureau of the Census, only 2.6 percent of families in the United States have money income of $50,000 or over. U. S. Bureau of the Census, *Current Population Reports*, series P-60, no. 118, "Money Income in 1977 of Families and Persons in the United States." [Washington, D.C.: U.S. Government Printing Office, 1979, p. 2, table A). For figures on income at these higher levels, see Smith and Franklin (1974).
[4] A dominant feeling, expressed directly and indirectly by teachers in this school, was boredom with their work. They did, however, in contrast to the working-class schools, almost always carry out lessons during class times.

REFERENCES

Althusser, L. Ideology and ideological state apparatuses. In L. Althusser, *Lenin and philosophy and other essays*. Ben Brewster, Trans. New York: Monthly Review Press, 1971.

Anyon, J. Elementary social studies textbooks and legitimating knowledge. *Theory and Research in Social Education*, 1978, 6, 40–55.

Anyon, J. Ideology and United States history textbooks. *Harvard Educational Review*, 1979, 49, 361–386.

Apple, M. W. *Ideology and curriculum*. Boston: Routledge and Kegan Paul, 1979.

Apple, M. W., & King, N. What do schools teach? *Curriculum Inquiry*, 1977, 6, 341–358.

Aronowitz, S. Marx, Braverman, and the logic of capital. *The Insurgent Sociologist*, 1978, 8, 126–146.

Benson, S. The clerking sisterhood: rationalization and the work culture of saleswomen in American department stores, 1890–1960. *Radical America*, 1978, 12, 41–55.

Berstein, B. *Class, codes and control, Vol. 3. Towards a theory of educational transmission*. 2nd ed. London: Routledge and Kegan Paul, 1977.

Bourdieu. P. and Passeron, J. *Reproduction in education, society, and culture.* Beverly Hills, Calif.: Sage, 1977.

Bowles, S. & Gintis, H. *Schooling in capitalist America: educational reform and the contradictions of economic life.* New York: Basic Books, 1976.

Braverman, H. *Labor and monopoly capital: the degradation of work in the twentieth century.* New York: Monthly Review Press, 1974.

Dreeben, R. *On what is learned in school.* Reading, Mass.: Addison-Wesley, 1968.

Jackson, P. *Life in classrooms.* Holt, Reinhart & Winston, 1968.

Lampman, R. J. *The share of top wealth-holders in national wealth, 1922–1956:* A study of the National Bureau of Economic Research. Princeton, N. J.: Princeton University Press, 1962.

Levison, A. *The working-class majority.* New York: Penguin Books, 1974.

New York Stock Exchange. *Census.* New York: New York Stock Exchange, 1975.

Rist, R. C. *The urban school: a factory for failure.* Cambridge, Mass.: MIT Press, 1973.

Sarasan, S. *The culture of school and the problem of change.* Boston: Allyn and Bacon, 1971.

Smith, J. D. and Franklin, S. The concentration of personal wealth, 1922–1969. *American Economic Review,* 1974, *64,* 162–167.

U.S. Bureau of the Census. *Current population reports.* Series P-60, no. 118. Money income in 1977 of families and persons in the United States. Washington, D.C.: U.S. Government Printing Office, 1979.

U.S. Bureau of the Census. *Statistical abstract of the United States: 1978.* Washington, D.C.: U.S. Government Printing Office, 1978.

Williams, R. *Marxism and literature,* New York: Oxford University Press, 1977.

Wright, E. O. *Class, crisis and the state.* London: New Left Books, 1978.

EXPLORATIONS

1. What do the everyday activities of college classrooms reveal about what the university and the instructors who teach there think is important for you to learn?

2. What is the "hidden curriculum" of Anyon's title?

3. What assumptions does Anyon seem to have about the purpose of schools? How would you define her own "curriculum" or agenda?

4. Place bell hooks in one of Anyon's classrooms and explain hook's reaction to being there.

5. Can you identify examples of the teaching practices Anyon describes in your own educational history? If so, describe them.

6. Anyon argues that there is probably a connection "between everyday activity in schools and classrooms and the unequal structure of economic relationships in which we work and live." Describe the everyday activities in an elementary, secondary, or college classroom with which

you are familiar. What do these activities tell you about what teachers and schools think is important for students to learn? What kinds of out-of-school activities do they seem to be preparing you for?

From The School Days
of an Indian Girl

ZITKALA-SA

*Also known as Gertrude Simmons or Gertrude Bonnin after
her marriage, Zitkala-Sa (1876–1938) defied her mother by
leaving the Yankton Sioux Agency in South Dakota for a
"white" education. While a student at Earlham College in
Indiana in 1896, she won an oratorical contest. Zitkala-Sa
later lived for a time in Boston, where she published stories
about American Indians and worked as an advocate for her
people. Her education led to her estrangement from her family and tribe; at the same time, she was never fully accepted in
the white world. She wrote in a letter that she felt "an eternal tug of war between being wild and becoming civilized."*

WRITING BEFORE READING

*Reflect on a time when the values or language of your home or com-
munity have been challenged in the classroom.*

I

The Land of Red Apples

There were eight in our party of bronzed children who were   1
going East with the missionaries. Among us were three young braves,
two tall girls, and we three little ones, Judéwin, Thowin, and I.

We had been very impatient to start on our journey to the Red   2
Apple Country, which, we were told, lay a little beyond the great circular horizon of the Western prairie. Under a sky of rosy apples we
dreamt of roaming as freely and happily as we had chased the cloud
shadows on the Dakota plains. We had anticipated much pleasure
from a ride on the iron horse, but the throngs of staring palefaces
disturbed and troubled us.

On the train, fair women, with tottering babies on each arm,   3
stopped their haste and scrutinized the children of absent mothers.
Large men, with heavy bundles in their hands, halted near by, and
riveted their glassy blue eyes upon us.

I sank deep into the corner of my seat, for I resented being   4
watched. Directly in front of me, children who were no larger than
I hung themselves upon the backs of their seats, with their bold

white faces toward me. Sometimes they took their forefingers out of their mouths and pointed at my moccasined feet. Their mothers, instead of reproving such rude curiosity, looked closely at me, and attracted their children's further notice to my blanket. This embarrassed me, and kept me constantly on the verge of tears.

I sat perfectly still, with my eyes downcast, daring only now and 5 then to shoot long glances around me. Chancing to turn to the window at my side, I was quite breathless upon seeing one familiar object. It was the telegraph pole which strode by at short paces. Very near my mother's dwelling, along the edge of a road thickly bordered with wild sunflowers, some poles like these had been planted by white men. Often I had stopped, on my way down the road, to hold my ear against the pole, and, hearing its low moaning, I used to wonder what the paleface had done to hurt it. Now I sat watching for each pole that glided by to be the last one.

In this way I had forgotten my uncomfortable surroundings, 6 when I heard one of my comrades call my name. I saw the missionary standing very near, tossing candies and gums into our midst. This amused us all, and we tried to see who could catch the most of the sweetmeats.

Though we rode several days inside of the iron horse, I do not 7 recall a single thing about our luncheons.

It was night when we reached the school grounds. The lights 8 from the windows of the large buildings fell upon some of the icicled trees that stood beneath them. We were led toward an open door, where the brightness of the lights within flooded out over the heads of the excited palefaces who blocked our way. My body trembled more from fear than from the snow I trod upon.

Entering the house, I stood close against the wall. The strong 9 glaring light in the large whitewashed room dazzled my eyes. The noisy hurrying of hard shoes upon a bare wooden floor increased the whirring in my ears. My only safety seemed to be in keeping next to the wall. As I was wondering in which direction to escape from all this confusion, two warm hands grasped me firmly, and in the same moment I was tossed high in midair. A rosy-cheeked paleface woman caught me in her arms. I was both frightened and insulted by such trifling. I stared into her eyes, wishing her to let me stand on my own feet, but she jumped me up and down with increasing enthusiasm. My mother had never made a plaything of her wee daughter. Remembering this I began to cry aloud.

They misunderstood the cause of my tears, and placed me at a 10 white table loaded with food. There our party were united again. As I did not hush my crying, one of the older ones whispered to me, "Wait until you are alone in the night."

It was very little I could swallow besides my sobs, that evening. 11

"Oh, I want my mother and my brother Dawée! I want to go   12
to my aunt!" I pleaded; but the ears of the palefaces could not hear
me.

From the table we were taken along an upward incline of wood-   13
en boxes, which I learned afterward to call a stairway. At the top was
a quiet hall, dimly lighted. Many narrow beds were in one straight
line down the entire length of the wall. In them lay sleeping brown
faces, which peeped just out of the coverings. I was tucked into bed
with one of the tall girls, because she talked to me in my mother
tongue and seemed to soothe me.

I had arrived in the wonderful land of rosy skies, but I was not   14
happy, as I had thought I should be. My long travel and the bewildering sights had exhausted me. I fell asleep, heaving deep, tired
sobs. My tears were left to dry themselves in streaks, because neither
my aunt nor my mother was near to wipe them away.

II

The Cutting of My Long Hair

The first day in the land of apples was a bitter-cold one; for the   15
snow still covered the ground, and the trees were bare. A large bell
rang for breakfast, its loud metallic voice crashing through the bel-
fry overhead and into our sensitive ears. The annoying clatter of
shoes on bare floors gave us no peace. The constant clash of harsh
noises, with an undercurrent of many voices murmuring an unknown
tongue, made a bedlam within which I was securely tied. And
though my spirit tore itself in struggling for its lost freedom, all was
useless.

A paleface woman, with white hair, came up after us. We were   16
placed in a line of girls who were marching into the dining room.
These were Indian girls, in stiff shoes and closely clinging dresses.
The small girls wore sleeved aprons and shingled hair. As I walked
noiselessly in my soft moccasins, I felt like sinking to the floor, for
my blanket had been stripped from my shoulders. I looked hard at
the Indian girls, who seemed not to care that they were even more
immodestly dressed than I, in their tightly fitting clothes. While we
marched in, the boys entered at an opposite door. I watched for the
three young braves who came in our party. I spied them in the rear
ranks, looking as uncomfortable as I felt.

A small bell was tapped, and each of the pupils drew a chair from   17
under the table. Supposing this act meant they were to be seated, I
pulled out mine and at once slipped into it from one side. But when
I turned my head, I saw that I was the only seated, and all the rest at

our table remained standing. Just as I began to rise, looking shyly around to see how chairs were to be used, a second bell was sounded. All were seated at last, and I had to crawl back into my chair again. I heard a man's voice at one end of the hall, and I looked around to see him. But all the others hung their heads over their plates. As I glanced at the long chain of tables, I caught the eyes of a paleface woman upon me. Immediately I dropped my eyes, wondering why I was so keenly watched by the strange woman. The man ceased his mutterings, and then a third bell was tapped. Every one picked up his knife and fork and began eating. I began crying instead, for by this time I was afraid to venture anything more.

But this eating by formula was not the hardest trial in that first   18 day. Late in the morning, my friend Judéwin gave me a terrible warning. Judéwin knew a few words of English; and she had overheard the paleface woman talk about cutting our long, heavy hair. Our mothers had taught us that only unskilled warriors who were captured had their hair shingled by the enemy. Among our people, short hair was worn by mourners, and shingled hair by cowards!

We discussed our fate some moments, and when Judéwin said,   19 "We have to submit, because they are strong," I rebelled.

"No, I will not submit! I will struggle first!" I answered.   20

I watched my chance, and when no one noticed I disappeared. I   21 crept up the stairs as quietly as I could in my squeaking shoes,—my moccasins had been exchanged for shoes. Along the hall I passed, without knowing whither I was going. Turning aside to an open door, I found a large room with three white beds in it. The windows were covered with dark green curtains, which made the room very dim. Thankful that no one was there, I directed my steps toward the corner farthest from the door. On my hands and knees I crawled under the bed, and cuddled myself in the dark corner.

From my hiding place I peered out, shuddering with fear when-   22 ever I heard footsteps near by. Though in the hall loud voices were calling my name, and I knew that even Judéwin was searching for me, I did not open my mouth to answer. Then the steps were quickened and the voices became excited. The sounds came nearer and nearer. Women and girls entered the room. I held my breath and watched them open closet doors and peep behind large trunks. Some one threw up the curtains, and the room was filled with sudden light. What caused them to stoop and look under the bed I do not know. I remember being dragged out, though I resisted by kicking and scratching wildly. In spite of myself, I was carried downstairs and tied fast in a chair.

I cried aloud, shaking my head all the while until I felt the cold   23 blades of the scissors against my neck, and heard them gnaw off one of my thick braids. Then I lost my spirit. Since the day I was taken

from my mother I had suffered extreme indignities. People had
stared at me. I had been tossed about in the air like a wooden pup-
pet. And now my long hair was shingled like a coward's! In my
anguish I moaned for my mother, but no one came to comfort me.
Not a soul reasoned quietly with me, as my own mother used to do;
for now I was only one of many little animals driven by a herder.

III

The Snow Episode

A short time after our arrival we three Dakotas were playing in a   24
snowdrift. We were all still deaf to the English language, excepting
Judéwin, who always heard such puzzling things. One morning we
learned through her ears that we were forbidden to fall lengthwise in
the snow, as we had been doing, to see our own impressions.
However, before many hours we had forgotten the order, and were
having great sport in the snow, when a shrill voice called us. Looking
up, we saw an imperative hand beckoning us into the house. We
shook the snow off ourselves, and started toward the woman as slowly as we dared.

Judéwin said: "Now the paleface is angry with us. She is going   25
to punish us for falling into the snow. If she looks straight into your
eyes and talks loudly, you must wait until she stops. Then, after a tiny
pause, say, 'No.'" The rest of the way we practiced upon the
little word "no."

As it happened, Thowin was summoned to judgment first. The   26
door shut behind her with a click.

Judéwin and I stood silently listening at the keyhole. The pale-   27
face woman talked in very severe tones. Her words fell from her lips
like crackling embers, and her inflection ran up like the small end of
a switch. I understood her voice better than the things she was saying. I was certain we had made her very impatient with us. Judéwin
heard enough of the words to realize all too late that she had taught
us the wrong reply.

"Oh, poor Thowin!" she gasped, as she put both hands over   28
her ears.

Just then I heard Thowin's tremulous answer, "No."   29

With an angry exclamation, the woman gave her a hard spank-   30
ing. Then she stopped to say something. Judéwin said it was this:
"Are you going to obey my word the next time?"

Thowin answered again with the only word at her command,   31
"No."

This time the woman meant her blows to smart, for the poor   32
frightened girl shrieked at the top of her voice. In the midst of the

whipping the blows ceased abruptly, and the woman asked another question: "Are you going to fall in the snow again?"

Thowin gave her bad password another trial. We heard he say 33 feebly, "No! No!"

With this the woman hid away her half-worn slipper, and led the 34 child out, stroking her black shorn head. Perhaps it occurred to her that brute force is not the solution for such a problem. She did nothing to Judéwin nor to me. She only returned to us our unhappy comrade, and left us alone in the room.

During the first two or three seasons misunderstandings as 35 ridiculous as this one of the snow episode frequently took place, bringing unjustifiable frights and punishments into our little lives.

Within a year I was able to express myself somewhat in broken 36 English. As soon as I comprehend a part of what was said and done, a mischievous spirit of revenge possessed me. One day I was called in from my play for some misconduct. I had disregarded a rule which seemed to me very needlessly binding. I was sent into the kitchen to mash the turnips for dinner. It was noon, and steaming dishes were hastily carried into the dining-room. I hated turnips, and their odor which came from the brown jar was offensive to me. With fire in my heart, I took the wooden tool that the paleface woman held out to me. I stood upon a step, and, grasping the handle with both hands, I bent in hot rage over the turnips. I worked my vengeance upon them. All were so busily occupied that no one noticed me. I saw that the turnips were in a pulp, and that further beating could not improve them; but the order was, "Mash these turnips," and mash them I would! I renewed my energy; and as I sent the masher into the bottom of the jar, I felt a satisfying sensation that the weight of my body had gone into it.

Just here a paleface woman came up to my table. As she looked 37 into the jar, she shoved my hands roughly aside. I stood fearless and angry. She placed her red hands upon the rim of the jar. Then she gave one lift and stride away from the table. But lo! the pulpy contents fell through the crumbled bottom to the floor! She spared me no scolding phrases that I had earned. I did not heed them. I felt triumphant in my revenge, though deep within me I was a wee bit sorry to have broken the jar.

As I sat eating my dinner, and saw that no turnips were served, 38 I whooped in my heart for having once asserted the rebellion within me.

IV

The Devil

Among the legends the old warriors used to tell me were many   39
stories of evil spirits. But I was taught to fear them no more than
those who stalked about in material guise. I never knew there was an
insolent chieftain among the bad spirits, who dared to array his
forces against the Great Spirit, until I heard this white man's legend
from a paleface woman.

Out of a large book she showed me a picture of the white man's   40
devil. I looked in horror upon the strong claws that grew out of his
fur-covered fingers. His feet were like his hands. Trailing at his heels
was a scaly tail tipped with a serpent's open jaws. His face was a
patchwork: he had bearded cheeks, like some I had seen palefaces
wear; his nose was an eagle's bill, and his sharp-pointed ears were
pricked up like those of a sly fox. Above them a pair of cow's horns
curved upward. I trembled with awe, and my heart throbbed in my
throat, as I looked at the king of evil spirits. Then I heard the paleface woman say that this terrible creature roamed loose in the world,
and that little girls who disobeyed school regulations were to be tor-
tured by him.

That night, I dreamt about this evil divinity. Once again I   41
seemed to be in my mother's cottage. An Indian woman had come
to visit my mother. On opposite sides of the kitchen stove, which
stood in the center of the small house, my mother and her guest
were seated in straight-backed chairs. I played with a train of empty
spools hitched together on a string. It was night, and the wick
burned feebly. Suddenly I heard some one turn our door-knob from
without.

My mother and the woman hushed their talk, and both looked   42
toward the door. It opened gradually. I waited behind the stove. The
hinges squeaked as the door was slowly, very slowly pushed inward.

Then in rushed the devil! He was tall! He looked exactly like the   43
picture I had seen of him in the white man's papers. He did not
speak to my mother, because he did not know the Indian language,
but his glittering yellow eyes were fastened upon me. He took long
strides around the stove, passing behind the woman's chair. I threw
down my spools, and ran to my mother. He did not fear her, but followed closely after me. Then I ran round and round the stove, crying aloud for help. But my mother and the woman seemed not to
know my danger. They sat still, looking quietly upon the devil's
chase after me. At last I grew dizzy. My head revolved as on a hidden pivot. My knees became numb, and doubled under my weight
like a pair of knife blades without a spring. Beside my mother's
chair I fell in a heap. Just as the devil stooped over me with out-

stretched claws my mother awoke from her quiet indifference, and lifted me on her lap. Whereupon the devil vanished, and I was awake.

On the following morning I took my revenge upon the devil. 44 Stealing into the room where a wall of shelves was filled with books, I drew forth The Stories of the Bible. With a broken slate pencil I carried in my apron pocket, I began by scratching out his wicked eyes. A few moments later, when I was ready to leave the room, there was a ragged hole in the page where the picture of the devil had once been.

V

Iron Routine

A loud-clamoring bell awakened us at half-past six in the cold 45 winter mornings. From happy dreams of Western rolling lands and unlassoed freedom we tumbled out upon chilly bare floors back again into a paleface day. We had short time to jump into our shoes and clothes, and wet our eyes with icy water, before a small hand bell was vigorously rung for roll call.

There were too many drowsy children and too numerous orders 46 for the day to waste a moment in any apology to nature for giving her children such a shock in the early morning. We rushed downstairs, bounding over two high steps at a time, to land in the assembly room.

A paleface woman, with a yellow-covered roll book open on her 47 arm and a gnawed pencil in her hand, appeared at the door. Her small, tired face was coldly lighted with a pair of large gray eyes.

She stood still in a halo of authority, while over the rim of her 48 spectacles her eyes pried nervously about the room. Having glanced at her long list of names and called out the first one, she tossed up her chin and peered through the crystals of her spectacles to make sure of the answer "Here."

Relentlessly her pencil black-marked our daily records if we were 49 not present to respond to our names, and no chum of ours had done it successfully for us. No matter if a dull headache or the painful cough of slow consumption had delayed the absentee, there was only time enough to mark the tardiness. It was next to impossible to leave the iron routine after the civilizing machine had once begun its day's buzzing; and as it was inbred in me to suffer in silence rather than to appeal to the ears of one whose open eyes could not see my pain, I have many time trudged in the day's harness heavy-footed, like a dumb sick brute.

Once I lost a dear classmate. I remember well how she used to 50 mope along at my side, until one morning she could not raise her head from her pillow. At her deathbed I stood weeping, as the pale-

face woman sat near her moistening the dry lips. Among the folds of
the bedclothes I saw the open pages of the white man's Bible. The
dying Indian girl talked disconnectedly of Jesus the Christ and the
paleface who was cooling her swollen hands and feet.

I grew bitter, and censured the woman for cruel neglect of our   51
physical ills. I despised the pencils that moved automatically, and the
one teaspoon which dealt out, from a large bottle, healing to a row
of variously ailing Indian children. I blamed the hard-working, well-
meaning, ignorant woman who was inculcating in our hearts her
superstitious ideas. Though I was sullen in all my little troubles, as
soon as I felt better I was ready again to smile upon the cruel
woman. Within a week I was again actively testing the chains which
tightly bound my individuality like a mummy for burial.

The melancholy of those black days has left so long a shadow   52
that it darkens the path of years that have since gone by. These sad
memories rise above those of smoothly grinding school days.
Perhaps my Indian nature is the moaning wind which stirs them now
for their present record. But, however tempestuous this is within me,
it comes out as the low voice of a curiously colored seashell, which
is only for those ears that are bent with compassion to hear it.

VI

Four Strange Summers

After my first three years of school, I roamed again in the   53
Western country through four strange summers.

During this time I seemed to hang in the heart of chaos, beyond   54
the touch or voice of human aid. My brother, being almost ten years
my senior, did not quite understand my feelings. My mother had
never gone inside of a schoolhouse, and so she was not capable of
comforting her daughter who could read and write. Even nature
seemed to have no place for me. I was neither a wee girl nor a tall
one; neither a wild Indian nor a tame one. This deplorable situation
was the effect of my brief course in the East, and the unsatisfactory
"teenth" in a girl's years.

It was under these trying conditions that, one bright afternoon,   55
as I sat restless and unhappy in my mother's cabin, I caught the
sound of the spirited step of my brother's pony on the road which
passed by our dwelling. Soon I heard the wheels of a light buck-
board, and Dawée's familiar "Ho!" to his pony. He alighted upon
the bare ground in front of our house. Tying his pony to one of the
projecting corner logs of the low-roofed cottage, he stepped upon
the wooden doorstep.

I met him there with a hurried greeting, and, as I passed by, he   56
looked a quiet "What?" into my eyes.

When he began talking with my mother, I slipped the rope from   57
the pony's bridle. Seizing the reins and bracing my feet against the
dashboard, I wheeled around in an instant. The pony was ever ready
to try his speed. Looking backward, I saw Dawée waving his hand to
me. I turned with the curve in the road and disappeared. I followed
the winding road which crawled upward between the bases of little
hillocks. Deep water-worn ditches ran parallel on either side. A
strong wind blew against my cheeks and fluttered my sleeves. The
pony reached the top of the highest hill, and began an even race on
the level lands. There was nothing moving within that great circular
horizon of the Dakota prairies save the tall grasses, over which the
wind blew and rolled off in long, shadowy waves.

Within this vast wigwam of blue and green I rode reckless and   58
insignificant. It satisfied my small consciousness to see the white
foam fly from the pony's mouth.

Suddenly, out of the earth a coyote came forth at a swinging trot   59
that was taking the cunning thief toward the hills and the village
beyond. Upon the moment's impulse, I gave him a long chase and
a wholesome fright. As I turned away to go back to the village, the
wolf sank down upon his haunches for rest, for it was a hot summer
day; and as I drove slowly homeward, I saw his sharp nose still pointed at me, until I vanished below the margin of the hilltops.

In a little while I came insight of my mother's house. Dawée   60
stood in the yard, laughing at an old warrior who was pointing his
forefinger, and again waving his whole hand, toward the hills. With
his blanket drawn over one shoulder, he talked and motioned excitedly. Dawée turned the old man by the shoulder and pointed me out
to him.

"Oh, han!" (Oh, yes) the warrior muttered, and went his way.   61
He had climbed the top of his favorite barren hill to survey the surrounding prairies, when he spied my chase after the coyote. His keen
eyes recognized the pony and driver. At once uneasy for my safety,
he had come running to my mother's cabin to give her warning.
I did not appreciate his kindly interest, for there was an unrest gnaw-
ing at my heart.

As soon as he went away, I asked Dawée about something else.   62

"No, my baby sister, I cannot take you with me to the party   63
tonight," he replied. Though I was not far from fifteen, and I felt
that before long I should enjoy all the privileges of my tall cousin,
Dawée persisted in calling me his baby sister.

That moonlight night, I cried in my mother's presence when I   64
heard the jolly young people pass by our cottage. They were no more
young braves in blankets and eagle plumes, nor Indian maids with

prettily painted cheeks. They had gone three years to school in the East, and had become civilized. The young men wore the white man's coat and trousers, with bright neckties. The girls wore tight muslin dresses, with ribbons at neck and waist. At these gatherings they talked English. I could speak English almost as well as my brother, but I was not properly dressed to be taken along. I had no hat, no ribbons, and no close-fitting gown. Since my return from school I had thrown away my shoes, and wore again the soft moccasins.

While Dawée was busily preparing to go I controlled my tears. 65 But when I heard him bounding away on his pony, I buried my face in my arms and cried hot tears.

My mother was troubled by my unhappiness. Coming to my 66 side, she offered me the only printed matter we had in our home. It was an Indian Bible, given her some years ago by a missionary. She tried to console me. "Here, my child, are the white man's papers. Read a little from them," she said most piously.

I took it from her hand, for her sake; but my enraged spirit felt 67 more like burning the book, which afforded me no help, and was a perfect delusion to my mother. I did not read it, but laid it unopened on the floor, where I sat on my feet. The dim yellow light of the braided muslin burning in a small vessel of oil flickered and sizzled in the awful silent storm which followed my rejection of the Bible.

Now my wrath against the fates consumed my tears before they 68 reached my eyes. I sat stony, with a bowed head. My mother threw a shawl over her head and shoulders, and stepped out into the night.

After an uncertain solitude, I was suddenly aroused by a loud cry 69 piercing the night. It was my mother's voice wailing among the barren hills which held the bones of buried warriors. She called aloud for her brothers' spirits to support her in her helpless misery. My fingers grew icy cold, as I realized that my unrestrained tears had betrayed my suffering to her, and she was grieving for me.

Before she returned, though I knew she was on her way, for she 70 had ceased her weeping, I extinguished the light, and leaned my head on the window sill.

Many schemes of running away from my surroundings hovered 71 about in my mind. A few more moons of such a turmoil drove me away to the eastern school. I rode on the white man's iron steed, thinking it would bring me back to my mother in a few winters, when I should be grown tall, and there would be congenial friends awaiting me.

VII

Incurring My Mother's Displeasure

In the second journey to the East I had not come without some   72
precautions. I had a secret interview with one of our best medicine
men, and when I left his wigwam I carried securely in my sleeve a
tiny bunch of magic roots. This possession assured me of friends
wherever I should go. So absolutely did I believe in its charms that
I wore it through all the school routine for more than a year. Then,
before I lost faith in the dead roots, I lost the little buckskin bag
containing all my good luck.

At the close of this second term of three years I was the proud   73
owner of my first diploma. The following autumn I ventured upon a
college career against my mother's will.

I had written for her approval, but in her reply I found no   74
encouragement. She called my notice to her neighbors' children,
who had completed their education in three years. They had
returned to their homes, and were then talking English with the
frontier settlers. Her few words hinted that I had better give up my
slow attempt to learn the white man's ways, and be content to roam
over the prairies and find my living upon wild roots. I silenced her
by deliberate disobedience.

Thus, homeless and heavy-hearted, I began anew my life among   75
strangers.

As I hid myself in my little room in the college dormitory, away   76
from the scornful and yet curious eyes of the students, I pined for
sympathy. Often I wept in secret, wishing I had gone West, to be
nourished by my mother's love, instead of remaining among a cold
race whose hearts were frozen hard with prejudice.

During the fall and winter seasons I scarcely had a real friend,   77
though by that time several of my classmates were courteous to me
at a safe distance.

My mother had not yet forgiven my rudeness to her, and I had   78
no moment for letter-writing. By daylight and lamplight, I spun with
reeds and thistles, until my hands were tired from their weaving, the
magic design which promised me the white man's respect.

At length, in the spring term, I entered an oratorical contest   79
among the various classes. As the day of competition approached, it
did not seem possible that the event was so near at hand, but it came.
In the chapel the classes assembled together, with their invited
guests. The high platform was carpeted, and gayly festooned with
college colors. A bright white light illumined the room, and outlined
clearly the great polished beams that arched the domed ceiling. The
assembled crowds filled the air with pulsating murmurs. When the

hour for speaking arrived all were hushed. But on the wall the old
clock which pointed out the trying moment ticked calmly on.

One after another I saw and heard the orators. Still, I could not   80
realize that they longed for the favorable decision of the judges as
much as I did. Each contestant received a loud burst of applause, and
some were cheered heartily. Too soon my turn came, and I paused a
moment behind the curtains for a deep breath. After my concluding
words, I heard the same applause that the others had called out.

Upon my retreating steps, I was astounded to receive from my   81
fellow-students a large bouquet of roses tied with flowing ribbons.
With the lovely flowers I fled from the stage. This friendly token was
a rebuke to me for the hard feelings I had borne them.

Later, the decision of the judges awarded me the first place.   82
Then there was a mad uproar in the hall, where my classmates sang
and shouted my name at the top of their lungs; and the disappoint-
ed students howled and brayed in fearfully dissonant tin trumpets. In
this excitement, happy students rushed forward to offer their congratulations. And I could not conceal a smile when they wished to
escort me in a procession to the students' parlor, where all were
going to calm themselves. Thanking them for the kind spirit which
prompted them to make such a proposition, I walked alone with the
night to my own little room.

A few weeks afterward, I appeared as the college representative   83
in another contest. This time the competition was among orators
from different colleges in our State. It was held at the State capital,
in one of the largest opera houses.

Here again was a strong prejudice against my people. In the   84
evening, as the great audience filled the house, the student bodies
began warring among themselves. Fortunately, I was spared witness-
ing any of the noisy wrangling before the contest began. The slurs
against the Indian that stained the lips of our opponents were already
burning like a dry fever within my breast.

But after the orations were delivered a deeper burn awaited me.   85
There, before that vast ocean of eyes, some college rowdies threw
out a large white flag, with a drawing of a most forlorn Indian girl
on it. Under this they had printed in bold black letter words that
ridiculed the college which was represented by a "squaw." Such
worse than barbarian rudeness embittered me. While we waited for
the verdict of the judges, I gleamed fiercely upon the throngs of
palefaces. My teeth were hard set, as I saw the white flag still floating insolently in the air.

Then anxiously we watched the man carry toward the stage the   86
envelope containing the final decision.

There were two prizes given, that night, and one of them was   87
mine!

The evil spirit laughed within me when the white flag dropped   88
out of sight, and the hands which hurled it hung limp in defeat.

Leaving the crowd as quickly as possible, I was soon in my room.   89
The rest of the night I sat in an armchair and gazed into the crackling fire. I laughed no more in triumph when thus alone. The little
taste of victory did not satisfy a hunger in my heart. In my mind I
saw my mother far way on the Western plains, and she was holding
a charge against me.

EXPLORATIONS

1. How are the "palefaces" seen through Zitkala-Sa's eyes? What image
   of "paleface" customs and manners does she give her readers?

2. What can we infer about Dakota life from this narrative?

3. What kind of "literacy" must Zitkala-Sa learn? For whose benefit is
   such literacy?

4. Zitkala-Sa obviously learned to write well, yet her story is one of loss
   and suffering. Speculate a bit about what it cost her to become literate
   in the world of the "paleface."

5. Like many of the writers in this book, Zitkala-Sa explores the tensions
   that can exist between the official, powerful languages of school and the
   often less powerful languages of communities that are on the margins
   of American society. Imagine that Zitkala-Sa and the rest of the writers
   in Part 3 were gathered for a conversation about literacy and the purposes of school in America. What might they say to each other? What
   common ground might be found between, for example, Cherríe
   Moraga, Zitkala-Sa, E. D. Hirsch, Mike Rose, and Philip Levine? Could
   they agree to the contents of "cultural literacy," or would such agreement be possible or even desirable?

America Skips School

BENJAMIN R. BARBER

Benjamin Barber (born 1939) teaches political science at Rutgers University in New Brunswick, New Jersey. In addition to numerous scholarly books and articles, Barber has published five plays and a novel. "America Skips School" appeared in the November 1993 issue of Harper's.

WRITING BEFORE READING

How relevant was what you studied in high school to your life outside the high school classroom?

On September 8, the day most of the nation's children were scheduled to return to school, the Department of Education Statistics issued a report, commissioned by Congress, on adult literacy and numeracy in the United States. The results? More than 90 million adult Americans lacked simple literacy. Fewer than 20 percent of those surveyed could compare two metaphors in a poem; not 4 percent could calculate the cost of carpeting at a given price for a room of a given size, using a calculator. As the DOE report was being issued, as if to echo its findings, two of the nation's largest school systems had delayed their openings: in New York, to remove asbestos from aging buildings; in Chicago, because of a battle over the budget.

Inspired by the report and the delays, pundits once again began chanting the familiar litany of the education crisis. We've heard it all many times before: 130,000 children bring guns along with their pencils and books to school each morning; juvenile arrests for murder increased by 85 percent from 1987 to 1991; more than 3,000 youngsters will drop out today and every day for the rest of the school year, until about 600,000 are lost by June—in many urban schools, perhaps half the enrollment. A lot of the dropouts will end up in prison, which is a surer bet for young black males than college: one in four will pass through the correctional system, and at least two out of three of those will be dropouts.

In quiet counterpoint to those staggering facts is another set of statistics: teachers make less than accountants, architects, doctors, lawyers, engineers, judges, health professionals, auditors, and surveyors. They can earn higher salaries teaching in Berlin, Tokyo, Ottawa, or Amsterdam than in New York or Chicago. American children are in school only about 180 days a year, as against 240 days or more for children in Europe or Japan. The richest school districts (school financing is local, not federal) spend twice as much per student as poorer ones do. The poorer ones seem almost beyond help: children with venereal disease or AIDS (2.5 million adolescents annually contract a sexually transmitted disease), gangs in the schoolyard, drugs in the classroom, children doing babies instead of homework, playground firefights featuring Uzis and Glocks.

Clearly, the social contract that obliges adults to pay taxes so that   4
children can be educated is in imminent danger of collapse. Yet for all the astonishing statistics, more astonishing still is that no one seems to be listening. The education crisis is kind of like violence on television: the worse it gets the more inert we become, and the more of it we require to rekindle our attention. We've had a "crisis" every dozen years or so at least since the launch of *Sputnik*, in 1957, when American schools were accused of falling behind the world standard in science education. Just ten years ago, the National Commission on Excellence in Education warned that America's pedagogical inattention was putting America "at risk." What the commission called "a rising tide of mediocrity" was imperiling "our very future as a Nation and a people." What was happening to education was an "act of war."

Since then, countless reports have been issued decrying the   5
condition of our educational system, the DOE report being only the most recent. They have come from every side, Republican as well as Democrat, from the private sector as well as the public. Yet for all the talk, little happens. At times, the schools look more like they are being dismantled than rebuilt. How can this be? If Americans over a broad political spectrum regard education as vital, why has nothing been done?

I have spent thirty years as a scholar examining the nature of   6
democracy, and even more as a citizen optimistically celebrating its possibilities, but today I am increasingly persuaded that the reason for the country's inaction is that Americans do not really care about education—the country has grown comfortable with the game of "let's pretend we care."

As America's educational system crumbles, the pundits, instead   7
of looking for solutions, search busily for scapegoats. Some assail the teachers—those "Profscam" pedagogues trained in the licentious Sixties who, as aging hippies, are supposedly still subverting the schools—for producing a dire illiteracy. Others turn on the kids themselves, so that at the same moment as we are transferring our responsibilities to the shoulders of the next generation, we are blaming them for our own generation's most conspicuous failures. Allan Bloom was typical of the many recent critics who have condemned

the young as vapid, lazy, selfish, complacent, self-seeking, materialistic, small-minded, apathetic, greedy, and, of course, illiterate. E. D.
Hirsch in his *Cultural Literacy* and Diane Ravitch and Chester E.
Finn Jr. in their *What Do Our Seventeen-Year-Olds Know?* have
lambasted the schools, the teachers, and the children for betraying
the adult generation from which they were to inherit, the critics
seemed confident, a precious cultural legacy.

How this captious literature reeks of hypocrisy! How sanctimo-   8
nious all the hand-wringing over still another "education crisis"
seems. Are we ourselves really so literate? Are our kids stupid or
smart for ignoring what we preach and copying what we practice?
The young, with their keen noses for hypocrisy, are in fact adept
readers—but not of books. They are society-smart rather than
school-smart, and what they read so acutely are the social signals
emanating from the world in which they will have to make a living.
Their teachers in that world, the nation's true pedagogues, are television, advertising, movies, politics, and the celebrity domains they
define. We prattle about deficient schools and the gullible youngsters
they turn out, so vulnerable to the siren song of drugs, but think
nothing of letting the advertisers into the classroom to fashion what
an *Advertising Age* essay calls "brand and product loyalties through
classroom-centered, peer-powered lifestyle patterning."

Our kids spend 900 hours a year in school (the ones who go   9
to school) and from 1,200 to 1,800 hours a year in front of the television set. From which are they likely to learn more? Critics such as
Hirsch and Ravitch want to find out what our seventeen-year-olds
know, but it's really pretty simple: they know exactly what our
forty-seven-year-olds know and teach them by example—on television, in the boardroom, around Washington, on Madison Avenue, in
Hollywood. The very first lesson smart kids learn is that it is much
more important to heed what society teaches implicitly by its deeds
and reward structures than what school teaches explicitly in its lesson plans and civic sermons. Here is a test for adults that may help
reveal what the kids see when they look at our world.

REAL-WORLD CULTURAL LITERACY

1. According to television, having fun in America means
   a) going blond
   b) drinking Pepsi
   c) playing Nintendo
   d) wearing Air Jordans
   e) reading Mark Twain

2. A good way to prepare for a high-income career and to acquire
   status in our society is to

a) win a slam-dunk contest
b) take over a company and sell off its assets
c) start a successful rock band
d) earn a professional degree
e) become a kindergarten teacher

3. Book publishers are financially rewarded today for publishing
   a) mega-cookbooks
   b) mega—cat books
   c) megabooks by Michael Crichton
   d) megabooks by John Grisham
   e) mini-books by Voltaire

4. A major California bank that advertised "no previous credit history required" in inviting Berkeley students to apply for Visa cards nonetheless turned down one group of applicants because
   a) their parents had poor credit histories
   b) they had never held jobs
   c) they had outstanding student loans
   d) they were "humanities majors"

5. Colleges and universities are financially rewarded today for
   a) supporting bowl-quality football games
   b) forging research relationships with large corporations
   c) sustaining professional programs in law and business
   d) stroking wealthy alumni
   e) fostering outstanding philosophy departments

6. Familiarity with *Henry IV, Part II* is likely to be of vital importance in
   a) planning a corporate takeover
   b) evaluating budget cuts in the Department of Education
   c) initiating a medical-malpractice lawsuit
   d) writing an impressive job résumé
   e) taking a test on what our seventeen-year-olds know

7. To help the young learn that "history is a living thing," Scholastic, Inc., a publisher of school magazines and paperbacks, recently distributed to 40,000 junior and senior highschool classrooms
   a) a complimentary video of the award-winning series *The Civil War*
   b) free copies of Plato's *Dialogues*
   c) an abridgment of Alexis de Tocqueville's *Democracy in America*
   d) a wall-size Periodic Table of the Elements

e) gratis copies of Billy Joel's hit single "We Didn't Start the Fire" (which recounts history via a vaguely chronological list of warbled celebrity names)

My sample of forty-seven-year-olds scored very well on the test. 10 Not surprisingly, so did their seventeen-year-old children. (For each question, either the last entry is correct or all responses are correct *except* the last one.) The results of the test reveal again the deep hypocrisy that runs through our lamentations about education. The illiteracy of the young turns out to be our own reflected back to us with embarrassing force. We honor ambition, we reward greed, we celebrate materialism, we worship acquisitiveness, we cherish success, and we commercialize the classroom—and then we bark at the young about the gentle arts of the spirit. We recommend history to the kids but rarely consult it ourselves. We make a fuss about ethics but are satisfied to see it taught as an "add-on," as in "ethics in medicine" or "ethics in business"—as if Sunday morning in church could compensate for uninterrupted sinning from Monday to Saturday.

The children are onto this game. They know that if we really val- 11 ued schooling, we'd pay teachers what we pay stockbrokers; if we valued books, we'd spend a little something on the libraries so that adults could read, too; if we valued citizenship, we'd give national service and civic education more than pilot status; if we valued children, we wouldn't let them be abused, manipulated, impoverished, and killed in their beds by gang-war cross fire and stray bullets. Schools can and should lead, but when they confront a society that in every instance tells a story exactly opposite to the one they are supposed to be teaching, their job becomes impossible. When the society undoes each workday what the school tries to do each day, schooling can't make much of a difference.

Inner-city children are not the only ones who are learning the 12 wrong lessons. TV sends the same messages to everyone, and the success of Donald Trump, Pete Rose, Henry Kravis, or George Steinbrenner makes them potent role models, whatever their values. Teen dropouts are not blind; teen drug sellers are not deaf; teen college students who avoid the humanities in favor of pre-business or pre-law are not stupid. Being apt pupils of reality, they learn their lessons well. If they see a man with a rubber arm and an empty head who can throw a ball at 95 miles per hour pulling down millions of dollars a year while a dedicated primary-school teacher is getting crumbs, they will avoid careers in teaching even if they can't make the major leagues. If they observe their government spending up to $35,000 a year to keep a young black behind bars but a fraction of that to keep him in school, they will write off school (and probably write off blacks as well).

Our children's illiteracy is merely our own, which they assume   13
with commendable prowess. They know what we have taught them
all too well: there is nothing in Homer or Virginia Woolf, in
Shakespeare or Toni Morrison, that will advantage them in climbing
to the top of the American heap. Academic credentials may still
count, but schooling in and of itself is for losers. Bookworms. Nerds.
Inner-city rappers and fraternity-house wise guys are in full agreement about that. The point is to start pulling down the big bucks.
Some kids just go into business earlier than others. Dropping out is
the national pastime, if by dropping out we mean giving up the
precious things of the mind and the spirit in which America shows so
little interest and for which it offers so little payback. While the
professors argue about whether to teach the ancient history of a
putatively white Athens or the ancient history of a putatively black
Egypt, the kids are watching televised political campaigns driven by
mindless image-mongering and inflammatory polemics that ignore
history altogether. Why, then, are we so surprised when our students
dismiss the debate over the origins of civilization, whether
Eurocentric or Afrocentric, and concentrate on cash-and-carry
careers? Isn't the choice a tribute not to their ignorance but to their
adaptive intelligence? Although we can hardly be proud of ourselves
for what we are teaching them, we should at least be proud of them
for how well they've learned our lessons.

Not all Americans have stopped caring about the schools,   14
however. In the final irony of the educational endgame, cynical
entrepreneurs like Chris Whittle are insinuating television into the
classroom itself, bribing impoverished school boards by offering free
TV sets on which they can show advertising for children—sold to
sponsors at premium rates. Whittle, the mergers and acquisitions
mogul of education, is trying to get rich off the poverty of public
schools and the fears of parents. Can he really believe advertising in
the schools enhances education? Or is he helping to corrupt public
schools in ways that will make parents even more anxious to use
vouchers for private schools—which might one day be run by
Whittle's latest entrepreneurial venture, the Edison Project.

According to Lifetime Learning Systems, an educational-   15
software company, "kids spend 40 percent of each day . . . where
traditional advertising can't reach them." Not to worry, says
Lifetime Learning in an *Advertising Age* promo: "Now, you can
enter the classroom through custom-made learning materials created with your specific marketing objectives in mind. Communicate
with young spenders directly and, through them, their teachers and
families as well." If we redefine young learners as "young
spenders," are the young really to be blamed for acting like mindless consumers? Can they become young spenders and still become

young critical thinkers, let alone informed citizens? If we are willing to give TV cartoons the government's imprimatur as "educational television" (as we did a few years ago, until the FCC changed its mind), can we blame kids for educating themselves on television trash?

Everyone can agree that we should educate our children to be   16
something more than young spenders molded by "lifestyle pattern-ing." But what should the goals of the classroom be? In recent years it has been fashionable to define the educational crisis in terms of global competition and minimal competence, as if schools were no more than vocational institutions. Although it has talked sensibly about education, the Clinton Administration has leaned toward this approach, under the tutelage of Secretary of Labor Robert Reich.

The classroom, however, should not be merely a trade school.   17
The fundamental task of education in a democracy is what Tocqueville once called once called the apprenticeship of liberty: learning to be free. I wonder whether Americans still believe liberty has to be learned and that its skills are worth learning. Or have they been deluded by two centuries of rhetoric into thinking that freedom is "natural" and can be taken for granted?

The claim that all men are born free, upon which America was   18
founded, is at best a promising fiction. In real life, as every parent knows, children are born fragile, born needy, born ignorant, born unformed, born weak, born foolish, born dependent—born in chains. We acquire our freedom over time, if at all. Embedded in families, clans, communities, and nations, we must learn to be free. We may be natural consumers and born narcissists, but citizens have to be made. Liberal-arts education actually means education in the arts of liberty; the "servile arts" were the trades learned by unfree men in the Middle Ages, the vocational education of their day. Perhaps this is why Thomas Jefferson preferred to memorialize his founding of the University of Virginia on his tombstone rather than his two terms as president; it is certainly why he viewed his Bill for the More General Diffusion of Knowledge in Virginia as a center-piece of his career (although it failed passage as legislation—times were perhaps not so different). John Adams, too, boasted regularly about Massachusetts's high literacy rates and publicly funded education.

Jefferson and Adams both understood that the Bill of Rights   19
offered little protection in a nation without informed citizens. Once educated, however, a people was safe from even the subtlest tyran-nies. Jefferson's democratic proclivities rested on his conviction that education could turn a people into a safe refuge—indeed "the only safe depository" for the ultimate powers of society. "Cherish

therefore the spirit of our people," he wrote to Edward Carrington in 1787, "and keep alive their attention. Do not be severe upon their errors, but reclaim them by enlightening them. If once they become inattentive to public affairs, you and I and Congress and Assemblies, judges and governors, shall all become wolves."

The logic of democracy begins with public education, proceeds 20 to informed citizenship, and comes to fruition in the securing of rights and liberties. We have been nominally democratic for so long that we presume it is our natural condition rather than the product of persistent effort and tenacious responsibility. We have decoupled rights from civic responsibilities and severed citizenship from education on the false assumption that citizens just happen. We have forgotten that the "public" in public schools means not just paid for by the public but procreative of the very idea of a public. Public schools are how a public—a citizenry—is forged and how young, selfish individuals turn into conscientious, community-minded citizens.

Among the several literacies that have attracted the anxious 21 attention of commentators, civic literacy has been the least visible. Yet this is the fundamental literacy by which we live in a civil society. It encompasses the competence to participate in democratic communities, the ability to think critically and act with deliberation in a pluralistic world, and the empathy to identify sufficiently with others to live with them despite conflicts of interest and differences in character. At the most elementary level, what our children suffer from most, whether they're hurling racial epithets from fraternity porches or shooting one another down in schoolyards, is the absence of civility. Security guards and metal detectors are poor surrogates for civility, and they make our schools look increasingly like prisons (though they may be less safe than prisons). Jefferson thought schools would produce free men: we prove him right by putting dropouts in jail.

Civility is a work of the imagination, for it is through the imag- 22 ination that we render others sufficiently like ourselves for them to become subjects of tolerance and respect, if not always affection. Democracy is anything but a "natural" form of association. It is an extraordinary and rare contrivance of cultivated imagination. Give the uneducated the right to participate in making collective decisions, and what results is not democracy but, as best, mob rule: the government of private prejudice once known as the tyranny of opinion. For Jefferson, the difference between the democratic temperance he admired in agrarian America and the rule of the rabble he condemned when viewing the social unrest of Europe's teeming cities was quite simply education. Madison had hoped to "filter" out popular passion through the device of representation. Jefferson saw in education a filter that could be installed within each individual, giving to each the capacity to rule prudently. Education creates a ruling aristocracy constrained by temperance and wisdom; when that education is public and universal, it is an aristocracy to which all can belong. At its best, the American dream of a free and equal society governed by judicious citizens has been this dream of an aristocracy of everyone.

To dream this dream of freedom is easy, but to secure it is difficult as well as expensive. Notwithstanding their lamentations, Americans do not appear ready to pay the price. There is no magic bullet for education. But I no longer can accept that the problem lies in the lack of consensus about remedies—in a dearth of solutions. There is no shortage of debate over how to repair our educational infrastructure. National standards or more local control? Vouchers or better public schools? More parental involvement or more teacher autonomy? A greater federal presence (only 5 or 6 percent of the nation's education budget is federally funded) or fairer local school taxes? More multicultural diversity or more emphasis on what Americans share in common? These are honest disputes. But I am convinced that the problem is simpler and more fundamental. Twenty years ago, writer and activist Frances Moore Lappé captured the essence of the world food crisis when she argued that starvation was caused not by a scarcity of food but by a global scarcity in democracy. The education crisis has the same genealogy. It stems from a dearth of democracy: an absence of democratic will and a consequent refusal to take our children, our schools, and our future seriously. 23

Most educators, even while they quarrel among themselves, will agree that a genuine commitment to any one of a number of different solutions could help enormously. Most agree that although money can't by itself solve problems, without money few problems can be solved. Money also can't win wars or put men in space, but it is the crucial facilitator. It is also how America has traditionally announced, We are serious about this! 24

If we were serious, we would raise teachers' salaries to levels that would attract the best young professionals in our society: starting lawyers get from $70,000 to $80,000—why don't starting kindergarten teachers get the same? Is their role in vouchsafing our future less significant? And although there is evidence suggesting that an increase in general educational expenditures doesn't translate automatically into better schools, there is also evidence that an increase aimed specifically at instructional service does. Can we really take in earnest the chattering devotion to excellence of a country so wedded in practice to mediocrity, a nation so ready to relegate teachers—conservators of our common future—to the professional backwaters? 25

If we were serious, we would upgrade physical facilities so that   26
every school met the minimum standards of our better suburban
institutions. Good buildings do not equal good education, but can
any education at all take place in leaky, broken-down habitats of the
kind described by Jonathan Kozol in his *Savage Inequalities?* If
money is not a critical factor, why are our most successful suburban
school districts funded at nearly twice the level of our inner-city
schools? Being even at the starting line cannot guarantee that the
runners will win or even finish the race, but not being even pretty
much assures failure. We would rectify the balance not by penalizing
wealthier communities but by bringing poorer communities up to
standard, perhaps by finding other sources of funding for our schools
besides property taxes.

If we were serious, we'd extend the school year by a month or   27
two so that learning could take place throughout the year. We'd
reduce class size (which means more teachers) and nurture more
cooperative learning so that kids could become actively responsible
for their own education and that of their classmates. Perhaps most
important, we'd raise standards and make teachers and students
responsible for them. There are two ways to breed success: to lower
standards so that everybody "passes" in a way that loses all meaning in the real world; and to raise standards and then meet them, so
that school success translates into success beyond the classroom.
From Confucian China to Imperial England, great nations have built
their success in the world upon an education of excellence. The challenge in a democracy is to find a way to maintain excellence while
extending educational opportunity to everyone.

Finally, if we were serious, parents, teachers, and students would   28
be the real players while administrators, politicians, and experts
would be secondary, at best advisers whose chief skill ought to be
knowing when and how to facilitate the work of teachers and then
get out of the way. If the Democrats can clean up federal government bureaucracy (the Gore plan), perhaps we can do the same for
educational bureaucracy. In New York up to half of the city's teachers occupy jobs outside the classroom. No other enterprise is run
that way: Half the soldiers at company headquarters? Half the cops
at stationhouse desks? Half the working force in the assistant manager's office? Once the teachers are back in the classroom, they will
need to be given more autonomy, more professional responsibility
for the success or failure of their students. And parents will have to
be drawn in not just because they have rights or because they are
politically potent but because they have responsibilities and their
children are unlikely to learn without parental engagement. How to
define the parental role in the classroom would become serious business for educators.

Some Americans will say this is unrealistic. Times are tough,   29
money's short, and the public is fed up with almost all of its public
institutions: the schools are just one more frustrating disappointment. With all the goodwill in the world, it is still hard to know how
schools can cur the ills that stem from the failure of so many other
institutions. Saying we want education to come first won't put it
first.

America, however, has historically been able to accomplish what   30
it sets its mind to. When we wish it and will it, what we wish and will
has happened. Our successes are willed; our failures seem to happen
when will is absent. There are, of course, those who benefit from the
bankruptcy of public education and the failure of democracy. But
their blame is no greater than our own: in a world where doing nothing has such dire consequences, complacency has become a greater
sin than malevolence.

In wartime, whenever we have know why we were fighting and   31
believed in the cause, we have prevailed. Because we believe in prof-
its, we are consummate salespersons and efficacious entrepreneurs.
Because we love sports, ours are the dream teams. Why can't a
Chicago junior high school be as good as the Chicago Bulls? Because
we cherish individuality and mobility, we have created a magnificent
(if costly) car culture and the world's largest automotive consumer
market. Even as our lower schools are among the worst in the
Western world, our graduate institutions are among the very best—
because professional training in medicine, law, and technology is vital
to our ambitions and because corporate America backs up state and
federal priorities in this crucial domain. Look at the things we do
well and observe how very well we do them: those are the things that
as a nation we have willed.

Then observe what we do badly and ask yourself, Is it because   32
the challenge is too great? Or is it because, finally, we aren't really
serious? Would we will an end to the carnage and do whatever it
took—more cops, state militias, federal marshals, the Marines?—if the
dying children were white and middle class? Or is it a disdain for the
young—white, brown, and black—that inures us to the pain? Why are
we so sensitive to the retirees whose future (however foreshortened)
we are quick to guarantee—don't worry, no reduced cost-of-living
allowances, no taxes on social security except for the well-off—and so
callous to the young? Have you noticed how health care is on every
politician's agenda and education on no one's?

To me, the conclusion is inescapable: we are not serious. We   33
have given up on the public schools because we have given up on the
kids; and we have given up on the kids because we have given up on
the future—perhaps because it looks too multicolored or too dim or
too hard. "Liberty," said Jean-Jacques Rousseau, "is a food easy to

eat but hard to digest." America is suffering from a bad case of indigestion. Finally, in giving up on the future, we have given up on democracy. Certainly there will be no liberty, no equality, no social justice without democracy, and there will be no democracy without citizens and the schools that forge civic identity and democratic responsibility. If I am wrong (I'd like to be), my error will be easy to discern, for before the year is out we will put education first on the nation's agenda. We will put it ahead of the deficit, for if the future is finished before it starts, the deficit doesn't matter. Ahead of defense, for without democracy, what liberties will be left to defend? Ahead of all the other public issues and public goods, for without public education there can be no public and hence no truly public issues or public goods to advance. When the polemics are spent and we are through hyperventilating about the crisis in education, there is only one question worth asking: are we serious? If we are, we can begin by honoring that old folk homily and put our money where for much too long our common American mouth has been. Our kids, for once, might be grateful.

EXPLORATIONS

1. How does Barber define literacy?

2. Barber claims that Americans are not serious about education. Do you agree or disagree with him? Why?

3. How does Barber portray American youth? Is this an accurate image? Why or why not?

4. Barber claims that the fundamental task of education is learning to be free. He calls this civic literacy, "the fundamental literacy by which we live in a civil society." What kinds of freedoms is Barber talking about?

5. Barber argues that if we were serious about education, we would put our money where our mouths are. Do you think Americans are serious about education? Drawing upon Barber's essay and other essays in Part 3, what would we have to do to collectively agree on the purposes of education?

The Student and the University

ALLAN BLOOM

Allan Bloom (1930–92) taught at the University of Chicago as a professor in the Committee on Social Thought. In 1987, he published the best-selling and controversial The Closing of the American Mind, *from which "The Student and the University" is excerpted. The book appeared about the same time as E.D. Hirsch's* Cultural Literacy. *Bloom's book drew criticism from those who believed that his vision of a liberal education, with its emphasis on the twenty or thirty most prestigious and selective universities, was elitist. On the other hand, the book was praised by those who believed that Bloom's ideas might help to unify college curricula that often seem fragmented and diluted.*

WRITING BEFORE READING

Did you ever imagine an "ideal" college education or have an idyllic vision of the college environment? What was that vision based on, and how have your college experiences complicated that vision?

What image does a first-rank college or university present today to a teen-ager leaving home for the first time, off to the adventure of a liberal education? He has four years of freedom to discover himself—a space between the intellectual wasteland he has left behind and the inevitable dreary professional training that awaits him after the baccalaureate. In this short time he must learn that there is a great world beyond the little one he knows, experience the exhilaration of it and digest enough of it to sustain himself in the intellectual deserts he is destined to traverse. He must do this, that is, if he is to have any hope of a higher life. These are the charmed years when he can, if he so chooses, become anything he wishes and when he has the opportunity to survey his alternatives, not merely those current in his time or provided by careers, but those available to him as a human being. The importance of these years for an American cannot be overestimated. They are civilization's only chance to get to him.

In looking at him we are forced to reflect on what he should learn if he is to be called educated; we must speculate on what the human potential to be fulfilled is. In the specialties we can avoid such speculation, and the avoidance of them is one of specialization's charms. But here it is a simple duty. What are we to teach this person? The answer may not be evident, but to attempt to answer the question is already to philosophize and to begin to educate. Such a concern in itself poses the question of the unity of man and the unity of the sciences. It is childishness to say, as some do, that everyone must be allowed to develop freely, that it is authoritarian to impose a point of view on the student. In that case, why have a university? If the response is "to provide an atmosphere for learning," we come back to our original questions at the second remove. Which atmosphere? Choices and reflection on the reasons for those choices are unavoidable. The university has to stand for something. The practical effects of unwillingness to think positively about the contents of a liberal education are, on the one hand, to ensure that all the vulgarities of the world outside the university will flourish within it, and, on the other, to impose a much harsher and more illiberal necessity on the student—the one given by the imperial and imperious demands of the specialized disciplines unfiltered by unifying thought.

The university now offers no distinctive visage to the young   3
person. He finds a democracy of the disciplines—which are there either because they are autochthonous or because they wandered in recently to perform some job that was demanded of the university. This democracy is really an anarchy, because there are no recognized rules for citizenship and no legitimate titles to rule. In short there is no vision, nor is there a set of competing visions, of what an educated human being is. The question has disappeared, for to pose it would be a threat to the peace. There is no organization of the sciences, no tree of knowledge. Out of chaos emerges dispiritedness, because it is impossible to make a reasonable choice. Better to give up on liberal education and get on with a specialty in which there is at least a prescribed curriculum and a prospective career. On the way the student can pick up in elective courses a little of whatever is thought to make one cultured. The student gets no intimation that great mysteries might be revealed to him, that new and higher motives of action might be discovered within him, that a different and more human way of life can be harmoniously constructed by what he is going to learn.

Simply, the university is not distinctive. Equality for us seems to   4
culminate in the unwillingness and incapacity to make claims of superiority, particularly in the domains in which such claims have always been made—art, religion and philosophy. When Weber found that he could not choose between certain high opposites—reason vs. revelation, Buddha vs. Jesus—he did not conclude that all things are equally good, that the distinction between high and low disappears. As a matter of fact he intended to revitalize the consideration of these great alternatives in showing the gravity and danger involved in choosing among them; they were to be heightened in contrast to the

trivial considerations of modern life that threatened to overgrow and
render indistinguishable the profound problems the confrontation
with which makes the bow of the soul taut. The serious
intellectual life was for him the battleground of the great decisions, all
of which are spiritual or "value" choices. One can no longer present
this or that particular view of the educated or civilized man as authoritative; therefore one must say that education consists in knowing,
really knowing, the small number of such views in their integrity. This
distinction between profound and superficial—which takes the place
of good and bad, true and false—provided a focus for serious study,
but it hardly held out against the naturally relaxed democratic tendency to say, "Oh, what's the use?" The first university disruptions
at Berkeley were explicitly directed against the multiversity smorgas-
bord and, I must confess, momentarily and partially engaged my sym-
pathies. It may have even been the case that there was some small element of longing for an education in the motivation of those students.
But nothing was done to guide or inform their energy, and the result
was merely to add multilife-styles to multidisciplines, the diversity of
perversity to the diversity of specialization. What we see so often happening in general happened here too; the insistent demand for greater
community ended in greater isolation. Old agreements, old habits,
old traditions were not so easily replaced.

Thus, when a student arrives at the university, he finds a bewil-   5
dering variety of departments and a bewildering variety of courses.
And there is no official guidance, no university-wide agreement,
about what he *should* study. Nor does he usually find readily available examples, either among students or professors, of a unified use
of the university's resources. It is easiest simply to make a career
choice and go about getting prepared for that career. The programs
designed for those having made such a choice render their students
immune to charms that might lead them out of the conventionally
respectable. The sirens sing *sotto voce* these days, and the young
already have enough wax in their ears to pass them by without
danger. These specialties can provide enough courses to take up
most of their time for four years in preparation for the inevitable
graduate study. With the few remaining courses they can do what
they please, taking a bit of this and a bit of that. No public career
these days—not doctor nor lawyer nor politician nor journalist nor
businessman nor entertainer—has much to do with humane learning.
An education, other than purely professional or technical, can even
seem to be an impediment. That is why a countervailing atmosphere
in the university would be necessary for the students to gain a taste
for intellectual pleasures and learn that they are viable.

The real problem is those students who come hoping to find out   6
what career they want to have, or are simply looking for an adven-

ture with themselves. There are plenty of things for them to do—courses and disciplines enough to spend many a lifetime on. Each department or great division of the university makes a pitch for itself, and each offers a course of study that will make the student an initiate. But how to choose among them? How do they relate to one another? The fact is they do not address one another. They are competing and contradictory, without being aware of it. The problem of the whole is urgently indicated by the very existence of the specialties, but it is never systematically posed. The net effect of the student's encounter with the college catalogue is bewilderment and very often demoralization. It is just a matter of chance whether he finds one or two professors who can give him an insight into one of the great visions of education that have been the distinguishing part of every civilized nation. Most professors are specialists, concerned only with their own fields, interested in the advancement of those fields in their own terms, or in their own personal advancement in a world where all the rewards are on the side of professional distinction. They have been entirely emancipated from the old structure of the university, which at least helped to indicate that they are incomplete, only parts of an unexamined and undiscovered whole. So the student must navigate among a collection of carnival barkers, each trying to lure him into a particular sideshow. This undecided student is an embarrassment to most universities, because he seems to be saying, "I am a whole human being. Help me to form myself in my wholeness and let me develop my real potential," and he is the one to whom they have nothing to say.

Cornell was, as in so many other things, in advance of its time 7
on this issue. The six-year Ph. D. program, richly supported by the Ford Foundation, was directed specifically to high school students who had already made "a firm career choice" and was intended to rush them through to the start of those careers. A sop was given to desolate humanists in the form of money to fund seminars that these young careerists could take on their way through the college of Arts and Sciences. For the rest, the educators could devote their energies to arranging and packaging the program without having to provide it with any substance. That kept them busy enough to avoid thinking about the nothingness of their endeavor. This has been the preferred mode of not looking the Beast in the Jungle in the face—structure, not content. The Cornell plan for dealing with the problem of liberal education was to suppress the students' longing for liberal education by encouraging their professionalism and their avarice, providing money and all the prestige the university had available to make careerism the centerpiece of the university.

The Cornell plan dared not state the radical truth, a well-kept 8
secret: the colleges do not have enough to teach their students, not

enough to justify keeping them four years, probably not even three years. If the focus is careers, there is hardly one specialty, outside the hardest of the hard natural sciences, which requires more than two years of preparatory training prior to graduate studies. The rest is just wasted time, or a period of ripening until the students are old enough for graduate studies. For many graduate careers, even less is really necessary. It is amazing how many undergraduates are poking around for courses to take, without any plan or question to ask, just filling up their college years. In fact, with rare exceptions, the courses are parts of specialties and not designed for general cultivation, or to investigate questions important for human beings as such. The so-called knowledge explosion and increasing specialization have not filled up the college years but emptied them. Those years are impediments; one wants to get beyond them. And in general the persons one finds in the professions need not have gone to college, if one is to judge by their tastes, their fund of learning or their interests. They might as well have spent their college years in the Peace Corps or the like. These great universities—which can split the atom, find cures for the most terrible diseases, conduct surveys of whole populations and produce massive dictionaries of lost languages—cannot generate a modest program of general education for undergraduate students. This is a parable for our times.

There are attempts to fill the vacuum painlessly with various   9
kinds of fancy packaging of what is already there—study abroad options, individualized majors, etc. Then there are Black Studies and Women's or Gender Studies, along with Learn Another Culture. Peace Studies are on their way to a similar prevalence. All this is designed to show that the university is with it and has something in addition to its traditional specialties. The latest item is computer literacy, the full cheapness of which is evidence only to those who think a bit about what literacy might mean. It would make some sense to promote literacy literacy, inasmuch as most high school graduates nowadays have difficulty reading and writing. And some institutions are quietly undertaking this worthwhile task. But they do not trumpet the fact, because this is merely a high school function that our current sad state of educational affairs has thrust upon them, about which they are not inclined to boast.

Now that the distractions of the sixties are over, and undergrad-   10
uate education has become more important again (because the graduate departments, aside from the professional schools, are in trouble due to the shortage of academic jobs), university officials have had somehow to deal with the undeniable fact that the students who enter are uncivilized, and that the universities have some responsibility for civilizing them. If one were to give a base interpretation of the schools' motives, one could allege that their concern

stems from shame and self-interest. It is becoming all too evident that liberal education—which is what the small band of prestigious institutions are supposed to provide, in contrast to the big state schools, which are thought simply to prepare specialists to meet the practical demands of a complex society—has no content, that a certain kind of fraud is being perpetrated. For a time the great moral consciousness alleged to have been fostered in students by the great universities, especially their vocation as gladiators who fight war and racism, seemed to fulfill the demands of the collective university conscience. They were doing something other than offering preliminary training for doctors and lawyers. Concern and compassion were thought to be the indefinable *X* that pervaded all the parts of the Arts and Sciences campus. But when that evanescent mist dissipated during the seventies, and the faculties found themselves face to face with ill-educated young people with no intellectual tastes—unaware that there even are such things, obsessed with getting on with their careers before having looked at life—and the universities offered no counterpoise, no alternative goals, a reaction set in.

Liberal education—since it has for so long been ill-defined, has 11 none of the crisp clarity or institutionalized prestige of the professions, but nevertheless perseveres and has money and respectability connected with it—has always been a battleground for those who are somewhat eccentric in relation to the specialties. It is in something like the condition of churches as opposed to, say, hospitals. Nobody is quite certain of what the religious institutions are supposed to do anymore, but they do have some kind of role either responding to a real human need or as the vestige of what was once a need, and they invite the exploitation of quacks, adventurers, cranks and fanatics. But they also solicit the warmest and most valiant efforts of persons of peculiar gravity and depth. In liberal education, too, the worst and the best fight it out, fakers vs. authentics, sophists vs. philosophers, for the favor of public opinion and for control over the study of man in our times. The most conspicuous participants in the struggle are administrators who are formally responsible for presenting some kind of public image of the education their colleges offer, persons with a political agenda or vulgarizers of what the specialties know, and real teachers of the humane disciplines who actually see their relation to the whole and urgently wish to preserve the awareness of it in their students' consciousness.

So, just as in the sixties universities were devoted to removing 12 requirements, in the eighties they are busy with attempts to put them back in, a much more difficult task. The word of the day is "core." It is generally agreed that "we went a bit far in the sixties," and that a little fine-tuning has now become clearly necessary.

There are two typical responses to the problem. The easiest and 13 most administratively satisfying solution is to make use of what is already there in the autonomous departments and simply force the students to cover the fields, i.e., take one or more courses in each of the general divisions of the university: natural science, social science and the humanities. The reigning ideology here is *breadth*, as was *openness* in the age of laxity. The courses are almost always the already existing introductory courses, which are of least interest to the major professors and merely assume the worth and reality of that which is to be studied. It is general education, in the sense in which a jack-of-all-trades is a generalist. He knows a bit of everything and is inferior to the specialist in each area. Students may wish to sample a variety of fields, and it may be good to encourage them to look around and see if there is something that attracts them in one of which they have no experience. But this is not a liberal education and does not satisfy any longing they have for one. It just teaches that there is no high-level generalism, and that what they are doing is preliminary to the real stuff and part of the childhood they are leaving behind. Thus they desire to get it over with and get on with what their professors do seriously. Without recognition of important questions of common concern, there cannot be serious liberal education, and attempts to establish it will be but failed gestures.

It is a more or less precise awareness of the inadequacy of this   14
approach to core curricula that motivates the second approach, which consists of what one might call composite courses. There are constructions developed especially for general-education purposes and usually require collaboration of professors drawn from several departments. These courses have titles like "Man in Nature," "War and Moral Responsibility," "The Arts and Creativity," "Culture and the Individual." Everything, of course, depends upon who plans them and who teaches them. They have the clear advantage of requiring some reflection on the general needs of students and force specialized professors to broaden their perspectives, at least for a moment. The dangers are trendiness, mere popularization and lack of substantive rigor. In general, the natural scientists do not collaborate in such endeavors, and hence these courses tend to be unbalanced. In short, they do not point beyond themselves and do not provide the student with independent means to pursue permanent questions independently, as, for example, the study of Aristotle or Kant as wholes once did. They tend to be bits of this and that. Liberal education should give the student the sense that learning must and can be both synoptic and precise. For this, a very small, detailed problem can be the best way, if it is framed so as to open out on the whole. Unless the course has the specific intention to lead to the permanent questions, to make the student aware of them and give him some competence in the important works that treat of them, it tends to be a pleasant diversion and a dead end—because it

has nothing to do with any program of further study he can imagine. If such programs engage the best energies of the best people in the university, they can be beneficial and provide some of the missing intellectual excitement for both professors and students. But they rarely do, and they are too cut off from the top, from what the various faculties see as their real business. Where the power is determines the life of the whole body. And the intellectual problems unresolved at the top cannot be resolved administratively below. The problem is the lack of any unity of the sciences and the loss of the will or the means even to discuss the issue. The illness above is the cause of the illness below, to which all the good-willed efforts of honest liberal educationists can at best be palliatives.

Of course, the only serious solution is the one that is almost 15 universally rejected: the good old Great Books approach, in which a liberal education means reading certain generally recognized classic texts, just reading them, letting them dictate what the questions are and the method of approaching them—not forcing them into categories we make up, not treating them as historical products, but trying to read them as their authors wished them to be read. I am perfectly well aware of, and actually agree with, the objections to the Great Books cult. It is amateurish; it encourages an autodidact's self-assurance without competence; one cannot read all of the Great Books carefully; if one only reads Great Books, one can never know what a great, as opposed to an ordinary, book is; there is no way of determining who is to decide what a Great Book or what the canon is; books are made the ends and not the means; the whole movement has a certain coarse evangelistic tone that is the opposite of good taste; it engenders a spurious intimacy with greatness; and so forth. But one thing is certain: wherever the Great Books make up a central part of the curriculum, the students are excited and satisfied, feel they are doing something that is independent and fulfilling, getting something from the university they cannot get elsewhere. The very fact of this special experience, which leads nowhere beyond itself, provides them with a new alternative and a respect for study itself. The advantage they get is an awareness of the classic—particularly important for our innocents; an acquaintance with what big questions were when there were still big questions; models, at the very least, of how to go about answering them; and, perhaps most important of all, a fund of shared experiences and thoughts on which to ground their friendships with one another. Programs based upon judicious use of great texts provide the royal road to students' hearts. Their gratitude at learning of Achilles or the categorical imperative is boundless. Alexander Koyré, the late historian of science, told me that his appreciation for America was great when—in the first course he taught at the University of Chicago, in 1940 at the beginning of his exile—a student spoke in his paper of Mr. Aristotle, unaware that he was not a contemporary. Koyré said that only an American could have the naive profundity to take Aristotle as living thought, unthinkable for most scholars. A good program of liberal education feeds the student's love of truth and passion to live a good life. It is the easiest thing in the world to devise courses of study, adapted to the particular conditions of each university, which thrill those who take them. The difficulty is in getting them accepted by the faculty.

None of the three great parts of the contemporary university is   16 enthusiastic about the Great Books approach to education. The natural scientists are benevolent toward other fields and toward liberal education, if it does not steal away their students and does not take too much time from their preparatory studies. But they themselves are interested primarily in the solution of the questions now important in their disciplines and are not particularly concerned with discussions of their foundations, inasmuch as they are so evidently successful. They are indifferent to Newton's conception of time or his disputes with Leibniz about calculus; Aristotle's teleology is an absurdity beneath consideration. Scientific progress, they believe, no longer depends on the kind of comprehensive reflection given to the nature of science by men like Bacon, Descartes, Hume, Kant and Marx. This is merely historical study, and for a long time now, even the greatest scientists have given up thinking about Galileo and Newton. Progress is undoubted. The difficulties about the truth of science raised by positivism, and those about the goodness of science raised by Rousseau and Nietzsche, have not really penetrated to the center of scientific consciousness. Hence, no Great Books, but incremental progress, is the theme for them.

Social scientists are in general hostile, because the classic texts   17 tend to deal with the human things the social sciences deal with, and they are very proud of having freed themselves from the shackles of such earlier thought to become truly scientific. And, unlike the natural scientists, they are insecure enough about their achievement to feel threatened by the works of earlier thinkers, perhaps a bit afraid that students will be seduced and fall back into the bad old ways. Moreover, with the possible exception of Weber and Freud, there are no social science books that can be said to be classic. This may be interpreted favorably to the social sciences by comparing them to the natural sciences, which can be said to be a living organism developing by the addition of little cells, a veritable body of knowledge proving itself to be such by the very fact of this almost unconscious growth, with thousands of parts oblivious to the whole, nevertheless contributing to it. This is in opposition to a work of imagination or of philosophy, where a single creator makes and surveys an artificial whole. But whether one interprets the absence of the classic in the social sciences in ways flattering or unflattering to them, the fact causes social scientists discomfort. I remember the professor who taught the introductory graduate courses in social science methodology, a famous historian, responding scornfully and angrily to a question I naively put to him about Thucydides with "Thucydides was a fool!"

More difficult to explain is the tepid reaction of humanists to 18 Great Books education, inasmuch as these books now belong almost exclusively to what are called the humanities. One would think that high esteem for the classic would reinforce the spiritual power of the humanities, at a time when their temporal power is at its lowest. And it is true that the most active proponents of liberal education and the study of classic texts are indeed usually humanists. But there is division among them. Some humanities disciplines are just crusty specialties that, although they depend on the status of classic books for their existence, are not really interested in them in their natural state—much philology, for example, is concerned with the languages but not what is said in them—and will and can do nothing to support their own infrastructure. Some humanities disciplines are eager to join the real sciences and transcend their roots in the now overcome mythic past. Some humanists make the legitimate complaints about lack of competence in the teaching and learning of Great Books, although their criticism is frequently undermined by the fact that they are only defending recent scholarly interpretation of the classics rather than a vital, authentic understanding. In their reaction there is a strong element of specialist's jealousy and narrowness. Finally, a large part of the story is just the general debilitation of the humanities, which is both symptom and cause of our present condition.

To repeat, the crisis of liberal education is a reflection of a crisis 19 at the peaks of learning, an incoherence and incompatibility among the first principles with which we interpret the world, an intellectual crisis of the greatest magnitude, which constitutes the crisis of our civilization. But perhaps it would be true to say that the crisis consists not so much in this incoherence but in our incapacity to discuss or even recognize it. Liberal education flourished when it prepared the way for the discussion of a unified view of nature and man's place in it, which the best minds debated on the highest level. It decayed when what lay beyond it were only specialties, the premises of which do not lead to any such vision. The highest is the partial intellect; there is no synopsis.

EXPLORATIONS

1. What does Bloom believe the university should stand for? What, in other words, does he see as the purposes of a liberal education? What do you think of Bloom's position?

2. How does Bloom portray American college students? Do you or students you know fit any of his descriptions?

3. How does Bloom define "intellectual pleasures"? How does his implied definition of "intellectual" compare with Royster's in "Perspectives on the Intellectual Tradition of Black Women"?

4. Bloom argues that the university curriculum is so fragmented that none of the courses seem to "speak to each other." Are there examples of this fragmentation at your college or university? Is this indeed a problem? Why or why not?

5. Bloom suggests that if colleges are only preparing students for professional careers, then in most cases four years of college are unnecessary. If Bloom is correct, what functions beside career training should colleges provide?

6. Bloom asserts that the students who enter college "are uncivilized, and that the universities have some responsibility for civilizing them." What does he mean? What do you think of this description of you and your classmates? What might someone like Zitkala-Sa or bell hooks or Paulo Freire say in response?

The Liberal Arts, the Campus, and the Biosphere: An Alternative to Bloom's Vision of Education

DAVID W. ORR

David W. Orr (1944–) is Professor of Environmental Studies at Oberlin College in Oberlin, Ohio. He is also cofounder of the Meadowcreek Project, a nonprofit environmental education organization. This essay is a chapter from his 1992 book Ecological Literacy: Education and the Transition to Postmodern World. *Orr is also coauthor of* The Global Predicament *and coeditor of the SUNY Press series* Environmental Public Policy.

WRITING BEFORE READING

Describe your interaction with and awareness of the natural world In your work, your education, and your personal life.

Debates about the content and purposes of education are most-   1
ly conducted among committees of the learned conditioned to such fare. Allan Bloom changed all of that in 1987 by writing a best-seller on the subject. Professor Bloom, as far as I can tell, believes that questions about the content of education (i.e., curriculum) were settled some time ago; perhaps once and for all with Plato, but certainly no later than Nietzsche. Subsequent elaborations, revisions, and refinements have worked great mischief with the high culture he purports to defend. Bloom's discontent focuses on American youth. He finds them empty, intellectually slack, and morally ignorant. The "soil" of their souls is "unfriendly" to the higher learning. And he thinks no more highly of their music and sexual relationships.

In Professor Bloom's ideal academy, students of a higher sort   2
would spend a great deal of time reading the Great Books, a list no longer universally admired. Bloom's avowed aim is to "reconstitute the idea of an educated human being and establish a liberal education again." But after 344 pages of verbal pyrotechnics—some illuminating the landscape, others merely the psyche of Professor Bloom—he leaves us only with some variation on the Great Books approach to education. The classics, he argues, "provide the royal road to the students' hearts . . . their gratitude [for being so

exposed is] . . . boundless." Exclusion of the classics, he thinks, has culminated in an "intellectual crisis of the greatest magnitude which constitutes the crisis of our civilization." Lesser minds might have related the crisis to more pedestrian causes such as violence, nuclear weapons, technology, overpopulation, or injustice. No matter. All of this was revealed to Professor Bloom while on the faculty at Cornell during the student uprising in 1969. One may reasonably infer that Professor Bloom and his Great Books were not at that moment treated kindly. One may also infer that Professor Bloom has neither forgiven nor forgotten.

Bloom has been widely attacked as a snob and as having totally   3
misunderstood what America is all about. In his defense, there is no reasonable case to be made against the inclusion of ancient wisdom in any good, liberal education. Nor can there be any good argument against the "idea of an educated human being." But questions about which ancient wisdom we might profitably consult, and about the intellectual and moral qualities of the educated person, have not been settled once and for all with Professor Bloom's book. At the end we know a great deal of what Professor Bloom is against, some of which is justified, but little of what he is for.

His vagueness about ends suggests that Professor Bloom,   4
without saying so, regards education as an end in itself. In a time of global turmoil, what transcendent purposes will Bloom's academy serve? In a time of great wrongs, what injustices does he wish to right? In an age of senseless violence, what civil disorders and dangers does he intend to resolve? In a time of anomie and purposelessness, what higher qualities of mind and character does he propose to cultivate? A careful reading of *The Closing of the American Mind* offers little insight about such matters. Rather, it is indicative of the closure of the purely academic mind to ecological issues.

For all of his conspicuous erudition, Professor Bloom seems to   5
regard the liberal arts as an abstraction. For example, rather than merely "reconstitute the idea" of educated human beings, why not actually educate a large number of them? Likewise, his reverence for the classics is not accompanied by any suggestion of how they might illuminate the major issues of the day. The effect is ironically to render them both sacred and unusable, except for purposes of conspicuous pedantry. It also distorts our understanding of the origins of some of humanity's best thinking. Many of what are now described as classics were produced by the friction of extraordinary minds wrestling with the problems of their day, which is to say that they were relevant in their time. Plato wrote *The Republic* in part as a response to the breakdown of civic order in fourth-century Athens.

Locke wrote his *Two Treatises* to justify the English civil war. Only in hindsight does their work appear to have the immaculate qualities that they certainly lacked at birth. The progress of human thought has been hard-fought, uneven, and erratic. We have reason to believe that it will continue to be so. If our descendants five centuries hence regard any books of our era as classics, they will be those that grappled with and illuminated the major issues of our time, in a manner that illuminates theirs. Beyond complaints about education, Professor Bloom does not offer an opinion about what these issues may be. He sounds rather like a fussy museum curator, irate over gum wrappers on the floor.

Amidst growing poverty, environmental deterioration, and violence in a nuclear-armed world, Professor Bloom is silent about how his version of the liberal arts would promote global justice, heal the breech with the natural world, promote peace, and restore meaning in a technocratic world. On the contrary, he arrogantly dismisses those concerned about such issues. Yet, ironically, if our era adds any "classics" to the archeology of human thought, they will more likely than not be written about these subjects. 6

It is now widely acknowledged that the classics of the Western tradition are deficient in certain respects. First, having been mostly composed by white males, they exclude the vast majority of human experience. Moreover, there are problems that this tradition has not successfully resolved, either because they are of recent origin, or because they were regarded as unimportant. In the latter category is the issue of the human role in the natural world. Search as one may through Plato, Aristotle, and the rest of the authors of the Great Books, there is not much said about it. With a few exceptions such as Hesiod, Cicero, Spinoza, and St. Francis (who wrote no "Great Book"), what wisdom we have from Western sources begins with the likes of Thoreau and George Perkins Marsh in the middle years of the last century. Whatever timeless qualities human nature may or may not have, Western culture has not offered much enlightenment on the appropriate relationship between humanity and its habitat. Nor does Professor Bloom. 7

Professor Bloom, I believe, has also missed something basic about education. Whitehead put it this way: "First-hand knowledge is the ultimate basis of intellectual life. . . . The second-handedness of the learned world is the secret of its mediocrity. It is tame because it has never been scared by the facts." An immersion in the classics, however valuable for some parts of intellectual development, risks no confrontation with the facts of life. The aim of education is not the ability to score well on tests, do well in Trivial Pursuit, or even to quote the right classic on the appropriate pedagogical occasion. The 8 aim of education is life lived to its fullest. A study of the classics is one tool among many to this end.

The purpose of a liberal education has to do with the develop- 9 ment of the whole person. J. Glenn Gray describes this person as "one who has fully grasped the simple fact that his self is fully impli- cated in those beings around him, human and nonhuman, and who has learned to care deeply about them." Accordingly, its function is the development of the capacity for clear thought and compassion in the recognition of the interrelatedness of life.

And what do these mean in an age of violence, injustice, eco- 10 logical deterioration, and nuclear weapons? What does wholeness mean in an age of specialization? It is perhaps easier to begin with what they do not mean. We do not lack for bad models: the careerist, the "itinerant professional vandal" devoid of any sense of place, the yuppie, the narrow specialist, the intellectual snob. In different ways, these all too common role models of the 1980s lack the capacity to relate their autobiography to the unfolding history of their time in a meaningful, positive way. They simply cannot speak to the urgent needs of the age, which is to say that they have been educated to be irrelevant. In Gray's words, they have not grasped "the simple fact" of their implicatedness, nor have they learned to "care deeply" about anything beyond themselves. To the extent that this has become the typical product of our educational institutions, it is an indictment of enormous gravity. Professor Bloom's emphasis on the classics and preservation of high culture does not remedy this dereliction in any obvious way.

It might be possible to dismiss Professor Bloom as a harmless 11 crank were it not for the wide impact of his book, and because he has become a spokesman for the powerful. The problem is not with Professor Bloom's ideas, which are toothless enough. The danger lies in the combination of vagueness, surliness, and the large number of things that he does not say. The result is that *Closing* can be cited by any number of ill-informed proponents of bad causes wanting to exit the twentieth century backwards. Bloom has not provided any coherent vision of the liberal arts relevant to our time. What he does offer is a sometimes insightful cultural critique in combination with a mummified curriculum with the distinct aroma of formaldehyde.

RECONSTRUCTION: THE TASK OF THE LIBERAL ARTS

The mission of the liberal arts in our time is not merely to incul- 12 cate a learned appreciation for the classics, as Bloom would have it, or to transmit "marketable skills," as any number of others propose, but to develop balanced, whole persons. Wholeness, first, requires the integration of the personhood of the student: the analytic mind with feelings, the intellect with manual competence. Failure to connect mind and feelings, in Gray's words, "divorces us from our own dispositions at the level where intellect and emotions fuse." A genuinely liberal education will also connect the head and the hands. Technical education and liberal arts have been consigned to different institutions that educate different parts of the anatomy. What passes for the higher learning deals with the neck up and only half of that, technical schools the remainder. This division creates the danger that students in each, in Gray's words, "miss a whole area of relation to the world." For liberal arts students, it also undermines an ancient source of good thought: the friction between an alert mind and practical experience. Abstract thought, "mere book learning," in Whitehead's words, divorced from practical reality and the facts of life, promotes pedantry and mediocrity. It also produces half-formed or deformed persons: thinkers who cannot do, and doers who cannot think. Students typically leave sixteen years of formal education without ever having mastered a particular skill or without any specific manual competence, as if the act of making anything other than term papers is without pedagogic or developmental value.

Second, an education in the liberal arts must overcome what 13 Whitehead termed "the fatal disconnection of subjects." The contemporary curriculum continues to divide reality into a cacophony of subjects that are seldom integrated into any coherent pattern. There is, as Whitehead reminds us, only one subject for education: "life in all its manifestations." Yet we routinely unleash specialists on the world, armed with expert knowledge but untempered by any inkling of the essential relatedness of things. Worse, specialization undermines the ability to communicate "plainly, in the common tongue." The academy, with its disciplines, divisions, and multiplying professional jargons, has come to resemble not so much a university as a cacophony of different jargons. I do not believe that Whitehead overstated the case. Disconnectedness in the form of excessive specialization is fatal to comprehension because it removes knowledge from its larger context. Collection of data supersedes understanding of connecting patterns, which is, I believe, the essence of wisdom. It is no accident that connectedness is central to the meaning of the Greek root words for both ecology and religion, *oikos* and *religio*.

A third task of the liberal arts is to provide a sober view of the 14 world, but without inducing despair. For many college freshmen, acquaintance with the realities of the late twentieth century comes as a shock. This is not the happy era they have heard described by a $120 billion-per-year advertising industry and by any number of feckless politicians. This is a time of danger, anomie, suffering, crack on the streets, changing climate, war, hunger, homelessness, spreading toxics, garbage barges plying the seven seas, desertification, poverty, and the permanent threat of Armageddon. Ours is the age of paradox. The modern obsession to control nature through science and technology is resulting in a less predictable and less bountiful natural world. Material progress was supposed to have created a more peaceful world. Instead, the twentieth century has been a time of unprecedented bloodshed in which two hundred million have died. Our economic growth has multiplied wants, not satisfactions. Amidst a staggering quantity of artifacts—what economists call abundance—there is growing poverty of the most desperate sort. How many student counseling services convey this sense of peril? Or obligation? The often-cited indifference and apathy of students is, I think, a reflection of the prior failure of educators and educational institutions to stand for anything beyond larger and larger endowments and an orderly campus. The result is a growing gap between the real world and the academy, and between the attitudes and aptitudes of its graduates and the needs of their time.

Finally, a genuine liberal arts education will equip a person to   15 live well in a place. To a great extent, formal education now prepares its graduates to reside, not to dwell. The difference is important. The resident is a temporary and rootless occupant who mostly needs to know where the banks and stores are in order to plug in. The inhabitant and a particular habitat cannot be separated without doing violence to both. The sum total of violence wrought by people who do not know who they are because they do not know where they are is the global environmental crisis. To reside is to live as a transient and as a stranger to one's place, and inevitably to some part of the self. The inhabitant and place mutually shape each other. Residents, shaped by outside forces, become merely "consumers" supplied by invisible networks that damage their places and those of others. The inhabitant and the local community are parts of a system that meets real needs for food, materials, economic support, and sociability. The resident's world, on the contrary, is a complicated system that defies order, logic, and control. The inhabitant is part of a complex order that strives for harmony between human demands and ecological processes. The resident lives in a constant blizzard of possibilities engineered by other residents. The life of the inhabitant is governed by the boundaries of sufficiency, organic harmony, and by the discipline of paying attention to minute particulars. For the resident, order begins from the top and proceeds downward as law and policy. For the inhabitant, order begins with the self and proceeds outward. Knowledge for the resident is theoretical and abstract, akin to training. For inhabitants, knowledge in the art of living aims toward wholeness. Those who dwell can only be skeptical of those who talk about being global citizens before they have attended to the minute particulars of living well in their place.

LIBERAL ARTS AND THE CAMPUS

This bring me to the place where learning occurs, the campus. 16 Do students in liberal arts colleges learn connectedness there or separation? Do they learn "implicatedness" or noninvolvement? And do they learn that they are "only cogs in an ecological mechanism," as Aldo Leopold put it, or that they are exempt from the duties of any larger citizenship in the community of life? A genuine liberal arts education will foster a sense of connectedness, implicatedness, and ecological citizenship, and will provide the competence to act on such knowledge. In what kind of place can such an education occur? The typical campus is the place where knowledge of other things is conveyed. Curriculum is mostly imported from other locations, times, and domains of abstraction. The campus as land, buildings, and relationships is thought to have no pedagogic value, and for those intending to be residents it need have none. It is supposed to be attractive and convenient, without also being useful and instructive. A "nice" campus is one whose lawns and landscapes are well-manicured and whose buildings are kept clean and good repair by a poorly paid maintenance crew. From distant and unknown places the campus is automatically supplied with food, water, electricity, toilet paper, and whatever else. Its waste and garbage are transported to other equally unknown places.

And what learning occurs on a "nice" campus? First, without 17 anyone saying as much, students learn the lesson of indifference to the ecology of their immediate place. Four years in a place called a campus culminates in no great understanding of the place, or in the art of living responsibly in that or any other place. I think it significant that students frequently refer to the outside world as the "real world," and do so without any feeling that this is not as it should be. The artificiality of the campus is not unrelated to the mediocrity of the learned world of which Whitehead complained. Students also learn indifference to the human ecology of the place and to certain kinds of people: those who clean the urinals, sweep the floors, haul out the garbage, and collect beer cans on Monday morning.

Indifference to a place is a matter of attention. The campus and   18
its region are seldom brought into focus as a matter of practical
study. To do so raises questions of the most basic sort. How does it
function as an ecosystem? From where does its food, energy, water,
and materials come and at what human and ecological cost? Where
does its waste and garbage go? At what costs? What relation does the
campus have to the surrounding region? What is the ecological history of the place? What ecological potentials does it have? What are
the dominant soil types? Flora and fauna? And what of its geology
and hydrology?

The study of place cultivates the habits of careful, close observa-   19
tion, and with it the ability to connect cause and effect. Aldo
Leopold described the capacity in these terms:

> Here is an abandoned field in which the ragweed is sparse and short.
> Does this tell us anything about why the mortgage was foreclosed?
> About how long ago? Would this field be a good place to look for quail?
> Does short ragweed have any connection with the human story behind
> yonder graveyard? If all the ragweed in this watershed were short,
> would that tell us anything about the future of floods in the stream?
> About the future prospects for bass or trout?

Second, students learn that it is sufficient only to learn about   20
injustice and ecological deterioration without having to do much
about them, which is to say, the lesson of hypocrisy. They hear that
the vital signs of the planet are in decline without learning to
question the *de facto* energy, food, materials, and waste policies of
the very institution that presumes to induct them into responsible
adulthood. Four years of consciousness-raising proceeds without
connection to those remedies close at hand. Hypocrisy undermines
the capacity for constructive action and so contributes to demoralization and despair.

Third, students learn that practical incompetence is *de rigueur*,   21
since they seldom are required to solve problems that have consequences except for their grade point average. They are not provided
opportunities to implement their stated values in practical ways or to
acquire the skills that would let them do so at a later time. Nor are
they asked to make anything, it being presumed that material and
mental creativity are unrelated. *Homo faber* and *Homo sapiens* are
two distinct species, the former being an inferior sort that subsisted
between the Neanderthal era and the founding of Harvard. The losses are not trivial: the satisfaction of good work and craftsmanship,
the lessons of diligence and discipline, and the discovery of personal
competence. After four years of the higher learning, students have
learned that it is all right to be incompetent and that practical com-

petence is decidedly inferior to the kind that helps to engineer lever-
aged buyouts and create tax breaks for people who do not need
them. This is a loss of incalculable proportions both to the personhood of the student and to the larger society. It is a loss to their
intellectual powers and moral development that can mature only by
interaction with real problems. It is a loss to the society burdened
with a growing percentage of incompetent people, ignorant of why
such competence is importance.

The conventional campus has become a place where indoor   22
learning occurs as a preparation for indoor careers. The young of our
advanced society are increasingly shaped by the shopping mall, the
freeway, the television, and the computer. They regard nature, if they
see it at all, as through a rearview mirror receding in the haze. We
should not be astonished, then, to discover rates of ecological literacy in decline, at the very time that that literacy is most needed.

THE UPSHOT:
THE CAMPUS AND THE BIOSPHERE

Every educational institution processes not only ideas and stu-   23
dents but resources, taking in food, energy, water, materials, and discarding organic and solid wastes. The sources (mines, wells, forests,
farms, feedlots) and sinks (landfills, toxic dumps, sewage outfalls) are
the least-discussed places in the contemporary curriculum. For the
most part, these flows occur out of sight and mind of both students
and faculty. Yet they are the most tangible connections between the
campus and the world beyond. They also provide an extraordinary
educational opportunity. The study of resource flows transcends disciplinary boundaries; it connects the foreground of experience with
the background of larger issues and more distant places; and it joins
empirical research on existing behavior and its consequences with
the study of other and more desirable possibilities.

The study of institutional resource flows is aimed to determine   24
how much of what comes from where, and with what human and
ecological consequences. How many kilowatt hours of electricity
from what power plants burning how much fuel extracted from
where? What are the sources of food in the campus dining hall? Was
it produced "sustainably" or not? Were farmers or laborers fairly
paid or not? What forests are cut down to supply the college with
paper? Were they replanted? Where does toxic waste from labs go?
Or solid wastes?

The study of actual resource flows must be coupled with the   25
study of alternatives·that may be more humane, ethically solvent,

ecologically sustainable, cheaper, and better for the regional econo-my. Are there other and better sources of food, energy, materials, water? The study of potentials must also address issues of conserva-tion. How much does the institution waste? How much energy, water, paper, and materials can be conserved? What is the potential for recycling paper, materials, glass, aluminum, and other materials? Can organic wastes be composted on-site or recycled through solar aquatic systems? At what cost? Can the institution shift its buying power from national marketing systems to support local economies? How? In what areas? How quickly? Can the landscape be designed for educational rather than decorative purposes? To what extent can good landscaping minimize energy spent for cooling and heating?

To address these and related questions, the Meadowcreek   26 Project conducted studies of the food systems of Hendrix College in Conway, Arkansas, and Oberlin College in Ohio. Both institutions are served by nationwide food-brokering networks that are not sus-tainable and that tend to undermine regional economies. In the Hendrix study, for example, students discovered that the college was buying only nine percent of its food within the state. Beef came from Amarillo, Texas; rice from Mississippi. Yet the college is located in a cattle and rice-farming region. In both studies, students uncovered ample opportunities for the institutions to expand purchases of local-ly grown products. Not infrequently, these are fresher, less likely to be contaminated with chemicals, and, not surprisingly, they are cheaper because shipping costs are lower. In conducting the research, which involved travel to the farms and feedlots throughout the United States that supply the campus, students confronted basic issues in agriculture, social ethics, environmental quality, economics, and politics. They were also involved in the analysis of existing buying patterns while having to develop feasible alternatives in cooperation with college officials. The results were action-oriented, interdisciplinary, and aimed to generate practical results. Both col-leges responded cooperatively in the implementation of plans to increase local buying. In the Hendrix case, in-state purchases dou-bled in the year following the study. Through video documentaries and articles in the campus newspaper, the studies became part of a wider campus dialogue. Finally, the willingness of both colleges to support local economies helps to bridge the gap between the insti-tutions and their locality in a way no public relations campaign could have done.

CONCLUSION

The study of institutional resource flows can lead to three 27
results. The first is a set of policies governing food, energy, water,
materials, architectural design, landscaping, and waste flows that
meet standards for sustainability. A campus energy policy, for example, would set standards for conservation, while directing a shift
toward the maximum use of both passive and active solar systems for
hot water, space conditioning, and electricity. A campus food policy
would give high priority to local and regional organic sources. A
materials policy would aim to minimize solid waste and recycling. An
architectural policy governing all new construction and renovation
would give priority to solar design and the use of nontoxic and
bioregionally available building materials. A landscape policy would
stress the use of trees for cooling and windbreaks, and as a means to
offset campus CO_2 emissions. Decorative landscaping would be
replaced by "edible landscaping." A campus waste policy, aimed
to close waste loops, would lead to the development of on-site
composting and the exploration of biological alternatives for handling waste water such as that being developed by John Todd.

The study of campus resource flows and the development of 28
campus policies would lead to a second and more important result:
the reinvigoration of a curriculum around the issues of human survival, a plausible foundation for the liberal arts. This emphasis would
become a permanent part of the curriculum through research projects, courses, seminars, and the establishment of interdisciplinary
programs in resource management or environmental studies. By
engaging the entire campus community in the study of resource
flows, debate about the possible meanings of sustainability, the
design of campus resource policies, and curriculum innovation, the
process carries with it the potential to enliven the educational
process. I can think of few disciplines throughout the humanities,
social sciences, and sciences without an important contribution to
this debate.

Third, the study and its implementation as policy and curriculum 29
would be an act of real leadership. Nearly every college and university claims to offer "excellence" in one way or another. Mostly the
word is invoked by unimaginative academic officials who want their
institution to be like some other. And for those so emulated, prestige, like barnacles on the hull of a ship, limit institutional velocity
and mobility. Real excellence in an age of cataclysmic potentials, consists neither in imitation nor timidity. College and university officials
with courage and vision have the power to lead in the transition to a
sustainable future. Within their communities, their institutions have

visibility, respect, and buying power. What they do matters to a large number of people. How they spend their institutional budget counts for a great deal in the regional economy. Through alumni, they reach present leaders; through students they reach those of the future. All of which is to say that colleges and universities are leverage institutions. They can help create a humane and livable future, rather than remaining passively on the sidelines, poised to study the outcome.

Not without irony, those who presume to defend the liberal arts 30 in the fashion of Allan Bloom have undersold them. A genuinely liberal education will produce whole persons with intellectual breadth, able to think at right angles to their major field; practical persons able to act competently; and persons of deep commitment, willing to roll up their sleeves and join the struggle to build a humane and sustainable world. They will not be merely well-read. Rather, they will be ecologically literate citizens able to distinguish health from its opposite and to live accordingly. Above all, they will make themselves relevant to the crisis of our age, which in its various manifestations is about the care, nurturing, and enhancement of life. And life is the only defensible foundation of a liberal education.

EXPLORATIONS

1. What purposes do you believe a liberal arts education should serve? Orr claims that "wholeness," or connecting the head and the hands, is essential for a liberal arts education. Do you agree or disagree? Explain your point of view.

2. Orr begins this chapter with a critique of Allan Bloom's *The Closing of the American Mind* and then moves to his own proposals for a liberal arts education. What advantages might he hope to gain by doing this? Does this help or hinder his argument? Why?

3. Orr suggests that university subjects are mostly disconnected from each other. Based on your experience, does this seem accurate? Why or why not?

4. Orr, like Barber, makes some specific claims about what shapes American youth. Do you agree with his views? Why or why not?

5. Explore the implications of Orr's general line of thought. What would an ecologically literate person know and do? What might a sustainable university look like?

FURTHER SUGGESTIONS FOR WRITING: ACADEMIC LITERACIES

The suggestions for writing that follow may appear complicated. What they do is offer you many options. These options are intended to stimulate your thinking about academic literacies, literacies that may determine students' success in college. As you read the options, consider which ones connect with your perceptions of and experiences with academic literacies. As you take notes, gather material, and collect specific information, think about a theme you may want to establish and how you will support and illustrate that theme in your rough draft. These assignments are designed for you to make significant insights into the academic world in which you are writing, insights that are worthwhile for you and your audience to take seriously.

1. **Analyzing Academic Literacy—Texts and Contexts:** This assignment asks you to turn your attention to what it means to be literate in certain rhetorical situations at your college or university. Specifically, it asks you to explore, analyze, and present a place in which literacy functions. You will be analyzing a particular place *and* the texts associated with that place. For instance, you might examine literacies expected and required of members of a particular academic discipline, for example, political science. One way you can learn about a discipline—perhaps the field you intend to major in—is to analyze a course offered in that discipline. Different academic disciplines require different ways of reading, writing, speaking, and listening. What might not be as obvious at first, however, is the way that many factors play a part in constructing rhetorical situations in a college classroom. Some of the factors you may want to consider are the number of students in a class, the assumptions that teachers and textbooks make about knowledge and learning, the course materials and class activities, the roles that teachers and students play, and even the physical arrangement of the classroom itself.

2. **Using Ethnographic Methods:** This assignment focuses on various literacies at work in a particular college setting and asks you to carry out a version of ethnographic research. This type of research requires that you make several visits to your selected site and record your observations as a participant/observer. You should also collect (or transcribe) examples of texts that are found in that space. For example, if you are examining your calculus class, pay attention to the textbooks, teaching methods, types of tests, use of classroom space, patterns of student interaction, and so on. If you are examining the types of literacy at work in the food court section in the student union, you might record the various menus and advertisements. The assignment encourages you to compile and select material that supports your point of view and your purposes for writing. You will also draw upon your experiences as a student and user of vari-

ous sites to analyze your raw data and perceptions as you shape your data in support of a coherent argument. As you draft and revise, filter this material with an eye toward showing and explaining convincingly to your audience the types of literacy at work in your site.

As you begin to gather information and plan your paper, consider the following suggestions and questions:

- Once you've decided on a site, do some brainstorming about it before you actually go visit. Enlist your memory to record what activities take place there, what it looks, smells, and feels like. Who uses it and at what times?

- Visit your site several times. Take a notebook along and describe (as concretely as possible) what you see. You might also bring a camera or a tape recorder. Record your impressions of how people are using that space. Collect materials. You are trying to compile a "thick description" of the site. Once you have a pile of raw data, start going through it to determine patterns and questions. (Clustering is one helpful strategy for finding patterns.) For instance, why do fast food vendors in the student union advertise their products as "low fat"? What sort of literacy does this advertising engage?

- In what ways is this place significant?

- To "understand" this place, what sorts of knowledge must you share with your readers?

- Why are certain communication strategies used effectively in one and not so effectively in another? Compare strategies in argumentation, for example, that work during a pickup basketball game but not in your first-year writing course?

- To what extent do such factors as race, class, gender, sexual orientation, appearance, age, disability, and experience determine who uses these places and from what positions of authority?

- What purposes do reading, writing, and speaking serve in your site? Writing, for instance, might serve a range of purposes, from self-expression and displaying knowledge to critical inquiry.

- What assumptions about language, teaching, learning, and audience are implied by the place and how it is arranged?

3. **Exploring the Purposes of Education:** Many of the selections in Part 3 are polemics that argue for particular visions of what "education" should be and do. On the one hand, we have Alan Bloom and E. D. Hirsch recommending "great books" or "cultural literacy" approaches to education, both of which are grounded in a very traditional, conservative idea of what "educated" people would know. On the other hand, we see that the violence described by Cherríe Moraga and Zitkala-Sa, the broad vision of intellectualism promoted by Jacqueline Jones Royster, and the "education as embrace" metaphor that Mike Rose gives us, are all implicitly at odds with Hirsch and

Bloom. For this assignment, write an essay that enters into a conversation with some of the writers in Part 3 and articulates your own vision of what a college education should be and do.

Writers like Bloom, Hirsch, David Orr, Royster, and Rose make their arguments in the contexts of current conversations about the purposes of education. For example, Orr constructs his vision of environmental literacy in opposition to Bloom's "great books" approach. It will be helpful, then, for you to summarize the positions taken by the writers you choose and your responses to these selections in your writer's notebook. Which essays do you find most compelling, and why? Which essays are you resisting, and why? It is equally important to draw on your own experience. While it is necessary to note the writers who have helped you think about the question and to show that you understand the positions of those writers with whom you disagree, it is crucial that you identify and articulate the personal experiences that have shaped your own views. "Personal" experience might include the literacies that you have brought with you to college, the literacies that have been shaped by families, home towns, prior experiences in school, and so on. As you plan your essay, consider some of the following questions:

- How should a formal education serve both the individual and the larger society?

- Which selections might help you make your point? With which selections do you want to argue?

- What do students need to know and be able to do in order to succeed in school, to become academically literate?

- How might schools or colleges best help students to become academically literate? At the same time, how might "academic literacy" be enriched by embracing the literacies that students bring with them to college?

- What literacies, aside from reading and writing, are important for college students to know?

4. **Collaborative Project:** Working with a small group or the whole class, place your essays in conversation with each other by putting together a "journal" or "book" that includes all of the essays that the individual members of the group have written. As a group, write an introduction that describes the issues raised by the writers, and include, if you want, brief biographies of the writers. Consider who, aside from the members of the group, might benefit from reading the collection. You might direct your journal toward another writing class that is considering the same issues, curriculum revision committees, or the dean of your college. If your group has computer access, consider developing a web page or another electronic version of the text.

4
PUBLIC LITERACIES

Public discourse is language shared by society as a whole. Public discourse also includes all the myths, legends, stories, and slogans through which society shapes us and by which we shape society. It includes the ways we talk about and understand the world—from public conversations about politics and education to casual chatter about sports or music. Public discourse takes all kinds of forms: magazines, newspapers, talk shows on radio and television, books, the Internet, political speeches and debates, advertising, sermons in churches and on street corners, and demonstrations. When you understand, question, manipulate, or simply participate in public discourse, you are practicing public literacy.

In his essay included in Part 3, Theodore R. Sizer argues that our shared knowledge of public discourse constitutes a public literacy that is often ignored by educators. He asks us to pay attention to the "shared symbol systems, the public literacy, that we already have" because this public literacy "is shaping, in an unprecedented way, a national culture." As you practice public literacies, you can also better participate in and influence the world around you.

You practice public literacies daily when you encounter, even casually, various forms of public discourse. You might interpret media messages in advertising or on television. You might also find yourself decoding the nuances of body language during a meeting or taking part in chat room or newsgroup conversations on the Internet. You also practice public literacy when you analyze how and why public spaces such as shopping malls are used.

Public literacies influence many of our decisions—the college or university we choose to attend, the bank we put our money in, the clubs and organizations we join, and even the brand of laundry detergent we purchase. The media and other forums for public discourse are so pervasive that they often pass unnoticed as subjects for study. The selections that follow ask you to pay attention to how shared symbol systems are used within the public sphere, while they also encourage you to participate in, respond to, and critique public discourse. Advertising, television, fashion, and even the physical arrangement of space within public buildings convey silent or ignored messages that nevertheless play influential roles in our everyday lives. In order to understand these discourses and to participate in them, you also need to be literate about the communities they represent.

EXPLORATION

Observe and record as many examples as possible of public discourse you are exposed to in a single day. Your list might include written examples (such as junk mail and the campus newspaper), visual examples (like television ads and billboards), and spoken examples (including the words of a manager training an employee or of the president of a campus organization giving a speech), as well as combinations of these types. Record what you see and hear as well as where the discourse takes place and how it is presented. Then, analyze the list considering the following questions: Are these instances of public discourse usually noticed? Why or why not? Did one example jump out at you? If so, why? Which examples were most notable? Why? In general, how do you think public discourse affects people? Be prepared to share your responses.

Public Literacy:
Puzzlements of a High School Watcher
THEODORE R. SIZER

*Theodore R. Sizer (1932–) is a professor in the
Department of Education at Brown University in
Providence, Rhode Island. He has published several books,
including* Horace's Compromise: The Dilemma of the
American High School, *which offers a program of reform for
American high schools.* "Public Literacy: Puzzlements of a
High School Watcher" *was originally published in* The
Right to Literacy, *an anthology of essays that grew out of
presentations given at the 1988 Right to Literacy conference
held in Columbus, Ohio. In this essay, Sizer points out the
common public literacy that Americans hold amidst our
diversity, and he asks us to consider why serious attention
has not been given to those common elements we share.*

WRITING BEFORE READING

*Consider the title of Sizer's essay. How do you think high schools
might be related to public literacy?*

To visit among American high schools is to be struck by 1
how similar these venerable social institutions are. Certainly, there is
variety, best explained by differences in social class and, to a small
extent, the race and the ethnicity of the students. The feel of a school
serving the poor is profoundly different from the feel of its cousin in a
Gold Coast suburb. However, it is the similarities that impress—the
ubiquitous routines, the seven-period day, the bells, homecoming,
school defined as English-math-science-social studies-language, each
purveyed to students in isolation from every other. There are the texts,
the sequence of topics, the testing, and, most important,
the assumptions about learning and teaching and schooling that
undergird these practices and the wry, usually genial cynicism of the
teachers. In a nation priding itself on its local schooling, the consistencies are surprising. And the consistencies are exhibited by the
students themselves—their clothing, lingo, enthusiasms, symbols.
Again, class counts here, as does geography. But the wonder is why the
differences are not far greater. Americans are mesmerized by their differences. Perhaps they should reflect a bit more on their similarities.

There is a wealth of shared knowledge reflected in high school 2
regimens. Kids can move from Bangor to Butte and lose few steps.

Not only are the language and the school routines relatively the same, but the nuances and the gestures of getting along remarkably transcend geography. The starker differences among Americans portrayed in basic training barrack scenes from World War II movies seem quaint today to most of us. The fact is that we clearly have a pervasive and powerful public literacy, a set of widely accepted symbols and ideas that give meaning to being American.

At a recent seminar my Brown University colleague Robert   3
Scholes neatly demonstrated this public literacy by asking us to examine carefully what we must already know if we are to understand a twenty-eight-second Budweiser beer television commercial. The spot portrayed a fledgling black baseball umpire. In the half minute he moves from a scruffy minor-league ballpark to a major-league stadium to a close play at third and the resultant tirade from an offended, beefy white manager to the predictable smoke-filled bar where, with a glamorous black woman dutifully at his side, he accepts the tip of a bottle across the room from that same manager. It's all about making it, with Bud. The segment is redolent with assumed meanings. Most foreigners would miss most of it, as Scholes found. We Americans share a culture so completely that we are barely aware of it.

During the week of 19 June 1988, a typical early-summer span,   4
the television sets that reside in more than 95% of America's 89 million homes were on some seven hours a day; 14.5 million households tuned in to *Night Court* and *Cheers; The Cosby Show* and *Sixty Minutes* drew barely fewer. Earlier that year, 37 million households watched the football Super Bowl. Shared experience, necessarily articulated in widely shared language and symbols, is a stunning reality. This shared experience shapes our expectations and discourse. It is no wonder that our adolescents are so much more alike than we, considering the expanse and the heterogeneous ethnicity of this country, might otherwise expect.

One might easily mock the results of this shared experience, this   5
American public literacy. It is better to test it undefensively and perhaps try to harness it. Our public literacy is characterized by at least four properties. First, it is centrally driven, usually for purposes of merchandising. Whether with jeans or biology textbooks, the name of the commercial game is national saturation. Only large companies survive in this big league, even if they appear to be little companies. For example, in the textbook field, Silver Burdett, Ginn, Allyn and Bacon, Simon and Schuster, and Prentice Hall are all Gulf and Western satraps. National symbols are expertly crafted. We have a substantial national curriculum, one with few professional educators' or elected school boards' fingerprints on it.

Second, our public literacy is commercial. The vehicle for our   6
shared culture emerges from the selling of things, usually products

or services of some sort but also people, in electoral campaigns, and even ideas, as Jim and Tammy Bakker and their kin would have us believe. Much of the message is about demands in the making, provoking us to want things we previously didn't even know about. Thus, it's expansive, broadening. If you've never tried oat bran, you haven't lived. Move up to a Buick.

Third, our public literacy simplifies, synthesizes, unifies, focuses. 7 *USA Today.* The McDonald's arches. Stylized logos. The *Harpers* short-essay format. The point is to be made simply, easily, quickly, and, above all, effectively. The sound bite. The powerful metaphor: an iron curtain. The utterly memorable modern version of Confucian analects. The reduction of a full life-style to the snapshot of a celebrity: *People* magazine.

Finally, our public literacy is pedagogically sophisticated, using 8 understandings about human learning and a range of technologies far beyond the school-teacher's ken. There are tie-ins—film to video to books to T-shirts. Clustered media characterize this pedagogy, the carefully coordinated use of sight and sound and print in artful, powerful combination. It is tough for your average French teacher to compete with MTV. As teachers, we school and college folk limp far behind our cousins in the communications industry.

The questions all this provokes are as demanding as they are 9 obvious. Is this shared experience, this public literacy, a good thing? It is tasteless? Is some of it, in fact, a vicious form of "acceptable" lying? Or is it modestly more benign, merely purveying corrupting fictions? Does it, with an artfulness that provokes acceptance and passivity, undermine habits of thoughtfulness? Is it undemocratic?

Why do we have it? Or, put more cogently, who wants it? (Public 10 acceptance to date seems to be almost universal.) Should it be changed? That is, should there be rules of public discourse, as well as rules of the road, or is the First Amendment the inevitable pro- tector of tawdriness and dishonesty, as well as free expression? Can, in fact, a public literacy be changed? What are the costs in trying to change it? Who should change it? Government? If so, by direct regulation, a national assessment of all the educating media? Or by indirection, through the tax code, with great business advantages given to alternative or public (not-for-profit) enterprises? Or do we leave change to the market, hoping that an aroused public will clean up mindlessness and worse in the common domain, somewhat as it appears to be doing to rid publicly shared air of cigarette-smoke pollution?

There must be answers to these questions. My concern here, 11 however, is not to pursue these but to express some puzzlements. Why aren't we talking much about this ubiquitous public literacy? The intense and visible concern for illiteracy, for the inability of many to read and to find meaning in that reading—as reflected in this conference—is as sincere and important as it is conventional; folks have to be able to read, understand, and articulate to survive in this society. But what of the shared symbol systems, the public literacy, that we already have? It is shaping, in an unprecedented way, a national culture. Its power seems greater in some important respects than the formal teaching in schools and colleges.

The academy itself accepts the megaculture, the machine for   12
public literacy, in a revealing way: it barely studies the matter. Higher education has been largely mute, for example, about the threat to academic freedom implicit in national testing or a de facto national-ized and virtually monopolistic textbook industry. The effects of television on American thought are remarkably little studied. We accept cultural gigantism, little reflecting on its meaning. By contrast, our savage little debates about critical theory rarely focus on the texts that saturate our cultural life but turn around intense little obscurities that, while perhaps of intellectual merit, have no cultural significance.

I am puzzled by how easily we rely on quick fixes in these   13
matters—acceptance of a single score on a forty-minute machine-graded test to rate a school or to rank a student against hundreds of thousands of others; a glib dismissal of the mass media, one resting on precious little empirical data; an avoidance of that army of people in the communications industry who are, in fact, teaching our people their shared values; concession to the encroachments on indi-vidual freedom implicit in the increasingly centralized character of our institutions. We aren't paying enough attention, and a charge of myopia against the academy is not too strong. However, there is not just inattention; there is in all too many quarters active hostility to studying the popular culture in general, much less its aspect as a form of literacy. Such concerns are considered soft, unworthy activ-ity for the bright person seeking tenure. It is both strange and sad.

The academy must recognize the reality of a public literacy, see   14
it in perspective, and study it carefully. We must adopt a rich defini-tion of this public literacy. As E. D. Hirsch has reminded us, it has a content, and we must see it as a content in context—gregarious, changeable, reflected and used in a rich variety of media. But content is only a part; no functioning literacy is merely facts; it is the ways of using those facts, of using style, of exhibiting habits. This use or exhibition arises from incentives, and the incentives that a culture presents its citizens shape their willingness to use and to be in the habit of using the values, content, and symbols that tie that culture together. Incentives arise from politics, both formal and informal, and the social system in which those politics proceed. Americans need to know more about the real content of our literacy, about its

exhibition, and about the incentives and the politics that produce such incentives, that provoke that exhibition. It is the duty of the academy to pursue these complex issues.

In sum, we have an unprecedented wide public literacy in this country. All those adolescents roiling through their schools' standardized routines and responding collectively to mass media's messages are evidence enough of that. Let us pay close attention to this new phenomenon, this product of affluence and technology. And if we find it wanting, let us be about changing it.

EXPLORATIONS

1. Consider the relationships between academic literacy and public literacy. What does the term "public literacy" mean and what does it encompass?

2. Sizer writes that the American culture we share is one that we "share so completely that we are barely aware of it." In Sizer's terms, what composes this culture? Why might an awareness of this culture be important?

3. Why, if public literacy is so important, does it go unexamined? What solutions to the problem does Sizer suggest?

4. Write a dialogue or short skit involving the characters of Sizer, Benjamin Barber, and David Orr. Set the scene for their interaction and set public discourse as their topic of discussion. Your dialogue or skit should reflect what they would say to one another if they met, for example, over lunch.

Masters of Desire :
The Culture of American Advertising
JACK SOLOMON

Jack Solomon is a professor of English at California State University. He has also published Discourse and Reference in the Nuclear Age *(1988) and* The Signs of Our Time *(1988), which is the source of this selection. In this reading, Solomon analyzes how advertisers exploit many of the shared values of American culture in order to sell their products as a part of the American dream.*

WRITING BEFORE READING

Has advertising or any ad in particular changed your lifestyle? Was the influence positive, negative, or both?

> Amongst democratic nations, men easily attain a certain equality
> of condition; but they can never attain as much as they desire.
>
> —*Alexis de Tocqueville*

On May 10, 1831, a young French aristocrat named Alexis de 1
Tocqueville arrived in New York City at the start of what would become one of the most famous visits to America in our history. He had come to observe firsthand the institutions of the freest, most egalitarian society of the age, but what he found was a paradox. For behind America's mythic promise of equal opportunity, Tocqueville discovered a desire for *unequal* social rewards, a ferocious competition for privilege and distinction. As he wrote in his monumental study, *Democracy in America*:

> When all privileges of birth and fortune are abolished, when all professions are accessible to all, and a man's own energies may place him at the top of any one of them, an easy and unbounded career seems open to his ambition. . . . But this is an erroneous notion, which is corrected by daily experience. [For when] men are nearly alike, and all follow the same track, it is very difficult for any one individual to walk quick and cleave a way through the same throng which surrounds and presses him.

Yet walking quick and cleaving a way is precisely what Americans 2
dream of. We Americans dream of rising above the crowd, of attaining a social summit beyond the reach of ordinary citizens. And therein lies the paradox.

The American dream, in other words, has two faces: the one 3
communally egalitarian and the other competitively elitist. This

contradiction is no accident; it is fundamental to the structure of American society. Even as America's great myth of equality celebrates the virtues of mom, apple pie, and the girl or boy next door, it also lures us to achieve social distinction, to rise above the crowd and bask alone in the glory. This land is your land and this land is my land, Woody Guthrie's populist anthem tells us, but we keep trying to increase the "my" at the expense of the "your." Rather than fostering contentment, the American dream breeds desire, a longing for a greater share of the pie. It is as if our society were a vast high-school football game, with the bulk of the participants noisily rooting in the stands while, deep down, each of them is wishing he or she could be the star quarterback or head cheerleader.

For the semiotician, the contradictory nature of the American 4 myth of equality is nowhere written so clearly as in the signs that American advertisers use to manipulate us into buying their wares. "Manipulate" is the word here, not "persuade"; for advertising campaigns are not sources of product information, they are exercises in behavior modification. Appealing to our subconscious emotions rather than to our conscious intellects, advertisements are designed to exploit the discontentments fostered by the American dream, the constant desire for social success and the material rewards that accompany it. America's consumer economy runs on desire, and advertising stokes the engines by transforming common objects— from peanut butter to political candidates—into signs of all the things that Americans covet most.

But by semiotically reading the signs that advertising agencies 5 manufacture to stimulate consumption, we can plot the precise state of desire in the audiences to which they are addressed. In this [essay], we'll look at a representative sample of ads and what they say about the emotional climate of the country and the fast-changing trends of American life. Because ours is a highly diverse, pluralistic society, various advertisements may say different things depending on their intended audiences, but in every case they say something about America, about the status of our hopes, fears, desires, and beliefs.

Let's begin with two ad campaigns conducted by the same com- 6 pany that bear out Alexis de Tocqueville's observations about the contradictory nature of American society: General Motors' campaigns for its Cadillac and Chevrolet lines. First, consider an early magazine ad for the Cadillac Allanté. Appearing as a full-color, four-page insert in *Time*, the ad seems to say "I'm special—and so is this car" even before we've begun to read it. Rather than being printed on the ordinary, flimsy pages of the magazine, the Allanté spread appears on glossy coated stock. The unwritten message here is that an extraordinary car deserves an extraordinary advertisement, and that both car and ad are aimed at an extraordinary consumer, or at least one who wishes to appear extraordinary compared to his more ordinary fellow citizens.

Ads of this kind work by creating symbolic associations between   7 their product and what is most coveted by the consumers to whom they are addressed. It is significant, then, that this ad insists that the Allanté is virtually an Italian rather than an American car, an automobile, as its copy runs, "Conceived and Commissioned by America's Luxury Car Leader, Cadillac" but "Designed and Handcrafted by Europe's Renowned Design Leader—Pininfarina, SpA, of Turin, Italy." This is not simply a piece of product information, it's a sign of the prestige that European luxury cars enjoy in today's automotive marketplace. Once the luxury car of choice for America's status drivers, Cadillac has fallen far behind its European competitors in the race for the prestige market. So the Allanté essentially represents Cadillac's decision, after years of resisting the trend toward European cars, to introduce its own European import—whose high cost is clearly printed on the last page of the ad. Although $54,700 is a lot of money to pay for a Cadillac, it's about what you'd expect to pay for a top-of-the-line Mercedes-Benz. That's precisely the point the ad is trying to make: the Allanté is no mere car. It's a potent status symbol you can associate with the other major status symbols of the 1980s.

American companies manufacture status symbols because   8 American consumers want them. As Alexis de Tocqueville recognized a century and a half ago, the competitive nature of democratic societies breeds a desire for social distinction, a yearning to rise above the crowd. But given the fact that those who do make it to the top in socially mobile societies have often risen from the lower ranks, they still look like everyone else. In the socially immobile societies of aristocratic Europe, generations of fixed social conditions produced subtle class signals. The accent of one's voice, the shape of one's nose, or even the set of one's chin, immediately communicated social status. Aside from the nasal bray and uptilted head of the Boston Brahmin, Americans do not have any native sets of personal status signals. If it weren't for his Mercedes-Benz and Manhattan townhouse, the parvenu Wall Street millionaire often couldn't be distinguished from the man who tailors his suits. Hence, the demand for status symbols, for the objects that mark one off as a social success, is particularly strong in democratic nations—stronger even than in aristocratic societies, where the aristocrat so often looks and sound different from everyone else.

Status symbols, then, are signs that identify their possessors'   9 place in a social hierarchy, markers of rank and prestige. We can all think of any number of status symbols—Rolls-Royces, Beverly Hills mansions, even Shar Pei puppies (whose rareness and expense has rocketed them beyond Russian wolfhounds as status pets and has even inspired whole lines of wrinkled-faced stuffed toys)—but how do we know that something *is* a status symbol? The explanation is quite simple: when an object (or puppy!) either costs a lot of money or requires influential connections to possess, anyone who possesses it must also possess the necessary means and influence to acquire it. The object itself really doesn't matter, since it ultimately disappears behind the presumed social potency of its owner. Semiotically, what matters is the signal it sends, its value as a sign of power. One traditional sign of social distinction is owning a country estate and enjoying the peace and privacy that attend it. Advertisements for Mercedes-Benz, Jaguar, and Audi automobiles thus frequently feature drivers motoring quietly along a country road, presumably on their way to or from their country houses.

Advertisers have been quick to exploit the status signals that 10 belong to body language as well. As Hegel observed in the early nineteenth century, it is an ancient aristocratic prerogative to be seen by the lower orders without having to look at them in return. Tilting his chin high in the air and gazing down at the world under hooded eyelids, the aristocrat invites observation while refusing to look back. We can find such a pose exploited in an advertisement for Cadillac Seville in which we see an elegantly dressed woman out for a drive with her husband in their new Cadillac. If we look closely at the woman's body language, we can see her glance inwardly with a satisfied smile on her face but not outward toward the camera that represents our gaze. She is glad to be seen by us in her Seville, but she isn't interested in looking at *us!*

Ads that are aimed at a broader market take the opposite 11 approach. If the American dream encourages the desire to "arrive," to vault above the mass, it also fosters a desire to be popular, to "belong." Populist commercials accordingly transform products into signs of belonging, utilizing such common icons as country music, small-town life, family picnics, and farmyards. All of these icons are incorporated in GM's "Heartbeat of America" campaign for its Chevrolet line. Unlike the Seville commercial, the faces in the Chevy ads look straight at us and smile. Dress is casual; the mood upbeat. Quick camera cuts take us from rustic to suburban to urban scenes, creating an American montage filmed from sea to shinning sea. We all "belong" in a Chevy.

Where price alone doesn't determine the market for a product, 12 advertisers can go either way. Both Johnnie Walker and Jack Daniel's are better-grade whiskies, but where a Johnnie Walker ad appeals to the buyer who wants a mark of aristocratic distinction in his liquor, a Jack Daniel's ad emphasizes the down-home, egalitar-

ian folksiness of its product. Johnnie Walker associates itself with
such conventional status symbols as sable coats, Rolls-Royces, and
black gold; Jack Daniel's gives us a Good Ol' Boy in overalls. In
fact, Jack Daniel's and Good Ol' Boy is an icon of backwoods
independence, recalling the days of the moonshiner and the Whisky
Rebellion of 1794. Evoking emotions quite at odds with those stim-
ulated in Johnnie Walker ads, the advertisers of Jack Daniel's have
chosen to transform their product into a sign of America's populist
tradition. The fact that both ads successfully sell whisky is itself a sign
of the dual nature of the American dream.

Beer is also pitched on two levels. Consider the difference   13
between the ways Budweiser and Michelob market their light beers.
But Light and Michelob Light cost and taste about the same, but
Budweiser tends to target the working class while Michelob has gone
after the upscale market. Bud commercials are set in working-class
bars that contrast with the sophisticated nightclubs and yuppie
watering holes of the Michelob campaign. "You're one of the
guys," Budweiser assures the assembly-line worker and the truck
driver, "this Bud's for you." Michelob, on the other hand, makes
no such appeal to the democratic instinct of sharing and belonging.
You don't share, you take, grabbing what you can in a competitive
dash to "have it all."

Populist advertising is particularly effective in the face of foreign   14
competition. When Americans feel threatened from the outside, they
tend to circle the wagons and temporarily forget their class differences. In the face of the Japanese automobile "invasion," Chrysler
runs populist commercials in which Lee Iacocca joins the simple folk
who buy his cars as the jingle "Born in America" blares in the background. Seeking to capitalize on the popularity of Bruce
Springsteen's *Born in the USA* album, these ads gloss over
Springsteen's ironic lyrics in a vast display of flag-waving.
Chevrolet's "Heartbeat of America" similarly attempts to woo
American motorists away from Japanese automobiles by appealing to
their patriotic sentiments.

The patriotic iconography of these campaigns also reflects the   15
general cultural mood of the early- to mid-1980s. After a period of
national anguish in the wake of the Vietnam War and the Iran
hostage crisis, America went on a patriotic binge. American athletic
triumphs in the Lake Placid and Los Angeles Olympics introduced a
sporting tone into the national celebration, often making international affairs appear like one great Olympiad in which America was
always going for the gold. In response, advertisers began to do their
own flag-waving.

The mood of advertising during this period was definitely   16
upbeat. Even deodorant commercials, which traditionally work on

our self-doubts and fears of social rejection, jumped on the band-wagon. In the guilty sixties, we had ads like the "Ice Blue Secret" campaign with its connotations of guilt and shame. In the feel-good Reagan eighties, "Sure" deodorant commercials featured images of triumphant Americans throwing up their arms in victory to reveal—no wet marks! Deodorant commercials once had the moral echo of Nathaniel Hawthorne's guilt-ridden *The Scarlet Letter:* in the early eighties they had all the moral subtlety of *Rocky IV*, reflecting the emotions of a Vietnam- weary nation eager to embrace the imagery of America Triumphant.

The commercials for Worlds of Wonder's Lazer Tag game   17
featured the futuristic finals of some Soviet-American Lazer Tag shootout ("Practice hard, America!") and carried the emotions of patriotism into an even more aggressive arena. Exploiting the hoopla that surrounded the victory over the Soviets in the hockey finals of the 1980 Olympics, the Lazer Tag ads pandered to an American desire for the sort of clean-cut nationalistic triumphs that the nuclear age has rendered almost impossible. Creating a fantasy setting where patriotic dreams are substituted for complicated realities, the Lazer Tag commercials sought to capture the imaginations of children caught up in the patriotic fervor of the early 1980s.

LIVE THE FANTASY

By reading the signs of American advertising, we can conclude   18
that America is a nation of fantasizers, often preferring the sign to the substance and easily enthralled by a veritable Fantasy Island of commercial illusions. Critics of Madison Avenue often complain that advertisers create consumer desire, but semioticians don't think the situation is that simple. Advertisers may give shape to consumer fan-tasies, but they need raw material to work with, the subconscious dreams and desires of the marketplace. As long as these desires remain unconscious, advertisers will be able to exploit them. But by bringing the fantasies to the surface, you can free yourself from advertising's often hypnotic grasp.

I can think of no company that has more successfully seized upon   19
the subconscious fantasies of the American marketplace—indeed the world marketplace—than McDonald's. By no means the first nor the only hamburger chain in the United States, McDonald's emerged victorious in the "burger wars" by transforming hamburgers into signs of all that was desirable in American life. Other chains like Wendy's, Burger King, and Jack-In-The-Box continue to advertise and sell widely, but no company approaches McDonald's transforma-tion of itself into a symbol of American culture.

McDonald's success can be traced to the precision of its adver-   20
tising. Instead of broadcasting a single "one-size-fits-all" campaign
at a time, McDonald's pitches its burgers simultaneously at different age groups, different classes, even different races (Budweiser
beer, incidentally, has succeeded in the same way). For children,
there is the Ronald McDonald campaign, which presents a fantasy
world that has little to do with hamburgers in any rational sense but
a great deal to do with the emotional desires of kids. Ronald
McDonald and his friends are signs that recall the Muppets, *Sesame
Street*, the circus, toys, storybook illustrations, even *Alice in
Wonderland*. Such signs do not signify hamburgers. Rather, they are
displayed in order to prompt in the child's mind an automatic association of fantasy, fun, and McDonald's.

The same approach is taken in ads aimed at older audiences—   21
teens, adults, and senior citizens. In the teen-oriented ads we may
catch a fleeting glimpse of a hamburger or two, but what we are really shown is a teenage fantasy: groups of hip and happy adolescents
singing, dancing, and cavorting together. Fearing loneliness more
than anything else, adolescents quickly respond to the group appeal
of such commercials. "Eat a Big Mac," these ads say, "and you
won't be stuck home alone on Saturday night."

To appeal to an older and more sophisticated audience no longer   22
so afraid of not belonging and more concerned with finding a place
to go out to at night, McDonald's has designed the elaborate
"Mac Tonight" commercials, which have for their backdrop a
nightlit urban skyline and at their center a cabaret pianist with a
moon-shaped head, a glad manner, and Blues Brothers shades. Such
signs prompt an association of McDonald's with nightclubs and
urban sophistication, persuading us that McDonald's is not only a
place for breakfast or lunch but for dinner too, as if it were a popular off-Broadway nightspot, a place to see and be seen. Even the
parody of Kurt Weill's "Mack the Knife" theme song the Mac the
Pianist performs is a sign, a subtle signal to the sophisticated
hamburger eater able to recognize the origin of the tune in Bertolt
Brecht's *Threepenny Opera*.

For yet older customers, McDonald's has designed a commer-   23
cial around the fact that it employs a large number of retirees and
seniors. In one such ad, we see an elderly man leaving his pretty
little cottage early in the morning to start work as "the new kid" at
McDonald's, and then we watch him during his first day on the job.
Of course he is a great success, outdoing everyone else with his energy and efficiency, and he returns home in the evening to a loving
wife and happy home. One would almost think that the ad was a kind
of moving "help wanted" sign (indeed, McDonald's *was* hiring
elderly employees at the time), but it's really just directed at con-

sumers. Older viewers can see themselves wanted and appreciated in the ad—and perhaps be distracted from the rationally uncomfortable fact that many senior citizens take such jobs because of financial need and thus may be unlikely to own the sort of home that one sees in the commercial. But realism isn't the point here. This is fantasy-land, a dream world promising instant gratification no matter what the facts of the matter may be.

Practically the only fantasy that McDonald's doesn't exploit is   24 the fantasy of sex. This is understandable, given McDonald's desire to present itself as a family restaurant. But everywhere else, sexual fantasies, which have always had an important place in American advertising, are beginning to dominate the advertising scene. You expect sexual come-ons in ads for perfume or cosmetics or jewelry— after all, that's what they're selling—but for room deodorizers? In a magazine ad for Claire Burke home fragrances, for example, we see a well-dressed couple cavorting about their bedroom in what looks like a cheery preparation for sado-masochistic exercises. Jordache and Calvin Klein pitch blue jeans as props for teenage sexuality. The phallic appeal of automobiles, traditionally an implicit feature in automotive advertising, becomes quite explicit in a Dodge com-mercial that shifts back and forth from shots of a young man in an automobile to teasing glimpses of a woman—his date—as she dresses in her apartment.

The very language of today's advertisements is charged with   25 sexuality. Products in the more innocent fifties were "new and improved," but everything in the eighties is "hot!"—as in "hot woman," or sexual heat. Cars are "hot." Movies are "hot." And ad for Valvoline pulses to the rhythm of a "heat wave, burning in my car." Sneakers get red hot in a magazine ad for Travel Fox athletic shoes in which we see male and female figures, clad only in Travel Fox shoes, apparently in the act of copulation—an ad that earned one of *Adweek's* annual "badvertising" awards for shoddy advertising.

The sexual explicitness of contemporary advertising is a sign not   26 so much of American sexual fantasies as of the lengths to which advertisers will go to get attention. Sex never fails as an attention-getter, and in a particularly competitive, and expensive, era for American marketing, advertisers like to bet on a sure thing. Ad people refer to the proliferation of TV, radio, newspaper, magazine, and billboard ads as "clutter," and nothing cuts through the clut-ter like sex.

By showing the flesh, advertisers work on the deepest, most   27 coercive human emotions of all. Much sexual coercion in advertis-ing, however, is a sign of a desperate need to make certain that clients are getting their money's worth. The appearance of adver-tisements that refer directly to the prefabricated fantasies of

Hollywood is a sign of a different sort of desperation: a desperation for ideas. With the rapid turnover of advertising campaigns mandated by the need to cut through the "clutter," advertisers may be hard pressed for new ad concepts, and so they are more and more frequently turning to already-established models. In the early 1980s, for instance, Pepsi-Cola ran a series of ads broadly alluding to Steven Spielberg's *E.T.* In one such ad, we see a young boy who, like the hero of *E.T.*, witnesses an extraterrestrial visit. The boy is led to a soft-drink machine where he pauses to drink a can of Pepsi as the spaceship he's spotted flies off into the universe. The relationship between the ad and the movie, accordingly, is a parasitical one, with the ad taking its life from the creative body of the film.

Pepsi did something similar in 1987 when it arranged with the producers of the movie *Top Gun* to promote the film's video release in Pepsi's television advertisements in exchange for the right to append a Pepsi ad to the video itself. This time, however, the parasitical relationship between ad and film was made explicit. Pepsi sales benefitted from the video, and the video's sales benefitted from Pepsi. It was a marriage made in corporate heaven.

The fact that Pepsi believed that it could stimulate consumption by appealing to the militaristic fantasies dramatized in *Top Gun* reflects similar fantasies in the "Pepsi Generation." Earlier generations saw Pepsi associated with high-school courtship rituals, with couples sipping sodas together at the corner drugstore. When the draft was on, young men fantasized about Peggy Sue, not Air Force Flight School. Military service was all too real a possibility to fantasize about. But in an era when military service is not a reality for most young Americans, Pepsi commercials featuring hotshot fly-boys drinking Pepsi while streaking about in their Air Force jets contribute to a youth culture that has forgotten what military service means. It all looks like such fun in the Pepsi ads, but what they conceal is the fact that military jets are weapons, not high-tech recreational vehicles.

For less militaristic dreamers, Madison Avenue has framed ad campaigns around the cultural prestige of high-tech machinery in its own right. This is especially the case with sports cars, whose high-tech appeal is so powerful that some people apparently fantasize about *being* sports cars. At least, this is the conclusion one might draw from a Porsche commercial that asked its audience, "If you were a car, what kind of car would you be?" As a candy-red Porsche speeds along a rain-slick forest road, the ad's voice-over describes all the specifications you'd want to have if you *were* a sports car. "If you were a car," the commercial concludes, "you'd be a Porsche."

In his essay "Car Commercials and *Miami Vice*," Todd Gitlin explains the semiotic appeal of such ads as those in the Porsche cam-

28

29

30

31

paign. Aired at the height of what may be called America's "myth of the entrepreneur," these commercials were aimed at young corporate managers who imaginatively identified with the "lone wolf" image of a Porsche speeding through the woods. Gitlin points out that such images cater to the fantasies of faceless corporate men who dream of entrepreneurial glory, of striking out on their own like John DeLorean and telling the boss to take his job and shove it. But as DeLorean's spectacular failure demonstrates, the life of the entrepreneur can be extremely risky. So rather than having to go it alone and take the risks that accompany entrepreneurial independence, the young executive can substitute fantasy for reality by climbing into his Porsche—or at least that's what Porsche's advertisers wanted him to believe.

But there is more at work in the Porsche ads than the fantasies 32 of corporate America. Ever since Arthur C. Clarke and Stanley Kubrick teamed up to present us with HAL 9000, the demented computer of *2001: A Space Odyssey*, the American imagination has been obsessed with the melding of man and machine. First there was television's *Six Million Dollar Man*, and then movieland's *Star Wars*, *Blade Runner*, and *Robocop*, fantasy visions of a future dominated by machines. Androids haunt our imagination as machines seize the initiative. *Time* magazine's "Man of the Year" for 1982 was a computer. Robot-built automobiles appeal to drivers who spend their days in front of computer screens—perhaps designing robots. When so much power and prestige is being given to high-tech machines, wouldn't you rather be a Porsche?

In short, the Porsche campaign is a sign of a new mythology that 33 is emerging before our eyes, a myth of the machine, which is replacing the myth of the human. The iconic figure of the little tramp caught up in the cogs of industrial production in Charlie Chaplin's *Modern Times* signified a humanistic revulsion to the age of the machine. Human beings, such icons said, were superior to machines. Human values should come first in the moral order of things. but as Edith Milton suggests in her essay "The Track of the Mutant," we are now coming to believe that machines are superior to human beings, that mechanical nature is superior to human nature. Rather than being threatened by machines, we long to merge with them. *The Six Million Dollar Man* is one iconic figure in the new mythology; Harrison Ford's sexual coupling with an android is another. In such an age it should come as little wonder that computer-synthesized Max Headroom should be a commercial spokesman for Coca-Cola, or that Federal Express should design a series of TV ads featuring mechanical-looking human beings revolving around strange and powerful machines.

FEAR AND TREMBLING IN THE MARKETPLACE

While advertisers play on and reflect back at us our fantasies   34
about everything from fighter pilots to robots, they also play on
darker imaginings. If dream and desire can be exploited in the quest
for sales, so can nightmare and fear.

The nightmare equivalent of America's populist desire to   35
"belong," for example, is the fear of not belonging, of social rejection, of being different. Advertisements for dandruff shampoos,
mouthwashes, deodorants, and laundry detergents ("Ring Around
the Collar!") accordingly exploit such fears, bullying us into
consumption. Although ads of this type are still around in the 1980s,
they were particularly common in the fifties and early sixties, reflecting a society still reeling from the witch-hunts of the McCarthy
years. When any sort of social eccentricity or difference could result
in a public denunciation or the loss of one's job or even liberty,
Americans were keen to conform and be like everyone else. No one
wanted to be "guilty" of smelling bad or of having a dirty collar.

"Guilt" ads characteristically work by creating narrative   36
situations in which someone is "accused" of some social "transgres-
sion," pronounced guilty, and then offered the sponsor's product as
a means of returning to "innocence." Such ads, in essence, are paro-
dies of ancient religious rituals of guilt and atonement, whereby
sinning humanity is offered salvation through the agency of priest and
church. In the world of advertising, a product takes the place of the
priest, but the logic of the situation is quite similar.

In commercials for Wisk detergent, for example, we witness the   37
drama of a hapless housewife and her husband as they are mocked by
the jeering voices of children shouting "Ring Around the Collar!"
"Oh, those dirty rings!" the housewife groans in despair. It's as if
she and her husband were being stoned by an angry crowd. But
there's hope, there's help, there's Wisk. Cleansing her soul of
sins as well as her husband's, the housewife launders his shirts with
Wisk, and behold, his collars are clean. Product salvation is only as
far as the supermarket.

The recent appearance of advertisements for hospitals treating   38
drug and alcohol addiction have raised the old genre of the guilt ad
to new heights (or lows, depending on your perspective). In such
ads, we see wives on the verge of leaving their husbands if they
don't do something about their drinking, and salesmen about to
lose their jobs. The man is guilty; he has sinned; but he upholds the
ritual of guilt and atonement by "confessing" to his wife or boss
and agreeing to go the hospital the ad is pitching.

If guilt looks backward in time to past transgressions, fear, like   39
desire, faces forward, trembling before the future. In the late 1980s,

a new kind of fear commercial appeared, one whose narrative played on the worries of young corporate managers struggling up the ladder of success. Representing the nightmare equivalent of the elitist desire to "arrive," ads of this sort created images of failure, storylines of corporate defeat. In one ad for Apple computers, for example, a group of junior executives sits around a table with the boss as he asks each executive how long it will take his or her department to complete some publishing jobs. "Two or three days," answers one nervous executive. "A week, on overtime," a tight-lipped woman responds. But one young up-and-comer can have everything ready tomorrow, today, or yesterday, because his department uses a Macintosh desktop publishing system. Guess who'll get the next promotion?

Fear stalks an ad for AT&T computer systems too. A boss and   40 four junior executives are dining in a posh restaurant. Icons of corporate power and prestige flood the screen—from the executives' formal evening wear to the fancy table setting—but there 's tension in the air. It seems that the junior managers have chosen a computer system that's incompatible with the firm's sales and marketing departments. A whole new system will have to be purchased, but the tone of the meeting suggests that it will be handled by a new group of managers. These guys are on the way out. They no longer "belong." Indeed, it's probably no accident that the ad takes place in a restaurant, given the joke that went around in the aftermath of the 1987 market crash. "What do you call a yuppie stockbroker?" the joke ran. "Hey, waiter!" Is the ad trying subtly to suggest that junior executives who choose the wrong computer systems are doomed to suffer the same fate?

For other markets, there are other fears. If McDonald's   41 presents senior citizens with bright fantasies of being useful and appreciated beyond retirement, companies like Secure Horizons dramatize senior citizens' fears of being caught short by a major illness. Running its ads in the wake of budgetary cuts in the Medicare system, Secure Horizons designed a series of commercials featuring a pleasant old man named Harry—who looks and sounds rather like Carroll O'Connor—who tells us the story of the scare he got during his wife's recent illness. Fearing that next time Medicare won't cover his bills, he has purchased supplemental health insurance from Secure Horizons and now securely tends his rooftop garden.

Among all the fears advertisers have exploited over the years, I   42 find the fear of not having a posh enough burial site the most arresting. Advertisers usually avoid any mention of death—who wants to associate a product with the grave?—but mortuary advertisers haven't much choice. Generally, they solve their problem by framing cemeteries as timeless parks presided over by priestly morticians, appealing to our desires for dignity and comfort in the face of bereavement. But in one television commercial for Forest Lawn we find a different approach. In this ad we are presented with the ghost of an old man telling us how he might have found a much nicer resting place than the run-down cemetery in which we find him had his wife only known that Forest Lawn was so "affordable." I presume the ad was supposed to be funny, but it's been pulled off the air. There are some fears that just won't bear joking about, some nightmares too dark to dramatize.

THE FUTURE OF AN ILLUSION

There are some signs in the advertising world that Americans are getting fed up with fantasy advertisements and want to hear some straight talk. Weary of extravagant product claims and irrelevant associations, consumers trained by years of advertising to distrust what they hear seem to be developing an immunity to commercials. At least, this is the semiotic message I read in the "new realism" advertisements of the eighties, ads that attempt to convince you that what you're seeing is the real thing, that the ad is giving you the straight dope, not advertising hype.   43

You can recognize the "new realism" by its camera techniques. The lighting is usually subdued to give the ad the effect of being filmed without studio lighting or special filters. The scene looks gray, as if the blinds were drawn. The camera shots are jerky and off-angle, often zooming in for sudden unflattering close-ups, as if the cameraman was an amateur with a home video recorder. In a "realistic" ad for AT&T, for example, we are treated to a monologue by a plump stockbroker—his plumpness intended as a sign that he's for real and not just another actor—who tells us about the problems he's had with his phone system (not AT&T's) as the camera jerks around, generally filming him from below as if the cameraman couldn't quite fit his equipment into the crammed office and had to film the scene on his knees. "This is no fancy advertisement," the ad tries to convince us, "this is sincere."   44

An ad for Miller draft beer tries the same approach, recreating the effect of an amateur videotape of a wedding celebration. Camera shots shift suddenly from group to group. The picture jumps. Bodies are poorly framed. The color is washed out. Like the beer it is pushing, the ad is supposed to strike us as being "as real as it gets."   45

Such ads reflect a desire for reality in the marketplace, a weariness with Madison Avenue illusions. But there's no illusion like the illusion of reality. Every special technique that advertisers use to   46 create their "reality effects" is, in fact, more unrealistic than the techniques of "illusory" ads. The world, in reality, doesn't jump around when you look at it. It doesn't appear in subdued gray tones. Our eyes don't have zoom lenses, and we don't look at things with our heads cocked to one side. The irony of the "new realism" is that it is more unrealistic, more artificial, than the ordinary run of television advertising.

But don't expect any truly realistic ads in the future, because a 47
realistic advertisement is a contradiction in terms. The logic of advertising is entirely semiotic: it substitutes signs for things, framed visions of consumer desire for the thing itself. The success of modern advertising, its penetration into every corner of American life, reflects a culture that has itself chosen illusion over reality. At a time when political candidates all have professional image-makers attached to their staffs, and the President of the United States is an actor who once sold shirt collars, all the cultural signs are pointing to more illusions in our lives rather than fewer—a fecund breeding ground for the world of the advertiser.

EXPLORATIONS

1. How does Solomon define the dual character of the American dream? What are its negative and positive aspects? How does advertising make use of the American dream?

2. What specific desires, fantasies, and fears does Solomon say advertisers use most effectively? What, for Solomon, is the value of recognizing both these desires and the ways in which advertisers manipulate them?

3. Solomon argues that advertising is designed to "manipulate," not "persuade." Do you think ads create needs and desires, or do they simply work on existing desires? Explain your point of view.

4. Locate and analyze a particular instance of public discourse for its explicit and implicit messages, looking critically at everything presented from the text to the images and their arrangement. What methods does the text use to make you want or need the product or service? How does it engage your interest or desire? Who is the audience? Where did you find the instance of public discourse? Is this location significant? What does the text actually say? What does it imply? Are those messages the same? Why or why not? Bring a copy of your chosen text to class and be prepared to present your analysis of it to the class.

Move Over, Boomers: The Busters Are Here—and They're Angry

LAURA ZINN

"Move Over Boomers" first appeared in the December 14, 1992, issue of Business Week. *In this article Zinn provides a market analysis of a specific audience—18- to 24-year olds—advising businesses on effective ways of marketing their products to appeal to this target audience.*

WRITING BEFORE READING

Describe an advertisement that you suspect was targeted at your demographic group—based on your age, your gender, your social class, or some other factor. How could you tell that the advertisement was meant to get your attention? Was it effective? Interesting? Offensive?

"The guy who has the job I want is 34 and has a wife and kids. So he's not leaving."

> —*Amy Ross, 24, who has a master's degree from Cornell University and now works as a traveling fabric salesperson*

"I'm very cynical about the Sixties: 'Peace, love, groovy, let's get high'—and look what happened. These people turned out to be worse than the people they rebelled against. They're materialistic hypocrites."

> —*Blan Holman, 23, free-lance environmental writer*

Hear that, baby boomers? That's the sound of the future coming up behind you. It's the sound of the 46 million Americans, aged 18 to 29, who make up the vanguard of the next generation.

Face it, you're not the future anymore. The idea will take some getting used to. As the largest demographic cohort in history moved through the years, boomers shaped much of postwar America—how it dressed, what it watched, read, listened to. Now, as they move into offices both corner and Oval, boomers will determine how America manages and governs.

But for the shape of things to come, look not at the boomers but at their successors. Call them by any of the many names they have already been saddled with—twentysomethings, Generation X, slackers, busters—they are entering the mainstream of American life. They're the ones who are studying on our campuses, slogging through first jobs—or just hoping to land a job, any job.

For all the talk of the baby bust, this is no small bunch. Compared 4
to those born from 1951 through 1962—the core of the baby boom—
this current crop of 18-to-29-year-olds is the second-largest group of
young adults in U. S. history. They're already starting to set tastes in
fashion and popular culture. They're the ones who will vote you into
office, buy your products, and work in your factories. They will give
birth to your grandchildren, nieces, and nephews.

TATTOOED AND PIERCED

So far, this group is having a tough time. Busters are the first 5
generation of latchkey children, products of dual-career households,
or, in some 50% of cases, of divorced or separated parents. They have
been entering the work force at a time of prolonged downsizing and
downturn, so they're likelier than the previous generation to be
unemployed, underemployed, and living at home with Mom and
Dad. They're alienated by a culture that has been dominated by
boomers for as long as they can remember. They're angry as they
look down a career path that's crowded with thirty- and fortysome-
things who are in no hurry to clear the way. And if they're angry
and alienated, they dress the part, with aggressively unpretty
fashions, pierced noses, and tattoos.

At the same time, though, they're ethnically diverse, and 6
they're more comfortable with diversity than any previous generation. Many of them don't give a hoot for the old-fashioned war
between the sexes, either, but instead tend to have lots of friends
of the opposite sex. Furthermore, as a generation that's been bombarded by multiple media since their cradle days, they're savvy—and
cynical—consumers.

To many older Americans, the Generation Xers have been a 7
virtually invisible subculture. They have been largely ignored by U. S.
media, businesses, and public institutions, which have spent years cov-
eting the baby boomers as audience, market and constituency.
"Marketers have been distracted by boomers going through their
household formations," says Scott L. Kauffman, 36, vice-president for
marketing, promotion, and development at *Entertainment Weekly.*
"Busters don't feel like anyone's paying attention to them."

MAGIC NUMBER

But that will have to change. For one thing, despite their many 8
hardships, consumers in their late teens and their twenties already
wield annual spending power of some $125 billion, according to

a survey by Roper Organization Inc. And the baby busters are essential to the success of many major categories, such as beer, fast food, cosmetics, and electronics. More important, within this decade, these consumers will be entering their peak earning years. With all the boomers blocking the road ahead, it may take the busters longer than some previous generations. But soon enough, they'll by setting up households by the millions, having families, and buying refrigerators, cars, homes—all the big-ticket items that drive an economy.

Indeed, it could well be the busters who lead the country out of recession according to the theory of the 25-year-old's powerful purse strings. Richard Hokenson, a demographer at Donaldson, Lufkin & Jenrette in New York, has been studying 25-year-olds' purchasing back to the 1950s. His theory: When a large number of young adults turn 25 at the same time, they buy a lot of consumer goods, pumping money into the economy and so stimulating demand across the board. Take 1986, when an unprecedented number of Americans turned 25. It was the best year for housing in the 1980s: 1.8 million units were built. And 1986 was also a record year for cars, with sales of 15.1 million cars and light trucks. 9

BIG GAP

Beginning next year, a bulge of 13 million kids who were born between October, 1968, and March, 1971, will start turning 25. They'll be the largest group of 25-year-olds since 1986. If Hokenson is right, then for three years starting next October, busters will by buying enough houses and durable goods to ignite a healthy recovery. 10

So who are these folks who will shape our destiny? The boomers who increasingly dominate the Establishment they once rebelled against will make a big mistake if they assume that the busters are just like they were at that age. "Most marketers today are boomers and much more likely to impose their values on this generation, to the point where busters are invisible," says Peter Kim, U. S. director for strategic planning at J. Walter Thompson North America. 11

At a recent convention of magazine publishers and editors, Karen Ritchie, senior vice-president at ad agency McCann-Erickson in Detroit, told the largely boomer audience that they were in danger of losing busters forever if they didn't pay attention to them now. "I told them that the media were not treating the next generation very well," says Ritchie. "They have never been addressed in any significant way and have very real reasons to be hostile." 12

And hostile they are. Busters resent the boomers, whom they see as having partied through the 1970s and 1980s, sticking the younger 13 generation with the check. "It will be me and my children that pay off the deficit," says Laura Romis, 23, a part-time bank teller and Ohio State University graduate who would like to be a journalist. "I blame the generations before us."

" McJOB"

Many busters said they have graduated from high school and   14
college into unemployment or underemployment. Unlike the trailing edge of baby boomers, who easily entered the expanding job market of the mid-1980s, busters often have to settle for what Douglas Coupland, thirtysomething author of the novel *Generation X*, calls "McJobs"—mundane and marginally challenging work that provides a paycheck and little else. Take Kristi Doherty, 22, a graduate of Lewis & Clark College. She wants to be an anthropologist, but she's clerking in a clothing store in Portland, Ore., and taking on babysitting jobs. "We were told since we were kids that if we worked hard, we would be successful." Instead, she says, "I worked hard, I had a high grade-point average, and I am 100% overqualified for my job."

This is the generation of diminished expectations—polar   15
opposites of the baby boomers, who grew up thinking anything was possible. In a general survey commissioned by Shearson Lehman Hutton Holdings Inc., 18-to-29-year-olds were the only age group to evaluate their own economic class as lower than their parents'. Of course, that's partly because they're early in their careers, says Sara Lipson, director of business development and market research at Shearson. "But the answer also reflects the sense that affluence is going to be harder to achieve, that the window of opportunity is closing on this generation." According to the Center for Labor Market Studies at Northeastern University, the current median income for households headed by adults under 30 is $24,500. That's a 21% drop in constant dollars from 1973.

BOOMER CASTOFFS

And as if a bleak economic situation wasn't enough, busters   16
don't have much emotional security, either. Boomers grew up in the post-Eisenhower era of the working dad and homemaker mom. "Boomers were told as kids, 'You're wonderful, you're the center of the universe,'" says Susan Hayward, senior vice-president of market research firm Yankelovich Partners Inc. "And boomers will feel that way until they're 90." Meanwhile, the busters' world

became progressively gloomier. "The economy began to fall apart, safety nets began to unravel, the loan guarantees were gone by the time they went to college, and they didn't have their mothers at home," says Hayward.

And where baby boomers had the sexual revolution, busters are   17
growing up in the age of AIDS. "People our age were forming their sexual identity with the understanding that we could die for our actions," says Adam Glickman, 26, co-founder of Condomania, a Los Angeles-based chain of eight condom stores. "No other generation has had to deal with this at this stage of their lives."

All this insecurity has created a painful paradox. "There's a   18
strong desire to be Establishment, but the recession is making it very hard to attain that," says Bradford Fay, 27, a research director at Roper. "The ironic thing is that the baby-boom generation had everything for the taking and at first rejected it. Here's a generation that very much wants those things but is having a very hard time getting them."

Except for their collective sense of foreboding, busters have   19
little in common with each other. Where boomers were united by pivotal events, such as the Vietnam War and Watergate, busters have been left largely unmoved by their era's low-cal war, Operation Desert Storm, and scandal-lite, Iran-*contra*.

They're also a racially diverse group, with 14% blacks, 12.3%   20
Hispanics, and 3.9% Asians, compared with 12.4%, 9.5%, and 3.3% respectively for the entire population. This diversity isn't always accepted—witness the rash of racial brawls on campuses. But the greater prevalence of minorities in this generation heavily influences the language, music, and dress that it adopts. And marketers use black cultural idioms such as hip hop—dance-oriented street music— as a kind of semaphore to reach Xers. "You see the African-American segment of the youth market leading the way," says Thomas Burrell, chairman of Burrell Advertising Inc. in Chicago, which does ads for McDonald's Corp. in African-American publications. "The groups aren't coming together physically, but you see the signals picked up through the media." Adds Keith Clinkscales, 28, publisher and editor-in-chief of *Urban Profile*, a magazine for black college students: "The mainstream has expanded. Now you have Madison Avenue copywriters enjoying the fruits of hip-hop and other parts of black culture."

Busters are also creating their own pop culture by borrowing   21
discarded boomer icons and mocking them while making them their own. Witness the renewed enthusiasm among young cable viewers for reruns of vapid TV shows made about two decades or more ago— *Gilligan's Island*, *The Brady Bunch*, and *The Dick Van Dyke Show*. It's all fascinating for trend-watchers. "This derisive viewing of

The Brady Bunch is not just motivated by a need to feel superior,"
says Mark Crispin Miller, professor of media studies at Johns
Hopkins University. "It's also motivated by a longing for the more
stable world of *The Brady Bunch*."

Busters' passion for boomer castoffs is also creeping into fash-   22
ion. This fall, the '70s-inspired "grunge" look has influenced
some of Seventh Avenue's younger designers. What's grunge?
You're showing your age. Grunge is slovenly, asexual, antifashion
fashion. The style has even surfaced in *Vogue*. In a special spread in
the magazine's December issue, a cast of waiflike models sports
long, lank hair, faded flannel shirts, clunky work boots, ripped
sweaters, old jeans and corduroys, long flowing skirts, pierces noses,
and a bleak "Fine, fire me, I don't care" look. "Grunge speaks to
a narrow band and to the exclusion of boomers," says
Entertainment Weekly's Kauffman.

JOLT-FUELED "RAVES"

Grunge music is similarly anomie-riddled and angry. Grunge   23
stars include Kurt Cobain and his group, Nirvana, whose 1991
album *Nevermind* sold 4.5 million copies in the U. S. Even harsher
are Soundgarden and Mudhoney. Then there are the spontaneous
dance marathons on the West Coast, called "raves," where music
from such groups as Nine Inch Nails makes up in speed what it lacks
in melody. Ravers take over vast warehouses or parking lots, where
they dance wildly in huge crowds, often fueled by supercaffeinated
Jolt cola, "smart drinks" of caffeine and protein mixers, and
Ecstasy, a combination of mild hallucinogens and speed. Busters also
dive into new magazines, such as *Details, Urban Profile, Spin*, and
YSB (*Young Sisters & Brothers*), that most boomers have probably
never heard of.

Grunge, anger, cultural dislocation, a secret yearning to belong: 24
They add up to a daunting cultural anthropology that marketers have
to confront if they want to reach twentysomethings. But it's worth
it. Busters do buy stuff: CDs, sweaters, jeans, boots, soda, beer,
cosmetics, electronics, cars, fast food, personal computers, mountain
bikes, and Rollerblades. In part because so many live at home—54%
of 18-to-24-year-olds in 1991, vs. 48% in 1980—they have lots of
discretionary income. Their brand preferences haven't yet been
entirely established, unlike those of aging boomers who are already
set in their ways. And like any group, they will appreciate being
courted—if the wooing is done right.

Finding the right tone can be tricky. For one thing, Xers were   25
often exposed to the temptations of consumer culture at an even

more tender age than boomers. Since so many busters grew up with working parents, they were given early shopping chores. Says Linda Cohen, publisher of *Sassy* magazine: "They're used to deciding what stereo is best, what car is cool, what vacation to go on. They are very savvy consumers."

That's good and bad for marketers. It's good because busters   26 are accustomed to shopping, bad because it means they are far more knowledgeable about and suspicious of advertising than earlier generations passing through their twenties. "Today's teens are media maniacs," says Sassy's Cohen. "Generation X has been brought up in the most overcommunicated society in the world." Adds James Truman, editor-in-chief of *Details*, whose readers' median age is 26: "They're tremendously cynical because they know the media is most often talking to them to sell them something."

"HEY, WE KNOW"

That combination of cynicism and responsibility even shows   27 up among supposedly carefree college students. Gary Flood, a vice-president for marketing at MasterCard International Inc., was surprised at how knowingly focus groups of students talked about getting a good credit rating. "Try some frivolous approach in selling them a credit card, or tell them to have a good time with the card with their friends, and it turns them off," Flood says. Instead, MasterCard is providing seminars on handling credit responsibly. Similarly, in a move that shows an understanding of buster concerns in the dour 1990s, MCI Communications Corp. has planned a promotion around a brochure it is publishing on the dos and don'ts of finding a first job.

At the same time, busters are turned off by marketing pitches   28 that take themselves too seriously. Not for them the 1980s-style yuppie ads that treat luxury cars or expensive cosmetics so reverentially. Busters respond best to messages that take a self-mocking tone. What works, says market researcher Judith Lander, is "advertising that is funny and hip and says, 'Hey, we know.'"

So how do you show you know? In one television ad for   29 Maybelline Inc.'s Expert Eyes Shadow, model Christy Turlington is shown looking coolly glamorous against a moonlit sky. A voice-over says: "Was it a strange celestial event . . . that gave her such bewitching eyes?" Then, Turlington, magically transported to her living room sofa, laughs and says: "Get over it." Says Sheri Colonel, executive vice-president at Maybelline's ad agency, Lintas New York: "We found we had to be irreverent, sassy, and surprising with this age group."

Another cosmetics maker, Revlon Inc., has ditched the gauzy, 30
worshipful ad approach in favor of a pitch that plays to diversity. In
ads for its Charlie perfume, Revlon shows a supermodel Cindy
Crawford playing basketball with a racially mixed group of young
men.

Taco Bell Worldwide also figured it had to use a playful approach 31
to pursue busters. The fast-food chain did a lot of market research to
determine the right tone, says Tim Ryan, senior vice-president for
marketing. His discovery: Busters "love music, they love to party,
and they love irreverence." Taco Bell's ad agency, Foote, Cone &
Belding, created a campaign that incorporates rockabilly music and
MTV-style shots of musicians playing in the desert.

Marketers also figure that busters like to think that they live life 32
on the edge. So one sure sign of an ad aimed at this group is imagery
of wild, death-defying stunts. "You're dealing with a group that really feels like it's seen it all," says Ann Glover, brand manager for
PepsiCo Inc.'s regular and Diet Mountain Dew soft drinks. "So the
challenge is how do you create a commercial that breaks through to
this person who thinks he knows everything?" Recent TV ads for the
$275 million Diet Dew brand attempt to reach 20-to-29-year-old
men by showing their ilk rollerblading down a volcano or kayaking
over a waterfall. Diet Dew advertises aggressively on MTV and on
Fox Broadcasting Co. shows such as *Melrose Place* and *In Living
Color* intended for busters.

HONESTY POLICY

Buster cynicism about blatant product pitches has also shaped 33
Nike Inc.'s marketing. Says Kate Bednarski, global marketing manager for the footwear maker's women's division: "That's one of
the reasons we decided to be as honest as possible, even though we
are a brand name and trying to sell a product."

Nike's ads for women's athletic shoes are all soft sell, showing 34
little footwear or apparel. Instead, they feature a lot of text and
depict women running, walking, or doing aerobics—always resolving
with an exhortation to go do some self-improving fitness activity—
sort of consciousness raising session in print. "I always read Nike ads
from start to finish," says Abby Levine, 23, a junior retail executive
in New York City. "They always have some words of encouragement."

Busters also resent all the lecturing they have gotten from 35
boomers, who, as Ritchie of McCann-Erickson notes, have grown
increasingly restrictive and reactionary as they approach middle age,
despite their revered memories of free love and political protest.

"The repressiveness of the baby boomers has really come to the fore in the last 10 years," Ritchie says.

Recent TV ads for the Isuzu Rodeo off-road vehicle tap into   36
busters' feelings of rebellion. One begins with a little girl in a class-room being urged by her teacher to color only between the lines. In the next shot, she's a twentysomething who abandons the traffic lanes and roars off the highway onto a dirt road. As a result of the campaign and its success with busters, the average age of Rodeo buyers has dropped into the low 30s, and overall sales have increased 60%, to 5,000 a month.

Not that busters don't have their own orthodoxies. They're   37
concerned about the environment: Ice cream maker Ben & Jerry's Homemade Inc. sells this point by informing customers of how it recycles packaging and buys blueberries from Indians in Maine.

BYE-BYE BIMBOS

And while they respond to sexy advertising, they're repelled by   38
anything that smacks of sexism. When August A. Busch IV became brand manager for Budweiser in July, 1991, the then-27-year-old told Anheuser-Busch Cos. wholesalers that research showed the typical bouncing-bimbo-filled beer ad "just doesn't cut through" to the 21-to-27-year-old drinkers he wanted to reach. Busch launched a campaign that displayed the kind of nonsexist irreverence that appeals to many Xers. One ad shows a granny teaching a rocker how to play his guitar better. Another series has busters receiving a slightly tongue-in-cheek lesson about the glorious tradition of Bud from older barmates. Busch's father, CEO August A. Busch III, was skeptical. "But he's looking through younger eyes," the father admitted. "He was right, and I was wrong." Through September, Anheuser-Busch posted a 1.3% gain in barrel shipments; the indus-try showed a 0.3% gain.

Marketers who get their messages right may be in for a pleasant   39
surprise. Like other demographers, Hokenson of Donaldson, Lufkin & Jenrette believes that a population cohort's size has a big influ-ence on its standard of living. Today's baby-bust generation, large as it is, still runs smaller than the boomer generation. That means it may not face the heavy competition boomers now encounter from their numerous brethren.

So, despite their struggles, busters may yet end up living better   40
than the boomers. That would be a rich irony: the overlooked gen-eration ultimately beating out the Me Generation in the race for prosperity.

—By Laura Zinn, with Christopher Power in New York,
Dori Jones Yang in Seattle,
Alice Z. Cuneo in San Francisco,
David Ross in New Haven,
and bureau reports.

EXPLORATIONS

1. Zinn analyzes a target audience, but who is Zinn's *own* target audience for this study and how does she appeal to *them*?

2. How does Zinn characterize Busters? What, according to Zinn, does or does not appeal to Busters? How does Zinn suggest products should be marketed to this target group? Can you think of any ads you have seen that either support or detract from Zinn's claims?

3. What do you think about Zinn's methods of audience analysis? Does it surprise you that such a "study" would be conducted? Do you think the analysis is a valid one?

4. With another student or in a small group, develop a marketing campaign for a new product. You will need to determine your target audience and how best to appeal to that audience. How do you go about making a product seem absolutely necessary to its targeted audience? Compose your own profile of that target audience.

Always Real: Coke Chillin' in The Hood

Scott Charles

Scott Charles, a twenty-eight-year-old returning student, is a psychology major at The Ohio State University. He was born and raised in Sacramento, California, where he most recently worked with high risk youth and teen parents for the California Department of Education. Charles's essay analyzes the ways in which Coca-Cola products are market-ed to the African American urban community.

WRITING BEFORE READING

How do you determine your target audience when you write an essay? Do you use any of the methods that advertisers use to analyze their audiences? Why or why not?

Four small words sum up the approach to Urban America that Coke has taken with its "Always Coca-Cola" campaign: *Get Your Chill On.* I recently came across these words in a full-page ad in the back of *VIBE* (a magazine published by Quincy Jones). The ad depicts a young black man and woman with their backs to one another, drinking out of contoured plastic Coke bottles. Behind this attractive couple is a massive fan, its blades representing 1:40 P.M. on a clock. While both of the people in the photograph are indepen-dently handsome—their heads centered for reasons of composition in the middle of the page—neither seems visibly perfected. They have the recognizable appeal usually reserved for those we interact with daily; not the air-brushed, ethnically blended qualities usually found in Madison Avenue advertising. Floating just above and to the right of the man is the red, buttonish Coca-Cola logo, with the words ALWAYS and REAL immediately above and below the icon, respec-tively. The phrase *Get Your Chill On*—the only other text found in the ad—provides encouragement at the top of the page. It is produced by bright red lettering of varying shape and size. Most is sans-serif. It provides the reader with a feeling of informality, of aesthetic rebellion, of undeniable hipness.

While there is nothing particularly impressive about any of the words—all short and containing one syllable—the message intended for its audience is powerful: "We are the cola of choice of the urban and/or black community!" Nothing makes this more clear than the words themselves. When combined in this particular order, these words address exclusively inner-city ears.

In order to fully appreciate the specificity of the ad, it is impor-   3
tant to understand the message. To get something *on* is to experience
it to its full potential. For example: *Getting your groove on* suggests
that you are intent on dancing; *getting your clown on* means that you
couldn't be any more embarrassing to others or yourself. It is the
ultimate in achievement. Once it's on, it's on. If a person has his or
her "chill on," he or she has surrendered completely to relaxation.
In the context of this ad, the phrase infers coolness both figuratively
and literally. The distinct use of this expression is generally limited to
the fraternity that is the young, urban, hip-hop generation. For the
purposes of this essay, I will consider hip-hop as a component of the
black community. Although it experiences the participation and
appreciation of a culturally diverse audience, it is an African American
innovation that is driven almost exclusively by the black community.
The reciprocation of influences and ideas that the collective black
community and hip-hop culture share has created an undeniable
marriage of the two.

HEY, BUT I'M DOWN!

Although the creative dialects of hip-hop culture often transcend   4
the boundaries of age, gender, and race, the significance of Coke's
intent should not be overlooked. Language in the black community
is often as exclusive to its residents as a national language is to those
indigenous to foreign countries. The cultural importance of African
American dialects dates back hundreds of years when slaves—after
being forced to abandon their native African languages—had to find
ways to communicate with one another without detection from slave
masters or hands. Because of the vast geography that the American
slave trade covered, it was necessary for these "secret" languages to
be widely understood and used by a great number of blacks. This
oral tradition continues today.

Today, however, the language of black America is in constant   5
motion. Just as in interpreting black codes from the underground
railroad, a person has to maintain a connection to those "in the
know" in order to stay abreast of the latest changes. What was in yesterday is out today. What was out of date the day before yesterday will
be reinvented to mean something completely different tomorrow.

The pressure to avoid detection has become even greater lately.   6
America's patronization of black America has led to a postArsenio-
dogbarking-RickiLake"Speaktothehand!"-"Don'tevengo-
there!"-Oprahfied-"Yougogirl" consciousness for many whites.
The increasing attention that Americans are paying to the hip-hop
culture (in hope of attaining new phrases to impress friends with) has

many blacks feeling intruded upon. Rarely are such expressions able to experience the longevity they once did. Even blacks who were once able to take their bilingual abilities for granted are finding it necessary to "keep their chops up." So when an expression avoids becoming generic it is embraced by blacks, and then used as a way to gauge "downness."

ALWAYS REAL

When Coke uses an expression that has not made it to the "blackese" graveyard, it achieves a level of credibility among many young black consumers. These four small words, "Get Your Chill On," speak volumes to the company's desire to specifically target this audience. The subtleties of the phrase would be lost upon those out of touch with the community—including many middle-class blacks. While the general public may gather that *chill* means to relax (as it too has been relegated to the "graveyard"), most fail to recognize the other things this phrase suggests. These fourteen letters, with their three spaces, say a lot to the reader: They say, " You know me!"; "I'm from around the way!"; "Say, 'black,' remember how we used to get down?!"   7

The icing on the cake came with Coke's placing "Always Real" in their ads. If readers were unsure before, they now know beyond a doubt that Coke is "down." Being "real" is the absolute criteria for being down. You cannot be down if you are at all pretentious—acting as though you came up some way other than hard. During the parting of two young black men, one of them will often implore the other to "Stay real!" For Coke, the use of the term suggests that—even though the company has made it big—it still remembers where it is from: It hasn't sold out. This means a great deal to an audience who, up until now, has been largely ignored by the products they consume.   8

Although PepsiCo used Ray Charles & "The Uh Huh Girls" to push its Diet Pepsi campaign, the truth is that few young black people can name any of his songs. Pepsi's intent, at a time when it had everything to lose as America's top pop, was to bring new "overclass" blacks into the feel-good fold, without alienating any of the well established drinkers it had captured during the "Cola Wars." For this purpose, Ray Charles, who had long been considered a "safe Negro"—since he is older and has not led police on any high-speed car chases, or been known to beat his wives—was a perfect tool. However, the spots alienated many in the community with the patriotic vibe that enshrouded some of the ads—an "American Experience" that most blacks don't feel a part of.   9

When Coca-Cola unveiled its new "Always Coca-Cola" 10
campaign in 1993 (*Beverage-World*, Fall '93), it made it clear that
it hoped to tap into the very lucrative black urban market. Realizing
that blacks spend $300 billion on goods and services each year, Coke
set out to develop new advertising that would appeal directly to this
group. It hired producers and songwriters Terry Coffey and Jon
Nettlesbey to create a soulful jingle that could reach urban audiences
without alienating others. The result is the beat-intensive groove
that has been used in more than thirty ads and put to a variety of
dance-oriented music, including rap, reggae, r&b, techno, and
house.

One of the ads that has been produced for this series features a 11
young black man between sixteen and nineteen years old riding a
public transit bus. As he boards—with his *Walkman* headphones
framing the shiny smoothness of his bald head as they cover his
ears—he is eyeballed by a young and gorgeous black woman. As he
coolly strides past, oblivious to her wanton desire, he hums the inde-
cipherable, yet recognizable, verse to Coke's jingle. Once he sits
down, however, he removes the headphones, and with a look of
complete (and almost orgasmic) satisfaction, he belts out the honey-
sweet hook: "Always Coca-Cola!"

Like a soul handshake, Coke uses the images in the ad as evi- 12
dence of its commitment to the cause. How else would it know the
visual "hot buttons" to push: the city bus; the brother's hip-hop
aesthetic, with his bald head and "don't give a f—k" vibe; the
"round the way" lust of the girl; and the fact that *nobody* knows the
words that lead up to "Always Coca-Cola."

THIS WILL BE OUR LITTLE SECRET

If Coke is truly "down," it is a discreet devotion. Most of its 13
"edgy" TV commercials that run endlessly on Black Entertainment
Television (BET), featuring Afrocentric themes, are rarely seen during national programming. Never during an episode of *Friends* does
the station break to the pulsing, Kente Cloth–drenched commercials
the Coke buys during reruns of *Roc* or *Sanford & Son* on BET. Seen
at these times are Coke's spots that represent the "polar opposite"
of the inner-city approach: The Snowbound Bears. The only print
ads that appear in non-black publications that even remotely resemble the urban campaign are those that feature professional athletes.
And even in these cases, the text refrains from the exclusive nature of
hip-hop language; generally the words are athletic or motivational.
Where contemporary black men are hostile and threatening, the
black athlete is conformed and is usually admirable enough to make

the average white American willing to live vicariously through him (even if those who receive the greatest ovation are the ones who play the most violently).

When Coke does use black faces in its mainstream TV ads, the 14 individuals tend to be light-complexioned and safe in appearance. Rap artists such as Pete Rock and C. L. Smooth, who are shown rapping in the studio in commercials for Sprite (a subsidiary of Coke), are nowhere to be found on Middle-America's televisions. Just as Pepsi had everything to lose when it first used a "safe Negro," Sprite has nothing to lose by using "rough" ones. The fact is that 7-Up has long sat at the head of the "un-cola" table, and seems unlikely to give up its seat. For Sprite, this leaves only the crumbs under the table—the Urban dweller.

While some might think that this fickle behavior on the part of 15 Coke could be seen as exploitation, it only serves to enforce the mystique that surrounds the company's appeal within the black community. The lasting message from Coke is the same as that exerted by many blacks attempting to experience financial success while maintaining cultural legitimacy: "Even though I appear to work for 'the man,' you know I'll always come home to the hood."

EXPLORATIONS

1. How does Charles support his claim that Coke targets the urban, hip-hop community? Does he believe that these ads are effective in reaching their desired audience? Why or why not?

2. Both Charles and Laura Zinn argue that companies analyze their targeted audiences. What are the key elements of such an analysis, and what appears to make such targeting successful?

3. How do the ads Charles discusses use language to appeal to the audience? How are images such as setting and dress used to promote the product?

4. Do the corporate tactics described by Charles coincide with those presented by Solomon? Is Coke selling the American dream, tapping into particular desires, or doing something else?

5. Describe the literacies Charles exhibits and discusses in this essay. How do they inform each other?

6. Bring in a copy of an advertisement that you feel is targeted toward a group you identify with. Work with your peer response group to analyze the audience and appeals in the ad. Remember to provide specific details to support any claims you might make.

The Incredible Shrinking Sound Bite

KIKU ADATTO

*Kiku Adatto has taught at Harvard University and writes fre-
quently about public discourse and its relationship to
American culture and the American political scene. "The
Incredible Shrinking Sound Bite" was originally published
in* The New Republic *on May 28, 1990. This article is the
basis for Adatto's 1993 book,* Picture Perfect, *in which she
compares the television coverage of the presidential campaigns of 1968 and 1988 and analyzes the rise of images in
American culture through the visual media of photography,
film, and television.*

WRITING BEFORE READING

*Is the character of a political candidate important to you? How do you
get information regarding a candidate's character? Is that information
reliable?*

Standing before a campaign rally in Pennsylvania, the 1968   1
Democratic vice presidential candidate, Edmund Muskie, tried to
speak, but a group of antiwar protesters drowned him out. Muskie
offered the hecklers a deal. He would give the platform to one of
their representatives if he could then speak without interruption.
Rick Brody, the students' choice, rose to the microphone where, to
cheers from the crowd, he denounced the candidates that the 1968
presidential campaign had to offer. "Wallace is no answer. Nixon's
no answer. And Humphrey's no answer. Sit out this election!"
When Brody finished, Muskie made his case for the Democratic ticket. That night Muskie's confrontation with the demonstrators
played prominently on the network news. NBC showed fifty-seven
seconds of Brody's speech, and more than a minute of Muskie's.

Twenty years later, things had changed. Throughout the entire   2
1988 campaign, no network allowed either presidential candidate to
speak uninterrupted on the evening news for as long as Rick Brody
spoke. By 1988 television's tolerance for the languid pace of political discourse, never great, had all but vanished. An analysis of all
weekday evening network newscasts (over 280) from Labor Day to
Election Day in 1968 and 1988 reveals that the average "sound
bite" fell from 42.3 seconds in 1968 to only 9.8 seconds in 1988.
Meanwhile the time the networks devoted to visuals of the candi-

dates, unaccompanied by their words, increased by more than 300 percent.

Since the Kennedy-Nixon debates of 1960, television has played 3 a pivotal role in presidential politics. The Nixon campaign of 1968 was the first to be managed and orchestrated to play on the evening news. With the decline of political parties and the direct appeal to voters in the primaries, presidential campaigns became more adept at conveying their messages through visual images, not only in political commercials but also in elaborately staged media events. By the time of Ronald Reagan, the actor turned president, Michael Deaver had perfected the techniques of the video presidency.

For television news, the politicians' mastery of television 4 imagery posed a temptation and a challenge. The temptation was to show the pictures. What network producer could resist the footage of Reagan at Normandy Beach, or of Bush in Boston Harbor? The challenge was to avoid being entangled in the artifice and imagery that the campaigns dispensed. In 1988 the networks tried to have it both ways—to meet the challenge even as they succumbed to the temptation. They showed the images that the campaigns sought to retain their objectivity by exposing the artifice of the images, by calling constant attention to their self-conscious design.

The language of political reporting was filled with accounts of 5 staging and backdrops, camera angles and scripts, sound bites and spin control, photo opportunities and media gurus. So attentive was television news to the way the campaigns constructed images for television that political reporters began to sound like theater critics, reporting more on the stagecraft than the substance of politics.

When Bush kicked off his campaign with a Labor Day appearance 6 at Disneyland, the networks covered the event as a performance for television. "In the war of the Labor Day visuals," CBS's Bob Schieffer reported, "George Bush pulled out the heavy artillery. A Disneyland backdrop and lots of pictures with the Disneyland gang." When Bruce Morton covered Dukakis riding in a tank, the story was the image. "In the trade of politics, it's called a visual," said Morton. "The idea is pictures are symbols that tell the voter important things about the candidate. If your candidate is seen in the polls as weak on defense, put him in a tank."

And when Bush showed up at a military base to observe the 7 destruction of a missile under an arms control treaty, ABC's Brit Hume began his report by telling his viewers that they were watching a media event. "Now, here was a photo opportunity, the vice president watching a Pershing missile burn off its fuel." He went on to describe how the event was staged for television. Standing in front of an open field, Hume reported, "The Army had even gone so far as to bulldoze acres of trees to make sure the vice president and the news media had a clear view. "

So familiar is the turn to theater criticism that it is difficult to 8 recall the transformation it represents. Even as they conveyed the first presidential campaign "made for television," TV reporters in 1968 continued to reflect the print journalist tradition from which they had descended. In the marriage of theater and politics, politics remained the focus of reporting. The media events of the day—mostly rallies and press conferences—were covered as political events, not as exercises in impression management.

By 1988 television displaced politics as the focus of coverage. 9 Like a gestalt shift, the images that once formed the background to political events—the setting and the stagecraft—now occupied the foreground. (Only 6 percent of reports in 1968 were devoted to theater criticism, compared with 52 percent in 1988.) And yet, for all their image-conscious coverage in 1988, reporters did not escape their entanglement. They showed the potent visuals even as they attempted to avoid the manipulation by "deconstructing" the imagery and revealing its artifice.

To be sure, theater criticism was not the only kind of political 10 reporting on network newscasts in 1988. Some notable "fact correction" pieces offered admirable exceptions. For example, after each presidential debate, ABC's Jim Wooten compared the candidates' claims with the facts. Not content with the canned images of the politicians, Wooten used television images to document discrepancies between the candidates' rhetoric and their records.

Most coverage simply exposed the contrivances of image-making. 11 But alerting the viewer to the construction of television images proved no substitute for fact correction. A superficial "balance" replaced objectivity as the measure of fairness, a balance consisting of equal time for media events, equal time for commercials. But this created a false symmetry, leaving both the press and the public hostage to the play of perceptions the campaigns dispensed.

Even the most critical versions of image-conscious coverage 12 could fail to puncture the pictures they showed. When Bush visited a flag factory in hopes of making patriotism a campaign issue, ABC's Hume reported that Bush was wrapping himself in the flag. "This campaign strives to match its pictures with its points. Today and for much of the past week, the pictures have been of George Bush with the American flag. If the point wasn't to make as issue of patriotism, then the question arises, what was it?" Yet only three days later, in an ABC report on independent voters in New Jersey, the media event that Hume reported with derision was transformed into an innocent visual of Bush. The criticism forgotten, the image played on.

Another striking contrast between the coverage of the 1968 and   13
1988 campaigns is the increased coverage of political commercials.
Although political ads played a prominent role in the 1968
campaign, the networks rarely showed excerpts on the news. During
the entire 1968 general election campaign, the evening news programs broadcast only two excerpts from candidates' commercials.
By 1988 the number had jumped to 125. In 1968 the only time a
negative ad was mentioned on the evening news was when CBS's
Walter Cronkite and NBC's Chet Huntley reported that a Nixon
campaign ad—showing a smiling Hubert Humphrey superimposed
on scenes of war and riot—was withdrawn after the Democrats cried
foul. Neither network showed the ad itself.

The networks might argue that in 1988 political ads loomed larg-   14
er in the campaign, and so required more coverage. But as with their
focus on media events, reporters ran the risk of becoming
conduits of the television images the campaigns dispensed. Even with
a critical narrative, showing commercials on the news gives free time
to paid media. And most of the time the narrative was not critical. The
networks rarely bothered to correct the distortions or misstatements
that the ads contained. Of the 125 excerpts shown on the evening
news in 1988, the reporter addressed the veracity of the commercials'
claim less than 8 percent of the time. The networks became, in effect,
electronic billboards for the candidates, showing political commercials
not only as breaking news but as stand-ins for the candidates, and file
footage aired interchangeably with news footage of the candidates.

The few cases where reporters corrected the facts illustrate how   15
the networks might have covered political commercials. ABC's
Richard Threlkeld ran excerpts from a Bush ad attacking Dukakis's
defense stand by freezing the frame and correcting each mistaken or
distorted claim. He also pointed out the exaggeration in a Dukakis
ad attacking Bush's record on Social Security. CBS's Leslie Stahl
corrected a deceptive statistic in Bush's revolving-door furlough ad,
noting: "Part of the ad is false. . . . Two hundred sixty-eight
murderers did not escape. . . . [T]he truth is only four first-degree
murderers escaped while on parole."

Stahl concluded her report by observing, "Dukakis left the   16
Bush attack ads unanswered for six weeks. Today campaign aides are
engaged in a round of finger-pointing at who is to blame." But the
networks also let the Bush furlough commercial run without challenge or correction. Before and even after her report, CBS ran
excerpts of the ad without correction. In all, network newscasts ran
excerpts from the revolving-door furlough ad ten times throughout
the campaign, only once correcting the deceptive statistic.

It might be argued that it is up to the candidate to reply to his 17 opponent's charges, not the press. But the networks' frequent use of political ads on the evening news created a strong disincentive for a candidate to challenge his opponent's ads. As Dukakis found, to attack a television ad as unfair or untrue it to invite the networks to run it again. In the final weeks before the election, the Dukakis campaign accused the Republicans of lying about his record on defense, and of using racist tactics in ads featuring Willie Horton, a black convict who raped and killed while on furlough from a Massachusetts prison. . . . In reporting Dukakis's complaint, all three networks ran excerpts of the ads in question, including the highly charged pictures of Horton and the revolving door of convicts. Dukakis's response thus gave Bush's potent visuals another free run on the evening news.

The networks might reply that the ads are news and thus need 18 to be shown, as long as they generate controversy in the campaign. But this rationale leaves them open to manipulation. Oddly enough, the networks were alive to this danger when confronted with the question of whether to air the videos the campaigns produced for the conventions. "I am not into tone poems," Lane Venardos, the executive producer in charge of convention coverage at CBS, told the *New York Times*. " We are not in the business of being propaganda arms of the political parties." But they seemed blind to the same danger during the campaign itself.

So successful was the Bush campaign at getting free time for its 19 ads on the evening news that, after the campaign, commercial advertisers adopted a similar strategy. In 1989 a pharmaceutical company used unauthorized footage of President Bush and Gorbachev to advertise a cold medication. "In the new year," the slogan ran, "may the only cold war in the world be the one being fought by us." Although two of the three networks refused to carry the commercial, dozens of network and local television news programs showed excerpts of the ad, generating millions of dollars of free airtime.

"I realized I started a trend," said Bush media consultant 20 Roger Ailes in the *New York Times*. "Now guys are out there trying to produce commercials for the evening news." When Humphrey and Nixon hired Madison Avenue experts to help in their campaigns, some worried that, in the television age, presidents would be sold like products. Little did they imagine that, twenty years later, products would be sold like presidents.

Along with the attention to commercials and stagecraft in 1988 21 came an unprecedented focus on the state managers themselves, the "media gurus," "handlers," and "spin-control artists." Only three reports featured media advisers in 1968, compared with twenty-six in 1988. And the numbers tell only part of the story.

The stance reporters have taken toward media advisers has changed dramatically over the past twenty years. In *The Selling of the President* (1969), Joe McGinniss exposed the growing role of media advisers with a sense of disillusion and outrage. By 1988 television reporters covered image-makers with deference, even admiration. In place of independent fact correction, reporters sought out media advisers as authorities in their own right to analyze the effectiveness and even defend the truthfulness of campaign commercials. They became "media gurus" not only for the candidates but for the networks as well.

For example, in an exchange with CBS anchor Dan Rather on Bush's debate performance, Stahl lavished admiration on the techniques of Bush's media advisers:

Stahl: "They told him not to look into the camera [She gestures toward the camera as she speaks.] You know when you look directly into a camera you are cold, apparently they have determined."

Rather [laughing]: "Bad news for anchormen I'd say. "

Stahl: " We have a lot to learn from this. Michael Dukakis kept talking right into the camera. [Stahl talks directly into her own camera to demonstrate.] And according to the Bush people that makes you look programmed, Dan. [Stahl laughs]. And they're very adept at these television symbols and television imagery. And according to our poll it worked."

Rather: "Do you believe it?"

Stahl: " Yes, I think I do, actually. "

So hypersensitive were the networks to television image-making in 1988 that minor mishaps—gaffes, slips of the tongue, even faulty microphones—became big news. Politicians were hardly without mishap in 1968, but these did not count as news. Only once in 1968 did a network even take note of a minor incident unrelated to the content of the campaign. In 1988 some twenty-nine reports highlighted trivial slips.

The emphasis on "failed images" reflected a kind of guerrilla warfare between the networks and the campaigns. The more the campaigns sought to control the images that appeared on the nightly news, the more the reporters tried to beat them at their own game, magnifying a minor mishap into a central feature on the media event.

Early in the 1988 campaign, for example, George Bush delivered a speech to a sympathetic audience of the American Legion, attacking his opponent's defense policies. In a slip, he declared that

September 7, rather than December 7, was the anniversary of Pearl Harbor. Murmurs and chuckles from the audience alerted him to his error, and he quickly corrected himself.

The audience was forgiving, but the networks were not. All three network anchors highlighted the slip on the evening news. Dan Rather introduced CBS's report on Bush by declaring solemnly, "Bush's talk to audiences in Louisville was overshadowed by a strange happening." On NBC Tom Brokaw reported, "He departed from his prepared script and left his listeners mystified." Peter Jennings introduced ABC's report by mentioning Bush's attack on Dukakis, adding, "What's more likely to be remembered about today's speech is a slip of the tongue."

Some of the slips the networks highlighted in 1988 were not even verbal gaffes or misstatements, but simply failures on the part of candidates to cater to the cameras. In a report on the travails of the Dukakis campaign, Sam Donaldson seized on Dukakis's failure to play to ABC's television camera as evidence of his campaign's ineffectiveness. Showing Dukakis playing a trumpet with a local marching band, Donaldson chided, "He played the trumpet with his back to the camera." As Dukakis played "Happy Days Are Here Again," Donaldson's voice was heard from off-camera calling, "We're over here, governor. "

One way of understanding the turn to image-conscious coverage in 1988 is to see how television news came to partake of the postwar modernist sensibility, particularly the pop art movement of the 1960s. Characteristic of this outlook is a self-conscious attention to art as performance, a focus on the process of image-making rather than on the ideas the images represent.

During the 1960s, when photography and television became potent forces for documentation and entertainment, they also became powerful influences on the work of artists. Photographers began to photograph the television set as part of the social landscape. Newspapers, photographs, and commercial products became part of the collage work of painters such as Robert Rauschenberg. Artists began to explore self-consciously their role in the image-making process.

For example, Lee Friedlander published a book of photography, *Self Portrait*, in which the artist's shadow or reflection was included in every frame. As critic Rob Slemmons notes, "By indicating the photographer is also a performer whose hand is impossible to hide, Friedlander set a precedent for disrupting the normal rules of photography." These "postmodernist" movements in art and photography foreshadowed the form television news would take by the late 1980s.

Andy Warhol once remarked, "The artificial fascinates me." In   37
1988 network reporters and producers, beguiled by the artifice of
the modern presidential campaign, might well have said the same.
Reporters alternated between reporting campaign images as if they
were facts and exposing their contrived nature. Like Warhol, whose
personality was always a presence in his work, reporters became part
of the campaign theater they covered—as producers, as performers,
and as critics. Like Warhol's reproductions of Campbell's soup
cans, the networks' use of candidates' commercials directed our
attention away from the content and toward the packaging.

The assumption that the creation of appearances is the essence of   38
political reality pervaded not only the reporting but the candidates'
self-understanding and conduct with the press. When Dan Quayle
sought to escape his image as a highly managed candidate,
he resolved publicly to become his own handler, his own "spin
doctor." "The so-called handlers story, part of it's true," he
confessed to network reporters. "But there will be no more handlers
stories, because I'm the handler and I'll do the spinning."
Surrounded by a group of reporters on his campaign plane, Quayle
announced, "I'm Doctor Spin, and I want you all to report that."

It may seem a strange way for a politician to talk, but not so   39
strange in a media-conscious environment in which authenticity
means being master of your own artificiality. Dukakis too sought to
reverse his political fortunes by seeking to be master of his own
image. This attempt was best captured in a commercial shown on
network news in which Dukakis stood beside a television set and
snapped off a Bush commercial attacking his stand on defense.
"I'm fed up with it," Dukakis declared. "Never seen anything like
it in twenty-five years of public life. George Bush's negative television ads, distorting my record, full of lies, and he knows it." The
commercial itself shows an image of an image—a Bush television
commercial showing (and ridiculing) the media event where Dukakis
rode in a tank. In his commercial, Dukakis complains that Bush's
commercial showing the tank ride misstates Dukakis's position on
defense.

As it appeared in excerpts on the evening news, Dukakis's com-   40
mercial displayed a quintessentially modernist image of artifice upon
artifice upon artifice: television news covering a Dukakis commercial
containing a Bush commercial containing a Dukakis media event. In
a political world governed by images of images, it seemed almost
natural that the authority of the candidate be depicted by his ability
to turn off the television set.

In the 1950s Edward R. Murrow noted that broadcast news was 41 "an incompatible combination of show business, advertising, and news." Still, in its first decades television news continued to reflect a sharp distinction between the news and entertainment divisions of the networks. But by the 1980s network news operations came to be seen as profit centers for the large corporations that owned them, run by people drawn less from journalism than from advertising and entertainment backgrounds. Commercialization led to further emphasis on entertainment values, which heightened the need for dramatic visuals, fast pacing, quick cutting, and short sound bites. Given new technological means to achieve these effects—portable video cameras, satellite hookups, and sophisticated video-editing equipment—the networks were not only disposed but equipped to capture the staged media events of the campaigns.

The search for dramatic visuals and the premium placed on 42 showmanship in the 1980s led to a new complicity between the White House image-makers and the networks. As Susan Zirinsky, a top CBS producer, acknowledged in Martin Schram's *The Great American Video Game,* "In a funny way, the [Reagan White House] advance men and I have the same thing at heart—we want the piece to look as good as [it] possibly can." In 1968 such complicity in stagecraft was scorned. Sanford Socolow, senior producer of the *CBS Evening News with Walter Cronkite,* recently observed, "If someone caught you doing that in 1968 you would have been fired."

In a moment of reflection in 1988, CBS's political correspon- 43 dents expressed their frustration with image-driven campaigns. "It may seem frivolous, even silly at times," said Schieffer. "But setting up pictures that drive home a message has become the number one priority of the modern-day campaign. The problem, of course, is while it is often entertaining, it is seldom enlightening."

Rather shared his colleague's discomfort. But what troubled him 44 about modern campaigns is equally troubling about television's campaign coverage. "With all this emphasis on the image," he asked, "what happens to the issues? What happens to the substance?"

EXPLORATIONS

1. What are some of the differences between the 1968 and 1988 campaigns? What is the "video presidency" and what implications does it have for our political debates?

2. How is campaign reporting like theater criticism? What does Adatto mean when she states that "Reporters alternated between reporting campaign images as if they were facts and exposing their contrived nature"?

3. How can "authenticity [mean] being master of your own artificiality"?

4. What effects do you think "sound bite" media have on voters?

5. How do politicians use the media to create an image? What function do political commercials serve?

Rock, Rap, and Movies
Bring You the News

JON KATZ

Jon Katz is a media critic for Rolling Stone, *where this article was originally published on March 5, 1992. Katz
explores the ways in which popular forms of entertainment
may actually present more important and newsworthy information than the traditional news media. Katz is also the
author of two novels,* The Suburban Detective *(1993) and*
Sign Off *(1991).*

WRITING BEFORE READING

*Where did you get your news today? Was it from your usual source?
Where would you go if you needed absolutely reliable information?*

It's a shame Oliver Stone wasn't running one of the networks   1
when the Bush administration decided journalists wouldn't cover
the Gulf War. Nobody denied that conspiracy. Stone would have
surely gone berserk, storming past the blue cabanas, over the berms,
and into the desert with his own camera-armed legions to bring back
riveting pictures and shocking notions, like war is hell.

It's a shame, too, that Sinéad O'Connor wasn't providing   2
network commentary in place of one more former general touting
new weapons. When she refused to have the national anthem played
at her concerts, she went further out on a limb than any of the major
news organizations did on behalf of their silenced correspondents.

Too bad, as well, that instead of one of those evening-news suits,   3
Bruce Springsteen isn't reporting on the economy. Springsteen
seemed to know years ago that the jobs weren't coming back. The
networks are still waiting for confirmation from the White House.

Straight news—the Old News—is pooped, confused, and broke.   4
Each Nielsen survey, each circulation report, each quarterly statement, reveals the cultural Darwinism ravaging the news industry.
The people watching and reading are aging and dying, and the
young no longer take their place. Virtually no major city daily has
gained in circulation in recent years (the *Washington Post* is one of
the few exceptions). In the last decade, network news has lost nearly half its audience. Advertising revenues are drying up.

In place of the Old News, something dramatic is evolving, a new   5
culture of information, a hybrid New News—dazzling, adolescent,

irresponsible, fearless, frightening, and powerful. The New News is a heady concoction, part Hollywood film and TV movie, part pop music and pop art, mixed with popular culture and celebrity magazines, tabloid telecasts, cable, and home video.

Increasingly, the New News is seizing the functions of main- 6 stream journalism, sparking conversations and setting the country's social and political agenda. It is revolutionizing the way information reaches people and moves among them. It is changing the way Americans evaluate politicians and, shortly, elect them.

Think of Walter Cronkite or Ted Koppel if you want to get an 7 image of the Old News. The voice is grave, resonant with the burden of transmitting serious matters—White House communications strategies, leaks from State Department sources, leading economic indicators. The stories are remote (from Yugoslavia, Nairobi, Beijing) or from institutions that feel as remote (Congress, Wall Street, the Supreme Court). The reporters of the Old News cluster there, talking to one another, mired in an agenda that seems increasingly obtuse and irrelevant.

In January 1992, the New News is absorbed with a different 8 agenda: on the eve of Martin Luther King's birthday, Public Enemy focuses the country's attention on his broken dream through its furious new video, an imagined enactment of the killing of Arizona state-government officials. In New York City, inner-city parents are taking their children to see *Juice* to educate them about the consequences of street violence. *JFK*—assaulted for weeks by the Old News as reckless and irresponsible—has prompted the chairman of a congressional committee that investigated the assassination to ask for the release of all government documents on the slaying. The kids on *Beverly Hills, 90210*—"The only show on TV that portrays teen life as it really is," says the editorial director of *16* magazine—are struggling with divorce, sex, and AIDS.

Meanwhile, the remnants of the Old News slowly begin to gath- 9 er in the bleak towns of New Hampshire for another presidential campaign. Only a few years ago, the three networks virtually hosted the presidential campaigns. Great media encampments took over entire motels in New Hampshire, with producers and technicians stuffed into trailers like a circus come to town. But ABC, CBS, NBC have already announced there will be no vast encampments on the primary trail or at the conventions this year. Day-to-day coverage will be left to cable. One network that has said it will offer more campaign coverage than it did in 1988 is MTV.

Once, the borders were clear and inviolate: newspapers, newscasts, 10 and newsmagazines covered serious events; pop culture entertained us.

But in the past generation, the culture sparked by rock and roll, then fused with TV and mutated by Hollywood, ran riot over the traditional boundaries between straight journalism and entertainment.

Now the list of issues addressed by the New News—far from the 11 front pages and evening newscasts—is growing steadily. We're exposed to gender conflict in *Thelma and Louise;* money blues, sexual conflicts, and working-class stress on *Roseanne;* motherhood, corporate takeovers, and journalistic ethics on *Murphy Brown.*

Bart Simpson's critique of society is more trenchant than that 12 of most newspaper columnists. Movies like *Boyz n the Hood* and *Straight Out of Brooklyn* and rappers like Public Enemy and Ice Cube deal with race more squarely than *Nightline.* No wonder Chuck D calls rap the CNN of black America.

In the same way that middle-class lacks rarely appear in the 13 traditional media, disaffected working-class whites don't seem to exist in the world Old News covers. Analysts looking for clues to David Duke's popularity would do better to listen to Guns n' Roses and Skid Row songs than to scan newscasts and newspapers for the source of white resentment.

The country's ascendant magazine is not a newsmagazine but a 14 New News magazine. *Entertainment Weekly* focuses on what editors used to call the back of the book—the arts and culture material once ghettoized behind the important stuff. But today, the back of the book is the book. In its January 17 cover story, "JFK: The Film and the Furor, What's Behind the Backlash," *EW* dramatically illustrated how popular culture and major stories have steadily converged on one another over the past three decades, redefining what news is and who gets to cover it.

It didn't happen overnight—more like thirty years. Bob 15 Dylan's vision of rock and roll helped mainstream music move from entertainment to political expression, an op-ed page for millions of kids who would never have dreamed of reading—or agreeing with—a newspaper editorial. Following in the tradition of shows like *All in the Family,* TV producers and writers broke free of the censors and produced broadcasts like *Hill Street Blues, St. Elsewhere,* and *L. A. Law,* presenting life more and more as viewers experienced it, not as the networks wanted it seen.

So did tabloid telecasts and made-for-TV movies, which drama- 16 tized, reenacted, and reinterpreted issues like sexism, child abuse, alcoholism, and homosexuality. Hollywood helped define Vietnam in *Apocalypse Now,* racial hatred in *Do the Right Thing,* the takeover culture in *Wall Street.* Emerging cable technology gave viewers and programmers vastly more choices, breaking open the New News.

Pop culture—America's most remarkable invention since the car—
had spawned a new information culture.

The modern news media—the Old News—was formed in the   17
years after World War II. Major newspapers and instantly powerful
network-news divisions chose Washington and New York as their
headquarters, and presidential politics, the economy, and foreign
affairs—the cold war, mostly—as their preeminent beats. In its heyday,
the Old news showed us the murder of John Kennedy, took us to the
moon, then helped drive a president from office and end a war.

Other stories—the sexual revolution, the role of race, dramatic   18
changes in the relationship between people and their jobs, the
evolution of pop culture, a rebirth of spiritualism—were covered spo-
radically and incompletely by the Old News. They often sprang up
away from well-staffed bureaus in a handful of major cities, thus
making them harder for Old News to cover. They were a sideline,
never the main event.

But for the New News—and for much of America—they were *the*   19
event. Women, blacks, Hispanics, gays, and Asians had launched an
ongoing political and cultural revolution against middle-class white
males, who continue to dominate most institutions, including the
news media. In some countries, revolutions are violent, bloody
affairs settled in the streets. In America, they are slugged out in
music videos, movies, and cable shows.

In the resulting turmoil, the Old News and the new have taken   20
off in opposite directions, diverging more and more dramatically in
content, packaging, and audience. Although Americans can watch, in
living color, a war or the description of an alleged rape, almost no
major daily deigns to use color photographs, and most anchors are
still white and male.

As Old News habits have ossified, its audience has evaporated.   21
Newspaper readership has been declining for thirty years. According
to a *Times Mirror* study, 71 percent of people between the ages of
seventy and seventy-nine read a daily newspaper, but only 40 percent
of people between the ages of eighteen and twenty-nine do. Of people under thirty who are married with children, only 30 percent read
a paper daily.

The median age of the *New York Times* subscriber is forty-two,   22
Time magazine's is thirty-eight. In contrast, *Entertainment
Weekly*'s is thirty-one, *Rolling Stone*'s is twenty-six. Among
shows that teenagers watch most often, *The Simpsons* and *Beverly
Hills, 90210* rank at the top; *60 Minutes* ranks 110th.

The Old News seems bewildered and paralyzed by the dazzling   23
new technologies competing for its audience, clucking like a cross

old lady chasing noisy kids away from her window. Editors and producers prefer "serious topics" to the New News culture. In the same way they once fussed over rock and roll, most newspapers and news shows were too busy attacking Nintendo addiction to notice that more than fifty million entertainment systems had taken up residence in American homes, literally redefining what a TV set was and what it did. In 1991, the Nintendo hot line got two million calls from players needing help in ascending yet another level of Tetris or Super Mario Bros. 3.

All the while, news organizations puzzled about why kids were 24 leaving in droves. Interactive video-jukebox systems and sports channels, round-the-clock local-news channels, video shopping, and scores of movie and entertainment channels helped to create a new video culture for the young, a profound change in leisure time that the Old News kissed off as a teen fad.

Stung by the mounting evidence that Americans' passions and 25 concerns increasingly lie elsewhere, Old News institutions do appear unnerved. They've launched promotional campaigns, experimented disdainfully with color, commissioned marketing studies. ("Perhaps we should start a kids' page?") But it's mostly fussing. Every time real change is broached—two years ago, CBS tried reenactments on *Saturday Night with Connie Chung*—the guardian crows of the old order shriek the innovators into submission.

The networks sneered as CNN haltingly began to construct the 26 most efficient and responsive electronic news-video-gathering machine in history. The newspaper industry's most dramatic response to the New News—*USA Today*—was greeted by the business with the same enthusiasm with which the human body greets a foreign invader. It was dubbed McPaper and dismissed as insubstantial, shallow, and, worst of all, TV-like.

Its owner, Gannett, which owns eighty-one newspapers and 27 admits to being alarmed about newspapers' shrinking and aging circulation, recently published a handbook for its editors. It says with shocking bluntness that papers have failed to recognize "key topics that shape readers' lives" and are filled with "dull, formula-based writing" and that newsrooms are "isolationist, elitist and afraid of change."

All the facts add up to a story that, Gannett's urgings notwith- 28 standing, journalism doesn't want to hear. The Old News has clung desperately to the view that the New News culture, like pornography, is nothing but trash and will eventually just go away. Yet journalistically, the New News is often superior to the old at spotting major stories and putting them into context.

All last summer, men and women were talking about men and women. Movies like *Thelma and Louise* and made-for-TV dramas like CBS's *Rape of Dr. Willis* clearly reflected the outrage that coalesced around the Anita Hill–Clarence Thomas confrontation. The view of men as insensitive, frequently hateful creatures who don't get it was also advanced in movies like *The Doctor*, in which a surgeon has to get cancer before he learns how to be compassionate, and *Regarding Henry*, whose hero learns the meaning of life only after he gets shot in the head. *Beauty and the Beast* might be the timeliest animated film ever made: the heroine is courageous and brainy; the two major male characters are a prince who's turned into a beast so that he can learn how to love and a macho man who is a beast, period. 29

If the white men in the U. S. Senate had spent more time at the movies and less watching Old News Sunday-morning talk shows, they might have heard the sound of thousands of women cheering when Thelma and Louise blew up that tanker truck. They might not have been so shocked when women all over the country exploded in fury at the Judiciary Committee's failure to explore Anita Hill's charges. 30

One of the most interesting scoops in the Thomas affair—an exclusive interview with the justice's wife—was secured by *People*. And just three weeks after the hearings, the characters on *Designing Women* spent an episode watching footage of the hearings and vigorously arguing both sides. For millions of Americans, it was a more relevant hashing of the matter than they would get on any Sunday-morning gasathon. 31

Other news stories have been foreshadowed by the New News. The FBI was so alarmed by the rap group N. W. A's "Fuck tha Police" that it cautioned local police departments against N. W. A's performing in their cities. Yet just two years later, in a stunning example of the new video culture's news-gathering potential, a bystander videotaped the brutal beating of Rodney King by the Los Angeles Police Department, the very force N. W. A was warning its listeners about. 32

There is, in fact, almost no story Old News has struggled to come to grips with more dramatically and unsuccessfully than race. America seems continually stunned by episodic explosions of racial hatred—by the murder of Yusuf Hawkins in New York, the violent black-Hasidic confrontations in Brooklyn last summer, the chord struck by David Duke. 33

Still overwhelmingly owned, staffed, and run by whites, and white males in particular, the media are stymied and discomfited by racial issues. After decades of ignoring brutal racism, they seem to 34 have lurched from one extreme to the other. Now they're so desperate to avoid the appearance of racism that they seem frozen by the subject.

The members of the media are able to quote demagogues and   35
activists, but they're unable to advance the country's understanding of ghetto fury, to portray and represent the view of the black middle class, or to explore white anger and confusion. Few issues in American life generate so much mythology, yet the intrigues of the White House chief of staff are covered in far greater detail. Spike Lee is far ahead of his mainstream journalistic competitors on racial issues. So is Ice Cube: "They have the authority / To Kill a minority / Fucking with me cause I'm a teenager / With a little bit of gold and a pager. "

Police advocates don't make many albums, but there's plenty   36
of white backlash to racial tensions evident in white rock, as well as worry about bleak economic futures. Perhaps the leading white working-class New News columnists at the moment are the members of Guns n' Roses, whose "Right Next Door to Hell," from *Use Your Illusion I,* is a national anthem for working-class anger:

> When your innocence dies
> You'll find the blues
> Seems all our heroes were born to lose
> Just walkin' through time
> You believe this heat
> Another empty house another dead-end street

Skid Row sounds like John Chancellor in comparison. From the   37
album and song *Slave to the Grind:* " You got me forced to crack my lids in two / I'm still stuck inside the rubber room / I gotta punch the clock that leads the blind / I'm just another gear in the assembly line."

Rap and rock—music listened to by the same kids the Old News   38
is fretting about losing—are describing a different world than the one reflected on evening newscasts and in daily papers. Washington journalists were abuzz for months in anticipation of the *Washington Post*'s seven-part series on Vice President Dan Quayle, reported and written by Old News royalty David Broder and Bob Woodward. But the tens of thousands of words lavished on Quayle told us more about the remote agenda of the Old News than it did about the vice president.

The most explosive assault the New News has made on the Old is   39
Oliver Stone's *JFK.* Its release has sparked less a free-for-all discussion of a recent historical event than a modern-day heresy trial. Stone set

out to upend conventional wisdom, centering his film on Jim
Garrison's largely discredited theories. It is unclear why so many
Americans remain skeptical about the Warren Commission's findings—only 19 percent believe in the lone-gunman theory, according to
polls—yet clearly they do. Whatever the accuracy of his theory, Stone—
whose *Platoon, Wall Street* and *Born on the Fourth of July* were
dramatically journalistic in their efforts to reflect different cultures at
crucial times—has tapped into this dark strain in American life.

The Old News condemns Stone as irresponsible because he is   40
advancing disproved theories and crackpot speculation as truth. The
Old News is crying foul, incensed that someone has crossed over
into their turf.

Yet it is Stone's movie, not years of columnizing by the Old   41
News, that is likely to force the release of Kennedy-assassination documents the government is keeping under wraps. The license Stone
took—and the risk—in reinventing a seminal story in the country's
history illustrates why the New News is gaining so dramatically on
the old: it is willing to heed and explore the passionate and sometimes frightening undercurrents in American life.

The United States is an odd country, a lot stranger than the stilt-   42
ed language or narrow conventions of the Old News can explain.
Remember the fascination with *Twin Peaks?* Americans seem to
know—though surely not from reading it or seeing it in most journalism—that their country is violent, troubled, and brooding, in
almost desperate need of mythological symbols like those advanced
by the cultural historian Joseph Campbell.

Elvis Presley's death and afterlife so boosted supermarket-   43
tabloid sales that they have become a permanent part of the New
News. As Greil Marcus shows in his new book *Dead Elvis*, Americans
are as obsessed with Presley's death as they are with Kennedy's
assassination.

We don't really know why, and how could we? Both stories fall   44
just this side of prostitution to most of the reporters assigned to
cover, say, the White House. Stone's assassination theories may or
may not have been correct, but his journalistic instinct was sure. He
hit one of the rawest nerves in American history, demonstrating at
the very least that to many Americans the Kennedy assassination is
far from a settled matter.

In their anger at Stone, the guardians of journalistic and cultural   45
propriety are saying that Americans aren't capable of drawing their
own conclusions, that only journalists operating in conventional ways
and within conventional boundaries can be entrusted with weighty or
controversial issues. The anger of the Old News demonstrates anew
one of its most self-destructive streaks—a patronizing contempt for

the young. Much of the criticism leveled at Stone suggests that Americans who weren't alive when Kennedy was shot are too ignorant or impressionable to see beyond Kevin Costner's earnest face, as though people under thirty can't grasp that a Hollywood film is one person's vision, not the provable truth.

A youthful audience is no guarantee that a New News product is journalistically superior; what is significant is that younger viewers and readers find conventional journalism of no particular use in their daily lives. In fact, given that the media make so much out of fairness and objectivity, it's a puzzle why so few people of any age trust it or its conclusions. 46

Mainstream journalism frequently checkmates itself. In worshiping balance over truth, objectivity over point of view, moderation over diversity, and credibility over creativity, the Old News gives consumers a clear choice. Consumers can have a balanced discussion, with every side of an issue neutralizing the other, or they can turn to singers, producers, and film-makers offering colorful, distinctive, often flawed but frequently powerful visions of their truth. More and more, Americans are making it clear which they prefer. 47

Younger audiences raised on New News traditions of outspokenness and hyperbole appear to understand that Public Enemy and Oliver Stone are not always to be taken literally. These New News communicators speak to states of mind, to anger at real issues like poverty and hopelessness, to disenchantment with jingoistic institutions, and to a common perception that mainstream news organizations don't tell the whole truth or at least don't much reflect their truth. 48

Stone's *JFK* will have to stand the ultimate capitalist media test, the same one every newspaper, TV station, magazine, and Nintendo dealer faces: people will buy it, watch it, read it, believe it. Or not. At least Stone has made it clear where he stands. 49

It's simply not possible to know yet whether the rise of the New News is good or bad, healthy or menacing. How about all of the above? The final form the Old News will take is unclear, and new News technology and content are still rapidly evolving. 50

This year Time Warner will unleash another Godzilla on the Old News—in New York, a twenty-four-hour local cable news channel will begin broadcasting. For the first time, *truly* local news—fires, high-school sports, board-of- education hearings on condom distribution—will be on TV. Advertisers like pharmacies, copy shops, and bridal salons will have an affordable electronic medium to advertise on. 51

Another billion-dollar shoe waiting to drop, ferociously opposed by its competitors, will come from the Baby Bells. Now that the fed- 52 eral courts have given the regional phone companies permission to enter the information market, they'll use computers and existing and future transmission technology to offer new kinds of electronic travel, shopping, banking, and commercial services, including news.

In the new world of twenty-four-hour electronic news, can print 53 or commercial broadcasting remain in the breaking-news business, as both so stubbornly insist on doing? Will newspapers ever stop running banner headlines over black-and-white photos that appeared live on TV twenty-four hours earlier? It seems they'd rather die.

The best vantage point from which to watch the dramatic colli- 54 sion of the competing news cultures will be living rooms across the country, as the Old News struggles to come to grips with its quadrennial Super Bowl-cum-Olympics—the presidential election. If the Old News is right, and only it can be trusted to capture and shape major events, then the country is heading straight for a civics nightmare in which challengers can't get coverage and issues can't be raised, because Americans, wired into their personal entertainment complexes, are too busy to think about who should occupy the White House.

This time around, CNN and C-SPAN will be on all the time, 55 for politicians desperate to communicate with their peers and for political junkies who want to see crucial votes or speeches. But fewer regular prime-time programs will be preempted. Except for the Democratic convention in New York, a cab ride across town, the anchors will be watching most of the campaign on studio monitors. A few troops—Sawyer, Chung—will be running around with their Star Trek earphones, but it will be a pathetic echo of the glory days for the Old News.

Maybe there's a better way. Maybe the New News should field 56 a team of its own this year. Don Henley could coanchor the convention coverage with Murphy Brown, prime-time TV's toughest news interviewer, not from a booth, but down on the convention floor, laying bare a process that would even consider reelecting a president who didn't know until December 17 that the recession wasn't over. Sinéad O'Connor, the Geto Boys, and Roseanne Arnold will do nightly commentary, maybe from the floor with working-stiff delegates. Spike Lee will air a series of documentaries on how race is being manipulated to win still another election, alternating with reports on how whites are getting screwed by the system, courtesy of Axl Rose, or perhaps an investigative special by Oliver Stone on how Ronald Reagan's election was the result of a conspiracy between the media, Hollywood filmmakers and jet-aircraft contractors.

EXPLORATIONS

1. What, according to Katz, are the characteristics of the "Old News" and the "New News"? Give an example of each and describe how they present the news differently.

2. What needs or desires does the New News fill? What issues does the New News address more effectively than the Old News? What are the potential dangers of the New News?

3. Why was the movie *JFK* so controversial? What do you think about movies that recreate or speculate about historical events? Are they misleading and dangerous, or entertaining and informative? Why do you think so?

4. Choose a song, a movie, or a television show that you would characterize as a New News forum. What issues does it cover? How is the information presented? How does the format allow the news to be expressed differently from the way it would be presented on the Old News? Would the issue be addressed by the Old News? Is the New News an effective way of presenting important information or does it trivialize crucial events?

Daytime Inquiries

ELAYNE RAPPING

*Elayne Rapping is a professor of communications at Adelphi
University in Garden City, New York. Rapping has written
numerous magazine articles analyzing television as a form of
public discourse. This article, which was originally published
in October 1991 in the* Progressive, *explores the forum of
daytime talk shows as an extension of the women's rights
movement of the 1960s and as an alternative news source for
issues that are relevant to women's lives. Rapping has also
written* The Looking Glass World of Non-fiction TV, *a book
published in 1987.*

WRITING BEFORE READING

*Would you consider being a guest on a talk show? Which one? What
subjects would you discuss?*

"On *Oprah* today: women who sleep with their sister's hus- 1
bands!"

"Donahue talks to women married to bisexuals!" 2

" Today—Sally Jessy Raphael talks with black women who have 3
bleached their hair blonde!"

These are only three of my personal favorites of the past televi- 4
sion season. Everyone's seen these promos and laughed at them.
"What next?" we wonder to each other with raised eyebrows. And
yet, these daytime talk shows are enormously popular and—more
often than we like to admit—hard to stop watching once you start.

As with so much else about today's media, the knee-jerk 5
response to this state of affairs is to hold one's nose, distance oneself from those who actually watch this stuff, and moan about the
degradation and sleaze with which we're bombarded. But this does-
n't tell us much about what's really going on in America—and
television's role in it. Worse, it blinds us to what's actually interesting about these shows, what they tell us about the way television
maneuvers discussions of controversial and contested topics.

It's no secret that television has *become* the public sphere for 6
Americans, the one central source of information and public debate
on matters of national import. Ninety-eight percent of us live in
homes in which the TV set is on, and therefore in one way or another being experienced and absorbed, an average of seven-and-a-half
hours a day; 67 percent of us get *all* our information from TV. This

is not a matter of laziness, stupidity, or even the seductive power of the tube. It is a tragic fact that illiteracy—actual and functional—is rampant. It is difficult if not impossible for more and more of us to read, even when we try. Television, in such cases, is a necessity, even a godsend.

In the early 1950s, when TV emerged as the dominant cultural form, it presented to us a middle-aged, middle-class, white-male image of authority. Network prime time *was* TV, and what it gave us, from dusk to bedtime, was a series of white middle-class fathers—Walter Cronkites and Ward Cleavers—assuring us night after night that they knew best, that all was in good hands, that we needn't worry about the many scary, confusing changes wrought by postwar capitalism. 7

Network prime time still plays that role, or tries to. The fathers sometimes are black now, the authority occasionally shared with mothers, a voice from the ideological fringes invited from time to time to be a "guest" (and behave appropriately or not get asked back). But prime time is still the home of Official, Authoritative Truth as presented by experts and institutional power brokers. Whatever oppositional voices are heard are always controlled by the Great White Father in charge, who get paid six- and seven-figure salaries for their trouble. 8

The money value of these guys to the media—the Koppels, the Jenningses—is so high because their jobs are increasingly difficult. TV, in a sense, was developed to put a reassuring, controlling facade over the structural fault lines of American life. 9

Ever since the 1960s, however, this has been harder and harder to manage. The breakdown of the family, the crises in education, religion, and the credibility of the state, the growing visibility and vocality of minority groups and ideas—all these took the country and media by storm. The most recent dramatic proof of the impact of social crises and the progressive movements they spawned is the amazing media hullabaloo over "multiculturalism" and "political correctness" on campuses. The Left, people of color, women, gays, and lesbians are apparently making the old white men extremely nervous. 10

At night, all of this tumult is being handled more or less as it has always been handled. Things seem to be under control. *MacNeil/Lehrer* and *Nightline* have their panels of experts, which now often include women, blacks, and—on rare occasions—"leftists" who really are leftists. But the structure of these shows makes it impossible seriously to challenge the host and, therefore, seriously to challenge TV hegemony. 11

A much juicier and, in many ways, more encouraging kind of ideological battle rages before 5 P.M., however. Daytime, women's 12 time, has always been delegated to "domestic matters." If Father Knew Best in the evening, on the soaps the women always ruled the roost and what mattered were family and relationships issues—sex, adultery, childbirth, marriage, and the negotiating of the social and domestic end of life in a class- and race-divided society.

This is still true on daytime. In fact, the soaps are more likely to treat such social issues as rape, incest, aging, and interracial relationships with depth and seriousness than any prime-time series. In the sexual division of labor, these matters of emotional and relational caretaking and socialization have always been seen as "women's domain." And so it goes in TV Land. Daytime equals women equals "soft" issues. Prime time equals men and the "hard" stuff.   13

Except that what used to be soft isn't so soft anymore. The social movement of the 1960s—especially feminism, with its insistence that "the personal is political"—changed all that. Everyone who isn't brain-dead knows—and feels with great intensity—that all the old rules for living one's life are up for grabs. Relations between sexes, the generations, the races, among co-workers, neighbors, family members—all of these are matters of confusion and anxiety.   14

What is the line, in the workplace, between being friendly and sexual harassment? How do we deal with our children, who are increasingly media-savvy and street-savvy and whose social environments are radically different from ours? What about sex education? Drugs? Condoms? Interracial dating? How do we handle social interactions with gay men and lesbians, now that more and more people are out and proud?   15

These are just the obvious issues. But they grow out of changes in the larger political and economic environments and they resonate into every crevice of our lives in far stranger, more confusing ways. In the breakdown of accepted views about things, and of the ties that kept us on the straight and narrow in spite of ourselves, unconventional behavior is both more common and more visible.   16

Women do, in fact, sleep with their sisters' husbands or find themselves married to bisexuals. Or perhaps they always did these things but never dreamed of discussing it, never saw it as a social topic, a matter for debate and disagreement about right and wrong. The same is true of something as seemingly trivial as one's choice of hair color. For black women, such tensions are rife, reflecting divisions brought on by political and cultural issues raised by black liberation movements.   17

The personal is ever more political, and inquiring minds not only want to know, they need to know. Or at least they need to talk and listen about these things. And so the coming of daytime talk shows, a financial gold mine for the media and a sensationalized, trivialized "political" event for confused and frightened people everywhere.   18

The political roots of this form are apparent. In structure, in   19
process, and in subject matter, they take their cues from an important
political institution of the 1960s: the women's consciousness-raising
movement. In those small groups, through which hundreds of thousands of women passed during a brief, highly charged four- or five-year
period starting in about 1968, we invented a democratic, emotionally
safe way of bringing out in the open things we never before spoke of.
We found we were not alone in our experiences and analyzed their
meanings.

Of course, the purpose of these consciousness-raising groups was   20
empowerment, political empowerment. The idea that the personal
was political led to a strategy for social change. We hoped that when
previously isolated and privatized women recognized common
sources of our unhappiness in the larger political world, we could
organize to change things.

The words "political" and "organize" do not, of course,   21
occur on daytime TV. The primary goal of talk shows as a television
form is to lure curious audiences and sell them products, not revolution. Thus the circuslike atmosphere and the need for bizarre and
giggle-inducing topics and participants.

Still, the influence of feminism (and other social and cultural   22
movements) is there, and the result is more interesting and contradictory because of it. Donahue, Oprah, and pals have reproduced, in
a plasticized format, the experience of being in a group and sharing
deeply personal and significant matters with others in the same boat.
Consciousness-raising, unfortunately, is long gone. But from 9 to
11 A.M. and from 3 to 5 P.M. on weekdays, there is a remarkable
facsimile thereof.

One reason these shows appeal is because, in line with the demo-   23
cratic thrust of 1960s feminism, their structure approaches the
nonhierarchical. The host is still the star, of course. But in terms of
authority, she or he is far from central. The physical set enforces this
fact. Audiences and participants sit in a circular form and—this is the
only TV format in which this happens—speak out, sometimes without being called on. They yell at each other and at the host, disagree
with experts, and come to no authoritative conclusions. There is
something exhilarating about watching people who are usually invisible—because of class, race, gender, status—having their say and,
often, being wholly disrespectful to their "betters."

The discussion of black women with blond hair, for example,   24
ignited a shouting match between those for whom such behavior
meant a disavowal of one's "blackness," a desire to "be white,"
and those who insisted it was simply a matter of choosing how one
wished to look, no different from the behavior of white women who
dye their hair or tan their bodies. The audience, selected from the

black community, took issue with everything that was said. Both participants and audience members attacked the "expert," a black writer committed to the natural—to BLACK IS BEAUTIFUL.

This is as close as television gets to open discourse on serious issues. But it is only possible because the issues discussed are not taken seriously by those in power. And that is why the sensationalism of these shows is double-edged. If they were more respectable in their style and choice of issues, they'd be reined in more. By allowing themselves to seem frivolous and trashy, they manage to carry on often-serious discussions without being cut off the air or cleaned up.

This may seem contradictory, but it's not. The truth is that the fringy, emotional matters brought up on Oprah, Donahue, Sally, and the others are almost always related in some way to deep cultural and structural problems in our society. Most of us, obviously, wouldn't go on these shows and spill our guts or open ourselves to others' judgments. But the people on these shows are an emotional vanguard, blowing the lid off the idea that America is anything like the place Ronald Reagan pretended to live in.

A typical recent program, for instance, featured a predictably weird ratings lure as topic: FAMILIES WHO DATE PRISONERS. It featured a family of sisters, and some other women, who sought out relationships with convicts. The chance for humor at guests' expense was not spared; Procter & Gamble doesn't care if people watch just to feel superior, as long as they watch. But in the course of the program, important political points came out.

Two issues were of particular interest. The "expert," a psychologist, pushed the protofeminist line that these women had low self-esteem—"women who love too much." Some admitted to it. Others, however, refused to accept that analysis, at least in their own cases. They stressed the prejudice against prisoners in society and went on to discuss the injustices of the criminal-justice system and to insist that their men were good people who had either made a mistake or were treated unfairly by the courts.

Our discomfort on watching what seems to be gross exhibitionism is understandable. We are taught, as children, that we don't air our dirty laundry in public. We learn to be hypocritical and evasive, to keep secret our own tragedies and sorrows, to feign shock when a public official is exposed for his or hers. It is not easy, even today, for most of us to reveal difficulties to neighbors. We are rightly self-protective. But the result of this sense of decorum is to isolate us, to keep us frightened and alone, unwilling to seek out help or share problems.

And so we sit at home, from Omaha to Orlando, and watch Oprah in order to get some sense of what it all means and how we might begin to handle it, whatever it is. These talk shows are safe. They let it all hang out. They don't judge anyone. They don't get shocked by anything. They admit they don't know what's right or wrong for anyone else. They are, for many people, a great relief.

Let me give one final example of how these shows operate as 31 forums for opposing views. A recent segment of *Donahue* concerned women and eating disorders. This show was a gem. It seems Phil had not yet gotten the word, or understood it, that eating disorders are serious matters from which women suffer and die. Nor had he grasped that this is a feminist issue, the result of highly sexist stereotypes imposed upon women who want to succeed at work or love.

Donahue's approach was to make light of the topic. His guests 32 were actresses from Henry Jaglom's film *Eating,* which concerns women, food, and body image, and he teased them about their own bouts with food compulsions. After all, they were all beautiful and thin; how bad could it be?

First, the call-in audience, then the studio audience, and finally 33 the actresses themselves, rebelled. Women called in to describe tearfully how they had been suicidal because of their weight. Others rebuked the host's frivolous attitude. Still others offered information about feminist counseling services and support groups. And finally, one by one, those downstage and then those on stage— the celebrities—rose to tell their stories of bulimia, anorexia, self-loathing, many with tears streaming down their faces.

Donahue was chastened and, I think, a bit scared. Ted Koppel 34 would never have allowed such a thing to happen. He would have several doctors, sociologists, or whatever, almost all of them white and male, answer *his* questions about what medical and academic professionals know about eating disorders. There would be no audience participation and very little dialogue among guests. Certainly none would yell or cry or show any other "excessive" emotional involvement in the matter. If they did, Koppel, the smoothest of network journalists, would easily take control and redirect the show. For that matter, only when such a subject as eating disorder is deemed nationally important by the media gatekeepers will it ever get on *Nightline* anyway. Daytime is less cautious.

I have been stressing the positive side of these shows primarily 35 because of their differences from their highbrow, prime-time counterparts, which are far more reactionary in form and content. It is, in the grand scheme of things as they are, a good thing to have these arenas of ideological interaction and open-endedness.

But, finally, these shows are a dead end, and they're meant to 36 be. They lead nowhere but to the drug store for more Excedrin. In fact, what's most infuriating about them is not that they are sleazy

or in bad taste. It is that they work to co-opt and contain real political change. What talk shows have done is take the best insights and
traditions of a more politicized time and declaw them. They are all
talk and no action. Unless someone yells something from the floor
(as a feminist did during the eating discussion), there will be no hint
that there is a world of political action, or of politics at all.

This makes perfect sense. It is the nature of the mass media in a   37
contradictory social environment to take progressive ideas, once they
gain strength, and contain them in the large, immobilizing structure
of the political status quo.

We are allowed to voice our woes. We are allowed to argue, cry,   38
shout, whatever. We are even allowed to hear about approved
services and institutions that might help with this or that specific
bruise or wound. But we are not allowed to rock the political or economic boat of television by suggesting that things could be different.
That would rightly upset the sponsors and network heads. Who
would buy their Excedrin if the headaches of American life went
away?

EXPLORATIONS

1. Why are daytime talk shows so popular? What is the target audience for
   these shows? How do the shows appeal to their audiences?

2. What kind of alternative news is offered through daytime talk shows?
   How are these shows different from the "white middle-class fathers"
   and the "Official, Authoritative Truth" of the network news? Do you
   think Jon Katz would include talk shows in his definition of New News?
   Why or why not?

3. According to Rapping, how can talk shows be simultaneously empowering and ineffectual at the same time?

4. In response to Rapping's article, write an analysis of a specific episode
   of a talk show you have seen. What was the topic of the show? Who
   were the invited guests? Who were the audience members? What roles
   were played by the host, the guests, and the audience? Did you learn
   anything useful about the topic? If so, what? Was the program valuable
   or not? Why or why not?

Report from El Dorado

Michael Ventura

Michael Ventura (1945–) resides in Los Angeles, California, where he cofounded and served as senior editor for the Los Angeles Weekly. *He has also served as arts editor for the* Austin Sun *and now works as a free-lance writer. Ventura says he writes "in the faith that those who read . . . complete what I write, taking what I write into territories I do not know." In "Report From El Dorado," a selection from his* Shadow Dancing in the U.S.A. *(1985), Ventura asks us to consider the media's role in constructing American culture.*

WRITING BEFORE READING

What do you think a media event is? What examples of a media event can you think of?

To go from a job you don't like to watching a screen on which others live more intensely than you . . . is American life, by and large.

This is our political ground. This is our artistic ground. This is what we've done with our immense resources. We have to stop calling it "entertainment" or "news" or "sports" and start calling it what it is: our most immediate environment.

This is a very, very different America from the America that built the industrial capacity to win the Second World War and to surge forward on the multiple momentums of that victory for thirty years. That was an America that worked at mostly menial tasks during the day (now we work at mostly clerical tasks) and had to look at each other at night.

I'm not suggesting a nostalgia for that time. It was repressive and bigoted to an extent that is largely forgotten today, to cite only two of its uglier aspects. But in that environment America meant America: the people and the land. the land was far bigger than what we'd done with the land.

This is no longer true. Now the environment of America is media. Not the land itself, but the image of the land. The focus is not on the people so much as it is on the interplay between people and screens. What we've done with the land is far more important now that the land—we're not even dealing with the land anymore, we're dealing with our manipulation and pollution of it.

And what we've done with the very concept of "image" is   6
taking on far more importance for many of us than the actual sights
and sounds of our lives.

For instance: Ronald Reagan stands on a cliff in Normandy to   7
commemorate the day U. S. Army Rangers scaled those cliffs in the
World War II invasion. Today's Rangers reenact the event while
some of the original Rangers, in their sixties now, look on. Except
that it is the wrong cliff. The cliff that was actually scaled is a bit further down the beach, but it's not as photogenic as this cliff, so this
cliff has been chosen for everybody to emote over. Some of the old
Rangers tell reporters that the historical cliff is over yonder, but the
old Rangers are swept up (as well they might be) in the ceremonies,
and nobody objects enough. This dislocation, this choice, this stance
that the real cliff is not important, today's photograph is more
important, is a media event. It insults the real event, and overpowers
it. Multiplied thousands of times over thousands of outlets of every
form and size, ensconced in textbooks as well as screenplays, in sales
presentations as well as legislative packages, in religious revivals as
well as performance-art pieces, this is the process that has displaced
what used to be called "culture."

"I'm not even sure it's a culture anymore. It's like this   8
careening hunger splattering out in all directions."

Jeff Nightbyrd was trying to define "culture" in the wee hours   9
at the Four Queens in Las Vegas. It was a conversation that had been
going on since we'd become friends working on the *Austin Sun* in
1974, trying to get our bearings now that the sixties were *really* over.
He'd spent that triple-time decade as an SDS organizer and editor
of *Rat*, and I'd hit Austin after a few years of roadroving, commune-
hopping, and intensive (often depressive) self-exploration—getting
by, as the song said, with a little help from my friends, as a lot of us
did then. This particular weekend Nightbyrd had come to Vegas from
Austin for a computer convention, and I had taken off from my duties
at the *L. A. Weekly* for some lessons in craps (at which Jeff is quite
good) and to further our rap. The slot machines clattered around us
in unison, almost comfortingly, the way the sound of a large shaky air
conditioner can be comforting in a cheap hotel room when you're
trying to remember to forget. We were, after all, trying to fathom an
old love: America.

There are worse places to indulge in this obsession than Las Vegas.   10
It is the most American, the most audacious, of cities. Consuming
unthinkable amounts of energy in the midst of an unlivable desert
(Death Valley is not far away), its decor is based on various cheap-to-
luxurious versions of a 1930s Busby Berkeley musical. Indeed, no

studio backlot could ever be more of a set, teeming with extras, people who come from all over America, and all over the world, to see the topless, tasteless shows, the Johnny Carson guests on parade doing their utterly predictable routines, the dealers and crap-table croupiers who combine total boredom with ruthless efficiency and milk us dry— yet at least these tourists are risking something they genuinely value: money. It's a quiz show turned into a way of life, where you can get a good Italian dinner at dawn. Even the half-lit hour of the wolf does-n't faze Las Vegas. How could it, when the town has survived the flash of atom bombs tested just over the horizon?

The history books will tell you that, ironically enough, the town 11 was founded by Mormons in 1855. Even their purity of vision couldn't bear the intensity of this desert, and they abandoned the place after just two years. But they had left a human imprint, and a decade later the U. S. Army built a fort here. The settlement hung on, and the railroad came through in 1905. During the Second World War the Mafia started to build the city as we know it now. Religious zealots, the Army, and the Mafia—quite a triad of found-ing fathers.

Yet one could go back even further, some 400 years, when the 12 first Europeans discovered the deserts of the American West— Spaniards who, as they slowly began to believe that there might be no end to these expansive wilds, became more and more certain that somewhere, somewhere to the north, lay El Dorado—a city of gold. Immeasurable wealth would be theirs, they believed, and eternal youth. What would they have thought if they had suddenly come upon modern Las Vegas, lying as it does in the midst of this bleached nowhere, glowing at night with a brilliance that would have fright-ened them? We have built our desert city to their measure—for they were gaudy and greedy, devout and vicious, jovial and frenzied, like this town. They had just wasted the entire Aztec civilization because their fantasies were so strong they couldn't see the ancient cultural marvels before their eyes. The Aztecs, awed and terrified, believed they were being murdered by gods; and in the midst of such strange-ness, the Spaniards took on godlike powers even in their own eyes. As many Europeans would in America, they took liberties here they would never have taken within sight of their home cathedrals. Their hungers dominated them, and in their own eyes the New World seemed as inexhaustible as their appetites. So when Nightbyrd described our present culture as "a careening hunger splattering out in all directions," he was also, if unintentionally, speaking about our past. Fittingly, we were sitting in the midst of a city that had been fantasized by those seekers of El Dorado 400 years ago. In that sense, America had Las Vegas a century before it had Plymouth

Rock. And our sensibility has been caught between the fantasies of the conquistadors and the obsessions of the Puritans ever since.

Yes, a fitting place to try to think about American culture.   13

"There are memories of culture," Nightbyrd was saying, "but   14 the things that have given people strength have dissolved. And because they've dissolved, people are into distractions. And distractions aren't culture."

Are there even memories? The media have taken over our mem-   15 ories. That day Nightbyrd had been driving through the small towns that dot this desert, towns for which Vegas is only a dull glow to the southwest. In a bar in one of those towns, "like that little bar in *The Right Stuff*," he'd seen pictures of cowboys on the wall. "Except that they weren't cowboys. They were movie stars. Guys who grew up in Glendale [John Wayne] and Santa Monica [Robert Redford]." Surely this desert had its own heroes once, in the old gold-mining towns where a few people still hang on, towns like Goldfield and Tonopah. Remembering those actual heroes would be "culture." Needing pictures of movie stars for want of the real thing is only a nostalgia for culture.

Nostalgia is not memory. Memory is specific. One has a rela-   16 tionship to a memory, and it may be a difficult relationship, because a memory always makes a demand upon the present. But nostalgia is vague, a sentimental wash that obscures memory and acts as a narcotic to dull the importance of the present.

Media as we know it now thrives on nostalgia and is hostile to   17 memory. In a television bio-pic, Helen Keller is impersonated by Mare Winningham. But the face of Helen Keller was marked by her enormous powers of concentration, while the face of Mare Winningham is merely cameo-pretty. A memory has been stolen. It takes a beauty in you to see the beauty in Helen Keller's face, while to cast the face of a Mare Winningham in the role is to suggest, powerfully, that one can come back from the depths unscathed. No small delusion is being sold here. Yet this is a minor instance in a world-wide, twenty-four-hour-a-day onslaught.

An onslaught that gathers momentum every twenty-four hours.   18 Remember that what drew us to Las Vegas was a computer fair. One of these new computers does interesting things with photographs. You can put a photograph into the computer digitally. This means the photograph is in there without a negative or print, each element of the image stored separately. In the computer, you can change any element of the photograph you wish, replacing it or combining it with elements from other photographs. In other words, you can take composites of different photographs and put them into a new photograph of your own composition. Combine this with computer drawing, and you can touch up shadows that don't match. When it comes out of the computer the finished product bears no evidence of tampering with any negative. The possibilities for history books and news stories are infinite. Whole new histories can now be written. Events which never happened can be full documented.

The neo-Nazis who are trying to convince people that the 19 Holocaust never happened will be able to show the readers of their newsletter an Auschwitz of well-fed, happy people being watched over by kindly S.S. men while tending gardens. And they will be able to make the accusation that photographs of the *real* Auschwitz were created in a computer by manipulative Jews. The Soviet Union can rewrite Czechoslovakia and Afghanistan, the United States can rewrite Vietnam, and atomic weapons proponents can prove that the average resident of Hiroshima was unharmed by the blast. On a less sinister, but equally disruptive, level, the writers of business prospectuses and real-estate brochures can have a field day.

Needless to say, when any photograph can be processed this way 20 then all photographs become suspect. It not only becomes easier to lie, it becomes far harder to tell the truth.

But why should this seem shocking when under the names 21 of "entertainment" and "advertising" we've been filming history, and every facet of daily life, in just this way for nearly a century now? It shouldn't surprise us that the ethics of our entertainment have taken over, and that we are viewing reality itself as a form of entertainment. And, as entertainment, reality can be rewritten, transformed, played with, in any fashion.

These considerations place us squarely at the center of our 22 world—and we have no choice, it's the only world there is anymore. *Electronic media has done for everyday reality what Einstein did for physics:* everything is shifting. Even the shifts are shifting. And a fact is not so crucial anymore, not so crucial as the process that turns a fact into an image. For we live with images as much as facts, and the images seem to impart more life than facts *precisely because they are so capable of transmutation, of transcendence, able to transcend their sources and their uses.* And all the while the images goad us on, so that we become partly images ourselves, imitating the properties of images as we surround ourselves with images.

This is most blatant in our idea of "a vacation"—an idea only 23 about 100 years old. To "vacation" is to enter an image. Las Vegas is only the most shrill embodiment of this phenomenon. People come here not so much to gamble (individual losses are comparatively light), nor for the glittery entertainment, but to step into an image, a daydream, a filmlike world where "everything" is promised. No matter that the Vegas definition of "everything" is

severely limited, what thrills tourists is the sense of being surrounded in "real life" by the same images that they see on TV. But the
same is true of the Grand Canyon, or Yellowstone National Park, or
Yosemite, or Death Valley, or virtually any of our "natural" attractions. What with all their roads, telephones, bars, cable-TV motels,
the visitors are carefully protected from having to *experience* the
place. They view its image, they camp out in its image, ski down or
climb up its image, take deep breaths of its image, let its image give
them a tan. Or, when they tour the cities, they ride the quaint trol-
ley cars of the city's image, they visit the Latin Quarter of its image,
they walk across the Brooklyn Bridge of its image—our recreation is
a *re*-creation of America into one big Disneyland.

And this is only one way we have stripped the very face of America   24
of any content, any reality, concentrating only on its power as image.
We also elect images, groom ourselves as images, make an image of our
home, our car, and now, with aerobics, of our very bodies. For in the
aerobics craze the flesh becomes a garment, susceptible to fashion.
So it becomes less *our* flesh, though the exercise may make it more
serviceable. It becomes "my" body, like "my" car, "my" house.
What, within us, is saying "my"? What is transforming body into
image? We shy away from asking. In this sense it can be said that after
the age of about twenty-five we no longer *have* bodies anymore—we
have possessions that are either more or less young, which we are
constantly trying to transform and through which we try to breathe.

It's not that all this transmutation of realities into un- or non-   25
or supra-realities is "bad," but that it's unconscious, compulsive,
reactive. We rarely make things more than they were; we simplify
them into less. Though surely the process *could*—at least theoreti-
cally—go both ways. Or so India's meditators and Zen's monks
say. But that would be to *increase* meaning, and we seem bent on the
elimination of meaning. We're Reagan's Rangers, climbing a cliff
that *is* a real cliff, except it's not the cliff we say it is, so that the
meaning of both cliffs—not to mention of our act of climbing—is
reduced.

As I look out onto a glowing city that is more than 400 years old   26
but was built only during the last forty years, as I watch it shine in
blinking neon in a desert that has seen the flash of atom bombs, it
becomes more and more plain to me that America is at war with
meaning. America is form opposed to content. Not just form *instead*
of content. Form opposed. Often violently. There are few things
resented so much among us as the suggestion that what we do
means. It *means* something to watch so much TV. It *means* something to be obsessed with sports. It *means* something to vacation by
indulging in images. It means something, and therefore it has

consequences. Other cultures have argued over their meanings. We tend to deny that there is any such thing, insisting instead that what you see is what you get and that's *it*. All we're doing is having a *good time*, all we're doing is making a buck, all we're doing is enjoying the spectacle, we insist. So that when we export American culture what we are really exporting is an attitude toward content. Media is the American war on content with all the stops out, with meaning in utter rout, frightened nuances dropping their weapons as they run.

"Media is the history that forgives," my friend Dave Johnson 27 told me on a drive through that same desert a few months later. We love to take a weekend every now and again and just *drive*. Maybe it started with reading *On the Road* when we were kids, or watching a great old TV show called *Route 66* about two guys who drove from town to town working at odd jobs and having adventures with intense women who, when asked who they were might say (as one did), "Suppose I said I was the Queen of Spain?" Or maybe it was all those rock 'n' roll songs about "the road"—the road, where we can blast our tapedecks as loud as we want, and watch the world go by without having to touch it, a trip through the greatest hologram there is, feeling like neither boys nor men but both and something more, embodiments of some ageless, restless principle of movement rooted deep in our prehistory. All of which is to say that we're just as stuck with the compulsion to enter the image as anybody, and that we love the luxuries of fossil fuel just as much as any other red-blooded, thickheaded Americans.

Those drives are our favorite time to talk, and, again, America is 28 our oldest flame. We never tire of speaking of her, nor of our other old girlfriends. For miles and miles of desert I thought of what Dave had said.

"Media is the history that forgives." A lovely way to put it, and 29 quite un-Western. We Westerners tend to think in sets of opposites: good/bad, right/wrong, me/you, past/present. These sets are often either antagonistic (East/West, commie/capitalist, Christian/heathen) or they set up a duality that instantly calls out to be bridged (man/woman). But Dave's comment sidesteps the dualities and suggests something more complex: a lyrical impulse is alive somewhere in all this media obfuscation. It is the impulse to redeem the past—in his word, to *forgive* history—by presenting it as we would have most liked it to be.

It is one thing to accuse the media of lying. They are, and they 30 know it, and they know we know, and we know they know that we know, and nothing changes. It is another to recognize the rampant lying shallowness of our media as a massive united longing for . . . innocence? For a sheltered childlike state in which we need not know about our world or our past. We are so desperate for this that we are willing to accept ignorance as a substitute for innocence. For there can be no doubt anymore that this society *knowingly* accepts its ignorance as innocence—we have seen so much in the last twenty years that now we know what we *don't* see. Whenever a TV show or a movie or a news broadcast leaves out crucial realities for the sake of sentimentality, we pretty much understand the nature of what's been left out and why.

But American media *forgives* the emptiness and injustice of our   31 daily life by presenting our daily life as innocent. Society, in turn, forgives American media for lying because if we accept the lie as truth then we needn't *do* anything, we needn't change.

I like Dave's line of thought because it suggests a motive—   32 literally, a motive force—for these rivers of glop that stream from the screens and loudspeakers of our era. Because, contrary to popular belief, profit is *not* the motive. That seems a rash statement to make in the vicinity of Las Vegas, but the profit motive merely begs the question: *why* is it profitable? Profit, in media, is simply a way of measuring attention. Why does what we call "media" attract so much attention?

The answer is that it is otherwise too crippling for individuals to   33 bear the strain of accepting the unbalanced, unrewarding, uninspiring existence that is advertised as "normal daily life" for most people who have to earn a living every day.

Do those words seem too strong? Consider: to go to a job you   34 don't value in itself but for its paycheck, while your kids go to a school that is less and less able to educate them; a large percentage of your pay is taken by the government for defenses that don't defend, welfare that doesn't aid, and the upkeep of a government that is impermeable to the influence of a single individual; while you are caught in a value system that judges you by what you own, in a society where it is taken for granted now that children can't communicate with their parents, that old people have to be shut away in homes, and that no neighborhood is *really* safe; while the highest medical costs in the world don't prevent us from having one of the worst health records in the West (for instance, New York has a far higher infant mortality rate than Hong Kong), and the air, water, and supermarket food are filled with God-knows-what; and to have, at the end of a busy yet uneventful life, little to show for enduring all this but a comfortable home if you've "done well" enough; yet to *know* all along that you're living in the freest, most powerful country in the world, though you haven't had time to exercise much freedom and don't personally have any power—this is to be living a life of slow attrition and maddening contradictions.

Add to this a social style that values cheerfulness more than any other attribute, and then it is not so strange or shocking that the average American family watches six to eight hours of network television a day. It is a cheap and sanctioned way to partake of this world without having actually to live in it. 35

Certainly they don't watch so much TV because they're bored—there's far too much tension in their lives to call them bored, and, in fact, many of the products advertised on their favorite programs feature drugs to calm them down. Nor is it because they're stupid—a people managing the most technically intricate daily life in history can hardly be written off as stupid; nor because they can't entertain themselves—they are not so different from the hundreds of generations of their forebears who entertained themselves very well as a matter of course. No, they are glued to the TV because one of the most fundamental messages of television is: "It's all right." 36

Every sitcom and drama says "It's all right." Those people on the tube go through the same—if highly stylized—frustrations, and are exposed to the same dangers as we are, yet they reappear magically every week (every day on the soap opera) ready for more, always hopeful, always cheery, never questioning the fundamental premise that this is the way a great culture behaves and that all the harassments are the temporary inconveniences of a beneficent society. It's going to get even *better*, but even now *it's all right*. The commercials, the Hollywood movies, the universal demand in every television drama or comedy that no character's hope can ever be exhausted, combine in a deafening chorus of: *It's all right.* 37

As a screenwriter I have been in many a film production meeting, and not once have I heard any producer or studio executive say, "We have to lie to the public." What I have heard, over and over, is, "They have to leave the theater feeling good." This, of course, easily (though not always) translates into lying—into simplifying emotions and events so that "it's all right." You may measure how deeply our people know "it" is *not* all right, not at all, by how much money they are willing to pay to be ceaselessly told that it is. The more they feel it's not the more they need to be told it is— hence Mr. Reagan's popularity. 38

Works that don't say "It's all right" don't get much media attention or make much money. 39

The culture itself is in the infantile position of needing to be assured, every day, that this way of life is good for you. Even the most disturbing news is dispensed in the most reassuring package. As 40 world news has gotten more and more disturbing, the trend in broadcast journalism has been to get more and more flimflam, to take it less seriously, to keep up the front of "It's really quite all right." This creates an enormous tension between the medium and its messages, because everybody knows that what's on the news is *not* all right. That is why such big money is paid to a newscaster with a calm, authoritative air who, by his presence alone, seems to resolve the contradictions of his medium. Walter Cronkite was the most popular newscaster in broadcast history because his very presence implied: "As long as I'm on the air, you can be sure that, no matter what I'm telling you, *it's still all right.*"

41 Which is to say that the media has found it profitable to do the mothering of the mass psyche. But it's a weak mother. It cannot nurture. All it can do is say it's all right, tuck us in, and hope for the best.

42 Today most serious, creative people exhaust themselves in a sideline commentary on this state of affairs, a commentary that usually gets sucked up into the media and spewed back out in a format that says "It's all right. What this guy's saying is quite all right, what this woman's singing is all right, all right." This is what "gaining recognition" virtually always means now in America: your work gets turned inside out so that its meaning becomes "It's all right."

43 Of course, most of what exists to *make media of,* to make images of, is more and more disorder. Media keeps saying, "It's all right" while being fixated upon the violent, the chaotic, and the terrifying. So the production of media becomes more and more schizoid, with two messages simultaneously being broadcast: "It's all right. We're dying. It's all right. We're all dying." The other crucial message— "We're dying"—runs right alongside *It's all right.*

44 Murder is the crux of much media "drama." But it's murder presented harmlessly, with trivial causes cited. Rare is the attempt, in all our thousands of murder dramas, to delve below the surface. We take for granted now, almost as an immutable principle of dramatic unity, that significant numbers of us want to kill significant numbers of the rest of us. And what are all the murders in our media but a way of saying "We are being killed, we are killing, we are dying"? Only a people dying and in the midst of death would need to see so much of it in such sanitized form *in order to make death harmless.* This is the way we choose to share our death.

45 Delete the word "entertainment" and say instead North Americans devote an enormous amount of time to the ritual of sharing death. If this were recognized as a ritual, and if the deaths were shared with a respect for the realities and the mysteries of death, this might be a very useful thing to do. But there is no respect for death

in our death-dependent media, there is only the compulsion to display death. As for the consumers, they consume these deaths like sugar pills. Their ritual goes on far beneath any level on which they'd be prepared to admit the word "ritual." So we engage in a ritual we pretend isn't happening, hovering around deaths that we say aren't real.

It is no coincidence that this practice has thrived while the 46 Pentagon uses the money of these death watchers to create weapons for death on a scale that is beyond the powers of human imagination—the very same human imagination that is stunting itself by watching ersatz deaths, as though intentionally crippling its capacity to envision the encroaching dangers. It is possible that the Pentagon's process could not go on without the dulling effects of this "entertainment."

When we're not watching our screens, we're listening to 47 music. And, of course, North Americans listen to love songs at every possible opportunity, through every possible orifice of media. People under the strain of such dislocating unrealities need to here "I love you, I love you," as often as they can. "I love you" or "I used to love you" or "I ought to love you" or "I need to love you" or "I want to love you." It is the fashion of pop-music critics to discount the words for the style, forgetting that most of the world's cultures have had songs about *everything*, songs about work, about the sky, about death, about the gods, about getting up in the morning, about animals, about children, about eating, about dreams—about everything, along with love. These were songs that everybody knew and sang. For a short time in the late sixties we moved toward such songs again, but that was a brief digression; since the First World War the music that most North Americans listen to has been a music of love lyrics that rarely go beyond adolescent yearnings. Either the song is steeped in the yearnings themselves, or it is saturated with a longing for the days when one could, shamelessly, feel like an adolescent. The beat has changed radically from decade to decade, but with brief exceptions that beat has carried the same pathetic load. (The beat, thankfully, has given us other gifts. We'll get to those later in this book.)

It can't be over-emphasized that these are entertainments of a 48 people whose basic imperative is the need not to think about their environment. The depth of their need may be measured by the hysterical popularity of this entertainment; it is also the measure of how little good it does them.

Media is not experience. In its most common form, media 49 substitutes a fantasy of experience or (in the case of news) an abbreviation of experience for the living fact. But in our culture the absorption of media has become a substitute for experience. We absorb media, we don't live it—there is a vast psychological difference, and it is a difference that is rarely brought up.

For example, in the 1940s, when one's environment was still 50 one's *environment*, an experience to be lived instead of a media-saturation to be absorbed, teenagers like Elvis Presley and Jerry Lee Lewis didn't learn their music primarily from the radio. Beginning when they were small boys they sneaked over to the black juke joints of Louisiana and Mississippi and Tennessee, where they weren't supposed to go, and they listened and learned. When Lewis and Presley began recording, even though they were barely twenty they had tremendous authority because they had experience—a raw experience of crossing foreign boundaries, of streets and sounds and peoples, of the night-to-night learning of ways that could not be taught at home.

This is very different from young musicians now who learn from 51 a product, not a living ground. Their music doesn't get to them till it's been sifted through elaborate corporate networks of production and distribution. It doesn't smack of the raw world that exists before "product" can even be thought of.

The young know this, of course. They sense the difference 52 intensely, and often react to it violently. So white kids from suburban media culture invented slam dancing (jumping up and down and slamming into each other) while black kids from the South Bronx, who have to deal with realities far more urgent than media, were elaborating the astounding graces of break dancing.

Slam dancing was a deadend. Break dancing, coming from a 53 living ground, goes out through media but becomes ultimately transformed into another living ground—the kids in the elementary school down the street in Santa Monica break dance. Which is to say, a grace has been added to their lives. A possibility of grace. With the vitality that comes from having originated from a living ground. The media here is taking its proper role as a channel, not as a world in itself. It's possible that these kids are being affected more in their bodies and their daily lives by the South Bronx subculture than by high-gloss films like *Gremlins* or *Indiana Jones and the Temple of Doom*. Even through all this static, life can speak to life.

Of course, break dancing inevitably gets hyped, and hence deval- 54 ued, by the entertainment industry, the way Elvis Presley ended up singing "Viva Las Vegas" as that town's most glamorous headlin-er. He went from being the numinous son of a living ground to being the charismatic product of a media empire—the paradigm of media's power to transform the transformers. The town veritably glows in the dark with the strength of media's mystique.

We do not yet know what life *is* in a media environment. We 55
have not yet evolved a contemporary culture that can supply that
definition—or rather, supply the constellation of concepts in which
that definition would live and grow. These seem such simple statements, but they are at the crux of the American dilemma now. An
important aspect of this dilemma is that we've barely begun a body
of thought and art which is focused on what is really *alive* in the
ground of a media-saturated daily life. For culture always proceeds
from two poles: one is the people of the land and the street; the
other is the thinker. You see this most starkly in revolutions: the
groundswell on the one hand, the thinker (the Jefferson, for
instance) on the other. Or religiously, the groundswell of belief that
is articulated by a Michelangelo or a Dante. The two poles can exist
without each other but they cannot be effective without each other.

Unless a body of thought connects with a living ground, there is 56
no possibility that this era will discover itself within its cacophony
and create, one day, a post-A.D. culture. It is ours to attempt the
thought and seek the ground—for all of us exist between those poles.
We are not only dying. We are living. And we are struggling to share
our lives, which is all, finally, that "culture" means.

EXPLORATIONS

1. Ventura describes reality as another form of entertainment. If this is so,
   why would an awareness of public literacy be important?

2. Ventura claims that we cannot define what life is like in a media environment. He goes on to state that we cannot understand American culture until we thoroughly understand the effects of media on us. Would
   Theodore Sizer or Jack Solomon agree? What about Benjamin Barber
   or David Orr?

3. Why would Ventura draw the conclusion that the media are not primarily aimed at making a profit but at reassuring us? Are the media reassuring?

4. Consider Ventura's argument as you watch your local news. Can you
   find evidence to support or modify Ventura's claims?

Enclosed. Encyclopedic. Endured.: One Week at the Mall of America

DAVID GUTERSON

David Guterson (1956–) is a high school teacher in Bainbridge Island, Washington, who has written a collection of short stories, The Country Ahead of Us, the Country Behind *(1989). He has also contributed to various periodicals, including* Harper's, *where "Enclosed. Encyclopedic. Endured.: One Week at the Mall of America" first appeared in August 1993. This selection explores the cultural implications of the spectacle presented by the Mall of America in Bloomington, Minnesota. Guterson's latest novel is* Snow Falling on Cedars *(1994).*

WRITING BEFORE READING

Have you ever gone to a mall to do something other than shop? If so, why did you go? What is the attraction of malls?

Last April, on a visit to the new Mall of America near Minneapolis, I carried with me the public-relations press kit provided for the benefit of reporters. In included an assortment of "fun facts" about the mall: 140,000 hot dogs sold each week, 10,000 permanent jobs, 44 escalators and 17 elevators, 12,750 parking places, 13,300 short tons of steel, $1 million in cash disbursed weekly from 8 automatic-teller machines. Opened in the summer of 1992, the mall was built on the 78-acre site of the former Metropolitan Stadium, a five-minute drive from the Minneapolis-St. Paul International Airport. With 4.2 million square feet of floor space— including twenty-two times the retail footage of the average American shopping center—the Mall of America was "the largest fully enclosed combination retail and family entertainment complex in the United States."

Eleven thousand articles, the press kit warned me, had already been written on the mall. Four hundred trees had been planted in its gardens, $625 million had been spent to build it, 350 stores had been leased. Three thousand bus tours were anticipated each year along with a half-million Canadian visitors and 200,000 Japanese tourists. Sales were projected at $650 million for 1993 and at $1 billion for 1996. Donny and Marie Osmond had visited the mall, as had Janet Jackson and Sally Jesse Raphael, Arnold Schwarzenegger, and the 1994 Winter Olympic Committee. The mall was five times larger than Red Square and twenty times larger than St. Peter's Basilica; it incorporated 2.3 miles of hallways and almost twice as much steel as the Eiffel Tower. It was also home to the nation's largest indoor theme park, a place called Knott's Camp Snoopy.

On the night I arrived, a Saturday, the mall was spotlit dramatically in the manner of a Las Vegas casino. It resembled, from the outside, a castle or fort, the Emerald City or Never-Never Land, impossibly large and vaguely unreal, an unbroken, windowless multi-storied edifice the size of an airport terminal. Surrounded by parking lots and new freeway ramps, monolithic and imposing in the manner of a walled city, it loomed brightly against the Minnesota night sky with the disturbing magnetism of a mirage. 3

I knew already that the Mall of America had been imagined by its creators not merely as a marketplace but as a national tourist attraction, an immense zone of entertainments. Such a conceit raised provocative questions, for our architecture testifies to our view of ourselves and to the condition of our souls. Large buildings stand as markers in the lives of nations and in the stream of a people's history. Thus I could only ask myself: Here was a new structure that had cost more than half a billion dollars to erect—what might it tell us about ourselves? If the Mall of America was part of America, what was that going to mean? 4

I passed through one of the mall's enormous entrance ways and took myself inside. Although from a distance the Mall of America had appeared menacing—exuding the ambience of a monstrous hallucination—within it turned out to be simply a shopping mall, certainly more vast than other malls but in tone and aspect, design and feel, not readily distinguishable from them. Its nuances were instantly familiar as the generic features of the American shopping mall at the tail end of the twentieth century: polished stone, polished tile, shiny chrome and brass, terrazzo floors, gazebos. From third-floor vistas, across vaulted spaces, the Mall of America felt endlessly textured—glass-enclosed elevators, neon-tube lighting, bridges, balconies, gas lamps, vaulted skylights—and densely crowded with hordes of people circumambulating in an endless promenade. Yet despite the mall's expansiveness, it elicited claustrophobia, sensory deprivation, and unnerving disorientation. Everywhere I went I spied other pilgrims who had found, like me, that the straight way was lost and that the YOU ARE HERE landmarks on the map kiosks referred to nothing in particular. 5

Getting lost, feeling lost, being lost—these states of mind are intentional features of the mall's psychological terrain. There are, one notices, no clocks or windows, nothing to distract the shopper's psyche from the alternate reality the mall conjures. Here we 6 are free to wander endlessly and to furtively watch our fellow wanderers, thousands upon thousands of milling strangers who have come with the intent of losing themselves in the mall's grand, stimulating design. For a few hours we share some common ground—a fantasy of infinite commodities and comforts—and then we drift apart forever. The mall exploits our acquisitive instincts without honoring our communal requirements, our eternal desire for discourse and intimacy, needs that until the twentieth century were traditionally met in our marketplaces but that are not met at all in giant shopping malls.

On this evening a few thousand young people had descended on the mall in pursuit of alcohol and entertainment. They had come to Gators, Hooters, and Knuckleheads, Puzzles, Fat Tuesday, and Ltl Ditty's. At Players, a sports bar, the woman beside me introduced herself as "the pregnant wife of an Iowa pig farmer" and explained that she had driven five hours with friends to "do the mall party scene together." She left and was replaced by Kathleen from Minnetonka, who claimed to have "a real shopping thing—I can't go a week without buying new clothes. I'm not fulfilled until I buy something."

Later a woman named Laura arrived, with whom Kathleen was acquainted. "I *am* the mall," she announced ecstatically upon discovering I was a reporter. "I'd move in here if I could bring my dog," she added. "This place is heaven, it's a *mecca*."

" We egg each other on," explained Kathleen, calmly puffing on a cigarette. "It's like, sort of, an addiction."

" You want the truth?" Laura asked. "I'm constantly suffering from megamall withdrawal. I come here all the time."

Kathleen: "It's a sickness. It's like cocaine or something; it's a drug."

Laura: "Kathleen's got this thing about buying, but I just need to *be* here. If I buy something it's an added bonus."

Kathleen: "She buys stuff all the time; don't listen."

Laura: "Seriously, I feel sorry for other malls. They're so small and *boring*."

Kathleen seemed to think about this: "Richdale Mall," she blurted finally. She rolled her eyes and gestured with her cigarette. "Oh, my God, Laura. Why did we even *go* there? "

There is, of course, nothing naturally abhorrent in the human impulse to dwell in marketplaces or the urge to buy, sell, and trade. Rural Americans traditionally looked forward to the excitement and sensuality of market day; Native Americans traveled long distances to barter and trade at sprawling, festive encampments. In Persian bazaars and in the ancient Greek agoras and the very soul of the community was preserved and could be seen, felt, heard, and smelled as it might be nowhere else. All over the planet the humblest of people have always gone to market with hope in their hearts and in expectation of something beyond mere goods—seeking a place where humanity is temporarily in ascendance, a palette for the senses, one another.

But the illicit possibilities of the marketplace also have long been acknowledged. The Persian bazaar was closed at sundown; the Greek agora was off-limits to those who had been charged with certain crimes. One myth of the Old West we still carry with us is that market day presupposes danger; the faithful were advised to make purchases quickly and repair without delay to the farm, lest their attraction to the pleasures of the marketplace erode their purity of spirit. 17

In our collective discourse the shopping mall appears with the tract house, the freeway, and the backyard barbecue as a product of the American postwar years, a testament to contemporary necessities and desires and an invention not only peculiarly American but peculiarly of our own era too. Yet the mall's varied and far-flung predecessors—the covered bazaars of the Middle East, the stately arcades of Victorian England, Italy's vaulted and skylit gallerias, Asia's monsoon-protected urban markets—all suggest that the rituals of indoor shopping, although in their nuances not often like our own, are nevertheless broadly known. The late twentieth-century American contribution has been to transform the enclosed bazaar into an economic institution that is vastly profitable yet socially enervated, one that redefines in fundamental ways the human relationship to the marketplace. At the Mall of America—an extreme example—we discover ourselves thoroughly lost among strangers in a marketplace designed to serve no community needs. 18

In the strict sense the Mall of America is not a marketplace at all—the soul of a community expressed as a *place*—but rather a tourist attraction. Its promoters have peddled it to the world at large as something more profound than a local marketplace and as a destination with deep implications. "I believe we can make Mall of America stand for all of America," asserted the mall's general manager, John Wheeler, in a promotional video entitled *There's a Place for Fun in Your Life.* "I believe there's a shopper in all of us," added the director of marketing, Maureen Hooley. The mall has memorialized its opening-day proceedings by producing a celebratory videotape: Ray Charles singing "America the Beautiful," a laser show followed by fireworks, "The Star-Spangled Banner" and "the Stars and Stripes Forever," the Gatlin Brothers, and Peter Graves. "Mall of America . . .," its narrator intoned. "The name alone 19 conjures up images of greatness, of a retail complex so magnificent it could only happen in America."

Indeed, on the day the mall opened, Miss America visited. The mall's logo—a red, white, and blue star bisected by a red, white, and blue ribbon—decorated everything from the mall itself to coffee mugs and the flanks of buses. The idea, director of tourism Colleen Hayes told me, was to position America's largest mall as an institution on the scale of Disneyland or the Grand Canyon, a place simultaneously iconic and totemic, a revered symbol of the United States and a mecca to which the faithful would flock in pursuit of all things purchasable.

On Sunday I wandered the hallways of the pleasure dome with the sensation that I had entered an M. C. Escher drawing—there was no such thing as up or down, and the escalators all ran backward. A 1993 Ford Probe GT was displayed as if popping out of a giant packing box; a full-size home, complete with artificial lawn, had been built in the mall's rotunda. At the Michael Ricker Pewter Gallery I came across a miniature tableau of a pewter dog peeing on a pewter man's leg; at Hologram Land I pondered 3-D hallucinations of the Medusa and Marilyn Monroe. I passed a kiosk called The Sportsman's Wife; I stood beside a life-size statue of the Hamm's Bear, carved out of pine and available for $1,395 at a store called Minnesot-ah! At Pueblo Spirit I examined a "dream catcher"—a small hoop made from deer sinew and willow twigs and designed to be hung over its owner's bed as a tactic for filtering bad dreams. For a while I sat in front of Glamour Shots and watched while women were groomed and brushed for photo sessions yielding high-fashion self-portraits at $34.95 each. There was no stopping, no slowing down. I passed Mug Me, Queen for a Day, and Barnyard Buddies, and stood in the Brookstone store examining a catalogue: a gopher "eliminator" for $40 (it's a vibrating, anodized-aluminum stake), a "no-stoop" shoehorn for $10, a nose-hair trimmer for $18. At the arcade inside Knott's Camp Snoopy I watched while teenagers played Guardians of the 'Hood, Total Carnage, Final Flight, and Varth Operation Thunderstorm; a small crowd of them had gathered around a lean, cool character who stood calmly shooting video cow-pokes in a game called Mad Dog McCree. Left thumb on his silver belt buckle, biceps pulsing, he banged away without remorse while dozens of his enemies crumpled and died in alleyways and dusty streets.

At Amazing Pictures a teenage boy had his photograph taken as a body-builder—his face smoothly grafted onto a rippling body—then proceeded to purchase this pleasing image on a poster, a sweatshirt, and a coffee mug. At Painted Tipi there was wild rice for sale, hand-harvested from Leech Lake, Minnesota. At Animalia I came across a polyresin figurine of a turtle retailing for $3,200. At Bloomingdale's I pondered a denim shirt with its sleeves ripped away, the sort of thing available at used-clothing stores (the "grunge look," a Bloomingdale's employee explained), on sale for $125. Finally, at a gift shop in Knott's Camp Snoopy, I came across a game called Electronic Mall Madness, put out by Milton Bradley. On the box, three twelve-year-old girls with good features happily vied to beat one another to the game-board mall's best sales.

At last I achieved an enforced self-arrest, anchoring myself against a bench while the mall tilted on its axis. Two pubescent girls in retainers and braces sat beside me sipping coffees topped with whipped cream and chocolate sprinkles, their shopping bags gathered tightly around their legs, their eyes fixed on the passing crowds. They came, they said, from Shakopee—"It's nowhere," one of them explained. The megamall, she added, was "a buzz at first, but now it seems pretty normal. 'Cept my parents are like Twenty Questions every time I want to come here. 'Specially since the shooting." 23

On a Sunday night, she elaborated, three people had been wounded when shots were fired in a dispute over a San Jose Sharks jacket. "In the *mall*," her friend reminded me. "Right here at megamall. A shooting." 24

"It's like nowhere's safe," the first added. 25

They sipped their coffees and explicated for me the plot of a film they saw as relevant, a horror movie called *Dawn of the Dead*, which they had each viewed a half-dozen times. In the film, they explained, apocalypse had come, and the survivors had repaired to a shopping mall as the most likely place to make their last stand in a poisoned, impossible world. And this would have been perfectly all right, they insisted, except that the place had also attracted hordes of the infamous living dead—sentient corpses who had not relinquished their attraction to indoor shopping. 26

I moved on and contemplated a computerized cash register in the infant's section of the Nordstrom store: "The Answer Is Yes!!!" its monitor reminded clerks. "Customer Service Is Our Number One Priority!" Then back at Bloomingdale's I contemplated a bank of televisions playing incessantly an advertisement for Egoïste, a men's cologne from Chanel. In the ad a woman on a wrought iron balcony tossed her black hair about and screamed long and passionately; then there were many women screaming passionately, too, and throwing balcony shutters open and closed, and this was all followed by a bottle of the cologne displayed where I could get a good look at it. The brief, strange drama repeated itself until I could no longer stand it. 27

America's first fully enclosed shopping center—Southdale Center, 28 in Edina, Minnesota—is a ten-minute drive from the Mall of America and thirty-six years its senior. (It is no coincidence that the Twin Cities area is such a prominent player in mall history: Minnesota is subject to the sort of severe weather that makes climate-controlled shopping seductive.) Opened in 1956, Southdale spawned an era of fervid mall construction and generated a vast new industry. Shopping centers proliferated so rapidly that by the end of 1992, says the National Research Bureau, there were nearly 39,000 of them operating everywhere across the country. But while malls recorded a much-ballyhooed success in the America of the 1970s and early 1980s, they gradually became less profitable to run as the exhausted and overwhelmed American worker inevitably lost interest in leisure shopping. Pressed for time and short on money, shoppers turned to factory outlet centers, catalogue purchasing, and "category killers" (specialty stores such as Home Depot and Price Club) at the expense of shopping malls. The industry, unnerved, re-invented itself, relying on smaller and more convenient local centers—especially the familiar neighborhood strip mall—and building far fewer large regional malls in an effort to stay afloat through troubled times. With the advent of cable television's Home Shopping Network and the proliferation of specialty catalogue retailers (whose access to computerized market research has made them, in the Nineties, powerful competitors), the mall industry reeled yet further. According to the International Council of Shopping Centers, new mall construction in 1992 was a third of what it had been in 1989, and the value of mall-construction contracts dropped 60 percent in the same three-year period.

Anticipating a future in which millions of Americans will prefer   29
to shop in the security of their living rooms—conveniently accessing online retail companies as a form of quiet evening entertainment— the mall industry, after less than forty years, experienced a full-blown mid-life crisis. It was necessary for the industry to re-invent itself once more, this time with a greater attentiveness to the qualities that would allow it to endure relentless change. Anxiety-ridden and sapped of vitality, mall builders fell back on an ancient truth, one capable of sustaining them through troubled seasons: they discovered what humanity had always understood, that shopping and frivolity go hand in hand and are inherently symbiotic. *If you build it fun, they will come.*

The new bread-and-circuses approach to mall building was first   30
ventured in 1985 by the four Ghermezian brothers—Raphael, Nader, Bahman, and Eskandar—builders of Canada's $750 million West Edmonton Mall, which included a water slide, an artificial lake, a miniature-golf course, a hockey rink, and forty-seven rides in an amusement park known as Fantasyland. The complex quickly generated sales revenues at twice the rate per square foot of retail space

that could be squeezed from a conventional outlet mall, mostly by developing its own shopping synergy: people came for a variety of reasons and to do a variety of things. West Edmonton's carnival atmosphere, it gradually emerged, lubricated pocketbooks and inspired the sort of impulse buying on which malls everywhere thrive. To put the matter another way, it was time for a shopping-and-pleasure palace to be attempted in the United States.

After selling the Mall of America concept to Minnesotans in 1985, the Ghermezians joined forces with their American counterparts—Mel and Herb Simon of Indianapolis, owners of the NBA's Indiana Pacers and the nation's second-largest developers of shopping malls. The idea, in the beginning, was to outdo West Edmonton by building a mall far larger and more expensive—something visionary, a wonder of the world—and to include such attractions as fashionable hotels, an elaborate tour de force aquarium, and a monorail to the Minneapolis-St. Paul airport. Eventually the project was downscaled substantially: a million square feet of floor space was eliminated, the construction budget was cut, and the aquarium and hotels were never built (reserved, said marketing director Maureen Hooley, for "phase two" of the mall's development). Japan's Mitsubishi Bank, Mitsui Trust, and Chuo Trust together put up a reported $400 million to finance the cost of construction, and Teachers Insurance and Annuity Association (the majority owner of the Mall of America) came through with another $225 million. At a total bill of $625 million, the mall was ultimately a less ambitious project than its forebear up north on the Canadian plains, and neither as large nor as gaudy. Reflecting the economy's downturn, the parent companies of three of the mall's anchor tenants—Sears, Mach's, and Bloomingdale's—were battling serious financial trouble and needed substantial transfusions from mall developers to have their stores ready by opening day.

The mall expects to spend millions on marketing itself during its initial year of operation and has lined up the usual corporate sponsors—Ford, Pepsi, US West—in an effort to build powerful alliances. Its public-relations representatives travel to towns such as Rapid City, South Dakota, and Sioux City, Iowa, in order to drum up interest within the Farm Belt. Northwest Airlines, another corporate sponsor, offers package deals from London and Tokyo and fare adjustments for those willing to come from Bismarck, North Dakota; Cedar Rapids, Iowa; and Kalamazoo or Grand Rapids, Michigan. Calling itself a "premier tourism destination," the mall draws from a primary tourist market that incorporates the eleven Midwest states (and two Canadian provinces) lying within a day's drive of its parking lots. It also estimates that in its first six month of operation, 5.3 million out of 16 million visitors came from beyond the Twin Cities metropolitan area.

The mall has forecast a much-doubted figure of 46 million annu- 33
al visits by 1996—four times the number of annual visits to
Disneyland, for example, and twelve times the visits to the Grand
Canyon. The number, Maureen Hooley explained, seems far less
absurd when one takes into account that mall pilgrims make far more
repeat visits—as many as eighty in a single year—than visitors to
theme parks such as Disneyland. Relentless advertising and shrewd
promotion, abetted by the work of journalists like myself, assure the
mall that visitors will come in droves—at least for the time being. The
national media have comported themselves as if the new mall were a
place of light and promise, full of hope and possibility. Meanwhile
the Twin Cities' media have been shameless: on opening night
Minneapolis's WCCO-TV aired a one-hour mall special, hosted by
local news anchors Don Shelby and Colleen Needles, and the *St.
Paul Pioneer Press* (which was named an "official" sponsor of the
opening) dedicated both a phone line and a weekly column to
answering esoteric mall questions. Not to be outdone, the
Minneapolis Star Tribune developed a special graphic to draw readers to mall stories and printed a vast Sunday supplement before
opening day under the heading A WHOLE NEW MALLGAME. By the
following Wednesday all perspective was in eclipse: the local press
reported that at 9:05 A.M., the mall's Victoria's Secret outlet had
recorded its first sale, a pair of blue/green silk men's boxer shorts;
that mall developers Mel and Herb Simon ate black-bean soup for
lunch at 12:30 P.M.; that Kimberly Levis, four years old, constructed
a rectangular column nineteen bricks high at the mall's Lego
Imagination Center; and that mall officials had retained a plumber
on standby in case difficulties arose with the mall's toilets.

From all of this coverage—and from the words you now read— 34
the mall gains status as a phenomenon worthy of our time and
consideration: place as celebrity. The media encourage us to visit our
megamall in the obligatory fashion we flock to *Jurassic Park*—
because it is there, all glitter and glow, a piece of the terrain, a
season's diversion, an assumption on the cultural landscape. All of
us will want to be in on the conversation and, despite ourselves, we
will go.

Lost in the fun house I shopped till I dropped, but the scale of the 35
mall eventually overwhelmed me and I was unable to make a
purchase. Finally I met Chuck Brand on a bench in Knott's Camp
Snoopy; he was seventy-two and, in his personal assessment of it, had
lost at least 25 percent of his mind. "It's fun being a doozy," he
confessed to me. "The security cops got me figured and keep their
distance. I don't get hassled for hanging out, not shopping.

Because the deal is, when you're seventy-two, man, you're just about all done shopping."

After forty-seven years of selling houses in Minneapolis, Chuck comes to the mall every day, He carries a business card with his picture on it, his company name and phone number deleted and replaced by his pager code. His wife drops him at the mall at 10:00 A.M. each morning and picks him up again at six; in between he sits and watches. "I can't sit home and do nothing," he insisted. When I stood to go he assured me he understood: I was young and had things I had to do. "Listen," he added, "thanks for talking to me, man, I've been sitting in this mall for four months now and nobody ever said nothing."

The next day I descended into the mall's enormous basement, where its business offices are located. "I'm sorry to have to bring this up," my prearranged mall guide, Michelle Biesiada, greeted me. "But you were seen talking to one of our housekeepers—one of the people who empty the garbage?—and really, you aren't supposed to do that."

Later we sat in the mall's security center, a subterranean computerized command post where two uniformed officers manned a bank of television screens. The Mall of America, it emerged, employed 109 surveillance cameras to monitor the various activities of its guests, and had plans to add yet more. There were cameras in the food courts and parking lots, in the hallways and in Knott's Camp Snoopy. From where we sat, it was possible to monitor thirty-six locations simultaneously; it was also possible, with the use of a zoom feature, to narrow in on an object as small as a hand, a license plate, or a wallet.

While we sat in the darkness of the security room, enjoying the voyeuristic pleasures it allowed (I, for one, felt a giddy sense of power), a security guard noted something of interest occurring in one of the parking lots. The guard engaged a camera's zoom feature, and soon we were given to understand that a couple of bored shoppers were enjoying themselves by fornicating in the front seat of a parked car. An officer was dispatched to knock on their door and discreetly suggest that they move themselves along; the Mall of America was no place for this. "If they want to have sex they'll have to go elsewhere," a security officer told me. "We don't have anything against sex, per se, but we don't want it happening our parking lots."

I left soon afterward for a tour of the mall's basement, a place of perpetual concrete corridors and home to a much-touted recyclery. Declaring itself "the most environmentally conscious shopping center in the industry," the Mall of America claims to recycle up to 80 percent of its considerable refuse and points to its "state-of-the-art" recycling system as a symbol of its dedication to Mother Earth. Yet Rick Doering of Browning-Ferris Industries—the company contracted to manage the mall's 700 tons of monthly garbage—described the on-site facility as primarily a public-relations gambit that actually recycles only a third of the mall's tenant waste and little of what is discarded by its thousands of visitors; further-more, he admitted, the venture is unprofitable to Browning-Ferris, which would find it far cheaper to recycle the mall's refuse some-where other than in its basement.

A third-floor "Recycle NOW Center," located next to Macy's   41
and featuring educational exhibits, is designed to enhance the mall's self-styled image as a national recycling leader. Yet while the mall's developers gave Macy's $35 million to cover most of its "build-out" expenses (the cost of transforming the mall's basic structure into finished, customer-ready floor space), Browning-Ferris got nothing in build-out costs and operates the center at a total loss, paying rent equivalent to that paid by the mall's retailers. As a result, the company has had to look for ways to keep its costs to a minimum, and the mall's garbage is now sorted by developmental-ly disabled adults working a conveyor belt in the basement. Doering and I stood watching them as they picked at a stream of paper and plastic bottles; when I asked about their pay, he flinched and grimaced, then deflected me toward another supervisor, who said that wages were based on daily productivity. Did this mean that they made less than minimum wage? I inquired. The answer was yes.

Upstairs once again, I hoped for relief from the basement's   42
oppressive, concrete gloom, but the mall felt densely crowded and with panicked urgency I made an effort to leave. I ended up instead at Knott's Camp Snoopy—the seven-acre theme park at the center of the complex—a place intended to alleviate claustrophobia by "bringing the outdoors indoors." Its interior landscape, the press kit claims, "was inspired by Minnesota's natural habitat—forests, meadows, river banks, and marshes . . ." And "everything you see, feel, smell and hear adds to the illusion that it's summertime, seventy degrees and you're outside enjoying the awesome splendor of the Minnesota woods."

Creators of this illusion had much to contend with, including   43
sixteen carnival-style midway rides, such as the Pepsi Ripsaw, the Screaming Yellow Eagle, Paul Bunyan's Log Chute by Brawny, Tumbler, Truckin', and Huff 'n' Puff; fifteen places for people to eat, such as Funnel Cakes, Stick Dogs and Campfire Burgers, Taters, Pizza Ovens, and Wilderness Barbecue; seven shops with names like Snoopy's Boutique, Joe Cool's Hot Shop, and Camp Snoopy Toys; and such assorted attractions as Pan for Gold, Hunter's Paradise Shooting Gallery, the Snoopy Fountain, and the video

arcade that includes the game Mad Dog McCree.

As if all this were not enough to cast a serious pall over the   44
Minnesota woods illusion, the theme park's designers had to
contend with the fact that they could use few plants native to
Minnesota. At a constant temperature of seventy degrees, the mall
lends itself almost exclusively to tropical varieties—orange jasmine,
black olive, oleander, hibiscus—and not at all to the conifers of
Minnesota, which require a cold dormancy period. Deferring
ineluctably to this troubling reality, Knott's Camp Snoopy brought
in 526 tons of plants—tropical rhododendrons, willow figs, buddhist
pines, azaleas—from such places as Florida, Georgia, and Mississippi.

Anne Pryor, a Camp Snoopy marketing representative, explained   45
to me that these plants were cared for via something called "integrated pest management," which meant the use of predators such as
ladybugs instead of pesticides. Yet every member of the landscape
staff I spoke to described a campaign of late-night pesticide spraying
as a means of controlling the theme park's enemies—mealybugs,
aphids, and spider mites. Two said they had argued for integrated
pest management as a more environmentally sound method of controlling insects but that to date it had not been tried.

Even granting that Camp Snoopy is what it claims to be—   46
an authentic version of Minnesota's north woods tended by
environmentally correct means—the question remains whether it
makes sense to place a forest in the middle of the country's largest
shopping complex. Isn't it true that if people want woods, they are
better off not going to a mall?

On Valentine's Day last February—cashing in on the promotional   47
scheme of a local radio station—ninety-two couples were married en
masse in a ceremony at the Mall of America. They rode the roller
coaster and the Screaming Yellow Eagle and were photographed
beside a frolicking Snoopy, who wore an immaculate tuxedo. "As we
stand here together at the Mall of America," presiding district judge
Richard Spicer declared, "we are reminded that there is a place for
fun in your life and you have found it in each other." Six months
earlier, the Reverend Leith Anderson of the Wooddale Church in
Eden Prairie conducted services in the mall's rotunda. Six thousand
people had congregated by 10:00 A.M., and Reverend Anderson
delivered a sermon entitled "The Unknown God of the Mall."
Characterizing the mall as a "direct descendant" of the ancient
Greek agora, the reverend pointed out that, like the Greeks before
us, we Americans have many gods. Afterward, of course, the flock
went shopping, much to the chagrin of Reverend Delton Krueger,
president of the Mall Area Religious Council, who told the
Minneapolis Star Tribune that as a site for church services, the mall

may trivialize religion. "A good many people in the churches," said Krueger, "feel a lot of the trouble in the world is because of materialism."

But a good many people in the mall business today apparently think   48
the trouble lies elsewhere. They are moving forward aggressively on the premise that the dawning era of electronic shopping does not preclude the building of shopping-and-pleasure palaces all around the globe. Japanese developers, in a joint venture with the Ghermezians known as International Malls Incorporated, are planning a $400 million Mall of Japan, with an ice rink, a water park, a fantasy-theme hotel, three breweries, waterfalls, and a sports center. We might shortly predict, too, a Mall of Europe, a Mall of New England, a Mall of California, and perhaps even a Mall of the World. The concept of shopping in a frivolous atmosphere, concocted to loosen consumers' wallets, is poised to proliferate globally. We will soon see monster malls everywhere, rooted in the soil of every nation and offering a preposterous, impossible variety of commodities and entertainments.

The new malls will be planets unto themselves, closed off from   49
this world in the manner of space stations or of science fiction's underground cities. Like the Mall of America and West Edmonton Mall—prototypes for a new generation of shopping centers—they will project a separate and distinct reality in which an "outdoor café" is not outdoors, a "bubbling brook" is a concrete watercourse, and a "serpentine street" is a hallway. Safe, surreal, and outside of time and space, they will offer the mind a potent dreamscape from which there is no present waking. This carefully controlled fantasy—now operable in Minnesota—is so powerful as to inspire psychological addiction or to elicit in visitors a catatonic obsession with the mall's various hallucinations. The new malls will be theatrical, high-tech illusions capable of attracting enormous crowds from distant points and foreign ports. Their psychology has not yet been tried pervasively on the scale of the Mall of America, nor has it been perfected. But in time our marketplaces, all over the world, will be in essential ways interchangeable, so thoroughly divorced from the communities in which they sit that they will appear to rest like permanently docked spaceships against the landscape, windowless and turned in upon their own affairs. The affluent will travel as tourists in each, visiting the holy sites and taking photographs in the catacombs of far-flung temples.

Just as Victorian England is acutely revealed beneath the   50
grandiose domes of its overwrought train stations, so is contemporary America well understood from the upper vistas of its shopping malls, places without either windows or clocks where the tempera-

ture is forever seventy degrees. It is facile to believe, from this vantage point, that the endless circumambulations of tens of thousands of strangers—all loaded down with the detritus of commerce—resemble anything akin to community. The shopping mall is not, as the architecture critic Witold Rybczynski has concluded, "poised to become a real urban place" with "a variety of commercial and noncommercial functions." On the contrary, it is poised to multiply around the world as an institution offering only a desolate substitute for the rich, communal lifeblood of the traditional marketplace, which will not survive its onslaught.

Standing on the Mall of America's roof, where I had ventured to inspect its massive ventilation units, I finally achieve a full sense of its vastness, of how it overwhelmed the surrounding terrain—the last sheep farm in sight, the Mississippi River incidental in the distance. Then I peered through the skylights down into Camp Snoopy, where throngs of my fellow citizens caroused happily in the vast entrails of the beast. 51

EXPLORATIONS

1. Guterson spent a week in the Mall of America reflecting on how space and design affect those who frequent the mall. Choose a public space to observe and analyze. Think about how space is used and arranged and about the rhetorical effects of spatial arrangements. For instance, while you're at your academic adviser's office, the grocery store, or the dentist's office, take a good look at your surroundings: the arrangement of counters, furniture, and space, the decor, the appearance of the employees, the music or other sounds. What does the aim of the arrangement seem to be? What is the goal of the space — to serve you quickly and get you out, to lure you into buying fattening and high-priced foods, or to make you feel comfortable? Or is it to make you feel you are in the presence of authority? What audience is such an arrangement aimed at and how does it work to influence that audience?

2. How does Guterson describe the atmosphere of the Mall of America, including the physical construction of the building, lighting, layout, etc.? How do these physical characteristics affect him and others that he interviews? What are some of the intended effects of the mall's physical characteristics? Why doesn't the mall have clocks or windows? How do these and other choices affect mall-goers?

3. How does the mall symbolize or package the "American" character? How do the unseen parts of the mall contradict its public image? How, in Guterson's analysis, does the mall represent American values and beliefs?

4. How does the mall market itself to a variety of audiences? What do you think of Guterson's characterization of the mall as primarily a tourist attraction or as the "embodiment of place as celebrity"?

5. What kinds of responses to the mall did the interviewed people have? Why do you think Guterson chose to interview these particular people

(a middle-aged woman, a few girls, a 72-year-old man)? Why might he have interviewed more women than men? What persuasive effects do these interviews have?

Receivers of the World's Attention

STEPHEN DOBYNS

Stephen Dobyns (1941–) was born in Orange, New Jersey,
received his B.A. from Wayne State University in Detroit,
Michigan, and his M.F.A. from the University of Iowa in
1967. Dobyns writes poetry and fiction, but considers him-
self first and foremost a poet. In 1984, Dobyns was the
National Poetry Series winner for his collection Black Dog,
Red Dog. *In this poem, Dobyns exhibits several of the*
themes that characterize his poetry: humor, attention to the
seemingly bizarre, and social and political criticism.

WRITING BEFORE READING

Reflect upon the title of this poem. What does it make you think of?
What do you think the poem might be about? After you have read the
poem, compare your reaction to your expectations.

It is the shoes that show the breaking point,   1
the complete collapse in their lives, the moment
when something just whacked them and after that

all became different. You have seen these shoes
singly or in pairs, isolated in intersections,   5
nestling by curbs on suburban streets, bordering

expressways or by the edge of a dirt road
in Montana or Maine, maybe on a sidewalk, even
hanging from overhead wires, a pair of sneakers

suspended from blue sky like a bird transfixed   10
smack in the air, sometimes a shiny black brogan,
sometimes a gymshoe missing its laces. Innocuous,

innocent, the only evidence that something
peculiar has happened. And you think of a person
who has stared at the newspaper for too long,   15

or has gotten too wrapped up with the news on TV,
or has spent too long listening to people
complaining about It, it being the world

and all its depredations: killings here,
famines there, the usual violent mumbo jumbo,   20
except these people have gotten stuck in that

413

cul de sac where they can't push it back
like the rest of us, can't buy a new sweater
or dress and say, Boy, I sure needed that,

and let the world slide off a little, give them   25
some room to swing their arms before the pictures
crowd in again: the face of someone screaming,

the ever increasing numbers of the dead
nudging ever closer, until there occurs
an explosion inside them, some kind of attack,   30

and all you know is this shoe in the roadway,
this smidgin of evidence that something for somebody
went wrong. How lucky that it hasn't happened

to you yet, that the world remains distant
and abstract, hasn't overwhelmed you yet,   35
that your shoes are still accounted for.

But for them something snapped. Then they were
picked up, patched back together and packed off
to heal themselves. Perhaps these are the people

you see in the malls sitting hour after hour,   40
watching the crowds file past, the endless
buying and selling. Someone drops them off

in the morning and picks them up at night.
Sometimes they sip tea from styrofoam cups
or nibble a hotdog or thin slice of pizza.   45

Sometimes they form part of the crowd watching
the baton twirling display or karate display
or some fellow showing off a vegetable scraper.

They are eager to return to us, become
part of us again, and they sit in the mall   50
as a place blessedly lacking past or future:

no one dies there, the world does not intrude there.
They almost feel like people again. No one
weeps there, no one gets angry, no one

yells at them or finds fault with them or tells them   55
to do something quick. They sit in their new shoes
studying the crowds and trying to fix themselves,

like trying to invent a new kind of smile
and upsidedown one or sideways like a scar.
And they sit very quietly because they know   60

if they jump or move quickly they will break apart
and the custodians in their gray coveralls
will gather around these broken fragments of glass

with a little water, a little ice like a spilled drink
and even their spirits will be yelled at, even   65
their tentative souls. So they just watch

and try to believe in a world like this one:
no extremes of sound or color, no extremes
of emotion, everything exactly in the middle,

and no death, no death anyplace, and no cruelty.   70
And sometimes it works, sometimes they truly
get better. You can wait in the parking lot

and might see a man toddling out through the exit,
his arms raised for balance, taking one step
then another, blinking into the bright light,   75

flinching a little at the sound of traffic.
If you shouted right now you could break him.
But who wants to do that? Isn't this when

you should hurry to welcome him, to embrace him?
Wouldn't he do the same for you if your positions   80
were reversed and you were the one creeping back

into the world? And they are glad to be back
if only for a short time, glad for the chance
to chuckle with their families and glance around

with wonder, to reenter their passionate stories   85
before the world again rears up and entangles them
with the statistics of its victims, enfolds them

with all the faces of the lost, before the world
wraps its string around them and sets them spinning
between one curb and the other, while behind them   90

as souvenirs of the world's attention—
a black running show, a torn cowboy boot,
a new black pump with the heel snapped off.

EXPLORATIONS

1. How does Dobyns's characterization of mall-goers compare to Guterson's? How does each piece affect you as a reader?

2. What purpose does the space of the mall serve in this poem?

3. Consider the structure of the poem. Why do you think Dobyns uses this particular structure to write about malls, shoes, the media, and other subjects?

4. How do you react to malls? Write a mall poem. If you have trouble getting started, try using Dobyns' poem as a model.

From John T. Molloy's
New Dress for Success

John T. Molloy

John T. Molloy is an author and clothing consultant who founded Dress for Success, Inc., a company founded on the belief that clothing plays a major role in a person's ability to succeed in the business world. The following excerpts are taken from a longer work, John T. Molloy's New Dress for Success, *which is a revised version of his 1977 original. He has also written a companion guide for women,* The Woman's Dress for Success.

WRITING BEFORE READING

Why are you wearing what you are wearing today?

INTRODUCTION: WHY MEN DRESS FOR FAILURE AND WHAT TO DO ABOUT IT

When I tell conservatively dressed businessmen that most men dress for failure, they generally agree. They all know men who wear ill-fitting polyester suits, wash-and-wear shirts and garish ties and they know that in their companies these men have no chance of getting to the top. However, when I tell them that many of them in their conservative suits, shirts and ties are dressing for failure as well, they are incredulous. They find it difficult to believe that dressed that way they could be doing their careers and their companies more damage than the fellows in their polyester suits, but the research is overwhelming; they are.

The reasons that businessmen dress for failure are many. The chief ones are:

1. They let their wives or their girl friends choose their clothing.
2. They let their favorite sales clerk choose their clothing.
3. They let designers choose their clothing.
4. They let one of the new breed of image consultants choose their clothing.
5. They let their backgrounds choose their clothing.

There is a way to avoid making any of those mistakes and to dress for success instead. Let research choose your clothing. My research is unique in concept, scope and results. It has been conducted over a period of twenty-six years and includes the opinions

416

and subconscious reactions of over sixty thousand executives in all phases of business, as well as those of a wide cross section of the general public.

This research is based on the very reasonable premise that the two 4 great behaviorists Pavlov and Skinner are right: We are preconditioned by our environment—and the clothing we wear is an integral part of that environment. The way we dress has a remarkable impact on the people we meet professionally or socially, and greatly (sometimes crucially) affects how they treat us.

It is possible, through the skillful manipulation of dress in any 5 particular situation, to evoke a favorable response to your personality and your needs.

And it is possible for me, based on the research I have done, to 6 teach you to dress for success.

I do not ask you to accept these conclusions immediately; I do 7 hope that you will accept them when you have finished this book.

I will never ask you to concede that it is fair or just or moral for 8 a man's success or failure to depend, to a large extent, on how he dresses. But that is very much the way the money-oriented sectors of our culture work; and it is my contention that in matters of individual striving, it is far more rewarding to let reality be your guide, to use the system rather than ignore or flout it.

Many critics charge that my approach to successful dress is snob- 9 bish, conservative, bland and conformist. They may further charge that I am encouraging the executive herd-instinct. To these charges I must plead guilty, for my research documents that in matters of clothing, conservative, class-conscious conformity is absolutely essential to the success of the American business and professional man. Executives do, in particular, constitute a herd, and those who understand how to cope rather than fight are much more likely to emerge as leaders than as casualties. . . .

DRESSING TO MATCH YOUR PRODUCT

When Gerald Ford was minority leader of the House of 10 Representatives, he sold his product—himself—excellently. He was Jerry, the nice guy, and he dressed like Jerry, the nice guy. When he became president, he had a different product to sell—leader of the country—but he did not change his image in the beginning of his presidency and was still projecting Jerry, the nice guy. As a result a great number of people looked on him with disdain. He had to change his image—and he did, successfully. But most of the damage had already been done. The image of Gerald Ford as an ineffective bumbler hung over his presidency like a black cloud. Every time he slipped or mishit a golf ball the press jumped all over him, in spite of the fact that he was probably the best athlete ever to occupy the White House.

Ronald Reagan, on the other hand, came from a casual   11
California show-business environment. But luckily for him, he had served first as governor of California and realized that he had to change his image when he got to Washington in the same way he had had to change his image when he first arrived in Sacramento. By the time he reached the White House, he looked every inch presidential. From his first day in office everyone, including the liberal media, treated him with a great deal more respect than they had President Ford. If historians agree that Ronald Reagan was a successful president, they will also agree that one of the main reasons for his success was that he was a master of controlling image and dressed to sell his product—leadership. If you want to sell any product, you must do the same.

I was once disseminating this advice to a group of salesmen   12
when one jumped up and said, "I sell computers. How do you dress like a computer?" I then did a very quick analysis of the audience. I first asked if there were men present who did not sell computers. Then I asked them what they knew about computers. They answered that computers are expensive, and efficient, yet they break down a lot.

I then told the salesman that he really was not selling a comput-   13
er. What his client was buying when he chose between computers was the reliability and integrity of the company. If the salesman worked for IBM, his integrity was already guaranteed by the company's reputation. However, if he worked for The Small Unknown Computer Company, the only way a buyer could judge the company was by looking carefully at him. Therefore, it is more important for the salesman representing a small company to dress in a way that announces that his is a very honest, reliable company that will back up its claims and give excellent service.

DO YOU KNOW WHAT YOUR TRUE PRODUCT IS?

The main problem with most salesmen dressing to suit their   14
product is that they do not know what their true product is. They assume that the product is what it physically is. This is wrong. Salesmen must dress to suit not what they are selling, but what people are buying. The difference can be large and crucial.

I was once hired by a Cadillac dealer to help dress his sales force.   15
He owned several dealerships throughout the country. One dealership dealt only with people who were quite rich. They were not

buying Cadillacs; they were buying basic transportation. Like most upper-middle-class people, these customers trusted people who looked as if they were in the same income bracket, so we put the salesmen in good, conservative upper-middle-class attire, and their sales increased.

Several months later the owner called me and said that he had dressed his salesmen in another dealership in the same way and was having trouble. When I visited the other dealership I discovered the reason. That dealership was selling primarily to people who had considerably less money. They were not buying Cadillacs either; they were buying prestige. So we dressed up that group of salesmen with high-power-prestige apparel that conveyed that they had made it big. Sales improved.

Incidentally, I found in both dealerships that the most successful salesmen had been dressing correctly before I got there. Although we are talking about a fairly subtle difference in the appearance between the salesmen in the two agencies, that slight difference made a substantial difference in sales, because the buyer's frame of mind was substantially different. Here then, is proof that the problem is not what is being sold; it is what is being bought.

With some products and sales methods, the point of customer attitude toward the person who sells the product is particularly significant. When working for insurance companies, I have found that salesmen who sell life insurance to people from the lower middle class had best not wear gray pinstripe suits, although they should look affluent. The very idea behind insurance (i.e., death) and the inevitable complexity and fine print of all policies scare lower-middle-class people, so if the salesman comes on as a very strong executive type, these people do not consider themselves able to hold a conversation with him. They are intimidated by his appearance and will turn him off long before he can close the sale. If he comes on as just a well-dressed neighbor, he fares much better.

HOW TO SELL DOOR-TO-DOOR

If a man is selling door-to-door, he can make one or two mistakes in trying to overcome the natural fear women have of strangers that will not let him get past the door. He can dress too much like a businessman or he can dress too little like businessman. It may seem to be a catch-22, but it isn't. If he dresses like a high-authority businessman in a three-piece pinstripe suit, most of the women will think he is too slick, too sharp, and will be afraid of being bamboozled, so they will not let him start his presentation. If, on the other hand, he wears an open shirt without a tie, they will wonder if he is really a legitimate businessman and will worry about his real purpose, and will not let him in.

A door-to-door salesman has two products to sell and the first   20
product he has to sell is himself. If he does not sell himself first, he never gets a chance to sell anything else.

There are two ways of getting women to open the door to you.   21
First, dress like a businessman but not an authority figure. Wear a beige, tan, light gray, medium-range blue or any soft nonauthorita-tive suit. Wear it with a colorful shirt and a bright tie that has been carefully coordinated with the shirt and the suit. Women associate dress with decency and are much more likely to open the door to a man who is dressed nicely. The second and even more effective way to open a door is to have your company put you in a jacket with a logo on it. It will announce to the women that you are a business-man without threatening them. Either tactic will work.

Salesmen selling to offices have a different problem. If they do   22
not wear high-authority garments, they either cannot get past recep-tionists and secretaries or are made to wait interminably because their importance will be judged by their clothing. Expensive power garments can cut that waiting time by one-third to one-half, so there is that much more time left for selling.

Today, IBM and its symbol-laden white shirt remain first-glance   23
indicators of success, prestige and reliability. But when IBM first started selling computers, the world of these expensive machines was a confusing, unreliable new field. The basic idea about computers in the minds of most people was that they were unreliable. The white shirt was a brilliant tactical move because it lent the look of reliabil-ity to the salesmen even if the product was trouble-prone.

Used-car salesmen face a similar problem. People are automati-   24
cally suspicious of them (perhaps with good reason), but I have found that by taking used-car salesmen out of their usually gaudy attire and putting them in blue blazers, gray pants, nondescript shirts and perhaps even a club tie with a small company logo or insignia, there is much less resistance to their sales pitch and people feel they are more credible. The look conveys a feeling of youth and inno-cence and it works.

When I am first invited to speak before business organizations,   25
I know that if the men present have never met me before, they will automatically have me stereotyped as a fashion designer or consul-tant—someone who is frilly and flighty and unimportant. My standard wardrobe for such appearances is a pinstripe suit, usually with a vest, and a very conservative tie. This clothing immediately suggests—accurately—that I am another businessman, just as they are, that I am a man of substance, and that I am serious. This is how I am able to off-set the negative connotations of my services before I even say a word.

After I have worked with an organization half a dozen times I   26
sometimes dress less conservatively. I usually wear two-piece suits
with white shirts and conservative ties, but often I open my jacket or
loosen my tie as a signal to my clients that I am open and friendly;
that is part of a consultant's job. When I speak before college
groups, I try to wear inexpensive outfits. At the beginning of the
presentation I tell the students how much my suit, shirt and tie cost,
and I explain to them that if I can appear before them and talk about
"Dressing for Success" with moderately priced clothing, they can use
the same clothing to go for an interview. There is nothing that works
as well as a personal example when selling a dress code to students
or others.

Clothing can also be used to enhance further the existing positive   27
associations of your business. If you work for a large, old corporation,
and you dress very conservatively, your clothing will reconfirm the
feeling in your clients that the company is still solid as a rock,
reputable and doing quite nicely.

I once knew a man in Washington who sold packaged political   28
campaigns. Since politicians are not known for giving much credence
to the ideas of others, he knew he had to come on as a supreme
authority figure. And he found that the best way to do it was to over-
whelm them. He was a large man to begin with, but he reinforced
his physique by wearing black suits and pinstripes, a white shirt and
black tie. And he overwhelmed people who were not accustomed to
being overwhelmed. He used a super-hard sell, and his clothing
added to his power and prestige.

DRESS CODES

In addition to conducting employee surveys, I continued to run   29
the image surveys that I have been running for corporations for
years, following the same procedure: I arrange to have a professional photographer take pictures of employees at two or three in the
afternoon on two days chosen at random. If we are dealing with a
department where the people do not work in an office, I arrange to
have their pictures taken when they are leaving the office to go into
the field. In addition, I visit the headquarters and as many branch
offices as I can during a six-month period. On those visits I walk
through the offices as unobtrusively as possible, taking notes about
the way people in various offices dress and how I think their dress
impacts their performance and the image of the company. The visits
I make to these offices—including the president's—are always unan-
nounced. If I'm going to be useful to the company, I must see the
clothing that their people normally wear to work.

After visiting at least one-fourth of the major offices of a client   30
company, I arrange to meet with the corporate officers in the largest
room they have, usually the boardroom. Before they come in, my
assistants arrange the photographs that we have collected, either
directly on the walls or on bulletin boards we hang on the walls. On
the top level we put the pictures of all the executives. We divide them
according to office and location. On the second level we put the
pictures of the professionals and managers of various departments—
legal, engineering and so on—and we put them directly underneath
the executives for whom they work. On the third level, we put the
pictures of all the people who work in these departments: the
accountants, the engineers, the lawyers, the managers, the under-
writer. On the fourth level we put the pictures of the clerical people
who work in these offices, and on the fifth level we put pictures of
blue-collar people who work at those locations. On the sixth level we
put the people who work in uniforms in various sections of the country. In the sixth set of pictures we always have two groups: the
pictures that the uniform company originally used when they were
selling the uniform, and pictures of the people in the field actually
wearing the uniform—which often looks very different. Naturally, as
soon as the executives walk into the room they look at the pictures.
Many of them, particularly those who have worked at corporate
headquarters for many years, find that a very enlightening and sometimes sobering experience.

It can also be a very dangerous experience because of what I call   31
the "Going to dress those slobs" reflex. Ninety percent of the time,
when the executives walk into a room wearing their $600-plus suits,
whether they learned to dress at their daddy's pinstripe knee, or
learned the rules in the school of hard knocks, they immediately
want to get everyone out there to dress as they do. Unless I restrain
them, they pick up the phone and start screaming at the man in
charge of the San Jose office, telling him he had better whip his
people into shape. I am so certain of their response that as they come
into the room, I have them promise that before they do anything we
will sit down and discuss the problem calmly.

I explain to them that America's most successful companies   32
have dress codes that match their management philosophy. For
example, IBM was founded by Mr. Watson, who came out of a
marketing and sales background. His experience taught him that
dressing conservatively opened doors and announced to the world
that he was a serious businessperson. That is probably the main reason it is not surprising that when Watson established a dress code for
his entire company it was a dress code that worked best for salesmen.
The conservative suits, white shirt and shined shoes worn by IBMers
say that they are serious professionals and that they represent a

reliable company. That is important today, but it was even more important in the early days of IBM when computers were less reliable and IBM had financial problems that hurt the credibility of their salespeople. By putting his men into conservative outfits Watson announced that IBM was a dependable, conservative company that would stand behind the large, delicate machines they sold. Undoubtedly, sending that message successfully was one of the reasons IBM succeeded. It has become one of the world's great companies because its dress code has always matched its philosophy and its management style.

When Pat Haggerty helped found Texas Instruments he set up 33 an entirely different dress code in that company. As an ex-naval officer he avoided anything that struck him as a uniform. He and the other founders of the company came to work with open collars and no ties. Mr. Haggerty believed that uniforms inhibited creativity, and would turn off the very people he wanted to attract.

Haggerty not only had a very casual dress code, he designed very 34 casual corporate offices. In fact, his corporate offices looked more like college campuses than industrial sites. He sent a series of nonverbal signals to the academic whiz kids and the technical geniuses that they would be welcomed, respected and cherished at Texas Instruments. No question about it, his message worked. Texas Instruments attracted a surprising number of those technical wizards and became one of the world's best engineering companies.

As you can see, both of the above dress codes fit the management 35 style, the philosophy, and the aims of the companies for which they were designed and, because they did they helped those companies succeed.

I go on to explain to them that their companies or the Fortune 36 500 companies whose dress codes they have copied were formed either in the late nineteenth or early twentieth century. They did not grow up overnight. They are products of pre-World War II thinking and management style.

Before World War II, education, at least a college education, was 37 generally limited to the upper class in America. Harvard was not filled with the best and the brightest, but the richest and the best-connected, and they ran America. There was a real gap between the socioeconomic and educational backgrounds of the workers and the bosses. Most blue-collar workers recognized this gap and accepted it as normal. The clothing worn by the men in corporate America at the time reflected the truth that existed in society and in the company. Society at the turn of the century consisted of two classes: people in charge and the people they were in charge of, the bosses and the workers.

Today, the distance between the classes has lessened. The rich 38 are not as rich or powerful as they once were. They still live very comfortable lives, but modest by comparison with the rich of just fifty or sixty years ago. And, although the poor are still poor and comparatively powerless, they are not as poor or as powerless as they once were. What is more, the sons and daughters of an average American today, or even a poor American today, have a much better chance of acquiring money and power than did their grandparents. Conversely, the sons and daughters of the rich have much less chance of achieving power than did their grandparents. It is not that they do not have an advantage and are not more likely to be influential in our society, it is that they are not the only ones who are going to be influential. Things have changed and for the better. However, the dress codes based on the autocratic social system that long ago disappeared still exist in most corporations and, in most, they are counterproductive.

I do not want to give the impression that if every company in   39
America developed a laid-back casual dress code as did Texas Instruments, they would improve their profit margin. They would not. The biggest problem in America is not good dress codes or bad dress codes, it is umbrella dress codes. Dress codes which put every-one in the company in the same uniform. Even when umbrella dress codes are successful you pay a price for them. If you look at America's best-known and most successful dress code company, IBM, you can see this. IBM, in spite of its reputation as a technical company, has never been considered by most technical people as an innovative company. They build good products and have the ability to market those products successfully, but their motto never really has been, "think"; it has been "sell and then think."

The problem with this is that in the long run the salvation of   40
IBM and every other high-tech company in America will depend on innovation in the creation of new products, not just on selling them. In order to do this successfully IBM is going to have to attract and hold creative people. I believe that IBM will have limited success in this area unless they change their image.

I speak at about thirty colleges a year and in the past two years,   41
whenever possible, I have interviewed the top engineering students in the schools where I spoke. These are the brilliant and innovative people, mainly young men, that every high-tech company—including IBM—would like to have working for them. Eight of the twenty students I interviewed told me they would not even consider inter-viewing with IBM. Seven others said that IBM was not their first choice and in most cases it was not even their second. Among the remaining five students, only two expressed any real desire to work for IBM. The reason most of these creative student engineers said they did not want to work for IBM was they believed that IBM did not encourage creative people. Whether IBM does or does not is not

really the question. The fact is, the students hold this belief and it affects IBM's ability to recruit them. It is not going to be easy for them to win these young people over. When I told the students that the experimental engineers at IBM that I interviewed said that they were as free at IBM to experiment as they were at any other company, and possibly freer, I do not think they believed me. Only one student openly challenged me, but the others I think were just polite enough to dance around the topic.

I am not suggesting that the executives or salespeople at IBM throw out their conservative suits and white shirts; that would be silly. I think that they should continue to dress the way they do. IBM is a very successful marketing company and to change the way their salesmen or executive dress would be counterproductive. However, instead of denying they have a dress code, IBM should admit that one exists for their salespeople and executives and then announce loudly and clearly that the other people at IBM have the freedom to dress in any way they want. They should make this announcement where the young engineers are likely to hear it. If I were IBM I would make it a point of running ads containing pictures of bearded and tieless experimental engineers wearing colored shirts. Instead of showing one face to the world, IBM should show several faces. They should make a major effort to convince the talented engineers of this world that there is a place for them at IBM.

Texas Instruments has a similar problem. Their umbrella dress code sends a message that engineers, and only engineers are really going to be influential at Texas Instruments. After interviewing several dozen people in marketing and sales, I came to the conclusion that most of them really did not believe that they were ever going to have a major say in how that company was run. Which means Texas Instruments must have a very difficult time attracting and keeping ambitious sales and marketing people—the people Texas Instruments needs most.

A company's dress code and its resulting image can have an effect not only on its ability to recruit and hold talented people and to develop specific areas in the company, it can have a direct effect on its sales. Apple Computer is a classic example of a company with a public image problem. Several years ago a friend of mine was hired to research why people bought various brands of personal computers. Since the two biggest personal computers on the market were IBM and Apple, he asked a number of people who purchased either one why they made their choice. The people who bought Apple generally chose it because they though it was simpler and easier to operate. Those who chose IBM chose it usually because they thought IBM was a large company and would stand behind its product. They had faith in the company. In ninety percent of the cases the people who bought personal computers did not have enough information to make a technical decision and they really were not making one. Several of those questioned in focus groups said they actually would have preferred purchasing the Apple Computer because they thought it was simpler, but were not sure that Apple was going to be around in a couple of years and therefore chose IBM.

When asked to describe IBM as a company and Apple computer   45
as a company, these people had two dramatically different pictures. IBM, in their minds, was a great giant who was too large to disappear. Apple, on the other hand, was a company run by whiz kid engineers who had been producing computers in the backs of garages just a few years ago. They knew it was bigger than that now, but they were not quite sure how bit it was. When asked to estimate the comparable size of IBM and Apple, they accurately estimated IBM's size and vastly underestimated Apple's.

In the middle of this research IBM announced it was pulling its   46
PC Junior off the market. My friend wondered if people would no longer think of IBM as the company that always stood behind its products; after all they had just given up on one. But the fact is that the numbers changed very little. Most of the people who had to choose between IBM and Apple still chose IBM when they were looking at the same price range, and still chose it for the same reasons. Their perception of the company had more effect on what they purchased than the reality of how the company acted in the marketplace.

During my meetings with the heads of large corporations, I am   47
always surprised to learn that they have given such little thought to the fact that their company should show the world not one face, but several. They should be interested in showing a different face to their employees than they do to their customers, and a different face to their customers than they do to their competitors. They should also realize that the way their employees dress has a major impact on their corporate image.

But the executives I talk with usually admit that when it comes   48
to *looking* at corporate dress, most of them simply ignore it. These same men who spend millions of dollars in developing logos and packaging their products don't spend a dime packaging their people. They say they have not done it because they do not think it has to be done. Most of them are happy with the way their people dress. When I ask them how they decide if their dress code is satisfactory, they tell me they rely on instinct, on what they feel good about. When I ask them if they would package their products or pick a logo based on the same instinct, the response is always no. They say those factors are too important to guess about—and usually, as soon as they make that statement, realize they have made a mistake. . . .

HOW TO DRESS UP YOUR OFFICE FOR SUCCESS

Obviously, professional qualifications are important for lawyers, 49
doctors, architects and others—including wardrobe consultants—
who are in business for themselves. But so are appearances, and the
only appearance that will help such men is the appearance of success,
prestige and power. I hope that I have by now established how
importantly clothing contributes to this look of success. Another
significant element in this look of success that can be controlled is
the physical setup of your office.

Unfortunately, most corporate executives have little control over 50
the look of their offices because the office arrangement, furniture
and decor are usually controlled by the companies for which they
work, at least to a considerable extent. Such control, however, is
absolutely crucial to any man who must bring in business, who must
bring in clients or patients from the outside, and especially professionals in business for themselves. Corporate executives would be
well advised to follow as many of my research-based tips as their
management will permit.

The impression that anyone from the outside will have of any 51
man will depend in no small measure on the setting in which he sees
that man functioning—his office. Men have realized for years that
offices are important. But most have not sought to systematize their
concern, to make their offices yield the ultimate benefits possible.

The people who sell office furniture are much more concerned 52
with selling the products they have been given to sell than with selling power. They are more interested in selling something new rather
than something useful. There are some decorators who are wizards
at office arrangement, furnishing and decor, but they are few and
very expensive.

HOW TO MAKE IT BIG

Like successful clothing, the successful office exudes the qualities 53
of the upper middle class. It is (or looks) spacious and uncrowded.
It is rich. It is well kept. It is tasteful. It is impressive. It is comfortable. It is private.

The most important aspect of any office is size; it should be as 54
large as possible. Obviously there are financial limitations attached to
this advice, but if you have a section consisting of several offices, as
most professional men do, and you must skimp, be sure to skimp
somewhere other than on your personal office.

About as important as your office's size and richness is its 55
address. The best addresses are generally the most expensive, and no

matter what city you work in, you should have the most prestigious address you can afford. This is even more important if some of your clients come from a distance. For years, most of my clients have been from New York, and I maintained an office on West 55th Street, right off Fifth Avenue. Knowledgeable New Yorkers know that this is a highly respectable location, but to the executive from Kansas City or the banker from Amarillo who may be considering my services, West 55th Street might at first suggest West 55th Street off Eighth Avenue where his best friend was mugged returning from the theater last year. So now, since more and more of my clients and prospective clients are from areas away from New York, I am moving to a Fifth Avenue office. To any man I want as a client, Fifth Avenue suggests prestige and substance. Any man to whom it doesn't say that, I can't help much anyway.

An office with a window or windows is better than an office without. An office with a window and a beautiful view is the best you can come by. If the view through your window is of an air shaft or similar atrocity, be very sure to keep your window covered.   56

The ideal office has two well-defined and separate areas: one in which the central object is your desk; and the other an informal conversation area, with a couch and/or chairs in a comfortable grouping. The best office for such an arrangement is L-shaped, but that is quite difficult to come by unless you have the money and ability to rearrange walls.   57

THE PRIORITY: THE DESK

After you have chosen your office, the most essential piece of furniture—and it should be chosen first—is your desk. The desk should be as large as possible with out crowding or dwarfing the office. A desk that overpowers the space into which it is put creates a strongly negative impression. Regardless of its style, a desk should be functional for your needs and work habits. It should be wood or have the look of wood and should be as expensive as you can afford. All types of metal desks should be generally avoided; they do not look as if they belong to a man of substance and power.   58

The next item to acquire is your desk chair. In most cases, the best chair is a large one that comes up to the back of the head. It should be a standard office chair, various styles of which will blend with any decor from antique to ultramodern. The only man who should avoid the large chair is the very small man. He should choose a chair proportional to his size because a large chair will make him look even smaller.   59

In front of your desk should be two comfortable chairs for visi-   60
tors. They should be of good quality, in either leather or Naugahyde,
preferably matching your desk chair. The most acceptable colors for
desk and visitors' chairs are deep maroon, deep green, dark, rich
brown or tan. At present, the most common and sought-after color
is black, but it is not as effective as the above colors because they give
off a much richer look.

WHERE VISITORS SHOULD SIT

Always place visitors' chairs in front of your desk, never at the   61
side. Somehow, when a visitor moves up to the side of your desk,
he invades your area of privacy and cuts down on your authority in
dealing with him. Sitting on the side is not as psychologically comfortable for him nor as effective for you. Keep the chairs in front of
the desk.

Depending on the space available for your second area, you   62
should at least have a couch (it can be small if necessary) and a
coffee-type table that fits in with the rest of the room's decor. If
you have an exceptionally large office, and if your work requires it,
you might also add a third area in which you would place a small
work or conference table with chairs around it. The best example
I've ever seen of this was an antique table with matching antique
chairs; it gave the powerful impression of a small boardroom in the
office.

The only other items of furniture that are completely acceptable   63
in most offices are bookcases, credenzas and filing cabinets. But if at
all possible, you should keep your filing cabinets in your secretary's
office or in some other area. Important men just do not have obtru-
sive filing cabinets in their offices. . . .

HOW TO "FRAME" YOURSELF
FOR MAXIMUM AUTHORITY

In the ideal office, the desk acts like a throne, giving you power   64
over those who come in. They should be impressed with your importance and authority. The best way to create this impression by instant
visual impact is to position your desk and yourself within a frame that
automatically turns you into its central element. The best elements
to create such a frame are either a window or pictures directly behind
the desk. The best frame is an open window with a beautiful view. If
you have such a view, use it as the central frame behind your desk.
Although most decorations ignore such considerations, if one has a

view of constant colors (not seasonal ones such as green trees), and these colors are followed through in the office, the dimensions of the office will seem to be extended.

If you do not have a window, or are unable to position your desk   65 in front of the window, paintings will accomplish the same effect. You must decide what painting, how large and how many, but regardless of these decisions the painting or paintings should be symmetrically positioned directly behind the desk, and not appear off-center or askew.

EXPLORATIONS

1. Why does Molloy think it important for businesses to hire image consultants? Why do you think Molloy's text is aimed primarily at businessmen?

2. Molloy speaks of dress as self-packaging and urges sales people to think of themselves as embodiments of their products. What does it mean to sell leadership or trustworthiness? Are such efforts ethical? Why or why not?

3. How does Molloy's analysis of office space compare to David Guterson's analysis of space in the Mall of America?

4. Think of a time when matters of dress have had great significance for you. Can you remember an instance when the way you dressed affected how you were treated, when you misjudged a situation and dressed inappropriately, or when you were influenced to trust someone or see him or her in a particular way because of the way he or she dressed? How do clothes represent values and beliefs? How do they play a role in stereotyping and categorizing people? You may want to think about dress as a form of literacy or in terms of its rhetorical or persuasive effect as Molloy outlines.

The Internet Is Four Inches Tall

M. KADI

*M. Kadi (1968–) is a free-lance computer consultant in the
San Francisco area whose work provides her with the raw
material for her essays about computer usage. She has written on various topics for h2so4, bOING, bOING, and
hotWired, an on-line journal for the magazine Wired. "The
Internet Is Four Inches Tall" was written for the 'zine
h2so4, a journal of literary, social, and political commentary
whose name is the chemical symbol for sulfuric acid, which
medieval alchemists considered to be the key to knowledge.
Kadi raises important questions about access and diversity as
they pertain to the Internet.*

WRITING BEFORE READING

*Have you ever surfed the Internet? If so, describe your experiences. If
not, what do you think it would be like?*

"Computer networking offers the soundest basis for world peace
that has yet been presented. Peace must be created on the bul-
wark of understanding. International computer networks will knit
together the peoples of the world in bonds of mutual respect; its
possibilities are vast, indeed."

— *Scientific American*

"Cyberspace is a new medium. Every night on Prodigy,
CompuServe, GEnie, and thousands of smaller computer bulletin
boards, people by the hundreds of thousands are logging on
to a great computer mediated gabfest, an interactive debate that
allows them to leap over barriers of time, place, sex, and social
status."

— *Time* Magazine

"The Internet is really about the rise of not merely a new technology, but a new culture—a global culture where time, space,
borders, and even personal identity are radically redefined."

— *Online Access* Magazine

"When you begin to explore the online world, you'll find a
wealth of publicly available resources and diverse communities."

— A 'Zine I Actually Like—so I'm
not going to tell you where I got this quote

"The first time you realize the super toy you wanted is really only   1
four inches tall you learn a hard lesson." Q: How big is the Internet?
A: Four inches tall. Blah. Blah. Blah. Everyone is equal on the Net.
Race, gender, sexual orientation are invisible and, being invisible,
foster communication. Barriers are broken down. The global community exists and is coming together. (Right here, right now.)

Diversity.   Community.   Global   Culture.   Information.   2
Knowledge. Communication. Doesn't this set your nostalgia alarm
off? Doesn't it sound like all that sixties love-in, utopian, narcissistic trash that we've had to listen to all our lives? Does this sound
familiar to anyone but me?

Computer bulletin board services offer up the glories of e-mail,   3
the thought provocation of newsgroups, the sharing of ideas implicit in public posting, and the interaction of real-time chats. The
fabulous, wonderful, limitless world of communication is just waiting for you to log on. Sure. Yeah. Right.

I confess, I am a dedicated cyberjunkie. It's fun. It's interest-   4
ing. It takes me places where I've never been before. I sign on once
a day, twice a day, three times a day, more and more; I read, I post, I
live. Writing an article on the ever-expanding, ever-entertaining, everpresent world of online existence would have been easy for me. But it
would have been familiar, perhaps dull; and it might have been a lie.
The world does not need another article on the miracle of online
reality; what we need, what I need, what this whole delirious, interconnected, global community of a world needs is a little reality check.

To some extent the following scenario will be misleading. There   5
are flat rate online services (Netcom for one) which offer significant
connectivity for a measly seventeen dollars a month. But I'm interested in the activities and behavior of the private service users who will
soon comprise a vast majority of online citizens. Furthermore, let's
face facts, the U. S. Government by and large foots the bill for the
Internet, through maintaining the structural (hardware) backbone,
including, among other things, funding to major universities. As surely as the Department of Defense started this whole thing, AT&T or
Ted Turner is going to end up running it so I don't think it's too
unrealistic to take a look at the Net as it exists in its commercial form[1]
in order to expose some of the realities lurking behind the regurgitat-
ed media rhetoric and the religious fanaticism of net junkies.

---

[1] Techno concession: I know that the big three commercial services are not considered part of the Internet proper, but they (Prodigy, CompuServe, and AOL) are
rapidly adding real Net access and considering AOL just bought Netcom . . . well, just
read the article.

TIME AND MONEY

The average person, the normal human, J. Individual, has an income. Big or small, how much of J. Individual's income is going to be spent on Computer Connectivity? Does 120 dollars a month sound reasonable? Well, you may find that number a bit too steep for your pocketbook, but the brutal fact is that 120 dollars is a "reasonable" amount to spend on monthly connectivity. The major online services have a monthly service charge of approximately $15. Fifteen dollars to join the global community, communicate with a diverse group of people, and access the world's largest repository of knowledge since the Alexandrian Library does not seem unreasonable, does it? But don't overlook the average per-hour connectivity rate of an additional $3 (which can skyrocket upwards of $10, depending on your modem speed and service). You might think that you are a crack whiz with your communications software—that you are rigorous and stringent and never, ever respond to e-mail or a forum while online, that you always use your capture functions and create macros, but let me tell you that no one, and I repeat, no one, is capable of logging on this efficiently every time. Thirty hours per month is a realistic estimate for online time spent by a single user engaging in activities beyond primitive e-mail. Now consider that the average, one-step-above-complete neophyte user has at least two distinct BBS accounts, and do the math: Total Monthly Cost: $120. Most likely, that's already more than the combined cost of your utility bills. How many people are prepared to double their monthly bills for the sole purpose of connectivity?

In case you think thirty hours a month is an outrageous estimate, think of it in terms of television. (OK, so you don't own a television, well, goody-for-you—imagine that you do!) Thirty hours, is, quite obviously, one hour a day. That's not so much. Thirty hours a month in front of a television is simply the evening news plus a weekly *Seinfeld/Frasier* hour. Thirty hours a month is less time than the average car-phone owner spends on the phone while commuting. Even a conscientious geek, logging on for e-mail and the up-to-the-minute news that only the net services can provide is probably going to spend thirty hours a month online. And, let's be truthful here, thirty hours a month ignores shareware downloads, computer illiteracy, real-time chatting, interactive game playing and any serious forum following, which by nature entail a significant amount of scrolling and/or downloading time.

If you are really and truly going to use the net services to connect with the global community, the hourly charges are going to add up pretty quickly. Take out a piece of paper, pretend you're writing a check, and print it out "One hundred and Twenty dollars—" and tell me again, how diverse is the online community?

That scenario aside, let's pretend that you're single, that you don't have children, that you rarely leave the house, that you don't have a TV and that money is not an issue. Meaning, pretend for a moment that you have as much time and as much money to spend online as you damn-well want. What do you actually do online?

Well, you download some cool shareware, you post technical questions in the computer user group forums, you check your stocks, you read the news and maybe some reviews—Hey, you've already passed that thirty hour limit! But, of course, "since computer networks make it easy to reach out and touch strangers who share a particular obsession or concern," you are participating in the online forums, discussion groups, and conferences.

Let's review the structure of forums. For the purposes of this essay, we will examine the smallest of the major user-friendly commercial services—America Online (AOL). There is no precise statistic available (at least none that the company will reveal—you have to do the research by Hand!!!) on exactly how many subject-specific discussion areas (folders) exist on AOL. Any online service is going to have zillions of posts pertaining to computer usage (e.g., the computer games area of AOL breaks into five hundred separate topics with over 100,000 individual posts), so let's look at a less popular area: the "Lifestyles and Interests" department.

For starters, there are fifty-seven initial categories within the Lifestyle and Interests area. One of these categories is Ham Radio. Ham Radio? How can there possible be 5,909[2] separate, individual posts about Ham Radio? [There are] 5,865 postings in the Biking (and that's just bicycles, not motorcycles) category. Genealogy—22,525 posts. The Gay and Lesbian category is slightly more substantial—22,525 posts. There are five separate categories for political and issue discussion. The big catch-all topic area, The Exchange, has over 100,000 posts. Basically, service wide (on the smallest service, remember) there are over a million posts.

So, you want to communicate with other people, join the online revolution, but obviously you can't wade through everything that's being discussed—you need to decide which topics interest you, which folders to browse. Within The Exchange alone (one of

---

[2] Statistics obtained in June 1994. Most of these numbers have increased by at least 20 percent since that time, owing to all the Internet hoopla in the media, the consumer desire to be "wired" as painlessly as possible, and AOL's guerrilla marketing tactics.

fifty-seven subdivisions within one of another fifty higher divisions) there are 1,492 separate topic-specific folders—each containing a rough average of fifty posts, but with many containing close to four hundred. (Note: AOL automatically empties folders when their post totals reach four hundred, so total post numbers do not reflect the overall historical totals for a given topic. Sometimes the posting is so frequent that the "shelf life" of a given post is no more than four weeks.)

So, there you are J. Individual, ready to start interacting with folks, sharing stories and communicating. You have narrowed yourself into a single folder, three tiers down in the AOL hierarchy, and now you must choose between nearly fifteen hundred folders. Of course, once you choose a few of these folders, you will then have to read all the posts in order to catch up, be current, and not merely repeat a previous post. 14

A polite post is no more than two paragraphs long (a screenful of text, which obviously has a number of intellectually negative implications). Let's say you choose ten folders (out of fifteen hundred). Each folder contains an average of fifty posts. Five hundred posts, at, say one paragraph each, and you're now looking at the equivalent of a two hundred page book. 15

Enough with the stats. Let me back up a minute and present you with some very disturbing, but rational, assumptions. J. Individual wants to join the online revolution, to connect and communicate. But, J. Individual is not going to read all one million posts on AOL. (After all, J. Individual has a second online service.) Exercising choice is J. Individual's god-given right as an American, and, by gosh, J. Individual is going to make some decisions. So, J. Individual is going to ignore all the support groups—after all, J. is a normal, well-adjusted person, and all of J.'s friends are normal, well-adjusted individuals. What does J. need to know about alcoholism or incest victims? J. Individual is white. So, J. Individual is going to ignore all the multicultural folders. J. couldn't give a hoot about gender issues; does not want to discuss religion or philosophy. Ultimately, J. Individual does not engage in topics which do not interest J. Individual. So, who is J. meeting? Why, people who are *just like* J. 16

J. Individual has now joined the electronic community. Surfed the Net. Found some friends. *Tuned in, turned on, and geeked out.* Traveled the Information Highway and, just off to the left of that great Infobahn, J. Individual has settled into an electronic suburb. 17

Are any of us so very different from J. Individual? It's my time and my money and I am not going to waste any of it reading posts by disgruntled Robert-Bly drum-beating men's-movement boys who think that they should have some say over whether or not I 18 choose to carry a child to term simply because a condom broke. I know where I stand. I'm an adult. I know what's up and I am not going to waste my money arguing with a bunch of Neanderthals.

Oh yeah; I am so connected, so enlightened, so open to the 19 opposing viewpoint. I'm out there, meeting all kinds of people from different economic backgrounds (who have $120 a month to burn), from all religions (yeah, right, like anyone actually discusses religion anymore from a user-standpoint), from all kinds of different ethnic backgrounds and with all kinds of sexual orientations (as if any of this ever comes up outside of the appropriate topic folder).

People are drawn to topics and folders that interest them and 20 therefore people will only meet people who are likewise interested in the same topics in the same folders. Rarely does anyone venture into a random folder just to see what others (The Others?) are talking about. This magazine being what it is, I can assume that the average white collar worker out in the burbs—but still, I think you and I are participating in the wide, wide world of online existence only insofar as our already existing interests and prejudices dictate.

Basically, between the monetary constraints and the sheer num- 21 ber of topics and individual posts, the great Information Highway is not a place where you will enter an "amazing web of new people, places, and ideas." One does not encounter people from "all walks of life" because there are too many people and too many folders. Diversity might be out there (and personally I don't think it is), but the simple fact is that the average person will not encounter it because with one brain, one job, one partner, one family, and one life, no one has the time!

Just in case these arguments based on time and money aren't 22 completely convincing, let me bring up a historical reference. Please take another look at the opening quote of this essay from *Scientific American*. Featured in their "50 Years Ago Today" column, where you read "computer networks," the original quote contained the word *television*. Amusing, isn't it?

Moving beyond the practical obstacles mentioned above, let's 23 assume that the Internet is the functional, incredible information tool that everyone says it is. Are we really prepared to use it?

WHO, WHAT, WHERE, WHEN, AND WHY?

School trained us to produce answers. It didn't matter if your 24 answer was right or wrong, the fact is that you did the answering while the teacher was the one asking the questions, writing down the equations, handing out the topics. You probably think that you came up with your own questions in college. But did you? Every class had its theme, its reading list, its issues; you chose topics for papers and projects keeping within the context set by your professors and the academic environment. Again, you were given questions, perhaps more thinly disguised than the questions posed to you in fourth grade, but questions nevertheless. And you answered them. Even people focusing on independent studies and those pursuing higher degrees, still do very little asking, simply because the more you study, the more questions there seem to be, patiently waiting for you to discover and answer them.

These questions exist because any contextual reality poses ques- 25 tions. The context in which you exist defines the question, as much as it defines the answer. School is a limited context. Even life is a limited context. Well, life was a limited context until this Information Highway thing happened to us. Maybe you think that this Infobahn is fabulous; fabulous because all that information is out there waiting to be restructured by you into those answers. School will be easier. Life will be easier. A simple tap-tap-tap on the ol' keyboard brings those answers out of the woodwork and off the Net into the privacy of your own home.

But this Information Highway is a two-way street and as it 26 brings the world into your home it brings you out into the world. In a world filled with a billion answers just waiting to be questioned, expect that you are rapidly losing a grip on your familiar context. This loss of context makes the task of formulating a coherent question next to impossible.

The questions aren't out there and they never will be. You must 27 make them.

Pure information has no meaning. I would venture to assert that 28 a pure fact has no meaning; no meaning, that is, without the context which every question implies. In less than fifteen minutes I could find out how much rain fell last year in Uzbekistan, but that fact, that answer, has no meaning for me because I don't have or imagine or know the context in which the question is meaningful.

No one ever taught me how to ask a question. I answered other 29 people's question, received a diploma, and now I have an education. I can tell you what I learned, and what I know. I can quantify and qualify the trivia which comprises my knowledge. But I can't do that with my ignorance. Ignorance, being traditionally "bad," is just lumped together and I have little or no skills for sorting through the vast territory of what I don't know. I have an awareness of it— but only in the sense that I am aware of what I don't know about the topics which I already know something about in the first place.

What I mean to say is, I don't know what I don't know about,   30
say, miners in China because I don't know anything about China,
or what kinds of minerals they have, or where the minerals are, or the
nature of mining as a whole. Worse yet, I don't have a very clear
sense of whether or not these would be beneficial, useful, enlightening things for me to know. I have little sense of what questions are
important enough for me to ask, so I don't know what answers,
what information to seek out on the Internet.

In this light, it would seem that a massive amount of self-   31
awareness is a prerequisite for using the Internet as an information
source—and very few people are remotely prepared for this task. I
believe that most people would simply panic in the face of their own
ignorance and entrench themselves even more firmly into the black
holes of their existing beliefs and prejudices. The information is
certainly out there, but whether or not any of us can actually learn
anything from it remains to be seen.

FLY, WORDS, AND BE FREE

The issues pertaining to time, money, and the fundamental use-   32
fulness of pure information are fairly straightforward when contrast-
ed with the issues raised by e-mail. E-mail is the first hook and the
last defense for the Internet and computer-mediated communication. I would like to reiterate that I am by no means a Luddite when
it comes to computer technology; in fact, because of this I may be
unqualified to discuss, or even grasp, the dark side of electronic communication in the form of e-mail. The general quality of e-mail sent
by one's three-dimensional[3] friends and family is short, usually
funny, and almost completely devoid of thoughtful communication.
I do not know if this is a result of the fact that your 3-D friends
already "know" you, and therefore brief quips are somehow more
revealing (as they reflect an immediate mental/emotional state) than
long, factual exposés, or if this brevity is a result of the medium
itself. I do not know if I, personally, will ever be able to sort this out,
owing to the nature of my friends, the majority of whom are, when
all is said and done (unlike myself, I might add), writers.

---

[3] So sue me for being a nerd. Personally, I find referring to friends one has made outside of the cyber world as one's "real" friends, or one's "objective" friends, to
be insulting and inaccurate. Certainly one's cyber friends are three-dimensional in a
final sense, but the "3-D" adjective is about the only term I have come up with
which doesn't carry the negative judgmental weight of other terms so over-used in
European philosophy. Feel free to write me if you've got a better suggestion. Better
yet, write me in the appropriate context: flox@netcom.com.

Writers have a reverence for pen and paper which does not carry 33
over well into ASCII. There is no glorified history for ASCII exchange
and perhaps because of this fact my friends do not treat the medium
as they would a handwritten letter. Ultimately, there is very little to
romanticize about e-mail. There is decidedly a lack of sensuality, and
perhaps some lack of realism. There is an undeniable connection
between writers and their written (literally) words. This connection is
transferred via a paper letter in a way that can never be transferable
electronically. A handwritten letter is physically touched by both the
sender and the receiver. When I receive an electronic missive, I receive
only an impression of the mind, but when I receive a handwritten
letter, I receive a piece, a moment, of another's physical (real?)
existence; I possess, I own, that letter, those words, that moment.

Certainly there is a near-mystical utopianism to the lack of 34
ownership of electronic words. There is probably even an evolution
of untold consequences. Personally, I do not think, as so many do,
that a great democracy of thought is upon us—but there is a change,
as ownership slips away. While this is somewhat exciting, or at least
intriguing, insofar as public communication goes, it is sad for private
correspondence. To abuse a well-known philosopher, there is a
leveling taking place: The Internet and the computer medium
render a public posting on the nature of footwear and a private
letter on the nature of one's life in the same format, and to some
extent this places both on the same level. I cannot help but think that
there is something negative in this.

Accessibility is another major issue in the e-mail/handwritten 35
letter debate. Text sent via the Net is instantly accessible, but it is
accessible only in a temporal sense. E-text is inaccessible in its lack of
presence, in its lack of objective physicality. Even beyond this, the
speed and omnipresence of the connection can blind one to the fact
that the author/writer/friend is not physically accessible. We might
think we are all connected, like an AT&T commercial, but on what
level are we connecting? A handwritten letter reminds you of the
writer's physical existence, and therefore reminds you of their physical absence; it reminds you that there is a critical, crucial component
of their very nature which is not accessible to you; e-mail makes us
forget the importance of physicality and plays into our modern belief
in the importance of time.

Finally, for me, there is a subtle and terrible irony lurking with- 36
in the Net: The Net, despite its speed, its exchange, ultimately reeks
of stasis. In negating physical distance, the immediacy of electronic
transfers devalues movement and the journey. In one minute,
a thought is in my head, and the next minute it is typed out, sent,
read, and in your head. The exchange may be present, but the jour-

ney is imperceptible. The Infobahn hype would have us believe that this phenomenon is a fast-paced dynamic exchange, but the feeling, when you've been at it long enough, is that this exchange of ideas lacks movement. Lacking movement and the journey, to me it loses all value.

Maybe this is prejudice. Words are not wine, they do not neces- 37 sarily require age to improve them. Furthermore, I have always hated the concept that Art comes only out of struggle and suffering. So, to say that e-mail words are weaker somehow because of the nature, or lack, of their journey, is to romanticize the struggle. I suppose I am anthropomorphizing text too much—but I somehow sense that one works harder to endow one's handwritten words with a certain strength, a certain soul, simply because those things are necessary in order to survive a journey. The ease of the e-mail journey means that your words don't need to be as well prepared, or as well equipped.

Electronic missives lack time, space, embodiment, and history 38 (in the sense of a collection of experiences). Lacking all these things, an electronic missive is almost in complete opposition to my existence and I can't help but wonder what, if anything, I am communicating.

EXPLORATIONS

1. What is Kadi's attitude toward the Internet as a form of media or public discourse? What does she characterize as myths of Internet culture?

2. How do you think the Internet compares to other forms of media? In what ways is it more or less powerful than other forms of media?

3. Who really has access to the Internet, and how does that access influence the on-line environment?

4. How does Kadi characterize the process used by "J. Individual" to surf the net? How does that process affect the usefulness of this form of media?

5. Do you think that the Internet can be a democratizing force? Why or why not? Does it provide mind-opening or mind-numbing experiences? How do your experiences on the Net relate to the issues Kadi raises?

Men, Women, and Computers

Barbara Kantrowitz

Barbara Kantrowitz is a senior writer for Newsweek, *where she has worked since 1985. This article, published in the issue for May 16, 1994, explores the differences between men's and women's attitudes towards computers and attempts to outline some possible reasons for these differences.*

WRITING BEFORE READING

People often conceal their identities or even create whole new personalities when they communicate on-line. Is this ethical behavior? Are there other public arenas where people alter their identities?

As a longtime "Star Trek" devotee, Janis Cortese was eager to be part of the Trekkie discussion group on the Internet. But when she first logged on, Cortese noticed that these fans of the final frontier devoted megabytes to such profound topics as whether Troi or Crusher had bigger breasts. In other words, the purveyors of this "Trek" dreck were all *guys*. Undeterred, Cortese, a physicist at California's Loma Linda University, figured she'd add her perspective to the electronic gathering place with her own momentous questions. Why was the male cast racially diverse while almost all the females were young, white and skinny? Then, she tossed in a few lustful thoughts about the male crew members.

After those seemingly innocuous observations, "I was chased off the net by rabid hounds," recalls Cortese. Before she could say "Fire phasers," the Trekkies had flooded her electronic mailbox with nasty messages—a practice called "flaming." Cortese retreated into her own galaxy by starting the all-female Starfleet Ladies Auxiliary and Embroidery/Baking Society. The private electronic forum, based in Houston, now has more than 40 members, including psychologists, physicians, students and secretaries. They started with Trektalk, but often chose to beam down and go where no man had ever wandered before—into the personal mode. When Julia Kosatka, a Houston computer scientist, got pregnant last year, she shared her thoughts with the group on weight gain, sex while expecting and everything else on her mind. Says Kosatka: "I'm part of one of the longest-running slumber parties in history."

From the Internet, to Silicon Valley to the PC sitting in the   3
family room, men and women often seem like two chips that pass in
the night. Sure, there are women who spout techno-speak in their
sleep and plenty of men who think a hard drive means four hours on
the freeway. But in general, computer culture is created, defined and
controlled by men. Women often feel about as welcome as a system
crash.

About a third of American families have at least one computer,   4
but most of those are purchased and used by males. It may be new
technology, but the old rules still apply. In part, it's that male-
machine bonding thing, reincarnated in the digital age. "Men tend
to be seduced by the technology itself," says Oliver Strimpel,
executive director of The Computer Museum in Boston. "They
tend to get into the faster-race-car syndrome," bragging about the
size of their discs or the speed of their microprocessors. To the truly
besotted, computers are a virtual religion, complete with icons (on-
screen graphics), relics (obsolete programs and machines) and
prophets (Microsoft's Bill Gates, outlaw hackers). This is not something to be trifled with by mere . . . females, who seem to think that
machines were meant to be *used*, like the microwave oven or the
dishwasher. Interesting and convenient on the job but not worthy of
obsession. Esther Dyson, editor of Release 1.0, an influential soft-
ware-industry newsletter, has been following the computer field for
two decades. Yet when she looks at her own computer, Dyson says
she still doesn't "really care about its innards. I just want it to
work."

Blame (a) culture (b) family (c) schools (d) all of the above.   5
Little boys are expected to roll around in the dirt and explore.
Perfect training for learning to use computers, which often requires
hours in front of the screen trying to figure out the messy arcanum
of a particular program. Girls get subtle messages—from society if
not from their parents—that they should keep their hands clean and
play with their dolls. Too often, they're discouraged from taking
science and math—not just by their schools but by parents as well
(how many mothers have patted their daughters on the head and
reassured them: "Oh, I wasn't good at math, either").

The gender gap is real and takes many forms.   6

BARBIE VS. NINTENDO

Girls' technophobia begins early. Last summer, Sarah Douglas,   7
a University of Oregon computer-science professor, took part in a
job fair for teenage girls that was supposed to introduce them to

nontraditional occupations. With great expectations, she set up her computer and loaded it with interesting programs. Not a single girl stopped by. When she asked why, the girls "told me computers were something their dads and their brothers used," Douglas sadly recalls. "Computer science is a very male profession . . . When girls get involved in that male world, they are pushed away and belittled. Pretty soon, the girls get frustrated and drop out."

Computer games usually involve lots of shooting and dying. Boy   8 stuff. What's out there for girls? "If you walk down the street and look in the computer store, you will see primarily male people as sales staff and as customers," says Jo Sanders, director of the gender-equity program at the Center for Advanced Study in Education at the City University of New York Graduate Center.

Boys and girls are equally interested in computers until about   9 the fifth grade, says University of Minnesota sociologist Ronald Anderson, who coauthored the recent report "Computers in American Schools." At that point, boys' use rises significantly and girls' use drops, Anderson says, probably because sex-role identification really kicks in. Many girls quickly put computers on the list of not-quite-feminine topics, like car engines and baseball batting averages. It didn't have to be this way. The very first computer programmer was a woman, Ada Lovelace, who worked with Charles Babbage on his mechanical computing machines in the mid-1800s. If she had become a role model, maybe hundreds of thousands of girls would have spent their teenage years locked in their bedrooms staring at screens. Instead, too many are doing their nails or worrying about their hair, says Marcelline Barron, an administrator at the Illinois Mathematics and Science Academy, a publicly funded coed boarding school for gifted students. "You're not thinking about calculus or physics when you're thinking about that," says Barron. "We have these kinds of expectations for young girls. They must be neat, they must be clean, they must be quiet."

Despite great strides by women in other formerly male fields,   10 such as law and medicine, women are turning away from the computer industry. Men earning computer-science degrees outnumber women 3 to 1 and the gap is growing, according to the National Science Foundation. Fifteen years ago, when computers were still new in schools, they hadn't yet been defined as so exclusively male. But now girls have gotten the message. It's not just the technical and cultural barrier. Sherry Turkle, a Massachusetts Institute of Technology sociologist who teaches a course on women and computers, says that computers have come to stand for "a world without emotion," an image that seems to scare off girls more than boys.

In the past decade, videogames have become a gateway to tech-   11
nology for many boys, but game manufacturers say few girls are
attracted to these small-screen shoot-'em-ups. It's not surprising
that the vast majority of videogame designers are men. They don't
call it Game *Boy* for nothing. Now some manufacturers are trying to
lure girls. In the next few months, Sega plans to introduce
"Berenstein Bears," which will offer players a choice of boy or girl
characters. A second game, "Crystal's Pony Tale," involves coloring (there's lots of pink in the background). Neither game requires
players to "die," a common videogame device that researchers say
girls dislike. Girls also tend to prefer nonlinear games, where there
is more than one way to proceed. "There's a whole issue with
speaking girls' language," says Michealene Cristini Risley, group
director of licensing and character development for Sega. The
company would like to hook girls at the age of 4, before they've
developed fears of technology.

Girls need freedom to explore and make mistakes. Betsy Zeller,   12
a 37-year-old engineering manager at Silicon Graphics, says that
when she discovered computers in college, "I swear I thought I'd
seen the face of God." Yet she had to fend off guys who would come
into the lab and want to help her work through problems or, worse
yet, do them for her. "I would tell them to get lost," she says. "I
wanted to do it myself." Most women either asked for or accepted
proffered help, just as they are more likely to ask for directions when
lost in a strange city. That may be the best way to avoid driving in
circles for hours, but it's not the best way to learn technical
subjects.

Schools are trying a number of approaches to interest girls in   13
computers. Douglas and her colleagues are participating in a men-
torship program where undergraduate girls spent a summer working
with female computer scientists. Studies have shown that girls are
more attracted to technology if they can work in groups; some
schools are experimenting with team projects that require computers
but are focused on putting out a product, like a newspaper or
pamphlet. At the middle- and high-school level, girls-only computer
classes are increasingly popular. Two months ago Roosevelt Middle
School in Eugene, Ore., set up girls-only hours at the computer lab.
Games were prohibited and artists were brought in to teach girls
how to be more creative with the computer. Students are also learning to use e-mail, which many girls love. Says Debbie Nehl, the
computer-lab supervisor: "They see it as high-tech note-passing."

POWER NETWORKS

As a relatively new industry, the leadership of computerdom 14
might be expected to be more gender-diverse. Wrong; few women
have advanced beyond middle-management ranks. According to a
study conducted last year by The San Jose Mercury News, there are
no women CEOs running major computer-manufacturing firms and
only a handful running software companies. Even women who have
succeeded say they are acutely conscious of the differences between
them and their male co-workers. "I don't talk the same as men,"
says Paula Hawthorn, an executive at Montage Software, in Oakland,
Calif. "I don't get the same credibility." The difference, she says,
"is with you all the time."

Women who work in very technical areas, such as programming, 15
are often the loneliest. Anita Borg, a computer-systems researcher,
remembers attending a 1987 conference where there were so few
women that the only time they ran into each other was in the
restroom. Their main topic of discussion: why there were so few
women at the conference. That bathroom cabal grew into Systers, an
on-line network for women with technical careers. There are now
1,740 women members from 19 countries representing 200 colleges
and universities and 150 companies. Systers is part mentoring and
part consciousness-raising. One graduate student, for example,
talked about how uncomfortable she felt sitting in her shared office
when a male graduate student and a professor put a picture of a nude
woman on a computer. The problem was resolved when a couple of
female faculty members, also on the Systers network, told their
offending colleagues that the image was not acceptable.

Women have been more successful in developing software, espe- 16
cially when their focus is products used by children. Jan Davidson, a
former teacher, started Davidson & Associates, in Torrance, Calif.,
with three programs in 1982. Now it's one of the country's biggest
developers of kids' software, with 350 employees and $58.6 million
in revenues. Multimedia will bring new opportunities for women.
The technology is so specialized that it requires a team— animators,
producers, scriptwriters, 3-D modelers—to create state-of-the-art
products. It's a far cry from the stereotype of the solitary male programmer, laboring long into the night with only takeout Chinese
food for company. At Mary Cron's Rymel Design Group in Palos
Verdes, Calif., most of the software artists and designers are women,
Cron says. "It's like a giant puzzle," she adds. "We like stuff we
can work on together. "

As more women develop software, they may also help create 17
products that will attract women consumers—a huge untapped

market. Heidi Roizen, a college English major, cofounded T/Maker Co. in Mountain View, Calif., a decade ago. She says that because women are often in charge of the family's budget, they are potential consumers of personal-finance programs. Women are also the most likely buyers of education and family-entertainment products, a fast-growing segment of the industry. "Women are more typically the household shopper," Roizen says. "They have tremendous buying power. "

WIRED WOMEN

The infobahn—a.k.a. the Information Superhighway—may be   18
the most hyped phenomenon in history—or it could be the road to the future. In any case, women want to get on. But the sign over the access road says CAUTION. MEN WORKING. WOMEN BEWARE. Despite hundreds of thousands of new users in the last year, men still dominate the Internet and commercial services such as Prodigy or CompuServe. The typical male conversation on line turns off many women. "A lot of time to be crude, it's a pissing contest," says Lisa Kimball, a partner in the Meta Network, a Washington, D. C. on-line service that is 40 percent female. Put-downs are an art form. When one woman complained recently in an Internet forum that she didn't like participating because she didn't have time to answer all her e-mail, she was swamped with angry responses, including this one (from a man): "Would you like some cheese with your whine?"

Some men say the on-line hostility comes from resentment over   19
women's slowly entering what has been an almost exclusively male domain. Many male techno-jocks "feel women are intruding into their inner sanctum," says André Bacard, a Silicon Valley, Calif., technology writer. They're not out to win sensitivity contests. "In the computer world, it's 'Listen, baby, if you don't like it, drop dead,' " says Bacard. "It's the way men talk to guys. Women aren' t used to that."

Even under more civilized circumstances, men and women have   20
different conversational styles, says Susan Herring, a University of Texas at Arlington professor who has studied women's participation on computer networks. Herring found that violations of long-established net etiquette—asking too many basic questions, for example, angered men. "The women were much more tolerant of people who didn't know what they were doing," Herring says. "What really annoyed women was the flaming and people boasting. The things that annoy women are things men do all the time."

Like hitting on women. Women have learned to tread their 21
keyboards carefully in chat forums because they often have to fend
off sexual advances that would make Bob Packwood blush. When
subscribers to America Online enter one of the service's forums,
their computer names appear at the top of the screen as a kind of
welcome. If they've chosen an obviously female name, chances are
they'll be bombarded with private messages seeking detailed
descriptions of their appearance or sexual preferences. "I couldn't
believe it," recalls 55-year-old Eva S. "I said, 'Come on, I'm a
grandmother. ' "

More and more women are signing on to networks that are 22
either coed and run by women, or are exclusively for women. Stacy
Horn started ECHO (for East Coast Hang Out) four years ago
because she was frustrated with the hostility on line. About 60 percent of ECHO's 2,000 subscribers are men; among ECHO's 50
forums, only two are strictly for women. "Flaming is nonexistent on
ECHO," Horn says. "New women get on line and they see that.
And then they're much more likely to jump in." Women's Wire
in San Francisco, started in January, has 850 subscribers, only 10
percent of them men—the reverse of most on-line services. "We
wanted to design a system in which women would help shape the
community and the rules of that community from the floor up,"
says cofounder Ellen Pack. The official policy is that there is no such
thing as a dumb question—and no flaming.

Male subscribers say Women's Wire has been a learning 23
experience for them, too. Maxwell Hoffmann, a 41-year-old computer company manager, says that many men think that only women
are overly emotional. But men lose it, too. A typical on-line fight
starts with two guys sending "emotionally charged flames going
back and forth" through cyberspace (not on Women's Wire). Then
it expands and "everybody starts flaming the guy. They scream at
each other and they're not listening."

If only men weren't so *emotional*, so *irrational*, could we all get 24
along on the net?

TOYS AND TOOLS

In one intriguing study by the Center for Children and 25
Technology, a New York think tank, men and women in technical
fields were asked to dream up machines of the future. Men typically
imagined devices that could help them "conquer the universe," says
Jan Hawkins, director of the center. She says women wanted
machines that met people's needs, "the perfect mother. "

Someday, gender-blind education and socialization may render   26
those differences obsolete. But in the meantime, researchers say both
visions are useful. If everyone approached technology the way
women do now, "we wouldn't be pushing envelopes," says
Cornelia Bruner, associate director of the center. "Most women,
even those who are technologically sophisticated, think of machines
as a means to an end." Men think of the machines as an extension
of their own power, as a way to "transcend physical limitations."
That may be why they are more likely to come up with great leaps in
technology, researchers say. Without that vision, the computer and
its attendant industry would not exist.

Ironically, gender differences could help women. "We're at a   27
cultural turning point," says MIT's Turkle. "There's an opportunity to remake the culture around the machine." Practicality is
now as valued as invention. If the computer industry wants to put
machines in the hands of the masses, that means women—along with
the great many men who have no interest in hot-rod computing. An
ad campaign for Compaq's popular Presario line emphasized the
machine's utility. After kissing her child good night, the mother in
the ad sits down at her Presario to work. As people start to view their
machines as creative tools, someday women may be just as comfortable with computers as men are.

EXPLORATIONS

1. How does Kantrowitz characterize the different attitudes that men and
   women have toward computers? What factors contribute to women's
   lack of interest in computers?

2. What strategies are companies and schools using to make computers
   more appealing to girls and women? What do you think about these
   strategies?

3. How do men's and women's differing conversational styles manifest
   themselves in on-line computer environments? What do these tensions
   in on-line conversations suggest about gender roles in our society?

4. Enter an on-line chat group and observe the conventions of conversation. What does it take to be literate in such a community? Pay special
   attention to gender relations as you write an analysis of what you
   observe.

Gender Gap in Cyberspace

DEBORAH TANNEN

Deborah Tannen is a professor of linguistics at Georgetown University and is the author of the best-selling books That's Not What I Meant! How Conversational Style Makes or Breaks Your Relationship with Others *(1986) and* You Just Don't Understand *(1990). Her most recent work is in* Gender and Discourse *(1994). In this article, published in the May 16, 1994, issue of* Newsweek, *Tannen explores the effects of gender on e-mail communication.*

WRITING BEFORE READING

How is e-mail communication different from letter writing or talking on the telephone?

I was a computer pioneer, but I'm still something of a novice. That paradox is telling.

I was the second person on my block to get a computer. The first was my colleague Ralph. It was 1980. Ralph got a Radio Shack TRS-80; I got a used Apple II+. He helped me get started and went on to become a maven, reading computer magazines, hungering for the new technology he read about, and buying and mastering it as quickly as he could afford. I hung on to old equipment far too long because I dislike giving up what I'm used to, fear making the wrong decision about what to buy and resent the time it take to install and learn a new system.

My first Apple came with videogames; I gave them away. Playing games on the computer didn't interest me. If I had free time I'd spend it talking on the telephone to friends.

Ralph got hooked. His wife was often annoyed by the hours he spent at his computer and the money he spent upgrading it. My marriage had no such strains—until I discovered e-mail. Then I got hooked. E-mail draws me the same way the phone does: it's a souped-up conversation.

E-mail deepened my friendship with Ralph. Though his office was next to mine, we rarely had extended conversations because he is shy. Face to face he mumbled so, I could barely tell he was speaking. But when we both got on e-mail, I started receiving long, self-revealing messages; we poured our hearts out to each other. A friend discovered that e-mail opened up that kind of communication

449

with her father. He would never talk much on the phone (as her mother would), but they have become close since they both got on line.

Why, I wondered, would some men find it easier to open up on e-mail? It's a combination of the technology (which they enjoy) and the obliqueness of the written word, just as many men will reveal feelings in dribs and drabs while riding in the car or doing something, which they'd never talk about sitting face to face. It's too intense, too bearing-down on them, and once you start you have to keep going. With a computer in between, it's safer.

It was on e-mail, in fact, that I described to Ralph how boys in groups often struggle to get the upper hand whereas girls tend to maintain an appearance of cooperation. And he pointed out that this explained why boys are more likely to be captivated by computers than girls are. Boys are typically motivated by a social structure that says if you don't dominate you will be dominated. Computers, by their nature, balk; you type a perfectly appropriate command and it refuses to do what it should. Many boys and men are incited by this defiance: "I'm going to whip this into line and teach it who's boss! I'll get it to do what I say!" (and if they work hard enough, they always can). Girls and women are more likely to respond, "This thing won't cooperate. Get it away from me!"

Although no one wants to think of herself as "typical"— how much nicer to be sui generis—my relationship to my computer is—gulp—fairly typical for a woman. Most women (with plenty of exceptions) aren't excited by tinkering with the technology, grappling with the challenge of eliminating bugs or getting the biggest and best computer. These dynamics appeal to many men's interest in making sure they're on the top side of the inevitable who's-up-who's-down struggle that life is for them. E-mail appeals to my view of life as a contest for connections to others. When I see that I have 15 messages I feel loved.

I once posted a technical question on a computer network for linguists and was flooded with long dispositions, some pages long. I was staggered by the generosity and the expertise, but wondered where these guys found the time—and why all the answers I got were from men.

Like coed classrooms and meetings, discussions on e-mail networks tend to be dominated by male voices, unless they're specifically women-only, like single-sex schools. On line, women don't have to worry about getting the floor (you just send a message when you feel like it), but, according to linguists Susan Herring and Laurel Sutton, who have studied this, they have the usual problems of having their messages ignored or attacked. The anonymity of public networks frees a small number of men to send long, vituperative, sarcastic messages that many other men either can tolerate or actually enjoy, but turn most women off.

The anonymity of networks leads to another sad part of the 11 e-mail story: there are men who deluge women with questions about their appearance and invitations to sex. On college campuses, as soon as women students log on, they are bombarded by references to sex, like going to work and finding pornographic posters adorning the walls.

Taking time: Most women want one thing from a computer—to 12 work. This is significant counterevidence to the claim that men want to focus on information while women are interested in rapport. That claim I found was often true in casual conversation, in which there is no particular information to be conveyed. But with computers, it is often women who are more focused on information, because they don't respond to the challenge of getting equipment to submit.

Once I had learned the basics, my interest in computers waned. 13 I use it to write books (though I never mastered having it do bibliographies or tables of contents) and write checks (but not balance my checkbook). Much as I'd like to use it to do more, I begrudge the time it would take to learn.

Ralph's computer expertise costs him a lot of time. Chivalry 14 requires that he rescue novices in need, and he is called upon by damsel novices far more often than knaves. More men would rather study the instruction booklet than ask directions, as it were, from another person. "When I do help men," Ralph wrote (on e-mail, of course), "they want to be more involved. I once installed a hard drive for a guy, and he wanted to be there with me, wielding the screwdriver and giving his own advice where he could." Women, he finds, usually are not interested in what he's doing; they just want him to get the computer to the point where they can do what they want.

Which pretty much explains how I managed to be a pioneer 15 without becoming an expert.

EXPLORATIONS

1. What exactly is the gender gap in cyberspace?
2. Even though she was the second person on her block to get a computer, Tannen says that she did not get "hooked." How does she account for her own lack of interest in computer technology?
3. Why does e-mail finally get Tannen involved in the computer culture?

4. How can e-mail affect the ways people communicate with each other? What does Tannen think characterizes the communication behaviors of men and women on e-mail?

5. Based on your own experience, do you think Tannen and Kantrowitz are oversimplifying when they characterize the conflicting motivations that men and women have for using computer technology? Why or why not?

FURTHER SUGGESTIONS FOR WRITING: PUBLIC LITERACIES

The assignments that follow offer many suggestions for writing. As is always the case with writers, you, the author, must exercise authority in determining which of the suggestions to follow, which to ignore, and which to put on the back burner while you determine the focus that your work will take and the needs of your intended audience. Use the following questions and suggestions for the purposes of invention.

1. **Analyzing Public Literacy:** Consider the multiple literacies at work in our culture. In this assignment, you will use the tools of rhetorical analysis to examine the ways in which a particular institution or organization represents itself, its products, or its services to the public. You should do primary research by collecting and analyzing these representations—brochures, books, ads, web sites, etc. Your paper should help your intended audience understand the significance of the institution or organization you are examining by providing cultural and historical contexts. To do so, you should expect to undertake additional research in the library, on the Internet, in the community or in other sites in order to gather enough information to fully and persuasively develop your analysis.

   Focus on a particular site, text, or set of texts representing a company, organization, or product. (Your junk mail might be potentially rich in this regard.) These texts might be brochures or flyers distributed by a particular campus organization, print or television ads for a company or product such as CompuServe or Diet Coke, or even the ways a business such as a local bank uses office design and employee appearance to represent itself. You could also analyze a news forum—a newspaper, news magazine, TV news show, talk show, movie, or song through which the news or a news event is presented. You can draw upon the ethnographic research techniques described in the *Further Suggestions for Writing* in Part 3, but your primary focus is on textual analysis and interpretation. As you begin your analysis, consider the following questions:

   - If you are analyzing an ad, pay attention to where you found it. Was it, for example, in a periodical or on a billboard, the Internet, or bus stop poster? How does the context affect the way in which it is perceived? Does an ad appearing in *The New York Times* have more authority than the same ad appearing in a neighborhood shopper? What language or visual images are incorporated into your text and for what purposes? How do words and images work together to create the desired representations? What implicit and explicit claims are made? How does the text appeal to its audience? What is the main purpose of the text and how does the text achieve that purpose? Why should people understand the ways in which advertisements work to persuade their audiences?

- If you are analyzing the rhetorical effects of the arrangement and use of space, notice the placement of furniture and counters, the decor, the colors used, the appearance of employees, and the music or other sounds that you hear. Think, for example of your dentist's office or of a retail store such as the Gap. What purposes do these elements serve and how do they affect the audience? What kind of image is presented and what does that image tell you about the purpose of the space? How can an awareness of such spaces be useful?

- If you are analyzing a news forum, consider who is presenting the news. What stories are chosen and why? How are those stories told? How are the presenters of the news trying to appeal to their audience? How are the music, graphics, stage sets, and the appearance of the anchor person used to create a particular look or image? How are these news forums trying to sell the news to the public? What implications does this have for the status of public knowledge? How might an awareness of the operation of the news media be helpful to us as voters and citizens?

2. **Taking Part in Public Discourse:** Most of the selections in Part 4 describe and analyze instances of the multiple literacies at work in contemporary American society. Theodore Sizer talks about public literacies; Jack Solomon discusses American advertising. Kiku Adatto and Jon Katz both uncover the literacies involved in the news media, while Barbara Kantrowitz describes how men and women develop, use, and value different literacies in regard to computer technology. Within these selections, many conflicts emerge concerning access to particular literacies and the proper uses of public discourse.

This assignment asks you to consider the assumptions behind public discourse and to take an advocacy role in articulating your point of view on a subject, situation, or location that articulates a public literacy that is, or should be, of interest to a wider audience. For instance, you might take up the controversy regarding cigarette advertising targeted toward children, or you might take a stand on the regulation of certain "public spaces" by skateboarders. The idea here is to examine the conventions, or public literacies, involved in these subjects, situations, or locations. Americans, in general, believe in the free use of public spaces, but when certain groups and certain activities come to dominate certain spaces (such as skateboarders using pedestrian walkways), suddenly those "free" spaces don't seem so free after all and policies are written that restrict use. Other topics you might consider include access to cyberspace; the usage and cultural significance of public parks, wilderness areas, or shopping malls; the use of facilities for the handicapped; the function of art in American culture—public art, museum art; and access to golf courses.

You can see from this list that the possibilities are endless. Your goal, however, in this assignment has a much tighter scope. You want to engage an issue you feel strongly about and then develop a piece of writing that addresses those people or institutions that should hear your point of view. You will need to determine the type of piece your work will become: If you are dealing with the skateboarding issue, you might prepare a proposal that recommends a compromise for the use of that space. You will also have to determine to whom that proposal will be addressed. Should it go to the president of the university? a committee in student government? a public official?

Your work might take a variety of forms: the proposal mentioned above, a letter to the editor, an op-ed for the local newspaper, a report, or a web site or home page on the Internet, to name just a few. The final goal of this assignment is to send your work out: to a magazine, to a newspaper, to the company you are taking issue with, to the university, or to post it on the Internet.

As you write, consider these points:

- Identify the groups involved and the potential conflicts at work in your analysis of a particular public literacy (for example, the conflict over equal access to desirable tee times between women golfers and country club boards of directors).

- What are the motives of these groups and how do those motives manifest themselves within the public discourse? (Women golfers want to have equal time and access to the golf course, therefore, they are protesting. The board of directors wants to maintain tradition, so they have kept restrictive rules in place).

- What assumptions are held about your instance of public literacy? (The members of the board might assume that women are slow or inadequate golfers.)

- Are there any points on which the groups involved agree? If so what are those points of agreement and why do they exist? (Both groups probably agree on the value of golf as a sport.)

- Which group do you identify with? Why? How did you come to identify with this group?

- What possible solutions to this conflict over public literacy can you offer?

Acknowledgments *(Continued from copyright page)*

"On Dumpster Diving." Copyright © 1993 by Lars Eighner. From TRAV-
ELS WITH LIZBETH: THREE YEARS ON THE ROAD AND ON
THE STREETS by Lars Eighner. Reprinted by permission of St.
Martin's Press, Inc.

"From Outside, In" originally appeared in *The Georgia Review*, volume
XLI, No. 2 (Summer 1987), © 1987 by the University of Georgia, ©
1987 by Barbara Mellix. Reprinted by permission of Barbara Mellix and
The Georgia Review.

"Aria: A Memoir of a Bilingual Childhood." Copyright © 1980 by Richard
Rodriguez. Reprinted by permission of Georges Borchardt, Inc. for the
author. Originally published in *American Scholar*.

"On Being White, Female, and Born in Bensonhurst" by Marianna
DeMarco Torgovnick. From CROSSING OCEAN PARKWAY by
Marianna DeMarco Torgovnick. Copyright © by and reprinted with
permission from Marianna DeMarco Torgovnick and The University of
Chicago Press. This selection first appeared in *Partisan Review*, vol. 57,
no. 3, 1990.

"Literacy and the Lesbian/Gay Learner" by Ellen Louise Hart. From THE
LESBIAN IN THE FRONT OF THE CLASSROOM, edited by Irene
Reti and Sarah Hope-Parmeter. Copyright © 1988. Reprinted by per-
mission of Ellen Louise Hart.

"Theme for English B" by Langston Hughes. From COLLECTED
POEMS by Langston Hughes. Copyright © 1994 by the Estate of
Langston Hughes. Reprinted by permission of Alfred A. Knopf, Inc.

"The Fourth Vision: Literate Language at Work" by Shirley Brice Heath.
Reprinted by permission of the Modern Language Association of
America from THE RIGHT TO LITERACY, ed. by Andrea Lunsford,
Helene Moglen and James Slevin. Copyright © 1990.

"Crossing Boundaries." Reprinted with the permission of The Free Press,
a division of Simon & Schuster from LIVES ON THE BOUNDARY:
THE STRUGGLES AND ACHIEVEMENTS OF AMERICA'S
UNDERPREPARED by Mike Rose. Copyright © 1989 by Mike Rose.

"It's the Poverty." Reprinted from Cherríe Moraga's *Loving in the War
Years*, with permission from the publisher, South End Press; 116 Saint
Botolph Street; Boston, MA 02115.

"Cultural Literacy" by E. D. Hirsch. Reprinted from *The American
Scholar*, volume 52, Number 2, Spring 1983. Copyright © 1983 by the
author.

"Final Exam: American Renaissance" from AN OREGON MESSAGE by
William Stafford. Copyright © 1987 by William Stafford. Reprinted by
permission of HarperCollins Pubishers, Inc.

"The Banking Concept of Education." PEDAGOGY OF THE
OPPRESSED by Paolo Freire. Copyright © 1970. Reprinted with the
permission of The Continuum Publishing Company.

"Perspectives on the Intellectual Tradition of Black Women Writers" by
Jacqueline Jones Royster. Reprinted by permission of the Modern

Language Association of America from THE RIGHT TO LITERACY, ed. by Andrea Lunsford, Helene Moglen and James Slevin. Copyright © 1990.

"Confronting Class in the Classroom" by bell hooks. Reprinted from TEACHING TO TRANSGRESS, by bell hooks, copyright © 1994 with the permission of the publisher, Routledge, New York.

"M. Degas Teaches Art & Science at Durfee Intermediate School" by Philip Levine. From WHAT WORKS IS by Philip Levine. Copyright © 1991 by Philip Levine. Reprinted by permission of Alfred A. Knopf, Inc.

"Social Class and the Hidden Curriculum of Work" by Jean Anyon. Reprinted from *Journal of Education*, Boston University School of Education (1980), vol. 162, with permission from The Trustees of Boston University and Jean Anyon, Chair of the Dept. of Education, Rutgers University.

"America Skips School" by Benjamin R. Barber. Copyright © 1993 by *Harper's Magazine*. All rights reserved. Reproduced from the November issue by special permission.

"The Student and the University." Reprinted with the permission of Simon & Schuster from THE CLOSING OF THE AMERICAN MIND by Allan Bloom. Copyright © 1987 by Allan Bloom.

"The Liberal Arts, the Campus, and the Biosphere," HARVARD EDU-CATIONAL REVIEW, 60:2, pp. 205-216. Copyright © 1990 by the President and Fellows of Harvard College. All rights reserved.

"Public Literacy: Puzzlements of a High School Watcher" by Theodore R. Sizer. Reprinted by permission of the Modern Language Association of America from THE RIGHT TO LITERACY edited by Andrea Lunsford, Helene Moglen, and James Sevin. Copyright © 1990.

"Masters of Desire: The Culture of American Advertising" by Jack Solomon. Reprinted by permission of The Putnam Publishing Group/Jeremy R. Tarcher, Inc. From THE SIGNS OF OUR TIMES by Jack Solomon. Copyright © 1988 by Jack Fisher Solomon, Ph.D.

"Move over Boomer: The Busters Are Here—and They're Angry. " Reprinted from December 14, 1992, issue of *Business Week* by special permission, copyright © 1992 by The McGraw-Hill Companies.

"The Incredible Shrinking Sound Bite" by Kiku Adatto, author of PIC-TURE PERFECT: THE ART AND ARTIFICE OF IMAGE MAK-ING. Basic Books, © 1994.

"Rock, Rap and Movies Bring You the News" by Jon Katz. From *Rolling Stone*, March 5, 1992. By Straight Arrow Publishers, Inc. 1992.

"Daytime Inquiries." Reprinted by permission from *The Progressive*; 409 East Main Street; Madison, WI 53703.

"Report from El Dorado" by Michael Ventura. Reprinted by permission of the Putnam Publishing Group/Jeremy P. Tarcher, Inc. From SHAD-OW DANCING IN THE USA by Michael Ventura. Copyright © 1985 by Michael Ventura.

"Enclosed. Encyclopedic. Endured.: One Week at the Mall of America." Copyright © 1993 by David Guterson. Reprinted by permission of Georges Borchardt, Inc. for the author.